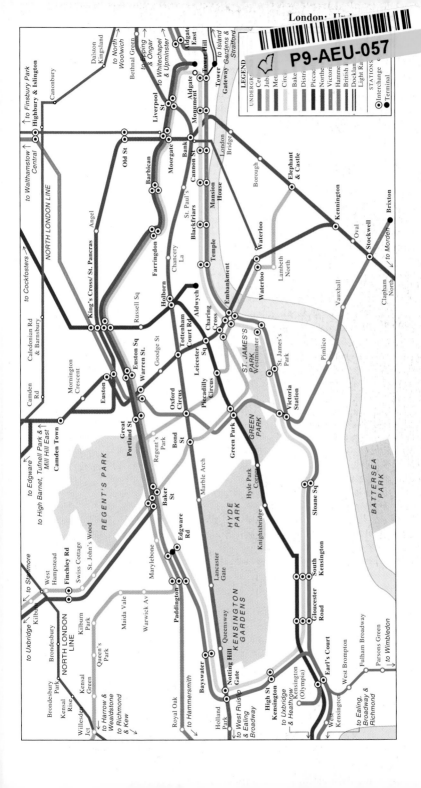

London: Westminster and Whitehall

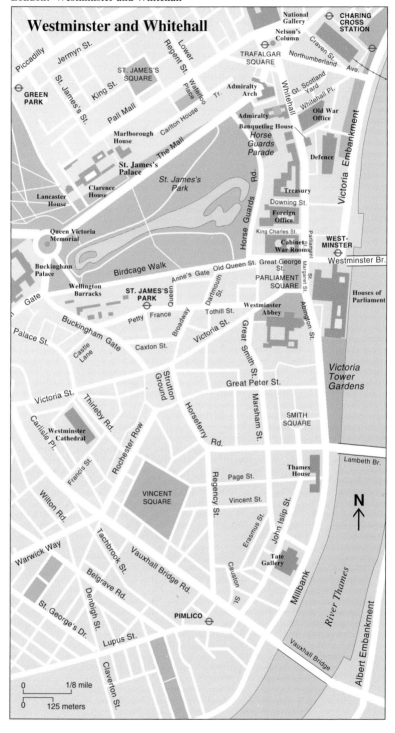

Westminster and Whitehall

Piccadilly
Jermyn St.
St. James's St.
King St.
ST. JAMES'S SQUARE
Regent St.
Lower Regent St.
Waterloo Place
Tr.
Pall Mall
Carlton House
The Mall
Marlborough House
St. James's Palace
Clarence House
Lancaster House
St. James's Park
Queen Victoria Memorial
Buckingham Palace
Wellington Barracks
ST. JAMES'S PARK
Gate
Palace St.
Castle Lane
Buckingham Gate
Petty France
Thirleby Rd.
Victoria St.
Carlisle Pl.
Westminster Cathedral
Francis St.
Wilton Rd.
Warwick Way
Tachbrook St.
Belgrave Rd.
Denbigh St.
St. George's Dr.
Lupus St.
Claverton St.
VINCENT SQUARE
Strutton Ground
Rochester Row
Caxton St.
Broadway
Tothill St.
Victoria St.
Great Smith St.
Westminster Abbey
Great Peter St.
Marsham St.
Horseferry Rd.
Page St.
Vincent St.
Erasmus St.
Caustop St.
John Islip St.
Tate Gallery
Regency St.
Vauxhall Bridge Rd.
VAUXHALL BRIDGE
PIMLICO
Millbank
SMITH SQUARE
Thames House
Lambeth Br.
River Thames
Albert Embankment
Victoria Tower Gardens
Houses of Parliament
Westminster Br.
WEST-MINSTER
Westminster Abbey
Abingdon St.
Margaret St.
PARLIAMENT SQUARE
Great George St.
Old Queen St.
Anne's Gate
Dartmouth St.
Queen Anne's Gate
Birdcage Walk
Foreign Office
Downing St.
Treasury
Cabinet War Rooms
King Charles St.
Horse Guards Rd.
Parliament St.
Defence
Old War Office
Whitehall Pl.
Victoria Embankment
Gt. Scotland Yard
Northumberland Ave.
Craven St.
TRAFALGAR SQUARE
Nelson's Column
National Gallery
CHARING CROSS STATION
Admiralty Arch
Admiralty
Banqueting House
Horse Guards Parade
Whitehall

GREEN PARK

N
↑

0   1/8 mile
0   125 meters

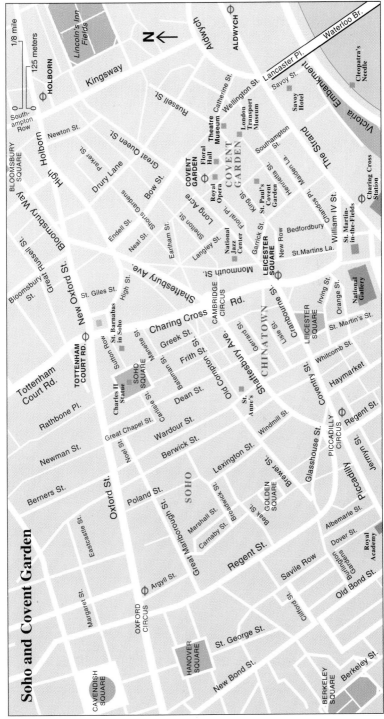

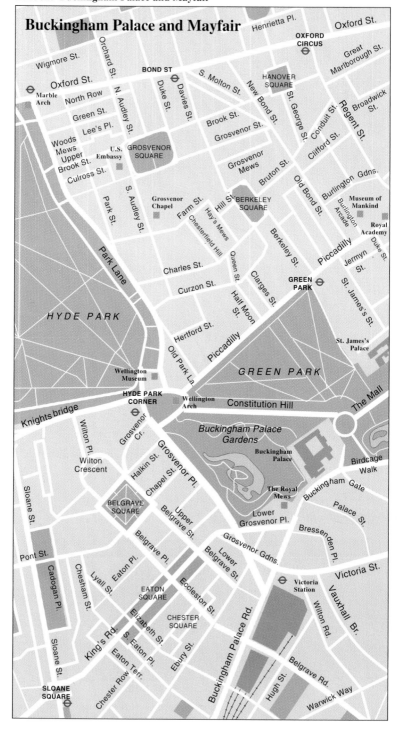

Buckingham Palace and Mayfair

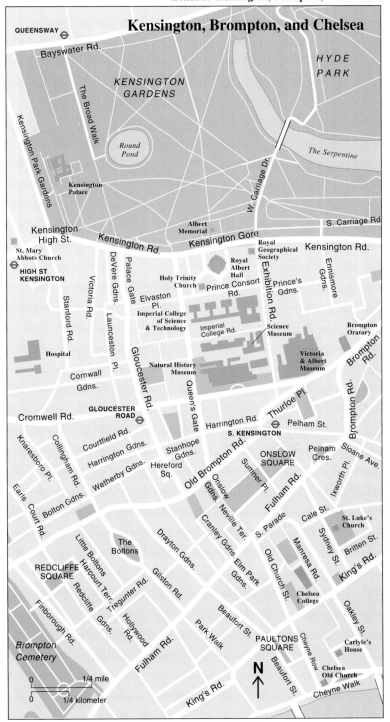

Kensington, Brompton, and Chelsea

QUEENSWAY

Bayswater Rd.

HYDE PARK

KENSINGTON GARDENS

The Broad Walk

Kensington Park Gardens

Round Pond

The Serpentine

W. Carriage Dr.

Kensington Palace

S. Carriage Rd

Albert Memorial

Kensington High St.

Kensington Rd.

Kensington Gore

Kensington Rd.

St. Mary Abbots Church

HIGH ST KENSINGTON

Royal Geographical Society

Royal Albert Hall

DeVere Gdns.

Palace Gate

Holy Trinity Church

Prince Consort Rd.

Exhibition Rd.

Prince's Gdns.

Ennismore Gdns.

Victoria Rd.

Stanford Rd.

Launceston Pl.

Elvaston Pl.

Imperial College of Science & Technology

Imperial College Rd.

Science Museum

Brompton Oratory

Hospital

Cornwall Gdns.

Gloucester Rd.

Natural History Museum

Queen's Gate

Victoria & Albert Museum

Brompton Rd.

Cromwell Rd.

GLOUCESTER ROAD

Thurloe Pl.

Brompton Rd.

Harrington Rd.

Pelham St.

S. KENSINGTON

Knaresboro Pl.

Collingham Rd.

Courtfield Rd.

Harrington Gdns.

Stanhope Gdns.

Hereford Sq.

Old Brompton Rd.

Onslow Gdns.

Summer Pl.

ONSLOW SQUARE

Pelham Cres.

Sloane Ave.

Ixworth Pl.

Earls Court Rd.

Wetherby Gdns.

Bolton Gdns.

Neville Ter.

Cranley Gdns. Elm Park Gdns.

Fulham Rd.

S. Parade

Cale St.

St. Luke's Church

Little Boltons

The Boltons

Drayton Gdns.

Old Church St.

Manresa Rd.

Sydney St.

Britten St.

King's Rd.

REDCLIFFE SQUARE

Harcourt Terr.

Redcliffe Gdns.

Tregunter Rd.

Gilston Rd.

Hollywood Rd.

Chelsea College

Oakley St.

Finborough Rd.

Park Walk

Beaufort St.

PAULTONS SQUARE

Cheyne Row

Carlyle's House

Brompton Cemetery

Fulham Rd.

King's Rd.

N

Beaufort St.

Chelsea Old Church

Cheyne Walk

0 1/4 mile

0 1/4 kilometer

The City

Leman St.
Commercial St.
Mansell St.
Middlesex St.
Widegate St.
ALDGATE EAST
Minories
Royal Mint St.
E. Smithfield
St. Katharine's Way
Tower Br. Approach
Tower Br.
Houndsditch
ALDGATE
Aldgate
Fenchurch St. Station
Pepys St.
TOWER HILL
TRINITY SQUARE
Tower Hill
The Tower
Tower Pier
Liverpool St. Station
St. Mary Axe
Fenchurch St.
St. Olave's
Seething La.
All Hallows
Sun St.
Bishopsgate
Old Broad St.
Leadenhall St.
Lloyd's
Leadenhall Market
Lime St.
Mincing La.
Mark La.
St. Dunstan's
Gt. Tower St.
Lower Thames St.
HMS Belfast
London Stock Exchange
Threadneedle St.
Cornhill
St. Mary at Hill
Eastcheap
The Monument
Monument St.
Billingsgate Market
St. Magnus Martyr
South Pl.
London Wall
Throgmorton Ave.
St. Margaret's
Lothbury St.
Bank of England
BANK
Lombard St.
King William St.
MONUMENT
London Br.
MOORGATE
FINSBURY CIRCUS
Moorgate
Princes St.
St. Mary Abchurch
Ropemaker St.
Chiswell St.
Moorfields
Coleman St.
Bassinghall Ave.
Mansion House
Poultry
St. Stephen Walbrook
Walbrook
Temple of Mithras
CANNON
Cloak La.
Cannon St. Station
Southwark Br.
Silk St.
Fore St.
Basinghall St.
Guildhall
King St.
St. Mary le Bow
Watling St.
St. Mary Aldermary
Cannon St.
MANSION HOUSE
Queen St.
Beech St.
Wood St.
Gresham St.
Milk St.
Cheapside
Bread St.
River Thames
Barbican Centre
St. Giles without Cripplegate
Museum of London
London Wall
St. Martin's-Le-Grand
New Chance
St. Paul's Cathedral
St. Andrew-by-the-Wardrobe
Queen Victoria St.
Upper Thames St.
St. Benet's
Aldersgate St.
St. Bartholomew the Great
Little Britain
Puddle Dock
Blackfriars Station
BARBICAN
Long Lane
West Smithfield
ST. PAUL'S
Old Bailey
Newgate St.
Warwick La.
Ludgate Hill
St. John St.
Giltspur St.
Holborn Viaduct Station
Holborn Viaduct
Snow Hill
Old Bailey
LUDGATE CIRCUS
New Bridge St.
BLACKFRIARS
Blackfriars Br.
FARRINGDON
Cowcross St.
Smithfield Market
Farringdon Rd.
Fleet La.
St. Bride St.
Fleet St.
GOUGH SQ.
Tudor St.
Temple Ave.
The Temple
Clerkenwell Rd.
Hatton Garden
Greville St.
Ely Pl.
Farringdon Rd.
Shoe Lane
New Fetter La.
Fetter La.
Temple Church
Middle Temple La.
Victoria Embankment

N

0   1/4 mile
0   1/4 km

LET'S GO:
London

"Its yearly revision by a new crop of Harvard students makes it as valuable as ever." —**The New York Times**

"Value-packed, unbeatable, accurate, and comprehensive." —**The Los Angeles Times**

"A world-wise traveling companion—always ready with friendly advice and helpful hints, all sprinkled with a bit of wit." —**The Philadelphia Inquirer**

"Lighthearted and sophisticated, informative and fun to read. [Let's Go] helps the novice traveler navigate like a knowledgeable old hand." —**Atlanta Journal-Constitution**

"All the essential information you need, from making a phone call to exchanging money to contacting your embassy. [Let's Go] provides maps to help you find your way from every train station to a full range of youth hostels and hotels." —**Minneapolis Star Tribune**

"Unbeatable: good sight-seeing advice; up-to-date-info on restaurants, hotels, and inns; a commitment to money-saving travel; and a wry style that brightens nearly every page." —**The Washington Post**

Let's Go researchers have to make it on their own.

"The writers seem to have experienced every rooster-packed bus and lunar-surfaced mattress about which they write." —**The New York Times**

"Retains the spirit of the student-written publication it is: candid, opinionated, resourceful, amusing info for the traveler of limited means but broad curiosity." —**Mademoiselle**

No other guidebook is as comprehensive.

"Whether you're touring the United States, Europe, Southeast Asia, or Central America, a Let's Go guide will clue you in to the cheapest, yet safe, hotels and hostels, food and transportation. Going beyond the call of duty, the guides reveal a country's latest news, cultural hints, and off-beat information that any tourist is likely to miss." —**Tulsa World**

Let's Go is completely revised each year.

"Up-to-date travel tips for touring four continents on skimpy budgets." —**Time**

"Inimitable.... Let's Go's 24 guides are updated yearly (as opposed to the general guidebook standard of every two to three years), and in a marvelously spunky way." —**The New York Times**

Let's Go Publications

Let's Go: Alaska & The Pacific Northwest
Let's Go: Britain & Ireland
Let's Go: California
Let's Go: Central America
Let's Go: Eastern Europe
Let's Go: Ecuador & The Galápagos Islands
Let's Go: Europe
Let's Go: France
Let's Go: Germany
Let's Go: Greece & Turkey
Let's Go: India & Nepal
Let's Go: Ireland
Let's Go: Israel & Egypt
Let's Go: Italy
Let's Go: London
Let's Go: Mexico
Let's Go: New York City
Let's Go: Paris
Let's Go: Rome
Let's Go: Southeast Asia
Let's Go: Spain & Portugal
Let's Go: Switzerland & Austria
Let's Go: USA
Let's Go: Washington, D.C.

Let's Go **Map Guide:** Boston
Let's Go **Map Guide:** London
Let's Go **Map Guide:** New York City
Let's Go **Map Guide:** Paris
Let's Go **Map Guide:** San Francisco
Let's Go **Map Guide:** Washington, D.C.

LET'S GO

The Budget Guide to
London
1997

Bruce L. Gottlieb
Editor

Andrew E. Nieland
Editor

St. Martin's Press ≈ New York

HELPING LET'S GO

If you want to share your discoveries, suggestions, or corrections, please drop us a line. We read every piece of correspondence, whether a postcard, a 10-page e-mail, or a coconut. All suggestions are passed along to our researcher-writers. Please note that mail received after May 1997 may be too late for the 1998 book, but will be retained for the following edition. **Address mail to:**

> **Let's Go: London**
> **67 Mt. Auburn Street**
> **Cambridge, MA 02138**
> **USA**

Visit Let's Go at **http://www.letsgo.com,** or send e-mail to:

> **Fanmail@letsgo.com**
> **Subject: "Let's Go: London"**

In addition to the invaluable travel advice our readers share with us, many are kind enough to offer their services as researchers or editors. Unfortunately, the charter of Let's Go, Inc. enables us to employ only currently enrolled Harvard-Radcliffe students.

About Let's Go

THIRTY-SIX YEARS OF WISDOM

Back in 1960, a few students at Harvard University banded together to produce a 20-page pamphlet offering a collection of tips on budget travel in Europe. This modest, mimeographed packet, offered as an extra to passengers on student charter flights to Europe, met with instant popularity. The following year, students traveling to Europe researched the first, full-fledged edition of *Let's Go: Europe*, a pocket-sized book featuring honest, irreverent writing and a decidedly youthful outlook on the world. Throughout the 60s, our guides reflected the times; the 1969 guide to America led off by inviting travelers to "dig the scene" at San Francisco's Haight-Ashbury. During the 70s and 80s, we gradually added regional guides and expanded coverage into the Middle East and Central America. With the addition of our in-depth city guides, handy map guides, and extensive coverage of Asia, the 90s are also proving to be a time of explosive growth for Let's Go, and there's certainly no end in sight. The first editions of *Let's Go: India & Nepal* and *Let's Go: Ecuador & The Galapagos Islands* hit the shelves this year, and work toward next year's series has already begun.

We've seen a lot in 37 years. *Let's Go: Europe* is now the world's bestselling international guide, translated into seven languages. And our new guides bring Let's Go's total number of titles, with their spirit of adventure and their reputation for honesty, accuracy, and editorial integrity, to 30. But some things never change: our guides are still researched, written, and produced entirely by students who know first-hand how to see the world on the cheap.

HOW WE DO IT

Each guide is completely revised and thoroughly updated every year by a well-traveled set of 200 students. Every winter, we recruit over 120 researchers and 60 editors to write the books anew. After several months of training, Researcher-Writers hit the road for seven weeks of exploration, from Anchorage to Ankara, Estonia to El Salvador, Iceland to Indonesia. Hired for their rare combination of budget travel sense, writing ability, stamina, and courage, these adventurous travelers know that train strikes, stolen luggage, food poisoning, and marriage proposals are all part of a day's work. Back at our offices, editors work from spring to fall, massaging copy written on Himalayan bus rides into witty yet informative prose. A student staff of typesetters, cartographers, publicists, and managers keeps our lively team together. In September, the collected efforts of the summer are delivered to our printer, who turns them into books in record time, so that you have the most up-to-date information available for *your* vacation. And even as you read this, work on next year's editions is well underway.

WHY WE DO IT

At Let's Go, our goal is to give you a great vacation. We don't think of budget travel as the last recourse of the destitute; we believe that it's the only way to travel. Living cheaply and simply brings you closer to the people and places you've been saving up to visit. Our books will ease your anxieties and answer your questions about the basics—so you can get off the beaten track and explore. Once you learn the ropes, we encourage you to put Let's Go away now and then to strike out on your own. As any seasoned traveler will tell you, the best discoveries are often those you make yourself. When you find something worth sharing, drop us a line. We're Let's Go Publications, 67 Mt. Auburn St., Cambridge, MA 02138, USA (e-mail: fanmail@letsgo.com).

HAPPY TRAVELS!

Contents

Stuck for cash? Don't panic. With Western Union, money is transferred to you in minutes. It's easy. All you've got to do is ask someone at home to give Western Union a call on US 1 800 3256000. Minutes later you can collect the cash.

WESTERN UNION | MONEY TRANSFER

The fastest way to send money worldwide.

Maps

Color Maps

Acknowledgements

Team London raises a stiff Pimms to: our reverend handler Sir Jake, who as a friend and editor receives the Order of the Booty for going far beyond the call of duty; Shonda and John, for endless patience and hospitality (congratulations, we'll see you next summer when 2 Thurloe is done); Michelle and the LG brass for taking a chance and for keeping the home fires burning; Eric Giroux and Wendy Weiden, daytrippers extraodinaire; Bozack, Natasha, Alice (Ah-LEE-chay), Ashley, Adeel, PD, and Brooke for help with nightlife research; Amy B. for taking us in; E-dawg and Ellie for their couch; Jane and Nikia for keeping us off the steam grates; Jumpin' Gene for the monitor; the B&I&I kids for tolerating us. Cheers.   **—The Both of Us**

Andrew of course deserves first mention—to him I am beholden for his preternatural tolerance, his unflagging good spirits, a strong LG brass? work ethic, a McDonald's milkshake, and rockin' good times. The Chelsea and Westminster A&E ward can take a hint from Slick Rick, while to UCL I tip my hat. KcM, Dave M., Hruscka, Dame Lex, DanO, Dave F., Mrs.-I'm-not-Smitty, and Liz Angell made the 2nd half worthwhile. Finally, my wonderful parents and the little Bear (who tolerates my inexplicable absence with a patience belying his years) are constantly missed and forever loved. And Natasher…I hardly know what to say, 'cept I couldn't say no to a lazy afternoon in Regent's Park or anywhere else.   **—BG**

Thanks and the biz to Bruce, my partner in crime past, present and always; as usual, it was a humbling and edifying experience, thanks for bringing me along and not dying of food poisoning. Tristanne and Mike, my LG mentors, for getting me in the game, *danke*. On the homefront: Lord Mayer (living proof that it don't take a Spence diploma to be a classy lassy), Lady Lex, Sully, Chumpie, Hrushka, Dave F., my agent SoRelle—I wish I'd known ya sooner. To Smitty, Murph, Liz, DanO, Mike, Ryan, EJS, Daves E&M, Lauren—we've only just begun. Everyone who lodged me—sorry about the snoring. To mom, dad, Jus, and James, who've never needed a resume to take on chance on me; blood is thicker than the mud, I miss and love you.   **—AEN**

How To Use This Book

A good travel guide—like the Wizard of Oz—strives to be all things to all people. If a friend were so eager to please you'd call him shallow, but please, for the love of God, don't judge us so harshly.

Contained herein is enough yellow-bound fun for a week, month, or year. History buffs, silver-suited swingers, Mods, rockers, Sloane Rangers, art majors on holiday, Royal watchers, and budding scholars "studying" in London will find something within to scratch that itch, if only they know where to look.

London: An Introduction provides a digestible *entreé* to the whirlwind world of London's wordmongers, politicians, musicians, builders, and nobles past and present. It won't pull you a First at University, but it might impress the person on the next barstool. The **Essentials** section is chock full of organizations and publishers just dyin' to save you a few bucks or smooth your journey, as well as advice lovingly gathered from the accumulated silt of years of *Let's Go* experience. Do yourself a favor and spend a few hours looking for the travel tip that will make your vacation. A stitch in time saves…well, whatever, you get the point.

Accommodations provides a list of recommended Bed & Breakfasts, hostels, and Halls of Residence in popular locations. Landing in London without a place to stay is a bit like landing on your bicycle and realizing it has no seat—be smart, make reservations. **Restaurants & Pubs** are organized by area and by type.

The accommodation, food, and drink entries are listed in order of quality. The **Let's Go Picks** (starred) are the budget restaurants and bunkhouses we liked best, and wouldn't want to miss for the world.

Sights and **Greater London** list the lurvliest attractions in a particular area, as well as list the city's best parks, gardens and views. In the beginning of the sights section you'll find our recommendations—they're new this year, so please, read them, use them, and write us to say that you love them too.

The **Shopping** section will point you towards that pair of patent leather jeans you've always wanted, as well as more traditional native garb. The **Entertainment** section contains enough clubs, theater, and music venues to keep it (your thang, that is) shakin' all night. Our **Bisexual, Gay, and Lesbian London** contains clubs, restaurants, and bars catering to guess who. If you've got a good reason, **Daytrippers** will help you take the easy way out, sending you to places almost as worthy as the Capital. But enough about us, London's calling, so get yer arse out there and swing.

A NOTE TO OUR READERS

The information for this book is gathered by *Let's Go*'s researchers during the late spring and summer months. Each listing is derived from the assigned researcher's opinion based upon his or her visit at a particular time. The opinions are expressed in a candid and forthright manner. Other travelers might disagree. Those traveling at a different time may have different experiences since prices, dates, hours, and conditions are always subject to change. You are urged to check beforehand to avoid inconvenience and surprises. Travel always involves a certain degree of risk, especially in low-cost areas. When traveling, especially on a budget, always take particular care to ensure your safety.

London: An Introduction

At first, London is kind to the expectations of visitors stuffing their mental baggage with bobbies and Beefeaters, nursery rhymes and "Masterpiece Theatre," Sherlock Holmes and history books. The Thamescape is still bounded by the over-familiar Big Ben in the west and the archetypal Tower Bridge in the east; St. Paul's and the Tower of London pop up in between. And the whole world and all its double-decker red buses *do* seem to spin around the mad whirl of Piccadilly Circus.

But even the most timid of tourists will notice that for some reason, those tube lines spider out a long way from the Circle Line—central London is just a speck on the Greater London map. Beyond Tower Bridge looms the glossy, pyramid-tipped Canary Wharf skyscraper, centerpiece of one of the world's largest and most controversial redevelopments. The Victorian doorway inscribed with an Anglican piety may belong to a Sikh or a Muslim in a city internalizing its imperial past. A glance between the bus fenders at peers and punks swirling around Piccadilly, or at a newsagent overflowing with music and style mags, reveals that "culture" means more than the Royal Opera.

■ History

Personal enterprise and ownership have defined London since its founding as the **Roman Empire's** farthest outpost. Although Roman officials laid out merely the skeleton of a town in 43 AD—a bridge, roads, a mint—the city soon became a thriving purchase and shipping hub for wool, wheat, and metals. Within just a few years, Tacitus described the new **Londinium** as "a great trading center, full of merchants." With the Romans for protection, the locals were able to concentrate on commerce. But in 61 AD, the Romans failed to prevent **Queen Boudicca**'s Iceni warriors from attacking, looting, and burning the town. The Queen was incensed that the Romans had seized the kingdom left her by her husband and whipped her in public. To protect it from future raids, the Romans built a large stone fort on the edge of the town. In 200 AD, they added a wall and a wooden stockade, but in 410, with Rome in decline, they left altogether.

London slipped into a period of decay. Celts, Saxons, and Danes squabbled over it until 886 AD, when **King Alfred the Great** of Wessex recaptured the city. The Danes managed to seize the city from Alfred's successor, Ethelred the Unready. In response, Ethelred enlisted the help of his better-prepared friend Olaf (later a saint), who led a fleet up the Thames to the bridge in 1014. Olaf tied ropes to the bridge supports and rowed away, pulling down the rickety bridge. The Danes fell into the Thames—and the nursery rhyme "London Bridge is Falling Down" was born.

William the Conqueror arrived in London after his brief engagement at Hastings in 1066. To protect his unruly subjects, and protect himself from them, he built the White Tower immediately after his Christmas Day coronation as King of England. Under more stable administration, the city began to rebuild itself economically and politically. It gained a municipal government under **Richard I,** and the right to elect a yearly mayor under **John I.** The merchant guilds, which arose after the Norman Conquest, took charge of elections and other municipal functions, set quality standards, and watched over sick and elderly workers.

Overseas trade and inland culture gained new momentum under **Elizabeth I**'s austere guidance. Joint stock ventures such as the Virginia Company sent the British flag fluttering across the seas. Playwrights and poets amused commoners in the outdoor theaters of Southwark. Coffeehouses cropped up, brewing business deals alongside literary and political discussions. Natural disasters ravaged the city—the Plague in 1665 and the **Great Fire** in 1666—but Londoners energetically rebuilt.

As Britannia's rule expanded under **Victoria,** London enthusiastically took up its position as the center of the Empire. The 1851 Great Exhibition and the Crystal Pal-

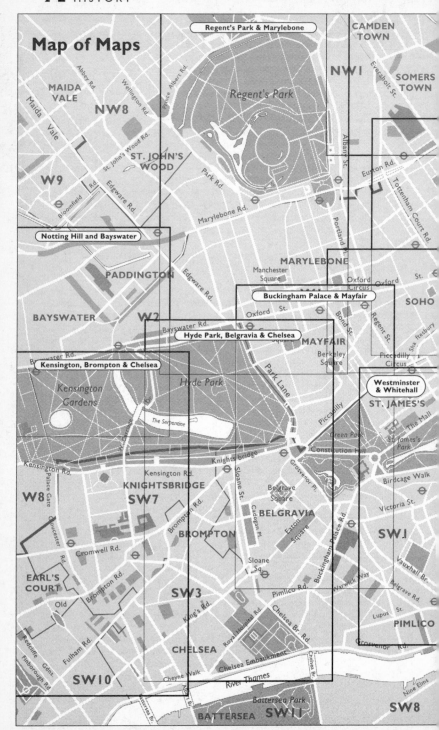

Map of Maps

Regent's Park & Marylebone

Notting Hill and Bayswater

Buckingham Palace & Mayfair

Hyde Park, Belgravia & Chelsea

Kensington, Brompton & Chelsea

Westminster & Whitehall

MAIDA VALE

NW8

CAMDEN TOWN

NW1

SOMERS TOWN

Regent's Park

ST. JOHN'S WOOD

W9

PADDINGTON

BAYSWATER

W2

MARYLEBONE

Manchester Square

Oxford Circus

SOHO

Oxford St.

MAYFAIR

Berkeley Square

Piccadilly Circus

ST. JAMES'S

Kensington Gardens

Hyde Park

The Serpentine

W8

KNIGHTSBRIDGE

SW7

BROMPTON

BELGRAVIA

Belgrave Square

St. James's Park

Birdcage Walk

Victoria St.

SW1

EARL'S COURT

Sloane Sq.

SW3

CHELSEA

PIMLICO

SW10

River Thames

Battersea Park

SW8

BATTERSEA

SW11

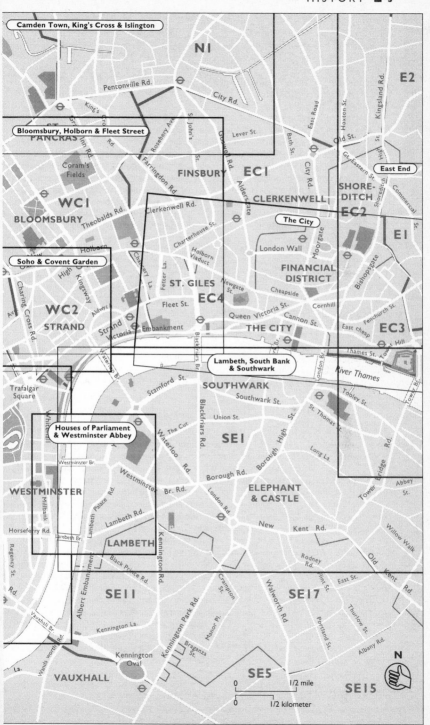

Camden Town, King's Cross & Islington

N1

Pentonville Rd.

City Rd.

E2

Kingsland Rd.

ST. Bloomsbury, Holborn & Fleet Street

PANCRAS

Lever St.

Old St.

East End

Coram's
Fields

FINSBURY

EC1

SHORE-
DITCH
EC2

WC1

CLERKENWELL

BLOOMSBURY   Theobalds Rd.

Clerkenwell Rd.

The City

E1

Soho & Covent Garden

Charterhouse St.

Holborn
Viaduct

London Wall

Moorgate

FINANCIAL
DISTRICT

WC2

ST. GILES
EC4

Fleet St.

Newgate
St.

Cheapside

Cornhill

STRAND

Strand

Queen Victoria St.   Cannon St.

East cheap

EC3

Victoria   Embankment

THE CITY

Trafalgar
Square

Lambeth, South Bank
& Southwark

River Thames

Stamford St.

SOUTHWARK

Southwark St.

Tooley St.

Houses of Parliament
& Westminster Abbey

The Cut

Union St.

St. Thomas St.

Westminster Br.

Blackfriars Rd.

SE1

Long La.

WESTMINSTER

Westminster   Br. Rd.

Borough Rd.

London Rd.

ELEPHANT
& CASTLE

Tower Bridge Rd.

Abbey
St.

Horseferry Rd.

Lambeth Rd.

New   Kent Rd.

Willow Walk

LAMBETH

Kennington Rd.

Rodney
Rd.

Old   Kent Rd.

Regency
St.

Black Prince Rd.

SE11

Crampton
St.

Walworth Rd.

SE17

East St.

Thurlow St.

Portland St.

Kennington La.

Braganza
St.

Manor Pl.

Albany Rd.

VAUXHALL

Kennington
Oval

SE5

0   1/2 mile

0   1/2 kilometer

SE15

N

ace in which it was housed symbolized British supremacy in industry and science, as did the South Kensington museums created under Prince Albert's patronage.

While the empire burgeoned, the city became increasingly **crowded.** Rampant growth in the 18th and 19th centuries worsened structural problems (horse-drawn traffic jams and street pollution) that the government was unable to address. Private enterprise stepped into the gap; the first underground **tube** line was financed entirely by private backers. But the London County Council, created in 1889, provided a more substantial public transit solution. It developed public motor-buses to reduce congestion and passed the Clean Air Act in 1935. The grimy, foggy streets that Holmes and Watson once rattled down would never be the same again.

The world wars of the 20th century tested the endurance and common spirit of Londoners. After WWI, the "Homes for Heroes" program, which failed to deliver fully its promise of adequate housing, nevertheless expanded the map of London fourfold. And, in WWII, Londoners rallied against the Germans and their bombs. "We would rather see London laid in ruins and ashes than that it should be tamely and abjectly enslaved," **Winston Churchill** declared in 1940. During the **Battle of Britain,** the city endured bombing every night except one for three straight months. When Hitler finally transferred the Luftwaffe to the Russian front, London emerged from the Blitz, battered but unbowed.

In 1944, the city gained the right to purchase all areas razed by the bombing; on this land they built hundreds of blocks of towering Council housing. In 1947 the Town and Country Planning Act provided for the creation of a "green belt" on the outskirts of the city. While the **London Building Act of 1939** limited heights of buildings to 100 ft. "unless the Council otherwise consent," the office blocks of central London seem to suggest that the Council has otherwise consented quite a bit. These days, Londoners have grown concerned about high-rise developments, regarding the "dream homes" in postwar blocks of flats as blighted. The council was overhauled in 1965, becoming the Greater London Council. Castigated by Conservatives as a den of the "loony left," the Council was controversially abolished in 1986 under Margaret Thatcher, leaving London with no single elected governing body. The functions formerly discharged by the GLC have since devolved onto local councils.

■ Politics

Ever since a few barons bullied King John into signing the *Magna Carta* in 1215, political and social change has occurred (relatively) calmly in Britain—give or take a 17th-century regicide. Politics has long been a civilized affair joined in by public-minded artists, writers, and scholars. William Pitt, Benjamin Disraeli, and Winston Churchill chastised opponents and praised friends with eloquence and grace.

Another salient feature of British politics is its **partisanship.** In the tumultuous 17th century, before organized partes even existed, the religious floundering of the Stewart monarchs divided MPs (members of Parliament) into **Tories,** who wished to preserve a steady line of succession regardless of religion, and the **Whigs,** who wanted an Anglican king regardless of the line of succession. As time passed, Tories became more generally conservative and loyal to the monarch, while the Whigs became a group of reformers and progressives. In the 19th century, the **Conservative** and **Liberal** Parties formed along these ideological lines. Today, the word Tory is still used to indicate a Conservative Party member. The dismal industrial conditions of the late 19th and early 20th centuries prompted not only moderate governmental regulation, but also clamors for change. Trades unions became increasingly organized, a phenomenon crystallized in the strike of the East London dockers in 1889, and continuing in today's London. In 1906, the almost two million trades union members found political voice in the newly formed **Labour** party, which finally bumped the **Liberal Party** off as the official second party after WWI.

There is no such thing as a minor **sex scandal** in London politics. The steamy **Profumo affair,** on which the film *Scandal* was based, involved some high-profile House of Lords types and a mistress allegedly shared by the Minister of Defense and a KGB agent. The British sex scandal fixation took an interesting turn before the 1992 election, when the revelation of an affair by Liberal Democrat leader Paddy Ashdown shot his opinion poll ratings up by 15%. In 1993, the peculiarities of British political scandal met the (equally peculiar) intricacies of British libel law; when the *New Statesman* suggested that **John Major** was having an affair with a Downing Street caterer, Major sued for libel, placing the magazine in a precarious financial position.

There are no set dates for Britain's general **parliamentary election.** The responsibility for setting a date falls on the prime minister, who must "request" that the queen dissolve the Parliament and hold an election at least every five years. The prime minister must give only three weeks notice, a rule which keeps elections short and inexpensive. The leader of the majority party is then formally invited by the Queen to form a government. Each of the parties has a specific means of nominating a candidate, involving party MPs and sometimes others. Candidates for Prime Minister are nominated by their specific parties and elected in a general election. The main opposition party is constantly poised to move into office. The Opposition leader (an officially paid position currently held by Tony Blair) forms a **"shadow cabinet"** that mirrors the Cabinet in government, and prepares to set up a ministry should they win a majority.

Though such a system is ostensibly a two-party one, **"third parties"** persist. The Liberal Democrats (LDs) were formed from the old Liberal Party and the Social Democratic Party, a moderate Labour splinter group. The LDs, led by Paddy Ashdown, champion a bill of rights and open government, as well as libertarian economics. Other important parties include the Greens, Sinn Fein, the Scottish Nationalist Party, Plaid Cymru (the Welsh nationalist party), and the Ulster Unionists.

It is **Parliament** that has served as the voice of authority ever since political power moved from the House of Lords to the House of Commons during the 19th century. It expanded male suffrage grudgingly, but made social welfare a priority. During the same period, British women, led by suffragette Emmeline Pankhurst, sought their own political rights; women gained full voting rights in 1928.

After WWII, the Labour Party introduced a **national health system,** fondly known as the NHS, nationalized industries, and initiated a period of vaguely social-democratic "consensus." Some 30 years later, politics took on a new direction, when **Margaret Thatcher** brought the country's movement towards socialism to an abrupt halt. She claimed to have revitalized the nation's economy, increased competitiveness, and created a new style of affluence for the money-managers. Her opponents counter that she left growing social tensions, staggering dole lines (Britain's form of welfare), and a tattered educational system in her wake. One of her most controversial (and last) actions as Prime Minister was to abolish local tax rates based on property value in favor of rates based on number of inhabitants over 18 per dwelling—a **poll tax.** Euphemistically referred to by the government as "Community Charge," this tax was an undeniably regressive form of legislation which has since been repealed.

Thatcher's replacement, **John Major,** was confirmed in a close general election in 1992. Elected as a right-winger, and as somebody who was neither Thatcher nor her nemesis Michael Hesseltine, Major is now a self-described centrist. This confusion about his stance is fundamental to his political profile: critics complain that he tries to please everyone and fails, of course, to entirely please even one of the many and multiplying factions. One thing few disagree on is the fact that Major has replaced Thatcher's voluble resistance to the **European Community** (EC) with cautious negotiation, a stance that has divided his party and gravely threatened their majority.

■ This Year's News

On February 9th, 1996, an explosion in the Docklands brought Britain's most inflammatory and persistent political problem to a full boil, as the **IRA** ended their 17-month cease-fire. Republicans blamed the British for stalling the peace process unnecessarily by demanding the surrender of IRA weapons before all-party peace talks could begin. Further bomb attacks in London and Manchester followed, and religiously motivated unrest again festered in Ireland. Nonetheless, both governments and Sinn Fein renewed their commitment to the peace process, although the events have lead many to suspect that a dangerous rift between Sinn Fein and more militant factions of the IRA had opened.

Around the same time, travelers faced an even more subtle danger while in London: the beef on their dinner plates. Scientists had warned of a link between bovine spongiform encephalopathy (BSE, affectionately known as **"mad cow disease"**) and Creutzfeldt-Jakob disease, a degenerative brain disorder in humans, since 1990. When the British government finally acknowledged this threat in March, panic ensued. The EU banned exports of British beef and beef consumption dropped substantially at first, but as prices plummeted and farmers howled, the combination of cheap meat and promises of heightened government vigilance returned the Sunday chop to most British tables.

The real fallout from the BSE scare occurred in the international arena, where the **European Union**'s ban further strained Britain's already uneasy role in the EU. Britons viewed the move as a sell out, a sign of the EU's lack of solidarity despite increased British cooperation. The most virulent Euro-skeptics (opponents of greater European unity) even toyed with the idea of complete withdrawal from the Union. The U.K.'s fury at this commercial backstabbing was matched by Europe's anger at a government they saw as having imposed, through sheer negligence, a serious health risk and financial calamity on the entire continent. Demonstrations grew so fierce that ferries on the continent carrying British citizens were stalled by French farmers, who burned effigies of John Major.

Though Britain's agreement to take further control measures have paved the way for a gradual easing and lift of the ban, the incident exemplifies the damned-if-you-do, damned-if-you-don't dilemma that the EU represents for Britain. Britain is daily learning that a leadership role in the new Europe will require a great deal of economic and political sacrifice, while increased isolationism will also prove costly—the City may lose its status as the world's largest international finance center if it fails to keep pace with the continental march towards a federal Europe. Currently, debate rages most fiercely over the impending introduction of a common European currency unit (the "Euro") which will commit Britain almost irrevocably to the monetary policy of a united Europe.

Meanwhile, 10 Downing St., London's hottest piece of real estate, goes on the market again as partisans gear up for a general parliamentary election, due before May

---

Gays in the British Military

British attitudes towards sexuality can be baffling: tabloids sport topless page-three girls, national television channels think little of having a series of "Out" films, London Underground is quite happy to supply transsexuals with one male and one female ID while they undergo conversion; and yet this is also a country with some of the strictest laws regulating sexuality. Section 28 of the criminal code, for example, bans local authorities from promoting homosexuality. Judiciaries have made their distaste for the law quite clear, and it is rarely applied.

This is also the way the "gays in the military" issue seems to be going. A recent appeal to Britain's Supreme Court, the Law Lords, has resulted in the law being upheld but a rebuke being administered to the government. Unlike the American system, for example—where the application of law depends on the interpretation of the constitution—in Britain, Parliament reigns supreme. This is mostly because there is no written constitution. Lord Chief Justice Brown thus ruled that the law could stand but that "the tide of history" suggested that it was unlikely that "the existing policy can survive for much longer." The Ministry of Defense has already indicated that it will commission a report to be headed by a distinguished civilian to recommend on the issue. The gay community can't quite claim total success but it can at least claim a moral victory.

1997. Most pundits feel that by the time the waves of summer tourists head to London, John Major's waning Conservative parliamentary majority, wracked by infighting will have disappeared, bringing **Tony Blair** and his Labour party into power. Blair's wife is a lawyer; his decision to send his child to a public (private) school drew fire from critics, and he's on a centrist quest to form a "New Labour" party free from the socialist vestiges of traditional labour politics. These traits have spawned numerous comparisons to U.S. president Clinton; indeed, the political climate in the U.K. this year is remarkably similar to that in the U.S. in 1992, when anti-incumbent fervor propelled Clinton to the White House.

■ Royal London

It's not easy being Queen. Lots of money, to be sure, but it seems that no one likes you any more. Every few years another book comes out with a list of reasons why England should finally abandon its monarchy. Commoners are outraged about the US$60 million the Royal Family receives per annum (though the Queen agreed to give up the royal tax exemption in 1992). Two of your boys found themselves in a couple of the most public bad marriages in the Western world, both recently ended in costly, embarrassing, and messy divorces. The British tabloids have recently taken off the gloves in their coverage of Royal foibles—the headlines scream news of the latest embarrassment and many have full-time Royal watchers.

The royal slump began in 1992, pronounced an *annus horribilis* by the Queen (which means a horrible year in Latin and has nothing whatsoever to do with hemorrhoids). The last few years have witnessed behavior which falls, how shall we say it..., short of elegant: divorce proceedings between Charles and Diana; the alleged discovery and broadcast of Charles' indiscretions with his lover Camilla Parker-Bowles by M15 while spying on Charles and Diana; the separation of Fergie and Andrew; a massive fire in the summer castle; Fergie's photographed romp with a Texas tycoon; and now the possibility of her serving as a consultant to a movie on the life of Victoria. Indeed, it is not entirely surprising that London bookmaking organization William Hill calculated that there is now a one-in-six chance that the Windsors will soon be out of a job.

Still, despite much complaint, the British seem to be unable to give the royals that greatest of insults, namely to ignore them. News that Charles and Diana were discussing divorce pushed news of an IRA cease-fire off of the front pages (this in the middle of a renewed series of IRA bombings). And despite the recent furor there are still many traditionalists who feel that the royals are a way of affirming a connection to a glorious history. Besides, there may be a more base motive than national pride for subsidizing the royal presence—queens and princes add to a mystique that draws millions of tourists to London each year. At some level, the tourist experience in London would be quite different were there no monarchy. *Maclean's* magazine makes an observation for Canadians which holds equally true for all foreigners: as non-taxpayers we get all the fun of watching the royals without spending a cent.

The current queen, **Elizabeth II,** is not to be confused with her mother, the **Queen Mum,** who was once queen, but is no longer. Elizabeth's children are **Charles, Prince of Wales** (next in line for the throne, has two children himself), **Andrew, Duke of York** (resting after a tumultuous marriage to the notorious Sarah Ferguson), **Anne,** and **Edward** (who's about to get hitched).

Charles and Diana were slated to be the King and Queen of England, but their marriage soon became an acrimonious embarrassment to the Crown. In December 1992 John Major, the Prime Minister, announced that the Royal couple would be separating. Both couples continued making embarrassing admissions to the tabloids about their various infidelities, until the Queen demanded that the warring partners divorce. After heated negotiations, in July 1996 Diana agreed to forfeit the title Her Royal Highness (HRH) in return for US$22.5 million and US$600,000 per year. The forfeiture of the HRH appellation means that she is formally obligated to curtsy to her royal sons, though *The Times* reports that in response to her question "Would you mind if I were not HRH?" her youngest, Prince Harry, has told her "I don't care what you are called, you're **mummy.**" Diana also applied to Major to be a roving **"ambassadress of love,"** who would travel the world providing succor. Buckingham Palace rejected the idea.

Recent peccadillos aside, the Queen is still the Queen, and unless your first name is Duke, getting to see her is not easy. Her public engagements (several hundred each year) are published daily in the Court Circular in *The Times, The Daily Telegraph,* and *The Independent.* You can see the Queen at one of the numerous annual pageants she attends, such as the **Trooping the Colour** ceremony during the middle of June. This is a celebration of the Queens "official birthday"—never mind that she was born on April 21. In October, at the **State Opening of Parliament,** another occasion not without a fancy robe or two, the Queen gives a speech prepared by the government that outlines proposed legislation for the new session. The Queen rides to and from Parliament via the Mall and Whitehall in the state coach. A large division of the Royal Family usually turns out for the **Remembrance Day Service** (Sun. nearest Nov. 11), held at the Cenotaph in Whitehall to honor the war dead. A more cheerful occasion is the distribution of Maundy Money, on **Maundy Thursday** (the day before Good Friday). In a demonstration of royal humility, the Queen distributes a special silver coin to randomly selected pensioners, the number of which equals her age (71 in 1997). Originally, this ancient ritual (which dates back to around the 12th century) involved the monarch washing the feet of the poor, but the Plague put an end to that.

■ Architecture

In the aftermath of the Great Fire of 1666, as most of London lay an ashy wasteland, ambitious young architect Christopher Wren presented his blueprints for a new city to Charles II. Wren envisioned broad avenues and spacious plazas: London would no longer be a medieval hodgepodge of streets and buildings. But the pragmatic king was well aware that the plan, which took no account of existing property lines, would incense local landowners. So he vetoed Wren's design and the city was rebuilt in the same piecemeal way that it had risen.

The Anglos and the Saxons began the confusing story of English building with a style that combined the severe Roman and simple Celtic approaches. They built small monasteries and churches with several towers and wooden or stone roofs. The Normans brought the first distinctive national style in the 11th century: churches with endlessly long naves and rectangular east wings. These Romanesque elements survive in the 12th-century church of St. Bartholomew the Great.

In the Middle Ages, Gothic architecture became the design of choice for clerical buildings. Ribbed vaulting, pointed arches, and flying buttresses became immensely popular. The predecessor to today's St. Paul's Cathedral was one of Europe's largest Gothic churches. In the early 17th century, Court Architect **Inigo Jones** introduced Italian stylings: English manor houses began to be laid out symmetrically and surrounded by manicured gardens. Inspired by Italian Andrea Palladio, Jones spread the Palladian style throughout England. He coated James I's Banqueting House in Whitehall with gleaming Portland stone, constructed the airy Covent Garden Piazza, and built the first classical church in England for Charles I's Spanish fiancée.

The **Great Fire of 1666** provided the next opportunity for large-scale construction. **Christopher Wren** built 51 new churches, flooding the skyline with a sea of spires leading up to St. Paul's, his masterwork. St. Paul's was Wren's final church—he used the earlier ones as experiments to work out anticipated design problems.

The lyrical styles begun by Jones and Wren continued to shape London's architecture for much of the next century. Other designers, like **James Gibbs, Colin Campbell,** and **William Kent,** refined their styles and integrated them with the new baroque trend sweeping the Continent. The tower and steeple plan of St. Martin's-in-the-Fields proved a popular model for Gibbs' colonial churches, particularly in the United States. Kent, a painter, designed the walls and pseudo-Pompeiian ceiling of

Kensington Palace, and the interior of the Palladian Chiswick House. Campbell built early mansions such as Burlington House, now home of the Royal Academy.

By the late 1700s, builders yearned for something more exotic. Tired of London's stout brick face, **John Nash** covered the town with fanciful terraces and stucco façades. He wanted to create a massive garden city for the nobility. His plan was never realized in full, but the romantic pediments, triumphal arches, and sweeping pavilions of Regent's Park provide a glimpse of his rich vision. The discovery of Pompeii and Lord Elgin's pilfering of the Parthenon inspired the next trend—mock Greek and Roman ruins. Architects **Robert Adam, William Chambers,** and **John Soane** went on columnic rampages, grafting Doric, Tuscan, Ionic, and Corinthian pillars onto a variety of unlikely structures.

This enthusiasm for Neoclassicism faded under the reign of Victoria. Victoria's dark propriety and the Romantics' flair combined to usher in a spirited Gothic revival: pubs, villas, and banks were oddly festooned with Italian Gothic pillars. The design contest for the new House of Commons in 1894 required that the style be Gothic or Elizabethan. An immense Gothic cathedral soon rose at St. Pancras Station. While many architects insisted on bringing back Gothic, others ushered in Italian Renaissance, French, and Dutch forms; still others latched onto Tudor, and some lonely pioneers discovered new building possibilities in iron and glass. **Sir Joseph Paxton** created the splendid Crystal Palace for the exposition of 1851. The inspirational (1600 ft. long) building burned down at the time of Edward's abdication.

After WWII, the face of building in London, perhaps exhausted by the demolition of the war, took a harsher turn. The 1951 Festival of Britain, a centennial celebration of the Great Exhibition and postwar "Tonic to the Nation," created such buildings as the Royal Festival Hall. The hopes of postwar utopian planning, and their varying degrees of fulfillment, are embodied in the vast and slightly interplanetary Barbican Centre. Then came the early 60s and a building boom in which the post-Blitz face of the City was established. Hulking monoliths now neighbor Victorian door pillars and spiraling chimneys. The medley of building continues: Modern, Neoclassical, and/or postmodern. Lloyd's of London's 1986 tower is remarkable for being decked on the *outside* with elevators and ducts. Contemporary London continues to be the city planner's nightmare—the frenetic development south of the Thames and in the Docklands will surely usher in new architectural styles.

■ Art

Religious art went out of vogue with the Reformation in the 16th century, distinguishing Britain from its still-Roman Catholic counterparts. An early republican revolution (Cromwell's in 1649) led to a more diverse group of British patrons—gentry and wealthy members of the bourgeoisie began commissioning artworks.

Despite these distinguishing marks, many of England's early stars were imported. In the 16th century, the German **Hans Holbein** worked in London as the official painter to the king. A century later, **Sir Anthony Van Dyck** played the same role, painting dramatic royal portraits of Charles I. Partly in reaction to these foreign artists who had helped shape the conventions of British painting, 18th-century painter and Londoner **William Hogarth** prided himself on his distinctly English sense of style. *A Harlot's Progress* and *A Rake's Progress,* two series of morally instructive engravings, established his reputation and broadened the audience for British art.

From the mid-18th to mid-19th century, portraiture continued to thrive under the influence of painters **Thomas Gainsborough** and **Joshua Reynolds.** The **Royal Academy** which Reynolds founded currently holds summer Academy exhibits in Piccadilly. The mid-18th century also saw the emergence of British landscape painting. London was home to **J.M.W. Turner,** who painted mythic, light-filled landscapes in both watercolor and oil paint. He is famed for the visual records of his travels, including a set of engravings entitled *Picturesque Views of England and Wales.* The Tate has a magnificent collection of Turner's work (see Tate Gallery, p. 218). In the same period, **John Constable** lovingly painted the smaller details of English landscape.

This period was followed by an eclectic visual feast ranging from **William Blake's** fantastical paintings and illustrations, to the jewel-like paintings of the Pre-Raphaelites **John Everett Millais, Dante Gabriel Rossetti,** and **Edward Burne-Jones,** to the Pop Art and later 'Op' Art of the 60s. Disturbing meat-filled portraits by **Francis Bacon** and the oddly unrealistic "realism" of **Lucien Freud** transformed Britain's tradition of portraiture in the last half of this century.

London is filled with art forms other than painting and engraving, including sculpture, photography, and constantly reinvented mixtures of media. Britain's sculptural tradition can be traced in London's architectural details, stone and brass tomb carvings, and abundant public monuments. Beginning in the 1930s, **Henry Moore's** rounded and abstracted human forms and **Barbara Hepworth's** carved elemental materials catapulted modern British sculpture into international fame. During the same period, **Bill Brandt's** photographs (collected in *The English at Home* and *Night in London*) described London in visual essays. British photography since then has ranged from the intensely personal work of radical feminist **Jo Spence** to **Nick Wapplington's** photos of working-class interiors and the families that live in them.

■ Literary London

Geoffrey Chaucer, the son of a well-to-do London wine merchant, initiated the tradition that British tales commence in London. The pilgrims in *Canterbury Tales* set off from the Tabard Inn in Southwark on the South Bank. Since then London has cast a long shadow over the British literary imagination.

Rowdy dramatist **Ben Jonson** held sway in the English court scene of the early 17th century. He planned balls for Queen Elizabeth and her friends, creating original music, choreography, and special effects. Meanwhile, **William Shakespeare** (and his colleagues **Marlowe, Jonson,** and **Webster**) catered to the 'jes folks in the circular theatres across the Thames, the heart of the red-light district.

Many writers found London a degenerate, morally disturbing place, though they could not resist incorporating it into their art. **John Donne,** who became Dean of St. Paul's in 1621, wrote poetry while meting out advice to his parishioners. He set his first and fourth satires in London, drawing attention to urban evils. As a market for books developed in the 1700s, literary society began to resemble today's marketplace of trends: it welcomed **Alexander Pope** as a prodigy at the age of 17, but his disillusionment came quickly. In London, "nothing is sacred…but villainy," he wrote in the epilogue to his *Satires*. Pope drank away his gloom with professional genius and renowned conversationalist **Samuel Johnson** in the Cheshire Cheese pub, while **James Boswell** scurried around collecting crumbs for his magnificent biography, the *Life of Johnson*. **Daniel Defoe, Henry Fielding,** and **Samuel Richardson** also explored themes of urban injustice, using journalism, satire, and sermons as their tools.

Poets of the Age of Reason fantasized about a city different from the crime-filled one that they unhap'ly inhabited, but few moved away. London remained a haven for publishing and literary cliques wrestling with ideas of social justice. In the early 18th century, **Joseph Addison** and **Richard Steele** attacked urban ills in a new way: the *Tatler* and *Spectator* delivered moral and political essays to subscribers.

As a gray haze settled over the city's houses and the beggars on the streets swelled into what **Marx** referred to as the capitalists' "reserve army," the wretchedness attracted the empathy and creative interest of a number of writers, most famously **Charles Dickens.** Dickens—whose name has elicited titters from generations of schoolboys—described his characters wendings through the nineteenth century's filthy back allies, poorhouses, and orphanages. These fictional characters served to warn readers that too much time in industrial London does wretched things to one's nerves. The Romantic poets had the same idea. They abandoned the classical idealization of the urban and left the city. **John Keats** and **William Wordsworth** lived in Hampstead and Westminster, both distant suburbs at the time. **Percy B. Shelley** wrote, "Hell is a city much like London," and **William Blake** doubted the existence of a new Jerusalem "amongst these dark Satanic mills."

By the close of the 19th century, when reforms began to mitigate the effects of industrialization, some writers turned to purely aesthetic issues. In the 1890s, **W.B. Yeats** joined the London Rhymers' Club. The relentlessly quotable **Oscar Wilde** proclaimed that art could only be useless. Fellow dramatist and Fabian socialist **George Bernard Shaw** allowed his politics to find expression in his vision of art—his plays were more didactic that decadent.

In 1921, Missouri-born T.S. Eliot turned London into an angst-ridden modern *Waste Land,* and "Unreal City." The poem follows a crowd over London Bridge into the City, wondering how many of them the war has "undone." Both Eliot and Yeats did their time in the high modernist Bloomsbury group. This erudite crowd included **Virginia Woolf, Vanessa and Clive Bell,** the multitalented **John Maynard Keynes, Lytton Strachey,** and **E.M. Forster** (recently re-popularized by Merchant-Ivory). Meanwhile, a concerned **George Orwell** was meeting street people and telling yarns of urban poverty in his ultimate tale of budget travel, *Down and Out in Paris and London.* Orwell put forth his disturbing and compelling critique of the direction of modern life in *1984;* much of this book is clearly a reflection of a Orwell's deep misgivings about city life.

Aside from Orwell's haunting account and **Anthony Burgess**'s description of the "ultra-violence" of future life in *A Clockwork Orange,* much of London's modern literature is witty and bright. **P.G. Wodehouse** wrote a clever and light novel for each of the 70-some years of his long life. **Kingsley Amis** and his now famous son **Martin** write well-loved satirical novels. London has become a publishing center for writers in English from the former colonies and other lands, such as **Salman Rushdie, V.S. Naipaul,** and **Timothy Mo.** While questions about London's future European and world status in the emerging order may be open for discussion, a survey of recent titles—Amis's *London Fields,* **V.S. Pritchett's** *London Perceived,* **Doris Lessing's** *London Observed*—tells us that it retains a distinguished place in the world's intellectual and literary life. Writers keep coming to this irresistible town—as a publishing center and an inexhaustible topic, they can't seem to avoid it.

Bad-Mouthed Bard

The 16th century provided England with perhaps its most famous literary figure. Those who equate Shakespeare with an English-class avalanche of whithers and wherefores would do well to know that the Bard held perhaps the filthiest feather ever to scrawl the English language. We provide a handy table for you to adapt his words to curses and putdowns you may wish to use in your everyday travels:

My, they're horny!	*they're* "as prime as goats, as hot as monkeys, as salt as wolves in pride."
to have sex	*to make the* "beast with two backs"
This guy's a fat pain-in-the-ass!	"This sanguine coward, this bed-presser, this horse-back-breaker, this huge hill of flesh."
You suck!	"The devil damn thee black, thou cream-faced loon."
A guy in a bar wants to fight you. You say...	"Brass, cur! Thou damned and luxurious mountain goat, thou offer'st me brass?"

■ The Media

In a culture not yet completely addicted to the telly, the influence of papers is enormous. **The Sun,** a daily Rupert Murdoch-owned tabloid better known for its **page-three pinup** than for its reporting, was widely credited with delivering victory to Margaret Thatcher in her re-election campaign (no, she did not pose). Ambitious English journalists aspire to finish their apprenticeships in the provinces and join "the Fleet Street hacks" (who now inhabit the old Wapping docks). With the exception of the Manchester-born **Guardian,** national papers originate from London.

The Financial Times, printed on pink paper, does more elegantly for the City what the *Wall Street Journal* does for Manhattan. **The Times,** for centuries a model of thoughtful discretion and mild infallibility, has gone downmarket and does a fair impression of *USA Today.* The **Daily Telegraph** (dubbed "Torygraph") is fairly conservative and old-fashioned, but rigorously fair. The **Independent** lives up to its name. Of the screaming tabloids, **The Daily Mail, The Daily Express,** and **The Evening Standard** (the only evening paper) make serious attempts at popular journalism, while **News of the World,** the **Star,** the **Daily Mirror,** and **Today** are as shrill and lewd as *The Sun.* The best international news shows up in *The Guardian, The Financial Times,* and *The Independent.*

On Sundays, *The Sunday Times, The Sunday Telegraph, Independent on Sunday,* and the highly polished *Observer* publish multi-section papers with glossy magazines, detailed arts, sports, and news coverage, together with a few more "soft bits" than their daily counterparts. Sunday papers, although they share close association with their sister dailies, are actually distinctly styled, separate newspapers.

The immensely popular **Viz** parodies modern prejudices and hypocrisies with unashamedly outrageous comic-strips. World affairs are covered with a surreptitious wit by **The Economist. The New Statesman** on the left and **The Spectator** on the right cover politics and the arts with verve and sense. England also boasts some of the best music rags in the world: **Melody Maker** and **New Musical Express** trace the latest trends with often hilarious wit (check these for concert news), **Q** covers a broader spectrum in excellent detail, while **Grammophone** focuses on classical music. The indispensable London journal **Time Out** is the most comprehensive calendar/guide to the city and features fascinating pieces on British life and culture.

The Shipping Forecast

The dominance of the BBC in all matters relating to broadcasting is no longer what it was, but both television and the radio remain shared national experiences. Some of the fiercest resistance against the wholescale privatization of the nations airwaves has come from traditionalists, such as the late Dennis Potter, who bemoaned the eradication of a common cultural patrimony. Given such fierce protection of the BBC, especially among the middle classes of Britain, it came as no surprise that the BBC's decision to move *The Shipping Forecast* from its traditional slot at 12:33am to 12:45am led to outrage in the leafy suburbs of Hampstead and the market towns of Tunsbridge Wells. "The BBC has totally lost sight of the concept of public service broadcasting," thundered the head of the self-appointed Radio 4 Watch.

To the outsider the debate will seem utterly baffling since the Shipping Forecast consists of a five-minute broadcast of weather warnings and the wind conditions at a series of navigation points around the British Isles. The announcer recites: "Viking, North Utsire, South Utsire," through to "Shannon, Rockall, Malin" and the aptly named "Channel Light Vessel Automatic" and supplies the appropriate weather warning. The whole thing culminates in "Sailing by" a suitably soporific piece of music—and that's it. Yet thousands have fallen to sleep with this nightly recital and they won't give up their favorite lullaby without making some very un-English fuss.

The **BBC** established its reputation for fairness and wit with its radio services: BBC1 has ceded responsibilities of news coverage to its cousin BBC4, but continues to feature rock and roll institution John Peel. BBC2 has easy listening and light talk shows; BBC3 broadcasts classical music (undoubtedly the finest station of its kind anywhere). AM is called Medium Wave (MW) in England. Each town and region in England is equipped with a variety of local commercial broadcasting services.

TV-owners in England have to pay a tax; this supports the advertisement-free activities of BBC TV. Close association with the government has not hampered innovation. Home of *Monty Python's Flying Circus,* BBC TV broadcasts on two national channels. BBC1 carries news at 1, 6, and 9pm as well as various Britcoms. Sheep-dog trials are telecast on BBC2, along with cultural programs. ITV, Britain's established commercial network, carries much comedy along with its own McNews. Channel 4, the newest channel, has highly respected arts programming and a fine news broadcast at 7pm on weeknights—Salman Rushdie once worked for it. At press time there were rumblings of the BBC picking up *The Simpsons,* currently available only on Sky TV, Britain's satellite network. Parliament was introduced to television in late 1989: try to catch a session of **Question Time,** the regular, refreshingly hostile, parliamentary interrogation of the prime minister.

▓ Music

England was long called "a land without music," a tag which is not entirely deserved. Morley, Weelkes, and Wilbye revamped madrigals; John Dowland wrote lachrymose works for lute. **Henry Purcell** was England's best-known composer for centuries; his opera *Dido and Aeneas* is still performed. London welcomed Handel, Mozart (who wrote his first symphony in Chelsea), and Haydn (whose last cluster of symphonies was named "London"). **Gilbert and Sullivan**'s operettas are loved for their puns, social satire, farce, and pomp. Though the pair allegedly hated each other, they collaborated on such gems as *The Mikado, H.M.S. Pinafore,* and *The Pirates of Penzance.* Serious music began a "second renaissance" under **Edward** *(Enigma Variations)* **Elgar,** whose bombast is outweighed by moments of quiet eloquence. Delius redid impressionism, while **Gustav** *(The Planets)* **Holst** adapted neoclassical methods and folk materials to his Romantic moods.

William Walton and **Ralph Vaughan Williams** brought musical modernism to England in the 20th century. **Benjamin Britten**'s *Peter Grimes* turned a broader audience on to opera, and his *Young Person's Guide to the Orchestra* continues to introduce classical music to young and old alike. **Michael Tippett** wrote operas, four symphonies, and the oratorio *A Child of Our Time,* for which he asked T.S. Eliot to write the words; Eliot told Tippett he could do better himself.

After WWII, imported American rock and jazz led to the first wave of "British Invasion" bands. **The Beatles** spun out the songs your mother should know and seemed at the front of every musical and cultural trend; the **Rolling Stones** became their nastier, harder-edged answer, while the **Kinks** voiced horror at the American vulgarity that seemed, to them, to have crushed Little England. **The Who** began as Kinks-like popsters, then expanded into "rock operas" like *Tommy* (lately a Broadway hit) and the better *Quadrophenia,* which chronicled the famous fights in Brighton between "rockers" (who liked leather jackets and America) and "mods" (who liked scooters, speed, androgyny, and the Who).

Psychedelic drugs and high hopes produced a flurry of great tunes by bands like the short-lived **Creation** from '66 to '68. White British adapters of African-American blues—most famously the **Yardbirds**—spawned guitar heroes such as **Eric Clapton** (Cream) and **Jimmy Page** (Led Zeppelin), who dominated mass markets in the early 70s. The same period's **"art-rock"** (Yes, Pink Floyd, Roxy Music) was at times exciting, at times dreadful. Working-class "skinheads" adopted the sounds and aggression of Jamaican reggae and ska; later skins would split into socialist, anti-racist and right-wing, neo-fascist factions, both propelled by stripped-down rock called "oi." While **David Bowie** flitted through personae, "pub rock" groups tried to return rock to the people—and in London, a King's Road entrepreneur organized the **Sex Pistols** to publicize his boutique, "Sex."

With "Sex"'s clothes and Johnny Rotten's snarl, the Pistols changed music and culture forever. **The Clash** made their punk explicitly anti-Thatcherite and political; the all-female **Slits** mixed theirs with reggae. "Do it yourself" was the order of the day: untouched, and often untouchable, by the big corporations, the second wave of punks started their own clubs, record labels, distributors, and studios, creating the International Pop Underground that persists to this day.

Industrial unemployment gave Northerners the time to form bands and a harsh landscape to inspire them. The fans who sent it up the charts were surprised to learn that the **Buzzcocks**' Pete Shelley wrote "Ever Fallen in Love?" about a man. **Joy Division** and **Factory Records** made Manchester echo with gloomily poetic rock and graphic design. Leeds's **Mekons** stayed true to punk's roots, and **Gang of Four**'s *Entertainment!* chewed up funk and reggae to spit out a profound Marxist critique of capital, work, and sex. Birmingham's **Au Pairs** asked feminist questions over a hooky backbeat, and that grim city's leftist ska bands, like the Selecter and the Specials, took their "two-tone" style to the people. **Elvis Costello, Squeeze,** and **the Jam** found that punk and ska had cleared the ground for smart pop, which stayed persistently and bitingly English even as it took over world charts.

Melancholy stylishness like **Felt** and **Eyeless in Gaza** passed sadly unnoticed through the 80s, but the **Smiths** of Manchester shook teens everywhere. Bristol's Subway Records sent **Flatmates, Razorcuts,** and **Rosehips** spinning winsomely across the land. **King of the Slums** bowed and scraped before the electric violin; sweetly-loud **My Bloody Valentine** were much-copied in the early 90s. Oxford's **Tallulah Gosh** idealized childhood in million-mile-an-hour pop; regrouped as **Heavenly,** they, and Bristol-based **Sarah Records,** inspired self-proclaimed "boys" and "girls" to cast aside volume and swagger for last-chance tries at innocence.

Even current dance trends spring from punk: the **Human League** and **Cabaret Voltaire** (whose native Sheffield had no clubs to play in) learned to play synths to make assaultive noise before they used them to shake up clubgoers. **Yaz, Depeche Mode,** and **New Order** soon joined them. A decade later, unemployed kids and easy access to the drug **Ecstasy** created rave culture's all-night, all-day, sweaty, anaesthetic gatherings and the faceless electronic music that accompanied them.

National trends are made and unmade by London-based music weeklies. An unknown band can make "single of the week," graduate to the papers' covers, sell 600,000 CDs, and then vanish. "Indie" bands like **Pulp** continue to wrestle with the same credibility problems as their American "alternative" counterparts. **Oasis,** vanguard of the more straight-ahead, shiny "Britpop" sound, have captured the sound and hype (minus the creativity) of the Beatles to win the hearts of tabloids and 14-year-olds alike.

Hip-hop's burgeoning popularity in Europe is reflected by British trip-hop bands like **Portishead** and **Tricky.** Despite this, London's sole momentous contribution to rap remains the fact that it served as the birthplace and childhood home of Ricky Walters, aka **Slick Rick (the Ruler).**

Essentials

The title above says it all. At best, the information below will get you to and from London cheaply and with minimum fuss; at worst, it will keep you out of prison and the hospital. Either way, it's fairly important. The chapter is divided into three self-explanatory sections: **Planning Your Trip, Getting There,** and **Once There.**

PLANNING YOUR TRIP

▓ When To Go

Traveling during the off-season will save you money. Airfares drop and domestic travel becomes less congested. You'll have more elbow room and will benefit from lower rates and prices. Hotel owners generally consider November to March the off-season, although business may be slow enough in October, April, and May for you to bargain for a discount. For sights, October to April is the off-season and opening hours are shortened. For climate information see p. 292.

▓ At-Home Resources

GOVERNMENT INFORMATION OFFICES

British Tourist Authority (BTA), 551 Fifth Ave, Suite 701, New York, NY 10176-0799 (tel. (800) 462 2748 or (212) 986 2200; http://www.budgetbritain.com). Lines open Mon.-Fri. 9am-7pm. Other U.S. branches in **Chicago, Atlanta,** and **Los Angeles.** In **Canada,** 111 Avenue Rd., Toronto, Ont. M5R 3J8 (tel. (416) 925 6326). Lines open Mon.-Fri. 9am-5pm. Publishes helpful student guides including *UK: The Guide,* and *Britain on a Budget.* Britrail's **British Travel Bookshop** (tel. (800) 677 8585), in BTA's New York office, sells guides and travel passes.

British Consulates: In the **U.S.,** British Embassy, 3100 Massachusetts Ave. NW, Washington, D.C. 20008 (tel. (202) 462-1340). Consulates at 845 Third Ave., New York, NY 10022 (tel. (212) 745-0200); Marquis One Tower #2700, 245 Peachtree Center Ave., Atlanta, GA 30303 (tel. (404) 524-5856); 33 North Dearborn St., Chicago, IL 60602 (tel. (312) 346-1810); First Interstate Bank Plaza #1990, 1000 Louisiana, Houston, TX 77002 (tel. (713) 659-6270); and 11766 Wilshire Blvd. #400, Los Angeles, CA 90025-6536 (tel. (310) 477-3322). Call the Embassy for additional consulate addresses. In **Canada,** British High Commission, 80 Elgin St., Ottawa, Ont. K1P 5K7 (tel. (613) 237-1530). In **Australia,** British High Commission, Commonwealth Ave., Yarralumla, Canberra, ACT 2600 (tel. (616) 270-6666). In **New Zealand,** British High Commission, 44 Hill St., Wellington 1 (tel. (644) 472-6049).

TRAVEL ORGANIZATIONS

American Automobile Association (AAA) Travel Related Services, 1000 AAA Dr. (mail stop 100), Heathrow, FL 32746-5080 (407-444-8411). Provides road maps and travel guides free to members. Offers emergency road services, travel services, and auto insurance (nonmembers pay a small fee). For emergency road services, call 800-222-4357; to become a member, call 800-926-4222 for the nearest office.

Council on International Educational Exchange (Council), 205 East 42nd St., New York, NY 10017-5706 (tel. (888) COUNCIL (268-6245); fax (212) 822-2699; e-mail info@ciee.org; http://www.ciee.org). A private, nonprofit organization, Council administers work, volunteer, and academic programs around the world. They also offer identity cards, including the ISIC and the GO25, and a range of publications, including the magazine *Student Travels* (free). Call or write for more information.

Federation of International Youth Travel Organizations (FIYTO), Bredgade 25H, DK-1260 Copenhagen K, Denmark (tel. (45) 33 33 96 00; fax 33 93 96 76; e-mail mailbox@fiyto.org), is an international organization promoting educational, cultural and social travel by young folk. FIYTO sponsors the GO25 Card.

International Student Travel Confederation, Herengracht 479, 1017 BS Amsterdam, The Netherlands (tel. (31) 20 421 2800; fax 20 421 2810; http://www.istc.org; e-mail istcinfo@istc.org). The ISTC is a nonprofit confederation of student travel organizations dedicated to developing, promoting, and facilitating travel by young people and students. International Student Rail Association (ISRA), Student Air Travel Association (SATA), ISIS Travel Insurance, and the International Association for Educational and Work Exchange Programs (IAEWEP) are members.

USEFUL PUBLICATIONS

In addition to this stylin' volume, Let's Go offers travelers the slim, sleek fold-out maps and textual highlights of *Let's Go Map Guide: London.* The following businesses and organizations also specialize in keeping travelers informed:

Blue Guides: Published in Britain by A&C Black Limited, 35 Bedford Row, London WC1R 4JH (tel. (0171) 242 0946; fax 831 8478); in the U.S. by W.W. Norton & Co. Inc., 500 Fifth Ave., New York, NY 10110; and in Canada by Penguin Books Canada Ltd., 2801 John St., Markham, Ontario L3R 1B4. Blue Guides provide excellent historical and cultural information as well as sightseeing routes, maps, tourist information, and pricey hotel listings. Titles include *England, Ireland, London, Literary Britain & Ireland,* and *Scotland.*

Bon Voyage!, 2069 W. Bullard Ave., Fresno, CA 93711-1200 (tel. (800) 995-9716, from abroad (209) 447-8441; e-mail 70754.3511@compuserve.com). Annual mail order catalog offers products for the luxury traveler and the diehard trekker. Books, travel accessories, luggage, electrical converters, maps, videos, and more. All merchandise may be returned for exchange or refund within 30 days of purchase and lower advertised prices will be matched and merchandise shipped free.

The College Connection, Inc., 1295 Prospect St. Suite A, La Jolla, CA 92037 (tel. (619) 551-9770; fax 551-9987; e-mail eurailnow@aol.com; http://www.eurail-pass.com). Publishes *The Passport,* a booklet listing hints about every aspect of traveling and studying abroad. This booklet is free to *Let's Go* readers; send your request by email or fax only. Also sells railpasses and discount flights.

Forsyth Travel Library, P.O. Box 480800, Kansas City, MO 64148 (tel. 800-367-7984; fax 816-942-6969; http://www.forsyth.com). A mail-order service stocking a wide range of city, area, and country maps, as well as guides to rail and ferry travel in Europe. Sells rail tickets and passes and offers reservation services. Sells the *Thomas Cook European Timetable* for trains, a complete guide to European train departures and arrivals (US$28 or $39 with full map of European train routes; postage $4.50 for Priority shipping). Free catalogue available.

Superintendent of Documents, U.S. Government Printing Office, P.O. Box 371954, Pittsburg, PA 15250-7954 (tel. (202) 512-1800; fax 512-2250). Open Mon.-Fri. 7:30am-4:30pm. Publishes *Your Trip Abroad* (US$1.25) and *Health Information for International Travel* (US$14). Postage is included in price.

Wide World Books and Maps, 1911 N. 45th St., Seattle, WA 98103 (tel. (206) 634-3453; fax 634-0558; email travelbk@mail.nwlink.com; http://nwlink.com/travelbk). A good selection of travel guides and hard-to-find maps.

COMPUTER RESOURCES

There is a vast amount of information available through the international computer network known as the **Internet.** Commercial providers such as America Online, CompuServe, and Prodigy offer many travel-related services to their subscribers. Among the most popular and accessible Internet resources are the **Usenet Newsgroups,** including: **soc.culture.british, rec.travel.europe,** and **rec.travel.air.** The easiest way to find information on the Internet is via the **WorldWide Web.** You can accomplish a search of what is available by pointing your browser to a service such as http://www.yahoo.com/. **The U.S. State Department Travel Warnings and Consular**

Information Sheets, for example, are available at http://www.stolaf.edu/network/travel-advisories.htlm. **City.Net** has an eclectic collection of travel related information available at http://www.city.net.

E-mail is probably the most cost-effective means of maintaining a long-distance relationship—those who will be absent for longer might want to inquire into getting access. Most universities provide students with free accounts and commercial providers such as Delphi also operate services in the U.K.

■ Paperwork

When you travel, always carry two or more forms of ID on your person, including at least one photo ID. Many establishments, especially banks, require several IDs before cashing traveler's checks. It is useful to carry extra passport-size photos to affix to the various IDs you will eventually acquire.

PASSPORTS

Before you leave, photocopy the page of your passport that contains your photograph and identifying information, especially your passport number. Carry this photocopy and, for further peace of mind, an expired passport or copy of your birth certificate, in a safe place apart from your passport and leave another copy at home. If you lose your passport, tell the local police and consulate immediately.

United States citizens may apply for a passport, valid for 10 years (five years if under 18) at any federal or state **courthouse** or **post office** authorized to accept passport applications, or at a **U.S. Passport Agency.** Refer to the "U.S. Government, State Department" section of the telephone directory, or call your local post office for addresses. Passports cost US$65 (under 18 US$40). You can **renew** your passport by mail or in person for US$55. Processing takes two to four weeks, but agencies offer a **rush service** (surcharge US$30) if you have proof that you're departing within 10 working days (e.g., an airplane ticket or itinerary). Abroad, a U.S. embassy or consulate can usually issue a new passport, given proof of citizenship. For more info, contact the U.S. Passport Information's **24-hour recorded message** (tel. (202) 647-0518).

Canadian citizens can pick up application forms in English and French at all **passport offices, post offices,** and most **travel agencies.** Citizens may apply in person at any one of 28 regional Passport Offices; a travel agent can direct you to the nearest location. Canadian citizens residing abroad should contact a Canadian embassy or consulate. The CDN$60 fee can also be paid in cash, money order, or certified check to Passport Office, Ottawa, Ont. K1A OG3. Processing takes approximately five business days for in-person applications and three weeks for mailed ones. Children under 16 may be included on a parent's passport, though some countries require children to carry their own passports. A passport is valid for five years and is not renewable. If a passport is lost abroad, Canadians must be able to prove citizenship with another document. For additional info, call (800) 567-6868 (24hr.; from Canada only) or call the Ottawa Passport Office at (819) 994-3500. In Metro Toronto, call (416) 973-3251. Montréalers should dial (514) 283-2152. Refer to the booklet *Bon Voyage, But...*(free at passport offices) for more help and a list of embassies and consulates abroad.

Australian citizens must apply for a passport in person at a post office, a passport office, or an Australian diplomatic mission overseas. An appointment may be necessary. Passport offices are located in Adelaide, Brisbane, Canberra City, Darwin, Hobart, Melbourne, Newcastle, Perth, and Sydney. A parent may file an application for a child who is under 18 and unmarried. Application fees are adjusted frequently. For more info, call toll-free (in Australia) 13 12 32.

New Zealand citizens can obtain application forms for passports at home from travel agents and Department of Internal Affairs Link Centres and overseas from New Zealand embassies, high commissions, and consulates. Completed applications may be lodged at Link Centres and at overseas posts, or forwarded to the Passport Office, PO Box 10-526, Wellington, New Zealand. Processing time is 10 working days from receipt of a correctly completed application. An urgent passport service is also available. The application fee for an adult passport is NZ$80 in New Zealand and NZ$130 overseas for applications lodged under the standard service.

South African citizens can apply for a passport at any Home Affairs Office. South African passports require a $12 fee and remain valid for 10 years. For further information, contact the nearest Department of Home Affairs Office.

ENTRANCE REQUIREMENTS

You must have a valid **passport** to enter Britain and to re-enter your country. Citizens of the U.S., Canada, Australia, and New Zealand may enter the U.K. without a visa. The standard **period of admission** is six months in Britain. To stay longer, you must show evidence that you can support yourself for an extended period of time and a medical examination is often required. Admission as a visitor from a non-EC nation does not include the right to work, which is authorized only by the possession of a work permit (see Alternatives to Tourism, p. 37). Entering Britain to study does not require a special visa, but immigration will want to see proof of acceptance by a British school, proof that the course of study will take up most of your time in the country, and proof that you can support yourself. Possession of a roundtrip airline ticket (proof that you'll eventually leave) is also advisable.

CUSTOMS

British Citizens or visitors arriving in the U.K. from outside the EU must declare any goods in excess of the following allowances: 200 cigarettes, 100 cigarillos, 50 cigars, or 250g tobacco; still table wine (2L); strong liqueurs over 22% volume (1L), or fortified or sparkling wine, other liqueurs (2L); perfume (60 cc/mL); toilet water (250 cc/mL); and UK£136 worth of all other goods including gifts and souvenirs. You must be over 17 to import liquor or tobacco. These allowances also apply to duty-free purchases within the EU, except for the last category, other goods, which then has an allowance of UK£71. Goods on which duty and tax are paid and are meant for personal use (regulated according to set guide levels) within the EU do not require any further customs duty. For information, contact Her Majesty's Customs and Excise, Custom House, Nettleton Road, Heathrow Airport, Hounslow, Middlesex TW6 2LA (tel. (0181) 910 3744; fax 910 3765).

Returning Home

Canadian citizens who remain abroad for at least one week may bring back up to CDN$500 worth of goods duty-free once per calendar year. Canadian citizens or residents who travel for a period between 48 hours and six days can bring back up to CDN$200 with the exception of tobacco and alcohol. You are permitted to ship goods except tobacco and alcohol home under this exemption as long as you declare them when you arrive. Citizens of legal age (which varies by province) may import in-person up to 200 cigarettes, 50 cigars, 400g loose tobacco, 400 tobacco sticks, 1.14L wine or alcohol, and 24 355mL cans/bottles of beer; the value of these products is included in the CDN$500. For more information, write to Canadian Customs, 2265 St. Laurent Blvd., Ottawa, Ontario K1G 4K3 (tel. (613) 993-0534).

Australian citizens may import AUS$400 (under 18 AUS$200) of goods, 1.125L of alcohol, and 250 cigarettes or 250g tobacco duty-free. You must be over 18 to import smokes or booze. There is no limit to the amount of Australian and/or foreign cash that may be brought into or taken out of the country. However, amounts of AUS$5000 or more, or the equivalent in foreign currency, must be reported. All foodstuffs and animal products must be declared on arrival. For information, contact the Regional Director, Australian Customs Service, GPO Box 8, Sydney NSW 2001 (tel. (02) 213-2000; fax 213-4000).

New Zealand citizens may bring home up to NZ$700 worth of goods duty-free if they are intended for personal use or are unsolicited gifts. The concession is 200 cigarettes (1 carton), 250g tobacco, 50 cigars, or a combination of all three not to

exceed 250g. You may also bring in 4.5L of beer or wine and 1.125L of liquor. Only travelers over 17 may bring tobacco or alcoholic beverages into the country. For more information, consult the *New Zealand Customs Guide for Travelers,* available from customs offices, or contact New Zealand Customs, 50 Anzac Ave., Box 29, Auckland (tel. (09) 377 35 20; fax 309 29 78).

South African citizens may import duty-free: 400 cigarettes, 50 cigars, 250g tobacco, 2L wine, 1L of spirits, 250mL toilet water, and 50mL perfume; and other items up to a value of SAR500. Amounts exceeding this limit but not SAR10,000 are dutiable at 20%. Certain items such as golf clubs and firearms require a duty higher than the standard 20%. Goods acquired abroad and sent to the Republic as unaccompanied baggage do not qualify for any allowances. You may not export or import South African bank notes in excess of SAR500. Persons who require specific information or advice concerning customs and excise duties can address their inquiries to the Commissioner for Customs and Excise, Private Bag X47, Pretoria 0001. This agency distributes the pamphlet *South African Customs Information* for visitors and residents traveling abroad. South Africans residing in the U.S. should contact the Embassy of South Africa, 3051 Massachusetts Ave., NW, Washington, D.C. 20008 (tel. (202) 232-4400; fax 244-9417) or the South African Home Annex, 3201 New Mexico Ave. #380, NW, Washington D.C. 20016 (tel. (202) 966-1650).

United States citizens returning home may bring US$400 worth of accompanying goods duty-free and must pay a 10% tax on the next US$1000. You must declare all purchases, so have sales slips ready. Goods are considered duty-free if they are for personal or household use (this includes gifts) and cannot include more than 100 cigars, 200 cigarettes (1 carton), and 1L of wine or liquor. You must be over 21 to bring liquor into the U.S. If you mail home personal goods of U.S. origin, you can avoid duty charges by marking the package "American goods returned." For more information, consult the brochure *Know Before You Go,* available from the U.S. Customs Service, Box 7407, Washington, D.C. 20044 (tel. (202) 927-6724).

DRIVING PERMITS AND INSURANCE

If you plan to drive a car while in the U.K., we recommend obtaining an **International Driving Permit (IDP).** Your IDP must be issued in your own country before you depart. U.S. license holders can obtain an International Driving Permit (US$10), valid for one year, at any **American Automobile Association (AAA)** office or by writing to the main office (see p. 15).

Canadian license holders can obtain an IDP (CDN$10) through any **Canadian Automobile Association (CAA)** branch office in Canada or CAA Central Ontario, 60 Commerce Valley Drive East, Thornhill, Ontario L3T 7P9 (tel. (416) 221-4300).

Most credit cards cover standard insurance. If you rent, lease, or borrow a car, you will need a **green card** or **International Insurance Certificate** to prove that you have liability insurance. Obtain it through the car rental agency; most of them include coverage in their prices. If you lease a car, you can obtain a green card from the dealer. Some travel agents offer the card and it may be available at the border. Verify whether your auto insurance applies abroad; even if it does, you will still need a green card to certify this to foreign officials. If you have a collision while in London, the accident will show up on your domestic records if you report it to your company. Rental agencies may require you to purchase theft insurance in some countries that they consider to have a high risk of auto theft.

■ Hostel Membership

For information specific to London hostels, see Accommodations, p. 78. If you have Internet access, check out the **Internet Guide to Hostelling** (http://hostels.com). Reservations for HI hostels may be made via the International Booking Network (IBN), a computerized system which allows you to book to and from HI hostels (more than 300 centers worldwide) months in advance for a nominal fee. Most every

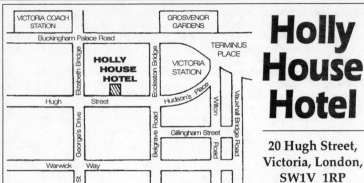

modern country has its own HI branch, all of whose hostels and memberships are part of the greater HI familiy. Credit card bookings may be made over the phone—contact your local hostelling organization for more details. To join the club, contact the organization below nearest you:

Hostelling International-American Youth Hostels (HI-AYH), 733 15th St. NW, Suite 840, Washington, D.C. 20005 (tel. (202) 783-6161; fax 783-6171; http://www.taponline.com/tap/travel/hostels/pages/hosthp.html). HI-AYH maintains 34 offices and over 150 hostels in the U.S. Twelve-month HI memberships: US$25, under 18 US$10, over 54 US$15, family US$35. Membership package includes *Hostelling USA: The Official Guide to Hostels in the United States.*

Hostelling International-Canada (HI-C), 400-205 Catherine St., Ottawa, Ontario K2P 1C3, Canada (tel. (613) 237-7884; fax 237-7868). Canada-wide membership/customer service line (800) 663-5777. Maintains 73 hostels throughout Canada. IBN Booking Centers in Edmonton, Montréal, Ottawa, and Vancouver. Membership fees: 1-yr., CDN$25, under 18 CDN$12, 2-yr., CDN$35, lifetime CDN$175.

Youth Hostels Association of England and Wales (YHA), Trevelyan House, 8 St. Stephen's Hill, St. Albans, Hertfordshire AL1 2DY, England (tel. (01727) 855 215; fax 844 126). Enrollment fees: UK£9.30, under 18 UK£3.20, UK£18.60 for both parents with children under 18 enrolled free, UK£9.30 for one parent with children under 18 enrolled free, UK£125.00 for lifetime membership.

An Óige (Irish Youth Hostel Association), 61 Mountjoy St., Dublin 7 (tel. (01) 830 4555; fax 830 5808; http://www.touchtel.ie). Membership fees: one year IR£7.50, under 18 IR£4, family IR£7.50 per adult with children under 16 free. Prices from IR£4.50-9.50 a night. 37 locations.

Youth Hostels Association of Northern Ireland (YHANI), 22 Donegall Rd., Belfast BT12 5JN, Northern Ireland (tel. (01232) 315435; fax 439699).

Australian Youth Hostels Association (AYHA), Level 3, 10 Mallett St., Camperdown NSW 2050 (tel. (02) 565 1699; fax 565 1325; e-mail YHA@zeta.org.au). Membership fees: AUS$42, renewal AUS$26, under 18 AUS$12.

Youth Hostels Association of New Zealand (YHANZ), P.O. Box 436, 173 Gloucester St., Christchurch 1 (tel. (643) 379 9970; fax 365 4476; e-mail hostel.operations@yha.org.nz; http://yha.org.nz/yha). Annual membership fee NZ$24.

Hostel Association of South Africa, P.O. Box 4402, Cape Town 8000 (tel. (21) 419 1853; fax 216937). 14 IBN-linked (and 36 total) hostels in South Africa. Membership: SAR45, Students SAR 30, Group SAR120, Family SAR90, Lifetime SAR225.

▨ Money Matters

CURRENCY AND EXCHANGE

US$1 = 0.64 British pounds	£1 = US$1.55
CDN$1 = £0.47	£1 = CDN$2.13
IR£1 = £1.04	£1 = IR£0.96
AUS$1 = £0.50	£1 = AUS$2.01
NZ$1 = £0.44	£1 = NZ$2.27
SAR1 = £0.15	£1 = SAR6.99

> **A Note on Prices and Currency:**
> The information in this book was researched in the summer of 1996. Since then, inflation may have raised the rates considerably. The exchange rates listed were compiled on August 2, 1996. Since rates fluctuate considerably, confirm them before you go by checking a national newspaper.

Nothing is certain in London but expense.
—William Sherstone, *Curiosities of Literature*

Even those lucky enough to have money may have trouble holding on to it as they make their way through the web of commissions and conversion rates. Remember

ESSENTIALS

that pounds will be less costly in Britain than at home. Even so, converting at least US$50 will allow you to breeze past expensive airport exchange counter lines.

Observe commission rates closely when abroad. Banks will ordinarily offer better rates than those of travel agencies, restaurants, hotels, and the dubious bureaux de change. Don't be lured by bureaux that scream "No Charge—No Commission." If it makes you wonder how they make their money, just look at the rates. Since you lose money with every transaction, convert in large sums (unless the currency is depreciating rapidly), but don't convert more than you need, because it may be difficult to change it back to your home currency, or to a new one. If you are using traveler's checks or bills, be sure to carry some in small denominations (US$50 or less), especially for times when you are forced to exchange money at disadvantageous rates.

The British pound sterling (£) is divided into 100 pence (p). Coins are issued in denominations of 1p, 2p, 5p, 10p, 20p, 50p, and £1; notes are issued in denominations of £5, £10, £20, and £50. If you hear the term "quid," don't stress, it's merely slang for £1 (as in 20 quid). And, if you are given Scottish money as change, don't worry, Scotland's pound notes are legal tender throughout the U.K.

Most banks are closed on Saturday, Sunday, and all public holidays. Britain enjoys "bank holidays" several times a year (see Appendix, p. 294, for dates). Usual bank hours in Britain are Mon.-Fri. 9:30am-3:30pm, although many banks, especially in central London, remain open until 5pm or on Saturday mornings.

Carrying cash around with you, even in a money belt, is risky; personal checks from home will probably not be acceptable no matter how many forms of identification you have (even some banks shy away from accepting checks).

TRAVELER'S CHECKS

Traveler's checks are one of the safest and least troublesome means of carrying funds. Several agencies and many banks sell them, usually for face value plus a 1% commission. (The American Automobile Association issues American Express checks commission-free to members). American Express and Visa are the most widely recognized, though other major checks are sold, exchanged, cashed, and refunded with almost equal ease. If you're ordering your checks, do so well in advance, especially if large sums are being requested.

Each agency provides refunds if your checks are lost or stolen; many provide additional services. (Note that you may need a police report verifying loss or theft.) Inquire about toll-free refund hotlines in London, emergency message relay services, and stolen credit card assistance when you purchase your checks.

You should expect a fair amount of red tape and delay in the event you lose your traveler's checks. To expedite things, keep your check receipts separate from your checks and store them in a safe place or with a traveling companion; record check numbers when you cash them and leave a list of check numbers with someone at home. Keep a separate supply of cash or traveler's checks for emergencies. Be sure never to countersign your checks until you're prepared to cash them. And always be sure to bring your passport with you when you plan to use the checks.

Traveler's checks are fairly easy to dispose of in English banks, who will exchange them for cash. London shopkeepers sometimes accept checks, but not reliably.

American Express: Call (800) 221-7282 in the U.S. and Canada; in the U.K. (0800) 52 13 13; in New Zealand (0800) 44 10 68; in Australia (008) 25 19 02). Elsewhere, call U.S. collect (801) 964-6665. American Express traveler's cheques come in pounds sterling. They are the most widely recognized worldwide and the easiest to replace if lost or stolen. Checks can be purchased for a small fee at American Express Travel Service Offices, banks, and American Automobile Association offices (commission-free for AAA members). Cardmembers can also purchase checks at American Express Dispensers at Travel Service Offices at airports and by ordering them via phone (tel. (800) ORDER-TC (673-3782)). American Express offices cash their checks commission-free (except where prohibited by national governments), although they often offer slightly worse rates than banks. Request

American Express booklet "Traveler's Companion," listing travel office addresses and stolen check hotlines for each European country. Traveler's checks are also available over America OnLine.

Citicorp: Call (800) 645-6556 in the U.S. and Canada; in the U.K. (0181) 297 4781; from elsewhere call U.S. collect (813) 623-1709. Sells both Citicorp and Citicorp Visa traveler's checks in British pounds. Commission is 1-2% on check purchases. Checkholders are automatically enrolled for 45 days in the Travel Assist Program (hotline (800) 250-4377 or collect (202) 296-8728) which provides travelers with English-speaking doctor, lawyer, and interpreter referrals as well as check refund assistance and general travel information. Citicorp's World Courier Service guarantees hand-delivery of traveler's checks when a refund location is not convenient. Call anytime.

Thomas Cook MasterCard: Call (800) 223-9920 in the U.S. and Canada; elsewhere call U.S. collect (609) 987-7300; from the U.K. call (0800) 622 101 free or (01733) 502 995 collect. Offers checks in British pounds. Commission 1-2% for purchases. Try buying the checks at a Thomas Cook office for potentially lower commissions. If you cash your checks at a Thomas Cook Office they will not charge you commission (whereas most banks will).

Visa: Call (800) 227-6811 in the U.S.; in the U.K. (0800) 895 492; from anywhere else in the world call (01733) 318 949 which is a pay call, but can reverse the charges. Call any of the above numbers and give your zip code, they will tell you the closest office which vends their traveler's checks. Any kind of Visa traveler's checks can be reported lost at the Visa number.

CREDIT CARDS

As in most major cities, a credit card (particularly someone else's) can be your best friend in London. Businesses, excepting the most budget, welcome plastic. Using major credit cards (**MasterCard** and **Visa** are the most widely accepted) you can instantly extract cash advances in pounds sterling from associated banks and teller machines throughout the city. Provided you pay your bill quickly, this is a great bargain because credit card companies get the wholesale exchange rate, which is generally 5% better than the retail rate used by banks and and even better than that used by other currency exchange establishments. **American Express** cards also work in some ATMs, as well as at AmEx offices and major airports. All such machines require a **Personal Identification Number (PIN),** which credit cards in the United States do not usually carry. You must ask American Express, MasterCard, or Visa to assign you one before you leave; without this PIN, you will be unable to withdraw cash with your credit card abroad. Keep in mind that MasterCard and Visa might be called "Access" and "Barclaycard" respectively in the Britain.

Credit cards are also invaluable in an emergency—such as an unexpected hospital bill or ticket home or the loss of traveler's checks—which may leave you temporarily without other resources. Furthermore, credit cards offer an array of other services, from insurance to emergency assistance—these, however, depend completely upon the issuer. Some even cover car rental collision insurance.

American Express (tel. (800) CASH-NOW(528-4800)) has a hefty annual fee (US$55) but offers a number of services. AmEx cardholders can cash personal checks at AmEx offices abroad. U.S. Assist, a 24-hour hotline offering medical and legal assistance in emergencies, is also available (tel. (800) 554-2639 in U.S. and Canada; from abroad call U.S. collect (301) 214-8228). Cardholders can also utilize the American Express Travel Service; benefits include assistance in changing airline, hotel, and car rental reservations, sending mailgrams and international cables, and holding your mail at one of the more than 1700 AmEx offices around the world.

MasterCard (tel. (800) 999-0454) and **Visa** (tel. (800) 336-8472) are issued in cooperation with individual banks and some other organizations.

CASH CARDS

Cash cards—popularly called ATM (Automated Teller Machine) cards—are widespread in Europe and elsewhere. Depending on the system that your bank at home uses, you will probably be able to access your own personal bank account whenever you're in need of funds. Happily, ATMs get the same wholesale exchange rate as credit cards . Despite these perks, do some research before relying too heavily on automation. There is often a limit on the amount of money you can withdraw per day and computer network failures are not uncommon. Be sure to memorize your PIN code in numeral form since machines abroad often don't have letters on the keys. Also, if your PIN is longer than four digits, be sure to ask your bank whether the first four digits will work, or whether you need a new number. A great many ATMs are outdoors; don't let anyone distract you while at the machine and use discretion as you walk away from the machine.

The two international money networks you should know about are **Cirrus** (U.S. tel. (800) 4-CIRRUS (424-7787)) and **PLUS** (U.S. tel. (800) 843-7587)). Both are widely available in London, often from the same machine. You may incur additional charges for non-domestic withdrawals, depending on your bank.

GETTING MONEY FROM HOME

One of the easiest ways to get money from home is to bring an **American Express** card. Green-card holders can draw cash from their checking accounts at any of AmEx's major offices and many of its representatives' offices, up to US$1000 every 21 days (no service charge or interest). AmEx also offers Express Cash from many ATMs. Express Cash withdrawals are automatically debited from the cardmember's specified bank account or line of credit. Green-card holders may withdraw up to $1000 in a seven day period with a 2% transaction fee (US$2.50 minimum). To enroll in Express Cash, cardmembers may call 1-800-CASH NOW (528-4800). Outside the U.S. call collect (904) 565-7875. Unless using the AmEx service, avoid cashing checks in foreign currencies; they usually take weeks and a US$30 fee to clear.

Money can also be wired abroad through international money transfer services operated by **Western Union** tel (800 325-6000). In the U.S., call Western Union any time at (800) CALL-CASH (225-5227) to cable money with your Visa or MasterCard within the domestic United States. Credit card transfers do not work overseas; you must send cash. The rates for sending cash are generally US$10 cheaper than with a credit card. The money is usually available in the country you're sending it to within an hour, although in some cases this may vary.

Sending money abroad via **Federal Express,** though reasonably reliable, and tax–free, is very illegal, and as risky as sending cash through regular mail. Few things can ruin a vacation faster than a drug charge. A tax-evasion charge might be one of them.

In emergencies, U.S. citizens can have money sent via the **State Department's Overseas Citizens Service,** American Citizens Services, Consular Affairs, Public Affairs Staff, Room 4831, U.S. Department of State, Washington, D.C. 20520 (tel. (202) 647-5225; at night and on Sundays and holidays (202) 647-4000); fax (202) 647-3000; http://travel.state.gov). For a fee of US$15, the State Department will forward money within hours to the nearest consular office, which will then disburse it according to instructions. The office serves only Americans in the direst of straits abroad. The quickest way to have the money sent is to cable the State Department through Western Union.

VALUE-ADDED TAX

Britain charges value-added tax (VAT), a national sales tax, on most goods and some services. VAT is 17.5% on many services (such as hairdressers, hotels, restaurants, and car rental agencies) and on all goods (except books, medicine, food, and children's clothes). The prices stated in *Let's Go* include VAT unless otherwise specified. Visitors to the U.K. can get a VAT refund through the **Retail Export Scheme.** Ask the shopkeeper for the appropriate form, which immigration officials will sign and stamp when you leave the country. To obtain the refund in cash, bring your stamped form to the Tax Free refund desk in the airport. To obtain the refund by check or credit card, send the form back in the envelope provided and the shop-keeper will then send your refund; note, however, that a service charge will be deducted from your refund. Many shops have a purchase minimum of £50-75 which you will have to meet before they fill out a VAT form for you; stores may try to fob you off because of the inconvenience, but insist and the prices you pay for goods will become much more reasonable. You must leave the country within three months of your purchase in order to claim a VAT refund.

OPENING A BANK ACCOUNT

For a long stay in London, an English **sterling bank account** may be a convenient way to manage funds. If you're planning on working for a year in the city, you should have no problems. The head branches of the five big U.K. banks are: **Barclays Bank,** 54 Lombard St., EC3 (tel. 699 5000); **Lloyd's Bank,** 71 Lombard St., EC3 (tel. 626 1500); **Midland Bank,** 27-32 Poultry, EC2 (tel. 260 8000); and **National Westminster Bank,** 41 Lothbury, EC2 (tel. 606 6060). (Bank tube for all.) **Abbey National,** head office at 201 Grafton Gate East, Central Milton Keynes (tel. (01908) 343 000), will refer you to your nearest branch or a special branch set up to deal with short-term customers. Decisions concerning opening accounts and extended credit priviledges are ultimately the discretion of the branch manager. In all cases you should contact your home bank a few months before coming to London. Obtain a letter of introduction from your bank and find out if it can make arrangements in advance for an account to be opened at a bank in the U.K., so that it is available for use on arrival. Once in London, it may be harder to have your home bank help you open an account. When opening an account here you must show your passport and your bank's letter of introduction, a letter from an employer confirming the tenure of employment in Britain and a regular salary, or a letter from your school (in Britain) confirming your status as a full-time student.

While proof of employment almost guarantees an account, students are screened rigorously. Students of American colleges studying abroad should contact their home school's bursar's office, which may have a special arrangement with a bank in London. When opening an account for a student, the bank generally requires a large deposit to be placed in the account, which could ideally support the student for the full period of study. Alternatively, they may accept proof that regular payments would be made into the account (e.g., from parents).

Once you have made your way through all the red tape, the bank will generally issue you a checkbook, a check guarantee card (vouching for checks of up to £50 or £100), and a cash machine card. They may be rather reticent about handing out credit cards to temporary visitors—which should not matter as long as you can arrange to have your own credit card bills paid back home. Note that Barclaycard acts as both a Visa card and a check guarantee card for Barclay's checks. If the obstacles prove too great, try a **building society,** the British version of a savings and loan—building societies are less likely to require proof of employment.

■ Safety and Security

Travelers can feel safer in London than in many large American cities. After all, even the bobbies are unarmed. It's hard to wander unwittingly into unnerving neighborhoods—these areas, in parts of Hackney, Tottenham, and South London, lie well away from central London.

To avoid getting robbed, keep all valuables on your person, preferably stowed away in a money belt or neck pouch, which hide your money from prying eyes.

Don't put money in a wallet in your back pocket. Women should sling purses over the shoulder and under the opposite arm. Carry all your treasured items (including your passport, railpass, traveler's checks and airline ticket) either in a money belt or neck pouch stashed securely inside your clothing. When sitting in public, keep your bags directly underfoot, or hooked under the leg of your chair if possible. Never count your money in public and carry as little as possible. Keep a sharp eye out for fast-fingered pick-pockets, dastardly con artists, and conniving packs of hustlers masquerading as angel-faced children. Be alert in public telephone booths. If you must say your calling-card number, do so very quietly. Wherever you stow your belongings, try to keep your valuables on your person. Making photocopies of important documents (passport, ID, driver's license, health insurance policy, traveler's checks, credit cards) will allow you to replace them in case they are lost or stolen. Carry one copy separate from the documents and leave another copy at home.

Unattended packages will be taken by thieves or the police (for fear of IRA bombs), so hold your parcels tight. Report any suspicious unattended packages.

At night, the areas around King's Cross/St. Pancras and Notting Hill Gate tube stations are a bit seedy and parks, heaths, and riverbanks in all areas should be avoided. Late trains on the tube out of central London are usually crowded and noisy. Waiting at less central stations, on the other hand, can be unsettling. On night buses, sit on the lower deck next to the driver, who has a radio. When walking after dark, stride purposefully on busy, well-lit roads. Keep to the right, facing oncoming traffic. Avoid shortcuts down alleys or across wasteground. Women may want to carry a rape alarm or whistle. For more safety tips, order Maggie and Gemma Moss's *Handbook for Women Travellers* (see Women and Travel, p. 32).

Especially when **traveling alone,** be sure that someone at home knows your itinerary. Never say that you're traveling alone. Steer clear of empty train compartments and avoid large Underground stations after dark. Ask managers of your hotel, hostel, or B&B for advice on specific areas and consider staying in places with a curfew or night attendant. Some cheap accommodations may entail more risk than savings; when traveling alone, you may want to forego dives and city outskirts.

For the love of god, look right! British drivers travel on the opposite side of the road, meaning that they'll be speeding towards pedestrians from a different direction than most visitors will expect. It's a testament to the competence of London drivers that more tourists aren't killed by stepping unwittingly into traffic. Don't go out like a sucker—signs at your feet tell you which way to look. Obey them.

Drugs and traveling can be a bad combination. If you carry **prescription drugs** while you travel, it is vital to have a copy of the prescriptions themselves readily accessible at country borders. As for **illegal drugs,** the safest bet is to avoid them. It may seem "square," but little can ruin a vacation faster than a narcotics charge.

In an emergency, call 999 (the emergency number for England), a free call. The operator will ask whether you require police, ambulance, or fire service.

Self defense classes, though expensive, may prove helpful. **Model Mugging,** a national organization with offices in several major US cities, teaches a very effective, comprehensive course on self-defense (course prices vary from US$400-500). Women's and men's courses are offered. Contact Lynn S. Auerbach on the East Coast (617-232-7900), Alice Tibits in the Midwest (612-645-6189), and Cori Couture on the West Coast (415-592-7300). **Community colleges** frequently offer self-defense courses at more affordable prices. For an official **Department of State Travel Advisory** on Ireland or the United Kingdom, call the 24-hour hotline at (202) 647-5225. To order publications, including a pamphlet entitled *A Safe Trip Abroad,* write them at Superinendant of Documents, U.S. Government Printing office, Washington, D.C. 20402 or call (202) 783-3238.

■ Health

AIDS AND HIV

All travelers must be concerned about sexually transmitted diseases (STDs), especially HIV infection; HIV is the virus that leads to AIDS (Acquired Immune Deficiency Syndrome). To protect yourself from HIV infection and other STDs while traveling, follow all the precautions that you should follow at home. Never have unprotected sex with people you do not know or with people, even those you know well, that you are not certain are HIV negative (on the basis of test results from six months after the person's last risky contact). For more information on AIDS, call the **U.S. Center for Disease Control's** 24-hour Hotline at (800) 342-2437. For similar advice with a British accent while in London, call the UK's 24-hour National AIDS Helpline (tel. (0800) 567 123). Council's brochure, *Travel Safe: AIDS and International Travel*, is available at all Council Travel offices (see p. 15).

BIRTH CONTROL AND ABORTION

If you are straight and sexually active, you will need to think about contraception. Women on the Pill should bring enough to allow for possible loss or extended stays and should bring a prescription, since forms of the Pill vary a good deal. If you use a diaphragm, be sure that you have enough contraceptive jelly on hand. Though condoms are increasingly available, you might want to bring your favorite national brand before you go; availability and quality vary.

Abortion is legal in Britain. Your consulate can give you a list of ob/gyn doctors who perform abortions. For general information on contraception, condoms, and abortion worldwide, contact the **International Planned Parenthood Federation,** European Regional Office, Regent's College Inner Circle, Regent's Park, London NW1 4NS (tel. (0171) 486 0741 fax 487 7950; e-mail ippinfo@ippf.attmail.com; http://www.oneworld.org/ippf/).

INSURANCE

Beware of unnecessary insurance coverage—your current policies might well extend to many travel-related accidents. **Medical insurance** often covers costs incurred abroad; check with your insurance company before you go. Canadians are protected by their home province's health insurance plan: check with the provincial Ministry of Health or Health Plan Headquarters. Your **homeowners' insurance** may cover theft during travel; homeowners are generally covered against loss of travel documents up to about US$500. ISIC, ITIC, Council, STA and AmEx provide varying levels of insurance. To supplement ISIC's insurance, **Council** (see p. 15) offers the inexpensive Trip-Safe plan with options covering medical treatment and hospitalization, accidents, baggage loss, and charter flights missed due to illness; they and **STA** also offer more comprehensive and expensive policies.

Remember that insurance companies usually require a copy of the police report for theft, or, in medical matters, evidence of having paid medical expenses before they will honor a claim, and may have time limits on filing for reimbursement. Have all documents written in English to avoid possible translating fees. Always carry policy numbers and proof of insurance. Note that some plans offer cash advances or guaranteed bills; check with your insurance carrier for specific restrictions.

■ Specific Concerns

WOMEN TRAVELERS

Women exploring any area on their own inevitably face additional safety concerns. In all situations it is best to trust your instincts: if you'd feel better somewhere else, don't hesitate to move on. You may want to consider staying in hostels which offer single rooms which lock from the inside, or religious organizations that offer rooms for women only. Stick to centrally located accommodations and avoid late-night treks or rides on the Underground. Remember that hitching is *never* safe for lone women, or even for two women traveling together.

To escape unwanted attention, foreign women in London should follow the example of local women; in many cases, the less you look like a tourist, the better off you'll be. Look as if you know where you're going and ask women or couples for directions if you're lost or if you feel uncomfortable. Your best answer to verbal harassment may be no answer at all. Seek out a police officer or a female passerby before a crisis erupts and don't hesitate to scream for help. *Always* carry change for the phone and extra money for a bus or taxi. Carry a whistle on your keychain and don't hesitate to use it in an emergency. **London Women's Aid** (tel. 251 6537) offers 24-hour support for victims of violence and the **London Rape Crisis Centre** (tel. 837 1600) hotline is answered Monday-Friday 6-10pm, Saturday-Sunday 10am-10pm. These warnings and suggestions shouldn't discourage women from traveling alone—avoid unnecessary risks, but keep your spirit of adventure.

The **WHEEL** (Women's Health, Education, Entertainment and Leisure) at Wesley House, 4 Wild Ct., WC2 (tel. 831 6946; tube: Holborn; open Monday-Friday 8am-10pm, Sat. 9am-10pm), is an umbrella organization that houses a variety of political, ethnic, leisure, and support groups for women. The **Audre Lorde Clinic,** at the Ambrose King Centre, Royal London Hospital, E1 (tel. 377 7312; tube: Whitechapel), and the **Bernhard Clinic,** Dept. of Gen. Medicine, Charing Cross Hospital, Fulham Palace Rd., W6 (tel. (0181) 846 1576; tube: Baron's Court or Hammersmith), are female-staffed facilities offering smear tests, screenings for STDs and vaginal infections, breast exams, HIV tests, advice, and counselling for lesbians. (Call the Audre Lorde Friday 10am-5pm or the Bernhard Wednesday 2-7pm for appointment.) **Lady Cabs** (tel. 272 3019 or 281 4803; fax 272 1992) is a north London-based women's taxi service (drivers are female, riders are both sexes). (Open Mon.-Thurs. 7:45am-12:30am, Fri. 7:45:am-1am, Sat. 8:30am-2am, Sun. 10am-midnight.) For more general information on women and travel, consult these publications:

Handbook For Women Travelers by Maggie and Gemma Moss (UK£9). Encyclopedic and well-written. From Piaktus Books, 5 Windmill St., London W1P 1HF (tel. (0171) 631 07 10).

A Journey of One's Own, by Thalia Zepatos (Eighth Mountain Press, US$17). The latest thing on the market, interesting and full of good advice, plus a specific and manageable bibliography of books and resources.

A Foxy Old Woman's Guide to Traveling Alone by Jay Ben-Lesser encompasses practically every specific concern, offering anecdotes and tips for anyone interested in solitary adventure. No experience necessary. Available in bookstores and from Crossing Press in Freedom, CA (tel. (800)-777-1048), US$11.

Women Travel: Adventures, Advice & Experience by Miranda Davies and Natania Jansz (Penguin, US$13). Info on specific foreign countries plus a decent bibliography and resource index. The sequel *More Women Travel* is US$15.

Women Going Places, a women's travel and resource guide emphasizing women-owned enterprises. Geared towards lesbians, but offers advice appropriate for all women. US$14 from Inland Book Company, 1436 W. Randolph St., Chicago, IL 60607 (tel. (800) 243-0138), or order from a local bookstore.

SENIOR TRAVELERS

A wide array of discounts (called **concessions**) are available with proof of senior citizen status. These are often denoted "OAP" (old-age pensioners).

AARP (American Association of Retired Persons), 601 E St., NW, Washington, D.C. 20049 (tel. (202) 434-2277). Members 50 and over receive benefits and services including the AARP Motoring Plan from AMOCO (tel. (800) 334-3300) and discounts on lodging, car rental, and sight-seeing. Annual fee US$8 per couple; lifetime membership US$75.

ESSENTIALS

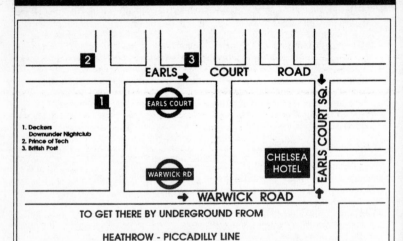

Elderhostel, 75 Federal St., 3rd Fl., Boston, MA 02110-1941 (tel. (617) 426-7788; fax 426-8351; http://www.elderhostel.org). Educational programs in over 20 countries for those 55 or over (spouse of any age).

Gateway Books, 2023 Clemens Road, Oakland, CA 94602 (tel. (510) 530-0299, credit card orders (800) 669-0773; fax (510) 530-0497; e-mail donmerwin@aol.com; http://www.hway.com/gateway/). Publishes *Adventures Abroad* (US$13) for the frugal senior considering a long stay or retiring abroad.

Pilot Books, 103 Cooper St., Babylon, NY 11702 (tel. (516) 422-2225). Publishes a large number of helpful guides including *The International Health Guide for Senior Citizens* (US$5, postage US$2) and *The Senior Citizens' Guide to Budget Travel in Europe* (US$6, postage US$2). Call or write for a complete list of titles.

Unbelievably Good Deals and Great Adventures That You Absolutely Can't Get Unless You're Over 50, by Joan Rattner Heilman. After you finish reading the title page, check inside for some great tips on senior discounts and the like. Contemporary Books, US$10.

BISEXUAL, GAY, AND LESBIAN TRAVELERS

The following organizations and publications provide general travel information. For information specific to London, see Bisexual, Gay, and Lesbian London, p. 228.

Are You Two...Together? A Gay and Lesbian Travel Guide to Europe. A travel guide with anecdotes and tips for gays and lesbians traveling in Europe. Includes lists of gay/lesbian organizations, gay/lesbian-oriented, and gay/lesbian-friendly establishments. Available in bookstores. Random House, $18.

Ferrari Guides, P.O. Box 37887, Phoenix, AZ 85069 (tel. (602) 863-2408; fax 439-3952; e-mail ferrari@q-net.com). Gay and lesbian travel guides. Available in bookstores or by mail (postage/handling US$4.50 for the first item, US$1 for each additional item mailed within the US. Overseas, call or write for shipping cost).

Giovanni's Room, 345 S. 12th St., Philadelphia, PA 19107 (tel. (215) 923-2960; fax 923-0813; e-mail gilphilp@netaxs.com). An international feminist, lesbian, and gay bookstore with mail-order service.

International Gay Travel Association, Box 4974, Key West, FL 33041 (tel. (800) 448-8550; fax (305) 296-6633; e-mail IGTA@aol.com; http://www.rainbowmall.com/igta). An organization of over 1100 companies serving gay and lesbian travelers worldwide. Call for lists of travel agents, accommodations, and events.

Spartacus International Gay Guides (US$33), published by Bruno Gmunder, Postfach 110729, D-10837 Berlin, Germany (tel. (30) 615 00 30; fax (30) 615-9134). Lists establishments around the world catering to gays. Also lists hotlines for gays in various countries and homosexuality laws for each country. Available in bookstores and in the U.S. by mail from Giovanni's Room (listed above).

The Pink Plaque Guide to London, by Michael Elliman and Frederick Roll. Walks covering some of London's more unconventional heroes and heroines. £8.

Women Going Places (US$14). International women's travel and resource guide emphasizing women-owned enterprises; geared toward lesbians (see p. 32).

DISABLED TRAVELERS

Transportation companies in Britain are remarkably conscientious about providing facilities and services to meet the needs of travelers with disabilities. Notify a bus or coach company of your plans ahead of time and they will have staff ready to assist you. **British Rail** offers a discounted railcard for £14; it is good for a year and entitles you to discounts of up to one-third on BR tickets. With advance notification, BR will set aside a convenient spot for your wheelchair. Not all stations are accessible; write for the pamphlet *British Rail and Disabled Travellers.* **National Express** (bus travel) also offers some discounts. Several **car rental agencies** can have hand-controlled cars available provided you give them advance notice. Britain imposes a six-month quarantine on all animals entering the country—this includes seeing-eye dogs (called "blind-dogs" in England). The owner must also obtain a veterinary certificate

ESSENTIALS

(consult the nearest British Consulate for details). You can write to the British Tourist Authority for free handbooks and access guides.

Useful guides to London for people with disabilities are Nicholson's *Access in London*, a guide to accommodations, transport, and accessibility compiled by researchers with disabilities, available in any well-stocked travel shop (about £3.50). *London for All* is a booklet on transport, tours, and hotels published by the London Tourist Board and available at tourist Information Centres. For **travel by Underground and Bus**, pick up the free booklet *Access Around London* from Tourist Information Centres and London Transport Information Centres, or by post from from the Unit for Disabled Passengers (London Transport, 172 Buckingham Palace Rd., London SW1W 9TN; tel. 918 3312; fax 918 3876). London Transport's 24-hour travel information hotline is also useful (tel. 222 1234). New this year are the dozen networks of **Mobility Buses** (tel. 918 3312) which are fully wheelchair accessible and available to anyone requiring extra space or time getting on and off. An increasing number of routes are served by **Low-Floor Buses** (tel. 918 3312 for specific information) which are accessible to those in wheelchairs and are also available to parents pushing prams. The **Stationlink** (tel. 918 3312) coaches are fully accessible low-floor buses which run at hourly intervals along a route between the main line terminals. In the last year the Underground has relented and now allows wheelchair users to ride the Tube, though would-be riders are warned that few, if any, of the ancient stations are easily navigated. The newer stations being built for the Jubilee and East London extensions will be fully wheelchair accessible.

The **"Arts Access"** section at the beginning of the London telephone books details special services available at theaters, cinemas, and concert halls around London. Call 936 3436 with Arts Access questions, or **Artsline**, 5 Crowndale Rd., NW1 (tel. 388 2227), for entertainment accessibility information (Mon.-Fri. 9:30am-5:30pm). **Shape** (tel. 700 8138) offers very cheap tickets to accessible arts events, as well as providing transport and escorts to these events.

For general information, phone the **Greater London Association for the Disabled** (tel. 274 0107). The following organizations can be helpful:

Access Project (PHSP), 39 Bradley Gardens, West Ealing, London W13 8HE, England. Distributes an access guide to London for a donation of £5. Researched by persons with disabilities. They cover traveling, accommodation, and access to sights and entertainment. Includes a "Loo Guide" with a list of wheelchair-accessible toilets.

Facts on File, 11 Penn Plaza, 15th Floor, New York, NY 10001 (tel. (212) 967-8800). Publishers of *Disability Resource*, a reference guide for travelers with disabilities (US$45 plus shipping). Retail bookstores or by mail order.

Graphic Language Press, P.O. Box 270, Cardiff by the Sea, CA 92007 (tel. (619) 944-9594). Publishers of *Wheelchair Through Europe* (US$13). Comprehensive advice for the wheelchair-bound traveler. Specifics on wheelchair-related resources and accessible sites in various cities throughout Europe.

Mobility International, USA (MIUSA), P.O. Box 10767, Eugene, OR 97440 (tel. (514) 343-1284 voice and TDD; fax 343-6812). International Headquarters in Brussels, rue de Manchester 25 Brussels, Belgium, B-1070 (tel. (322) 410 6297; fax 410 6874). Contacts in 30 countries. Information on travel programs, international work camps, accommodations, access guides, and organized tours for those with physical disabilities. Membership US$25 per year, newsletter US$15. Sells the periodically updated and expanded *A World of Options: A Guide to International Educational Exchange, Community Service, and Travel for Persons with Disabilities* (US$14, nonmembers US$16). In addition, MIUSA offers a courses that teach strategies helpful for travelers with disabilities. Call for details.

Society for the Advancement of Travel for the Handicapped (SATH), 347 Fifth Ave., #610, New York, NY 10016 (tel. (212) 447-7284; fax (212) 725-8253). Publishes quarterly travel newsletter *SATH News* and information booklets (free for members, US$13 each for nonmembers) with advice on trip planning for people with disabilities. Annual membership US$45, students and seniors US$25.

The following organizations arrange tours or trips for disabled travelers:

Directions Unlimited, 720 N. Bedford Rd., Bedford Hills, NY 10507 (tel. (800) 533-5343; in NY (914) 241-1700; fax 241-0243). Specializes in arranging individual and group vacations, tours, and cruises for the physically disabled.

Flying Wheels Travel Service, 143 W. Bridge St., Owatonne, MN 55060 (tel. (800) 535-6790; fax 451-1685). Arranges trips in the USA and abroad for groups and individuals in wheelchairs or with other sorts of limited mobility.

The Guided Tour Inc., Elkins Park House, Suite 114B, 7900 Old York Road, Elkins Park, PA 19027-2339 (tel. (800) 783-5841 or (215) 782-1370; fax 635-2637). Organizes travel programs for persons with developmental and physical challenges and those requiring renal dialysis. Call, fax, or write for a free brochure.

TRAVELERS WITH CHILDREN

Children under two generally fly for 10% of the adult airfare on international flights (this does not necessarily include a seat). International fares are usually discounted 25% for children from two to eleven. Most sights and many accomodations in Britain and Ireland have reduced fees for children, sometimes listed under the name "concessions." Always have children carry a passport or other ID in case of emergency or if they get lost. You might want to refer to **Backpacking with Babies and Small Children** (US$10), published by Wilderness Press, 2440 Bancroft Way, Berkeley, CA 94704 (tel. (800) 443-7227 or (510) 843-8080; fax 548-1355). Another good resource is **Take Your Kids to Europe,** by Cynthia W. Harriman (US$14), published by Mason-Grant Publications, P.O. Box 6547, Portsmouth, NH 03802 (tel. (603) 436-1608; fax 427-0015; e-mail charriman@masongrant.com).

KOSHER AND VEGETARIAN TRAVELERS

See the Food introduction and listings under "Vegetarian" in Food and Drink, p. 77.

The European Vegetarian Guide to Restaurants and Hotels (US$145, plus $1.75 shipping) is available from the Vegetarian Times Bookshelf (tel. (800) 435-9610, orders only).

The International Vegetarian Travel Guide (UK£2) was last published in 1991. Order back copies from the Vegetarian Society of the UK (VSUK), Parkdale, Dunham Rd., Altringham, Cheshire WA14 4QG (tel. (0161) 928 0793; fax 926 9182). VSUK also publishes other titles, including *The European Vegetarian Guide to Hotels and Restaurants.*

The Jewish Travel Guide (US$12, postage US$1.75) lists synagogues, kosher restaurants, and Jewish institutions in over 80 countries. It is available in the U.S. from Sepher-Hermon Press, 1265 46th St., Brooklyn, NY 11219 (tel. (718) 972-9010; US$14 plus US$2.50 shipping).

▓ Packing

Pack light; the rest is commentary. Remember that you can buy anything you'll need in London. One tried-and-true method of packing is to set out everything you think you'll need, then pack half of it—and pack twice the money, if you can.

For a long stay in London you might prefer a suitcase to a conspicuous backpack. If you'll be on the move frequently, go with the pack. Bring along a small daypack for carrying lunch, a camera, and valuables. Keep your money, passport, and other valuables with you in a purse, neck pouch, or money belt. Label every article of baggage both inside and out with your name and address. For added security, bring a combination lock for your main bag and for London hostel lockers.

Nothing will serve you more loyally in London than comfortable walking shoes and a folding umbrella. Bring a light sweater (even in summer), an alarm clock, and a raincoat. Despite its rainy reputation, London gets gruelingly sunny in summer—pack sunglasses. A single-sheet sleeping sack is free in all London HI hostels.

Any electrical gadget will need an adapter and a converter. The voltage in England is 240 volts AC. (North American appliances are 110 volts AC.) Converters and adapters are available worldwide in department and hardware stores (US$10-15).

If you take expensive **cameras** or equipment abroad, it's best to register everything with customs at the airport before departure. If you're coming from the U.S., buy a supply of film before you leave; it's more expensive in Britain. Unless you're shooting with 1000 ASA or more, airport security x-rays should not harm your pictures. Pack film in your carry-on, since the x-rays employed on checked baggage are much stronger. Though fiercely contested, many allege that x-rays damage floppy disks—if you're bringing a laptop or notebook computer, you may want to have both computer and floppy discs hand-inspected, lest stray x-rays wipe out your as-yet-unpublished chef-d'oeuvre. Officials may ask you to turn it on, so be sure the batteries are fully loaded. A warning: Lost baggage is common and not always retrieved. Keep all valuables in your carry-on.

■ Alternatives to Tourism

If the often madcap, train-changing, site-switching pace of tourism loses its appeal, consider a longer stay in London. Study, work, or volunteering will help you get a better sense of parts of the city that are often hidden to the short-term visitor.

STUDY

It's not difficult to spend a summer, a term, or a year studying in London under the auspices of a well-established program. Enrolling as a full-time student, however, is somewhat more difficult; the requirements for admission can be hard to meet unless you attended a British secondary school and often only a limited number of foreign students are accepted each year. **Council** sponsors over 40 study abroad programs throughout the world. Contact them for more information (see p. 15). There is a study abroad website at **http//www.studyabroad.com/liteimage.html.**

American Institute for Foreign Study, College Division, 102 Greenwich Ave., Greenwich, CT 06830 (tel. (800) 727-2437; for high school students (800) 888-2247; http://www.aifs.org). Organizes year, semester, quarter, and summer programs for study in foreign universities. Open to adults. Minority and AIFS International scholarships available. Also offers Au Pair in Europe for those aged 18-26 who provide child care in exchange for room and board for families in London.

Association of Commonwealth Universities, John Foster House, 36 Gordon Square, London WC1H OPF, England (tel. (0171) 387 85 72). Administers scholarship programs such as the British Marshalls and publishes information about Commonwealth universities.

Institute of International Education (IIE), 809 United Nations Plaza, New York, NY 10017-3580 (tel. (212) 984-5413 for recorded information; fax 984-5358). For book orders: IIE Books, Institute of International Educations, P.O. Box 371, Annapolis Junction, MD 20701 (tel. (800) 445-0443; fax (301) 953-2838; e-mail iiebooks@iie.org.). A nonprofit international and cultural exchange agency. IIE's library of study abroad resources is open to the public Tues.-Thurs. 11am-3:45pm. Publishes *Academic Year Abroad* (US$43 plus US$4 shipping), detailing over 2300 semester and year-long programs worldwide, and *Vacation Study Abroad* (US$37 plus US$4 shipping), which lists over 1800 short-term, summer, and language school programs. Write for a list of publications.

InterStudy Programmes, 42 Milson St., Bath BA1 1DN (tel. (01225) 464 769; fax (01255) 444 104). In the U.S., call toll-free (800) 663-1999. Offers semester- and year-long programs in Britain and Ireland; handles all details between program institution and your home institution, including housing and credit transfer.

UKCOSA/United Kingdom Council for International Education, 9-17 St. Albans Place, London N1 0NX (tel. (0171) 226 3762; fax 226 3373). Advises prospective and current students on immigration, finance, and more.

Universities and Colleges Admissions Services, P.O. Box 28, Cheltenham, Glos. GL50 3SA (tel. (01242) 227788). Provides information and handles applications for admission to all full-time undergraduate courses in universities and their affiliated colleges in the United Kingdom. Write to them for an application and the extremely informative UCAS *Handbook.*

UNH Cambridge Summer Program, University of New Hampshire, 95 Main St., Hamilton Smith Hall, Durham, NH 03824 (tel. (603) 862 3962; fax 862 3962; e-mail Cambridge.Program@UNH.edu). Sponsors a 6-wk. program in July and Aug. at Gonville and Caius College, one of the 30 colleges comprising Cambridge University. A distinguished British and American faculty; courses in English, history, and the humanities. Transfer credit for U.S. students. Applicants must have completed first undergraduate year.

WORK

Becoming a part of the economy may be the best way to immerse yourself in a foreign culture. You may not earn as much as you would at home, but you should manage to cover your living expenses and possibly your airfare. A range of short-term opportunities are available, although obtaining a work permit may be difficult. If you are a full-time student at a U.S. university, one easy way to get a job abroad is through work permit programs run by the **Council on International Educations Exchange (Council)** and its member organizations (see p. 15). For a US$200 application fee, Council can procure three- to six-month work permits (and a handbook to help you find work and housing) for Britain. Each country has an office to help with finding accommodations, openings, and connections.

Many books exist which list work-abroad opportunities. Note especially the excellent guides put out by **Vacation Work** (see below). In order to avoid scams from fraudulent employment agencies which demand large fees and provide no results, educate yourself using publications from the following sources.

Addison-Wesley, Jacob Way, Reading, MA 01867 (tel. (800) 822-6339). Published *International Jobs: Where They Are, How to Get Them* in 1993-1994 (US$16).

Vacation Work Publications, 9 Park End St., Oxford OX1 1HJ (tel. (01865) 24 19 78; fax 79 08 85). Publishes a wide variety of guides with job listings and information for the working traveller. Opportunities for summer or full-time work in countries all over the world. Write for a catalogue of their publications.

World Trade Academy Press, Suite 509, 50 E. 42nd St., New York, NY 10017-5480 (tel. (212) 752-0329). Publishes *The Directory of American Firms Operating in Foreign Countries* (1996) for US$200 and *The Directory of Foreign Firms Operating in the United States* (1995) for $150. These may be found in bookstores or libraries and serve as helpful resources for those wishing to work abroad.

Permits

Unless you're a citizen of a Common Market or British Commonwealth nation, you'll have a tough time finding a legal paying job. Citizens of British Commonwealth nations (including Canada, Australia, and New Zealand) between the ages of 17 and 27 may work in Britain during a visit if the employment they take is "incidental to their holiday" by obtaining a working holiday visa. Commonwealth citizens with a U.K.-born parent may apply for a certificate of entitlement to the right of abode, which allows them to live and work in Britain without other formalities.

Officially, you can hold a job in European countries only with a work permit, applied for by your prospective employer (or by you, with supporting papers from the employer). The real catch-22 is that normally you must physically enter the country in order to have immigration officials validate your work permit papers and note your status in your passport. This means that if you can't set up a job from afar and have the work permit sent to you, you must enter the country to look for a job, find

ESSENTIALS

an employer and have them start the permit process, then *leave* the country until the permit is sent to you (up to six weeks), and finally return and start work.

Finding a Job

While casual jobs—bar, restaurant, and hotel reception work, for example—are readily available (look in shop windows and for the advertisements posted in the windows of local tobacconists), wages are unlikely to be more than £3-4 per hour. Most students here do not work during term-time, so part-time jobs that fit in with a daytime study schedule may be harder to find. Advice can be found at a local university's work-abroad resource center.

VOLUNTEERING

Not surprisingly, people everywhere are willing to let you work for them for free, allowing great opportunities to go places and meet people. You may receive room and board in exchange for your labor and the work can be fascinating. The following organizations and publications can help you to explore possibilities. Organizations that arrange placement often charge high application fees in addition to workcamps' charges for room and board.

Council (see p. 15) offers 2- to 4-wk. environmental or community service projects in over 30 countries around the globe through its Voluntary Services Department (US$195 placement fee). Participants must be at least 18yr. old.

Service Civil International Voluntary Service (SCI-VS), 5474 Walnut Level Rd., Crozet, VA 22932 (tel. (804) 823-1826; fax 823-5027; e-mail sciivsusa@igc.apc.org). Arranges placement in workcamps in Europe (ages 18 and over). Local organizations sponsor groups for physical or social work. Registration fees US$50-250, depending on the camp location.

Volunteers for Peace, 43 Tiffany Rd., Belmont, VT 05730 (tel. (802) 259-2759; fax 259-2922; e-mail vfp@vermontel.com; http://www.vermontel.com/lvfp/home. htm). A nonprofit organization that arranges for speedy placement in over 800 workcamps in more than 60 countries in Europe, Africa, Asia, and the Americas. Many camps last for 2 to 3 wks. and are comprised of 10 to 15 people. Most complete and up-to-date listings provided in the annual *International Workcamp Directory* (US$12). Registration fee US$175. Some workcamps are open to 16- and 17-yr. olds for US$200. Free newsletter.

GETTING THERE

■ Budget Travel Agencies

The following budget travel organizations typically offer discounted flights for students and youths, railpasses, ISICs and other identification cards, hostel memberships, travel gear, travel guides, and general expertise in budget travel. Students and people under 26 ("youth") with proper ID qualify for enticing reduced airfares.

Council Travel (http://www.ciee.org/cts/ctshome.htm), the travel division of Council, is a full-service travel agency specializing in youth and budget travel. They offer railpasses, discount airfares, hosteling cards, guidebooks, budget tours, travel gear, and student (ISIC), youth (GO25), and teacher (ITIC) identity cards. U.S. offices include: Emory Village, 1561 N. Decatur Rd., **Atlanta,** GA 30307 (tel. (404) 377-9997); 2000 Guadalupe, **Austin,** TX 78705 (tel. (512) 472-4931); 273 Newbury St., **Boston,** MA 02116 (tel. (617) 266-1926); 1138 13th St., **Boulder,** CO 80302 (tel. (303) 447-8101); 1153 N. Dearborn, **Chicago,** IL 60610 (tel. (312) 951-0585); 10904 Lindbrook Dr., **Los Angeles,** CA 90024 (tel. (310) 208-3551); 1501 University Ave. SE, **Minneapolis,** MN 55414 (tel. (612) 379-2323); 205 E. 42nd St., **New York,** NY 10017 (tel. (212) 822-2700); 953 Garnet Ave., **San Diego,** CA

92109 (tel. (619) 270-6401); 530 Bush St., **San Francisco,** CA 94108 (tel. (415) 421-3473); 4311½ University Way, **Seattle,** WA 98105 (tel. (206) 632-2448); and 3300 M St. NW, **Washington, D.C.** 20007 (tel. (202) 337-6464). **For U.S. cities not listed,** call 800-2-COUNCIL (226-8624). Also 28A Poland St. (Oxford Circus), **London,** W1V 3DB (tel. (0171) 437 7767).

CTS Travel, 220 Kensington High St., London, W8 (tel. 937 3366 for travel in Europe, 937 3388 for travel world-wide). Tube: High St. Kensington. Specializes in student/youth travel and discount flights. Open Mon.-Fri. 9:30am-6pm, Sat. 10am-5pm. Also at 44 Goodge St., W1 (tel. 637 4199; tube: Goodge St.).

Let's Go Travel, Harvard Student Agencies, 67 Mt. Auburn St., Cambridge, MA 02138 (800-5-LETS GO (553-8746) or tel. (617) 495-9649). Railpasses, HI-AYH memberships, ISICs, ITICs, FIYTO cards, guidebooks (including all of the *Let's Go* guides and Map Guides), maps, bargain flights, and a complete line of budget travel gear. All items available by mail; call or write for a catalog.

Bed & Breakfast (GB), P.O. Box 66, Henley-on-Thames, Oxon, England RG9 1XS (tel. (01491) 578 803; fax 410 806); in the U.S., Hometours (tel. (800) 367-4668). The U.K.'s most comprehensive B&B service, covering London and the British Isles for £14.50 and up per night. Telephone and fax reservation service. Write for free annual mini-guide *How To Book a Bed & Breakfast in Britain,* which includes information on prices, reservations, and host locations.

Campus Travel, 52 Grosvenor Gardens, London SW1W OAG. Campus Travel is a large supplier of student travel products in the U.K., with 37 branches throughout the country. They supply student cards, book trips on planes, trains, and boats, and provide a full range of travel-related products and services. In London, call for tele-sales and bookings in Europe (tel. 730 3402), North America (tel. 730 2101), or worldwide (tel. 730 8111). In Manchester call (0161) 273 1721. In Scotland dial (0131) 668 3303).

Eurolines, 52 Grosvenor Gardens Victoria, London SW1W 0AU (tel. (01582) 404 511 main office, or (0171) 730 8235 in London). Specializes in coach travel all over

Europe, including Eastern Europe. Open April-Oct. Mon.-Sat. 8am-8pm, June 18-Sept. 10 Sun. 10-4, all other times Mon.-Sat. 8am-6pm.

Rail Europe Inc., 226 Westchester Ave., White Plains, NY 10604 (tel. (800) 438-7245; fax 432-1329; http://www.raileurope.com). Sells all Eurail products and passes, national railpasses, and point-to-point tickets. Up-to-date information on all rail travel in Europe, including Eurostar, the English Channel train.

STA Travel, 6560 Scottsdale Rd. #F100, Scottsdale, AZ 85253 (tel. (800) 777-0112 nationwide; fax (602) 922-0793). A student and youth travel organization with over 100 offices worldwide offering discount airfares for young travelers, railpasses, accommodations, tours, insurance, and ISICs. In the U.K., 6 Wrights La., **London** W8 6TA (tel. (0171) 938 47 11 for North American travel). In New Zealand, 10 High St., **Auckland** (tel. (09) 309 97 23). In Australia, 222 Faraday St., **Melbourne** VIC 3050 (tel. (03) 349 69 11).

Students Flights Inc, 5010 East Shea Blvd. #A104, Scottsdale, AZ 85254 (tel. (602) 951-1177; fax 951 1216); **Los Angeles,** CA 90045 (tel. (310) 338-8616); 1450 City Councillors St., #1450, **Montréal,** Qué. H3A 2E6 (tel. (800) 361-7799 or (514) 845-9137; fax 845-9137); **Toronto,** Ont. (tel. (416) 415-1060). Over 100 offices worldwide, most in Italy. The official representative of the Italian state railways in the US; also sells Eurail.

Travel CUTS (Canadian Universities Travel Services Limited), 187 College St., Toronto, Ont. M5T 1P7 (tel. (416) 979-2406; fax 979-8167; e-mail mail@travelcuts). Canada's national student travel bureau and equivalent of Council, with 40 offices across Canada. Also in the U.K., 295-A Regent St., **London** W1R 7YA (tel. (0171) 637 3161). Discounted domestic and international airfares open to all; special student fares to all destinations with valid ISIC. Issues ISIC, FIYTO, GO25, and HI hostel cards, as well as railpasses. Offers free *Student Traveller* magazine, as well as information on the Student Work Abroad Program (SWAP).

■ By Plane

The first challenge to the budget traveler is getting there. The **airline industry** attempts to squeeze every dollar from customers; finding a cheap airfare in their deliberately mysterious and confusing jungle will be easier if you understand the airlines' systems better than most people do. Call every toll-free number and don't be afraid to ask about discounts. Have several knowledgeable **travel agents** guide you; better yet, have an agent who specializes in the region(s) you will be travelling to guide you. Travel agents may not want to spend time finding the cheapest fares (for which they receive the lowest commissions) but, if you travel often, you should definitely find an agent who will cater to you and your needs and track down deals in exchange for your frequent business. **TravelHUB** (http://www.travelhub.com) will help you search for travel agencies on the web.

Students and "youth" (people under 26) should never need to pay full price for a ticket. Seniors can also get great deals; many airlines offer senior traveler clubs or airline passes and discounts for their companions as well. Sunday newspapers often have travel sections that list bargain fares from the local airport. Australians should consult the Saturday travel section of the *Sydney Morning Herald,* as well as the ethnic press, where special deals may be advertised. Outsmart airline reps with the phone-book-sized *Official Airline Guide* (check your local library; at US$397, the tome costs as much as some flights), a monthly guide listing nearly every scheduled flight in the world (with prices) and toll-free phone numbers for all the airlines which allow you to call in reservations directly. *The Airline Passenger's Guerrilla Handbook* (US$15; last published in 1990) is a more renegade resource. On the web, try the **Air Traveler's Handbook** (http://www.cis.ohio-state.edu/hypertext/faq/usenet/travel/air/handbook/top.html), for comprehensive info on air travel.

Most airfares peak between mid-June and early September. Midweek (Mon.-Thurs. morning) roundtrip flights run about US$40-50 cheaper than on weekends. Traveling from hubs such as New York, Atlanta, Dallas, Chicago, Los Angeles, San Francisco, Vancouver, Toronto, Sydney, Melbourne, Brisbane, Auckland, or Wellington to Lon-

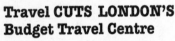 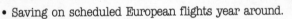

don, Frankfurt, Paris, Brussels, Luxembourg, Rome, or Amsterdam will win a more competitive fare than from smaller cities. Return-date flexibility is usually not an option for the budget traveler; traveling with an "open return" ticket can be pricier than fixing a return date and paying to change it. Whenever flying internationally, pick up your ticket well in advance of the departure date, have the flight confirmed within 72 hours of departure, and arrive at the airport at least three hours before your flight.

COMMERCIAL AIRLINES

The commercial airlines' lowest regular offer is the **APEX** (Advance Purchase Excursion Fare); specials advertised in newspapers may be cheaper, but have more restrictions and fewer available seats. APEX fares provide you with confirmed reservations and allow "open-jaw" tickets (landing in and returning from different cities). Generally, reservations must be made seven to 21 days in advance, with seven- to 14-day minimum and up to 90-day maximum stay limits, and hefty cancellation and change penalties (fees rise in summer). Book APEX fares early during peak season; by May you will have a hard time getting the departure date you want.

Even if you pay an airline's lowest published fare, you may waste hundreds of dollars. For the adventurous or the bargain-hungry, there are other, perhaps more inconvenient or time-consuming options but, before shopping around, it is a good idea to find out the average commercial price in order to measure just how great a "bargain" you are being offered.

TICKET CONSOLIDATORS

Ticket consolidators resell unsold tickets on commercial and charter airlines at unpublished fares. Consolidator flights are the best deals if you are traveling: on short notice, you bypass advance purchase requirements, since you aren't tangled in airline bureaucracy; on a high-priced trip; to an offbeat destination; or in the peak season, when published fares are jacked way up. There is rarely a maximum age or stay limit but, unlike tickets bought through an airline, you won't be able to use your tickets on another flight if you miss yours and you will have to go back to the consolidator to get a refund, rather than the airline. Keep in mind that these tickets are often for coach seats on connecting (not direct) flights on foreign airlines and that frequent-flyer miles may not be credited. Decide what you can (and can't) live with (out) before shopping.

Consolidators come in three varieties: wholesale only, who sell only to travel agencies; specialty agencies (both wholesale and retail); and **"bucket shops"** or discount retail agencies. You, as a private consumer, can deal directly only with the latter, but you have access to a larger market if you use a travel agent, who can also get tickets from wholesale consolidators. Look for bucket shops' tiny ads in weekend papers (in the U.S., the *Sunday New York Times* is best). In London, the Air Travel Advisory Bureau (tel. (0171) 6365000) provides a list of consolidators.

Be a smart and careful shopper. Among the many reputable and trustworthy companies are, unfortunately, some shady wheeler-dealers. Contact the local Better Business Bureau to find out how long the company has been in business and its track record. Although not necessary, it is preferable to deal with consolidators close to home so you can visit in person, if necessary. Ask to receive your tickets as quickly as possible so you have time to fix any problems. Get the company's policy in writing: insist on a **receipt** that gives full details about the tickets, refunds, and restrictions and record who you talked to and when. It may be worth paying with a credit card (despite the 2-5% fee) so you can stop payment if you never receive your tickets. Beware the "bait and switch" gag: shyster firms will advertise a super-low fare and then tell a caller that it has been sold. Although this is a viable excuse, if they can't offer you a price near the advertised fare on *any* date, it is a scam to lure in customers—report them to the Better Business Bureau. Ask also about accommodations and car rental discounts; some consolidators have fingers in many pies.

START IN DOWNTOWN LONDON AND IN 3 HEURES, ARRIVEZ AU CENTRE DE PARIS.

Imagine traveling directly between London and Paris with no connections to run for; no busses to board, no taxis to hail. In fact, the only thing you have to change is the tongue you speak upon arrival.

That's exactly what you'll experience aboard the high-speed Eurostar passenger train.

Board the Eurostar at the center of one city, travel through the new Channel Tunnel, and arrive directly in the center of the other. Simple as that. And at speeds of up to 200 miles per hour, the entire trip lasts just three short hours. We can also get you between London and Brussels in three and a quarter.

For more information, simply contact your travel agent or Rail Europe at 1-800-EUROSTAR.

If a quick, comfortable trip between London and Paris is on your itinerary, you'll find we speak your language perfectly.

CALL 1-800-EUROSTAR.

For cheap fares to London, try **Airfare Busters,** offices in Washington, D.C. (tel. (800) 776-0481), Boca Raton, FL (tel. (800) 881-3273), and Houston, TX (tel. (713) 232-8783); **Pennsylvania Travel,** Paoli, PA (tel. (800) 331-0947); **Cheap Tickets,** offices in Los Angeles, CA, San Francisco, CA, Honolulu, HI, Overland Park, KS, and New York, NY (tel. (800) 377-1000); **Moment's Notice,** New York, NY (tel. (718) 234-6295; fax 234-6450), for air tickets, tours, and hotels (US$25 annual fee); **Rebel,** Valencia, CA (tel. (800) 227-3235) or Orlando, FL (tel. (800) 732-3588); or **Discount Travel International,** New York, NY (tel. (212) 362-3636; fax 362-3236). For a processing fee, depending on the number of travelers and the itinerary, **Travel Avenue,** Chicago, IL (tel. (800) 333-3335) will search for the lowest international airfare available and even give you a rebate on fares over US$300.

Kelly Monaghan's *Consolidators: Air Travel's Bargain Basement* (US$7 plus US$2 shipping) from the Intrepid Traveler, P.O. Box 438, New York, NY 10034 (e-mail intreptrav@aol.com), is an valuable source for more information and lists of consolidators by location and destination. Cyber-resources include **World Wide** (http:// www.tmn.com/wwwanderer/wwwa) and Edward Hasbrouck's incredibly informative **Airline ticket consolidators and bucket shops** (http://www.gnn.com/gnn/wic/ wics/trav.97.html).

STAND-BY FLIGHTS

Airhitch, 2641 Broadway, Third Floor, New York, NY 10025 (tel. (800) 326-2009 or (212) 864-2000) and Los Angeles, CA (tel. (310) 726-5000), will add a certain thrill to the prospect of when you will leave and where exactly you will end up. Complete flexibility on both sides of the Atlantic is necessary; flights cost US$169 each way when departing from the Northeast, US$269 from the West Coast or Northwest, and US$229 from the Southeast and Midwest. The snag is that you buy not a ticket, but the promise that you will get to a destination near where you're intending to go within a window of time (usually 5 days) from a location in a region you've specified. You call in before your date-range to hear all of your flight options for the next seven days and your probability of boarding. You then decide which flights you want to try to make and present a voucher at the airport which grants you the right to board a flight on a space-available basis. This procedure must be followed again for the return trip. Be aware that you may only receive a refund if all available flights which departed within your date and destination-range were full. There are several offices in Europe, so you can wait to register for your return; the main one is in Paris (tel. (1) 47 00 16 30). **Air-Tech, Ltd.,** 584 Broadway #1007, New York, NY 10012 (tel. (212) 219-7000; fax 219-0066) offers a very similar service. Their Travel Window is one to four days; rates to and from Europe (continually updated; call and verify) are: Northeast US$169, West Coast US$249, Midwest/Southeast US$199. Upon registration and payment, Air-Tech sends you a FlightPass with a contact date falling soon before your Travel Window, when you are to call them for flight instructions. Note that the service is one-way—you must go through the same procedure to return—and that *no refunds* are granted unless the company fails to get you a seat before your Travel Window expires. Air-Tech also arranges courier flights and regular confirmed-reserved flights at discount rates. Be sure to read all the fine print in your agreements with either company—a call to The Better Business Bureau of New York City may be worthwhile. Be warned that it's difficult to receive refunds, and that clients' vouchers won't be honored if an airline fails to receive payment in time.

CHARTER FLIGHTS

The theory behind a **charter** is that a tour operator contracts with an airline (usually one specializing in charters) to fly extra loads of passengers to peak-season destinations. Charter flights fly less frequently than major airlines and have more restrictions, particularly on refunds. They are also almost always fully booked and schedules and itineraries may change or be cancelled at the last moment (as late as 48 hours before the trip and without a full refund); you'll be much better off purchasing a ticket on a

ESSENTIALS

regularly scheduled airline. As always, pay with a credit card if you can; consider traveler's insurance against trip interruption.

Eleventh-hour **discount clubs** and **fare brokers** offer members savings on European travel, including charter flights and tour packages. Research your options carefully. **Last Minute Travel Club,** 1249 Boylston St., Boston, MA 02215 (tel. (800) 527-8646 or (617) 267-9800), and **Discount Travel International,** New York, NY (tel. (212) 362-3636; fax 362-3236), are among the few travel clubs that don't charge a membership fee. Others include **Moment's Notice,** New York, NY (tel. (718) 234-6295; fax (718) 234 6450) for air tickets, tours, and hotels (US$25 annual fee); **Travelers Advantage,** Stanford, CT (tel. (800) 835-8747; US$49 annual fee); and **Travel Avenue** (tel. (800) 333-3335; see **Ticket Consolidators,** above). Study these organizations' contracts closely—don't end up with an unwanted overnight layover.

COURIER COMPANIES AND FREIGHTERS

Those who travel light should consider flying to London as a **courier.** The company hiring you will use your checked luggage space for freight; you're only allowed to bring carry-ons. You are responsible for the safe delivery of the baggage claim slips (given to you by a courier company representative) to the representative waiting for you when you arrive—don't screw up or you will be blacklisted as a courier. You will probably never see the cargo you are transporting—the company handles it all—and airport officials know that couriers are not responsible for the baggage checked for them. Restrictions to watch for: you must be over 18, have a valid passport, and procure your own visa (if necessary); most flights are rountrip only with short fixed-length stays (usually one week); only single tickets are issued (but a companion may be able to get a next-day flight); and most flights are from New York. Rountrip fares to Western Europe from the U.S. range from US$250-400 (during the off-season) to US$400-550 (during the summer). **NOW Voyager,** 74 Varick St. #307, New York, NY 10013 (tel. (212) 431-1616), acts as an agent for many courier flights worldwide primarily from New York. They offer special last-minute deals to London for as little as US$200 rountrip plus a US$50 registration fee. Also try **Halbart Express,** 147-05 176th St., Jamaica, NY 11434 (tel. (718) 656-5000).

You can also go directly through courier companies in New York, or check your bookstore or library for handbooks such as *Air Courier Bargains* (US$15, plus$3.50 shipping from the Intrepid Traveler, P.O. Box 438, New York, NY 10034). *The Courier Air Travel Handbook* (US$10 plus US$3.50 shipping) explains how to travel as an air courier and contains names, phone numbers, and contact points of courier companies. It can be ordered directly from Bookmasters, Inc., P.O. Box 2039, Mansfield, OH 44905 (tel. (800) 507-2665).

A final caveat for the budget conscious: don't get caught up in the seemingly great deals. Always read the fine print; check for restrictions and hidden fees. There are cheap fares waiting to be unearthed, but you can't get something for nothing.

If you really have travel time to spare, **Ford's Travel Guides,** 19448 Londelius St., Northridge, CA 91324 (tel. (818) 701-7414; fax (818) 701-7415) lists **freighter companies** that'll take passengers worldwide. Ask for their *Freighter Travel Guide and Waterways of the World* (US$16, plus US$2.50 postage if mailed outside the U.S.).

■ By Train

In May 1994, the **Channel Tunnel** (Chunnel) was completed, physically connecting England and France, to the horror of some. This union is symbolized by the attendants on the new *Eurostar* trains. They speak fluent English while sporting uniforms created by the French designer Balmain. *Eurostar* operates rather like an airline with similar discounts, reservations, and restrictions. Major railpasses are not tickets to ride, they entitle you to discounts, as does being a youth. Call (800) EUROSTAR (387 6782) to purchase your ticket. In the U.K., call (01233) 617 575 for more information.

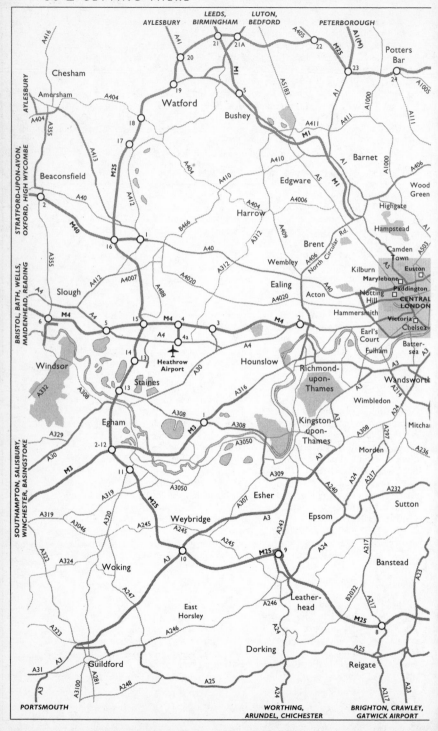

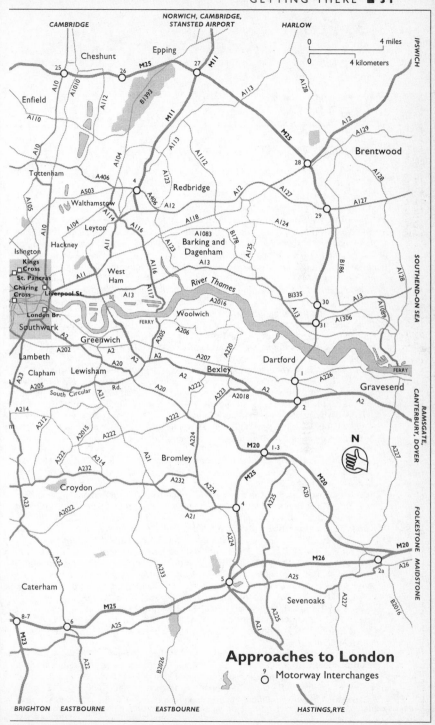

Approaches to London

○ Motorway Interchanges

■ By Ferry

To get between Britain and the Continent consider crossing the English Channel by **ferry** (Stena Sealink Line, Head Office, Charter House, Park St., Ashford, Kent TN24 8EX, England (tel. (01233) 647047)).

ONCE THERE

■ Emergencies and Help

Emergency medical care, psychological counseling, crash housing, and sympathetic support can often be found in London free of charge.

Britons receive largely free health care from the National Health Service (NHS). Foreign visitors do not, of course, get such favorable terms, but are nevertheless eligible for some free treatment, including: outpatient treatment in the Accident and Emergency (A&E) ward of an NHS hospital; treatment of communicable diseases (such as V.D., typhoid, or anthrax); and "compulsory" mental treatment. Unfortunately, many of the hospitals are shrinking their operations and no longer offer 24-hour care, so make sure you check where you are going before rushing out for help.

AIDS: National AIDS Helpline (tel. (0800) 567 123; 24hr.). Toll-free for information on testing, health care, or simply to answer questions and listen (for more on AIDS/HIV and travelling, see AIDS and HIV, p. 30).

Alcoholics Anonymous: London Helpline (tel. 352 3001) answered daily 10am-10pm; answering machine from 10pm-10am.

Automobile Breakdown: AA Breakdown service, tel. (0800) 887 766; 24-hr. RAC Breakdown Service, tel. (08000) 828 282.

British Diabetic Association: 10 Queen Anne St., London, W1M OBD (tel. (0171) 323 1531). Offers information on diabetic treatment and services and free travel guides specifically for diabetic concerns covering much of the world. Careline (tel. 636 6112) open Mon.-Fri. 9am-5pm to answer questions and concerns.

Citizen's Advice Bureaux: Holborn Library, 32-38 Theobald's Rd., WC1 (tel. 404 1497). Tube: Holborn. Several branches dot London and offer advice on anything from housing advice to silencing your neighbor's doberman. Open Mon.-Wed. and Fri. 2-4pm, Thurs. 5-7pm.

Dental Care: Eastman Dental Hospital, 256 Gray's Inn Rd., WC1 (tel. 915 1000; fax 915 1012). Phone for emergency treatment availability and times. Tube: Chancery La. or King's Cross.

Discrimination: Liberty: the National Council for Civil Liberties, 21 Tabard St., SE1 4LA. Tube: Borough. Advice on dealing with discrimination excluding education and housing issues, by letter only.

Domestic Violence/Rape: Women's Aid, 52-54 Featherstone St., EC1 (tel. 251 6537). 24-hr. helpline provides aid, advice, and emergency shelter for victims of domestic and sexual abuse. **The London Rape Crisis Centre's Rape Crisis Hotline,** P.O. Box 69, WC1 (tel. 837 1600). Allows you, emergency or not, to talk to another woman, receive legal or medical information, or obtain referrals. They'll send someone to accompany you to the police, doctors, clinics, and courts upon request. Phones answered Mon.-Fri. 6-10pm, Sat.-Sun. 10am-10pm.

Emergency (Medical, Police, and Fire): Dial 999; no coins required.

Family Planning Association: 2-12 Pentonville Rd., N1 (tel. 837 5432). Tube: Angel. Informational services: contraception, pregnancy test and abortion referral. Open Mon.-Fri. 9am-5pm.

Gay and Lesbian Information: see Gay and Lesbian London, p. 259.

Hospitals: In an emergency, you can be treated at no charge in the A&E ward of a hospital. You have to pay for routine medical care unless you work legally in Britain, in which case NHS tax will be deducted from your wages and you will not be charged. Socialized medicine has lowered fees here, so don't ignore any health problem merely because you are low on cash. The following have 24-hr. walk-in A&E (also known as casualty) departments: **Chelsea & Westminster Hospital,** 369 Fulham Rd., SW10 (tel. 746 8000; tube: South Kensington or Fulham Broadway); **Royal London Hospital,** Whitechapel Rd., E1 (tel. 377 7000; tube: Whitechapel); **Royal Free Hospital,** Pond St., NW3 (tel. 794 0500; tube: Belsize Park or BR: Hampstead Heath); **Charing Cross Hospital,** Fulham Palace Rd. (entrance St. Dunstan's Rd.), W6 (tel. (0181) 846 1234; tube: Baron's Ct. or Hammersmith); **St. Thomas' Hospital,** Lambeth Palace Rd., SE1 (tel. 928 9292; tube: Westminster); **University College Hospital,** Gower St. (entrance on Grafton Way), WC1 (tel. 380 9857; tube: Euston or Warren St.). For others, look under "Hospitals" in the gray Businesses and Services phone book.

Information for Travelers with Disabilities: Phone **RADAR** (tel. 250 3222) Mon.-Fri. 10am-4pm Mon.-Fri. or the **Greater London Association for the Disabled** (tel. 274 0107) Mon. 9am-5pm, Tues.-Fri. 2pm-5pm for general info.

Legal Advice: Release, 388 Old St., EC1 (tel. 729 9904; 24-hr. emergency number 603 8654). Tube: Liverpool St. or Old St. Specializes in criminal law and advising those who have been arrested on drug charges. Open by appointment only Mon.-Fri. 10am-6pm. **Legal Aid Board,** 29-37 Red Lion St., WC1 (tel. 813 5300). Tube: Holborn. Provides representation (upon a solicitor's referral) for minimal fees. Open Mon.-Fri. 9am-5pm.

Narcotics Anonymous: (tel. 730 0009). Hotline answered daily 10am-8pm, open till 10pm Mon., Tues. and Thurs.

Victim Support National: Cranmer House, 39 Brixton Rd., SW9 (tel. 735 9166). Tube: Oval. Trained volunteers based in 378 local schemes in England, Wales, and Northern Ireland offer emotional support, information, and practical help to victims of crime. Details available from the national office (open Mon.-Fri. 9am-5:30pm, answering machine at other times).

Pharmacies: Every police station keeps a list of emergency doctors and chemists in its area. Listings under "Chemists" in the Yellow Pages. **Bliss Chemists** at Marble Arch (5 Marble Arch, W1; tel. 723 6116) is open daily, including public holidays, 9am-midnight.

Police: Stations in every district of London, including: Headquarters, New Scotland Yard, Broadway, SW1 (tel. 230 1212; tube: St. James's Park); West End Central, 10 Vine St., W1 (tel. 437 1212; tube: Piccadilly Circus); King's Cross, 76 King's Cross Rd., WC1 (tel. 704 1212; tube: King's Cross); Kensington, 72 Earl's Court Rd., W8 (tel. 376 6212; tube: Earl's Ct.).

Police Complaints: If the problem is the police, contact the **Police Complaint Authority,** 10 Great George St., SW1 (tel. 273 6450). Be sure to note the offending officer's number (worn on the shoulder).

Shelter: *Sleeping in the open is not only uncomfortable, it is highly dangerous.* Several organizations provide emergency shelter in London. The **Salvation Army** has a battery of emergency hostels: the **Booth House** (Whitechapel Rd., E1 (tel. 247 3401; tube: Whitechapel) and **Parkway** (12 Inverness Terr., W2 (tel. 229 9223; tube: Bayswater) are men-only. **Hopetown** (60 Old Montague St., E1; tel. 247 1004) is women only; all will do their best to accommodate you or refer you to a place that will. The **Piccadilly Advice Centre** (100 Shaftesbury Ave., W1 (tel. 434 1877; fax. 734 8678); tube: Piccadilly Circus) provides advice, information, and referrals to the "young, homeless, or new to London." Call to ask about soup-runs (free food) and night shelters (open daily 2-6pm and 7-9pm). The **Shelter Nightline** (tel. (0800) 446 441), a volunteer-run helpline, offers free advice on emergency accommodations (open Mon.-Fri. 6pm-9am, Sat.-Sun. 24hr).

Samaritans: 46 Marshall St., W1 (tel. 734 2800). Tube: Oxford Circus. Highly respected 24-hr. crisis hotline provides a listening (rather than advice) for suicidal depression and other problems.

Sexual Health: Jefferiss Wing Centre for Sexual Health, St. Mary's Hospital, Praed St., W2 (tel. 725 6619). Tube: Paddington. Free and confidential sexual health services. Drop-in for free condoms and dental dams, STDs testing, and AIDS and HIV tests and counselling. Open Mon. 8:45am-7pm, Tues. and Fri. 8:45am-6pm, Wed. 10:45am-6pm, Thurs. 8am-6pm, Sat. 10am-noon.

Women's Health: see Women Travelers, p. 30.

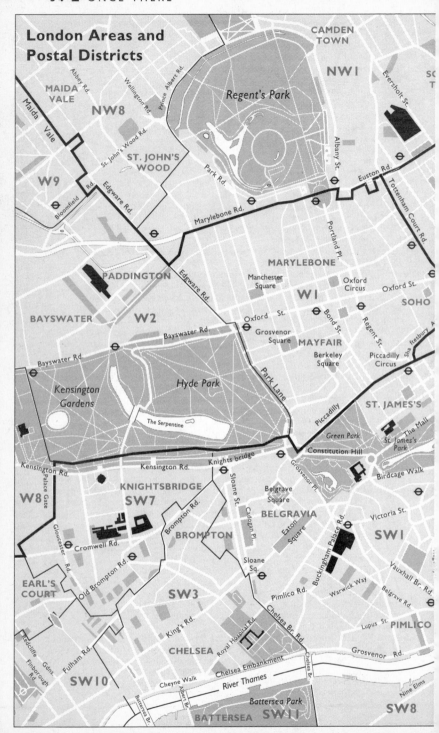

London Areas and Postal Districts

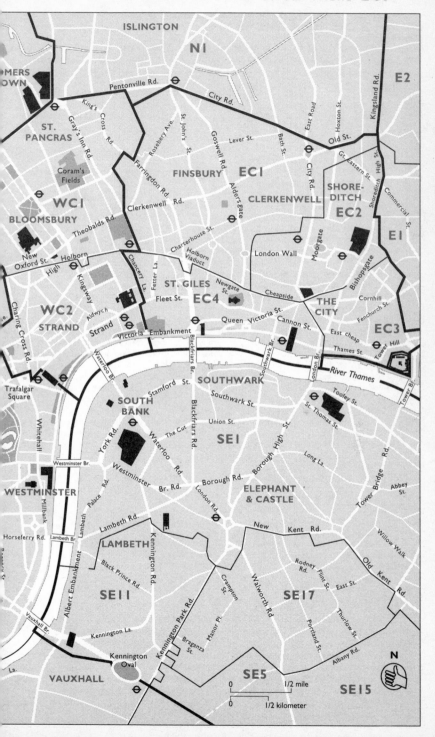

ISLINGTON

N1

MERS
OWN

Pentonville Rd.

City Rd.

E2

King's Cross Rd.

Kingsland Rd.

ST.
PANCRAS

Gray's Inn Rd.

East Road

Old St.

Hoxton St.

Gt. Eastern St.

Shoreditch High St.

Commercial St.

St. John's St.

Rosebery Ave.

Farringdon Rd.

Goswell Rd.

Lever St.

Bath St.

City Rd.

FINSBURY

EC1

SHORE-
DITCH

Coram's
Fields

WC1

CLERKENWELL

EC2

E1

BLOOMSBURY

Clerkenwell Rd.

Aldersgate

Theobalds Rd.

Charterhouse St.

London Wall

Moorgate

Bishopsgate

New
Oxford St.

Holborn

Holborn
Viaduct

High

Chancery La.

Fetter La.

ST. GILES

Newgate St.

Cheapside

Cornhill

Fenchurch St.

Kingsway

Fleet St.

EC4

Queen Victoria St.

THE
CITY

East cheap

EC3

WC2

Aldwych

STRAND

Strand

Cannon St.

Thames St.

Tower Hill

Charing Cross Rd.

Victoria Embankment

Blackfriars Br.

Southwark Br.

London Br.

River Thames

Tower Br.

Waterloo Br.

Trafalgar
Square

SOUTHWARK

Tooley St.

Whitehall

SOUTH
BANK

Stamford St.

Southwark St.

St. Thomas St.

York Rd.

Waterloo Rd.

The Cut

Blackfriars Rd.

Union St.

SE1

Long La.

Tower Bridge Rd.

Abbey St.

Westminster Br.

Westminster

Br. Rd.

Borough Rd.

Borough High St.

London Rd.

ELEPHANT
& CASTLE

WESTMINSTER

Palace Rd.

Lambeth

Millbank

Horseferry Rd.

Lambeth Br.

Lambeth Rd.

Kennington Rd.

New

Kent Rd.

Willow Walk

LAMBETH

Black Prince Rd.

Rodney
Rd.

Flint St.

Old Kent Rd.

Albert Embankment

SE11

Kennington Park Rd.

Crampton St.

Manor Pl.

Walworth Rd.

East St.

Portland St.

Thurlow St.

SE17

Albany Rd.

Vauxhall Br.

Kennington La.

Braganza
St.

N

Kennington
Oval

SE5

SE15

VAUXHALL

La.

0   1/2 mile

0   1/2 kilometer

■ Tourist Offices

London Tourist Board Information Centre: Victoria Station Forecourt, SW1 (tel. (0839) 123 432; recorded message only; 39-49p/min., available within U.K. only.). Tube: Victoria. Information on London and England, a well-stocked bookshop, theater and tour bookings, and an accommodations service (a hefty £5 booking fee, plus 15% refundable deposit). Expect long waits at peak hours, around noon. Their cheapest rooms cost £22, most run £25-30. Victoria Station center open April.-Nov. daily 8am-7pm; Dec.-March Mon.-Sat. 8am-7pm, Sun. 8am-5pm. Additional tourist offices located at **Heathrow Airport** (open April-Nov. daily 9am-6pm; Dec.-March 9am-5pm), **Liverpool St. Underground Station** (open Mon. 8:15am-7pm, Tues.-Sat. 8:15am-6pm, Sun 8:30am-4:45pm), and **Selfridges** department stores during store hours (see Department Stores, p. 249).

British Travel Centre: 12 Regent St., SW. Tube: Piccadilly Circus. Down Regent St. from the Lower Regent St. tube exit. Run by the British Tourist Authority (tel. (0181) 846 9000) and ideal for travelers bound for destinations outside of London. Combines the services of the BTA, British Rail, and a Traveller's Exchange with an accommodations service. £5 surcharge for booking and a required deposit (either 1 night's stay or 15% of the total stay depending on the place; does not book for hostels). Also sells maps, theater tickets, books, and pamphlets translated into many languages. Pleasantly relaxed compared to LTB, but equally long queues. Open Mon.-Fri. 9am-6:30pm, Sat. 9am-5pm, Sun. 10am-4pm; Nov.-April Mon.-Fri. 9am-6:30pm, Sat. and Sun. 10am-4pm.

City of London Information Centre: St. Paul's Churchyard, EC4 (tel. 606 3030). Tube: St. Paul's. Specializes in information about the City of London but answers questions on all of London. Helpful, knowledgeable staff. Open daily 9:15am-5pm; Nov.-March Mon.-Fri. 9:15am-5pm, Sat. 9:15am-12:30pm.

London Transport Information Offices: (24-hr. information line, tel. 222 1234). At Euston (Mon.-Sat. 7:15am-6pm, Sun 8:30am-5pm); Victoria (Mon.-Sat. 8am-7pm, Sun. 8:45am-7pm); King's Cross (Mon.-Sat. 8am-6pm, Sun. 8:30am-5pm); Liverpool St. (Mon.-Sat. 8am-6pm, Sun. 8:30am-4:40pm); Oxford Circus (Mon.-Sat. 8:45am-6pm); Piccadilly (daily 8:45am-6pm); St. James's Park (Mon.-Fri. 8:30am-5:30pm); Heathrow 123 station (Mon.-Sat. 7:15am-7pm, Sun. 8:15am-7pm); Heathrow Terminal 1 (Mon.-Sat. 7:15am-10pm, Sun. 8:15am-10pm); Heathrow Terminal 2 (Mon.-Sat. 7:15am-5pm, Sun. 8:15am-5pm); Heathrow Terminal 4 (Mon.-Sat. 6am-3pm, Sun. 7:15am-3pm); Hammersmith (Mon.-Fri 7:15am-6pm, Sat. 8:15am-6pm); and West Croydon Bus Station (Mon. 7am-7pm, Tues.-Fri. 7:30am-7pm, Sat. 8am-6:30pm). Helpful agents can give advice on travel by underground or bus. Free maps. Booths sell helpful brochures, guidebooks, and the museum Whitecard (see Museums, p. 214).

Greenwich Tourist Information Centre, 48 Greenwich Church St., SE10 (tel. (0181) 858 6376). Offers information on sights in Greenwich and surrounding areas. Open daily 10:15am-4:45pm.

Islington Tourist Information Centre, 44 Duncan St., N1 (tel. 278 8787). Information on Islington and other North London sights. Open Mon.-Sat. 10am-5pm.

Southwark Tourist Information Centre, Hay's Galleria, Tooley St., SE1. Helpful advice in navigating the newly dynamic areas south of the muddy Thames. Open Mon.-Fri. 11am-5:30pm, Sat. and Sun. noon-5:30pm.

■ Embassies and High Commissions

If anything goes seriously wrong, inquire first at your country's consulate. Consulary offices are housed within each country's London embassy or high commission. The distinction between an embassy and a consulate is significant: an embassy houses the ambassador's office and staff; you won't gain access unless you know someone inside. All facilities for dealing with nationals are in the consulate. If your passport is lost or stolen, go to the consulate as soon as possible to get a replacement. The consulate keeps lists of local lawyers and doctors, will notify family members of accidents, and has information on how to proceed with legal problems, but its functions end there. Don't ask the consulate to pay for your hotel or medical bills, investigate crimes, obtain work permits, post bail, or interfere with standard legal proceedings. If you are arrested during your stay, there is little, if anything, that your own government can do to help you, so behave yourself. All embassies and High Commissions close on English holidays.

United States Embassy: 24 Grosvenor Sq., W1 (tel. 499 9000). Tube: Bond St. Phones answered 24hr.

Australian High Commission: Australia House, The Strand, WC2 (tel. 379 4334; in emergency, tel. 438 8181). Tube: Aldwych or Temple. Visa info (0891) 600 333. Passport info dial main line between 2-4pm. Open Mon.-Fri. 9:30am-3:30pm.

Canadian High Commission: MacDonald House, 1 Grosvenor Sq., W1 (tel. 258 6600). Tube: Bond St. or Oxford Circus. Visas Mon.-Fri. 8-11am.

Irish Embassy: 17 Grosvenor Pl., SW1 (tel. 235 2171). Tube: Hyde Park Corner. Open Mon.-Fri. 9:30am-1pm and 2:15-5pm.

New Zealand High Commission: New Zealand House, 80 Haymarket, SW1 (tel. 930 8422). Tube: Charing Cross. Open Mon.-Fri. 10am-noon and 2-4pm.

South African High Commission: South Africa House, Trafalgar Sq., WC2 (tel. 451 7299). Tube: Charing Cross. Open 10am-noon and 2-4pm.

■ Getting In and Out of London

FROM THE AIRPORT

With planes landing every 47 seconds, **Heathrow Airport** (tel. (0181) 759 4321) in Hounslow, Middlesex, is the world's busiest international airport. The bureau de change in each terminal are open daily. The most recognizable bureaux are the red **Thomas Cook** booths which are found in every terminal. The easiest way to reach central London from Heathrow is by **Underground** (Piccadilly line, about 45min. to central London), with one stop for terminals 1, 2, and 3 and another for terminal 4. To reach **Victoria Station,** transfer at Gloucester Rd. or South Kensington to a District Line or Circle Line train heading east. At Victoria, you'll find a blue **Tourist Information Centre** with an accommodations service, currency exchange, and help with transportation connections (see Getting Around, p. 64).

London Regional Transport's **Airbus** (tel. 222 1234) makes the one-hour trip from Heathrow to central points in the city. The Airbus A1 runs to Victoria, stopping at Hyde Park Corner, Harrods, and the Earl's Ct. tube station. Airbus A2 runs to Russell Sq., with stops at Euston Station, Baker St. station, Marble Arch, Paddington station, Queensway station, Notting Hill Gate station, and Holland Park. (Both buses run daily 6:15am-8:30pm; £6, children £4.) **Airbus Direct** is a faster bus service (same prices as Airbus) which stops only in the center of the City and at Hyde Park Corner.

Gatwick Airport in West Sussex (tel. (0293) 535 353) is London's second-busiest airport. Heathrow is not close to the city and Gatwick is even farther. A number of 24-hour restaurants and bureaux de change are located in both the North and South Terminals. From Gatwick, take the **BR Gatwick Express** (tel. 928 2113) for recorded schedule) train to Victoria Station (daily 5:30am-11pm every 15min., 11pm-1am and 4-5:30am every 30min., 1-4am every hr. on the hr.; 35min.; 1-mo. open return £15, day return £8.50-10). **National Express coaches** run between Gatwick and Victoria (5:30am-10pm every hr.; 1hr.; £7.50, return £11).

Taxis which congregate outside the terminals charge a fee based upon distance which is designed for short hops in the city. Fares from central London to Heathrow run at least £30; from central London to Gatwick, expect to pay £50-60. Travelers who are too loaded down with bulky bags to negotiate the stairs and escalators entailed by public transport should consider using **Airport Transfers,** a private chauffeur service (tel. 403 2228). For a flat rate, London Airways will take up to four people from either airport to any central London destination (£15/car from Heathrow, £30/car from Gatwick).

Flights from the U.S. go into both Gatwick and Heathrow. Double check which airport your flight serves before you leave. Major international flights are now arriving in upstart **Stansted Airport,** northeast of London in Stansted, Essex (tel. (01279) 680 500). Stansted is served by British Rail's **Stansted Express** (tel. (01223) 311 999) to Liverpool St. Station (every 30min. Mon.-Fri. 5am-11pm, Sat. 5:30am-11pm, Sun. 7am-11pm; 41min.; £10, under 15 £5).

FROM THE TRAIN STATIONS

British Rail (BR) trains leave London from several stations on the perimeter of Central London. All BR stations are served by Tube as well. To begin your journey you must first find out which of the stations your train will be leaving from. This can be a surprisingly difficult task at times. British Rail, once owned by the government, is in the process of being split up and sold off to private corporations. The practical effect on travelers is that there is no single number one may call to get information on how to get from here to there. Instead, the traveler should call one of the following six numbers depending upon desired destination:

To East Anglia, Essex, Southern England, Northeast, and South London: tel. 928 5100. Open 24hr.

To the South Midlands, West of England, South Wales, West London, and Republic of Ireland via Fishguard: tel. 262 6767. Open Mon.-Sat. 7am-10:30pm and Sun. 8am-10:30pm.

To the East and West Midlands, North Wales, Northwest England, Scotland via West Coast, Northwest London, Northern Ireland, and Republic of Ireland via Holyhead: tel. 387 7070. Open 24hr.

To East and Northeast England, Scotland via East Coast, and North London: tel. 278 2477. Open Mon.-Sat. 7am-10:30pm and Sun. 8am-10:30pm.

To Europe: tel. 834 2345 or by Eurostar (thru the Chunnel) tel. (0345) 881 881.

Any of the tourist information centers run by the London Tourist Board or the British Tourist Authority can help you navigate the difficult maze that is the newly deregulated British Rail (see Tourist Offices and Embassies, p. 56).

To get a **Young Person's Railcard** (£16), you must be under 24 or a full-time student in the U.K. A **Senior Railcard** for persons over 60 also costs £16. Both will save you one-third on off-peak travel for one year. A **Network Card** gives the same discount for travel in the Network South East area. The **Network Rover** allows unlimited travel on Network Southeast for the daytripper (3 days on weekend £47; 7 days £69; children ½-price). Ask at any mainline station.

FROM THE BUS STATIONS

Victoria Coach Station (tube: Victoria), located on Buckingham Palace Rd., is the hub of Britain's coach network. **National Express coaches** (tel. (0990) 808080) service an expansive network which links cities big and small. Coaches are considerably less expensive than trains but also take longer. National Express offers a **Discount Coach Card** (£7) to students, youths 16-25, seniors, and disabled persons (30% discount). Other coach companies compete with National Express; their routes often overlap and prices are almost identical.

Much of the commuting area around London, including Hampton Court and Windsor, is served by **Green Line** coaches, which leave frequently from Eccleston Bridge behind Victoria Station. (For information, call (0181) 668 7261 Mon.-Fri. 8am-8:30pm, Sat.-Sun. 9am-5pm; or try the information kiosk on Eccleston Bridge.) Purchase tickets from the driver. Prices for day returns are higher before 9am Monday through Friday. Green Line discounts include the one-day **Rover** ticket (£7, children and seniors £4, valid on almost every Green Line coach and London Country bus Mon.-Fri. after 9am, Sat.-Sun. all day).

HITCHHIKING AND RIDE SHARING

Women, even in a group, should never hitchhike. Men should consider all of the risks involved before hitching. Anyone who values safety will take a train or bus out of London. Hitchers often check the University of London Union's ride board, on the ground floor of 1 Malet St., WC1 (tube: Russell Sq.), or ask at youth hostels for possibilities. Hitching can be quite difficult within central London and reasonably easy from places like Cambridge and Oxford to the city. Let's Go does not recommend hitchhiking as a safe means of transportation.

Freewheelers is a **"lift agency"** which can match you up to a driver going your way. Membership (£10/year) is required. Each match-up costs £3. The price for the trip itself is agreed between the passenger and driver based on fuel costs, approximately 3½p/mi. The agency requires that members abide by a safety procedure to confirm each other's identity and keeps records of all members and matches made. Single-sex matching can be arranged. But Freewheelers does not take responsibility for members' safety—you are still getting in a car with a stranger. For more details, call (0191) 222 0090, fax (0191) 221 0066, e-mail freewheelers@freewheelers.co.uk, http://www.freewheelers.co.uk/freewheelers, or write to Freewheelers, Ltd., 25 Low Friar St., Newcastle upon Tyne, NE1 5UE.

■ Orientation

Greater London is a colossal aggregate of distinct villages and anonymous suburbs, of ancient settlements and modern developments. As London grew, it swallowed adjacent cities and nearby villages and chewed up the counties of Kent, Surrey, Essex, Hertfordshire, and Middlesex. "The City" now refers to the ancient, and much smaller, "City of London," which covers but one of the 620-sq.-mi. of Greater London. London is divided into boroughs and into postal code areas. The borough name and postal code appear at the bottom of most street signs. Areas or neighborhoods are more vaguely delineated, but correspond roughly to the numbered postal areas; the district names are used frequently in non-postal discourse.

Most of the sightseer's London falls within the five central boroughs: the **City of London,** the **City of Westminster, Kensington and Chelsea, Camden,** and **Islington.** This region north of the river Thames is bounded roughly by the Underground's Circle line. The center of most visits to London is usually the **West End,** an area primarily within the borough of the City of Westminster. The West End incorporates the elegant Georgian façades of Mayfair, the crowded shopping streets around Oxford Street, the vibrant labyrinth of gay- and fashion-conscious Soho, and the chic market in Covent Garden. All distances in London are measured from **Charing Cross,** the official center of London, on the south side of Trafalgar Square.

East of the West End, toward the City of London, lies **Holborn,** the center of legal activity, and **Fleet Street,** until recently the center of British journalism. Though the **City of London** is no longer the hub of central London, it continues to function as the metropolis' financial heart. Here St. Paul's Cathedral is skirted by newer, taller buildings. The Tower of London, at the eastern boundary of the City, stands between central London and the vast **Docklands** building site stretching down the Thames— once port to the Empire, now the face of a new commercial Britain.

Northeast of the West End, **Bloomsbury** harbors the British Museum, the core of London University, and scores of bookshops and art galleries. North and northwest of the West End, tidy terraces cling to the streets bordering Regent's Park in the districts of **Marylebone, Camden Town,** and **St. John's Wood. Islington** to the northeast harbors an artsy intellectual image and houses a growing gay community. One stage farther north, **Hampstead** and **Highgate** are separated from each other by the enormous Hampstead Heath. Two of London's most expensive residential areas, they command exceptional views of the city. Lying west of the West End, the faded squares of Paddington and Bayswater give way to Notting Hill, home each August bank holiday to the largest street carnival in Europe.

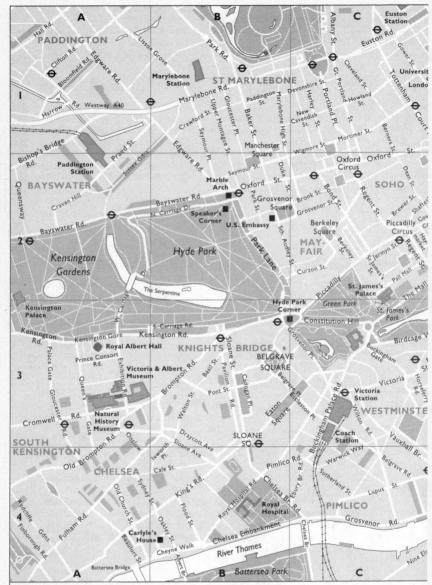

Central London: Major Street Finder

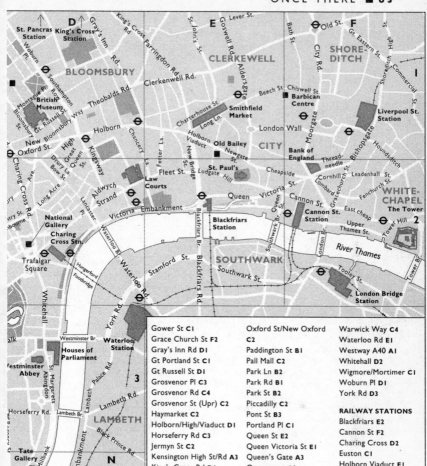

Gower St **C1**
Grace Church St **F2**
Gray's Inn Rd **D1**
Gt Portland St **C1**
Gt Russell St **D1**
Grosvenor Pl **C3**
Grosvenor Rd **C4**
Grosvenor St (Upr) **C2**
Haymarket **C2**
Holborn/High/Viaduct **D1**
Horseferry Rd **C3**
Jermyn St **C2**
Kensington High St/Rd **A3**
King's Cross Rd **D1**
King's Rd **B4**
Kingsway **D2**
Knightsbridge **B3**
Lambeth Palace Rd **D3**
Lisson Grove **A1**
Lombard St **F2**
London Wall **E1**
Long Acre/Grt Queen **D2**
Long Ln **E1**
Ludgate Hill **E2**
Marylebone High St **B1**
Marylebone Rd **B1**
Millbank **D4**
Montague Pl **D1**
Moorgate **F1**
New Bridge St **E2**
New Cavendish **C1**
Newgate St **E1**
Nine Elms Ln **C4**
Oakley St **B4**
Old St **F1**
Old Brompton Rd **A4**
Onslow Sq/St **A3**

Oxford St/New Oxford **C2**
Paddington St **B1**
Pall Mall **C2**
Park Ln **B2**
Park Rd **B1**
Park St **B2**
Piccadilly **C2**
Pont St **B3**
Portland Pl **C1**
Queen St **E2**
Queen Victoria St **E1**
Queen's Gate **A3**
Queensway **A2**
Redcliffe Gdns **A4**
Regent St **C2**
Royal Hospital Rd **B4**
St. James's St **C2**
Seymour Pl **A1**
Seymour St **A2**
Shaftesbury Ave **C2**
Sloane/Lwr Sloane **B3**
Southampton Row **D1**
Southwark Bridge Rd **E2**
Southwark Rd **E2**
St. Margarets/Abingdon **D3**
Stamford St **E2**
Strand **D2**
Sydney St **A4**
Thames St(Upr&Lwr) **F2**
The Mall **C2**
Theobald's Rd **D1**
Threadneedle St **F2**
Tottenham Ct Rd **C1**
Vauxhall Br. Rd **C4**
Victoria Embankment **D2**
Victoria St **C3**

Warwick Way **C4**
Waterloo Rd **E1**
Westway A40 **A1**
Whitehall **D2**
Wigmore/Mortimer **C1**
Woburn Pl **D1**
York Rd **D3**

RAILWAY STATIONS
Blackfriars **E2**
Cannon St **F2**
Charing Cross **D2**
Euston **C1**
Holborn Viaduct **E1**
King's Cross **D1**
Liverpool St **F1**
London Bridge **F2**
Marylebone **B1**
Paddington **A2**
St Pancras **D1**
Victoria **C3**
Waterloo East **E3**
Waterloo **D3**

BRIDGES
Albert **B4**
Battersea **A4**
Blackfriars **E2**
Chelsea **C4**
Hungerford Footbridge **D2**
Lambeth **D3**
London Bridge **F2**
Southwark **E2**
Tower Bridge **F2**
Waterloo **D2**
Westminster **D3**

Edgware Rd **A1**
Euston Rd **C1**
Exhibition Rd **A3**
Farringdon Rd **E1**
Fenchurch/Aldgate **F2**
Fleet St **E2**
Fulham Rd **A4**
Gloucester Pl **B1**
Gloucester Rd **A3**
Goswell Rd **E1**

South and southwest of the West End, still in the City of Westminster, is the actual district known as **Westminster.** This is England's royal, legislative, and ecclesiastical center, home of Buckingham Palace, the Houses of Parliament, and Westminster Abbey. Belgravia, packed with embassies, nestles between Westminster and the semi-gracious borough of **Kensington** and **Chelsea.** The shops of Knightsbridge and Kensington High Street, the excellent museums of South Kensington, the "posers" stalking King's Road in Chelsea, and the Australians and the large gay male population in Earl's Court ensure that this borough has no single image.

London's suburbs extend for mi. in all directions. To the southwest, **Kew** luxuriates in its exquisite botanical gardens. In adjacent **Richmond** the expansive deer park brings wildlife to the capital. Towards the southeast, **Greenwich** takes pride in its rich navigational and astronomical history on the privileged path of the Prime Meridian. **Brixton,** just south of the river, is home to a large African and Caribbean community. Farther south lies the residential suburb of **Wimbledon,** site of the famed tennis tournament. Far out on the fringes of northeast greater London, ancient **Epping Forest** manages to preserve a degree of wildness and straddles the eastern and western hemispheres.

At times you'll need the ingenuity of Sherlock Holmes to find one of London's more obscure addresses. Some homeowners favor names rather than numbers and the owner of a house on a corner is free to choose either street name as an address. Numbering starts at the end of the street nearest the center of London, but note that house numbers on opposite sides of large streets increase at different rates; house no. 211 may face no. 342. Numbers occasionally go up one side of the street and down the other. Some streets abruptly change names, disappear, and then materialize again after a hundred yards, while others twist through and around greens. You might find yourself in a tangle of Eaton Mews, Eaton Square, Eaton Gate, Eaton Place, and Eaton Terrace. There are 31 variations on Victoria Road and 40 streets named Wellington. To navigate this mess, get a comprehensive street map or guide with a complete index, such as **London A to Z** ("A to Zed," as streetwise Londoners call it), *ABC Street Atlas,* or Nicholson's *London Streetfinder* (from £2). Even if you only intend to stay in London for a week or so, the outlay is well worth it.

Postal code prefixes, which often appear on London street signs and in street addresses, may help you find your way. The letters stand for compass directions, with reference to the central district (itself divided into WC and EC, for West Central and East Central). All districts that border this central district are numbered "1." There are no S or NE codes.

■ Getting Around

London's public transit system, operated by **London Regional Transport (LRT),** is impressively comprehensive. The **Underground** (known as "the tube") is supplemented by **buses,** the **Docklands Light Railway (DLR),** and by **British Rail (BR).** Because government subsidies for public transport are very low, London's public transport system is one of the most expensive systems to ride when compared to other world capitals. Nevertheless, London Transport is the busiest system in Western Europe and public transport is always cheaper than a taxi.

In general, fares on all modes of public transportation in Britain are either "single" (one way) or "return" (rountrip). When riding the tube or buses, a return ticket costs exactly twice as much as a single. BR offers significant savings for "day returns" (both legs traveled same day) and slightly less spectacular savings on "period returns" (requiring you to return within a specific number of days).

Information on both buses and the tube is available on the **24-hour help line** (tel. 222 1234). The line is busy in the early mornings but you should get an operator within two to three minutes during all other times. Pick up free maps and guides at **London Transport's Information Centres.** Look for a lowercase "i" beside the distinctive "roundel" logo at information windows and on signs (see Government information Offices, p. 15). For recorded information on how the buses and Underground trains are currently running, phone 222 1200 (24hr.). London Transport's **lost property office** (tel. 486 2496) lies just down the road from Holmes and Watson at 200 Baker St., W1 (tube: Baker St.; open Mon.-Fri. 9:30am-2pm). Allow two working days for articles lost on buses or the tube to reach the office.

London is divided into six concentric transport zones. Central London, including most of the major sights, is covered by zone 1; Heathrow Airport is zone 6. Fares depend on the distance of the journey and the number of zones crossed. The **Travelcard,** because of its price and flexibility of both its duration and the zones it covers, is a must for budget travelers. It can be bought for one day, one week, or one month's worth of travel. One-day Travelcards have certain restrictions: they cannot be used before 9:30am Monday-Friday, and are not valid on night buses (adult **one-day Travelcard,** zones 1 and 2, £3). The one-week and one-month Travelcards can be used at any time and are valid for Night Bus travel. You will need a passport-sized photo in order to purchase a one-week or one-month Travelcard. Photo booths can be found in major tube stations, including Victoria, Leicester Sq., Earl's Ct., and Oxford Circus (about £3 for 4 pictures). Most tourists will find the zones 1&2 cards the most useful and economical. All Travelcards can be used on the Underground, regular buses, British Rail, and the Docklands Light Railway. Travelcards can be purchased at Underground ticket offices, London Transport Information Centres, and PASS agents throughout the city; credit cards are accepted. (Adult **1-wk. Travelcard,** zones 1&2, £14.80; **adult 1-mo. Travelcard,** zones 1&2, £56.90.) **Weekend travelcards** (adult, zones 1&2, £4.50) consist of two valid one-day travelcards for Saturday and Sunday (or any two consecutive days on a holiday weekend) which cannot be used on Night buses. A valid Travelcard will save you money on tube and BR trains regardless of zone—ask for an extension ticket before boarding.

Travel agents in your home country can sell you Travelcards or vouchers for Travelcards before you leave. Prices in your country's currency are calculated in April and, based upon April's exchange rate, cost the same as buying with pounds. Of course, as the exchange rates fluctuate, buying in home currency may be a bit of a bargain or a loss, though these alterations are apt to be small. Travelcards purchased abroad can be for two to six days (whereas only one- and seven-day travelcards are available in London) which may mean savings if you're here for a short trip.

UNDERGROUND

The color-coded **Underground** railway system, or the **tube,** is the easiest way to get around London, with 273 stations (give or take) on 11 lines (Bakerloo, Central, Circle, District, East London, Hammersmith and City, Jubilee, Metropolitan, Northern, Piccadilly, and Victoria). Call the 24-hr. tube info line for help (tel. 222 1234). Small but invaluable "Journey Planner" maps are available at all stations. The stylization reduces above-ground geographic accuracy, but greatly increases lucidity.

Fares depend on the number of zones passed through—a journey wholly within central zone 1 will cost much less than a trip to a distant suburb. On Sundays and Bank Holidays (see Appendix, p. 294), trains run less frequently. All transfers are free. Bicycles are allowed on the above-ground sections of the Circle, District, Metropolitan, and Piccadilly lines for a child's fare except during morning and evening rush hours. A single adult ticket will cost between £1.10-3.20, with most central London trips costing £1.10-1.40. Return tickets cost exactly double the price of a single ticket. If you plan to make more than two trips in a day a Travelcard will save you money. You may also consider buying a **Carnet** (£10), which is a booklet entitling you to 10 one-way trips within Zone 1, if you'll be using the tube sporadically.

You can buy your ticket either from the ticket window or from a machine. The ticket allows you to go through the automatic gates; keep it until you reach your final destination, where the exit gates will collect it. Be aware that inspectors are becoming rather strict about enforcing the tube's new on-the-spot £10 fine for travel without a valid ticket. Acting the befuddled foreigner may not get you off the hook.

Most tube lines' **last trains** leave Central London between midnight and 12:30am; service resumes around 6am. The gap in service is bridged by Night Buses. The tube,

unremittingly packed during rush hour (Mon.-Fri. roughly 7-10am and 4:30-7:30pm), earns its share of flak due to delays, dirt, and diverted trains; the Northern line has been nicknamed "the misery line" because of its rush hour bedlam. Bear in mind that some distant suburban stations close on Sundays and other off-peak periods. Smoking is not allowed anywhere in or on the tube.

Some of London's deepest tube stations were used as air-raid shelters during the Blitz. At the worst of the bombing, as many as 175,000 people took shelter in them in one night; some were unable or unwilling to leave for days on end. While some stations may still bring bomb shelters to mind (indeed many remain virtually unchanged since then), others are quite jazzy with their intricate, colorful mosaics, often cryptically related to their name. London Transport continues its tradition of stylish poster art by commissioning paintings from contemporary artists for its "By Tube" posters and has expanded to posting poems by writers from Middle English scrawlers to contemporary versifiers.

Many stations feature labyrinthine tunnels and steep staircases so, if you're carrying a lot of luggage, you might fare better on a longer route that requires fewer transfers. Fitness zealots may wish to tackle the 331-step climb at Hampstead station, London's deepest. If you find yourself suffering from vertigo on the endless escalator, take heart from the example set by wooden-legged "Bumper" Harris. When London Transport installed the first escalators at Earl's Court in 1911, they hired Bumper to ascend and descend all day, thereby encouraging weak-kneed passengers. And remember to stand to the right and walk on the left on escalators, or risk a rude tumbling from commuters in full stride.

BUSES

The way to see London is from the top of a bus—the top of a bus, gentlemen.

—William Gladstone

If you're in a hurry, don't take a bus. Take the tube; it's faster, easier, and generally more consistent. However, being shuttled about underground tunnels can hardly match the majesty of rolling along the street enthroned on the front seats on top deck of a double-decker. Riding the buses is a great way to orient yourself to the city's layout and to soak up its atmosphere and its sights. A number of buses in central London provide excellent sight-seeing opportunities at discount rates. **Bus 11** originating in at Liverpool Street station, takes in St. Paul's, Fleet Street, the Strand, Trafalgar Square, Westminster, Sloane Square, and all of King's Road. **Bus 14** originates in Riverside-Putney and coasts down Fulham Road, past the South Kensington museums, Knightsbridge, Hyde Park Corner, Piccadilly Circus and Leicester Square, and terminates on Tottenham Court Road in Soho.

Unfortunately, double-decker **Routemaster** buses, with their conductors and open rear platforms, are being replaced to save money. On modern double-deckers and on single-deck "hoppa" buses, you pay your fare to the driver as you board and you must have exact change. On Routemasters, take a seat and wait for the conductor, who can tell you the fare and let you know when to get off. Smoking is not permitted on London's buses. **Bus stops** are marked with route information; at busy intersections or complicated one-way systems, maps tell where to board each bus. A warning: each stop is marked with route numbers and only those buses stop there. On stops marked "request," buses stop only if you flag them down (to get on) or pull the bell cord (to get off). While waiting, you must form a queue (line up); bus conductors may refuse some passengers at the stop with withering looks of scorn during crowded periods. Service is notoriously sporadic during the daytime; it is perfectly common to wait 20 minutes, only to be greeted by a procession of three buses in a row. Regular buses run from about 6am to midnight.

Night buses (the "N" routes) now run frequently throughout London from 11:30pm until the first day buses get going. When the tube goes to sleep (last trains run between midnight and 12:30am), night buses provide an inexpensive and conve-

ESSENTIALS

nient alternative to taxis. All night bus routes pass through Trafalgar Square and many stop at Victoria as well. London Transport's information offices put out a free brochure about night buses, which includes times of the last British Rail and Underground trains. Call London Transport's 24-hour information line (tel. 222 1234) for fares and schedules, see Tourist Offices for office location and hours (p. 15).

The bus network is divided into four zones. In and around central London, one-way **fares** range from 50p to about £1.20, depending on the number of zones you pass through. Be sure to carry change to pay your fare; drivers will not accept big bills. Travelcards purchased for the Underground are valid on buses; armed with a Travelcard, you can hop on or off as often as you like. Weekly and monthly **bus passes** are are generally less practical than the Travelcard; only slightly more expensive than a bus pass, a Travelcard is also valid on the Underground and the DLR.

If you're planning on utilizing the bus network, London Transport issues a free bus map for London called the *All-London Bus Guide,* which is available at most tube stations and LRT information offices. The *Central Bus Guide* is a more manageable pamphlet, describing only bus routes in zone 1. If you require more detailed information about bus routes, there are 35 different *Local Bus Guides* which will help you navigate specific regions and/or neighborhoods. To find out whether buses are running on schedule, or whether routes have changed, call 222 1200. To acquire free local guides, call 371 0247.

Wheelchair accessible **Mobility Bus** routes, numbered in the 800s and 900s, service most of London. **Stationlink,** a wheelchair accessible bus, travels hourly between the major train stations. For information on either service, call 918 3312. For more information, see Disabled Travelers (p. 33).

BRITISH RAIL

Most of London is fully served by buses and the tube. Some districts, however, notably southeast London, are most easily reached by train. The BR is speedy and runs frequently to suburbs and daytrip areas around London, functioning as a commuter rail that is often cheaper than the tube. Its old-fashioned compartments are roomy and comfortable. The North London Link, stretching across north London from North Woolwich to Richmond, often deposits travelers closer to sights (such as Keats's house) than the tube: trains (every 20min.) scoot from Hampstead Heath to Kew in 25 minutes. However, BR is used by most visitors for its service from Gatwick Airport to Victoria (see Getting In and Out of London, p. 57).

TAXICABS

In order to earn a license, London taxicab drivers must pass a rigorous exam called "The Knowledge" to demonstrate that they know the city's streets by heart; the route taken by a cabbie is virtually certain to be the shortest and quickest. Although the London cab appears clumsy and vaguely old-fashioned, these specialized vehicles comfortably seat five and are able to dart in and out of traffic jams unperturbed. Most of the distinctively shaped cabs are black, although a few come in other colors, including *Financial Times* pink and *Evening Standard* newsprint pattern.

You are most likely to find cabs at large hotels or at major intersections, but cabs abound throughout Central London and are easy to hail except during rain. A taxi is available if its yellow light is aglow. You can catch a cab yourself or call a radio dispatcher for one (tel. 272 0272 or 253 5000, or look in the Yellow Pages under "Taxi"); beware that you may be charged extra for ordering a cab by phone. Drivers are required to charge according to the meter for trips under 6 mi., but for longer distances you must negotiate the price. A 10% tip is expected, with a surplus charge for extra baggage or passengers. Taxis in London are notoriously expensive. If you believe that you have been overcharged, get the driver's number.

Apart from the licensed cabs, there are countless **"minicab"** companies, listed in the Yellow Pages. *Ladycabs* (tel. 272 3019) has only female cabbies. (Open Mon.-Thur. 7:45am-12:30am, Fri 7:45:am-1am, Sat 8:30am-2am, Sun 10am-midnight.) Be sure to ask the price when you order a minicab, and reconfirm it. Reclaim **lost property** (tel. 833 0996) you have left in a taxi at 15 Penton St., N1 (tube: Angel; open Mon.-Fri. 9am-4pm).

The cheapest way to get to and from the airports (besides public transportation of course) is to call a cab company which will dispatch an ordinary car (not the snazzy and distinctive London cabs) for a set fee (see Getting In and Out of London, p. 57).

DOCKLANDS LIGHT RAILWAY

The **Docklands Light Railway** (DLR), London's newest transport system, connects the flashy developments of the old docks with the City of London. Call the 24-hour **Docklands Travel Hotline** (tel. 918 4000) for information. The semi-automatic trains run on elevated tracks, providing an unusual perspective on both the dilapidation and the frenetic construction in the area. DLR cars are a little smaller and lighter than their plain vanilla Tube counterparts. The tube's zone system applies to the DLR; DLR lines appear on all tube maps. Fares are the same as for the tube; Travelcards apply. There are three lines, the **red line** running north-south (connecting with the tube at Bow Church and Stratford), the **green line** running west-east to merge with the red line (connecting with the tube at Bank, Shadwell, and Tower Hill/Gateway), and the new **Beckton** line, which starts at Poplar Station (on the red line) and extends five mi. to the east. The expansion of the transportation services required by the Docklands is expected to cost over £4 billion. The rail cars run Mon.-Fri. 5:30am-12:30am, Sat. 6:30am-12:30am, and Sun 7:30am-11:30pm. The area is also served by a network of busses which run during the same hours and have similar prices to the DLR rail cars. The N50 night bus from Trafalgar serves the Docklands area late at night.

BICYCLES

London's roads are in excellent condition, but on weekdays both the volume and temper of its traffic may seem homicidal. However, bicycling has its advantages and there are few better ways to spend a Sunday than pedaling through the parks of the city. Great deals on second-hand bikes can be found at the **General Auction** (see below). Also check outdoor markets, classified ads, and the University of London's bulletin board at 1 Malet St., WC1 (tube: Russell Sq.). Bikes are allowed on BR trains and on the above-ground sections of the Circle, District, Metropolitan, Hammersmith and City lines (Mon.-Fri. before 7:30am, 9:30am-4:30pm and after 7pm; Sat.-Sun. all day). Many London cyclists wear breathing masks while riding to lessen the effects of the miasmal fumes polluting the London streets. The *Green Screen* (£6) is a cheaper and less-effective mask, while the *Respro* (£20-25) is the mask of choice for cyclists in the know; both are available at virtually all bike shops.

Brixton Cycles Co-op, 435-7 Coldharbour La., SW9 (tel. 733 6055). Tube: Brixton. A veritable mecca of mountain bikes for the hard-core crunchers of London. Besides loads of literature on the latest bike races, routes, and bike-a-thon fundraisers in and outside the city, they also have a great message board where Brixtonians advertise for roommates, funk drummers, and political rallies. Open Mon.-Wed., Fri.-Sat. 9am-6pm, Thurs. 9am-7pm.

General Auctions, 63 Garrat La., Wandsworth, SW18 (tel. (0181) 874 2955). Tube: Tooting Broadway, then Bus 44 or 220. Police auction as many as 50-100 used bikes here every Mon. at 11am. Prices range from £5 to £400, working bikes begin at £40. Examine bikes Sat. 10am-3pm, Mon. 9-11am. Examine the £1 ones with particular care.

Mountain Bike and Ski, 18 Gillingham St., SW1 (tel. 834 8933). Tube: Victoria. From the station, go down Wilton Rd. and turn right on Gillingham St. Mountain bikes £7/day, £13/weekend, plus £1/day for insurance. £150 deposit required or £50 if you buy insurance. Open Mon.-Thurs. and Sat. 9:30am-5:30pm, Fri. 9:30am-6:30pm. MC, Visa.

On Your Bike, 5254 Tooley St., SE1 (tel. 357 6958). Tube: London Bridge. 3-speeds £8/day. Mountain bikes £15/day, £25/weekend. Tandems £60/week. Will take credit card imprint, passport, driver's license, or check for value of bike as deposit. Open. Mon.-Fri. 9am-pm, Sat. 9:30am-5:30pm, Sun. 11am-4pm. MC, Visa.

Scootabout Ltd., 1-3 Leek St., WC1 (tel. 833 4607). Tube: King's Cross. Serious touring motorcycles (500cc) from £45/day, £225/wk., including helmet, insurance, and unlimited miles. It's not a motorcycle, baby, it's a chopper. Credit card or £500 deposit required. Open Mon.-Fri. 9am-5pm.

CARS

London is not the place to go pouncing about in your Mini—parking is next to impossible, traffic is deplorable, gas is painfully expensive, and the gear shift (not to mention your car) is on the left. When all's said and done, you can bike, bus, tube, or walk quicker and cheaper. **Renting a car** will not save you time, money, or hassle compared to public transport in London. Big rental firms like Avis and Hertz may be convenient, but they are quite expensive. Small cheap companies can be dodgy. Drivers must usually be over 21 and under 70. Make sure you understand the insurance agreement before you rent; some agreements require you to pay for damages that you may not have caused. If you are paying by credit card, check to see what kind of insurance your company provides free of charge. You have been warned.

BOATS

The **River Thames** no longer commands as much traffic as in the Middle Ages, but if you venture out in a boat you can still sense the pulse of a major lifeline. **Catamaran Cruisers** (tel. 839 3572) offers cruises with commentary. Tours run from Charing Cross to Greenwich pier (every 30min. 10:30am-5:15pm; £5.75, return £6.80, children ½-price; day pass £8, children £4).

The following destinations are served by **Westminster Pier** (tube: Westminster): **Greenwich** (tel. 930 4097), **Hampton Court, Kew** and **Richmond** (tel. (0181) 940 3891), and the **Thames Barrier** (tel. 930 3373). For more information on these worthy destinations, see Greater London (p. 195).

Regent's Canal runs along the north rim of Regent's Park and sets the stage for many a leisurely walk or boat trip. **Jason's Trip** (tel. 286 3428) runs barges from Little Venice to Camden Lock (£4.50, return £5.50) at 10:30am, 12:30, and 2:30pm. On weekends they also have a barge at 4:30pm.

Call the London Tourist Board's **help line** for more information on boat tours and transportation at (0839) 123 432.

■ Keeping in Touch

MAIL

Airmail from London to anywhere in the world is speedy and dependable. A letter will reach the East Coast of the U.S. or urban Canada in about a week and may arrive in as few as three days. **Surface mail,** while much cheaper than airmail, takes up to three months to arrive. It is adequate for getting rid of books or clothing you no longer need in your travels (see Customs, p. 17). In summer 1996, an airmail letter to destinations outside Europe cost 42p, a postcard 36p. The cheapest way to write overseas is by aerograms, which are sold in packs of six for £2, making them cheaper than postcards. Single aerograms are 36p. Postage in the U.K. is 26p.

If you have no fixed address while in London, you can receive mail through the British post offices' **Poste Restante** (General Delivery) service. If you were sending a letter to Mick Sweet in Nottingham, you'd mark the envelope "HOLD," and address it like this: "Mick SWEET, Poste Restante, Nottingham, England NG1 2BN." Include the county and the postal code if you know them. Try to have your Poste Restante

sent to the largest post office in a region. When in London, send mail to Poste Restante, Trafalgar Square Post Office, 24-28 William IV St., London WC2N 4DL (tel. 930 9580; tube: Charing Cross; open Mon.-Thurs., Sat. 8am-8pm, Fri. 8:30am-8pm)—all general delivery with unspecified post office ends up here.

Postcards and aerograms sent from the U.S. cost US50¢. Airmailed letter under 5oz. can be sent to the UK for US60¢. Many U.S. city post offices offer Express Mail service, which sends packages up to 66lbs. to Britain in 40 to 72 hours (under 5oz. US$16.50, and it's straight up from there). Private mail services provide the fastest, most reliable overseas delivery. **DHL, Federal Express,** and **Airborne Express** can get mail from North America to London in two days.

American Express also receives and holds mail for up to 30 days, after which they return it to the sender. If you want to have it held longer, just write "Hold for x days" on the envelope. The envelope should be addressed with your name in capital letters; "Client Letter Service" should be written below your name. The London office at 445 Oxford St. (tel. 496 8891; open Mon.-Sat. 9:30am-5:30pm) provides this service free of charge for Amex cardholders and Traveler's Cheques users and can refer you to other London offices which do the same.

TELEPHONES

For a list of country codes, see p. 292. Within London, if you are dialing from one 0171 or 0181 number to another, you don't need to dial the prefix. If you are dialing from 0171 to 0181 or vice versa (or from another phone code in Britain), you do. If dialing from outside Britain, you need only dial 171 or 181. **In Let's Go: London, numbers have 0171 codes unless otherwise noted.**

The new, polite British payphone (known locally as the "callbox") lights up with the words "Insert Money" when you lift the receiver. Payphones do not accept coins smaller than 10p and they don't give change, so use 10p and 20p coins. When the initial time period is exhausted, a series of beeps warns you to insert more money and the digital display ticks off your credit in penny increments.

More convenient than carrying tons of pocket-destroying English change is the **British Telecom (BT) Phonecard,** available in denominations of £2, £4, £10, and £20. The entire country is in the process of changing from an older version of the card (inserted larger edge first) to a newer version (inserted skinnier end first). It's rare to find a phone that accepts both; keep an eye out for which cards the phones in your area take and buy accordingly. Both old and new cards are available everywhere: main post offices, almost any newsagent, or the W.H. Smith and John Menzies stationery chains stock them. BT calls are charged in 10p units. It costs £1.30 per minute to use a BT Phone card to call the U.S. If you use the private line of an acquaintance who is a BT residential customer, prices will be far more affordable.

For international calls, dial the international code (00), the country code, the city code (if necessary), and then the local number. BT publishes a simple pamphlet telling visitors how to make international calls from any phone (available at tourist offices and most hotels, printed in several languages). Consider calling through U.S. long-distance companies, which offer significantly cheaper rates. To access a U.S. AT&T operator from Britain, dial their **USA Direct** number (0800) 89 00 11. You can then call collect or with an AT&T calling card. The first minute (if calling the US) will be billed at US$4.40 and US$1.30 ever minute thereafter. Using an **MCI** (tel. (0800) 89 02 22) or **Sprint** (tel. (0800) 89 08 77) calling card may reduce your costs, but not by much. The first minute (to the US) costs about US$4.20, additional minutes cost $1.20-1.30. Calling collect costs much more. For Canadian Calling Card holders, **Canada Direct** is (0800) 89 00 16.

Get **reduced rates** for most international calls from Britain (Mon.-Fri. 8pm-8am, Sat.-Sun. all day; to Australia and N.Z., daily midnight-7am and 2:30-7:30pm). Within Britain, three rate periods exist: the lowest (Mon.-Fri. 6pm-8am, all day Sat.-Sun.); middle (Mon.-Fri. 8-9am and 1-6pm); and most expensive (Mon.-Fri. 9am-1pm).

Important numbers in Britain include **999** for police, fire, or ambulance emergencies, **100** for the telephone operator, **192** for London and Britain directory inquiries,

155 for the international operator, and **153** for international directory assistance. Directory assistance is free from public phones only. Translation assistance for international calls is available at (0181) 889 6363. Area codes for individual British cities are listed in telephone directories. Telephone area codes range from three to six digits, and local telephone numbers range from three to seven. The code **(0800)** indicates a toll-free number. If you call an advertised number beginning with **0898, 0836,** or **0077,** be aware that you will be charged at an extortionary rate.

Let's Go Picks

Gettin' bevvied: All pubs are created equal, but these are better. **The Three Grey-hounds** is wackier than it sounds (p. 125); the **Riki-Tik** is tops for super-duper drink specials and flavoured vodka—go ask Alice (p. 125); the **Crown and Anchor** packs 'em in, makes 'em happy, makes 'em awfully chatty—go ask Alice again (p. 126); the **Lamb and Flag** anchors Covent Garden (p. 126); the **Dog and Duck**'ll make you go barking quackers (p. 125); and **Belgo Centraal** serves a wicked Hoegaarten—go ask Andrew (p. 106). **Repertory cinemas** serve booze, which is damn near the best idea that we've ever encountered. Lax **open container laws** make outdoor spaces like Leicester Sq. the world's largest beer garden come 11pm.

Top six sights of all time: Hampton Court Palace has kings and queens and scatalog-ical fun (p. 207); **Kew Gardens** is mudluscious and puddle-wonderful (p. 205); **Hyde Park/Kensington Gardens** is prettier than yo' mama (p. 155); **Westminster Abbey** is full of our favorite corpses (p. 135); **St. Paul's** is where the Anglican God lives, it's so *very* that we can't bring ourselves to be crass about it (p. 182). **Windsor Castle** is spectacular, too (p. 209).

Our favorite London corpses: Karl Marx was wrong but we still love him; **Sigmund Freud** ditto; Dear **Sir Issac Newton**, thanks for calculus…, guess you got what you deserved; the **Unknown Warrior** and his bretheren saved the free world from the Huns (twice); **Charmaine** is really, really crazy—trust us; **Jeremy Bentham** is also dead despite his best efforts; **Sir Christopher Wren**'s monument surrounds you, while **William Shakespeare** has shuffled off his mortal coil.

Best stores: Topman/Topshop'll have you looking like Jarvis Cocker in minutes (p. 251); **Sam Walker** never lets a classic die (p. 250); **Harrods** costs too damn much (p. 249); **Honest Jon's** is nuthin' but a G thang (p. 256); **G. Smith and Sons Snuff Shop** is cheaper than the white stuff (p. 257); **Black Market** pushes beats 'n the biz (p. 255); and **Shelly's** sells funk-ified black shoes (p. 253).

Passive Entertainment: Barbican knows that the play's the thing (p. 230); the **Prince Charles Cinema** doesn't want to be a tampon in your pants (p. 234); **Speaker's Corner** offers raving derelicts and also…raving derelicts (p. 243); **Vidal Sassoon**—let's just say, if we don't look good, they don't look good (p. 243); the **Young Vic** journeys into night (p. 233); and the **Everyman Cinema** will make you a member for 40p (p. 234).

London movies we love: Trainspotting—alright, it's a Scottish movie, but Begbie goes TNT, kung-fu psycho in a London pub; **A Clockwork Orange** will make your yarbels ring-a-ting-ting; **National Lampoon's European Vacation**—"Look, kids. Big Ben. Parliament." **A Fish Called Wanda** makes us want to learn Russian and get the keys to a Thameside apartment; **Greystoke: The Legend of Tarzan, Lord of the Apes; Sammy and Rosie Get Laid; The Tall Guy; Family Ties Goes On Vacation** and sweet Malory falls in love while Tina Yothers gets lost in the hedge maze at Hampton Court Palace; and Antonioni's classic **Blow Up.**

Accommodations

To sleep in London, however, is an art which a foreigner must acquire by time and habit.

—Robert Southey, 1807

No matter where you plan to stay it is essential to plan ahead, especially in July and August when London's hotels are bursting with visitors. It is often worth the price of a phone call—or a fax if you have access to one—to secure a confirmed booking. The proprietor should specify the deposit amount (usually one night's stay). The hotel will advise the best way to make the deposit. More and more hotels and most HI hostels accept credit card reservations over the phone, so if you don't have the time to make written reservations, it's well worth calling ahead. The **Tourist Information Centre Accommodations Service** at Victoria Station can help you find a room (see Tourist Offices and Embassies, p. 56).

In the listings below, the accommodations near the top of the listing for each region generally offer more pleasant lodgings at a better price than those at the bottom of the listing. Starred listings are the few, the proud, the Let's Go Picks—those exceptional values which deserve special mention.

TYPES OF ACCOMMODATION

Traveling through London on a budget does not consign one to a tippy bunkbed in a dank room filled with tossing, snoring extras from a B-grade movie. Rather, London offers a wide range of accommodation types which will suit travelers with different social needs, attachments to privacy, and capacities for roughing it. There are three major categories of accommodation in the following listings: Hostels, B&Bs, and Halls of Residence.

Hostels are low-priced dorm-style accommodations generally geared towards young travelers. If you are traveling alone or in a small group a hostel will be your cheapest bunking option. You will be sleeping on a bed in a room with at least three fellow travelers (who may be strangers and who may snore) and, in rare cases, as many as 10 or 15 fellow travelers. Some hostels offer private rooms for two at a slightly higher cost per person. Many offer rooms of varying sizes for slightly different prices. You will be sharing a bathroom with your new roommates and sometimes with travelers from several rooms. The communal aspects of hostels provide a way to meet other travelers interested in roughing it. Hostels are places where globetrotters can swap information and meet new traveling companions. This social dimension is a selling point as important as hostels' low prices.

There are two flavors of hostel: **Hostelling International (HI) hostels** and **private hostels.** HI hostels generally cost more than private ones (around £15-20 per night), but are usually cleaner and often have spectacular locations in historic buildings or in parks and green spaces. The HI hostels require membership (see HI Hostels listings below for more information) and some have curfews. The staff in HI hostels are usually extremely knowledgable about the area and many can arrange activities for guests. Bathrooms and other common spaces unfailingly sparkle. On the other hand many travelers prefer the less expensive private hostels which tend to attract a more bohemian crowd. At their worst, private hostels can be a nightmare of beer-soaked mattresses and vomiting bunkmates in a frat-house circus. At their best, private hostels can be a home away from home, filled with friendly, happy travelers eager to welcome you into their family. Both descriptions can be accurate portraits of the same hostel, depending upon what makes you feel comfortable.

Bed & Breakfasts are smallish hotels run by a family or a proprietor who will provide—surprise!—a bed to sleep in and breakfast to eat. The term "B&B" encompasses budget hotels of varying quality and personality. Some are nothing more than budget hotels that serve breakfast—don't expect snug, quaint lodgings. Rooms in these lesser-quality B&Bs are small, dreary, and provide few amenities (although you can usually count on a sink and tea/coffee-making facilities). However, some B&Bs are quite cozy, sporting warm comforters, charming decorative details, friendly management, and the occasional pet. As the character of B&Bs can be so divergent, it is advisable to investigate all of your options before choosing a hotel. A **basic room** means that you share the use of a shower and toilet in the hall. An **en suite room,** which contains both a private shower and toilet (or "W.C."), costs several pounds more. Occasionally an en suite room will have either a shower or a toilet (not both), so be sure to check. Be warned, however, that in-room showers are often awkward prefab units jammed into a corner. **Family room** in B&B lingo generally means a quad or quint with at least one double bed and some single beds. A group of two or more may find that a room in a moderately-priced B&B costs less than staying in some hostels.

Most B&Bs (and some hostels) serve the full **English breakfast**—eggs, bacon, toasted toast, fried toast, baked beans, a peculiarly prepared tomato (baked or stewed) and tea or coffee. **Continental breakfast,** on the other hand, means only some form of bread and hot beverage.

B&Bs generally take reservations (by phone, fax, or letter) with one night's deposit unless we state otherwise. Most accept credit cards. If you are making reservations in person be sure to look at a room before agreeing to take it—test the bed, faucets, and toilet. If you arrive on a hotel's doorstep in the afternoon or evening looking for a night's lodging, **haggling** over the price can often save you a few quid—after all if you don't take the room it'll likely go empty. Some proprietors grant **rate reductions** for stays over a week or during the off season. Off season is from October through March (although September, April, and May are slow enough that you may be able to wrangle a few pounds' discount). In winter, be sure to check whether the room will be heated. If you don't like climbing stairs, keep in mind that "first floor" means second floor to Americans—few B&Bs in the budget range have lifts (elevators).

London's colleges and universities rent out rooms in their **Halls of Residence** over the summer. If you have a student ID, you can often find stupendous bargains—in some cases, you can get a private single for the same price that you would pay for a bed in a hostel dorm. Rates are a bit higher for those without student ID, but are still an affordable option for those traveling alone. Rooms tend to be fairly spartan—standard student digs—but clean. Many Halls of Residence are filled with large groups of adults or teens in London as part of a course or conference. Generally the halls offer rooms to individuals for two or three months over the summer, so calling or writing ahead is advisable. Some halls reserve a few rooms for travelers throughout the year.

ACCOMMODATION DISTRICTS

When contemplating where to stay, tourists should take into consideration what sorts of fun they'll be having in London. Some districts are better for those interested in being close to the sights, others are more geared toward those who seek the nightlife, baby. What follows is a thumbnail sketch of the areas in which tourists are most likely to bunk down. Keep in mind that London is not very well served by public transportation after midnight, so if you're staying in the outskirts you'll have to swallow a huge wait for a night bus or an expensive cab ride.

Bloomsbury. Quiet residential streets lined with B&Bs, a few Halls of Residence, and a few hostels. Close to the massive British Museum. This moderately expensive area is within walking distance of Drummond St. (home of outstanding Indian restaurants) to the north and Covent Garden (an exciting nightlife and shopping district) to the south. The West End theatres are within reach, either a longish walk or short bus ride away.

Near Victoria Station. Contains a wide variety of B&Bs and a few hostels as well. **Belgrave Rd.** is covered with cheap B&Bs of varying quality, while the more elegant (and pricey) **Ebury St.** offers more luxurious accommodations. The area around Victoria is near Buckingham Palace and some of the region's bigger museums and is also fairly close to major sights such as Westminster Abbey, Parliament, and Whitehall. Theatre and nightlife districts are not very far.

Paddington and Bayswater. These neighborhoods don't contain any of London's major sights, but they're a reasonable distance from nearly all of them. The Bayswater/Queensway area sustains a raucous, touristy pub scene, as well as a number of decent restaurants. Whiteley's, London's first large, indoor shopping mall, is within walking distance. Lovely Hyde Park and Kensington Gdns. are just to the south. Nightlife districts like Soho and Covent Garden are quite a distance.

Earl's Court. Emerging from the tube station onto Earl's Court Rd., travelers carrying bags will be harassed by hustlers hawking the area's budget accommodations (though authorities are cracking down on such activities). The beautiful Victorian area feeds on the budget tourist trade, spewing forth travel agencies, souvenir shops, and currency exchanges. Some streets seem to have only B&Bs and hostels on them. The area has a vibrant gay and lesbian population. It is also a tremendously popular destination for Aussie travelers cooling their heels in London. This is the destination of choice for backpackers looking for dirt-cheap hostels.

Kensington and Chelsea. Elegance comes at a price, and unfortunately the level of elegance in Kensington and Chelsea puts it almost out of the budget traveler's reach. Still there are a few B&Bs and hostels which offer outstanding value and allow a visitor to stay in this graceful area for an affordable price. Hyde Park and Kensington Gardens are just to the north, as are the fantastic museums (V&A, Natural History, and Science) which line the Park's southern border. Some of the city's best, and priciest, shopping is nearby. West End theatres and nightlife are a moderately long bus or tube ride away.

North London and Belsize Park. This huge area contains a few pleasant B&Bs, a few hostels, and a number of residence halls. The prices tend to offer outstanding value even though the long, expensive commute tends to diminish the savings. Some areas of North London can be fairly dreary, though Belsize Park and Hampstead are enclaves of wealth and comfort.

HI/YHA HOSTELS

Each of the Hostelling International/YHA hostels in London requires a **Hostelling International** or **Youth Hostel Association membership card.** Overseas visitors can buy one at YHA London Headquarters or at the hostels themselves for £9.30. An **International Guest Pass** (£1.55) permits residents of places other than England and Wales to stay at hostel rates without joining the hostel association. After you purchase six Guest Passes, you attain full membership. A membership card for residents of England and Wales costs £9.30, under 18 £3.20. (See also Essentials, p. 21.)

The cheerful staff members, often international travelers themselves, keep London HI/YHA hostels clean and refreshingly well managed. They can also often provide a range of helpful information on the environs of the hostel. Plan ahead, since London hostels are exceptionally crowded. During the summer, beds fill up months in advance. In recent years, hostels have not always been able to accommodate every written request for reservations, much less on-the-spot inquiries. But hostels frequently hold some beds free until a few days before—it's always worth checking. To secure a place, show up as early as possible and expect to stand in line. With a Visa or Mastercard, you can book in advance by phone. Or you can write to the warden of the individual hostel. There is a new **central reservations number** for all London hostels (tel. 248 6547; open Mon.-Sat. 9:30am-5:30pm).

For hostel information, visit or call the jumbo-market **YHA London Information Office and Adventure Shop,** 14 Southampton St., WC2 (tel. 836 1036; tube: Covent Garden; office open Mon.-Fri. 10am-6pm, Sat. 9am-6pm; shop open Mon.-Wed. 10am-6pm, Thurs.-Fri. 10am-7pm, Sat. 9am-6:30pm). Cardholders receive a 10% discount on anything in the Adventure Shop.

All hostels are equipped with large **lockers** that require a padlock. Bring your own or purchase one from the hostel for £2.50. London hostels do not charge for a sheet or sleeping bag. Most have laundry facilities and some kitchen equipment. Theatre tickets and discounted attraction tickets are available.

Oxford Street, 14-18 Noel St., W1 (tel. 734 1618; fax 734 1657). Tube: Oxford Circus. Walk east on Oxford St. and turn right on Poland St.; hostel stands next to a 1989 mural entitled "Ode to the West Wind." For accommodations any closer to the Soho action, you'd have to camp out in the basement of a sex club (*Let's Go* does not recommend this). Facilities include spacious TV lounge with plenty of comfortable chairs, fully equipped kitchen with microwave, and currency exchange. 24-hr. security; no curfew. 90 beds in small, clean rooms of 2-4 with pink walls. Rooms have large storage lockers, but you must bring your own padlock. Superb location makes up for the expense: £17.30, under 18 £14.10. Continental breakfast £2.70. Book at least 3-4 wks. in advance, very few walk-ins accepted; full payment required to secure a reservation. No children. Reception open 7am-11pm. MC, Visa.

Hampstead Heath, 4 Wellgarth Rd., NW11 (tel. (0181) 458 9054; fax 209 0546). Tube: Golders Green, then bus #210 or 268 toward Hampstead, or on foot by turning left from the station onto North End Rd. and then left again onto Wellgarth Rd (6min.). A beautiful, sprawling hostel in a former nursing school that looks like a convent. Serenely positioned at the edge of the Hampstead Heath extension. This is more like a hotel than a hostel. Kitchen and laundry facilities. The big bonus is the lovely backyard and outdoor walkway covered with clinging grape vines. Video games and pool table. 24-hr. security and check-in. No curfew. 200 beds in surprisingly sumptuous 4-bed dorms. £14.40, under 18 £12.30. £1 student discount. Restaurant (breakfast £2.80). MC, Visa, Switch.

City of London, 36 Carter La., EC4 (tel. 236 4965; fax 236 7681). Tube: St. Paul's. From the City Information Centre on the opposite side of St. Paul's Cathedral, go left down Godliman St., and then take the first right onto Carter Lane. Sleep in quiet comfort a stone's throw from St. Paul's. Antiseptic cleanliness and a full range of services, including secure luggage storage, currency exchange, laundry facilities, theatre box office, and 24-hr. security make this hostel a convenient base for excursions in and outside of ye olde City. Rooms contain between 1 and 15 beds; the average room has 5 beds. Larger rooms feature the less-than-ideal triple-decker bunk beds ubiquitous in London hostels. Reception open 7am-11pm. Single-sex rooms only. 5- to 8-bed dorm £19.75, under 18 £16.55. 10- to 15-bed dorm £16, under 18 £12.50. Single or double £22.75, under 18 £19.15. Triple or quad £20.15, under 18 £17.10. Special weekly rates available Sept.-Feb. A canteen offers inexpensive set lunches and dinners (3-course dinner £4.15). Best to call at least a week in advance, especially for the 10-15 bedders. MC, Visa.

Earl's Court, 38 Bolton Gdns., SW5 (tel. 373 7083; fax 835 2034). Tube: Earl's Ct. Exit from the tube station onto Earl's Court Rd. and turn right; Bolton Gdns. is the 5th street on your left. A converted townhouse in a leafy residential neighborhood. 155 beds in rooms of 4-16. Continental breakfast. Comfortable lounge has TV, video games, and soda machine. Currency exchange. Reception open 7am-11pm. 24-hr. security. No curfew. Meals available in the large, well-designed cafeteria 5-8pm. Kitchen and laundry access. Bunk beds are sturdy and comfortable. All rooms single-sex. £17.70, under 18 £15.55.

Highgate, 84 Highgate West Hill, N6 (tel. (0181) 340 1831, fax 341 0376). Tube: Archway. From the Archway stop take Bus 210, 271, or 143 to Highgate Village, or, on foot, use the Highgate Hill exit and walk up the hill, which leads to Highgate Village (¾mi.). At Highgate Village, turn left onto South Grove (where the triangular bus bay is), a street that becomes St. Michael's Terr. and merges with Highgate West Hill. About 35min. from central London. An unassuming Georgian house set along a residential street in the middle of historic Highgate village. One of the more "traditional," rough-it kind of hostels, where 20 people sometimes share 1 shower and 1 toilet. This is the smallest and cheapest hostel of the London YHA chain. Out-of-the-way location and idyllic neighborhood make for a homey hostel. 70 beds, 4-16 beds/room. Clean bathrooms have flowered curtains and pink floors. Rolling hill-garden outside that just overlooks the city. TV lounge, kitchen facilities. Midnight curfew; no lockout. Reception open 8:45-10am, 1-7pm, and 8-11:30pm, but

ACCOMMODATIONS

small staff sometimes closes it throughout the day, particularly in winter. £12.55, under 18 £8.80. Breakfast, served early, £2.80. MC, Visa.

Holland House, Holland Walk, W8 (tel. 937 0748; fax 376 0667). Tube: High St. Ken. This handsome Jacobean mansion and fairly nondescript modern addition house some 200 beds. The reception is large and drearily functional, but the rooms are clean and spacious. Bunk-beds are grouped in threes using the standard, purpose-built hostel beds. Laundry and kitchen facilities. 24-hr. access. HI membership required. Adults £17.50, under 18s £15.55. The restaurant offers a set dinner for £4.15 from 5-8pm each evening. Major credit cards accepted.

Rotherhithe, Island Yard, Salter Rd., SE1 (tel. 232 2114; fax 237 2919). Tube: Rotherhithe on the East London line; transfer onto this line from District or Hammersmith lines at Whitechapel or transfer from the Docklands Light Railway at Shadwell. A 15-min. walk down Brunel Rd., then onto Salter. Welcome to *2001, A Space Odyssey.* Chrome, glass, and white stucco make this modern 320-bed hostel a trip into futuristic living. Sunset over the Thames is perfectly visible from the hostel's glass-enclosed staircases, but one problem: being in the Docklands means you're in the boondocks. There is nearby transportation into the city, but it's still a schlep (around 30min.). Complete facilities include a restaurant, a roomy lounge with video games, and a bar with Belgian brew on tap. Tightly packed but immaculate rooms. Breakfast included. No curfew. 2-bed dorm £22.75, under 18 £19.15. 4-bed dorm £20.15, under 18 £17.10. 6-bed dorm £19.75, under 18 £16.55. 10-bed dorm £14.45, under 18 £11.40. Wheelchair accessible. MC, Visa.

Epping Forest, Wellington Hall, High Beach, Loughton, Essex 1G10 (tel./fax (0181) 508 5161). Tube: Loughton (zone 6, 45min. from central London), then a brisk 35-min. walk. (Follow Station Rd. as it crosses Epping High Rd. and becomes Forest Rd. Continue along Forest Rd. as it becomes Earl's Path, straight through the roundabout, keep right until the King's Oak pub, turn left and then right at the "Wellington Hall" sign; the hostel will be on your left.) A cab from the tube station costs £3 per carload. A retreat from London havoc and prices. Set in the heart of 6000 remote acres of ancient woodland. £6.75, students £5.57, under 18 £4.60. Simple washing facilities and no laundry, but large kitchen. Don't make the long journey for nothing—call ahead. Open Feb.-Dec.

PRIVATE HOSTELS

▓ Bloomsbury

Central University of Iowa Hostel, 7 Bedford Pl., WC1 (tel. 580 1121; fax 580 5638). Tube: Holborn or Russell Sq. From Russell Sq., head left and turn left onto Southampton Row, then turn right onto Russell Sq.; Bedford Pl. is the first left. On a quiet B&B-lined street near the British Museum. Bright, spartan rooms with bunk beds, new wood furniture, and bookshelves. Clientele, like the hostel, tend to be bright and clean. Reception open 8am-10pm. Continental breakfast. Laundry facilities, towels and linen, and a TV lounge provided. No curfew. Single £20. Double £18. Triple/quad £16. Open mid-May to end of July.

Astor's Museum Inn, 27 Montague St., WC1 (tel. 580 5360; fax 636 7948). Tube: Holborn, Tottenham Ct. Rd., or Russell Sq. Off Bloomsbury Sq. The prime location across the street from the British Museum and musical, free-wheeling clientele compensates for standard dorms with slightly saggy bunk beds. Kitchen facilities, cable TV lounge, and game room. If they're full, they'll direct you to 1 of 3 other Astor's hostels and pay for your tube or cab fare. Bathrooms feature "London's only glowing toilet" and slightly low-tech showers. Reception open 24hr. No curfew. Continental breakfast. Adequate linens provided. Coed dorms almost inevitable. 4-bed dorm £15; 6- to 8-bed dorm £14; 10-bed dorm £13. Discounts available Oct.-March. Book about a month ahead. MC, Visa.

Tonbridge School Clubs, Ltd., corner of Judd and Cromer St., WC1 (tel. 837 4406). Tube: King's Cross/St. Pancras. Follow Euston Rd. to the site of the new British Library and turn left onto Judd St.; the hostel is 3 blocks down. Students with non-British passports only. For the true budget traveler, a clean place for sleep and hot showers. No frills and no privacy, but dirt cheap. Men sleep in basement gym, women in karate-club hall. Blankets and foam pads provided. Ground-floor room offers inner-city atmosphere and use of pool tables, TV, video games. Storage space for backpacks during the day, but safety is not guaranteed. Men are advised to call ahead. Lockout 9:30am-10pm; use caution when walking in the area at night. Midnight curfew. £5.

■ Paddington, Bayswater, & Notting Hill Gate

Palace Hotel, 31 Palace Ct., W2 (tel. 221 5628; fax 243 8157). Tube: Notting Hill Gate or Queensway. From Notting Hill Gate, walk east until Notting Hill Gate turns into Bayswater, then turn left onto Palace Ct. From Queensway, walk west on Bayswater and take a right onto Palace Ct. The hostel is on your left. 70 beds. Young community atmosphere and bright dorm rooms make this great deal an excellent social space for enthusiastic hostelers. Snapshots of former guests posted on the walls testify to the good vibes. No curfew. Airy rooms with tall windows all house 8 beds. Shower facilities are immaculate. Single-sex rooms often available. Linens and comforters cleaned daily. Continental breakfast. £12. Weekly: £70. Winter discounts. Cash only.

Quest Hotel, 45 Queensborough Terr., W2 (tel. 229 7782). Tube: Queensway. From the tube, take a left onto Bayswater; walk for 2 blocks and turn left onto Queensborough Terr. The hostel, a terraced house, is on your left. 95 beds. Communal, clean, and sociable; staff throws one theme party a month—recent ones include a toga and a Pulp Fiction party. Walls are covered with fantastic murals painted by previous guests. Includes continental breakfast (English breakfast £2). Clean sheets provided daily. Pool room and kitchen. No curfew. 2-bed dorm (one available) £17, 4- to 8-bed dorms (coed and 1 women-only) £12-14. 2 have terraces facing the street. Weekly: winter only, £63. Key deposit £3. MC, Visa.

Centre d'Echanges Internationaux, 61-69 Chepstow Pl. at the Centre Français de Londres, W2 (tel. 221 8134; fax 221 0642). Tube: Notting Hill Gate or Bayswater. From Notting Hill Gate, head up Pembridge Gdns., turn right on Pembridge Sq., then turn left on Chepstow Place. From Bayswater, head west on Moscow Rd., then turn right onto Chepstow Place. Bilingual staff welcomes international clientele, half of whom hail from France. Rooms are clean if somewhat spartan. Study rooms, coffee and soda machines, pay phone, TV room, laundry. The hostel's recently renovated pink restaurant serves dinners from £1.30-4. Elevators, but narrow hallways prevent the hostel from being entirely wheelchair accessible. No curfew. 24-hr. reception. 2-bed dorm £21. 3-bed dorm £18. 8- to 12-bed dorm £15. Single £26.50. Double £42. Sheets, lockers, and breakfast included. Off-season discounts. Reservations are strongly recommended; you can call ahead to inquire about vacancies but only a deposit will hold your reservation (must cancel 48hr. in advance to receive deposit back). AmEx, MC, Visa.

■ Kensington, Chelsea, & Earl's Court

★Albert Hotel, 191 Queens Gate, SW7 (tel. 584 3019; fax 823 8520). Tube: Gloucester Rd, or bus 2 from South Kensington. A substantial walk from the tube; take a right on Cromwell and a left on Queen's Gate. The hotel is approximately ¼mi. up Queen's Gate on your right, deliciously close to Hyde Park. The bus, which stops by the Royal Albert Hall on Kensington Gore, is much quicker. Beautiful, gothic entrance leads into elegant, wood-paneled hostel with sweeping staircases. You are located in one of London's most elegant districts. Backpackers lounge on sunny balconies. Rooms range from large dorms to intimate twins, most with bath. Continental breakfast. 24-hr. reception. No lockout or curfew. 4- to 6-bed dorm £12.50-13. Dorm (single-sex or coed) £10. Single £26. Twin £35. Weekly: dorm only, £60. Laundry. Linen provided. Luggage storage £1/day. Reserve ahead with 1 night's deposit. No credit cards.

★**Curzon House Hotel,** 58 Courtfield Gdns., SW5 (tel. 581 2116; fax 835 1319). Tube: Gloucester Rd. Turn right onto Gloucester Rd., right again on Courtfield Rd., and right on Courtfield Gdns. Your lodgings will cost a bit more, but you will be amply repaid in cleanliness and friendliness. Tidy and cool; recently installed new showers. TV lounge features langour-inducing couches. Most rooms have tall ceilings and mammoth windows that overlook a gracious park; no bunkbeds here. Continental breakfast. Kitchen. Luggage storage. 4-bed dorm (single-sex only) £15. Single £28. Double £18. Triple £18. Quad £17, with bath £18. Weekly and seasonal discounts—as low as £65/wk. in winter. Visa, MC.

Court Hotel, 194-196 Earl's Ct. Rd., SW5 (tel. 373 0027; fax 912 9500). Tube: Earl's Ct. Sister hostel at 17 Kempsford Gardens (tel. 373 2174). Very clean Australian-managed hostel is quiet inside despite being located off a very noisy road. Many travelers like it so much they never seem to leave. All single, double, and twin rooms have TV and tea/coffee set. Full kitchen facilities and spacious TV lounge. Safe available for valuables. 3 to 4-bed dorm (single-sex only) £13. Single £26. Double £30. Twin £32. Weekly: dorm £77, single £168, double £175. Linen provided. Off-season and long-term discounts. Key deposit £10. Shower 10p/2min. Reservations not accepted; call for availability.

O'Callaghan's Hotel, 205 Earl's Ct. Rd., SW5 (tel. 370 3000, fax 370-2623). Tube: Earl's Court. This hotel offers a cheap, barebones place to hit the hay; guests like the relaxed atmosphere as well as the prices. 32 beds in neatly blue-painted rooms. 24-hr. reception. Garishly colored rooms have big windows and bunk beds. Dorm £12. Double £30. Weekly: dorm £60; double £180.

Chelsea Hotel, 33-41 Earl's Ct. Sq., SW5 (tel. 244 6892 or 7395; fax 244 6891). Tube: Earl's Ct. Turn right onto Earl's Ct. Rd., then right again at Earl's Ct. Sq. 300 dorm beds in a mammoth succession of connected houses. Vegetating party-hungry backpackers zone out in the lounge, or lounge about on the balcony. Slightly ramshackle but a center of the Earl's Court hotel social scene. A great place to meet a large group of people, but other hostels offer better facilities. Stark rooms generally feature bunk beds. May be a line for the bathrooms. 24-hr. reception. No lockout or curfew. Laundry. Fax available. Continental breakfast. Sheets provided. Dorm £10. Double £13.50, with shower £14.50. Triple £13. Quad £12. £1 winter discount. Weekly: 7 nights for the price of 6. Luggage storage £1/day.; store valuables in downstairs safe for 50p. Reserve ahead in writing.

Ayer's Rock Hotel, 16 Longridge Rd. (tel. 373 2944; fax 370 2623). Tube: Earl's Ct. Fairly basic accommodations. Large reception and lounge area (they're the same). Opportunities to stay for free in return for working a few hours each day—it beats singin' for your supper. Also runs virtually identical hostel, the **Table Mountain,** up the street, which handles overflow. 4- to 6-bed dorm £12. Double/twin £30. Weekly: dorms £60. Winter rates £2 cheaper per day.

▓ Near Victoria Station

★**Victoria Hotel,** 71 Belgrave Rd. SW1 (tel. 834 3077; fax 932 0693). Tube: Victoria or Pimlico. Closer to Pimlico. From the station, take the Bessborough St. (south side) exit and go left along Lupus St., then take a right at St. George's Sq. Belgrave Rd. starts on the other side. A clean, bohemian hostel with cool TV room and broad video selection. 70 beds. Wire sculptures dangle in the reception area. Bright red bunk beds brighten the standard rooms. Lots of long term guests make this hostel feel like a home. Shower stalls are a bit dark, but generally clean. Continental breakfast. Cozy kitchen, TV lounge, pool table lounge. Luggage storage. Reception 24hr. 5-bed dorm (coed) £14; 6-bed dorm (coed) £13.50; 6-bed dorm (women only, 1 available) £14; 8-bed dorm (coed) £12.50-14. Visa, MC, Delta.

Elizabeth House (YWCA Hostel), 118 Warwick Way, SW1 (tel. 630 0741; fax 630 0740). Tube: Victoria. Turn left onto Buckingham Palace Rd., then left onto the Elizabeth St. Bridge, which turns into St. George's Dr. Hostel is at intersection with Warwick Way. Not for women only—students and families with children over 5 welcome as well. Beautiful lobby and new carpets defy the YWCA's usual blandness. Friendly staff also helps diminish the institutional atmosphere. Large, spartanly furnished rooms. Continental breakfast. TV lounges. Dorms single-sex with big cushy beds. 3 to 4-bed dorm £15. Single £21. Double £42, with bath £45. 24-hr. reception. Weekly: dorm £100; single £135; double £270, with bath £290. Try to reserve at least a month ahead (£10 deposit).

O'Callaghans III, 92 Ebury St. (tel. 730 6776). From Victoria Station make a left onto Buckingham Palace Rd., then a right onto Eccleston St., then a left onto Ebury St. Like its sister hostel in Earl's Court, this joint doesn't aim to impress. Downstairs rooms feel like a bomb shelter what with piled mattresses and furniture. Still, it's a clean, very friendly hangout that provides some of the cheapest accommodations around. Plush red carpets along the staircases manage to add a vaguely regal feel. Luggage storage. Higher rates for single-night stays. 4- to 6-bed dorm £10. Twin, double, or triple £15.

■ Near North London

International Student House, 229 Great Portland St., W1 (tel. 631 8300 or 8310; fax 636 5565). Tube: Great Portland St. At the foot of Regent's Park, across the street from the tube station's rotunda. 60s exterior hides a thriving international metropolis with its own films, concerts, discos, study groups, athletic contests, expeditions, and parties. Over 500 beds. Well-maintained rooms with sturdy furnishings. Many in the 2nd building at 10 York Terrace East enjoy views of Regent's Park. The Una Mundo bar in the lobby has a huge TV and serves £1.35 pints from noon-11pm during the week and noon-2am on Fri. and Sat. Continental breakfast. Lockable cupboards in dorms, laundry facilities, money changing services (£3 flat fee). No curfew. Dorm £10. Single £24. Double £19. Triple £14. Quad £14. Rooms with WC and telephones £4 extra. Reserve through main office on Great Portland St. usually at least 1 month ahead, earlier during academic year. MC, Visa. Foreign currencies accepted.

Barbican YMCA, 2 Fann St., EC2 (tel. 628 0697; fax 638 2420). Tube: Barbican. Turn left out of the station then right onto Fann St. 240 rooms and 26 nationalities represented says it all: institutional feeling offset by international flair. Residents hang out in smartly decorated lobby or upstairs in café/TV room. Spacious fitness center with free weights, nautilus machines, treadmills and bikes provides a compelling perk for long term guests. Café open 8-10pm. No curfew. Single £23. Double £40. Breakfast included. Short term (1-4 wk.) weekly: single £135; double £236; two meals/day included. Long-term stay (12wks. or more): single £111.14 first week, £100.56 weeks 2-4, £91 thereafter; twin £190.50 first week, £169.34 weeks 2-4, £154 thereafter. Two meals/day. Must call 24hr. ahead for short-term stay, 2 months in advance for long-term. MC, Visa.

HALLS OF RESIDENCE

■ Bloomsbury

★High Holborn Residence, 178 High Holborn, WC1 (tel. 379 5589; fax 379 5640). Throw your tube pass in the trash! This 2-year-old London School of Economics hall provides an amazing combination of comfort and affordability, a stone's throw from the Bloomsbury, Covent Garden, and Leicester Sq. areas. Singles are spacious and immaculately furnished. You could eat off the bathroom floors, if so inclined. Usually booked far in advance, but they keep some singles available for walk-in customers. Continental breakfast, lounge and bar, laundry facilities. Reception open daily 7am-11pm. Single £25. Twin £43, with bath £47. Discounts for longer stays. Open July to mid-September.

Carr Saunders Hall, 18-24 Fitzroy St., W1 (tel. 323 9712; fax 580 4718). Tube: Warren St. Turn right off Tottenham Ct. Rd. onto Grafton Way, then left onto Fitzroy St. A newer London School of Economics building. 134 single study bedrooms, 12 doubles. Reception open 8:30am-11:30pm. English breakfast. Single £22. Double £42. Under 12 half-price. Self-catering apartments for 2-5 people also available across the street in the **Fitzroy/Maple Flats**; all are fully furnished, complete with cooking utensils, crockery, and bed linen. Weekly rates: 2-person flat £238; 3-person £350; 4-person £448; 5-person £539. Under 16 half-price. Book ahead, secure with credit card. Visa, MC.

Connaught Hall, 36-45 Tavistock Sq., WC1 (tel. 387 6181; fax 383 4109). Tube: Russell Sq. Head left from the station and turn right onto Woburn Pl.; the 1st left is Tavistock Sq. Graceful London University Hall often filled by academic groups. Quiet atmosphere. 200 small, single study bedrooms on long, narrow, typical college dorm hallways with sinks, wardrobes, desks, and tea-making facilities. Reception open daily 8am-11pm. English breakfast. Laundromat, reading rooms, private garden, and an elegant green marble lobby. Single £20. Reservations recommended. Open July-Aug. and Easter.

Passfield Hall, 1-7 Endsleigh Pl., WC1 (tel. 387 3584 or 387 7743; fax 387 0419). Tube: Euston. Head left on Euston Rd., then take the 1st right onto Gordon St. Endsleigh Pl. is the 2nd left. An LSE hall between Gordon and Tavistock Sq. Hordes of summer students. 100 singles, 34 doubles, 10 triples; rooms vary in size, but all have desks and a phone that can only receive incoming calls. Single £19. Double £35. Under 12 half-price. Laundry. Kitchen. English breakfast. Call by March/April for July. Secure booking with a credit card. Open July-Sept. and Easter 8am-midnight. MC, Visa.

John Adams Hall, 15-23 Endsleigh St., WC1 (tel. 387 4086; fax 383 0164). Tube: Euston. Heading right on Euston Rd., take 1st right onto Gordon St. and 1st left onto Endsleigh Gdns.; Endsleigh St. is the 2nd right. Elegant Georgian building belongs to London University. Some rooms have small wrought-iron balconies overlooking street. 124 singles, 22 doubles. Singles are small and simple, with a desk, wardrobe, and sink. Reception open Mon.-Fri. 8am-1pm and 2-10pm, Sat. 8am-1:30pm and 5:30-10pm, Sun. 9am-1:30pm and 5:30-10pm. English breakfast. Laundry facilities, TV lounge, ping-pong table, 5 pianos, and quiet reading room. Single £21.40, 5 or more days £19. Double £37, 5 or more days £33. Open July-Aug. and Easter, but a few rooms kept free for travelers all year. MC, Visa.

Hughes Parry Hall, 29 Cartwright Gdns., WC1 (tel. 387 1477). Tube: Russell Sq. Head right from the station, turn left onto Marchmont St., and Cartwright Gardens will appear just past Tavistock Pl. Another mammoth modern London University hall with 13 floors of 300 smallish sparse singles outfitted with desks and fairly large wardrobes. Squash and tennis, laundry facilities, libraries, TV lounge, bar (pint £1.40), 24-hr. porter. Reception open Mon.-Fri. 8:30am-5:30pm. Single with breakfast £18.50, with breakfast and dinner £22. Reservations with deposit. Open July-Aug. and Easter. Visa, MC, Access.

Commonwealth Hall, 1-11 Cartwright Gdns., WC1 (tel. 387 0311). Tube: Russell Sq. (See directions to Hughes Hall, above.) Not too different from Hughes Parry Hall. 420 small singles with institutional decor. Most have large windows—ask for a room overlooking Cartwright Gardens. Squash and tennis, kitchen and laundry facilities, ping pong, (satellite) TV lounges, library, music rooms, and a pleasant bar (pint £1.40). 24-hr. porter, no curfew. Singles with breakfast £18.50, with breakfast and dinner £22.50. A reservation (but no deposit) is required. Open July-Aug. No credit cards.

Canterbury Hall, 12-28 Cartwright Gdns., WC1 (tel. 387 5526). (See directions to Hughes Hall above.) Dejà vu—it's just like Commonwealth and Hughes Parry Halls, although smaller and older. Organized groups hog most of the 230 small singles. Better than its neighboring halls because there's 1 bathroom (with bathtub) for every 2 singles. No curfew. English breakfast. Squash courts, tennis courts, 2 TV lounges, laundry facilities. Single £21.15, with bath £23.15. Open July-early Sept., Easter, and Christmas. Best to call by end of March for July reservations.

■ Kensington, Chelsea, & Earl's Court

The **King's Campus Vacation Bureau,** (write to 127 Stanford Street, SE1 9NQ; call the college switchboard at 836 5454 and ask for the vacation bureau), controls bookings for a number of residence halls where students at **King's College** of the University of London live during the academic year. Generally the office deals with large groups on organized trips, but they will place individuals if beds are available. Rooms are available from early June to mid-September. All have 24-hour security and offer breakfast, linen, soap, towel, and laundry facilities. Some of the King's halls offer student discounts, but this may be discontinued in 1997. All offer a 10% discount for stays over seven days. Remember: these are dorm rooms and generally are not as elegant or tasteful as many private B&Bs. It's a good idea to bring thongs with you for the bathroom. The college will be opening a set of self-catering flats in Sept. 1996. These are totally brand spanking new and are likely to be quite comfortable. Call after Sept. and ask for prices.

Wellington Hall, 71 Vincent Sq., Westminster, SW1 (tel. 834 4740; fax 233 7709). Tube: Victoria. Walk 1 long block along Vauxhall Bridge Rd.; turn left on Rochester Row. Charming Edwardian hall on pleasant, quiet square. Convenient to Westminster, Big Ben, Buckingham Palace, and the Tate Gallery, this hall is the most central and expensive of the King's College halls. Memorable oak panels and stained-glass windows in dining room. Spacious rooms come with desks. English breakfast. 2 lounges, library, conference room, and bar. Single £23. Twin £35. Discounts for longer stays. Rooms generally available June-Sept. and Easter.

Lightfoot Hall, Manresa Rd. at King's Rd., SW3 (tel. 333 4898 or 351 6011 for booking; fax 333 4901). Tube: Sloane Sq. or South Kensington. From South Kensington, take Bus 49; from Sloane Sq., take Bus 319. Prime location between Chelsea and Kensington. Rooms in a modern, institutional block. Continental breakfast. Access to clean, functional kitchens and fridges. Satellite TV. Bar. Twin £21. Double £33. Rooms may be available during school year.

Other halls of residence not affiliated with King's College which let rooms include:

Queen Alexandra's House, Kensington Gore, SW7 (tel. 589 3635 or fax 589-3177). Tube: South Kensington, or Bus 52 to Royal Albert Hall; the hostel is just behind the Royal Albert Hall. Women only. Magnificent Victorian building with ornate bars and staircases running through the lobby. Continental breakfast. Kitchen, laundry, sitting room, and 20 piano-laden music rooms. Cozy rooms, mostly singles, £23. Although the hall is officially only open to guests from mid-July to mid-Aug., a few beds may be open during the off-season; call ahead. Write weeks in advance for a booking form.

Fieldcourt House, 31-32 Courtfield Gdns., SW5 (tel. 373 0153). Tube: Gloucester Rd. Turn left onto Cromwell Rd. Stay on Cromwell Rd. and turn left on Collingham Rd., then right onto Courtfield Gdns. Clean reception with unpolished, but comfy, TV lounge. Dorm rooms large and spare, with high ceilings. Each room has a microwave and kitchens are downstairs. Reception open 24hr. 5-bed dorm £10. 6-bed dorm £9. Single £15. Double £28. Triple £39. Quad £48. Weekly and winter discounts. Major credit cards.

More House, 53 Cromwell Rd., SW7 (tel. 584 2040). Tube: Gloucester Rd. Exit left onto Gloucester Rd. then turn right on Cromwell Rd. Unmarked Victorian building across from Natural History Museum. Though it doubles as the West London Catholic Chaplaincy Center, the atmosphere is not particularly religious. Occasional Monty Python screenings in a somewhat dated lounge. A non-profit "bar" downstairs serves some of the cheapest pints in London. Continental breakfast. Laundry and kitchen facilities available. Dorm £14. Single £23. Double £38. Triple £43. Weekly: single £100; double £150. £5 supplement for 1-night stays, 10% discount after a week. Reserve ahead with a £10 non-refundable deposit deductible from final bill. Open July-Aug. No credit cards.

■ North London

Hampstead Campus, Kidderpore Ave., NW3 (tel. 435 3564; fax 431 4402). Tube: Finchley Rd. or West Hampstead, or Bus 13, 28, 82, or 113 to the Platt's Lane stop on Finchley Rd. Turn onto Platt's Lane then take an immediate right on Kidderpore Ave. Reserve through **King's Campus Vacation Bureau** (see Kensington, Chelsea, and Earl's Ct., p. 81). Beautiful surroundings and singles at dorm room prices, in a style familiar to anyone who's set foot in a university dorm built between 1960 and 1980. 24-hr. security. Game rooms, music room, kitchen, and TV lounge. Single £14. Twin £25. MC, Visa, Delta.

Walter Sickert Hall, 29 Graham St., N1 (tel. 477 8822). Tube: Angel. Exit the station heading left. Turn left onto City Rd.; Graham St. will be on the left after an 8-min. walk. Right in Islington. This converted office building opened as a new City University dorm in March 1994. Fresh blue carpeting and white-painted halls. All rooms come with private toilet and shower, hot pot, and phone, and the furnishings include desks and bookshelves. About 220 units. Continental breakfast delivered to the room every morning. TV rooms, laundry facilities, 24-hr. security. Office-building feel prevents sense of hostel community but ensures clean living situation. Single £30, with TV £35. Prices subject to change, so call ahead. Open July-Sept. with a few rooms available during winter months.

University of North London, Arcade Hall, 385-401 Holloway Rd., N7 (tel. 607 5415; fax 609 0052) Tube: Holloway Rd. Head left from the tube station, dorms located above the Hog's Head Pub and Fatty Arbuckles diner. The University of North London offers single rooms in 4- to 6-person flats. Each flat has own kitchen and bathroom, both of which are functional if not sparkling. The cinderblock hallways are a fairly dreary staple of college architecture. Book 4 weeks in advance because low prices make these rooms very popular. Single bed £10, with linen £17.63. Open July 1 to mid-Sept.

BED AND BREAKFAST HOTELS

BED AND BREAKFAST AGENCIES

Bed & Breakfast (GB), P.O. Box 66, Henley-on-Thames, Oxon, England RG9 1XS (tel. (01491) 578 803; fax (01491) 410 806). Comprehensive UK B&B booking service (see Budget Travel Agencies, p. 41).

Primrose Hill Agency, 14 Edis St., NW1 8LG, (tel. 722 6869; fax 916 2240). Gail O' Farrell books charming accommodations in 10 homes in the beautiful Hampstead and Primrose hill areas. From £20-37 per person per night.

London Home-to-Home, 19 Mt. Park Crescent, Ealing, London W5 2RN (tel./fax (0181) 566 7976). Anita Harrison and Rosemary Richardson put 15 years of experience to work booking you in one of around 40 London homes. £22-27/person for West London areas like Hammersmith and Chiswick, higher for more central locales. Family rooms. 2-night min. stay.

■ Bloomsbury

GOWER STREET

Budget hotels line one side of Gower St. (tube: Goodge St.). From the tube station head left on Tottenham Ct. Rd., turn right onto Torrington Rd., and take the third right onto Gower St. These hotels tend be smaller and more intimate than some of their peers, exuding charm and personality. With the British Museum just down the street and loads of fabulous eateries around the tube station, Gower St. B&Bs offer a great combination of comfort and convenience in Bloomsbury.

★**Arosfa Hotel,** 83 Gower St., WC1 (tel./fax 636 2115). The name is Welsh for "place to rest," and the charming couple who have turned this B&B around over the last 2 years ensure it lives up to its name. All furnishings and fixtures are close to new, the rooms are spacious, and the facilities are all immaculate. Single £27. Double £40, with bath £50. Triple £53, with bath £63. Quad £63, with bath £73.

★**Arran House,** 77-79 Gower St., WC1 (tel. 636 2186 or 637 1140; fax 436 5328). The relatively large rooms come with TVs and hot pots and are embellished with various precious details such as elegant moulding, Japanese lanterns, and non-working fireplaces. Well-lit hallways decorated with old stage and theatre prints. Spotless bathrooms. Visitors have access to the lovely garden (4 singles overlook the garden, be sure to inquire), laundry facilities, and a cable TV lounge that feels like a private living room. Show your *Let's Go 1997,* for these prices. Single £31, with shower £36, with bath £41. Double £46, with shower £51, with bath £61. Triple £61, with shower £66, with bath £70. Quad £67, with shower £72, with bath £82. Quint £76. Eat all you want of the full English breakfast. MC, Visa.

Ridgemount Hotel, 65-67 Gower St., WC1 (tel. 636 1141 or 580 7060). Bright rooms with cheery pink bedspreads on firm beds. Owners have recently doubled capacity by taking over the hotel next door; on-going renovations have improved the quality of the hospitality. Radiantly clean throughout. Rooms with TV. Laundry facilities, garden in back, and free tea and coffee in the TV lounge. Full English breakfast. Single £28, with bath £38. Double £40, with bath £51. Triple £50, with bath £66. Quad £64, with bath £74. Call well in advance. No credit cards.

The Langland Hotel, 29-31 Gower St., WC1 (tel. 636 5801; fax 580 2227). Clean, spacious rooms, although sparsely furnished. Some with TV, some with shower. Cable TV lounge. Single £30. Double £40, with shower £50. Triple £60, with shower £70. Quad £70. Winter discounts. English breakfast. MC, Visa.

Garth Hotel, 69 Gower St., WC1 (tel. 636 5761; fax 637 4854). Some rooms charmingly furnished, others (mostly smaller) more standard. Hot pot available upon request. Hallways and dining room are decorated with old wooden signs from inns and pubs—read the fine print for amusement. TV lounge. Full English breakfast or traditional Japanese breakfast. Single £34, with shower £37, with bath £39.50. Double £47, with shower £55. Triple with shower £75. Quad with shower £88. Weekly rates about £5 cheaper per night. Winter discounts available. Book about 2 weeks ahead. Visa, MC, AmEx.

RUSSELL SQUARE

The grass grows a little greener and the traffic jams a little less on the other side of the British Museum—but the rates run a little higher. (Tube: Holborn or Russell Sq.)

Celtic Hotel, 62 Guilford St., WC1 (tel. 837 9258 or 837 6737). Go left when exiting the station. Take a left onto Herbrand St., and then left again onto Guilford. Family-run establishment providing basic, sparsely furnished rooms and clean facilities. Pastel color scheme gives the place a fresh feel, balancing out the darkly lit walkways. For safety's sake, they don't give room keys, but will open the door for guests 24-hr. Streetside rooms can be a bit noisy. TV lounge. English breakfast. Single £32.50. Double £44.50. Triple £63. Quad £72. Quint £90. Discounts for stays of over 2 weeks.

Ruskin Hotel, 23-24 Montague St., WC1 (tel. 636 7388; fax 323 1662). From the Holborn tube station take Southampton Row, then the 2nd left onto Great Russell St.; Montague St. is the 2nd right. Meticulously clean and well-kept rooms sport vaguely institutional motel-type furnishings, hot pots, and hairdryers. TV lounge with books and elegant glass lamps. Prime position across the street from one side of the British Museum. Pretty garden in back makes up for the mismatched carpet and pinkish bedspreads in the rooms. English breakfast. Single £39. Double £55, with bath £68. Triple £68, with bath £78. AmEx, MC, Visa.

Cosmo/Bedford House Hotel, 27 Bloomsbury Sq., WC1 (tel. 636 0577; fax 636 4661). From the Holborn tube station take Southampton Row, then the 2nd left onto Bloomsbury Pl.; the hotel is on your right. Clean, comfortable rooms with color TVs. Furnishings are a bit worn. Rooms in the back overlook a tree-filled garden, while some in the front have small balconies looking out onto the square. TV lounge with beverage machines and saggy brown sofas. Breakfast included. Single £30. Double £48. Triple £65. AmEx, Diner's Club.

CARTWRIGHT GARDENS

Accommodations encircle the crescent-shaped Cartwright Gardens (tube: Russell Sq.). From the tube station, follow Marchmont St. for two blocks until Cartwright Gardens appears on the left. Enjoy the pleasant neighborhood feel provided by the private garden in the center; only local B&B guests and University hall residents have access to the gated lawns and tennis courts, adding another bonus to already excellent accommodations.

Euro Hotel, 51-53 and 58-60 Cartwright Gdns., WC1 (tel. 387 4321; fax 383 5044). Large rooms with cable TV, radio, hot pot, phone, and sink. White walls and furnishings give the rooms a bright, airy feel. Immaculate bathroom facilities—3 showers and 2 toilets for only 9 rooms on each floor. Full English breakfast in the hardwood-floored dining room/lounge/reception room. Single £39.50. Double £54.50. Triple £66. Quad £76. Children under 13 free Sat.-Sun., otherwise £9.50. 10% discount for stays of a week or longer, flexible winter discounts.

Jenkins Hotel, 45 Cartwright Gdns., WC1 (tel. 387 2067; fax 383 3139). Petite, genteel, family-run B&B featured in the Agatha Christie TV series *Poirot.* Tidy rooms with pastel wallpaper, floral prints, phones, teapots, TV, hairdryers, and fridges. Some rooms boast (non-working) coal fireplaces. English breakfast. Single £39, with bath £52. Double £52, with bath £63. Triple with bath £76. Winter discount available. Book ahead. MC, Visa.

Mentone Hotel, 54-55 Cartwright Gdns., WC1 (tel. 387 3927; fax 388 4671). Pleasingly decorated with prints galore. Meticulous proprietess keeps rooms sparkling throughout continuing refurbishment. All rooms with color TV and tea/coffee makers. Single £38, with bath £48. Double £48, with bath £60. Triple with bath £68. Quads with bath £72. Reduced rates Dec.-April. MC, Visa.

Crescent Hotel, 49-50 Cartwright Gdns., WC1 (tel. 387 1515; fax 383 2054). Family-run with care for 30 years. Attractive and homey. Tea/coffee makers in each room, hair dryers and alarm clocks on request. Color TVs in each room. Also TV lounge/sitting room. English breakfast. Single £37, with shower £42, with bath £53. Twin/double with bath £68. Family rooms available. Discounts for stays over one week. MC, Visa.

George Hotel 60 Cartwright Gdns., WC1 (tel. 387 8777; fax 387 8666). Newly independent "spin-off" of the Euro Hotel. Like when Joannie and Chachi left *Happy Days,* but no '"Fonz." Similar rooms, but lower prices usually warrant lower expectations. "*Heeey*!" Single, £35.50. Double £49.50, with shower £56, with bath £63. Triple £63, with shower £69, with bath £77. Quad £76.

ARGYLE SQUARE

The area due south of the King's Cross/St. Pancras rail complex has been revitalized as the station prepares to become a Chunnel terminus (tube: King's Cross/St. Pancras). The budget hotels lining **Argyle St.,** directly south of the tube station, draw a brisk tourist crowd with their rock bottom prices. On the fringe of Bloomsbury, any sights are quite a walk away, but the tube station is well connected, serving five lines. There is a bit of a night scene around the station, but be cautious of King's Cross to the northeast (a notorious red-light district), and exercise caution at night.

★Alhambra Hotel, 17-19 Argyle St., WC1 (tel. 837 9575; fax 916 2476). The singles in the main building are clean and modest. En suite rooms in the newly refurbished annex are pricier and posher. TVs in all rooms and cornflakes in the English breakfast delight the American and French couch potatoes who pack this place in the summer. Single £25, with bath £30. Double £35, with shower £40, with bath £45.

Hotel Apollo, 43 Argyle St., WC1 (tel. 837 5489; fax 916 1862). Bright white with blue trim, this hotel stands out from the others on the street. Rooms come with sinks, lace curtains, TVs, and relatively new furnishings. English breakfast. Single £25. Double £35, with shower £42-45. Winter discounts available.

■ Near Victoria Station

The number of hotels lining the streets in this area must be seen to be believed. Many of the major thoroughfares seem to be populated solely by budget hotels. Naturally, competition is fierce—try to take advantage of this. Show reluctance to take a room, and you may see prices plummet. If your first choice is full, shop around. Don't be afraid to ask to see the room you'll be staying in before agreeing to take it, many

B&B's have rooms of widely differing quality. Also, don't be surprised if the proprietor asks you to pay up front for your first night. They have been burned too many times by over-eager reservation makers who fail to show up.

BELGRAVE ROAD

In an area chock full of budget hotels, this is the main drag. Be advised, B&Bs on Belgrave tend to be a bit less luxurious than those in the other areas around Victoria station, though they are priced accordingly. From the Victoria tube station (Victoria St. exit), head left past the bus bays and around the corner onto Buckingham Palace Rd. Turn left onto Eccleston Bridge, which becomes Belgrave Rd. Beware that addresses higher than 45 are quite a long walk down Belgrave Rd., which continues on the other side of Warwick Sq. A ride on Bus 24 from Victoria Station or a tube hop over to Pimlico Station is advisable.

★**Melbourne House,** 79 Belgrave Rd., SW1 (tel. 828 3516; fax 828 7120). Past Warwick Sq. Closer to Pimlico than Victoria; from Pimlico station take the Bessborough St. (south side) exit and go left along Lupus St. Turn right at St. George's Sq.; Belgrave Rd. starts on the other side of the square. The 2nd generation B&B proprietors, who live on the premises, are justifiably proud of the cleanliness of their rooms. The modern, private custom-designed showers have smashing water pressure and glass doors. Air fresheners add the perfect olfactory complement to the sparkling bedrooms, all of which come with TV, phone, and hot pot. English breakfast with cereal option. Singles £22-28, with bath £40-45. Doubles with bath £58-65. Triples with bath £75-80. 2-room quads with bath £80-90. Winter discount. Book ahead. MC, Visa.

Luna and Simone Hotel, 47-49 Belgrave Rd., SW1 (tel. 834 5897; fax 828 2474), past Warwick Sq. Bus 24 stops at the doorstep, or walk from Pimlico. Immaculate and well-maintained; the building is constantly being refurbished. The rooms, decorated in shades of blue, all come with TV, phones, hairdryers, and firm mattresses. English breakfast. Luggage storage. Single £28, with bath £42. Double £40, with bath £54. Triple £54, with bath £65. Winter discounts. MC, Visa.

Marne Hotel, 34 Belgrave Rd., SW1 (tel. 834 5195; fax 976 6180). Close to Victoria. With 6-month advance notice, friendly management will arrange home stays for students in association with Homestay U.K. Some of the high-ceilinged rooms are adorned with lush brocade wallpaper. All rooms with TV. Showers cramped but functional. Cat allergists beware—proprietor has 3 furballs running around. English breakfast. Laundry facilities. Single from £25. Double £35, with bath £50. Triple £50, with bath £60. Discounts for stays over 5 nights in winter. AmEx, Diners, MC, Visa.

Alexander Hotel, 13 Belgrave Rd., SW1 (tel. 834 9738; fax 630 9630). White and gold paisley and velvet wallpaper wins high awards for camp. Pretty, newly decorated downstairs rooms. Upstairs rooms dark and cozy, with nicked wood furnishings. All come with TV, radio, and private bath. New TV lounge with great couches. English breakfast. Single with shower £35. Double with shower £55. Triple with shower £65. MC, Visa.

Easton Hotel, 36-40 Belgrave Rd., SW1 (tel. 834 5938; fax 976 6560). Sunny rooms, some with TV. Lounge with bar. White-painted stairwells are a bit scuffed. The dining room has the ambiance of a fast food restaurant—the seats are attached to the tables, which are bolted to the floor. English breakfast. Single £28, with bath £38. Double £38, with bath £48. Triple £48, with bath £56. Quad with bath £66. 3-room quint with bath £75. AmEx, Diners, MC, Visa.

Belgrave House Hotel, 30-32 Belgrave Rd., SW1 (tel. 834 8620). Red leather furniture and chandelier in lobby give a quasi-hotel feel. Large, dark rooms, most with TV. Private shower cubicles have doors. One of the cheaper hotels along the street. Continental breakfast. Single £25, with shower £30. Double £35, with shower £40. Triple £45. Quad £60. Winter discounts. Reservations needed.

Stanley House Hotel, 19-21 Belgrave Rd., SW1 (tel. 834 5042 or 834 8439). Clean rooms and helpful management make this a fine choice. Nearer to the station than many on Belgrave Rd. Single £26, with shower £35. Twin £40, with shower £49. Triple with shower £60. Mention *Let's Go* for a 10% discount.

Dover Hotel, 44 Belgrave Rd., SW1 (tel. 821 9085; fax 834 6425). Small rooms include the full line up of extras: Satellite TV, clock/radio, phone, hairdryer, tea/coffee maker, and bath. Generic nature prints on wall are either scenes from Japan or North America—they're such hazy, misty archetypes of their form that one cannot tell. Private showers with sliding glass doors. Bathrooms are basically clean. All rooms en suite. Single £45. Doubles from £60. Triples from £66. Quads from £80. Quints from £90. Continental breakfast. AmEx, Diners, MC, Visa.

ST. GEORGE'S DRIVE

Running parallel to Belgrave Rd., St. George's Drive (tube: Victoria or Pimlico), tends to be quieter than its neighbor. From Buckingham Palace Rd., continue one block further past Eccleston Bridge. Turn left at Elizabeth Bridge, which turns into St. George's Drive. From Belgrave Rd., walk one block farther down Buckingham Palace Rd. before turning left onto Elizabeth St., which becomes St. George's Dr. B&Bs also line **Warwick Way,** which crosses both Belgrave Rd. and St. George's Dr. near Victoria.

Georgian House Hotel, 35 St. George's Dr., SW1 (tel. 834 1438; fax 976 6085). Terrific discounts on "student rooms" on the 3rd and 4th floors (you don't even need to be a student, just be willing to walk up the long flights of stairs). Fresh lilies greet you in the reception area. Spacious rooms decorated with personality—some with ceiling mouldings, some with striped curtains, some with blond wood furnishings, some with armchairs. Showers vary as well, ranging from metal stalls in the corner to newly refurbished bathing units. Lounge has mad velvet going on. All rooms come with TV, phone, and hot pot. Huge English breakfast includes fruit and cereal. Ask about rooms in the annex (about a block away) which are older but slightly cheaper. Single £28, students £18, with bath £32-39. Double with bath £47-53, students £31. Triples with bath £56-65, students £42. Quad £70, students £50. MC, Visa.

Colliers Hotel, 95-97 Warwick Way, SW1 (tel. 834 6931 or 828 0210; fax 834 8439). Well-lit hallways and plain but bright rooms, with peach walls and fire-engine-red bedspreads. Some new showers, some old. TV in each room, beverage machine in the entrance. English breakfast. Single £25, with bath £28. Double £34. Triple £42. Weekly rates. Senior discount. Diners, MC, Visa, Access.

For a hotel off the noisy main thoroughfares, but still within walking distance of Victoria Station, try one of these:

★**Oxford House,** 92-94 Cambridge St., SW1 (tel. 834 6467; fax 834 0225), close to the church. From St. George's Dr. (see directions above to St. George's), turn right onto Clarendon St., then take the 1st left onto Cambridge St. A true B&B, guests are welcomed into the family. Set in a quiet residential area, it's more home-like than most B&Bs in the vicinity. Proprietors live here, and the smell of their delicious dinners often pervades the house. Bask next to the cat in the cushy, plant-filled TV lounge or go outside to pet the Kader family's 2 rabbits. Commodious rooms with flowered wallpaper. Firm beds, new pastel double-lined shower curtains. Fabulously well prepared English breakfast. Single £30-32. Double £40-42. Triple £51-54. Quad £68-72. Reserve 3-4 weeks ahead.

Windsor Guest House, 36 Alderney St., SW1 (tel. 828 7922). From the Victoria Station end of St. George's Dr., take the 1st right onto Hugh St., then the 2nd left onto Alderney St. Also convenient to Victoria Coach Station. Simple B&B at an almost unbeatable price. Spacious rooms with TV and relatively new industrial carpeting; note, however, that some rooms don't have closets. Brown tiled bathrooms. English breakfast served in a room that doubles as a TV lounge. Single £22. Double £32. Triple £42. No credit cards.

Melita House Hotel, 33-35 Charlwood St., SW1 (tel. 828 0471 or 834 1387; fax 932 0988). 2nd left off Belgrave Rd. from Pimlico station, or Bus 24 from Victoria, which stops around the corner on Belgrave Rd. French spoken. Pale pink walls make the rooms fairly pleasant, although the private bathrooms are rather small. TV in each room. Full English breakfast served in the wood-paneled dining room. Single £30, with bath £40. Double £45, with bath £57. Family room £60-90. Discounts for stays over 1 week. MC, Visa.

EBURY STREET

Historic Ebury Street lies west of Victoria Station in the heart of Belgravia, between Victoria and Sloane Sq. tube stations. Those who can afford to stay here will enjoy a peaceful respite away from the bustle of the station while remaining close to many of London's major sights. From Victoria, take Buckingham Palace Rd. and turn right onto Eccleston St., then take the second left onto Ebury St.

Eaton House Hotel, 125 Ebury St., SW1 (tel./fax 730 8781). Kind hosts (former tour guides) serve up Belgravian comfort without Belgravian prices. Spanish spoken eagerly. Large, pastel rooms have sleek dark wood chairs, TV, and tea/coffee maker. English breakfast, no smoking in breakfast room. Single £35. Double £46. Triple £60. 10% discount in winter. AmEx, MC, Visa.

Collin House, 104 Ebury St. SW1 (tel. 730 8031) Super-clean rooms are pretty big for the area. Pine headboards and lovely breakfast room give this a very homey feel. Full breakfast. Single with shower £38. Double £52, with bath £62. Triple with bath £80. Major credit cards.

Westminster House, 96 Ebury St., SW1 (tel. and fax 730 4302). Large bathrooms are ultra-clean, with glass doors on the showers. Modestly sized rooms have gorgeous tufted velvet headboards, TV, and tea/coffee makers. English breakfast included. Single £40. Double £50, with bath £60. Triple with bath £70. Quad with bath £80. Discounts for stays over 1 week. Major credit cards.

Astors Hotel, 110-112 Ebury St., SW1 (tel. 730 3811; fax 823 6728). Young Euro-clientele relaxes in floral elegance. Upmarket rooms are clean and color-coordinated. All have TV, washbasin, soap, and fresh towels. English breakfast. Single £40, with bath £55. Double/twin £54, with bath £64. Triple with bath £84. Discounts for cash. MC, Visa.

▓ Paddington and Bayswater

B&Bs, some slightly decrepit, cluster around Norfolk Sq. and Sussex Gdns. (Tube: Paddington, unless otherwise noted.)

★Hyde Park Rooms Hotel, 137 Sussex Gdns., W2 (tel. 723 0225 or 723 0965). Recently renovated rooms are bright and airy. Larger rooms have puffy double beds. All come with TV and washbasin. An astounding value, particularly when compared to nearby hotels with similar rates. English breakfast. Single £20-24, with bath £30-36. Double £30-36, with bath £45. Triple £45, with bath £54. Occasional discount for small children. Visa, MC, and AmEx.

Dean's Court Hotel, 57 Inverness, W2 (tel. 229 2961; fax 727 1190). This hotel offers outstanding value—clean, functional rooms with firm mattresses, a filling breakfast, full-pressure showers, and a friendly atmosphere. The **New Kent** next door offers the same rooms at the same prices and the same management. Well over half the beds are in the share rooms (an unbeatable bargain). All rooms without facilities. English breakfast. Twin/double £36-48. Triple £48. Share rooms £12.50, £69/week.

Compton House Hotel and Millard's Hotel, 148-152 Sussex Gdns., W2 (tel. 723 2939; fax 723 6225). Turn left when you exit Paddington Station, then make a left onto Spring St. and another left on Sussex Gdns. Not quite what comes to mind when one normally thinks "Compton"—a clean, if careworn, establishment. Carpeted stairwells lead to spacious rooms, all with full tea/coffee set, washbasin, closet, and TV. Selected rooms house especially large beds. Single £22-25, with bath £35-38. Double £35, with bath £44-48. Triple £51, with bath £63. Winter and long-term discounts available. MC, Visa.

Barry House Hotel, 12 Sussex Pl., W2 (tel. 723 7340; fax 723 9775; http://www.traveling.com/london/barry.htm). One of the UK's first on-line B&Bs—visit their website if you're so inclined. Bright, smallish cyber-rooms with TVs, phones, and kettles, some with desks. English breakfast. Safe available for valuables. Single £30, with bath £38. Double with bath £55-62. Triple with bath £72-75. Quad £88. Family, winter (Nov.-Feb.) and long stay discounts available. All major cards.

Garden Court Hotel, 30-31 Kensington Gdns. Sq., W2 (tel. 229 2553; fax 727 2749). Tube: Bayswater. Just south of Westbourne Grove, relatively convenient to Hyde Park and Portobello. A larger hotel with TVs, phones, and hairdryers in every room. Firm yet bouncy mattresses add to the "real" hotel ambience. English breakfast. A plush common area with unlimited coffee/tea and TV keeps guests comfortable. Single £32, with bath £45. Double £48, with bath £58. Triple £63, with bath £72. Family £70, with bath £82. One night's deposit required. MC, Visa.

Lords Hotel, 20-22 Leinster Sq., W2 (tel. 229 8877; fax 229 8377). Tube: Bayswater. Halls have high ceilings and new wallpaper. Basic rooms are clean—some have balconies. Phone and radio in each room. Frequented by German students. Continental breakfast. Single £26, with bath £40. Double £38, with bath £55. Triple £48, with bath £66. Quad £58, with bath £75. Discounts Nov.-March. Secure booking with credit card or deposit. Visa, MC.

Hyde Park House, 48 St. Petersburgh Pl., W2 (tel. 229 1687). Tube: Queensway or Bayswater. From Queensway, take a right onto Bayswater, then turn right again onto St. Petersburgh Pl. From Bayswater, take an immediate left when exiting the station (onto Moscow Rd.), and then turn left again onto St. Petersburgh Pl. Just north of the new West End Synagogue and just east of the hulking St. Matthew's church, this inconspicuous B&B blends right into its quiet residential surroundings. Family-run. Cozy sun-filled rooms with TVs, washbasins, and an occasional fridge. Continental breakfast. Kitchen. Single £26. Double £38. Triple £55. Quad £65. 5-person family room £70. Reservation with deposit. No credit cards.

Ruddimans Hotel, 160 Sussex Gdns., W2 (tel. 723 1026; fax. 262 2983). Unfinished wood paneling renders somewhat dark rooms cozy and warm. 24-hr. reception. White-glove clean, with washbasins and TVs in rooms. Not much space to move around, though; bathrooms are miniscule. Single £25, with bath £35. Double £40, with bath £48. Triples £48, with bath £57. Quad (2 twin beds and a double bed) with bath £67. No credit cards.

■ Earl's Court

The Piccadilly tube line travels directly between Heathrow and Earl's Court. Underground exits are on Earl's Court Rd. and Warwick Rd., which run parallel to each other: turn right from the Warwick St. exit to reach Philbeach Gdns; turn right from the Earl's Court exit to Earl's Court Sq. or to Barkston Gdns., where the hotels are more pleasant but more expensive.

★York House Hotel, 27-29 Philbeach Gdns., SW5 (tel. 373 7519; fax 370 4641). French, Spanish, and Arabic are spoken in this dependable hotel. Special features include a modish 60s-style TV lounge and a lovely garden. Hallway facilities are extraordinarily clean, as are the rooms. English breakfast. Single £26. Double £42, with bath £58. Triple £52, with bath £68. Quad £59. Major credit cards.

Mowbray Court Hotel, 28-32 Penywern Rd., SW5 (tel. 373 8285 or 370 3690; fax 370 5693). Distinctive striped reception area leads to a lounge decorated in 70s swinger style, complete with full bar and cigarette machine. Manager-brother team Tony and Peter greet everyone who walks through the door. This place is expensive, but staff this helpful is a rarity in London; wake-up calls, tour arrangements, taxicabs, theatre bookings, and dry cleaning are all available. Rooms are equipped with firm mattresses, towels, shampoo, hair dryer, TV, radio, trouser press, telephone, the Bible, and *The Teachings of Buddha*. Superb continental breakfast. Suites with kitchens are on the way. In-room safes cost £2/day. A lift serves all floors. Single £40, with bath £45. Double £50, with bath £56. Triple £60, with bath £66. Family rooms for 4 people £66, with bath £72; for 5 £80, with bath £85; for 6

£90, with bath £96. Negotiable discounts. Reserve ahead if possible; no deposit required. Major credit cards.

Oxford Hotel, 24 Penywern Rd., SW5 (tel. 370 5162 or 370 5163; fax 373 8256). Musty orange bedspreads are mitigated by soaring ceilings and flamboyant mouldings. The windowless lounge features color TV. The stylish dining room has been recently refurbished to include a bar. Extra guests may be put in the annex 3 doors down. Single £28, with bath and TV £40. Double £42, with bath and TV £50. Triple £50, with bath and TV £55. Quad £60, with bath and TV £64. Quint with bath and TV £68. Winter and weekly rates may be 10-15% lower. Reserve ahead. No credit cards.

Beaver Hotel, 57-59 Philbeach Gdns., SW5 (tel. 373 4553; fax 373 4555). Rooms with facilities are too expensive to mention, but if you don't mind hall showers and you've been aching for a touch of luxury, look here. Plush lounge with polished wood floors and remote-control TV—a second lounge upstairs lounge is non-smoking. All rooms have desks, phones, firm mattresses, and coordinated linens. Located on an absolutely beautiful street. Single £28. Double £40. Breakfast served in lovely room. Reserve several weeks ahead. AmEx, MC, Visa.

Half Moon Hotel, 10 Earl's Ct. Sq., SW5 (tel. 373 9956; fax 373 8456). Graceful mirrors on every landing and inexpensive, adequate rooms. Welcome amenities include hair-dryer, telephone, and TV (w/Sky and CNN) in every room. Continental breakfast. Single £20-25, with shower £30-35. Double £30-35, with shower £45. Triple £42, with shower £60.

Lord Jim Hotel, 23-25 Penywern Rd., SW5 (tel. 370 6071; fax 373 8919). If you don't mind small bedrooms and closed spaces, this hotel offers prices about £5-10 lower than competitors. Large-windowed lounge with TV. Super-clean rooms include phone, TV, and hairdryer. Continental breakfast. Single £20-25, with shower £40. Double £28-35, with shower £48. Triple £39-55. Major credit cards.

Philbeach Hotel, 30-31 Philbeach Gdns., SW5 (tel. 373 1244 or 373 4544; fax 244 0149). The largest gay B&B in England, popular with both men and women. Elegant lounge done in deep reds and jewel-tone teals sports Asian porcelain and varnished wood mouldings. A gorgeous garden and an award-winning restaurant ("Wilde About Oscar," see p. 260) complement the fairly sumptuous rooms. Continental breakfast. Single £45-50. Double £55-65, with bath £60. One week advance booking recommended. Major credit cards.

Rasool Court Hotel, 19-21 Penywern Rd., SW5 (tel. 373 8900; fax 244 6835). Top-floor rooms have unique sloping ceilings. Curious red lounge has red curtains, red couches, and red chairs. All rooms include TV, phone, desk, closet, and colorful wall-hangings. Single £26, with shower £ 29, with bath £32. Double £37, with shower £40, with bath £43. Triple with shower £49, with bath £54. Continental breakfast. Reserve 3-4 weeks in advance; 1 night's deposit required. Major credit cards.

Manor Hotel, 23 Nevern Place (tel. 370 4164; fax 244 6610). A real hunter's palace. Plush red staircase runs beneath a knight's armor and a deer's head. Simple rooms with soft beds; nothing too fancy, but you'll get your money's worth. Single £25, with shower £35. Double £36, with shower £50. Triple £49, with shower £60.

Hotel Halifax, 65 Philbeach Gdns., SW5 (tel. 373 4153). You can't miss the bright yellow-and-white gate of this small gay hotel. Mostly men. Color TVs, radios, and basins in large, well-appointed rooms with firm mattresses. Continental breakfast plus cereal and a boiled egg. Single £30-45. Double £45-56. Some rooms come with a bathroom. Full payment upon arrival. Two weeks notice usually secures reservations.

Hunter's Lodge Hotel, 38 Trebovir Rd. SW5 (tel. 373 7331; fax 460-3524) A pleasant, clean, small B&B. The name is fairly inexplicable, but the lobby is nice and the rooms quite liveable. Single £25, with bath £30. Double/twin £30, with bath £45. Triple £36, with bath £55. Shared rooms £10.

▓ Kensington and Chelsea

These hotels will prove convenient for those who wish to visit the stunning array of museums that line the southwest side of Hyde Park. Prices are higher, but the appointments at these hotels are so outstanding that several rank among the best values in London. There are few hard-core, Europe-on-£10-a-day backpackers staying in the following listings—but if you require a slightly more luxurious room, these hotels deliver at astoundingly affordable prices. Vicarage Gate lies off Kensington Church St.

★**Abbey House Hotel,** 11 Vicarage Gate, W8 (tel. 727 2594). Tube: Notting Hill Gate. A superbly elegant entrance makes you feel like royalty when you come in. The owner or one of his 2 assistants will spend 20min. after you check in giving you a supremely helpful introduction to London, and are always available for advice on all things tourist. After a series of renovations, the hotel has achieved a level of comfort that can't be rivaled at these prices. A new tea room provides free hot beverages 24hr. a day. Palatial rooms with color TVs, washbasin, fresh towels and soap, and billowing curtains. Bathrooms (none en suite) decorated with Laura Ashley furnishings. English breakfast. Single £34. Double £55. Triple £66. Quad £76. Quint £86. Winter discounts. Weekly rates. Book ahead 1 month. No credit cards.

★**Vicarage Hotel,** 10 Vicarage Gate, W8 (tel. 229 4030; fax 792 5989). Tube: Notting Hill Gate. The immaculate stone entrance combines Greek marble columns with Victorian, Sherlock Holmesian lights. Once inside, you ascend a sweeping staircase surrounded by classy red velvet-striped wallpaper and gold framing. The stately breakfast room is only surpassed by the small, comfortable, and immaculate bedrooms, which contain fancy wooden wardrobes and antique mirrors. Ample English breakfast. Single £36. Double £58. Triple £70. Quad £80. Negotiable winter rates. Reserve 1 month ahead. No credit cards.

Swiss House, 171 Old Brompton Rd., SW5 (tel. 373 2769; fax 373 4983). A beautiful B&B with light, spacious rooms and a swell garden. Fluffy duvets, ruffled curtains, and matching carpets in every room. TV, telephone, towels, and soap included. Some hall toilets graced with plants and potpourri—a gentle touch. Continental breakfast. Single £36, with bath £53. Double/twin with bath £68. Extra bed £12. 10% discount if staying over a week.

Reeves Hotel for Women, 48 Shepherd's Bush Green, W12 (tel. (0181) 740 1158). Tube: Goldhawk Rd., head right down Goldhawk Rd., which turns into Shepherd's Bush Green as it runs along Shepherd's Bush Common. The women-only hotel will be on the right. 5 doubles and 7 singles available in the first hotel in Britain owned, managed, and run by women for women travelers. Rooms are inviting and comfortably furnished; all come with TV and hot pot. The breakfast room, tastefully decorated with modern fixtures, sits next to a cozy, fully licensed women-only bar (open every night to guests, open to non-residents Fri. 7:30pm-midnight). Garden patio in the back. Substantial continental breakfast may be ordered to room at no extra charge. Parking available. Single £25, with bath £35. Double £45, with bath £55. MC, Visa (5% surcharge for credit card payments).

Still farther south you can stay in trendy **Chelsea,** but you'll have trouble finding many moderately priced hotels south of King's Rd. Be aware that Chelsea is not well served by the Tube, though busses pass through frequently.

★**Oakley Hotel,** 73 Oakley St., SW3 (tel. 352 5599 or 6610; fax 727 1190). Tube: Sloane Sq. or Victoria, then bus 11, 19, or 22; or Kensington, then bus 49. Turn left onto Oakley St. from King's Rd. at the Chelsea Fire Station. Just steps away from Cadogan Pier, Albert Bridge, Battersea Park, and shopping on King's Rd., this hotel is one of the best bargains in London. Lovely bedrooms with large windows, matching bedspreads, and lots of fresh air. Powerful showers. Comfortable lounge with TV and VCR doubles as a dining room. Incredibly amiable staff invites guests to use the kitchen facilities at any hour of the day or night. English breakfast. 4-bed dorms (women only) £12.50, £69/week. Single £25. Twin £38, with bath £48. Triple £48, with bath £60. Quad £56, but if used for 5 people then £66. Winter and long-term discounts. Reserve ahead several weeks. No credit cards.

The area around **Cromwell and Gloucester Rd.** is less staid than the adjacent South Kensington and Chelsea neighborhoods and remains relatively convenient to the

Kensington museums and attractions (tube: Gloucester Rd.). Be aware that Cromwell Rd., though centrally located, is a very busy, noisy, and dirty street.

Hotel Europe, 131-137 Cromwell Rd., SW7 (tel. 370 2336/7/8; fax 244 6985). On a busy street, the number of employees, the bar, the large dining room, and a sizable lounge complex give the feel of a hotel, not a B&B. Continental breakfast. Single £30, with bath £35. Double £40, with bath £45. Triple £45, with bath £55. Discounts Nov. to mid-March. AmEx, MC, Visa.

Sorbonne Hotel, 39 Cromwell Rd., SW7 (tel. 589 6636 or 589 6637; fax 581-1313). Also very hotelly. Convenient access to the V&A and Harrods. Most rooms have TV, hair dryer, and phone; en suite rooms add a small fridge. Fake plants lend an atrium feel to some rooms. Continental breakfast. Laundry and ironing available. Single £30, with bath £45. Double £42, with bath £55. Triple £45, with bath £65. Family £72. No children under 5 allowed.

■ Belsize Park

This affluent suburb in North London is full of tree-lined residential streets. It is quite removed from both the historic district and the bumpin' nightlife scene but the values are unbeatable if you're willing to get a Travelcard and commute a bit.

Dillons Hotel, 21 Belsize Pk., NW3 (tel. 794 3360; fax 586 1104). Tube: Belsize Park or Swiss Cottage. Or head right on Haverstock Hill and take the 2nd left onto Belsize Ave., which becomes Belsize Pk. Spacious B&B in an affluent, tree-lined suburb. Conveniently located right around the corner from a lane of shops, little restaurants, a laundromat, and a post office. 15 large and well-furnished rooms. Cheery yellow breakfast room and deluxe, but small, TV lounge. Continental breakfast. Single £24, with shower £30. Double £34, with bath £40. Every 7th night free. Book a month ahead. One-night deposit needed.

Buckland Hotel, 6 Buckland Crescent (tel. 722 5574; fax 722 5594). Tube: Swiss Cottage. Exit station and head straight, then right onto Buckland Crescent. A Victorian-style B&B with 16 modest rooms and 1970s decor. Convenient to Finchley road shops. A bit expensive for a single traveler but a swell deal for groups of 4. Price is very negotiable. Single £27, with bath £32. Double with bath £55. Groups of 4 or more £13/person. Deposit required. Visa, MC, AmEx, Access.

CAMPING

Camping in London sounds like a made-for-TV movie starring Charlie Sheen, Mr. T, and Burt Convy. Still, this is the cheapest way to travel and the showers and toilets are similar to the ones in most hostels. In summer months, the few campsites near London fill up. You'll have to make reservations one to two weeks in advance.

Tent City—Acton, Old Oak Common Lane, East Acton, W3 (tel. (0181) 743 5708 in winter or (0181) 749 9074 in summer; fax (0181) 749 9074). Tube: East Acton. Turn left out of station and left on Wulfstan Rd., Tent city is a 10-min. walk. You can pitch your own tent, or sleep in one of the dormitory-size big top tents (no bearded ladies though). Extremely friendly campsite, full of backpackers. Showers, snack bar, baggage storage, laundry, and cooking facilities. Deservedly popular—basic but cheap. £5.50/person, children £2.50. Discounts for extended stays. Open June 1-Sept. 7.

Tent City—Hackney, Millfields Rd., Hackney Marshes, E5 (tel. (0181) 985 7656). Bus 38 from Victoria or Piccadilly Circus to Clapton Pond, and walk down Millfields Rd.; or Bus 22a from Liverpool St. to Mandeville St., and cross bridge to Hackney Marshes. 4mi. from London. An expanse of flat green lawn in the midst of London's East End where you may pitch your own or rest under their big top tents. Free hot showers, baggage storage, shop, snack bar, laundry, and cooking facilities.

No caravans. A bit less convenient by public transport than the Acton location. £5/person, children £2.50. Open June-Aug. 24hr.

Crystal Palace Caravan Club Site, Crystal Palace Parade, SE19 (tel. (0181) 778 7155). Tube: Brixton, then Bus 2A or 3. BR to Crystal Palace. 8mi. from London. Wonderfully close to the healthful activities at the Crystal Palace National Sports Centre. Showers and laundry facilities. Unlike Tent City you must bring your own tent. 21-day max. stay. Wheelchair accessible. £3.50/person, children £1.20. All visitors (even pedestrians) must pay additional parking fees: caravan £7, tent with car £5, tent with motorcycle £2.50, tent with walkers £1. Lower fees Oct.-April. Open year-round.

LONG-TERM STAYS

Anyone who's seen *Trainspotting* will be wary, and rightfully so, about the London real-estate game. Getting what you paid for is hard, and true bargains are even thinner on the ground. Take a cue from Frances Begbie: pull strings and stay with "friends" as often as you can. Consider renting a **bed-sit,** anything from a studio apartment to a small room in a private house, with access to a kitchen and bathroom. Bed-sits run at the very least £40 per week, and most landlords won't lease for less than a month. You will generally be required to pay a month's rent in advance, and put up a month's rent for a deposit.

Begin your search at the wonderful **University of London Accommodations Office,** University of London Senate House, Room B, Malet St., WC1 (tel. 636 2818; fax 580 2619; tube: Russell Sq). They put out lists of private accommodations available for summer stays beginning in June, and have similar lists of University-affiliated housing for the summer, Christmas and Easter holidays. Bear in mind: summer lets don't usually begin until late June, and Easter constitutes a six-week period from mid-Mar. to April. For year-round service the office boasts the largest accommodations posting boards in the London area, and the helpful staff gives free advice on the intricacies of London flatting, from tenant/landlord responsibilities to inventories and deposits—before you sign anything, come here. (Open Mon.-Fri. 9:30am-5:30pm.)

Do-it-yourselfers willing to put in some time and footwork should rush to the newsagent the morning that London's **ad papers** are published, and immediately begin calling. **Loot** (tel. 328 1771; £1.30) is published daily, while the **London Weekly Advertiser** (tel. (0181) 532 2000; 80p) and **To Let** (tel. (0181) 994 9444; £1) come out on Wednesdays. All allow private clients to **place ads for free.** Check their extensive listings and consider placing an ad of your own. Bulletin boards in small grocery shops frequently list available rooms and flats, as do the classified sections of the major newspapers. Call as early as possible when responding to advertisements in one of the larger papers. Beware of ads placed by accommodations agencies; they often try to sell you something more expensive when you call.

Slackers will find it easier to enlist the aid of an **Accommodations agency,** but at what cost—they generally charge one or two weeks' rent as a fee, and it's in their interest to find high-priced accommodations. **Jenny Jones Accommodations Agency,** 40 S. Molton St., W1 (tel. 493 4801; tube: Bond St.) charges the fee to the landlord instead of the tenant and has bed-sits starting from £50 for something suburban. You may have to check several times for a central location (£70-80). Check which transport zone the flat is in; this will determine the bus or tube fare you'll be charged during your stay. (Open Mon.-Fri. 9:30am-2pm and 2:30-5:15pm.) **Universal Aunts,** P.O. Box 304, SW4 0NN (tel. 738 8937; fax 622 1914) has central locations for about £75-150 plus a service charge.

★**International Student House,** 229 Great Portland St., W1 (tel. 631 8300 or 8310; fax 636 5565). Tube: Great Portland St. At the foot of Regent's Park, across the street from the tube station's rotunda. 60s exterior hides a thriving international metropolis with its own films, concerts, discos, study groups, athletic contests, expeditions, and parties. No curfew. Over 500 beds in well-maintained rooms with sturdy furnishings. Many in the second building at 10 York Terrace East enjoy views of Regent's Park. The Una Mundo bar in the lobby has a huge TV and serves £1.35 pints Sun.-Thurs. from noon-11pm and Fri. and Sat. from noon-2am. This privately run non-profit organization, in addition to offering short-term stays, also offers very reasonable rates to students who will be staying over 3 months. Must have letter from a university to be eligible. No kitchen facilites are a big drawback. Weekly: dorm £38, singles £80.50, double £63, triple £49. The first month's rate will be between £3-10 higher, depending upon type of room. MC, Visa. Foreign currencies accepted.

Lee Abbey International Students' Club, 57-67 Lexham Gdns., W8 (tel. 373 7242, fax 244 8702). Tube: Earl's Ct. Left onto the Earl's Court Rd., cross Cromwell Rd., then right on Lexham Gardens. The club is on your right. A Christian group-run hotel with international crowd and no religious restrictions. You must be at least 18 to stay here. Student status is required during the school year. Some rooms recently updated—the more modern are quite pleasant but in the older ones some of the decor has passed its prime. Some rooms en suite. Linens provided. English breakfast, evening meal, and lunch on Sat. and Sun. included. Single £25.25. Double £18.35, with bath £19. Weekly: single £144-176.75, double £128-137. Inquire about reservations 1 month in advance.

YWCA Park House, 227 Earl's Court Rd., SW5 (tel. 373 2851). This high-security block provides long-term stays for single women 16-25. 6-month min. stay, 3-year max. stay. Requires an interview and selection process which takes 3-7 days. 117 beds. Guests rent single bedrooms in 2- to 3-bedroom flats with living room, kitchen, and bathroom. Male visitors allowed between 10am-11:30pm. Feels like a women's college dorm. Telephones, laundry, and TV. £65/week.

Centre d'Echanges Internationaux, 61-69 Chepstow Pl. at the Centre Français de Londres, W2 (tel. 221 8134; fax 221 0642). Tube: Notting Hill Gate or Bayswater. From Notting Hill Gate, head up Pembridge Gdns., turn right on Pembridge Sq., then turn left on Chepstow Place. From Bayswater, head west on Moscow Rd., then turn right onto Chepstow Place. Bilingual staff welcomes international clientele, half of whom hail from France. Rooms are clean if somewhat spartan. No curfew. 24-hr. reception. Study rooms, coffee and soda machines, pay phone, TV room, laundry. Stays over 8 weeks qualify you for very reasonable weekly rates: dorm £52; single £120; twin £100; triple £86. The hostel's recently renovated pink restaurant serves dinners from £1.30-4. Elevators, but narrow hallways prevent the hostel from being entirely wheelchair accessible. Write first to enquire about availability and eligibility requirements. AmEx, MC, Visa.

ACCOMMODATIONS

Food and Drink

Once upon a time, British cuisine was something of a joke among international know-it-alls. "Going to England?" one's well-traveled friends might say, "Stick to McDonald's, heh-heh-heh." Well, smart guys, now the joke's on you. While British cooking persists in all its boiled glory, cuisines from around the world have recently breathed new life into English kitchens. The introduction of Lebanese, Greek, Indian, Chinese, Thai, Italian, Cypriot, African, and West Indian flavors has spiced London up considerably.

Of these different cuisines, London is perhaps most famous for its **Indian restaurants,** most of which are quiet and dimly lit. Dishes here are spicier (and often smaller) than their milder American counterparts. In general, Indian restaurants are cheaper around Westbourne Grove and Euston Square, and cheaper still on Brick Lane in the East End. Though spellings vary among restaurants, **bhell poori** in the title means strictly vegetarian; **Balti** means your order will be brought to the table in the same dish used to cook it; **Tandoori** is a method of cooking ingredients in a traditional Indian grill; and you will be asked to pay extra for orders of rice and *nan,* the traditional bread which complements Indian meals. **Bangledeshi** cuisine is essentially synonymous with Indian, due to a great deal of social and political history which is not, in the context of Food and Drink, germane.

London's wealth of international restaurants shouldn't deter you from sampling Britain's own infamous cuisine. **Pubs** have always offered cheap, filling English classics like meat pastries ("Cornish pasties" and "pies"), potatoes, and shepherd's pie (a meat mixture topped with mashed potatoes and baked). Recently, the Renaissance in cuisine has infiltrated even the most pubby pubs. Quality has improved markedly; some wood-paneled ale joints offer gourmet options like vegetable pancakes with ricotta and spinach ragout. Other cheap, quick dining options include **Fish-and-chip shops** and **kebab shops,** which may be found on nearly every corner. They vary little in price but can be oceans apart in quality. Look for queues out the door and hop in line. **Sandwich shops** are handy for a quick bite and differ little from their kind in any country. Many serve filling, inexpensive breakfast foods all day. Be warned—visitors may not share the British worship of **mayonnaise,** which is rivaled only by a love of **pure, rich butter.** You'll have to ask several times to get a sandwich without gobs of buttery goodness or mayonnaisey love.

In **restaurants,** watch the fine print: a perfectly inexpensive entrée may be only one item on a bill supplemented with side dishes, shamefully priced drinks, VAT, minimum per-person charges, and an occasional 50p–£2 cover charge. You don't have to tip in those restaurants that include service charge (10-12½%) on the bill. The menu or the bill should clearly state whether service has been included in the total. And if the service has disappointed you, you can complain to the manager and then legally subtract part or all of the service charge. When the service charge is not included in the bill, you should tip about 10%.

For a cheaper alternative to restaurant dining, try a meal in a **caff**—the traditional British equivalent of a U.S. diner. Caffs serve an odd mix of inexpensive English and Italian specialties (£4.50-6 for a full meal). Interiors may be dingy, and tables may be shared, but the food is often very good.

If you want regular **coffee,** ask for a **filter coffee. White coffee** is coffee with a good deal of milk in it, what Americans call café au lait. As for **tea,** Brits assume it is taken with milk, so if you drink plain tea (or black coffee), specify this clearly. Because most people add milk, coffee in England tends to be brewed strong and dark. Iced coffee is unheard of in London, even in summertime. (If you see it on a menu, it is referring to a shake-like coffee and ice cream drink.) Restaurants have to provide non-smoking sections, though you might find the rule honored mostly in the breach. In most eateries, smoking is permitted at any table (with the exception of vegetarian and whole food restaurants, where it is usually banned entirely).

Open-air markets pop up all over central London, vending fresh produce and raw fish at lower prices than stores. **Groceries** and **supermarkets** provide by far the cheapest option for a filling snack. Budget travelers should remember that it is always cheaper to eat take-away, rather than having a sit-down meal. Almost all restaurants have **take-away** service; by eating your meal elsewhere, you can sometimes save up to 40% on service and VAT charges.

The restaurants are arranged both by type and by location. Restaurants—By Type provides a list of restaurants cross-referenced by food and location. Every restaurant listed in this section is followed by an abbreviated neighborhood label; turn to Restaurants—By Location for the full write-up. In the listings by location, the restaurants towards the top of the list tend to offer a better combination of taste, ambience, and value than the ones towards the bottom of the list. Starred restaurants are **Let's Go Picks,** and represent the restaurants that we wouldn't miss on a trip to London. The following is a code to the abbreviated neighborhood labels

B	Brixton	*H*	Hampstead
B&E	Bloomsbury and Euston	*HSK*	High St. Kensington
B&Q	Bayswater and Queensway	*I*	Islington
C	Chelsea	*K&HP*	Knightsbridge and Hyde Park Corner
CG	Covent Garden		
CH	Chinatown	*NH&LG*	Notting Hill and Ladbroke Grove
City	The City		
CT	Camden Town	*S&PC*	Soho and Piccadilly Circus
D	Docklands	*SK*	South Kensington
EC	Earl's Court	*ST*	South of the Thames
EE	East End	*V*	Victoria
		W&E	Windsor and Eton

FOOD AND DRINK

RESTAURANTS—BY TYPE

AFRICAN

Asmara Restaurant, *B*
The Bel Air, *NH&LG*
Calabash Restaurant, *CG*
★Le Petit Prince, *CT*

AMERICAN

Chorister's, *City*
Kim's Cafe, *B*

ASIAN/PACIFIC REGIONAL

Golden Triangle Vietnamese Restaurant, *CG*
Hotei, *S&PC*
Makan, *NH&LG*
The New Culture Revolution, *I*
Penang, *B&Q*
Rasa Sayang, *S&PC*
★Wagamama, *B&E*

BREAKFAST

Benjy's, *EC*

Prost Restaurant, *NH&LG*
Vingt Quatre, *SK*
The Well, *V*

CAFÉS AND SANDWICH SHOPS

Al's Café, *City*
Aroma, *CG*
Barbican Grill, *City*
Beverly Hills Bakery, *K&HP*
Café Deco, *EC*
Café Emm, *S&PC*
Café Floris, *SK*
Café Pushkar, *B*
Cecil's Bakery, *B*
Chelsea Bun Diner, *C*
Choristers, *City*
Coffee Cup, *H*
The Coffee Gallery, *B&E*
The Courtyard Coffee Shop, *W&E*
Crank's, *CG and B&E*
Delice de France, *EC*
★Entre Nous, *C*
Farmer's Kitchen, *D*

Field's Sandwiches, *City*
Frank's Café, *CG*
Freshly Maid Café, *ST*
Gallery Café, *NH&LG*
The Gallery Café Bar, *City*
Gambarti, *B&E*
Glad's Café, *W&E*
Kim's Café, *B*
Knightsbridge Express, *K&HP*
Leigh St. Café, *B&E*
Marie's Café, *ST*
Marino's, *B&E*
Mima's Café, *K&HP*
Monmouth Coffee Company, *CG*National Film Theatre Coffee Bar, *ST*
★Neal's Yard Bakery Co-op, *CG*
★Neal's Yard Salad Bar, *CG*
Neal's Yard World Food Café, *CG*
October Gallery Café, *B&E*
Patisserie Valerie, *S&PC*
Phoenix, *B*
Presto, *S&PC*
St. Georges of Mayfair Sandwich Shop, *D*
Spreads of Covent Garden, *CG*
The Star Café, *S&PC*
Stop Gap, *B*
★Troubador Coffee House, *EC*
The Well, *V*
★Wren Café at St. James, *S&PC*

CARIBBEAN

The Bel Air, *NH&LG*
★Jacaranda, *B*

CHINESE

Camden Friends Restaurant, *CT*
Chuen Cheng Ku, *CH*
The Dragon Inn, *CH*
Harbour City, *CH*
Hong Kong Chinese Restaurant, *EC*
Hung's, *CH*
Kowloon Restaurant, *CH*
Lido Chinese Restaurant, *CH*
Lok Ho Fook, *CH*
Stick and Bowl, *HSK*
Wong Kei, *CH*

CLASSIC ENGLISH

See also Pubs, p. 124.
★Chelsea Kitchen, *C*
Cockney's, *NH&LG*
Neal's Yard Dairy, *CG*
Norman's, *B&Q*
The Pier Tavern, *D*
★The Stockpot, *S&PC*
The Two Brewers, *W&E*
The Waterman's Arms, *W&E*

FISH AND CHIPS

Alpha One Fish Bar, *S&PC*
The Fryer's Delight, *B&E*
Geale's, *NH&LG*
The Hi-Tide Fish&Chips Restaurant, *EC*
The Rock&Sole Plaice, *CG*
Upper St. Fish Shop, *I*

FRENCH

Ambrosiana Crêperie, *SK*
Café Deco, *EC*
★Le Crêperie de Hampstead, *H*
Delice de France, *EC*
Entre Nous, *C*
Jules Rotisserie, *SK, C*
Kramps Crêperie, *EC*
★Le Mercury, *I*
Mange 2, *City*
★Le Petit Prince, *CT*
South Bank Brasserie, *ST*

GREEK AND MIDDLE EASTERN

Cosma's Taverna, *B&E*
Gaby's Continental Bar, *S&PC*
Jimmy's Greek Taverna, *S&PC*
Manzara, *NH&LG*
★Nontas, *CT*
Phoenicia, *HSK*
★Sofra, *CG*

INDIAN/SOUTH ASIAN

Aladin Balti House, *EE*
Ambala Sweet Centre, *B&E*
★Bengal Cuisine, *EE*
Bharat, *CT*
Chutney's, *B&E*
Diwana Bhel Poori House, *B&E*
Eastern Eye, *EE*
Govinda's, *S&PC*
Great Nepalese Restaurant, *B&E*
Gupta Sweet Center, *B&E*
Indian Veg Bhelpoori House, *I*
★Khan's, *B&Q*
Khan's of Kensington, *SK*
★Mandeer, *S&PC*
Muhib, *EE*
Nazrul, *EE*
Rasa Sayang, *S&PC*
★Rhavi Shankar Bhel Poori House, *B&E*
Shampan, *EE*
Sheraz, *EE*
West End Tandoori, *S&PC*

ITALIAN

Arco Bar, *K&HP*

Asmara Restaurant, *B*
Bella Pasta, *SK*
Café Pasta, *HSK*
Calzone, *H*
Ciaccio, *V*
Cosmoba, *B&E*
Il Falconiere, *SK*
Frank's Café, *CG*
★Lorelei, *S&PC*
Mamma Conchetta, *CT*
Marine Ices, *CT*
Mille Pini Restaurant, *B&E*
O, Sole Mio, *V*
Parson's Restaurant, *SK*
Piazza Bar, *S&PC*
Pollo, *S&PC*
Ristorante Avanti, *CT*
Trattoria Aquilino, *I*
Trattoria Mondello, *B&E*

KOSHER/DELI

Al's Deli, *H*
The Nosherie, *City*

OPEN LATE

Alpha One Fish Bar, *S&PC*
Lido Chinese Restaurant, *CH*
Lord's Food and Wine, *K&HP*
Nyam's, *B*
Piazza Bar, *S&PC*
Vingt Quatre, *SK*

PIZZA

Gourmet Pizza Company, *ST*
Parkway Pizzeria, *CT*
Piazza Bar, *S&PC*
Pizzeria Franco, *B*

RUSSIAN

Borshtch 'n' Tears, *K&HP*

S.AMERICAN/ PORTUGEUSE/ TAPAS/

Bar Gansa, *CT*
Blanco's Restaurant, *EC*
★Café Olé, *I*
Lisboa Patisserie, *NH&LG*
Montesol, *H*
Nando's, *EC*
O'Porto Patisserie, *NH&LG*
La Piragua, *I*

SWEETS

Ambala Sweet Centre, *B&E*
Beverly Hills Bakery, *K&HP*
Canadian Muffin Co., *K&HP*
Gupta Sweet Centre, *B&E*
Lisboa Patisserie, *NH&LG*
Marine Ices, *CT*
Michael's The Eton Bakery, *W&E*
O'Porto Patisserie, *NH&LG*
Patisserie Valerie, *S&PC*
Perry's Bakery, *EC*
Rumbold's Bakery, *H*
Thompson's Bakery, *B*

THAI

Jewel of Siam, *B&Q*
Penang, *B&Q*
Tuk Tuk, *I*

VEGETARIAN

Alara Wholefoods, *B&E*
Café Pushkar, *B*
The Cherry Orchard Café, *EE*
Chutney's, *B&E*
Crank's, *CG, B&E*
Diwana Bhel Poori House, *B&E*
Food for Thought, *CG*
Futures!, *City*
Gaby's Continental Bar, *S&PC*
Gallery Café, *NH&LG*
Govinda's, *S&PC*
The Grain Shop, *NH&LG*
Indian Veg Bhelpoori House, *I*
★Jacaranda, *B*
★Mandeer, *S&PC*
Mildred's, *S&PC*
★Neal's Yard Bakery Co-op, *CG*
★Neal's Yard Salad Bar, *CG*
★The Place Below, *City*
★Rhavi Shankar Bhel Poori House, *B&E*
Woolley's Wholefood and Take Away, *B&E*
★The Wren at St. James's, *S&PC*

OTHER EATS

Belgo Centraal, *CG*
★The Fire Station, *ST*
Henry J. Bean's Bar and Grill, *C*
Jazz Bistro, *City*
My Old Dutch Pancake House, *C*
Mezzo, *S&PC*
Roxy Café Cantina, *I*
Ruby in the Dust, *CT*

FOOD AND DRINK

> ### Flakes and Smarties
>
> Few people travel to Britain for its food yet there are delights to be had, especially of the processed variety. Tea can't be drunk without a few biscuits and McVitties purveys the most. Chocolate Hobnobs, Jaffa Cakes and Digestive Biscuits are all national institutions—one nibble and you're nobbled, as the ad says.
>
> Britain has a greater variety of candy for sale than most countries. Brands to watch out for include Flake by Cadbury (with its racy commercials), Kit-Kat, and the ever-popular Smarties. Watch out for the orange ones—they're made of orange chocolate.
>
> Potato chips, or crisps as they are known in England, are not just salted, but come in flavors ranging from Prawn Cocktail, Beef, Chicken, Fruit 'n Spice, and the more traditional Salt & Vinegar.
>
> All this sugar and salt can be washed down with pineapple and grapefruit flavored soda Lilt or the ever popular Ribena, a red currant syrup which has to be diluted with water. This latter beverage belongs to a family of drinks known as squash, all of which are diluted before consumption.
>
> But the food that expatriate Britons miss most is Marmite, a yeast extract which is spread on bread. Unless you've been fed this as a baby you'll never understand it, but it's worth the experience.

RESTAURANTS—BY NEIGHBORHOOD

■ The West End

Soho, Piccadilly, and Covent Garden offer an inexhaustible world of dining options. Take-away is always less expensive, and sandwich bars and cafés will gladly send you off with a substantial meal for under £3. The entire West End is easily accessed by Piccadilly Circus, Leicester Square, Covent Garden, Tottenham Court Road, and Charing Cross tube stations. Pay special attention to closing times; some vegetarian eateries close quite early.

SOHO AND PICCADILLY CIRCUS

Scads of unimpressive pizza and fast food joints cluster around Piccadilly Circus. A trip a few blocks down Shaftesbury Ave. and left onto Wardour or Dean St. rewards the hungry with the smart cafés and cheaper sandwich shops of Soho. **Old Compton St.,** Soho's main drag, lies off Wardour St. one block north of and parallel to Shaftesbury Ave. For fresh fruit, check out old **Berwick Market** on Berwick St.

★**Mandeer,** 21 Hanway Place W1 (tel. 323 0660 or 580 3470). Tube: Tottenham Ct. Road. Color me Ayurvedic! Hidden in the upper reaches of Soho, Mandeer offers some of the best Indian food around, and the chance to learn about owner Ramesh Patel's Science of Life. The owners came to London to study and could not find the tasty, healthy vegetarian cuisine of their home province in Northern India—so they started their own restaurant which soon became the center of a Bohemian expatriate community. Food is exceedingly fresh, primarily organic, and all vegetarian. In accordance with Hindu philosophy, kitchen doors remain open so you can observe the calm chefs in their immaculate culinary workshop. The best deal in the house is the lunch buffet; for under £4 you get 3 heaping portions and rice. The restaurant is just a tad more expensive, but still affordable and well worth it. Try the Pani puri or kachori (£3.15) for starters, and don't miss the vadi and onion (£3.65). Management insists that "all you need is love and an open mind." Ask to see Mr. Patel's Guajarati poetry. Open Mon.-Sat. for lunch (self-service) noon-3pm, dinner 5:30-10pm.

★**The Stockpot,** 18 Old Compton St., W1 (tel. 287 1066), by Cambridge Circus. Tube: Leicester Sq. or Piccadilly. Beloved by locals, who pack the sidewalk tables, it's the cheapest place in Soho to soak up some style. Menus are handwritten daily but always represent a simply marvelous value. Omelettes £2.10-2.25. Entrées £2.10-4.85. Divine apple crumble in hot custard 85p. Open Mon.-Tues. 11:30am-11:30pm, Wed.-Sat. 11:30am-11:45pm, Sun. noon-11pm. Also at 40 Panton St.

★**The Wren Café at St. James's,** 35 Jermyn St., SW1 (tel. 437 9419). Tube: Piccadilly Circus or Green Park. Also accessible from Piccadilly. Wholefood/vegetarian delights served in the shadow of a Christopher Wren church. Tranquil and gorgeous for lunch or tea and cake in the shady courtyard. Casserole of the day with brown rice £3.50. Whole meal scones 75p. Pot of tea 80p. Open Mon.-Sat. 8am-7pm, Sun. 10am-5pm.

★**Lorelei,** 21 Bateman St., W1 (tel. 734 0954). Tube: Tottenham Ct. Rd., Leicester Sq., or Piccadilly Circus. While other Soho Italian joints lure travelers in with seductive decor and clientele, only to drown them with outrageous prices and hidden covers, this unassuming bistro works its magic on the food, keeping it affordable and delicious. Mushroom pizza £3.90. The *Poorman* (tomato, garlic, and oregano) was designed with the budget diner in mind (£2.90). Open Mon.-Sat. noon-11pm.

Govinda's, 9 Soho St., W1 (tel. 437 3662). Tube: Tottenham Ct. Rd. Welcome proof that there's more to Hare Krishna than minimalist hairstyles and flowers in the airport. The International Society for Krishna Consciousness serves deliciously wholesome vegetarian Indian food for very little money. No eggs, meat, or seafood are used, though some dishes contain milk or cream. The cafeteria-style, all-you-can-eat buffet provides full stomachs and spiritual fulfillment for a mere £5. Open Mon.-Sat. noon-8pm.

Mildred's, 58 Greek St., W1 (tel. 494 1634). Tube: Tottenham Ct. Rd. or Leicester Sq. Small, simple, and cozy, this restaurant has a menu that changes daily. You can always order the stir fry vegetables with rice (£4.10) and the falafel with tahini (£4.10). The art on the wall, like the menu, is in a constant state of flux, but the clientele remains the same—young, artsy Soho diners gorging themselves with healthy food. Anything take away is 40p less. Open Mon.-Sat. noon-11pm, Sun. 12:30-6:30pm.

Pollo, 20 Old Compton St., W1 (tel. 734 5917). Tube: Leicester Sq. or Piccadilly Circus. Founded 40 years ago, this restaurant/madhouse serves some of the best Italian values in Soho. Delicious, generous servings of a variety of pastas and a host of sauces (£3.10-3.40), great homemade *tiramisu* (£2.40). Thurs.-Sat., make reservations for parties over four, otherwise long waits. Open Mon.-Sat. noon-midnight.

Alpha One Fish Bar, 43 Old Compton St., W1 (tel. 437 7344). Tube: Leicester Sq. or Piccadilly Circus. Good, greasy fun in a slightly uptown chippie replete with brocaded chairs and neon. Cod with chips (£3.70, take-away discounts). The fish is delivered fresh every day from Scotland. Open Mon.-Thurs. 11:30am-1am, Fri.-Sat. 11:30am-2am, Sun. 11:30-midnight.

Presto, 4-6 Old Compton St., W1 (tel. 437 4006). Tube: Leicester Sq. A 35-year-old hyper-trendy caff where Derek Jarman ate at least once every day. Especially popular with gays and young folks, Presto fills with locals each night at suppertime. Harried waitstaff serves up pastas (£3.20-3.50). Jarman favored the spaghetti carbonara (£3.20). Breakfast from £2.50. Open Mon.-Fri. 11am-11:30pm, Sat. 11am-12:30am. MC, Visa.

The Star Café & Bar, 22 Great Chapel St., W1 (tel. 437 8778). Tube: Oxford Circus. A British approximation of the red checkered tableclothed American diner. Pasta of the day £3 take-away. Come after 3pm and guzzle £1.50 bottles of Becks until they close. Open Mon.-Fri. noon-6pm.

Jimmy's Greek Taverna, 23 Frith St., W1 (tel. 437 9521). Tube: Piccadilly Circus or Tottenham Ct. Rd. Below street level, Jimmy's is fun, hot, and sweaty, and portions are heaping. Colorful tablecloths and congenial atmosphere. Tasty vegetarian *moussaka* (£4.50) and chicken kebab (£5). All come with rice, chips and salad. Don't miss the sticky baklava (£1.50). Make reservations for parties over 4. Open Mon.-Sat. 12:30-3pm and 5:30-11pm.

Café Emm, 17 Frith St., W1 (tel. 437 0723). Tube: Leicester Sq. Most patrons of this cozy café overlook the wood-paneled interior and soothing atmosphere— they're busy clamoring for the 2 outdoor tables. A pleasingly cheap and palatable way to sample Soho café-culture, all dishes on the revolving special menu, from dazzling variety of chicken to stuffed peppers, are £5. Last orders 30min. before close. Open Mon.-Thurs. noon-3pm, 5:30-11pm, Fri. noon-3pm, 5:30pm-1am, Sat. 5pm-1am, Sun. 5-11pm.

Mezzo, 100 Wardour St., W1 (tel. 314 4000). Tube: Leicester Sq. Ultra-swank, 2-story mega-restaurant on the former site of the renowned Marquee Club. Doormen, cigarette girls—the whole nine. Priced accordingly, but come between 5:30-7:00pm and get a 2-course meal in the upstairs "mezzonine"—choose delicacies like eggplant and spring garlic soup or red cooked pork belly with bok choy and spring onions for only £7. Open Mon-Thurs. and Sun. noon-1am, Fri.-Sat. noon-2:30am. Major credit cards.

Patisserie Valerie, 44 Old Compton St., W1 (tel. 437 3466). Tube: Leicester Sq. Opened in 1926, this place introduced continental patisserie to the English. An immediate success, it became the meeting place for starving artists and bohemians. It still bustles today with a mixed crowd of young and old who come to enjoy the fresh tarts, cakes, breads, and truffles. Tasty sandwiches with salad also available (£2.80-4.50). Open Mon.-Fri. 8am-8pm, Sat. 8am-7pm, Sun. 10am-6pm.

Hotei, 39 Great Windmill St., W1 (tel. 434 9913). Tube: Piccadilly Circus. Take away, or sit at one of the 9 stools for Osaka-style snack food. Watch servers clad in smashing black and red kimonettes prepare your food before your eyes. Fill up on noodles prepared with vegetables, prawns, or hot Korean pickles (£2.30-4.10/serving). Open Mon.-Sat. 11am-11pm.

West End Tandoori, 5 Old Compton St., W1 (tel. 734 1057). Tube: Leicester Sq. A steaming dumbwaiter, unusual lighting, and languid Indian music add to the serene atmosphere. Chicken curry £4.85, vegetarian dishes £3.50-3.75. Service charge 10%. Open Mon.-Thurs. noon-2:30pm and 5:30pm-midnight, Fri.-Sat. noon-1am, Sun. noon-midnight. Major credit cards.

Rasa Sayang, 10 Frith St., W1 (tel. 734 8720). Tube: Leicester Sq. Unusual Malaysian and Singaporean food in a slickly decorated restaurant. While the main dishes are a bit pricey, bargain specials abound—the lunch special includes an entree with beer, wine, or soda (£5), or chomp to your heart's content at the £6.50 all-you-can-eat weekend buffet (Sat. 1-5pm and Sun. 1-7pm). Open Mon.-Thurs. noon-2:45pm and 6-11:30pm, Fri. noon-2:45pm and 6pm-1am, Sat. 1pm-1am, Sun. 1pm-10pm. Major credit cards.

Gaby's Continental Bar, 30 Charing Cross Rd., WC2 (tel. 836 4233). Tube: Leicester Sq. Right next to tube station. A bit cramped, this tiny deli-type restaurant serves great Middle Eastern and vegetarian food. Hefty falafel sandwich and a large selection of salads, around £2. Take away discounts. Open Mon.-Sat. 9am-midnight, Sun. 11am-10pm.

Piazza Bar, 146 Charing Cross Rd., WC2. Tube: Tottenham Ct. Rd. or Leicester Sq. Given the impressionistic murals of London, dirt-cheap prices, and 24hr. service, you'd feel guilty complaining about the food. Fortunately, you won't have to. The pasta (with salad and bread; £2.50 noon-4pm, then £2.90), pizza (£1.50/slice), and fresh-cut sandwiches (£2 and up) all pass muster. Open daily 24 hrs.

CHINATOWN

Dozens of traditional, inexpensive restaurants are crammed into London's Chinatown (tube: Leicester Sq.), which occupies the few blocks between Shaftesbury Ave. and Leicester Sq. **Gerrard St.,** the pedestrian-only backbone of Chinatown, is one block south of Shaftesbury Ave. Because of the Hong Kong connection, Cantonese cooking and language dominate. Most restaurants serve *dim sum* every afternoon, and many keep their doors open incredibly late. The **Golden Gate Cake Shop,** 13 Macclesfield St., W1, off Gerrard St. (open daily 10am-7pm), and the bakery at the **Kowloon Restaurant** (see below) sell pork buns and other delectable Chinese pastries. An automatic 10% service charge is standard.

Lok Ho Fook, 4-5 Gerrard St., W1 (tel. 437 2001). A busy place with good prices. Cream-colored table cloths create welcoming atmosphere. Extensive offerings with lots of seafood, noodles, and a slew of vegetarian dishes. Vegetarian hot and sour soup £1.55. Noodles, fried or in soup, £2.80. *Dim sum* is made fresh when you order and not strolled around on carts. Helpful staff will aid the novice in selection (before 6pm £1.35-2.55). Open daily noon-11:45pm. Major credit cards.

Kowloon Restaurant, 21-22 Gerrard St., W1 (tel. 437 0148). Meal-sized portions of vermiculli, wheat, or Ho-fun rice noodles (£2.50-5) served steaming and cheap in this Chinatown institution. Satisfy your sweet tooth in the bakery. Open daily noon-11:45pm.

Harbour City, 46 Gerrard St. W1 (tel. 439 7859). A wonderful place for *dim sum* (served noon-5pm daily), though there are no carts. Food is light and expertly prepared. The *cheung fun* (£2.20-2.60), a rice noodle surrounding various fillings in sweet soy sauce, are delectable. *Dim sum* £1.60-2.60/dish. Open Mon-Thurs. noon-11:30, Fri.-Sat. noon-midnight, Sun 11am-11pm.

Hung's, 27 Wardour St., W1 (tel. 287 6578). Open kitchen serves big bowls of steaming soups and noodles. Try the fried vermicelli noodles Singapore style (£3.80), or, for truly adventurous carnivores, ask for the beef tripe (cow stomach) on noodles. Open Mon.-Sat. noon-4:30am, Sun. 11am-4:30am.

The Dragon Inn, 12 Gerrard St., W1 (tel. 494 0870). Plain, diner-like setting, and traditional Cantonese home cooking. Delicious *dim sum* dishes are served from 11am-5pm daily. Try the stir-fried vegetables with oyster sauce (£4.50). Noodles from £3.80. Open 11am-11:45pm daily. Major credit cards.

Wong Kei, 41-43 Wardour St., W1 (tel. 437 3071). Three stories of endlessly harried waiters and the best value Chinese food in Soho. A waterfall trickles on the first floor and dumbwaiters zoom food up to the other floors. Solo diners should expect to share tables. Roasted pork and egg rice £2.40. Set dinner of sweet and sour pork, chicken in black beans, vegetable and rice £5.80. Open Mon.-Sat. noon-11:30pm, Sun. noon-10:30pm. Cash only.

Chuen Cheng Ku, 17 Wardour St., W1 (tel. 437 1398). Some consider it one of the planet's best restaurants. Certainly it has one of the longest menus. *Dim sum* dishes (served 11am-6pm) £1.75. Dried and fried *Ho-Fun* noodles £4.50. Long menu concentrates on seafood. Open daily 11am-midnight. Major credit cards.

Lido Chinese Restaurant, 41 Gerard St., W1 (tel. 437 4431). Elegant dark wood paneling and wall-set aquariums make this a serene but pricey place to recover from a night of Soho revelry. Chicken, beef, and vegetable dishes (£4.50-6) and *dim sum* (£1.50) into the early morning. Open daily 11:30am-4:30am. Major credit cards.

COVENT GARDEN

Covent Garden offers an enticing array of eateries to playgoers and tourists in the heart of London's theater district. Although this is a nicer area, don't let expensive looks deceive you. Good food at reasonable prices can be found. Tucked away from the tourist labyrinth, **Neal's Yard** (off Neal St.) overflows with sumptuous vegetarian joints amongst herbal healers and colorful window boxes. Beware that these restaurants, and many others in the area, close relatively early; keep an eye out for the inconspicuous brasseries that dot the area when searching for late evening dining options (tube: Covent Garden).

★**Neal's Yard Bakery Co-op,** 6 Neal's Yard, WC2 (tel. 836 5199). Only organic flour and filtered water are used in the delicious breads here. A small, open-air counter offers a plethora of baked goods, sandwiches, and salads—all vegetarian with many vegan options. Large 3-seed loaf £1.95. Bean burger £1.90, take-away £1.60. 50% discount on day-olds. No smoking. Open Mon.-Sat. 10:30am-5pm.

★**Sofra,** 36 Tavistock St., WC2 (tel. 240 3773). This Turkish restaurant serves the freshest of foods in a cool Mediterranean atmosphere to match. Plenty of vegetarian as well as carnivorous dishes. Try the mixed *meze*—a selection of various Turkish appetizers including *tabouli, falafel, hummus, imam bayildi,* and *kisir* (£9.45, junior platter £5). £5 set dinner includes your choice of hummus, tabouli, or a soup and salad combo, and a main course of grilled chicken, lamb, or *kofa*. Attentive and friendly waitstaff. Live music by a Turkish guitarist adds to the ambience.

Another location at 18 Shepard St. (tel. 493 3320), as well as several other cafés and take-away sites. Open daily noon-midnight.

★**Neal's Yard Salad Bar,** 2 Neal's Yard, WC2 (tel. 836 3233). Take-away or sit outside at this simple vegetarian's fantasyland. Get a plateful of the hearty and wholesome hot vegetable dishes made of grains and veggies (usually one has cheese) for £2.60. Tempting mix 'n' match salads from £1.90. Deliciously tangy frozen yogurt and vanilla-honey ice cream come from nearby Neal's Yard Dairy; small cone £1.20. Open daily 10am-8pm.

Food for Thought, 31 Neal St., WC2 (tel. 836 0239). Verdant foliage decorates this tiny basement restaurant offering large servings of excellent vegetarian food at moderate prices. Soups, salads, and stir-fries. Tasty daily specials from £2.80. Take-away or sit among the slightly cramped wooden tables. Open Mon.-Sat. 9:30am-9pm, Sun. noon-4:30pm.

Neal's Yard World Food Café, 14-15 Neal's Yard, WC2 (tel. 379 0298). Above the blue Remedies shop. In this airy upstairs café, you know you're eating fresh vegetarian food because you can see it being prepared—the kitchen is the center of the restaurant. World meals such as Indian, West African, Mexican, and Turkish £6, or order à la carte. Open Mon.-Thurs. noon-7:30pm, Fri.-Sat. noon-5pm.

Crank's, 1 The Market, WC2 (tel. 379 6508). This branch of the popular and affordable vegetarian chain has a terrace overlooking one of London's most happening piazzas. Golden grilled polenta with roasted vegetables £5.25. Full service meals on the piazza and in the evenings. Eight London locations, but still not chain-like. Open Mon.-Thurs. 9am-11pm, Fri. and Sat. 9am-11:30pm, Sun. 10am-8pm.

Belgo Centraal, 50 Earlham St., WC2 (tel. 813 2233). Friendly waiters in monk's cowls, bizarre 21st century beerhall interior, and great specials on mussels with Belgian beer make this one of Covent Garden's most popular restaurants. During lunchtime, a fiver buys your choice of mussels or wild boar sausage and a beer (including the inimitable *Hoegaarten*). Between 6-8pm, the price of a similar set meal is determined by the time your order (e.g. £6.26 at 6:26pm), so come early. Open Mon.-Sat. noon-11:30pm, Sun. noon-10:30pm.

Monmouth Coffee Company, 27 Monmouth St., WC2 (tel. 379 4337). Can't decide on a roast? Sit in the back sampling room, and taste the many brews (25p per taste). Or slide into one of the 4 small wood booths with a full cup (£1.10, 80p take-away). Some of the best coffee in Britain. No smoking policy lets you really taste your java. Café/sampling room open Mon.-Sat. 9am-6pm, Sun. 11am-4:30pm (no pastries on Sun.). Shop open Mon.-Sat. 9am-6:30pm, Sun. 11am-5pm.

Neal's Yard Dairy, 17 Shorts Gdns., WC2 (tel. 379 7646). Not for the lactose intolerant: a world-class, cheese shop selling fresh cheeses from the British Isles. In close contact with dairies in Britain and Ireland, they make regular buying trips to the farms. Daredevils can feast on the unpasteurized Cooleeney cheese from Tipperary, Ireland (£5.65 per lb.). Don't miss the fresh milk and homemade yogurt (£1.25 for about a quart). Cheesy. Open Mon.-Sat. 9am-7pm, Sun 10am-5pm.

The Rock and Sole Plaice, 47 Endell St., WC2 (tel. 836 3785). Fortunately, the fish (£3) and chunky chips (£1-1.20) are better than the puns. Sit under the trees at wooden picnic tables lined up along the sidewalk outside and enjoy. If ye be lacking sealegs have the spicy sausage and chips (£1.70 take-away). Open daily 11:30am-11:00pm.

Spreads of Covent Garden, 15a New Row, WC2 (tel. 379 0849). This cramped pre-theater establishment is packed on Sat. evenings and at lunchtime. The triple-decker B.C.L.T. (£3.55 with chips) puts a hearty twist (the C is for cheese) on a classic. Unbelievable deals for vegetarians: lasagna £2.45, veggie burgers and omelettes under £2.50. Take-away discount is a little under £1. Open Mon.-Sat. 8am-8:30pm, Sun. 9am-7pm.

Frank's Café, 52 Neal. St., WC2 (tel. 836 6345). An old and very unpretentious Italian café with a mural of Amalti covering the wall. Serves delicious homemade pastas at bargain prices (£2.80-3.80). Also pizzas, risottos, and breakfast foods available all day. Cappuccino £1. Take away discount. Open daily 8am-8pm.

Golden Triangle Vietnamese Restaurant, 16 Great Newport St., WC2 (tel. 379 6330). Airy venue provides affordable elegance. Try the mouthwatering *thit ga kho,* chicken with ginger and wine sauce (£4.30), or the *tom sot ga chua,* stir-fried prawns with spring onion and chili (£5.60). Friendly staff helps diners unfamiliar with Vietnamese cuisine negotiate the menu. Open Mon.-Thurs. noon-3pm and 5:30-11pm, Fri.-Sun. noon-11pm. AmEx, MC. Visa.

Calabash Restaurant, 38 King St., WC2 (tel. 836 1976). In the basement of the Africa Centre, taste the fruit of the motherland at reasonable prices. The savory pan-African menu feature *doro wat* (chicken in hot pepper sauce served with eggs and rice or *ingera* bread) £6.75. Open Mon.-Fri. 12:30-3pm and 6-11:30pm, Sat. 6-11:30pm.

Aroma, 36a St. Martin's La., WC2 (tel. 836 5110). Next door to the London Coliseum. A bright, modern café with a young and trendy crowd—a favorite with the hyper-trendy food writers at *Time Out,* if that tells you anything. Various frozen desserts, like iced coffee with Häagen Daz ice cream (£2.25). Fresh sandwiches for take away or sitting £2-3. Fruit salads and juices also available. Take-away 20-30p cheaper. Open Mon.-Fri. 8am-11pm, Sat. 9am-11pm, Sun. noon-9pm.

▓ Bloomsbury and Euston

Superb Greek, Italian, and vegetarian restaurants line **Goodge Street**, conveniently close to the British Museum. Northwest of Bloomsbury, around Euston Sq., a vast number of the city's best and most traditional Indian restaurants ply their trade. Try to avoid the restaurants on Woburn Pl., Southampton Row, and Great Russell St., which cater to swarms of tourists.

NEAR GOODGE STREET

This food-filled neighborhood (tube: Goodge St.) offers the gamut of culinary temptations: upscale French cuisine, informal Mediterranean fare, and modest sandwich shops and cafés. **Goodge St.** (to the right of the tube station) and **Tottenham St.** (to the left of the station) are the major avenues, but those who meander down side streets will make delicious discoveries.

Crank's Restaurant/Take-Away, 9-11 Tottenham St., W1 (tel. 631 3912). Another branch of London's original health food restaurant, founded in 1961, now an eight-store chain. Crisp blond wood and white brick interior; frosted glass atrium ceiling in rear. Large vegetarian and vegan dishes made with fresh ingredients, including free-range eggs and organic flour. Cool jazz soundtrack makes this the perfect place for a relaxing late afternoon break. Entrees ranging from vegetarian lasagna to polenta with roast vegetable with 2 side salads £4.95. Take-away available. No smoking. Open Mon.-Fri. 8am-7:30pm, Sat. 9am-7:30pm.

Trattoria Mondello, 36 Goodge St., W1 (tel. 637 9037). An array of zesty, but pricier, Sicilian dishes served in a rustic, seaside-style dining room with open-beam ceilings and discreet seating alcoves. Diverse clientele. Pastas come as a side or main dish, but the side serving is generous; try the *spaghetti al salmone* £4.50. Cappuccino £1. Open Mon.-Wed. noon-3pm and 5:30-11:30pm, Thurs.-Sat. noon-3pm and 5:30pm-midnight. Major credit cards.

Cosma's Taverna, 29 Goodge St., W1 (tel. 636 1877). Dark and smoky, with a simulated grape arbor and paintings of Grecian scenes on the walls. Where Mike Dukakis used to get down in London, but don't let that discourage you: the disco-ball-equipped basement *taverna* provides a perfect stage for an evening of *Ouzo*-fueled (£1.60) debauchery, complete with plate-smashing and belly-dancing. Tasty lamb kebab £5.90. *Ouzo* £1.60. *Moussaka* £5.50. Open daily 11:30am-3pm and 5:30pm-2am. Major credit cards.

The Coffee Gallery, 23 Museum St. (tel. 436 0455). Tube: Tottenham Ct. Rd. or Holborn. Sandwich prices (mozzarella, tomato, and basil (£2.80) are comparable to the other caffs flanking the British Museum, but the crowd here is fresher and the atmosphere is miles ahead. Within the bright blue walls is a gallery of ceramics and paintings in which delicious, fresh Italian garden food is served. The menu changes daily. Open Mon.-Fri. 8am-5:30pm, Sat. 10am-5:30pm.

Marino's, 31 Rathbone Pl., W1 (tel. 636 8965). From Goodge St. turn left onto Charlotte St., which turns into Rathbone Pl. Restaurant and sandwich bar bustling with a young, hip crowd. Large seating area, yet maintains a café feel. Perfect for lunch, an afternoon snack, or a cappuccino to read the paper by. Pizzas, omelettes, and grilled meats (£3.20-4.65). Salads and sandwiches (£1.60 and up). Take-away available. Open Mon.-Fri. 7am-7pm, Sat. 7am-4pm.

AROUND RUSSELL SQUARE

Immediately around Russell Square and the British Museum, eateries are predictably dull and overpriced. A few blocks to the east, on **Theobald's Rd.** and **Lamb's Conduit,** non-touristy cafés and bakeries line the walkways.

★**Wagamama,** 4A Streatham St., WC1 (tel. 323 9223). Tube: Tottenham Ct. Rd. Go down New Oxford St. and left onto Bloomsbury St. Streatham St. is the 1st right. "Positive Eating+Positive Living." Fast food with a high-tech twist: waitstaff take your orders on hand-held electronic radios that transmit directly to the kitchen. Strangers slurping happily from their massive bowls of ramen sit elbow-to-elbow at long tables, like extras from *Tampopo.* Pan-fried noodles, rice dishes, and vegetarian soup bases also available. Noodles in various combinations and permutations £3.80-5.70. Not the place for a long, quiet meal: average turnover time is 20 min. No smoking. Open Mon.-Fri. noon-2:30pm and 6-11pm, Sat. 12:30-3pm and 6-11pm, Sun. 12:30-3pm and 6-11pm. Cash only.

Woolley's Salad Shop and Sandwich Bar, 33 Theobald's Rd., WC1 (tel. 405 3028). Tube: Holborn. Healthy and delicious picnic fare for take-away, mostly vegetarian. Mix and match their 10 fresh salads in a variety of sizes (70p-£6.30 for a huge party pot). The adjoining sandwich shop offers everything from chicken sag to smoked salmon lovingly swaddled in fresh rolls, 80p-£2.30. Creative jacket potatoes (with ratatouille £2.40). Dried fruit, nuts, herbal tea, and muesli also for sale. One pretty white table in the pedestrian alleyway, if no one else takes it. Open Mon.-Fri. 7am-3:30pm.

Mille Pini Restaurant, 33 Boswell St., WC1 (tel. 242 2434). Tube: Holborn. Take Southampton Row and turn right onto Theobald's Row. Boswell St. is the second left. Wine racks on the walls and chandelier lights (each bulb with its own private lampshade) provide the decor; sepia-tone floor tiles add a rustic feel. Terrific brick-oven pizza, pasta (all £4.20-4.80), and homemade pastries. Divine *tiramisu* £2.40. Mon.-Fri. noon-3pm and 6-11pm, Sat. 6pm-midnight, Sun. 6-11pm.

Leigh St. Café, 16 Leigh St., WC1 (tel. 387 3393). Tube: Russell Sq. A bright student- and local-filled café serving creative sandwiches and pastries. Elegant decor and marble tables inside, enclosed garden seating in back. Sandwiches from 70p, and a selections of pastas changing daily (£3.25). Take-away available. Open daily 7:30am-8pm.

Alara Wholefoods, 58/60 Marchmont, WC1 (tel. 837 1172). Tube: Russell Sq. A good staple store offering dried fruit, nuts, grains, and a little wholefood propaganda. Lots of heathy foods for the cupboard, and the take-away kitchen in the back is practically giving away jacket potatoes (from 90p) and generous slices of quiche (£1.55). You can chomp at the table on the sidewalk in front. Open Mon.-Fri. 9am-7pm, Sat. 10am-6pm.

The Fryer's Delight, 19 Theobald's Rd., WC1 (tel. 405 4114). Tube: Holborn. One of the best chippies around. Popular with British Library scholars and assorted locals. Retro buffs will gladly pay some extra pence to submerge themselves in authentic orange, red, and blue formica. Large portions of fish and chips £3 take-away. Walk out with a Cornish pastie or a chicken pie for £1. Open Mon.-Sat. noon-10pm, until 11pm for take-away.

Gambarti, 38 Lamb's Conduit St., WC1 (tel. 405 7950). Tube: Russell Sq. Fresh, green café with hanging plants and a red tiled floor. Enjoy an English breakfast (£2.65) or sandwiches (85p-£1.30) in the rustic interior or outside on the pedestrian walkway. Vegetarian options and Danish pastries. Friendly service, but take-away is cheaper. Mon.-Fri. 7am-10pm.

October Gallery Café, 24 Old Gloucester St., WC1 (tel. 242 7367). Tube: Holborn. Take Southampton Row and turn right at Theobald's Rd. Old Gloucester St. is the first left. A high-ceilinged café with wood floors and wicker seats. Adjacent to the October Gallery (see Bloomsbury, p. 168). Exciting menu changes daily and reflects the multi-cultural artwork on display. Recent offerings included Roman Style chicken, cooked from an ancient Roman recipe recovered by the British Museum(£3.50). Open Mon.-Fri. 12:30-2:30pm, but closed in Aug.

Cosmoba, 9 Cosmo Pl., WC1 (tel. 837 0904). Tube: Russell Sq. On this pedestrian thoroughfare off of Old Gloucester, this simple restaurant has welcomed the hungry of Bloomsbury with low prices and friendly Italian hospitality for nearly 40 years. Choose from spaghetti, tagliatelle, or penne with a variety of sauces (£3.15-4.85). Also succulent specials like *pollo arabiata* (chicken escaloppe in cream, brandy, and black pepper). Perfect cappuccinos £1. Open Mon.-Sat. 11:30am-3pm and 5:30-11pm. MC, Visa.

NEAR EUSTON

Restaurants specializing in Western and Southern Indian cuisine cluster along **Drummond St.** (tube: Warren St. or Euston Sq.). Many are *bhel poori,* or vegetarian. From the Warren St. tube station, head up Hampstead Rd. until it meets Drummond St. From the Euston Sq. station, take N. Gower St. until Drummond St. crosses it.

★**Rhavi Shankar Bhel Poori House,** 133-135 Drummond St., NW1 (tel. 338 6458). Tube: Euston Sq. Bright, cheery atmosphere; decorated with a very light, tasteful touch. Most entrées £2.50-3.80. *Paper dose* (paper-thin crispy rice pancake served with rich vegetable filling, tangy *sambhar* sauce, and coconut chutney) £3.70 and renowned *samosas* (3 for £1.70). Delectable *chapati.* Daily specials (£2-3) are an absolute godsend to hungry travelers who crave good Indian vegetarian grub. Open daily noon-10:45pm.

Chutney's, 124 Drummond St., NW1 (tel. 338 0604). Tube: Warren St. A cheerful café serving vegetarian dishes from Western and Southern India. Bright paintings in deep royal hues and spiral brass lamps decorate the walls. Appropriately, the chutneys are delicious. Organic wines for vegetarians and vegans (£7 per bottle). Delicious mango milkshakes £2. All you can eat lunch buffet Mon.-Sat. noon-2:45pm and Sun. noon-10:30pm (£5). *Dosas* (filled pancakes) £3.50-4.30. Take-away available 6-11:30pm. Open Mon.-Sat. noon-2:45pm and 6-11:30pm, Sun. noon-10:30pm. Visa, MC, Access.

Diwana Bhel Poori House, 121 Drummond St., NW1 (tel. 387 5556). Tube: Warren St. Tasty Indian vegetarian food in a clean and airy restaurant. Strict vegetarians (including liberal kosher eaters) will find this place a dining haven. Spicy sauces and chutneys make for a very creative use of vegetables. The specialty is *Thali* (an assortment of vegetables, rices, sauces, breads, and desserts) £3.80-4.10. Lunch buffet, noon-2:30pm, includes 4 vegetable dishes, rice, savouries, and dessert (£4). BYOB. Open daily noon-11:30pm. Also at 50 Westbourne Grove (tube: Bayswater). Major credit cards.

Great Nepalese Restaurant, 48 Eversholt St., NW1 (tel. 338 6737). Tube: Euston. From the station head left up Eversholt St. Walls covered with accolades from food critics and restaurant guides, as well as a photo of an Indian ghurka who received the V.C. Try Nepalese specialties like *bhutuwa* chicken, prepared with ginger, garlic, spice, and green herbs (£4.25). Also delicious vegetarian dishes like *aloo bodi tama* (potato, bamboo shoots, beans) £2.70. Food is spicy but the staff is sweet in this family-owned restaurant. It lives up to its unexciting but accurate title. Don't pass up the Nepalese Rum (£1.65) poured from the bottle shaped like the *kukri* knife—the national weapon of Nepal. 10% discount for take-away. Open Mon.-Sat. noon-2:45pm and 6-11:45pm, Sun. noon-2:30pm and 6-11:30pm.

Gupta Sweet Centre, 100 Drummond St., NW1 (tel. 380 1590). Tube: Warren St. Excellent Indian sweets and savories to take away. Delicious *chum-chum* (sweet cottage cheese) 30p. Samosa 30p. A refreshingly neighborly sort of shop that hasn't gone industrial in any way; you'll forget you're in London. Open Mon.-Thurs. 11am-7pm, Fri.-Sat. 10am-7pm, Sun. noon-7pm.

Ambala Sweet Centre, 112 Drummond St., NW1 (tel. 387 7886). The original shop of the 32-shop chain has been selling to sweet tooths since 1965. Check out the ever-popular *habshi halwa* (sticky nuts, milk, sugar; £3.30 per lb.). The *sohan salwa* (£2.70 per lb.) is like English toffee but better—and a thick circle of it will leave you only 60-70p poorer. Open daily 9am-10:30pm.

■ Victoria, Kensington, and Chelsea

VICTORIA

Culinary prospects in the areas immediately surrounding the Victoria station mega-plex may seem a bit grim. The avenues radiating north and east from the station (Buckingham Palace Rd., Victoria Rd., and Vauxhall Bridge Rd.) are populated with mediocre sandwich shops and chain restaurants catering to desperate and famished (i.e. non-discriminating) tourists. Follow the suits and count on local office workers to find the cheapest lunch spots. Those willing to take a short stroll will be rewarded by the three spots we've found.

Ciaccio, 5 Warwick Way, SW1 (tel. 828 1342). An intimate Italian eatery whose prices and spices make it a giant for budget eaters. Pick a container of pasta and one of about 10 sauces (pesto, veggie, tomato and meat), and they'll heat it up in the microwave for £1.39-2.50. Handsome portions make for an unbeatable value. Open Mon.-Fri. 10am-6pm, Sat. 9:30am-5pm.

The Well, 2 Eccleston Place, SW1 (tel. 730-7303). A large open eatery dispensing sandwiches (£1.55-1.80) and good cheer (free). Breakfast especially cheap— eggs, bacon and sundry other breakfast goodies a mere 65p each. Open Mon.-Fri. 9am-6pm, Sat. 9:30am-5pm.

O Sole Mio, 39 Churton St. (tel. 976 6887). Yeah, like the song. Basement eatery serves healthy portions of pasta at reasonable prices (£5.30-6); pizza's a good deal too (£5.70-6). Open Mon.-Fri. noon-3pm, 6:30-11:30pm and Sat. 6:30-11:30pm.

KNIGHTSBRIDGE AND HYDE PARK CORNER

Epicurean stomachs-on-a-budget teased by the sumptuous outlay of the Harrods food court may growl with disappointment at the dearth of affordable eateries near Knightsbridge (tube: Knightsbridge). **Knightsbridge Green,** which connects Bromp-ton Rd. and Knightsbridge Rd. just past their divergence, offers several sandwich shops, in addition to fresh fruit and vegetable stands where you can procure provisions for a picnic.

Mima's Café, 9 Knightsbridge Green, SW1 (tel. 589 6820). Understandably packed during lunch hours. Practically every sandwich under the sun, each £2.50 or less, including Scottish roast beef and chicken and sweet corn. Huge salads £4-6. Open Mon.-Sat. 6am-5:30pm.

Knightsbridge Express, 17 Knightsbridge Green, SW1 (tel. 589 3039). Proprietor George looks after the crowds who pack this upbeat eatery during lunch hours. The upstairs seating area is more placid. Most sandwiches £1.20-2.40. Pasta platters £3.40. Open Mon.-Sat. 6am-5pm.

Arco Bar, 46 Hans Crescent, SW1 (tel. 584 6454). Crowds pack in for cheap Italian food. Large portions of pasta only £4.40. Generously filled sandwiches on excellent bread £1.30-2.20 take-away. Open Mon.-Fri. 7am-6pm, Sat. 8am-6pm.

Borshtch 'n' Tears, 46 Beauchamp Pl., SW3 (tel. 589 5003). Dining here can prove an evening's entertainment (though it's anything but cheap). The management of this Russian restaurant scoffs at English reserve. Blinis & smoked salmon £6. Entrées £7-12. Try a shot from one of the 16 different vodkas in Baron Benno von Borshtch's bewildering collection (around £2.50). Live music nightly. Last orders at 1am. Cover £1. Service charge 10%. Open daily 6pm-2am.

Beverly Hills Bakery, 3 Egerton Terrace, SW3 (tel. 584 4401). A cozy café and bak-ery whose name proves that the rich everywhere identify with each other. Every-thing baked on the premises with natural ingredients. Key lime pie, carrot cake, and cheese cake slices £2.20, £1.80 take-away. Muffins £1, 12 muffins £4.50. Espresso 80p take-away. Open Mon.-Sat. 7:30am-6:30pm, Sun. 8am-6pm.

Lord's Food and Wine, 209 Brompton Rd., SW7 (tel. 589 8851). A 24-hr. supermar-ket offering cheap, tasty take-away. Serves a wicked good whole roast chicken for only £4; potato with hoummus £1.59. Open all the time.

SOUTH KENSINGTON

This is the unofficial French quarter of London; also it is one of the ritziest areas in the city. As one would expect, South Ken (as it's called by those in the know) is not brimming with bargains. For budget dining, **Old Brompton Rd.** and **Fulham Rd.** are the main thoroughfares in this graceful area of London, Fulham Rd. is especially lively in the evenings. South Kensington tube station lies closest, but some of the restaurants below require a substantial hike from there; others can be easily reached from the Earl's Ct. tube station. Old Brompton Rd. is served by Buses 74 and C1; Fulham Road by Buses 14, 45a, and 211.

Café Floris, 4 Harrington Rd., SW7 (tel. 589 3276). A bustling caff offering delicious sandwiches and filling breakfasts. Double egg on toast is £2, sandwiches are £1.20-2. You' re paying something of a premium for eating in South Ken, but it's a better value than anything for miles. Open daily 7am-7pm.

Ambrosiana Crêperie, 194 Fulham Rd., SW10 (tel. 351 0070). Airy storefront with small tables. Gourmet but friendly. Savory crepes £4.60-5.80 (try the combination of salami, asparagus, onions, and cheese). Sweet crepes slightly cheaper (peaches, *creme de caçao*, and ice cream £3.65). Mon. and Thurs. all crepes half-price. Open Mon.-Fri. noon-3pm and 6-11:30pm, Sat.-Sun. noon-11:30pm.

Jules Rotisserie, 6-8 Bute St., SW7 (tel. 584 0600; fax 584 0614). This lively, pleasant restaurant with indoor and outdoor seating serves delicious roasted free-range poultry. Quarter chicken with potatoes and green salad £5.95. Fresh orange juice £1.30. More elegant franchise has recently opened at 338 King's Rd. (tel. 351 0041). Open daily 11:30am-11:30pm.

Vingt Quatre, 325 Fulham Rd., SW10 (tel. 376 7224). Open 24-7, just as the name implies (if you're a cunning linguist). Hyper-modern brushed steel tables and chairs give a strangely space-age feel to this pricey diner. Full English breakfast £4.75 for small, £6.75 for large. Burgers £5.75. Drinks served noon-midnight. Cover charge varies between 50p-£1. Never closes.

Il Falconiere, 84 Old Brompton Rd., SW7 (tel. 589 2401). A bit of Italy on Old Brompton Rd.—sidewalk tables and blindingly white tablecloths. A full meal proves quite expensive. Pasta £4-5.50. Salmon salad £5.50. Veal in lemon sauce £6.50. £1 cover charge. Open Mon.-Sat. noon-2:45pm and 6-11:45pm. Major credit cards.

Khan's of Kensington, 3 Harrington Rd., SW 7 (tel. 581 2900 or 584 4114). This restaurant proves that elegant decor, attentive service, and delicately prepared dishes are too often associated with criminally small portions. Still, the food here tastes great and the atmosphere is more than pleasant—if you're willing to tighten your belt and loosen your wallet, this is one of the best Indian restaurants in town. Tandoori lamb chops £6.25. Vegetarian tandoori mushroom *masala* £5. Open Mon.-Sat. noon-2:30pm and 5:30-11:30pm, Sun. 1-3:30pm and 6:30-11:30pm. Major credit cards.

Parson's Restaurant, 311 Fulham Rd., SW10 (tel. 352 0651). Lovely wood floors and tables give an airy open feel. In the summer the ceiling opens like a sun-roof and you can pretend that you're in a convertible. Huge pasta specials (£4.25-4.65) come with a free second helping and free refills on coffee. Open daily noon-1am, last orders at 12:30am (midnight on Sun.).

Bella Pasta, 60 Old Brompton Rd. SW7 (tel. 584 4028). The nicest store in a popular chain. Cool 2-tiered seating that flows into street. This is considered fast food for Kensington, but it's still elegant. Pastas £5-7. Open Mon.-Thurs. 10:30am-11:30pm, Fri. and Sat. 10:30am-midnight, Sun. 10:30am-11pm. AmEx, MC, Visa.

Canadian Muffin Co., 353 Fulham Rd. (tel. 351 0015). Forget scones and bite into a real North American muffin—with café latte, of course. Try the piña colada muffin or traditional blueberry muffins £1. Jacket potatoes £2. Open 8am-8pm.

HIGH ST. KENSINGTON

There are few appealing options for eating in the area. If you've got more time than you have money, walk uphill to Notting Hill Gate, where the range of food options is noticeably wider and less expensive.

Phoenicia, 11-13 Abingdon Rd., W8 (tel. 937 0184). Save this acclaimed Lebanese restaurant for a special night. Small and down-to-earth; food in huge helpings. All-you-can-eat luncheon buffet (£10, Sun. £12) served 12:15-2:30pm (until 3:30pm on Sun.). Healthy vegetarian display. Cover charge £1.50 doesn't apply to buffet. Service charge 15%. Open daily noon-midnight. Visa, Delta.

Stick and Bowl, 31 Kensington High St., W8 (tel. 937 2778). Cheap, quick, and good Chinese cuisine. When you're done, your waiter may politely kick you off your bar stool to accommodate the waiting crowd. Crispy beef £3.50. Try a special mixed dish for £4 (includes spring roll, sweet-and-sour pork, fried rice and vegetables, and one exploding prawn). Special dishes made upon request. Min. £2. Open daily 11:30am-1pm.

Cafe Pasta, 229 Kensington High St., W8 (tel. 937 6314). This chain offers healthy portions at reasonable prices to the beautiful people. Pastas around £5. Open Mon.-Sat. 9am-11:30pm, Sun. 9am-11pm.

CHELSEA

When hunger pangs strike during a promenade down **King's Road,** you can either sate your desires on the spot or consider a jaunt down a neighboring thoroughfare, where affordable restaurants abound. Buses 11 and 22 run the length of King's Rd. from the Victoria or Sloane Sq. tube stations. Almost every destination along King's Rd. requires a bus ride or a considerable walk. Alternately, turn right onto Sydney St. or Edith Grove and head towards Fulham Rd., which runs parallel to King's Rd., to access South Kensington's cornucopia of culinary delights (p. 111).

★**The Stockpot,** 273 King's Rd., SW3 (tel. 823 3175). Random food selection in an average atmosphere. The minimum per person is £2.20, but most meals won't cost you more than that anyway. The food here runs from the simple (spaghetti bolognese £2) to the gourmet (prawn and avocado salad £4.20), but the common thread is low, low prices. You won't go away hungry here. Gorgeous cakes only £1.30-1.40. Open Mon.-Sat. 8am-midnight, Sun. 10am-midnight.

★**Chelsea Kitchen,** 98 King's Rd., SW3 (tel. 589 1330). 5-to 10min. walk from the tube. Locals rave about the eclectic menu of cheap, filling, tasty food: turkey and mushroom pie, *spaghetti bolognese,* and a Spanish omelette are each £2.60 or less. Cozy booth seating. When the weather is amenable, grab one of the front tables and watch the Sloan Rangers pass you by. Set menu £4.70. Breakfast served 8-11:25am. Open Mon.-Sat. 8am-midnight, Sun. 9am-11:30pm.

★**Entre Nous,** 488 King's Rd., SW3 (tel. 352 4227). Cosmopolitan sun-filled French atmosphere at budget prices. Tremendously sized portions despite the chic atmosphere. Huge sandwiches on crusty bread £1.20-3. Salads £2.80-3.50. Specials (around £3) are a phenomenal value—mounds and mounds of delicious food. Open Mon.-Fri. 8am-6pm, Sat. 10am-6pm.

My Old Dutch Pancake House, 221 King's Rd., SW3 (tel. 376 5650). Saturated with things Dutch, the restaurant is kitschy and fun. Huge pancakes (more like crepes than flapjacks), both sweet and savory, served on huge windmill dishes. Stick to simple ingredients—the more elaborate combinations are sometimes less than successful. Cheese, onion, and mushroom pancake £5. Set lunch menu, available weekdays noon-4pm, offers a pancake with your choice of three toppings, a waffle with whipped cream and sauce, and tea or coffee (£6). Pancakes half-price Mon. 6-11pm. Open Mon. noon-11pm, Tues.-Thurs. 11am-11:30pm, Fri.-Sat. 11am-midnight, Sun. 11am-11pm. Visa, MC, Eurocard, Diners.

Chelsea Bun Diner, 9a Limerston St., SW10 (tel. 352 3635), just off King's Rd. Vast selection of expensive sandwiches overflowing with gourmet fillings like smoked salmon and avocado (£1.30-4) and veggie lasagne (£5). In summer, the glass windows in front open out into the street for delightful *al fresco* dining. £3.90 special includes soup and entrée (choice of pasta or meat) and tea or coffee. Huge breakfast special £3.35 (2 eggs, bacon, sausage, tomato, toast, and tea or coffee), super deals on breakfast between 7-10am. BYOB. Open daily 7am-midnight.

Henry J. Bean's Bar and Grill, 195-97 King's Rd., SW3 (tel. 352 9255). This large, pseudo-American frontier tavern is worth patronizing for one reason—the huge, glorious beer garden outside, the nicest place to relax on King's Rd. Luncheon special: £5 for main course, salad, and "fries" Mon.-Fri. noon-3pm. £5.25 for burger or blackened chicken sandwich anytime. Open daily noon-11pm.

▓ Earl's Court

Earl's Court and **Gloucester Road** eateries cater generously to their tourist traffic (tube: Earl's Ct. unless stated otherwise). Earl's Court, a take-away carnival, revolves around cheap and palatable food. Groceries in this area charge reasonable prices; shops stay open late at night and on Sunday. The closer you get to the high-rise hotels around Gloucester Rd. Station, the more expensive restaurants become. Look for the scores of coffee shops and Indian restaurants on Gloucester Rd. north of Cromwell Rd. (especially near Elvaston Pl.).

★**Troubador Coffee House,** 265 Old Brompton Rd., SW5 (tel. 370 1434), near Earl's Ct. and Old Brompton Rd. junction. Copper pots, pitchforks, and mandolins are suspended from the ceiling, and whirring espresso machines steam up the windows in this enjoyable community café. Formerly a bastion of countercultural activity—Bob Dylan and Paul Simon played here early in their careers, and many artists still see the downstairs basement as a testing ground for new material. Assorted snacks, soups, and sandwiches, under £4. Liquor available with food orders. Vast selection of coffee drinks. Live music (see Entertainment, p. 239). Open daily 9:30am-11pm. Check *Time Out* or call for who's performing.

The Hi-Tide Fish and Chips Restaurant, 7 Kenway Rd., SW5 (tel. 373 9170). Tube: Earl's Ct. Delicious fish and chips. A simple restaurant with a row of 5 booths, and a little more space downstairs. Fish from Billingsgate Market. Don't know the difference between cod, rock, plaice, and haddock? Read the back of the menu, which tells all. Large chunk of cod and chips £3.70, £2.90 take-away. Open Mon.-Sat. noon-midnight, Sun. 5-11pm.

Perry's Bakery, 151 Earl's Court Rd., SW5 (tel. 370 4825). Amiable Bulgarian-Israeli management prides itself on a somewhat eclectic menu and phenomenal fresh baked goods. Jazz always playing in the background. Flaky *borekas* (pastry filled with cheese) make a filling snack (with spinach £1.40). Straight from Israel come *Mitzli* juices (60p) and falafel (£2) with know-how. For breakfast enjoy their croissant plus all-you-can-drink tea or coffee for £2. *Challah* loaves £1.50. For dinner enjoy a combo plate of the day's special for less than £3. Nice Barry White pictures too. Open daily 6am-midnight.

Benjy's, 157 Earl's Court Rd., SW5 (tel. 373 0245). Crowded with hungry hostelers who weren't sated by their included "breakfast." Simple decor and noteworthy all-day breakfast specials. Load up for the day (or night) with the "Builder Breakfast" (bacon, egg, chips, beans, toast, 2 sausages) £3.40. The "vegetarian" suits smaller appetites (toast, 2 eggs, baked beans) £3. All fixed breakfasts come with all-you-can-drink tea or coffee. Open daily 7am-9:30pm.

Blanco's Restaurant, 314 Earl's Court Rd., SW5 (tel. 370 3101). A comfortable *tapas* bar. Red and black tiles, upright chairs, and vaguely Spanish prints on the wall. Many drink here once the pubs close. *Tapas* £2-5. Grilled trout £5.50. Veal escalope £7. Pint of lager £2.30. Open Mon.-Sat. 10am-1am, Sun. 10am-midnight.

Hong Kong Chinese Restaurant, 14 Hogarth Place, SW5 (tel. 373 2407). Only a second away from Earl's Ct. on a street saturated with inexpensive and occasionally strange (e.g. Ashbee's Austro-Anglo wine cellar) ethnic restaurants. Clean, sleek, and friendly, Hong Kong keeps almost all dishes under the £5 mark. Noodle dishes are generous at £3.50. Smiling service. Take-away available. Open daily noon-11:30pm.

Café Deco, 62 Gloucester Rd., SW7 (tel. 225 3286). Tube: Gloucester Rd. Chrome and marble decor attracts French students from a nearby language school. The food must make them feel right at home; delicate fresh fruit tarts (apple, peach, and pear £1.25; raspberry or strawberry £2.35) and croissants (50p) are the *spécialités de la maison.* Cappuccino £1.18; take-away 80p. Open daily 8am-8pm.

Nando's, 204 Earl's Court Rd., SW5 (tel. 259 2544). A South African-born Portuguese fast-food chain that serves spicy budget-oriented chicken dishes to those tired of burgers. Don't worry that it's quick-serve—you can watch your chicken being grilled right in front of you. Half chicken and chips £5. Also in Camden (tel. 424 9040) and Ealing Common (tel. 992 2290). Open daily 11:30am-11:45pm

Kramps Crêperie, 6 Kenway Rd., SW5 (tel. 244 8759). Crepes cooked right in front of you in a confusedly Spanish and French atmosphere. Pretty flower plate designs and colorful candlelights. Open kitchen. Cheese, tomato, oregano crêpe £4.40. Homemade sangría £6/liter.

Delice de France, 1 Kynance Pl. off Gloucester Rd. (tel. 581 5884). Tube: Gloucester Rd. Left out of station, cross Cromwell Rd. Kynance Pl. will be on your left. This sandwich shop is exactly what the name connotes: a pseudo-Parisian café nestled on a quiet street, with fresh bread and hefty sandwiches. Filled baguettes £1.85-2.41. Open Mon.-Fri. 7am-7pm, Sat.-Sun. 7:30am-6pm.

■ Notting Hill and Ladbroke Grove

The many restaurants dotting the streets that radiate out from the Notting Hill Gate and Ladbroke Grove stations exude a certain "goodness" that is not readily found elsewhere. Dishes from around the globe can be found in the area's hearty, reasonably priced restaurants. Stylish coffeehouses and pastry shops cluster near the Ladbroke Grove station. **Portobello Rd.** is lined with budget eateries.

★**Manzara,** 24 Pembridge Rd., W11 (tel. 727 3062). Tube: Notting Hill Gate. Ostensibly a take-away shop, Manzara actually seats 40 people. A wonderfully cheap place to get your grub on after a stroll through the Portobello market. In the afternoon, pizzas are £3, and sandwiches are £1. In the evenings, they offer a £6 all-you-can-eat array of Greek and Turkish specialties. Chomp! Take-away discount. Open daily 8am-midnight.

★**The Grain Shop,** 269a Portobello Rd., W11 (tel. 229 5571). Tube: Ladbroke Grove. Step inside this narrow shop and you'll be amazed by the surprisingly large array of tasty foods in this take-away joint. Organic whole grain breads baked daily on the premises (75p-£1.80/fresh loaf). Also you may direct the staff to fill various sized containers with any combination of the 6 hot vegetarian dishes—large £4.10, medium £3, small £2. Delicious pastries made from organic flour and free range eggs. Danish 95p, cheese croissant 60p, cakes £1.35, huge vegan brownies £1. Groceries also available, many organic. Open Mon.-Sat. 10am-6pm.

Gallery Café, 74 Tavistock Rd., W11 (tel. 221 5844). Tube: Ladbroke Grove. A mellow vegetarian café just off 269 Portobello Rd. Lunch specials include portions of lasagne, moussaka, or lentils with curry sauce and salad £4.25, small £3.25. Many locals lunch here daily. Take-away discount. Open daily 9am-5pm.

The Bel Air, 23 All Saints Rd., W11 (tel. 229 7961). Tube: Westbourne Park or Ladbroke Grove. Behind a rust-red exterior, this candlelit restaurant serves well-prepared West Indian and African dishes to a mix of funk and jazz. Jamaican jerk chicken £4.50. Fried plantains £2. Open daily 2:30pm-midnight.

Cockney's, 314 Portobello Rd. W10 (tel. (0181) 960 9409). Tube: Ladbroke Grove. After streets of varied ethnic eateries, this stalwart of English cuisine seems downright exotic. If the cheap, no-nonsense pie and mash (£1.50) can't hold you, try a portion of eel (£2). Who said British food was boring? Open Mon.-Thurs. 11:30am-5:30pm, Fri. 11:30am-7pm.

Lisboa Patisserie, 57 Golborne Rd. W10 (tel. (0181) 968 5242). Join the energetic locals sitting in this marble-floored Portuguese patisserie. All food is made in the kitchen below. Loads of traditional Portuguese pastels; *pastel bata* (custard tart) melts in your mouth (60p). Glass of coffee 65p. Open daily 8am-8pm.

Makan, 270 Portobello Rd., W10 (tel (0181) 960 5169). Exotic and delightful smells waft out of this Malaysian take-away joint. A wide variety of dishes, from chicken curry to *sambul* prepared with squid or spicy eggplant, around £4. Take-away discount 80p. Open Mon.-Sat. 10am-8pm.

Geale's, 2 Farmer St., W8 (tel. 727 7969). Tube: Notting Hill Gate. Spirited locals crowd this reputable wood-paneled restaurant. Geale's has won various awards for their consistently crisp fish and chips. Fresh haddock, cod, and plaice from Grimsby in the North are the house specialties. Market price usually £4.75-6.50. Try the salmon fish cakes as a starter (£2.40). Often a wait—sit it out in the bar upstairs. Take-away available. Cover 15p. Open Tues.-Sat. noon-3pm and 6-11pm.

O'Porto Patisserie, 62a Golborne Rd., W10 (tel. (0181) 968 8839). Tube: Ladbroke Grove. A thriving enclave of Portuguese culture, this *pastelaria* serves delectable pastries crafted from Iberian ingredients. Locals of Portuguese and North African descent mingle with city kids and Portobello strays around crowded tables. Sandwiches sold on traditional Portuguese breads and rolls filled with chicken, fish, or parma ham £1.40-1.75. Miraculously, these inexpensive baked goods can make a full meal. Open daily 8am-8pm.

Prost Restaurant, 35 Pembridge Rd., W11 (tel. 727 9620). Tube: Notting Hill Gate. Delicate food in an upmarket and intimate setting. Entrees here might exceed your price limit, but Sunday brunch is a classy and affordable option. Ask for a table upstairs by the window, where you can admire the heavy curtains and rich green decor. Hot English breakfast includes 2 fried eggs, bacon, sausage, and a grilled tomato (£4). Try the chicken breast filled with roquefort cheese (£7). Open Mon.-Fri. 5:30-11pm, Sat.-Sun. 10:30am-11pm. Major credit cards.

■ Bayswater and Queensway

The culinary options in this area tend to be less scintillating than those in the neighboring Notting Hill/Ladbroke Grove area; if you crave nuanced flavors and sophisticated ambience, consider dining there. However, the famished traveler should have no trouble finding a solid, inexpensive meal in Bayswater or Queensway. Check out one of the countless kebab and fish-and-chip shops that dot the streets, or head to **Westbourne Grove** (tube: Bayswater or Royal Oak) for large concentrations of competent South Asian restaurants.

★**Khan's,** 13-15 Westbourne Grove, W2 (tel. 727 5240). Tube: Bayswater. Cavernous, noisy, and crowded, Khan's persists as the best bargain around for delicious Indian cuisine. The menu explains to diners that the distinctive flavor of each dish "cannot come from the rancid ambiguity called curry powder," but only from "spices separately prepared each day." They're not kidding—the chicken *saag* (chicken cooked with spinach £2.95) contains piquant spices that are well complemented by flat *nan* bread (£1.10) or rice (£1.35). If you dip into one of the chutneys sitting expectantly on your table when you arrive, you will be charged 30p per person. Chicken *tikka masala* £3.50. Vegetable curry £2.20. Open daily noon-3pm and 6pm-midnight. Major credit cards.

Penang, 41 Hereford Rd., W2 (tel. 229 2982). Tube: Bayswater. The standard interior hides magnificent Malaysian and Thai cuisine. Tangy lemon chicken £4. *Sayor lodeh* (mixed vegetables cooked in savory coconut milk gravy) has a well-deserved reputation (£3). Beef, pork, and curry dishes also available. Open Mon.-Sat. 6-11:30pm, Sun. 6-11pm. AmEx, MC, Visa.

Norman's, 7 Porchester St. W2 (tel. 727-0278). Tube: Bayswater, Porchester is just off Queensway north of the station. Plain food at plain prices is the pithiest description we can give. Roast chicken plate £4. Open Mon.Sat. 9am-11pm, Sun. 9am-9:30pm.

Jewel of Siam, 39 Hereford Rd., W2 (tel. 229 4363). Tube: Bayswater. Well-prepared Thai food in a contrived yet endearing setting. Entrees are pricey, but sumptuous appetizers (£3.50-4.50) and noodle lunch specials (under £5) are quite satisfying. Excellent *pad thai* (fried noodles with prawns, shrimp, beansprouts, ground peanut, and egg) £5.10. Vegetarian options affordable and savory £3.50-4.50. Take it away to one of the nearby parks for a 10% discount, or duck downstairs to dodge the £1.50 cover charge. Open Mon.-Fri. noon-2:30pm and 6pm-11pm, Sat. 6pm-11pm, Sun. 6pm-10:30pm. AmEx, MC, Visa.

■ The City of London

Restaurants in this area tend to cater exclusively to either businessmen or to the construction workers who build and renovate their offices. The former are scattered throughout the area—benches and stools filled with suits are generally bad signs for budget travelers. Remember: these blokes have no time, but money to burn. Cheap lunch-time haunts line **Whitecross St.,** which is accessed by following Beech St. east from the Barbican. The best way to have a cheap dinner here is to bring it yourself— the City is traditionally a ghost-town after office hours, and the nightspots springing up here are strictly executive class.

★**The Place Below,** in St. Mary-le-Bow Church crypt, Cheapside, EC2 (tel. 329 0789). Tube: St. Paul's. Attractive and generous vegetarian dishes served to the hippest of City executives in the unexpectedly light atmosphere of a stone church basement. Makes for a religious dining experience, so to speak. Second dining room moonlights as an ecclesiastical court, where the Archbishop of Canterbury still settles cases pertaining to Anglican law and swears in new bishops a few times a year. Menu changes daily. Quiche and salad £5.55. Savory tomato, almond, and saffron soup £2.40. Meals about £1.50 cheaper take-away and 11:30am-noon. Open Mon.-Fri. 7:30am-2:30pm.

Jazz Bistro, 340 Farringdon St., EC1 (236 8112). Tube: Farringdon. Exit right on Cowcross, left on Farringdon. Exciting jazz bar/restaurant with a suave Latin American feel. Rusty wooden walls and towering plants provide exotic jungle-like background for nightly jazz performers, who often play way past 11pm, the unofficial city pub bedtime. Meals are as excellent as the tunes. Spicy Mexican dishes for lunch (£4-6) induce loco behavior for the rest of the day. Open noon-1am. £3 standard cover well worth it.

The Gallery Café Bar, Unit 1, 9 Leather La., EC1 (tel. 404 5432). Tube: Chancery La. A sleek café with floor-to-ceiling glass windows and marble tables. Serves up unbelievable desserts to hip clientele. Sandwiches from £1, homemade pizza slices from £1.50. Open Mon.-Fri. 7am-4pm.

Al's Café, 11-13 Exmouth Market, EC1 (tel. 837 4821). Tube: Farringdon. Exit right from station, restaurant on corner of Farringdon St. and Exmouth Market. Set against the shops of Exmouth Market, this stylish café/bar is a favorite hangout for trendy magazine journalists, as well as for young, brooding intellectuals. Bagel with smoked salmon £1.90. Free jazz Fri. 7-11pm. Open Mon.-Fri. 7am-11pm, Sat.-Sun. 10am-8pm.

Barbican Grill, 117 Whitecross St., EC1 (tel. 256 6842). Tube: Moorgate. This pleasantly managed, unassuming caff serves up amazing bargains for its budget-minded student and workingman crowd. Chicken, chips, and peas for £3.20. Sandwiches with everything from chicken to salmon £2.10 or less. Open Mon.-Fri. 6:30am-4:30pm, Sat. 6:45-11:45am.

Field's Sandwiches, 5 St. John St., EC1 (tel. 608 2235). Tube: Barbican. The wooden shelves packed with bric-a-brac lend this sandwich shop a charm its brethren lack, while high ceilings prevent take-away claustrophobia. Lasagna £2.20, sandwiches 60p-£1.20, pork pies 60p. Open Mon-Fri. 10am-5pm.

The Nosherie, 12 Greville St., EC1 (tel. 242 1591). Tube: Chancery La. Inset among the jewellers of Hatton Garden, this unassuming deli serves both classic New York-style deli and exotic international dishes. Indonesian salads are especially delicious. Fish and chips £2.50. Jacket potatoes from £1.35. Minimum charge £3 per person noon-3pm. Open Mon.-Fri. 6:30am-6:30pm, Sat. 8am-4pm.

Futures!, 8 Botolph Alley, EC3 (tel. 623 4529). Tube: Monument. Off Botolph La. Fresh take-away vegetarian breakfast and lunch prepared in a petite kitchen open to view. Daily main dishes, like stir-fry with rice or chili vegetables £3.40. Spinach pizza £1.85. open Mon.-Fri. 7:30am-10am and 11:30am-3pm. If you're in the mood for Futures! food and want to sit down, stop by their snazzy, more expensive Futures!! branch in Exchange Sq. (behind Liverpool Station).

Choristers, 36 Carter La. EC 4 (tel. 329 3811). Tube: St. Paul's. Located in City of London Youth hostel. Not for the gourmet, but this fast-food style eatery will give you a cheap, decent meal in a smoke-free zone. Menu changes daily, but price stays the same at £4.15 for 3 courses. Lunch served noon-2pm and dinner 5-8pm.

Mange 2, 3 Cowcross St., EC1 (tel. 250 0035). Tube: Farringdon. Exit left onto Cowcross. This is the place to go if you're in the mood to splurge. Very trendy, surreal interior with funky decorations and wonderfully fresh food. Meat, fish, and vegetables purchased daily at Smithfield market across the street. Inside, luscious red walls and 10ft. candles surround small tables with high back chairs—the Addams Family dining room with pizazz. Jazz every evening in bar 6:30-10:30pm. Dinner menu £17 (not including service charge) for a 2-course meal, £20 for 3 courses. Bar has its own menu with cheaper but smaller portions. Lunch £6-9. Open Mon.-Fri. noon-3pm and 6:30-10:30pm.

■ The East End

It's easy to feel as if one were lost in the streets of Bangladesh, Ireland, or olde Europe when moseying around the East End. One wildly popular Indian-Bangledeshi style is **Balti** which means that the portion you order is brought to you in the individual vessel (the Balti) in which it was cooked. **Brick Lane** is home to a suburb collection of Bangledeshi restaurants, probably the longest string outside of Dhaka.

★**Bengal Cuisine,** 12 Brick La., E1 (tel. 377 8405). Tube: Aldgate East. First along a string of many, this restaurant distinguishes itself through quick service and tasty dishes. The spices (all brought in directly from India) are combined in wonderful dishes that make this Curry Club member something special. Ornate tapestries from Bangladesh (for sale, inquire if interested) lend a more elegant tone to the pink table cloth setting. Chicken curries £3.35-4.45. All you can eat of a delicious buffet weekends noon-6pm (£7 adults, £4 children). 10% student discount on weekends. Open daily noon-midnight.

Nazrul, 130 Brick La., E1 (tel. 247 2505). Tube: Aldgate East. Although the velvet booths are inviting, the rapid service means that you don't have to linger long if you're pressed for time. Nazrul recently added Balti cooking to the menu and was voted a member of the "Curry Club." Considering the size of the portions, prices are terrifically cheap; balti menu £3-4. No bar, but BYOB. Open Mon.-Thurs. noon-3pm and 5:30pm-midnight, Fri.-Sat. noon-3pm and 5:30pm-1am, Sun. noon-midnight.

Shampan, 79 Brick La., E1 (tel. 375 0475). Tube: Aldgate East. A tad more expensive and with a more refined, quiet interior than its neighbors, but still very reasonable. A favorite of food critics. Surrounding plants and immaculate interior invites diverse clientele. Balti dishes from £5.25, seafood dishes £5. Open daily noon-3pm and 6pm-midnight. Visa, MC, Delta.

The Cherry Orchard Café, 247 Globe Rd., E2 (tel. (0181) 980 6678). Tube: Bethnal Green. A lovely un-Chekhovian restaurant run by Buddhists. Walls in the pleasant interior are a shocking orange and turquoise; the outdoor garden is lovely if the weather is nice. The strictly vegetarian menu changes daily. Delicious hot entrees around £3.50. Open Mon. 11am-3pm, Tues.-Fri. 11am-7pm.

Sheraz, 13 Brick La., E1 (tel. 247 5755). Tube: Aldgate East. One of the gateways into Brick Lane, this upscale restaurant now cooks Kashmiri food as well as Balti specialties. Generically elegant interior makes for quieter atmosphere than in other Bangledeshi restaurants up the street. Entrées averaging £4-6, although 10% student discount given if meal is paid for in cash. Fully stocked bar. Open daily noon-3pm and 6pm-midnight. Major credit cards.

Aladin Balti House, 132 Brick La., E1 (tel. 247 8210). Must be good if it's the hangout for the local Bangladeshi mayor, his cronies, and the Prince of Wales. Owner Toimus Ali once fed the future king at an East End community meeting, and if you are nice to Mr. Ali, he'll play you an LBC recording of Prince Charles mentioning the restaurant. Big mark of distinction for a joint with linoleum on the floor. 5% student discount if you spend more than £15. Balti dishes from £3. Open 11:30am-11:30pm, Fri. and Sat. nights until midnight.

Eastern Eye, 63a Brick La., E1 (tel. 375 1696). Tube: Aldgate East. Plain on the outside and pretty on the inside, this Tandoori restaurant specializes in Balti dishes (from £5). The dense foliage inside makes this the Bangledeshi equivalent of an 80s fern bar. Chicken or lamb *tikka* £5. Halal food available. Open daily noon-midnight, although the restaurant occasionally closes during the late afternoon until 5:30pm. Major credit cards.

Muhib, 73 Brick Lane E1 (tel. 247 7122). Tube: Aldgate East. Billed as the cheapest food on the street, chef will prepare anything not on menu. Red velvet benches and chairs make one think of Vegas; photo of Taj Mahal is not as evocative. Moderately sized portions begin as low as £2.50. Open daily noon–3pm and 6-11pm.

▓ Islington

Dress smartly for a meal in one of the many bistros that line **Upper St.,** which runs to the right as you exit the tube station (tube: Angel). Be careful when seeking specific addresses, though, since Upper St. numbers ascend on one side of the street and descend on the other. Unfortunately, few budget restaurants can be found in this cutting-edge area; candle-lit tables and expensive menus, not budget fares, have become uniform for Islington's trendy restaurants. Cheaper nosh lurks in the take-away sandwich shops, bakeries, and chip shops of the less upscale Chapel Market (the 1st left off Liverpool Rd.).

★**Café Olé,** 119 Upper St., N1 (tel. 226 6991). A hip Italian/Spanish bar/café adorned with colorful ceramic plates and painted floral borders on the salmon walls. Bustling with Islington trendies of all ages, the atmosphere remains comfortable. Endless breakfast: egg, bacon, sausage, tomato, mushroom, black pudding, bubble and squeak, and toast £3.80. Vegetarian breakfast also available. Lunch menu offers pasta (£4-4.50) and salads (£3.50), in addition to sandwiches (£1-2.50). The selection of pastas and salads expands at dinner; all are around £5. Open Mon.-Sat. 8am-11pm.

★**LeMercury,** 140a Upper St., N1 (tel. 354 4088). Tube: Angel or Highbury and Islington. This French restaurant has the quintessential Islington candle-lit effect, but it also has 3 stories of space overlooking the action of Upper St. and outstanding prices to boot. All main courses £5.45 (try the salmon). Delicate flavors and healthy portions. Lunch is a super value at £4. Crowds drawn to a great deal make it a bit loud during dinner. Open Mon.-Sat. 11am-11pm, Sun. noon-11:30pm.

Indian Veg Bhelpoori House, 92-93 Chapel Market, N1 (tel. 837 4607 or 833 1167). One of the best bargains in London. All-you-can-eat lunch or dinner buffet of 18 vegetarian dishes and chutneys for a startling £3. If it's good enough for Miss Asia, who dined here with Miss Philippines in 1992, it's good enough for you. Open daily noon-midnight. MC, Visa.

La Piragua, 176 Upper St., N1 (tel. 354 2843). Tube: Angel or Highbury and Islington. Welcome to South America—all of it! Colombian, Chilean, Venezuelan, and Argentinian dishes complement an extensive Latin American wine list. Low-key beige walls with pictures of the owner's hometown Patagonia make this an intimate gathering place for food or wine. Long tables packed with tables of chattering people. £5-9 for main courses. Try the *pastel de choco* (fried chicken with minced beef, olives, raisins, covered with sweet corn). Open daily noon-1am.

The New Culture Revolution, 42 Duncan St., N1 (tel. 833 9083). Exit right from the station and take the first right onto Duncan St. A dumpling and noodle bar with slick lacquer tables and chairs. The small store front masks a spacious interior. Dumplings and noodles come either fried or in soup base, cooked with a variety of different meats, fish, or vegetables. Soups are lightly seasoned; the fried dishes are zestier. Dumplings and noodles hover around £5. Open Mon.-Fri. noon-2:30pm and 6-11pm, Sat. 1-11pm. AmEx, MC, Visa.

Roxy Cafe Cantina, 297 Upper St. (tel. 226-5746). Open, multi-level seating in this popular Mexican restaurant. All main dishes £6, except fajitas £7. Open Mon.-Sat. noon-midnight, Sun. noon-11pm.

Trattoria Aquilino, 31 Camden Passage, N1 (tel. 226 5454). This intimate restaurant, with its extensive menu of homemade pasta, is a gem. The native Italian staff jumps to the diner's every request. Posh appearance belies good prices. Pastas £2.60-4.40. *Pollo parmigiana* £4.85. Generous portions. Best for lunch or early dinner—there is a £6 minimum after 6pm. 10% service charge. Open Mon.-Sat. 12:30-2:30pm and 6:30-11:30pm. Cash only.

Upper St. Fish Shop, 324 Upper St., N1 (tel. 359 1401). A well-known fish and chips joint offering specials varied according to the day's catch. Comfortable wood-paneled and red-check-tableclothed interior, but there is a £5 minimum for eating in. Fish and chips £7. They also prepare non-fried fish for around £7-9. Open Mon. 6pm-10:15pm, Tues.-Thurs. noon-2:15pm and 6-10:15pm, Fri. noon-2:15pm and 5:30-10:15pm, Sat. noon-3pm and 5:30-10:15pm

Tuk Tuk, 330 Upper St., N1 (tel. 266 0837). Bright blue exterior hides a sleek Thai restaurant with black metal chairs and speckled red tables. A moped taxi sticks its nose out of a ceiling corner. *Pad thai* £4.95. Noodle or rice dishes £4.50-5.95. Open Mon.Fri. noon-3pm, 6pm-11pm; Sat. 6-11pm, Sun. 6-10pm. AmEx, MC Visa.

■ Camden Town

Camden Town can be a bit grotty, especially in the wake of the weekend markets. Glamourous cafés and international restaurants, however, are interspersed along the main drag, **Camden High Street,** which runs south from the Camden Town tube station to Mornington Crescent, and north to Chalk Farm, becoming **Chalk Farm Road.** Note that many pubs in the area offer standard pub grub which will keep body and soul together at a reasonable price. (Tube: Camden Town, unless otherwise noted.)

★**Le Petit Prince,** 5 Holmes Rd., NW5 (tel. 267 0752). Tube: Kentish Town. French/ Algerian cuisine served in a whimsically decorated café/bar/restaurant. Illustrations from Saint-Exupéry's *Le Petit Prince* dot the walls, which are painted to simulate a cartoon-purple night sky. Lighting fixtures are draped with charming painted screens. Generous plantain sauté starter £3. Vegetarian couscous £5. Lamb, chicken, and fish dishes are slightly more expensive, but come with unlimited couscous and vegetable broth. Lunch menu includes crepes (£4.25-4.40) and a coriander, guacamole, and melted goat cheese sandwich (£4). Live acoustic music some Fri. nights. Open daily noon-3pm and 7-11:30pm.

★**Nontas,** 14-16 Camden High St., NW1 (tel. 387 4579). Tube: Mornington Crescent or Camden Town. This wonderfully intimate restaurant is one of the best Greek venues in the city. The incomparable *meze* (£8.75) offers a seemingly endless selection of dips, meats, and cheeses. Other Hellenic fare includes kebabs (£5.40-5.70). *Ouzerie* in front, with plush chairs and petite tables, serves luscious pastries, like *baklava* (£1.05) and Turkish coffee (75p). If the weather seems nice, ask to sit in the back garden. Don't take a vegetarian here unless you can placate them with 95p spirits (rum, whiskey, etc…). Open Mon.-Sat. noon-3pm and 6-11:30pm. *Ouzerie* open Mon.-Sat. 8:30-11:30pm. AmEx, MC, Visa.

★**Captain Nemo,** 171 Kentish Town Rd., NW1 (tel. 485 3658). Tube: Kentish Town. Seemingly unassuming Chinese/chippie take-away combo rocks your world with their tangy, delicious chips in curry sauce (£1.20). Arguably the best use of grease and potato in London, they're good to the last slurp. We'd travel 10,000 leagues under the sea for a crack at these heavenly spuds. Open Mon.-Fri. noon-3pm and 5:30pm-midnight, Sat.-Sun. 5:30pm-midnight.

Bar Gansa, 2 Inverness St., NW1 (tel. 267 8909). Exit the station to the right and head right; Inverness is the first left. A small *tapas* bar with bright walls, festive Spanish candles, and Mediterranean ornaments. Happy, glossy people of all ages linger over their food, coffee, and wine. Ham, eggs, and chips (£4) and other breakfast fare available till as late as 1:30pm. *Tapas* £2-3.50. Limited outdoor seating. Fresh veggies procured daily from the nearby outdoor produce market. Open Mon.-Thurs. 10:30am-11:45pm, Fri.-Sat. 10:30am-midnight, Sun. 10:30am-11pm.

Ruby in the Dust, 102 Camden High St., NW1 (tel. 485 2744). Young crowd drawn to the bright decor and jazzy milieu. Patrons have such a good time that you can hear them up and down the street. Burgers or tuna steak £6. Wide selection for vegetarians, veggie burger £5.55. Selection of newspapers hang from the wall if you're feeling antisocial. Also at 70 Upper St., Islington. Open daily 10am-midnight. Downstairs club open on weekend evenings. MC, Visa.

Parkway Pizzeria, 64 Parkway, NW1 (tel. 485 0678). Exit the station to the right, then head left along Camden High St., Parkway is the immediate right. A pizzeria off the main thoroughfare which local food critics routinely praise. Parquet floor and cool Art Deco mirrors. A basic pizza costs £3.70; fully loaded with various combinations of exotic toppings like pine nuts, leeks, olives, anchovies, and capers costs £5.35. Take-away available. £3 min. when the restaurant is full. Open daily noon-midnight.

Mamma Conchetta, 10 Kentish Town Rd., NW1 (tel. 813 0056). Homey *ristorante* and pizzeria, with fresh flowers on the small wooden tables and painted china on the walls. One wall is a false house façade, complete with two shuttered windows. Newly built café next door provides quick taste of Italy if you don't have time to sit in the restaurant. Pizza £4-5.50, pasta £4.80-5.20. Open Mon.-Fri. noon-3pm and 6-11pm, Sat.-Sun. noon-11pm. MC, Visa.

Camden Friends Restaurant, 51a Camden High St., NW1 (tel. 387 2835). Tube: Mornington Crescent or Camden Town. Wash down Pekingese cuisine in this small, friendly establishment (with this somewhat puzzling name could it be otherwise?). Chicken dishes all less than £5.10. Vegetarian dishes £3.50-4.40. Open Mon.-Sat. noon-2:30pm and 6pm-midnight, Sun. 6pm-midnight. AmEx, MC, Visa.

Bharat, 23 Camden High St., NW1 (tel. 388 4553). If on Sun. morning you have a yen for spicy food, the all-you-can-eat Sun. buffet at £4.50 is your bit o' heaven. Of equally notable value is the set dinner, which includes a starter, a chicken or lamb dish, vegetable curry, bread or rice, vanilla ice cream, and coffee, for £5.50. Open daily noon-3pm and 6pm-midnight. AmEx, MC, Visa.

Marine Ices, 8 Haverstock Hill, NW3 (tel. 485 3132). Tube: Chalk Farm. Head left from the station. Superb Italian ice cream (£1/scoop) and sundaes. Epic concoctions like *Vesuvius* (£5.50). Ice-cream counter open Mon.-Sat. 10:30am-11pm, Sun. 11am-10pm. Attached restaurant offers pizza (£5) and other entrees (£8-9). Open Mon.-Fri. noon-3pm, 5:30-11pm, Sat.noon-11pm, Sun. noon-10pm.

Restorante Avanti, 38 Middle Yard, Camden Lock Place, NW1 (tel. 284 1890). A quiet, waterfront pizzeria except on Sun. market days when it becomes a reed in a torrent of bargain-hounds. Big bay windows afford pleasant view of Camden's canals and locks. Pizza £3.90-6. Any of the pizzas with beer only £5. 10% student discount with ID. Open Mon.-Fri. noon-3pm, Wed.-Thurs. 6-10pm, Fri. 6-11pm, Sat. noon-11pm, Sun. noon-6pm. MC, Visa. Wheelchair accessible.

■ Hampstead

This affluent district in northern London has an artsy bent. Traditional teahouses for lunching ladies still do well amid a number of pricey brasseries and cafés and many new or redone restaurants. The food served in local restaurants is almost as important as the show-off space they provide for the ritzy young crowd. The station (tube: Hampstead) is on the corner of Heath St. and Hampstead High St.

★**Le Crêperie de Hampstead,** 77 Hampstead High St., NW3. Outside the King William IV pub. A Hampstead institution and a moveable feast. Paper-thin Brittany crêpes made in front of your eyes by a real French crepe-maker in the tiniest van imaginable. Both sweet fillings (including banana and Grand Marnier) and savory (spinach and garlic cream, mushroom, and cheese) £2-3. Open Mon.-Sat. 1-11pm, Sun. 1:30-11pm.

Coffee Cup, 74 Hampstead High St., NW3 (tel. 435 7565). The place to be seen if you're young, rich, and trendy. Arguably the center of Hampstead's evening social scene. Marble tables on the sidewalk are packed by noon and stay that way until midnight. Not surprisingly, menu items are uniformly small and tasty (samosas £3). Open Mon.-Sat. 8am-midnight, Sun. 9am-midnight.

Calzone, 66 Heath St., NW3 (tel.794 6775). Petite bistro serves up quality pizza, calzones, and a great view of the beautiful people strolling along Heath St. The simple entrees (£4.75 and up) have been Hampstead favorites for years. Open daily noon-11:30pm.

Rumbold's Bakery, 45 South End Rd., NW3 (tel. 794 2344), across from the BR Hampstead Heath station. Handy for visitors to Keats House, which is just around the corner, and worth every step. First-rate pastries, often still warm from the oven. Chocolate croissant drizzled with chocolate and dusted with powdered sugar 75p. Apricot danish with fresh apricot slices in the middle and a honey glaze 70p. Gourmet sandwiches too. Open Mon.-Sat. 8am-5pm.

Al's Deli, down the alley of the Hampstead Market fruit stall next to 78 Hampstead High St., NW3. Cheap and cheerful and a Hampstead institution. One of the cheapest lunches in Hampstead. Workers lunch on the benches across from the counter. Sandwiches and pastries under £1. Open Mon.-Sat. 7am-5pm.

Montesol, 42 Hampstead High St., NW3 (tel. 435 7632). If you're coming just for the Spanish *tapas* (£3-5) and neatly-painted geometric figures on the walls, then you're in for more than you bargained. This is another bastion of Hampstead evening activity. Open daily noon-midnight.

▩ South of the Thames

Currently the locus of massive new economic and cultural development, the regions south of the Thames are experiencing a new vibrancy and vivacity. Unfortunately for the budget diner, the upscale nature of the development means that while exciting eateries abound, few are affordable. Nonetheless, **Lower Marsh,** just inland from the river and west off of **Waterloo Rd.,** has managed to dodge the tide of progress, and has several tasty greasy spoons to fill you up for under £3. The **Gabriel's Wharf** complex has a nice atmosphere offset by high prices and is a good place to grab a light lunch or a relaxing snack. (Tube: Waterloo, or Embankment and cross the Hungerford footbridge, unless indicated.)

★**The Fire Station,** 150 Waterloo Rd., SE1 (tel. 620 2226). A spacious converted Edwardian fire station (a former rave venue) houses an exquisite restaurant with a cactus terrace and an open kitchen. Delectable dishes crafted from seasonal ingredients without using microwaves or freezers. Chalkboard menu changes twice daily. Main dishes, from filet of sole to boar sausages, are exquisite but a bit pricey (£7-9), come between 6-7pm and get your choice of any two courses for £10. Full menu served Mon.-Sat. noon-3:30pm and 6-11pm, Sun. noon-5pm. The excellent bar serves a wide variety of drinks and draft beers Mon.-Sat. noon-11pm, Sun. noon-5:30pm. AmEx, MC, Visa.

Freshly Maid Café, 79 Lower Marsh (tel. 928 5426). One of the cheapest cafés in London with fresh and tasty food. The specialty is the *moussaka* served with chips and Greek salad £2.60. Also a huge selection from the grill—chicken burgers as low as £1. Small diner-type seating area. Open Mon.-Fri. 6am-7pm.

Marie's Café, 90 Lower Marsh (tel. 928 1050). Join the regulars who queue to get into this English/Thai style caff. Sit at one of the dozen tiny red diner booths to a heaping plate of Thai food. 3 different Thai dishes each day like pad thai or vegetarian curry with rice (£2.90 each). Traditional English dishes as well. Open Mon.-Fri. 7am-5pm, Sat. 7am-3pm.

Gourmet Pizza Company, Gabriel's Wharf, Upper Ground, SE1 (tel. 928 3188). A chain restaurant in bustling Gabriel's Wharf. Outdoor seating on the waterfront. Various crazy pizza flavors, including English breakfast, chinese duck, prawn, and smoked salmon (£4.70-8.35). Open daily noon-10:45pm. AmEx, Visa.

South Bank Brasserie, Gabriel's Wharf, 56 Upper Ground, SE1 (tel. 620 0596). Superb location in a waterfront Victorian building with a wide view of the Thames and St. Paul's. Salads and pastas are tasty and affordable. Chicken breast and chips £8. Open Mon.-Sat. 11am-1am, Sun. 11am-10:30pm.

▩ Brixton

The area within a three-block radius of the Brixton tube station has a wealth of budget dining options. **Brixton Market** is a perfect place to purchase fruits and vegetables, but you don't have to stray far from the action in the marketplace to enjoy an affordable sit-down meal. **Brixton Wholefoods,** 59 Atlantic Road (tel. 737 2210), sells a potpourri of grains, coffees, spices, juices, candies, and nuts (open Mon. and Fri. 9:30am-6pm, Tues.-Thurs. and Sat. 9:30am-5:30pm).

★**Jacaranda,** 11-13 Brixton Station Road, SW9 (tel. 274 8383). A budgeteer's delight— low prices and tasty grub. Main dishes like Jamaican style peas and rice served with salad or vegetarian gumbo with rice and okra all under £5. 5 kinds of foccacia, £3 each. Mon.-Fri. 10am-7pm, Sat.-Sun. 10am-6pm.

Pizzeria Franco, 4 Market Row, Electric La., SW9 (tel. 738 3021). A tiny restaurant in the heart of the vast market. One of London's most famous pizzerias, this bistro serves tasty oven-baked foundations (including mussels, mushrooms, and eggplant) topped with spicy tomato sauce, herbs, and different cheeses (£3.70-5.90). Most pizzas under £5. Open Mon.-Tues. and Thurs.-Sat. 8:30-11:30am for "morning coffee," (double espresso £1.20); full menu 11:30am-5pm.

Cecil's Bakery, 411a Brixton Rd., SW9 (tel. 737 0885). Everything is fresh-baked on the premises. Homemade vegetable and meat patties (82p veg., 90p meat) and other hot foods—curries, jerk chicken, and fish (large £3.80, small £2.80). Specialty is hard dough (£1) as well as the enormous selection of Guyanese and English pastries. Dirt-cheap but ultra-tasty scones 38p. Open daily 8am-5:30pm.

Asmara Restaurant, 386 Coldharbour La., SW9 (tel. 737 4144). This chandelier-bedecked restaurant projects an atmosphere of humble elegance and serves an eclectic mix of Ethiopian and Italian dishes. Pasta *alla carbonera* £3.50. Spicy chicken stew £4.50. Open Mon.-Sat. 11am-12:30am, Sun. 5pm-12:30am. MC, Visa.

Nyam's, 423 Coldharbour La., SW9 (tel. 737 3581). Cheap grub, low prices, and central location make this swangin' take-away a perfect place to quash the munchies, however late they strike. Chicken and chips, £1.60. Open daily 24hr.

Phoenix, 441 Coldharbour La., SW9 (tel. 733 4430). Simple dishes and friendly management make a good place to lunch. Straightforward diner ambience, but Coldharbour locale guarantees that your fellow diners will be hip. No sandwich above £2, and they come loaded on thick hard dough bread from area bakeries. Hot meals like chicken cutlet with veggies £2.50. Open Mon.-Sat. 6:30am-5pm.

Thompson's Bakery, 14d Market Row, SW9 (tel. 673 2249). This tiny and simple bakery smells divine, dahlin,' and sells bread which manages to be soft and dense at once. Buy a loaf of the sweet harddough bread with raisins and sink your teeth into heaven (£1). Or pick up a huge, round loaf of the plain hard dough and you'll be fed for days (£1.20). Open Mon., Tues., Thurs.-Sat. 9am-5pm, Wed. 9am-1pm.

Café Pushkar, Brixton Market, 16c Market Row, SW9 (tel. 738 6161). A great vegetarian staple amid the Brixton Market. Not high cuisine, but the daily hot specials are cheap and filling. Casserole of the day with two salads, £4, between 2-5pm, £3.50 for students and UB40s. Open Mon.-Tues. and Thurs.-Sat. 9am-5pm.

Kim's Café, Brixton Market, 15 Market Row, SW9 (tel. 924 9105). Casual diner garishly decked in red and green—looks like an old American fast food joint. Affable management and crowd of regulars makes you feel right at home. Chicken curry £3. Gigantic English breakfast £3.50. Open daily 8:30am-5pm.

Stop Gap, 500a Brighton Terrace, SW9 (tel. 737 5204). Right behind Red Records on Brixton Rd. Extremely affordable sandwich bar carries all the basics (75p-£2.75). Jerk chicken £3.89. Less carnivorous large salads £3.20. No tables. Open daily Mon.-Thurs. 7:30am-midnight, Fri.-Sat. 24hr.

■ Docklands

The Docklands plays host to hundreds of thousands of hungry corporate types during the weekdays. Naturally, it has a great number of the somewhat bland, though not quite cheap, sandwich shops which follow downtown corporate centers around the world, as well as a smattering of more expensive watering-holes catering to those expense-account execs requiring a three-martini lunch or post-office round of gin & tonics. The area around **Canary Wharf** (DLR: Canary Wharf) is a good spot to pick up a quick bite. In the bowels of the complex is a **slick modern grocery store** featuring ready-to-eat meals at reasonable prices. Also see the pub listings for Docklands, these riverside establishments (many are hundreds of years old) offer grub in less sterile surroundings than the newer section of Docklands.

St. Georges of Mayfair Sandwich Shop, Turnberry Quay, E14 (tel. 537 4678). DLR: Crossharbour. Across the path from London Arena. A cheap, delicious alternative to Docklands' more pricey restaurants. Join the junior executives and office workers who form along queue during the lunch hour. Fresh display of exotic salads, meats, and desserts will make choosing a sandwich difficult. Tandoori chicken slices in sandwich £1.90. Open Mon.-Fri. 8am-5pm.

Farmer's Kitchen, Pier St., E14 (tel. 515 5901). DLR: Crossharbour or Mudchute. Located next to Mudchute Farm stables. Offers cheap food for hungry visitors. Salad and sandwich £1.20. Open daily 10am-5pm.

The Pier Tavern, 299 Manchester Rd., E14 (tel. 515 0960). Tube: DLR Island Gardens. Exit right from the station and follow Manchester St. as it curves around until corner of Pier St. Serves standard bar food in a quasi-upscale atmosphere. Cheap student dishes (Ham, eggs, and chips £3.95). Wheelchair accessible. Open Mon.-Thurs. 11:30am-3pm and 6:30-11pm, Fri. 11:30am-11pm, Sat. noon-11pm, Sun. noon-10:30pm. Serves food noon-2:30pm and 6-9pm. AmEx, MC, Visa.

■ Windsor and Eton

The Waterman's Arms, just over the bridge into Eton and to the left at Brocas St. next to the Eton College Boat House (tel. (01753) 861 001). A traditional public house (circa 1542) and a favorite of the locals. Delicious cod, chips, and salad £4.15. Guinness £2.05 per pint. Open Mon.-Thurs. 11am-2:30pm and 6-11pm, Fri.-Sat. 11am-3pm and 6-11pm, Sun. noon-3pm and 7-10:30pm.

Michael's The Eton Bakery, 43 Eton High St. (tel. (01753) 864 725). Eton High St. is the continuation of the bridge from Windsor. An old-time, neighborhood bakery selling fresh n' cheap baked goods. Large loaves of farmhouse bread £1. Mixed fruit pies £1.50, tarts 32p. Buy stale bread to feed the ducks (10p). Take-away only. Open Mon.-Fri. 7:30am-5pm, Sat. 7:30am-4:30pm.

The Courtyard Coffee Shop, 8 King George V Pl. (tel. (01753) 858 338), turn left out of the Riverside station. A little place in Royal Windsor. Homemade scones, soup, and quiche. Fresh sandwiches £1.75-2.90. Sit in the outdoor courtyard or inside for English cream tea (£3.50). Open Mon.-Fri. 8am-5pm, Sat.-Sun. 8am6pm.

The Two Brewers, 34 Park St. (tel. (01753) 855 426). Pub just outside of the entrance to the Great Park—a perfect place to pick up a delicious take-away ploughman's lunch (£3.50) or sandwich (£1.50-2). Open Mon.-Sat. 10:30am-11pm, Sun. noon-10:30pm.

Glad's Café, 4 River St. (tel. (01753) 830 254). Burgers, meat (£1.50) and veggie (£1.60). Spicy kebab rolls £2.50. Sit on the river's bank or lounge on the spacious patio in front. Open Mon.-Thurs. 9am-6pm, Fri.-Sat. 9am-1am, Sun. 9am-9pm.

GROCERIES AND SUPERMARKETS

Tesco and **Sainsbury's** are the two largest chains of supermarkets. Larger branches come complete with bakery, café, and housewares. Other chains include **Europa, Spar,** and **Asda.** If you're willing to spend a bit more, then you might consider **Marks and Spencer,** which introduced Britain to the concept of baby tomatoes, potatoes, and more cute produce. And if you're willing to splurge, the foodhalls of **Harrods** and **Fortnum and Mason's** are attractions in their own right.

PUBS AND BARS

"Did you ever taste beer?"
"I had a sip of it once," said the small servant.
"Here's a state of things!" cried Mr. Swiveller, "She never tasted it—it
can't be tasted in a sip!"
— Charles Dickens, *The Old Curiosity Shop*

London, like much else in life, is much more fun after a few beers. In recognition of this phenomenon, the social institution that is the English pub was created centuries ago, coddling tipplers of all affiliations with its mahogany paneling, soft velvet stools, and brass accents. Sir William Harcourt observed that, "As much of the history of England has been brought about in public houses as in the House of Commons," and this historic import has waned little through the centuries. While taverns and inns no longer serve as staging posts for coaches and horses, pubs remain meeting-places, signposts, and bastions of Britannia. And even if you don't see or make history, pubs provide an excellent place to get bloody pissed.

As the face of the British pub continues to change, they are beginning to offer a full bar selection, but still specialize in beverages of the beer family. If you thirst for cocktails, hi-balls, or mixed drinks, you're better off visiting a **bar.** London bars offer later hours, less traditional decor, and higher prices—visit them during happy hour (around 5:30-7:30pm) for the best drink deals. The listings below include both bars and pubs; names alone should indicate which is which.

Let crowd and atmosphere, rather than price, be your guide in selecting a pub. The difference (per pint) between drinking like a lord—in a classy, "expensive" pub—and drinking like a pauper—in a sleazy dive—is seldom more than 40p, and in London, 40p don't buy 30p. Pubs closely reflect their neighborhoods: touristy (and over-priced) near the inner-city train stations (Paddington, Victoria, etc.), stylish and trendy in the West End, gritty and cheap in the East, and suit-packed in the City. Once you've found a good pub, don't be afraid to leave—making a circuit, or **pub crawl,** is fun, and lets you experience the diversity of a neighborhood's nightlife.

The "last order" bells which ring through the streets of London at 10:50pm, testifying to the lamentable truth that British pubs close miserably early. Don't let these bells ring your evening's death knell, however. Take a tip from the locals and begin drinking when the pubs open at 11am. Or hustle to a bar or a club before 11pm when they begin to charge a cover (or raise an existing one). Though further relaxation of liquor laws was pending at press time, pubs may open only 12 hours per day. Most serve from 11am to 11pm Monday through Saturday in order to get lunchtime and afternoon business. Sundays are less free-flowing, with most pubs open noon-10:30pm.

Beer is the standard pub drink. Many pubs are "tied" to a particular brewery and only sell that brewery's ales. **Free Houses** sell a wider range of brands. In either case, beer is "pulled" from the tap in a dizzying variety of ways. All draughts, ales, and stouts are served "warm"—at room temperature—and by the pint or half-pint. Beware the so-called "half-pint"—though it costs half as much as a full pint, it mysteriously contains less than half the volume. **Bitter** is the staple of English beer, named for the sharp hoppy aftertaste. **"Real ale,"** naturally carbonated (unlike most beer) and drawn from a barrel, retains its full flavor. Brown, mild, pale, and India pale ale all have a relatively heavy flavor with noticeable hop. **Stout** is rich, dark, creamy, and virtually synonymous with the Irish superstout **Guinness.** If you can't stand the heat, try a **lager,** the European equivalent of American beer. Bottled beer is always more expensive than draft, and American beers, where available, cost 30% more than German and British brews. **Cider,** English wine, is a potent apple drink. Among the more complex liquids appearing at a pub near you are the **shandy,** a refreshing combination of beer and fizzy lemonade; **black and tan,** beer and stout layered like a parfait;

black velvet, a mating of Guinness and Champagne, and **snakebite,** a murky mix of lager and cider, with two drops of grenadine.

Those who don't drink alcohol should savor the pub experience all the same; fruit juices, colas, and sometimes low-alcohol beers are served. Buy all drinks at the bar—pub barkeeps are not usually tipped, unless you're trying to chat them up. Prices vary greatly with area and even clientele. Generally, a pint will set you back £1.80-2.35. Along with food and drink, pubs often host traditional games, including darts, pool, and bar billiards, an ingenious derivative of billiards played from only one end of the table. More recently, a brash and bewildering proliferation of video games, fruit (slot) machines, and extortionary CD jukeboxes have invaded pubs.

Look before you buy pub food. Pubs now serve anything from curry to burgers, some of which can be quite good. Quality and prices vary greatly with virtually no relation between the two. **Steak and kidney pie** or **pudding** is a mixture of steak and kidney, mushrooms, and pastry or pudding crust. A **cornish pasty** is filled with potato, onion, and often meat. **Shepherd's pie** consists of minced beef or lamb with onion, saddled with mashed potatoes, and baked. A **ploughman's lunch** means portions of bread, cheese, and pickled onions. **Mash** is British for "mashed potatoes." It comes coated with "liquor," (a parsley-flavored green sauce), with sausages **(bangers and mash),** or with cabbage **(bubble and squeak).**

For a selection of gay pubs, see Bisexual, Gay, and Lesbian London, p. 259.

▓ Soho and Piccadilly

The Dog and Duck, 8 Bateman St., W1 (tel. 437 4447). Tube: Tottenham Ct. Rd. Frequent winner of the Best Pub in Soho award, its size keeps the crowd down. Local TV and advertising professionals crowd in at lunch for the inexpensive pints (£1.85-2.10). Evenings bring locals, theater-goers, actors on the way home, and, yes, some tourists. Open Mon.-Fri. noon-11pm, Sat. 6-11pm, Sun. 7-10:30pm.

The Three Greyhounds, 25 Greek St., W1 (tel. 287 0754). Tube: Leicester Sq. This tiny, medieval-styled pub, provides welcome respite from the endless cafés and posturing of Soho. 1996 winner of the Best Pub in Soho award. Open Mon.-Sat. 11am-11pm, Sun. noon-3pm and 7-10:30pm.

The Porcupine, 48 Charing Cross Rd., WC2 (836 0054). Tube: Leicester Sq. The West End's most schizophrenic pub: young folks on the first floor generate smoke and noise while partying to clubby dance music. Meanwhile their parents peck at tasty pre-theater pub meals (£4.50-7) upstairs. Pints: lager £2.30, bitter £2.05. Open Mon.-Sat. noon-11pm, Sun. noon-10:30pm. Major credit cards.

Riki Tik, 23-24 Bateman St., W1 (tel. 437 1977). Tube: Leicester Square, Tottenham Ct. Rd., or Piccadilly Circus. A hyped, hip, and tremendously swinging bar specializing in orgasmic flavored vodka shots (try the white chocolate, £2.40). The decor is George Jetson on acid, the crowd is swish, and the drink prices are exorbitant. Come during happy hour (5;30-7:30pm) when the deliciously fruity cocktails are a near-bargain at £6.50/pitcher. Open Mon.-Sat. noon-1am. Get there before the pubs close, or you'll be asked to pay a £3 cover. MC, Visa.

The Dog House, 187 Wardour St., W1 (tel. 434 2116). Tube: Tottenham Court Road. Decor, a colorful riff on the "Dogs Playing Poker" motif, complements the mellow clientele surprisingly well. Prices are just so-ho, but excellent cocktail and food specials abound during the 5:30-7:30pm happy hour. Open Mon.-Fri. 5:30-11pm, Sat. 6-11pm.

The Salisbury, 90 St. Martin's La., WC2 (tel. 836 5863). Tube: Leicester Sq. A Victorian pub with a blindingly polished decor; ornate glass and gilt bewilder as the beers slip down. Business people and tourists by day, a younger crowd by night—they all like the pints of Theakston's Bitter Ale from Yorkshire (£2.05). Open Mon.-Sat. noon-11pm, Sun. noon-10:30pm. Major credit cards.

Sherlock Holmes, 10 Northumberland St., WC2 (tel. 930 2644). Tube: Charing Cross. Upstairs replicates Holmes' 221b Baker St. den. Hosts of relics to thrill tourists as well as the Holmes fiend—tobacco in the slipper, correspondence affixed to the mantelpiece with a dagger, and the Hound of the Baskervilles' head. Inexpensive and cozy—if you can bear the kitsch (e.g., Sherlock Holmes Ales at £1.81/pint). Open Mon.-Sat. 11am-11pm, Sun noon-10:30pm.

■ Covent Garden

The nightlife in Covent Garden is as busy and exciting as the daylife. The multitude of pubs and bars fill up early and stay packed late with a young, exuberant crowd of international tourists and Londoners.

Lamb and Flag, 33 Rose St., WC2, off Garrick St. (tel. 497 9504). Tube: Covent Garden or Leicester Sq. Rose St. is off Long Acre, which runs between the 2 tube stops. A traditional old English pub, with no music and still separated into 2 sections—the public bar for the working class, and the saloon bar for the businessmen, though today the classes mix. It's filled with regulars who know each other and have been comin' 'ere for 'ears. Look for their names on the brass plaques on the bar. Live jazz upstairs Sun. from 7:30pm. Open Mon.-Thurs. 11am-11pm, Fri. and Sat. 11am-10:45pm, Sun. noon-10:30pm.

Crown and Anchor, 22 Neal St., WC2 (tel. 836 5439). Tube: Covent Garden. One of Covent Garden's most popular pubs. The crowd perches on kegs or sits on the cobbles outside, forming a mellow oasis in the midst of Neal St.'s bustling pedestrian zone. Open Mon.-Sat. 11am-11pm, Sun. noon-10:30pm.

Belushi's, 9 Russell St., WC2 (tel. 240 3411). Tube: Covent Garden. More of a bar than a pub. The upbeat Aussie and Kiwi barmen and barmaids serve Budweiser and dance to the horrid pop music of the early 80s, making for an unrepentantly cheesy, but howlingly good time. Watch out for the 2-min. specials; they've been known to call Jäger shots for 50p. Open daily 11am-midnight.

Freud Café Bar Gallery, 198 Shaftesbury Ave., WC2 (tel. 240 9933). Tube: Tottenham Ct. Rd. or Covent Garden. Find comfort in this downstairs café-bar-gallery where you'll be surrounded by old concrete-slab walls, slate tables, and month-long art shows (bar has its own curator). The music is ambient—lots of soothing, funky tunes. Home of famous Freud's lemonade (£2). By night Freud's gracefully morphs from café to bar. Cheaper than an hour on the couch, a beer here (£2-3) represents therapy nonetheless. Open daily 11am-11pm.

Outback Inn, 11 Henrietta St. and 33 Maiden Lane, WC2 (tel. 379 5555). A block long and 2½ stories deep, this outback watering hole on steroids packs in fun-loving backpackers from the land down under every night. If you've ever been to a frat party anywhere you'll know what to expect from the nightly live and DJed music. Oh what a night, indeed. Australian/Kiwi beers imported. Open Mon.-Sat. noon-11pm, Sun. noon-10:30pm.

Roundhouse, 1 Garrick St., WC2 (tel. 836 9838). Tube: Leicester Sq. or Covent Garden. This pub is pleasant in the afternoons and late evenings, but the flood of office workers arriving shortly after 5pm will prevent visitors from seating themselves or breathing fresh air. In summer, the crowd spills outside. Pints £2.05-2.25. Open Mon.-Sat. 11am-11pm, Sun. 11am-10:30pm.

The White Hart, 191 Drury La., WC2 (tel. 242 3135). Established in 1201, this is the oldest licensed pub in England. Traditional pub fare is served along with hand-pulled ales. Pool tables and big screen TV to boot! Shake your money-maker on Fri. Disco nights. Open Mon.-Sat. 11am-11pm.

Nag's Head, 10 James St., WC2. Tube: Covent Garden. A favorite of London's theatre elite. Always crowded, you may need a partner to get in—sometimes they'll call "couples only." The round, light beige booths recall airport lounges. Open Mon-Sat. 11am-11pm, Sun. noon-10:30pm. Credit cards for food only.

Maple Leaf, 41 Maiden Lane, WC2 (tel. 240 2843). Tube: Covent Garden. Maiden Lane is parallel to the Strand and 1 block away. "The only place outside North America with Molson on tap (£2.30/pint)" says it all, eh? Start a rousing chorus of "O Canada" and make some new friends. Mon.-Fri. 1-11pm, Sat-Sun. noon-11pm.

Globe, 37 Bow St., WC2 (tel. 836 0219). Tube: Covent Garden. Turn right from the tube onto Long Acre, then right again on Bow St. A classic pub near the Royal Opera House—join orchestra members and kill the ringing in your ears. Depicted in Hitchcock's *Frenzy*. Open daily 11am-11pm.

■ Kensington and Chelsea

World's End Distillery, 459 King's Rd. near World's End Pass before Edith Grove (tel. 376 8946). Tube: Sloane Sq. This pub isn't wedged into a street corner like most others; it stands alone, grandiose and cathedralesque. If the universe collapsed and nothing but the World's End remained, we would not weep. Rather, we'd lounge in a soft leather booth and play one of the many board games offered here, or sit on a green velvet stool and peruse one of the old books shelved near the candlelit mirror. Open Mon.-Sat. 11am-11pm, Sun. noon-3pm, 7pm-10:30pm.

The Chelsea Potter, 119 King's Rd., SW3 (tel. 352 9479). Tube: Victoria then Bus 11, 19, or 22. This pub's name reflects its history as a haven for ramshackle Chelsea artists throwing pots and living on their trust funds. Noisy outdoor tables. Pints of Foster's £2.15. Open Mon.-Sat. 11am-11pm and Sun. noon-10:30pm.

The Goat in Boots, 333 Fulham Rd. Tube: South Ken. then take Onslow to Fulham and walk for about 20min. Open multi-level bar attracts a young, fun-lovin' crowd. Drink specials each night, like £1 shots on Weds., even from the 26 flavored vodkas (usually £2.50). Open Mon-Sat. 11:30am-11pm, Sun. noon-10:30pm.

Cadogan Arms, 218 King's Rd. near Old Church St., SW3 (tel. 352 1645). Tube: Sloane Sq. or Victoria, then Bus 11, 19, or 22. A quiet retreat from the trendiness and business that is the King's Road. Swell TV setup and pool table. Large burgers £3-4. Open Mon.-Sat. 11am-11pm, Sun. noon-11pm.

The King's Head and Eight Bells, 50 Cheyne Walk, SW3. Take Bus 11 down King's Rd., get off at Oakley St., walk toward the river, and turn right on Cheyne Walk. Richly textured 16th-century pub where Thomas More would have a jar with his dangerous friend Henry VIII. Carlyle's house is just around the corner.

■ Earl's Court

The King's Head, 17 Hogarth Pl., SW5 (tel. 244 6722). Tube: Earl's Ct. From Earl's Ct. Rd., head east on Childs Walk or Hogarth Pl. The place to get loose. Billions of lusty tourists packed into a classic pub, with smoky atmosphere and all. Another link in the Earl's Court hangout circuit. Besides real ale, this pub has a passable wine list. Pint o' real ale £2.20. Open daily 11am-11pm.

The Prince of Teck, 161 Earl's Ct. Rd., SW5 (tel. 373 3107). Tube: Earl's Ct. An atmosphere like Venus—hot and oppressive. Some love it, some loathe it; either way, you'll sweat. Aussie headquarters. Door sign says it all: "G'day and welcome to the land of Oz." Open Mon.-Sat. 11am-11pm, Sun. noon-3pm and 7-10:30pm.

The Scarsdale, 23a Edward Sq., W8. Tube: Earl's Ct. Walk up Earl's Ct. Rd. 3 blocks past Cromwell Rd., and turn left at Pembroke Sq. When you see people sitting outside in a sea of flowers and ivy, contentedly throwing back a few pints as they talk without the interruption of beeping fruit machines and screeching jukeboxes, well, you've found it. Don't be thrown off by the fact that it looks like a house. Open daily noon-11pm.

■ Bloomsbury

The Old Crown, 33 New Oxford St., WC1 (tel. 836 9121). Tube: Tottenham Ct. Rd. A thoroughly untraditional pub. Cream-colored walls, faded pine-green bar, green plants, and funky brass crowns which suspend light fixtures from the ceiling. The lively crowd spills out onto the outdoor seating, creating a babble of voices above the cool jazz playing in the background; quieter seating upstairs. Open Mon.-Sat. noon-11pm. Major credit cards.

Lord John Russell Pub, 91 Marchmont St., WC1 (tel. 388 0500). Tube: Russell Sq. The exact point where the bustle of Marchmont St. flows into the residential calm of nearby Cartwright Gardens. Drink a well-drawn pint of Director's bitter (£2.05) under the watchful eye of the Lord John Russell football club. Ploughman's lunch £3.75. Open Mon.-Sat. 11:30am-11pm, Sun. noon-10:30pm.

The Lamb, 94 Lamb's Conduit St., WC1 (tel. 405 0713). Tube: Russell Sq. E.M. Forster and other Bloomsbury luminaries used to tipple here. Discreet cut-glass "snob screens"—holdovers from Victorian times—render this pub ideal for dangerous liaisons and illicit assignations. Several tables for limited outdoor seating, and a no-smoking room tastefully decorated with old Vanity Fair caricatures. Hot food served noon-2:30pm. Open Mon.-Sat. 11am-11pm, Sun. noon-4pm.

Calthorpe Arms, 252 Gray's Inn Rd., WC1 (tel.278 1207) Tube: King's Cross/St. Pancras. Locals young and old envelop this spacious, airy pub. Out of the way location and mellow atmosphere make pints of Young's brew even more of a bargain at £1.64 (bitter) and £1.98 (premium lager). Open Mon.-Wed. 11am-3pm, 5-11pm, Thurs.-Sat. 11am-11pm, Sun. 11am-10:30pm.

Princess Louise, 208 High Holborn, WC1 (tel. 405 8816). Tube: Holborn. This big pub isn't big enough to contain the jovial crowd that assembles after office hours. Built in 1872 and refurbished in 1891, the pub retains its ornate Victorian grandeur—beautiful tiles and etched mirrors line the walls. Fancy plasterwork columns support a decadent scarlet ceiling trimmed in gold. 8-10 real ales at all times. Pint of bitter £1.75-1.85. Open Mon.-Fri. 11am-11pm, Sat. noon-3pm and 6-11pm, Sun. noon-2pm and 7-10:30pm.

The Water Rats, 328 Grays Inn Rd., WC1 (tel. 278 3879). Tube: King's Cross/St. Pancras. Ordinary appearance belies radical historical connections—this used to be one of Marx and Engels' favorite haunts. Moonlights as the Splash Club at nights, a venue for indie rock, punk, and occasional acoustic gigs. 3 bands a night. Cover £5, concessions £3.50. Bands start at 8pm. Open daily noon-midnight.

Museum Tavern, 49 Great Russell St., WC1 (tel. 242 8987). Tube: Tottenham Ct. Rd. High coffered ceiling; spacious, plush atmosphere. Karl Marx sipped *Bier* here after banging out *Das Kapital* across the street in the British Museum reading room. The Star Tavern, which formerly occupied this site, was one of Casanova's rendezvous spots. Tourists, businessmen, and daytime regulars mingle over the 16 beers on tap. Open Mon.-Sat. 11am-11pm, Sun. noon-10:30pm, but no alcohol between 3-7pm.

Grafton Arms, 72 Grafton Way, W1 (tel. 387 7923). Tube: Warren St. Off the tourist trail, near Regent's Park. One of the best central London pubs for a relaxed pint. Caters to a lively London University student crowd. 8 real ales. Standard pub fare sold all day. Wine bar on rooftop patio. Open Mon.-Sat. 11am-11pm, Sun. 11am-3pm and 7-10:30pm. MC, Visa.

The City of London

Black Friar, 174 Queen Victoria St., EC4 (tel. 236 5650). Tube: Blackfriars. Directly across from the station. One of the most exquisite and fascinating pubs in all of London. The edifice's past purpose as a 12th-century Dominican friary is celebrated not only in the pub's name but in the intriguing arches, mosaics, and reliefs that line the pub's walls. Each relief describes some aspect of the daily life of the "merry monks," but the real treasure is found in the "side chapel" (located in back), where dimly lit candles hang from monk-shaped brass holders against arches and mini-columns. Prices unfortunately reflect pub's popularity. Average pint £2. Open Mon.-Wed. 11:30am-10:30pm and Thurs.-Fri. 11:30am-11pm.

Ye Olde Cheshire Cheese, Wine Office Ct. by 145 Fleet St., EC4 (tel. 353 6170). Tube: Blackfriars or St. Paul's. On Fleet St., watch out for Wine Office Ct. on the right; small sign indicates the alley. Classic 1600s bar where Dr. Johnson and Dickens, as well as little-known Americans Mark Twain and Theodore Roosevelt, hung out. Today it's hot among businessmen and theatre-goers. Note "Gentlemen Only" sign over first room on right, where famed Polly the Parrot insulted female drinkers in 3 languages. Open Mon.-Sat. 11:30am-11pm, Sun. noon-3pm.

The Shakespeare, 2 Goswell Rd., EC1 (tel. 253 6166). Tube: Barbican. Upstairs always flooded with hip student crowd from YMCA across the street and business-people getting soused during and after work. Lunch served 11:30am-2:45pm, dinner 6:30-10pm. A pint of the Bard's Brew (£1.60) makes a cheap and refreshing, if ephemeral, souvenir of your trip to the City. Open Mon.-Sat. 11am-11pm, Sun. noon-10:30pm. MC, Visa, Switch.

Fuego Bar y Tapas, 1 Pudding La., EC3 (tel. 929 3366). Tube: Monument. Turn right on Eastcheap St., then another right onto Pudding La. This snazzy executive

watering hole compensates for lack of windowspace and cavernous basement location with neat lighting and lively evening events. Elevated walkway makes for
great, smoky disco experience. Spanish music Tues.-Wed. nights, disco Thurs.-Fri.
nights. Lunch £10 for starter and main course. Dinner main course £6.90-10. Open
Mon.-Fri. 11:30am-2am.

La Baguette at the Kings Head, 49 Chiswell St., EC1 (tel. 606 9158). Tube: Barbican. Head straight from tube exit through tunnel. A dignified cross between a Las
Vegas casino and an airport executive lounge. Kings Head is distinguished from all
other slot machine-filled city pubs by its outstanding baguette shop in the rear of
the pub. French bread baked daily on premises. Most popular sandwiches include
tuna and ham (£2.35). Open Mon.-Sat. 11am-11pm, Sun. noon-10:30pm.

■ The East End

The Blind Beggar, 337 Whitechapel Rd., E1 (tel. 247 3798). Tube: Whitechapel.
You may be sitting where George Cornell sat when he was gunned down by rival
Bethnal Green gangster Ronnie Kray in 1966. Keep your head low. Spacious pub
with conservatory and garden. Open Mon.-Sat. 11am-11pm, Sun. noon-10:30pm.

White Hart, 359 Bethnal Green, E2 (tel. 729 1090). Tube: Bethnal Green. A bastion
of East End Irishness lustily exhibiting its Irish soul. Dublin music and sport playing
on TV makes you feel just like ya weere baaack in tha olde couuntry. So does the
extraordinarily cheap beer. Pint of Guinness £1.50.

The Old Blue Anchor, 133 Whitechapel Rd., E1 (tel. 247 4926). A local bar replete
with a ships helm on the wall, velvet chairs, and twangy stuff comin' o'er the
speakers. Open Mon.-Sat. 11am-11pm, Sun. noon-3pm.

The Black Bull, 199 Whitechapel Rd., E1 (tel. 247-6707). A woody place filled with
football fans (a Newcastle sign hangs in the corner so Arsenal fans 'ad best steer
clear). Open Mon.-Sat. 11am-11pm, Sun. noon-3pm.

■ Camden Town

The Engineer, 65 Gloucester Ave., NW (tel. 722 0950). Tube: Chalk Farm. Classic
pub design with bright, flowery atmosphere that makes everybody feel relaxed.
Primrose Hill crowd does not object to pricey menu, but one beer in such a cheery
joint won't kill you. Beer £2. Open daily noon-11pm. Major credit cards. Wheelchair accessible.

Lock Tavern, 35 Chalk Farm Rd., NW1 (tel. 284 0723). Tube: Chalk Farm or Camden Town. A high-ceilinged pub decorated with theater bills. Roof patio offers a
view of the action at Camden Market. Lively, mixed crowd. Beer £1.90. Open
Mon.-Fri. 11am-11pm, Sat.-Sun. 11am-midnight.

Engine Room, 78-9 Chalk Farm Rd., NW1 (tel. 916 0595). Tube: Chalk Farm. Frequented by local band members. Painted black outside, with grafitti art on the windows; inside, the walls are plastered with old music posters, vinyl platters, and
movie ads. Pool table. Cheap pub grub. Open Mon.-Thurs. 11am-11pm, Fri. 11am-
midnight, Sat. noon-midnight, Sun. noon-11pm.

Harvey Floorbanger's, 202 Camden High St., NW1 (tel. 284 1513). Tube: Camden
Town. Sausages come in meat and vegetarian formulations (£3-5). Attracts a crowd
that appreciates grunge and indie rock. Open Mon.-Sat. 11am-11pm, Sun. noon-
11pm.

Edinboro Castle, 57 Mornington Terr., NW1 (tel. 387 8916). Tube: Camden Town.
Exit to the right and head left down Camden High St. Turn right on Delancey St.
and follow it until it intersects with Mornington Terr. A friendly neighborhood
place tucked away from the bustle of Camden's main drag. Pool table. Large outdoor patio often crowded with deflated or elated sports teams from nearby
Regent's Park. Barbecue in summer. Pints £1.90. Open Mon.-Sat. 11am-11pm, Sun.
noon-10:30pm.

FOOD AND DRINK

■ Islington

Slug and Lettuce, 1 Islington Green, N1 (tel. 226 3864). Tube: Angel. Upper St. changes to Islington Green as it passes the Green. Serves pretty elaborate food for a pub (spinach and ricotta pancakes covered with tomato sauce and mozarella, £5) but this is Islington. Open Mon.-Sat. 11am-11pm, Sun. 11am-10:30pm.

Minogues, 80 Liverpool Rd., N1 (tel. 354 4440). Tube: Angel. Liverpool branches left off of Upper St. directly across from the station. If you can't make the journey across the Irish Sea, throw back a Guinness (£2.10) at one of London's most traditional and friendly Irish pubs. Live music Thurs.-Sun. morning and Sun. nights. Open daily 11am-midnight, but really closes when the beer runs out. Visa, Access.

Filthy MacNasty's Whiskey Café, 68 Amwell St. (tel. 837 6067). Tube: Angel. Exit the station left, then right to Pentonville Rd. and turn left at Claremont Sq, which turns into to Amwell. "In drink you're mine all the time... In drink, in drink" bellow the patrons of this famously small Irish pub. Celtic drawings line the fire-colored walls; former Pogues singer Shane MacGowan frequently appears for last call. Renowned location for traditional Irish music. Live shows Thurs.-Sun. all day. Open daily 11am-11pm. Wheelchair accessible.

Finnegan's Wake, 2 Essex Rd., N1 (tel. 226 1483). Tube: Angel. Essex Rd. splits off from Essex by Islington Green. Pool-tabled pub with comedy club downstairs on Mon., Fri., and Sat. nights. Live Irish music on Thurs. and Sun. All new material by local professionals, but watch out: humor takes many forms. Show gets going about 9pm. Open daily 11am-11pm

Camden Head, 2 Camden Walk, N1 (tel. 359 0851). Tube: Angel. Just past the tip of the Islington green. A beautiful pub with cut-glass windows and plush seats, founded in 1749. Popular with the younger set. Wed. and Sat. the outdoor patio bustles with thirsty visitors taking a break from bargain-hunting at the market. Beer £2.05. Open Mon.-Sat. 11am-11pm, Sun. noon-10:30pm.

All-Bar-One, 1 Liverpool St., N1 (tel. 226 3414). Tube: Angel. Only the choppy wood floors testify to this trendy, smooth pub's previous existence as a powerhouse indie dance club. Beer starts at £2. Open Mon.-Sat. 11am-11pm, Sun. noon-10:30pm.

■ Hampstead and Highgate

King of Bohemia, 10 Hampstead High St. NW3 (tel. 435 6513). Most pubby of Hampstead High St. hangouts, but still has yuppie, upscale clientele that swarm to outdoor seating in summer. Library-like, elegant seating in back is also a pleasant area to tipple. Open Mon.-Sat. 10am-11pm, Sun. noon-3pm and 7-10:30pm.

Bar Room Bar, 48 Rossyln Hill, NW3 (tel. 435 0808). Hampstead High St. turns into Rossyln Hill. This is an "art gallery bar," where exotic paintings and sculptures for sale hang from chic beige walls. Artsy clientele matches funky design. The rear garden, also lined with exquisite murals and shadowed by the gothic church next door, makes for wonderful, quiet evening drinking. Open Mon.-Sat. 11am-11pm, Sun. 11am-10:30pm.

The Holly Bush, 22 Holly Mount, NW3 (tel. 435 2892). Tube: Hampstead. From the tube climb Holly Hill and watch for the sharp right turn. The quintessential snug Hampstead pub in a quaint cul-de-sac. A maze of glass and wood serving pints from £1.55. Open Mon.-Fri. noon-3pm and 5:30-11pm, Sat. noon-4pm and 6-11pm, Sun. noon-3pm and 7-10:30pm.

The Flask Tavern, 77 Highgate West Hill, N6 (tel. (0181) 340 7260). Tube: Archway. Near the youth hostel. Enormously popular on summer evenings and at Sun. noontime for its vast terrace seating. Drink a toast to Karl Marx, Yehudi Menuhin, or any other Highgate luminary whose name flits through your giddy brain. Open Mon.-Sat. 11am-11pm, Sun noon-3pm and 7-10:30pm.

King William IV, 77 Hampstead High St., NW3 (tel. 435 5747). Tube: Hampstead. Outside: the famed Crêperie de Hampstead (see Restaurants, p. 120). Inside: the famed gay pub, attracting all ages. Open Mon.-Sat. noon-11pm, Sun. noon-10:30pm.

The Angel, 37 Highgate High St. (tel. (0181) 340 4305). Tube: Archway or Highgate. The management of this pool-tabled bar is dying to pack in a young happening crowd and performs tricks to do it. £4 for 8-oz. steak; special meal and drink nights (like shots 90p). Open Mon.-Sat.noon-11pm, Sun. noon-10:30pm.

Spaniards Inn, Spaniards End, NW3 (tel. (0181) 455 3276). Tube: Hampstead, then Bus 210 along Spaniards Rd. Upscale pub on north edge of Hampstead Heath. Pub has provided garden in summer and hearth in winter since 1585. Infamous patrons have included highwayman Dick Turpin and the Gordon rioters—drink carefully. Open Mon.-Sat. 11am-11pm, Sun. noon-10:30pm.

Archway Tavern, 1 Archway Close, N19 (tel. 272 2840). Tube: Archway. Across the street from station. The exterior of this smoky pub could easily be mistaken for the Munsters' House, but the inside is much more Seamus than Herman: come before 8pm and allow the £1.39 pints of Guinness to wreck your pool game. Live Irish music Fri.-Sat. with £2 cover. Open Mon.-Sat. 11am-11pm, Sun. noon-3pm.

■ Hammersmith and Putney

There is, in fact, reason to travel to Hammersmith or Putney for a drink: the pubs listed here are all on the waterfront, and have outdoor seating with expansive views of the Thames. The Victorian bridges arching across the river are often lit beautifully at night, making this area a popular evening destination. To get to any of the pubs on **Upper Mall,** come out of the station and head west on Blacks Road. Walk for five minutes, take any left (Angel Walk, Bridge Avenue), and you'll hit the river. To reach **Lower Richmond Road** pubs, take the tube to Putney Bridge (District Line) and cross the Putney Bridge. After you cross, Lower Richmond is on your right.

The Dove, 19 Upper Mall, SW6 (tel. (0181) 748 5405). Tube: Hammersmith. Make the trip to the 300-year-old tavern for a delicious lunch overlooking the Thames. Harvest pie £2.25, 7 different Thai dishes served at night £4-6. Pints £1.90. Open Mon.-Sat. 11am-11pm, Sun. noon-3pm and 7-10:30pm.

The Rutland Ale House, 15 Upper Mall, SW6 (tel. (0181) 748 5586). Tube: Hammersmith. Red neon sign reflects onto the Thames. Crowded with younger locals, looking good and feelin' fine. Lots of pub food served til 8pm. Try the kidney pie with fries and vegetables £5. Open Mon.-Sat. 11am-11pm, Sun. noon-10:30pm.

Half Moon, 93 Lower Richmond Rd., SW15 (tel. (0181) 780 9383). Tube: Putney Bridge. A no-nonsense pub about a block off of the Thames known for daily live tunes in the back room (cover £3-6). Bitter £1.65. Open Mon.-Sat. 11am-11pm, Sun. noon-10:30pm.

Star and Garter, 4 Lower Richmond Rd., SW15 (tel. (0181) 788 0345). Tube: Putney Bridge. A veritable monument of a riverside pub. Cavernous lounge nearly always full of students and under-25s. If you exchange your glass for a plastic cup you can take your ale for a walk along the Thames. Traditional Sunday roasts £4.90. Open Mon-Sat. 11am-11pm, Sun. noon-10:30pm.

■ South of the Thames and Brixton

The Brixtonian, 11 Dorrell Pl., SW9 (tel. 978 8870). Tube: Brixton. A cozy, artsy bar removed from the movin' and groovin' of the market area. Green picnic tables on the pedestrian walk outside are ideal for a quiet, slow drink with a loved one. Open Mon.-Sat. noon-1am, Sun. 2pm-midnight.

Babushka, 173 Blackfriars Road, SE1 (tel. 928 3693). Tube: Waterloo. Much attention paid to decor, perhaps in response to the clientele's upscale pretensions. High ceilings. Bottled beers £1.90-2, wine £1.80 per glass. Spirits served. Live music (mostly jazz) Wed. 6-9:30pm. Open Mon.-Wed. 11am-11pm, Thurs.-Sat. 11am-midnight, Sun. noon-10:30pm. Access, Visa.

Bar Central, 131 Waterloo Rd., SE1 (tel. 928 5086). Tube: Waterloo. Near the Old Vic. An electric blue façade welcomes the thirsty to this cosmopolitan full bar and brasserie. Open daily noon-11pm.

George Inn, 77 Borough High St., SE1 (tel. 407 2056). Tube: London Bridge. A fine 17th-century galleried inn; the older equivalent of Victoria coach station. Now it's the last stop of the day for the suits of the South Bank, not to mention a major tourist haven. But yea! still neat for a walk through history. Open Mon.-Sat. 11am-11pm, Sun. noon–10:30pm. Major credit cards.

■ Docklands

These four riverside pubs have seen almost two millennia among them. They are located away from the area's huge glass and steel monuments to commerce, and are reminders that the Docklands once—in an earlier incarnation which gave it its name—served as the entry point to the city Joseph Chamberlin declared the clearinghouse of the world.

Prospect of Whitby, 57 Wapping Wall, E1, London Docks (tel. 481 1095). Tube: Wapping. 600-year old pub with sweet riverside terrace. Open ceilings and a rustic flagstone bar pale next to glorious Thamescape. Riverside terrace and prohibitive upstairs restaurant. Very touristy. Open daily 11am-3pm and 6:30-11pm.

The Angel, 101 Bermondsey Wall, SE16 (tel. 252 0327). Tube: Rotherhithe. Sip a soda from this 17th-century pub's balcony while overlooking the spectacular Tower Bridge and flood-lit city. You may be drinking above one of the pub's trap doors formerly used for smuggling. Upstairs dining room is out of budget travel bounds (although sublime view just might have you shelling out). Open Mon.-Sat. 11am-11pm, Sun 11am-10:30pm.

The Dickens Inn, St. Katherine's Way, E1 (tel. 488-2208). Tube: London Tower or DLR: Tower Gateway. Before entering the Dickens to have a drink, imagine 18th-century spice traders milling about on one of the Inn's 3-story balconies. Today the flower-sprayed exterior is a nice place to stop if you're checking out the Crown Jewels nearby. Bar food £2.45-4.25. Open daily 11am-11pm. AmEx, Diners, MC, Visa.

Grapes, 76 Narrow St. (tel. 987 4396). Another famous river pub that has seen the ebb and flow of Docklands activity for over 500 years. Dickens wrote about it in *My Mutual Friend.* Pint around £2. Open Mon.-Fri. noon-3pm, Sat. 7pm-11pm, Sun. noon-4pm and 7pm-10:30pm.

TEA

One should always eat muffins quite calmly. It is the only way to eat them.
—Oscar Wilde, *The Importance of Being Earnest*

English "tea" refers to both a drink and a social ritual. Tea the drink is the preferred remedy for exhaustion, ennui, a row with one's partner, a rainy morning, or a slow afternoon. English tea is served strong and milky; if you want it any other way, say so. (Aficionados always pour the milk before the tea so as not to scald it.)

Tea the social ritual centers around a meal. Afternoon **high tea** includes cooked meats, salad, sandwiches, and pastries. "Tea" in the north of England refers to the evening meal, often served with a huge pot of tea. **Cream tea,** a specialty of Cornwall and Devon, includes toast, shortbread, crumpets (a much tastier sort of English muffin), scones, and jam, accompanied by delicious clotted cream (a cross between whipped cream and butter). Most Brits take short tea breaks each day, mornings ("elevenses") and afternoons (around 4pm).

London hotels serve afternoon set teas, often hybrids of cream and high tea, which are expensive and sometimes disappointing. You might order single items from the menu instead of the full set to avoid a sugar overdose. Cafés often serve a simpler tea (pot of tea, scone, preserves, and butter) for a lower price.

Louis, 32 Heath St., NW3 (tel. 435 9908). Tube: Hampstead. This intimate Hungarian confectionary and tea room thrills with finger-licking Florentines (a candy conglomerate of almonds, cherries, and chocolate) £1.30. A variety of cakes, tarts, and teas are also available. Open daily 10am-6:30pm.

Georgian Restaurant, Harrods, Knightsbridge, SW1 (tel. 225 6800). Tube: Knightsbridge. A carefully staged event. Revel in bourgeois satisfaction as you enjoy your expensive repast inside or on the terrace (£12.75). Beautiful view of downtown Knightsbridge. Tea served Mon.-Fri. 3-5:15pm, Sat. 3:45-5:15pm.

The Muffin Man, 12 Wrights La., W8 (tel 937 6652). Tube: High St. Kensington. Everything you dreamed a tearoom could be. Set cream tea £3.80. Min. £1.50 from 12:30-2:30pm. Open Mon.-Sat. 8am-5:30pm.

St. James Restaurant, at Fortnum & Mason's (see Department Stores, p. 249). Floors below, the madding crowd scrambles to purchase some of London's most famous teas, while you sip in this splendid enclave of glass and porcelain. Set tea £10.50, with champagne £15. Open Mon.-Sat. 3-5:30pm.

The Orangery Tea Room, Kensington Palace, Kensington Gardens, W8 (tel. 376 0239). Tube: High St. Kensington. Light meals and tea served in the marvelously airy Orangery built for Queen Anne in 1705. Two fruit scones with clotted cream and jam £3.15. Pot of tea £1.40. Trundle through the gardens afterward, smacking your lips. Open daily 10am-6pm.

The Savoy, Strand, WC2 (tel. 836 4343). The elegance of this music-accompanied tea is well worth the splurge. Starve yourself before you go, then graciously wolf down the delicious tarts, scones, and sandwiches as the bemused waitstaff refills your tray time after time. Strict dress code—no jeans or shorts. If gentlemen "forget" their jacket, they'll be forced to borrow a garish red number from the cloakroom. Set tea £16.50. Tea served daily 3-5:30pm. Book ahead on Saturday and Sunday.

WINE BARS

John Mortimer's fictional barrister Horace Rumpole, who drinks every afternoon at Pommeroy's Wine Bar, habitually orders a bottle of "Château Thames Embankment." Unlike Rumpole's brand, much of the wine served in London's sleek wine bars lives up to neither its price nor its pedigree. Nevertheless, we'd be remiss not to mention two stalwarts of the City-based wine bar scene. **Simpson's,** Ball Court, off 38½ Cornhill, EC3 (tel. 626 9985; Tube: Bank) allows you to rub elbows with sharp-dressed banking brass, but make sure not to step on their briefcases piled high at each entrance. Their wine of the day costs £2.30/glass (open Mon.-Fri. 11am-4pm, restaurant Mon.-Fri. 11:30am-3pm). At **Balls Brothers,** 2 Old Change Ct., St. Paul's Churchyard, EC4 (tel. 236 9921; Tube: St. Paul's), celebrate a secular communion in the shadow of St. Paul's Cathedral. The dignified interior of this venerable London chain matches the plush, elegant taste of its red wines. Glasses of wine from £2.45. Open Mon.-Fri. 11:30am-9pm.

Sights

Those who journey to London in expectation of friendly, rosy-cheeked, frumpy, tea-drinking, Queen-loving gardeners may be astounded to find that London is equally the province of slinkily-dressed, buff young things who spend their nights lounging around murky Soho cafes. London is an irrepressibly international city, the center of rave culture, the Britpop explosion, and countless other ripples which float swingers the world over. At the same time, those expecting non-stop hedonism may run head-long into an exquisitely British sense of propriety, morality, and culture. Pubs close at eleven, the nation would be outraged if Diana or Charles were to live with a signifi-cant other outside of wedlock, MPs resign over the smallest sexual peccadillos, and some of the hottest pick-up scenes are at the bookstores. Drunken revelers returning from a late night may pass fur-hatted guards on their way to work wearing the blazing scarlet coats which colonial militiamen found such easy targets in 1775. Despite an off-and-on embrace of the avant-garde, change comes slowly to London.

But London is no paradox, simply because we should presume no coherent way of living among the 7,000,000 people who call London home. Rather, there are many Londons, various of which will appeal to differently-minded visitors. Those seeking **Royal London** will be busy bees indeed. If visions of stiff guards, flashy heraldry, bur-nished armor, and the like make your engine race we recommend the **Changing of the Guard** at **Buckingham Palace** (p. 145), **Hampton Court Palace** (p. 207), **Wind-sor Castle** (p. 209), and the **Tower of London** (p. 184). For an account of the Royal Family's recent struggles see p. 7.

No visit would be complete without time spent luxuriating in **Green London:** Lon-don's glorious parks and gardens. **Hyde Park and Kensington Gardens** (see p. 155), **Kew Gardens** (p. 205), **St. James's Park** (p. 144), and the gardens at **Hampton Court Palace** (p. 207) deserve special mention. For a complete list of the more nota-ble gardens and parks see the listings beginning on p. 212.

England is remarkable for its homegrown religion and remarkable churches—architecture buffs will not want to miss the glorious places of worship which make up **Anglican London.** The oldest district—the City—is dotted with a number of churches open to visitors. A lovely day may be spent walking from church to church (see The City of London, p. 176). Any tour of the City churches should include Wren's favorite, **St. Stephen Walbrook.** The two most famous houses of worship—gargantuan **St. Paul's** (p. 182) and ancient **Westminster Abbey** (p. 135)—demand several hours each.

Everything that ever was is technically history. By this criterion all of London is **His-toric London**—but not all of it is interesting. London fortunately has much history which is interesting. History buffs should begin their travels at the **Museum of Lon-don** (see p. 225) which gives an engaging account of the city's past. The **Tower of London**'s walls have borne witness to much of the City's, and country's, turbulent past—from Guinivere's flight from an oversexed Mordred to the murder of the young Princes (p. 184). **Westminster Abbey** (p. 135) is the national repository of famous British corpses, the closest you may ever be to the great men of history. Today power has shifted from the Royals to the common folk—**Whitehall** (p. 143) and **Parliament** (p. 141) contain the literal seats of power. The **Docklands** (p. 200) and **South Bank** (p. 190) are both massive new building projects; both are designed to represent the London of the Future.

Cultural London may sound forbidding and boring, but it need not be. **Dickens** and **Keats** buffs will want to visit the museums which occupy their idols' former domiciles (see p. 195 for Keats and p. 169 for Dickens). The **British Library's** new digs will showcase rare manuscripts and fascinating exhibits—though completion may be delayed til 1998 and the Library may remain in the **British Museum** (p. 168). London is a world famous **theater** venue (see p. 228). Students especially should take advantage of the many theater discounts.

Finally, London is a mecca for swingers everywhere. In the 1960s, Time magazine dubbed **"Swingin' London"** the center of a debaucherous new youth movement. Today's city guards this hedonistic flame—rave culture began here and London's clubs are second to none. Though pubs close absurdly early, there is more fun to be had after 11am here than almost anywhere on earth (see Nightclubbing, p. 240). **Soho** (p. 150) is center of the night scene—cafés and nightclubs swing like bloody pendulums into the wee hours. **Camden** (p. 162) and **Brixton** (p. 194) rage as well.

■ Touring

> The characteristic of London is that you never go where you wish nor do
> what you wish, and that you always wish to be somewhere else than
> where you are.
>
> —Sydney Smith, 1818

You can begin to familiarize yourself with the eclectic wonders of London through a good city tour. The **Original London Sightseeing Tour** (tel. (0181) 877 1722) provides a convenient, albeit cursory, overview of London's attractions from a double-decker bus. Tours lasting two hours depart from Baker St., Haymarket (near Piccadilly Circus), Marble Arch, Embankment, and near Victoria Station. Route includes views of Buckingham Palace, the Houses of Parliament, Westminster Abbey, the Tower of London, St. Paul's, and Piccadilly Circus. A ticket allows you to ride the buses for a 24-hour period—permitting visitors to hop off at major sights and hop on a later bus to finish the tour. Other companies have a hop-on hop-off policy, but be sure to ask how often buses circle through the route—Original London coaches come every five to 10 minutes (tours daily 9am-5:30pm, £10, under 16 £5).

Walking tours can fill in the specifics of London that bus tours run right over. With a good guide, a tour can be as entertaining as it is informative. Among the best are **The Original London Walks** (tel. 624 3978; £4.50, students £3.50, accompanied children under 15 free) which cover a specific topic such as Legal London, Jack the Ripper, or Spies and Spycatchers. The two-hour tours are led by well regarded guides; many consider this company to be the best in London. **Historical Tours of London** (tel. (0181) 668 4019; £4.50, concessions £3.50) also leads popular tours. Leaflets for these and others are available in hotels and tourist information centers. For meeting times, see the "Around Town" section of *Time Out* magazine.

If glancing at London from the top of a bus is unsatisfactory and hoofing it seems daunting, a tour led by **The London Bicycle Tour Company** (tel. 928 6838) may be the happy medium. They offer a Sunday tour of the East End. It departs from Gabriel's Wharf, 56 Upper Ground, SE1 (Easter-Oct. Sat and Sun. 2pm; approximately 3½hr.; £10, independent bike £8/day; ask about student discount; tube: Waterloo.)

The double-decker **Bus 11** (which is free to Travelcard holders, otherwise standard bus fare) cruises between the city's main sights. It is a very affordable alternative to the commercial tour buses, though it doesn't feature the commercial tour guides' somewhat engaging chatter. The 11 chugs between Chelsea, Sloane Sq., Victoria Station, Westminster Abbey and Houses of Parliament, Whitehall, Trafalgar Sq., St. Paul's, and various stops in the City.

■ Westminster Abbey

> Think how many royal bones
> Sleep within this heap of stones;
> For here they lie, had realms and lands,
> That now want strength to stir their hands.
>
> —Francis Beaumont

Neither a cathedral nor a parish church, Westminster Abbey (tube: Westminster) is a "royal peculiar," controlled directly by the Crown and outside the jurisdiction of the

SIGHTS

Church of England. As both the site of every royal coronation since 1066 and the final resting place for an imposing assortment of sovereigns, politicians, poets, and artists, the Abbey's significance extends far beyond the religious. Westminster today functions as a hybrid national church and honor roll (as well as an important magnet for tourism). Burial in the abbey is the greatest and rarest of honors in Britain—over the last 200 years, space has become so limited that many coffins stand upright under the pavement. Residents have not been known to complain.

Although the Abbey was consecrated by King Edward the Confessor on December 28, 1065, only the Pyx Chamber and the Norman Undercroft (now the Westminster Abbey Treasure Museum, see below) survive from the original structure. Most of the present Abbey was erected under the direction of Henry III during the 13th century. However, what we see today is not Henry's legacy either—most of the stone visible in the Abbey today is actually refacing that dates from the 18th century. The stones which make the two **West Front Towers,** designed and built by Sir Christopher Wren and his Baroque pupil, Nicholas Hawksmoor, are of similar vintage. The North Entrance, completed after 1850, is the youngest part of the Abbey. The entrance's Victorian stonework includes carved figures of dragons and griffins. Work on the cathedral has continued into this decade—1995 saw an end to over 22 years of cleaning the Abbey's soot-stained stones.

In the Abbey's narrow **nave,** the highest in all of England, a slab of Belgian marble marks the **Grave of the Unknown Warrior.** Here the body of a World War I soldier is buried in soil from the bloody battlefields of France. A piece of green marble engraved with the words "Remember Winston Churchill" sits nearby, rather than among fellow prime ministers in Statesmen's Aisle. Parliament placed it here 25 years after the Battle of Britain, perhaps prompted by pangs of regret that Churchill's body lay buried in Bladon and not in the Abbey's hall of fame.

At the foot of the **Organ Loft,** found in the crossing, a memorial to Sir Isaac Newton sits next to the grave of Lord Kelvin. Franklin Roosevelt, David Lloyd George, Lord and Lady Baden-Powell of Boy Scout fame, and the presumptive David Livingstone are remembered in the nave. "Rare Ben Jonson" is buried upright; on his deathbed he proclaimed, "Six feet long by two feet wide is too much for me. Two feet by two feet will do for all I want." On the hour, the Dean of the Abbey climbs the stairs of the pulpit and offers a prayer for his distinguished captive audience.

To see rest of the abbey, referred to as the **Royal Chapels,** visitors must enter through a gate at the end of the north aisle of the nave and pay admission (see below). Visitors follow a route through the Royal Chapels which passes the monuments in the order described *passim.* **Musicians' Aisle,** just beyond this gate, contains the Abbey's most accomplished organists, John Blow and Henry Purcell, as well as memorials to Elgar, Britten, Vaughan Williams, and William Walton.

The cluttered **Statesmen's Aisle,** in the early Gothic north transept, has the most eclectic group of memorials. Prime Ministers Disraeli and Gladstone couldn't stand each other in life, but in death their figures symmetrically flank a large memorial to Sir Peter Warren, alongside Peel, Castlereagh, Palmerston, and others. Sir Francis Vere's Elizabethan tomb in the southeast corner of the transept features the cracked shells of his armor held above his body. A strange paving stone in front of the memorial bears no exalted name, only the strange inscription, "Stone coffin underneath."

The **High Altar,** directly south of the north transept, has been the scene of coronations and royal weddings since 1066. Anne of Cleves, Henry VIII's fourth wife, lies in a tomb on the south side of the sanctuary, just before the altar. A series of crowded choir chapels fills the space east of the north transept.

Beyond these chapels stands the **Chapel of Henry VII** (built 1503-12), perhaps England's most outstanding piece of the period. Every one of its magnificently carved wooden stalls, reserved for the Knights of the Order of the Bath, features a colorful headpiece bearing the chosen personal statement of its occupant. The lower sides of the seats, which fold up to support those standing during long services, were the only part of the design left to the carpenters' discretion; they feature cartoon-like images of wives beating up their husbands and other pagan stories. Lord Nelson's

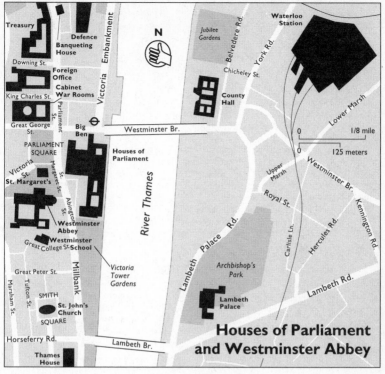

Houses of Parliament and Westminster Abbey

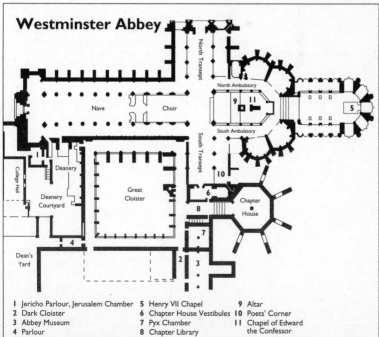

Westminster Abbey

1 Jericho Parlour, Jerusalem Chamber
2 Dark Cloister
3 Abbey Museum
4 Parlour
5 Henry VII Chapel
6 Chapter House Vestibules
7 Pyx Chamber
8 Chapter Library
9 Altar
10 Poets' Corner
11 Chapel of Edward the Confessor

stall was no. 20, on the south side. Latter-day members of the order include Americans Ronald Reagan and Norman Schwarzkopf. The chapel walls sport 95 saints, including the once-lovely Bernadette, who grew a beard overnight after praying to be saved from a multitude of suitors. The chapel's elaborate ceiling was hand-carved after it had been erected. Henry VII and his wife Elizabeth lie at the very end of the chapel. Charles II exhumed Oliver Cromwell's body from this part of the Abbey in 1661 then had the corpse hanged, beheaded, and left to rot on a post outside. Today a simpler and more tasteful memorial to Cromwell remains. Protestant Queen Elizabeth I (in the north aisle) and the Catholic cousin she had beheaded, Mary, Queen of Scots (in the south aisle), are buried on opposite sides of the Henry VII chapel. Both, the verger insists, "put Britain back on its feet again."

The **Royal Air Force (RAF) Chapel,** at the far east end, commemorates the Battle of Britain. A hole in the wall in the northeast corner of the Air Force memorial, damage from a German bomb, has deliberately been left unrepaired. Many may find themselves a little choked up when surrounded by the stained glass panels celebrating the few to whom so many owe so much.

Behind the High Altar, in the **Chapel of St. Edward the Confessor,** rests the Coronation Chair, on which all but two (Edward V and Edward VIII) English monarchs since 1308 have been crowned. The chair rests on the ancient **Stone of Scone** ("skoon"), rumored to be inextricably linked to the government of Britain. The legendary stone (some say it was the biblical Jacob's pillow) was used in the coronation of ancient Scottish kings; James I took it to London to represent the Union, and in the 1950s it was reclaimed for several months by daring Scottish nationalists (see "Stoned," below). During WWII, it was hidden from possible capture by Hitler—rumor has it that only Churchill, Roosevelt, the Prime Minister of Canada, and the two workers who moved the stone knew of its whereabouts. The chair sits next to the 7ft.-long State Sword and the shield of Edward III. On July 4, 1996 Prime Minister Major announced that—700 years after being taken from Scotland —the stone will return home and visit the Abbey only for coronations.

Numerous monarchs are interred in the chapel, from Henry III (d. 1272) to George II (d. 1760). Edward I had himself placed in an unsealed crypt here, in case he was needed again to fight the Scots; his mummy was carried as a standard by the English army as it tried to conquer Scotland. An engraving by William Blake commemorates the moment in 1774 when the Royal Society of Antiquaries opened this coffin in order to assess the body's state of preservation. Sick persons hoping to be cured would spend nights at the base of the Shrine of St. Edward the Confessor, at the center of the chapel. The king purportedly wielded healing powers during his life and dispensed free medical care to hundreds.

Visitors uninterested in the graves of arcane English monarchs may find the names on the graves and plaques in the **Poets' Corner** more compelling. This shrine celebrates those who've died, been canonized, and later anthologized. It begins with Geoffrey Chaucer, who was originally buried in the abbey in 1400—the short Gothic tomb you see today in the east wall of the transept was not erected until 1556. The lower classes of the dead poets' society, and those leading "unconventional" lifestyles, often had to wait a while before getting a permanent spot in the Abbey; even the Bard remained on the waiting list until 125 years after his mortal coil was shuffled off. Oscar Wilde was honored with a long overdue monument in Poet's Corner in 1995, the centenary of his conviction for homosexual activities. Floor panels commemorate Tennyson, T.S. Eliot, Dylan Thomas, Henry James, Lewis Carroll, Lord Byron, W.H. Auden, and poets of World War I, all at the foot of Chaucer's tomb. Each one bears an appropriate description or image for puzzle solvers: D.H. Lawrence's publishing mark (a phoenix) or T.S. Eliot's symbol of death.

The south wall bears tributes to Edmund Spenser and John Milton. A partition wall divides the south transept, its east side graced with the graves of Samuel Johnson and actor David Garrick, its west side with busts of William Wordsworth, Samuel Taylor Coleridge, and Robert Burns, in addition to a full-length William Shakespeare which overshadows the tiny plaques memorializing the Brontë sisters. On the west wall of the transept, Handel's massive memorial looms over his grave next to the resting place of prolific Charles Dickens. On this side of the wall, you'll also find the grave of Rudyard Kipling and a memorial to that morbid Dorset farm boy, Thomas Hardy. Two non-wordsmiths are inexplicably included here: Old Parr, who reportedly lived to the age of 152, and "Spot" Ward, who once healed George II of a thumb injury.

The Abbey's tranquil **cloister** reposes in a special peace of its own. The entrance in the northeast corner dates from the 13th century, the rest of it from the 14th. The **Chapter House,** east down a passageway off the cloister, has one of the best-preserved medieval tile floors in Europe. The windows in the ceiling depict scenes from the Abbey's history. The King's Great Council used the room as its chamber in 1257 and the House of Commons used it as a meetingplace in the 16th century. Even today, the government and not the abbey administers the Chapter House and the adjacent **Pyx Chamber,** once the Royal Treasury and now a plate museum.

Royal effigies (used instead of actual corpses for lying-in-state ceremonies) rest in the **Westminster Abbey Treasure Museum.** The oldest, that of Edward III, has a lip permanently warped by the stroke that killed him. Those who knew Admiral Nelson found his effigy almost supernaturally accurate—perhaps because his mistress arranged his hair. The museum also includes an exhibit on the history of the Abbey as well as some historical oddities, including a Middle English lease to Chaucer and the much-abused sword of Henry V. (Chapter House and Pyx Chamber open 10:30am-4pm. Admission £2.50, concessions £1.90.)

Enter through the cloisters on Great College St. to visit the 900-year-old **College Garden,** the oldest garden in England. (Open April-Sept. Tues. and Thurs. 10am-6pm; Oct.-March Tues. and Thurs. 10am-4pm. Admission 20p. Concerts on Thurs. during July-Aug. 12:30-2pm.)

Those who enjoy amazingly informative discussions about architecture, fun gossip about the dead, and just a little sermonizing should take the excellent, all-inclusive Abbey Guided Super Tour (1½hr., £7), which takes visitors to otherwise inaccessible

Stoned

On Christmas Day, 1950, daring Scottish patriot Ian Hamilton—posing as a visitor—hid himself in Westminster Abbey until it closed. He meant to steal the 200-kg Stone of Scone and return it to Scotland. As he approached the door near Poet's Corner to let in his three accomplices, a night watchman detected his presence inside the Abbey. Hamilton (now a prominent Scottish MP) talked fast enough to convince the watchman that he had involuntarily been locked in.

That same night the foursome forcibly entered the Abbey and pulled the stone out of its wooden container. In removing it, they inadvertently broke the famed rock into two uneven pieces. Hamilton sent his girlfriend, Kay, driving off to Scotland with the smaller piece, while he returned to deal with the larger piece. The remaining two accomplices had been instructed to drag the larger piece towards the cars, but when he returned Hamilton found only the stone and no sign of his buddies. He lugged the piece to his car, and, while driving out of London, happened across his wayward accomplices.

Unfortunately, the car's engine could not handle the weight, and the three were forced to ditch the stone in a field. Returning two weeks later to recover the stone, Hamilton found the site guarded by gypsies. To take the stone across the border into Scotland, he agreed to join the gypsy troupe.

The stone was repaired in a Glasgow workyard, but the patriots were frustrated that they could not display their nationalistic symbol in a public place. On April 11, 1951 Hamilton & Co. carried the stone to the altar at Arbroath Abbey where it was discovered and returned to England.

The final chapter of the story is that now-deceased Glasgow councilor Bertie Gray claimed, before he died, that the stone was copied and that the stone currently in Westminster Abbey is a fake. The British authorities dispute his claim.

SIGHTS

parts of the Abbey. (Tours depart from the Enquiry Desk in the nave Mon.-Thurs. at 10, 10:30, 11am, 2, 2:30, and 3pm; Fri. at 10, 11am, 2, and 3pm; Sat. at 10, 11am, and 12:30pm.) To book one, inquire at the Abbey desk, call 222 7110, or (if you want to be absolutely sure) write to Super Tours, 20 Dean's Yard, SW1P 3PA. Portable tape-recorded commentaries in assorted tongues are available for £6. (Westminster Abbey nave open Mon.-Sat. 7:30am-6pm, Wed. also 6-7:45pm, Sun. in between services; free. Royal chapels (most of the Abbey) open Mon.-Fri. 9am-4:45pm, Wed. also 6-7:45pm, Sat. 9am-2:45pm and 3:45-5:45pm; last admission to royal Chapels 1hr. before closing (7:15pm on Wed.); admission £4, concessions £2, children £1; **photography** permitted Wed. 6-7:45pm only; on Wed. the last admission to the Royal Chapels is at 7:15pm and costs only £2, concessions £1.)

Music lovers can catch **Evensong** which is sung at 5pm on weekdays (except Wed. when it is said) and 3pm on weekends. Organ recitals are given on Tuesday during the summer at 6:30pm (£5, concessions £3; call 222-5152 or write the Concert Secretary, 20 Dean's Yard, SW1P 3PA.)

■ Westminster

The old city of Westminster, now a borough of London, once served as haven to a seething nest of criminals seeking sanctuary in the Abbey. A slum clearance program during Victoria's reign transformed the region into the array of brick and marble it is today. For the past 1000 years, Westminster has been the center of political and religious power in England. On weekdays, the streets still bear the traffic of civil service workers, who desert the high-rise canyons on weekends, leaving it to the crowds of tourists who flock here to see some of London's more monumental architecture.

In the literal shadow of Westminster Abbey, **St. Margaret's** is the church which tourists point to and say "Is that the Abbey?" in surprised tones, until the more imposing Abbey which sits behind become visible. St. Margaret's has served as the parish church of the House of Commons since 1614, when Protestant MPs feared Westminster Abbey was about to become Catholic. John Milton, Samuel Pepys, and Winston Churchill were married here. The stained-glass window to the north of the entrance depicts a blind Milton dictating *Paradise Lost* to one of his dutiful daughters, while the stunning east window, made in Holland in 1501, honors the marriage of Catherine of Aragon to Prince Arthur. The post-WWII John Piper windows on the south side provide a marked contrast; entitled "Spring in London," they are appropriately composed in shades of gray. Beneath the high altar lies the headless body of Sir Walter Raleigh, who was executed across the street in 1618. The inscription on his memorial respectfully asks readers not to "reflect on his errors." (Open daily 9:30am-5pm when services are not being held.)

On the south side of the abbey cluster the buildings of the hoity-toity **Westminster School,** founded as a part of the Abbey. References to the school date as far back as the 14th century, but Queen Elizabeth officially founded it in 1560. The arch in Dean's Yard is pitted with the carved initials of England's most privileged schoolboys, among them Ben Jonson, John Dryden, John Locke, and Christopher Wren.

The 14th-century **Jewel Tower,** a surviving tower of the medieval Westminster Palace, stands by the southeastern end of the Abbey, across from the Houses of Parliament. Formerly Parliament's outsized filing cabinet, and later the Weights and Measures office, it now contains eclectic exhibits ranging from bits of the original Westminster Hall to a Norman sword dredged from the moat. The moat, as it happens, was built for protection in less stable days but also to provide fish for the king's table. (Tower open April-Sept. daily 10am-1pm and 2-6pm; Oct.-March 10am-1pm and 2-4pm. Admission £1.50, concessions £1.10.)

The **Victoria Tower Gardens,** a narrow spit of land along the Thames immediately south of the Houses of Parliament, offers a pleasant view of the river. Militant suffragettes Emmeline Pankhurst and her daughter are memorialized in the northwest corner of the gardens. In the center is Auguste Rodin's famous *The Burghers of Calais.* Just northeast of the Houses of Parliament, a dramatic statue of Boudicca commands attention at the corner of Victoria Embankment and Bridge Street. Immortalized for your viewing pleasure, the valiant Queen Boudicca led the local Iceni tribe in an English revolt against the Romans in 60 AD.

Four assertive corner towers distinguish former church **St. John the Evangelist,** now a chamber music concert hall in nearby Smith Square, off Millbank at the south end of the Victoria Tower Gardens. Queen Anne, whose imagination was taxed by her leading role in the design of 50 new churches, supposedly upended a footstool and told Thomas Archer to build the church in its image. Dickens likened Archer's effort to a "petrified monster." Chamber music, choral, and orchestral concerts take place daily; tickets range from £4-15, with concessions starting as low as £3. (Box office tel. 222 1061; call ahead for details and concert times.) Any flurry of activity around the square is likely to be connected with no. 31, where the **Central Office of the Conservative Party** lurks, ready to swing into re-action down the road in Parliament.

At Ashley Place, a few blocks down Victoria St. from Westminster proper is **Westminster Cathedral.** Not to be confused with the Anglican abbey, the Cathedral is the headquarters of the Roman Catholic church in Britain. The architecture is Christian Byzantine, in pointed contrast to the Gothic abbey. The structure was completed in 1903, but the interior has yet to be finished, and the blackened brick of the domes contrasts dramatically with the swirling marble of the lower walls. A lift carries visitors to the top of the rocket-like, striped brick bell tower for a decent view of the Houses of Parliament, the river, and Kensington. (Lift open daily 9am-5pm. Admission to lift £2, concessions £1, families £5. Cathedral open daily 7am-7pm. Cathedral admission is free.)

■ The Houses of Parliament

The Houses of Parliament (tube: Westminster), oft-imagined in foggy silhouette against the Thames, have become London's visual trademark (check out the front cover of this book for an example). For the classic view captured by Claude Monet, walk about halfway over Westminster Bridge, preferably at dusk. Like the government offices along Whitehall, the Houses of Parliament occupy the former site of a royal palace. Only Jewel Tower (see Westminster, p. 140) and Westminster Hall (to the left of St. Stephen's entrance on St. Margaret St.) survive from the original palace, which was destroyed by a fire on October 16, 1834. **Sir Charles Barry** and **A.W.N. Pugin** won a competition for the design of the new houses. From 1840 to 1888, Barry built a hulking, symmetrical block that Pugin ornamented with tortured imitations of late medieval decoration—"Tudor details on a classic body," Pugin later sneered, before dying of insanity.

The immense complex blankets eight acres and includes more than 1000 rooms and 100 staircases. Space is nevertheless so inadequate that Members of Parliament (MPs) cannot have private offices or staff, and the archives—the original copies of every Act of Parliament passed since 1497—are stuffed into **Victoria Tower,** the large tower to the south. A flag flown from the tower (a signal light after dusk) indicates that Parliament is in session.

Much like Charlie from *Charlie's Angels,* you can hear **Big Ben** but you can't see him; he's actually neither the northernmost tower nor the clock but the 14-ton bell that tolls the hours. Ben is most likely named after the robustly proportioned Sir Benjamin Hall, who served as Commissioner of Works when the bell was cast and hung in 1858. Over the years Big Ben (the bell) has developed a crack. Each of the Roman numerals on the clock face measures 2 ft. in length; the minute hands, 14 ft. The mechanism moving the hands is still wound manually. The familiar 16-note tune that precedes the top-of-the-hour toll is a selection from Handel's *Messiah.*

Unfortunately, access to Westminster Hall and the Houses of Parliament has been restricted since a bomb killed an MP in 1979. To get a **guided tour** (Mon.-Thurs.) or a seat at **Question Time** when the Prime Minister attends (Tues. and Thurs. 3:15-3:30pm), you need to obtain tickets—available on a limited basis from your embassy—or an introduction from an MP. Because demand for these tickets is extremely high, the most likely way of getting into the building is to queue for a seat at a debate when Parliament is in session. As a rough guide, the Houses are not in session during Easter week, summer recess (late July to mid-Oct.), and a three-week winter recess during Christmas time.

However, tours for overseas visitors can also be arranged by sending a written request to the Public Information Office, 1 Derby Gate, Westminster, SW1. The **House of Commons Visitors' Gallery** (for "Distinguished and Ordinary Strangers") is open during extraordinary hours (Mon.-Thurs. 2:30-10pm, Fri. 9:30am-3pm and recently Wed. 9:30am-close of business). The **House of Lords Visitors' Gallery** is often easier to access (open Mon.-Wed. 2:30pm-late, Thurs. 3pm-late, and occasionally Fri. 11am-4pm), though the Lords perform, ahem…, less important work for the country. These hours are very rough guidelines—the MPs leave when they're done with business and begin when they feel like it. Visitors should arrive early and be prepared to wait in the long queues by St. Stephen's Gate (on the left for Commons, on the right for Lords; free). Those willing to sacrifice the roar of the debate for smaller, more focused business can attend meetings of any of the various committees by jumping the queue and going straight up to the entrance. For times of committee meetings each week, call the House of Commons Information Office (tel. 219 4272). Both houses' business is announced daily in the major newspapers and in a weekly schedule by St. Stephen's Gate.

After entering St. Stephen's Gate and submitting to an elaborate security check, you will be standing in **St. Stephen's Hall.** This chapel is where the House of Commons used to sit. In the floor are four brass markers where the Speaker's Chair stood. Charles I, in his ill-fated attempt to arrest five MPs, sat here in the place of the Speaker in 1641. No sovereign has entered the Commons since.

To the left from the Central Lobby are the **Chambers of the House of Commons.** Destroyed during the Blitz, the rebuilt chamber is modest, even anticlimactic. Most traditional features still remain, such as two red lines fixed two sword-lengths apart, which (for safety's sake) debating members may not cross. The Government party (the party with the most MPs in the House) sits to the Speaker's right, and the Opposition sits to his left. There are not enough benches in the chamber to seat all 650 members, which adds a sense of huddled drama to the few occasions when all are present. Members vote by filing into **division lobbies** parallel to the chamber: ayes to the west, nays to the east.

To enter the Lords' Gallery, go back through the Central Lobby and pass through the Peers' corridor—never passing up a chance to gloat, the MPs have bedecked the passage with scenes of Charles I's downfall. The ostentation of the **House of Lords,** dominated by the sovereign's Throne of State under a gilt canopy, contrasts with the sober, green-upholstered Commons' Chamber. Elaborate wall carvings divert attention from the speakers on the floor. The Lord Chancellor presides over the House from his seat on the **Woolsack,** stuffed with wool from all nations of the Kingdom and Commonwealth—harking back to a time when wool, like the Lords, was more vital to Britain. The woolsack may first appear to be a small white pillow on the throne where no one sits, but actually it's the red behemoth the size of a Volkswagen bug. The poor Lord Chancellor looks lost on this huge wash of red, propped up only by a small, insufficient pillow. Next to him rests the almost 6-ft. **Mace** which is brought in to open the House each morning.

Outside the Houses is the **Old Palace Yard,** site of the untimely demises of Sir Walter Raleigh and the Gunpowder Plotter Guy Fawkes (the palace's cellars are still ceremonially searched before every opening of Parliament). To the north squats **Westminster Hall** (rebuilt around 1400), where high treason trials, including those of Thomas More, Fawkes, and Charles I, were held until 1825. The **New Palace Yard** is a good place to espy your favorite MPs as they enter the complex through the Members' entrance just north of Westminster Hall.

▓ Whitehall

Whitehall was born in 1245 as York Place, residence for the Archbishops of York. Cardinal Wolsey enlarged York Place into a palace he thought fit for a king. Henry VIII agreed and later moved into his new London apartments of state, rechristened Whitehall, in 1530. This gargantuan palace stretched all the way to Somerset House on the Strand, but William II resented an unnamed diplomat's description of Whitehall as "the biggest, most hideous place in all Europe," and relocated to a shiny new Kensington Palace. The rejected palace burned in 1698, and since then "Whitehall" (tube: Westminster or Charing Cross), stretching from Parliament St. to Trafalgar Sq., has become the home and a synonym for the British civil service.

Conveniently enough, **Ten Downing Street** lies just steps up Parliament St. from the Houses. Sir George Downing, ex-Ambassador to The Hague (and the second person to graduate from Harvard College), built this house in 1681. Prime Minister Sir Robert Walpole, who is best remembered for his role in a series of vicious political satires, made it his official residence in 1732. The exterior of "Number Ten" is decidedly unimpressive, especially from a distance, but behind the famous door spreads an extensive political network. The Chancellor of the Exchequer forecasts economic recovery from No. 11 Downing St. and the Chief Whip of the House of Commons plans Party campaigns at No. 12. Visitors have long been banned from entering Downing St.

The **Cabinet War Rooms** lurk at the end of King Charles St., near Horse Guards Rd. (see Museums, p. 223). The formal **Cenotaph** honoring the war dead, usually decked with wreaths, stands where Parliament St. turns into Whitehall.

Just off Whitehall, at 6 Derby Gate, **New Scotland Yard** will probably fall short of crime-hounds' expectations. The second of three incarnations of the lair of those unimaginative detectives humbled by Sherlock Holmes and Hercule Poirot is nothing more than two buildings connected by an arch that currently contain government offices. The original Yard was at the top of Whitehall, on Great Scotland Yard, and the current New Scotland Yard is on Victoria St.

Henry VIII's **wine cellar** was one of the few parts of the palace spared in the fire of 1698. In 1953, the government erected the massive Ministry of Defense Building (nicknamed the Quadragon) just to the north, over Henry's cache. The cellar had to be relocated deeper into the ground to accommodate the new structure. Technically, visitors may view the cellar, but permission is dauntingly difficult to obtain (apply in writing to the Department of the Environment or the Ministry of Defense with a compelling story). Near the statue of General Gordon in the gardens behind the Ministry of Defense Building, you'll find the remnants of Queen Mary's terrace, built for Queen Mary II. The bottom of the steps leading from the terrace mark the 17th-century water level, reminding observers of the extent to which river transport determined the locations of 16th- and 17th-century buildings.

The 1622 **Banqueting House** (corner of Horse Guards Ave. and Whitehall), one of the few intact masterpieces of Inigo Jones, drips with beauty and irony, recalling the tumultuous times of the Stuart monarchy. James I and Charles I held feasts and staged elaborate masques, thinly-disguised pieces of theatrical propaganda, in the main hall. The 60ft.-high ceiling was commissioned by Charles I; the scenes Ruebens painted are allegorical representations of the divine strength of the English monarch. But not even the hall's considerable beauty could quell the cries of Cromwell's men. The party ended on January 27, 1649 when King Charles I, draped in black velvet, stepped out of a first floor window to the scaffold where he was beheaded. The weather vane on the roof tells another tale of Stuart misfortune— James II placed it there to see if the wind was favorable for his rival to the throne William of Orange's voyage from the Netherlands. From 1724 to 1890, the Banqueting House served as a Chapel Royal. These days the hall sees no executions, just harmless state dinners (behind bulletproof glass) and the occasional concert (tel. 930 4179; open Mon.-Sat. 10am-5pm, last admit 4:30; closed for government functions; admission £3, concessions £2.25, children £2.).

For folks who can't get enough of mounted, betassled guards, another battery of the **Queen's Life Guard** mark time on the west side of Whitehall north of Downing St. Monday to Saturday at 11am and Sunday at 10am, the arrival of more mounted troops, lots of barking in incoherent English, and shuffling horses mark Whitehall's **Changing of the Guard,** a less crowded and impressive version of the Buckingham Palace spectacle (see Buckingham Palace, p. 145). Daily at 4pm, the barking occurs again, this time accompanied by dismounting and strutting, and is called the **Inspection of the Guard.** The Changing and Inspection don't occur on June Saturdays, when the Guard is gearing up for Trooping the Colour (below). Note that many of the guards now wear UN medals after having served in Bosnia in 1995; the Queen's Cavalry serve six-month tours of duty with UN peace-keeping forces. Through the gates lies Horse Guards Parade, a large court (opening onto St. James's Park) from which the bureaucratic array of different architectural styles that make up Whitehall can be seen. The **Armistice Day Parade** (closest Sun. to Nov. 11) and the **Belgian Army Veteran's Parade** (closest Sun. to July 15) are launched annually from this sight. In addition, **Beating the Retreat,** a must for lovers of pomp and circumstance, takes place here June 4-5, 1997 (call 414 2271 for dates and ticket information). Beating the Retreat is merely a warm-up for **Trooping the Colour,** in which the Queen gives the royal salute to the Root Guards. Trooping the Colour takes place on June 14, 1997.

■ The Mall and St. James's

Just north of Buckingham Palace and the Mall, up Stable Yard or Marlborough Rd., stands **St. James's Palace,** the residence of the monarchy from 1660 to 1668 and again from 1715 to 1837 (tube: Green Park). The scene of many a three-volume novel and Regency romance, over the years this palace has hosted tens of thousands of the young girls whose families "presented" them at Court. Ambassadors and the elite set of barristers known as "Queen's Counsel" are still received "into the Court of St. James's." Only Henry VIII's gateway and clock tower and a pair of parading guards at the foot of St. James's St. still hark back to the Tudor palace; the guards' bayoneted rifles are a little too modern for comfort.

Today the Queen Mum inhabits St. James, where she can keep a motherly eye on her daughter, the Queen, who bunks just down the road at Buckingham. St. James's Palace is closed to the public, except for Inigo Jones's **Queen's Chapel,** built in 1626, which is open for Sunday services at 8:30 and 11am (Oct.-July). King Charles I slept for four hours in the palace's guardroom before crossing St. James's Park to be executed at the Banqueting House (see Whitehall, p. 135).

Henry VIII declared **St. James's Park** London's first royal park in 1532. The fenced-off peninsula at the east end of the park's pond, **Duck Island,** is the mating ground for thousands of waterfowl. St. James's is also a good place to discover that lawn chairs in England are not free—chairs have been hired out here since the 18th century (rental 70p for a 4-hr. sit, don't find the attendants, just sit and they'll find you). For a good view of the guards who change at Buckingham Palace, wait between the Victoria Memorial and St. James's Palace from about 10:40 to 11:25am. You might miss the band (it usually travels down Birdcage walk from Wellington Barracks), but you will also avoid the swarm of tourists.

The high-rent district around the palace has also taken the moniker St. James's. Bordered by St. James's Park and Green Park to the south and Piccadilly to the north, it begins at an equestrian statue of notorious madman George III on Cockspur St. off Trafalgar Sq. **St. James's Street,** next to St. James's Palace, runs into stately **Pall Mall** (both rhyme with "pal")—the name derives from "pail-mail," a 17th-century predecessor of croquet. Until Buckingham Palace was built, today's **Mall** was merely an endless playing field for the King. Lined with double rows of plane trees, the Mall grandly traverses the space from Trafalgar Sq. to Buckingham Palace (tube: Charing Cross). Two monuments to Queen Victoria contribute to the Mall's grandeur: the golden horses of the **Queen Victoria Memorial,** near Buckingham Palace, and the massive **Admiralty Arch** opening onto Trafalgar Sq.

Along the north side of the Mall lie the imposing façades of grand houses, starting with **Carlton House Terrace,** demolished, rebuilt, and remodeled since John Nash erected it along the Mall as part of the 18th-century Regent's Park route; the statue on the terrace memorializes the "Grand Old Duke of York." The building became the office of the Free French Forces from 1940 to 1945 under the leadership of General Charles de Gaulle. It now contains the Royal Society of Distinguished Scientists and, the area's newest and most attention-grabbing neighbor, the *avant-garde* **Institute of Contemporary Arts** (see Museums, p. 214, Film, p. 233, and Theatre, p. 228). The hipper-than-thou ICA was established in 1947 to provide British artists with the kinds of resources and facilities then available only at the Museum of Modern Art in New York and has been located in Carlton House since 1968.

Pall Mall and St. James's St., together with **Jermyn Street,** parallel to Pall Mall to the north, flank the traditional stomping grounds of the upper-class English clubman. At 70-72 Jermyn he will buy his shirts from Turnbull and Asser (one of Churchill's custom-made "siren suits" is on display). His bowler will be from Lock & Co. Hatters (ask politely to see their sinister-looking head measuring device), and his bespoke shoes will be the craft of John Lobb. Berry & Co. wine merchants supply the madeira, and Cuban cigars should really be bought at Robert Lewis, where Churchill indulged his habit for 60 years. "I am the sort of man easily pleased by the best of everything," claimed Sir Winston. Revel in the patrician solemnity of the area at **Alfred Dunhill,** 30 Duke Street (entrance on Jermyn)—lurking upstairs above the staid merchandise is a riotously sublime collection of smoking vessels from the world over (tel. 499 9566; open Mon.-Sat. 9:30am-6pm).

These Regency storefronts rub elbows with a number of famous London coffeehouses-turned-clubs. The coffeehouses of the early 18th century, whose political life was painted vividly by Addison and Steele in their journal *The Spectator,* were transformed by the 19th century into exclusive clubs for political and literary men of a particular social station. The chief Tory club, the Carlton, at 69 St. James's St., was bombed by the IRA not long ago. The chief Liberal club, the Reform at 104 Pall Mall, served as a social center of Parliamentary power. In 1823, a Prime Minister and the presidents of the Royal Academy and the Royal Society founded the Athenaeum, on Waterloo Pl., for scientific, literary, and artistic men. Gibbon, Hume, and Garrick belonged to the Whig Brooks, founded in 1764 (60 St. James's St.).

Around the corner from St. James's Palace stand royal medallists Spink's, and Christie, Manson, and Wodds Fine Art Auctioneers—better known as **Christie's,** 8 King St. (tel. 839 9060; tube: Green Park). The pamphlets describing the furniture, historical documents, and artworks being auctioned are lovely but cost £6-27. Auctions, open to the public, are held most weekdays at 10:30am. Amuse yourself on a rainy afternoon by watching the dealers do their bidding.

Between aristocratic Jermyn St. and Piccadilly, you can enter **St. James's Church** (tube: Green Park or Piccadilly Circus), a postwar reconstruction by Sir Albert Richardson of what Wren considered his best parish church. The work of Grinling Gibbons, Wren's master-carver, can be seen in the delightful flowers, garlands, and cherubs. Blake was baptized here, which will delight fans of innocence and experience alike.

▓ Buckingham Palace

> I must say, notwithstanding the expense which has been incurred in building the palace, no sovereign in Europe, I may even add, perhaps no private gentleman, is so ill-lodged as the king of this country.
> —Duke of Wellington, 1828

When a freshly crowned Victoria moved from St. James's Palace in 1837, Buckingham Palace, built in 1825 by John Nash, had faulty drains and a host of other leaky difficulties (tube: Victoria, and walk up Buckingham Palace Rd.; Green Park and St. James's Park are also convenient). Home improvements were made, and now, when the flag is flying, the Queen is at home—and you can visit her home.

After a recent debate about the proper way to subsidize the monarchy's senselessly posh existence—spurred by the need for funds to rebuild Windsor castle, which went up in flames in November 1992—Buckingham Palace finally opened to the public. Sort of. The doors were opened for a limited number of years—at press time it was unclear whether this window of opportunity would extend to 1997. Avid Royal-watchers should call Buckingham Palace (tel. 930 4832) to determine whether tours are running during their visit. If available, they will probably take place only in July and August. Not all of the Palace is laid open; the tour is well roped off from the State Rooms—the principal rooms used for ceremonies and official entertaining. But visitors are able to stroll through the Blue Drawing Room, the Throne Room, the Picture Gallery (filled with pictures by Rubens, Rembrandt, and Van Dyck), and the Music Room (where Mendelsohn played for Queen Victoria), as well as other stately rooms.

In the opulent **White Drawing Room,** notice the large mirror to the left of the fireplace; it conceals a door used by the Royal Family to make a grand appearance before formal dinners. Critics of the palace suggest it looks less like the home or even the office of the Queen and more like a museum, thus diminishing much of the excitement of seeing a monarch's digs. Indeed, the monarch scuttles off to Balmoral to avoid the plague of tourists descending upon her immaculate residence.

The 20th-century façade on the Mall is only big, not beautiful—the Palace's best side, the garden front, is seldom seen by ordinary visitors as it is protected by the 40-acre spread where the Queen holds garden parties. The most visible facade is patrolled by a set of very recognizable guards. Their fur hats look as if they were designed for guards with heads four times bigger—but no teasing, the guards carry modern assault rifles with bayonet.

If you happen to visit the palace on an off month, try to catch the chart-topping Kodak Moment for London tourists—the **Changing of the Guard,** which takes place daily from April to late August, and only on alternate days from September to March. This cutback in the winter spectacle is attributed to budget constraints, but is generally interpreted as an attempt on the army's part to manipulate public opinion in favor of increased spending on the military. The "Old Guard" marches from St. James's Palace down the Mall to Buckingham Palace, leaving at approximately 11:10am. The "New Guard" begins marching as early as 10:20am. When they meet at the central gates of the palace, the officers of the regiments then touch hands, symbolically exchanging keys, et voilà—the guard is officially changed. The soldiers gradually split up to relieve the guards currently protecting the palace. The ceremony moves to the beat of royal band music and the menacing clicks of thousands of cameras. In wet weather or on pressing state holidays, the Changing of the Guard does not occur. To witness the spectacle, show up well before 11:30am and stand directly in front of the palace. You can also watch along the routes of the troops prior to their arrival at the palace (10:40-11:25am) between the Victoria Memorial and St. James's Palace or along Birdcage Walk.

In the extravagant **Trooping the Colour** ceremony, held on the Queen's official birthday, June 14, 1997, the colors of a chosen regiment are paraded ceremonially before her and her family. The parade in honor of the Queen brings out luminaries mounted on horses while somewhat less influential types putter about in limousines with little golden crowns on top. The actual ceremony takes place at Horse Guards Parade, followed by a procession down the Mall to the palace, where she reviews her Household Cavalry and appears on the balcony for a Royal Air Force fly-by. The best view of all this is on TV, but you might catch a glimpse of the Queen in person as she rides down the Mall. Tickets for the event must be obtained through the mail. Write well in advance to the Household Division HQ, Horse Guards, SW1. If you don't get a ticket for the event, you should ask for tickets to one of the rehearsals on the two preceding Saturdays. Since the Queen does not need to rehearse, these tend to be noticeably less crowded.

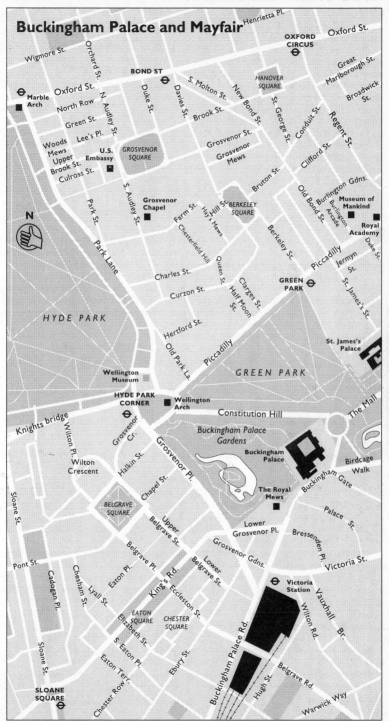

Buckingham Palace and Mayfair

Henrietta Pl.

Wigmore St.

Orchard St.

Oxford St.

OXFORD CIRCUS

Oxford St.

BOND ST

HANOVER SQUARE

Great Marlborough St.

S. Molton St.

Davies St.

New Bond St.

Broadwick St.

Marble Arch

Oxford St.

North Row

Duke St.

Brook St.

St. George St.

Conduit St.

Regent St.

Green St.

N. Audley St.

Grosvenor St.

Bruton St.

Clifford St.

Woods Mews

Lee's Pl.

GROSVENOR SQUARE

Grosvenor Mews

Old Bond St.

Burlington Gdns.

Museum of Mankind

Upper Brook St.

U.S. Embassy

Culross St.

S. Audley St.

Berkeley St.

Burlington Arcade

Royal Academy

Park St.

Grosvenor Chapel

Farm St.

Hay's Hill St.

BERKELEY SQUARE

Piccadilly

Jermyn St.

Duke St.

N

Park Lane

Chesterfield Hill

Charles St.

Queen St.

Clarges St.

GREEN PARK

St. James's St.

HYDE PARK

Curzon St.

Half Moon St.

Hertford St.

Old Park La.

Piccadilly

GREEN PARK

St. James's Palace

Wellington Museum

HYDE PARK CORNER

Wellington Arch

Constitution Hill

The Mall

Knights bridge

Wilton Pl.

Grosvenor Cr.

Grosvenor Pl.

Buckingham Palace Gardens

Buckingham Palace

Birdcage Walk

Wilton Crescent

Halkin St.

Chapel St.

Buckingham Gate

The Royal Mews

Palace St.

Sloane St.

BELGRAVE SQUARE

Upper Belgrave St.

Lower Grosvenor Pl.

Bressenden Pl.

Pont St.

Belgrave Pl.

Eaton Pl.

Lower Belgrave St.

Grosvenor Gdns.

Victoria St.

Cadogan Pl.

Chesham St.

Lyall St.

King's Rd.

Eccleston St.

Victoria Station

Vauxhall Br.

Chesham Pl.

EATON SQUARE

Elizabeth St.

CHESTER SQUARE

Wilton Rd.

Sloane St.

S. Eaton Pl.

Ebury St.

Buckingham Palace Rd.

Hugh St.

Belgrave Rd.

SLOANE SQUARE

Eaton Terr.

Chester Row

Warwick Way

Down the left side of the palace, off Buckingham Gate, an enclosed passageway leads to the **Queen's Gallery.** Selected treasures from the royal collection fill the rooms of this modern suite. The exhibition changes every few months, but you can usually catch a few of Charles I's Italian masters, George IV's Dutch still-lifes, Prince Albert's primitives, and occasionally some Leonardo da Vinci drawings from Windsor. 'Til January 1997 a wonderful display of da Vinci's drawings will be on display. Other planned exhibits include a bit on the young Victoria and Albert. (Open daily 9:30am-4:30pm, last admission 4pm. Admission £3.50, over 60 £2.50, under 17 £2.)

Also off Buckingham Gate stands the curious **Royal Mews Museum** which houses the royal coaches and other historic royal riding implements. (Open Oct.-March Wed. noon-4pm; April-July Tues.-Thurs. noon-4pm; Aug.-Sept. Tues.-Thurs. from 10:30am-4pm. Admission £3.50, under 17 £2, over 60 £2.50, family of 4 £10.) A combined pass for the Gallery and Mews may be purchased (admission £6, under 17 £3, over 60 £4, family of 4 £15).

Nearby, you can drop in on the **Guards Museum** at Wellington Barracks on Birdcage Walk, off Buckingham Gate (open Mon.-Thurs. and Sat.-Sun. 10am-4pm; admission £2, concessions £1). The courtyard outside Wellington Barracks is probably the only place where you'll ever see the Guards at relative ease. Go around 10 or 10:30am and you're likely to see them hanging around preparing for the Changing.

▓ Trafalgar Square and Charing Cross

Unlike many squares in London, **Trafalgar Square** (tube: Charing Cross), sloping down from the National Gallery at the center of a vicious traffic roundabout, has been public land ever since the razing of several hundred houses made way for its construction in the 1830s. **Nelson's Column,** a fluted granite pillar, commands the square, with four majestic, beloved lions guarding the base. The monument and square commemorate Admiral Horatio Nelson, killed during his triumph over Napoleon's navy off Trafalgar (the monument's reliefs were cast from French cannons). Floodlights bathe the square after dark, when it fills up with eager tourists and club kids trying to catch the right night bus home. Enthusiastic, even rambunctious, New Year's celebrations take place here, featuring universal indiscriminate kissing.

At the head of the square squats the ordering façade of the **National Gallery,** Britain's collection of Old Masters (see Museums, p. 216). A competition to design a new extension to the gallery ended in Prince Charles's denouncement of the winning entry as a "monstrous carbuncle" on the face of London and the subsequent selection of a new architect. Philadelphian Robert Venturi's wing to the west of the main building is now open; the mock columns and pillars that echo the old building and even Nelson's Column are much discussed and generally liked.

The church of **St. Martin-in-the-Fields,** on the northeastern corner of the square opposite the National Gallery, dates from the 1720s. Designer James Gibbs topped its templar classicism with a Gothic steeple. The interior, despite the gilded and chubby cherubim, is simple, its walls relatively uncluttered with monuments. St. Martin, which has its own world-renowned chamber orchestra, sponsors lunchtime and evening concerts, as well as a summer festival in mid-July (lunchtime concerts begin 1:05pm; box office in the bookshop open Mon.-Sat. 11:30am-7:30pm, Sun. noon-6pm; phone bookings (tel. 839 8362) Mon.-Fri. 10am-4pm; see Entertainment, p. 235, for more information). The crypt has been cleared of all those dreary coffins to make room for a gallery, a book shop, a brass rubbing center (where you can learn about and actually do your own rubbing), and a café that serves cappuccino with baroque flair (open daily 10am-8pm).

The original **Charing Cross,** last of 13 crosses set up to mark the stages of Queen Eleanor's royal funeral procession in 1291 ("charing" comes from "beloved queen" in French), was actually located at the top of Whitehall, immediately south of the present Trafalgar Square. Like many things, it was destroyed by Cromwell, and a replica now stands outside Charing Cross Station, just uphill from the Victoria Embankment. While the spot is still the geographical center of the city (all distances to

© 1996 AT&T.

Someone back home *really* misses you.
Please call.

With **AT&T Direct**℠ Service it's easy to call back to the States from virtually anywhere your travels take you. Just dial the **AT&T Direct** Access Number for the country *you are in* from the chart below. You'll have English-language voice prompts or an AT&T Operator to guide your call. And our clearest,* fastest connections** will help you reach whoever it is that misses you most back home.

AUSTRIA●◊ 022-903-011	GREECE● 00-800-1311	NETHERLANDS● ...06-022-9111
BELGIUM● 0-800-100-10	INDIA✖..........................000-117	RUSSIA●▲▶ (Moscow).755-5042
CZECH REP▲ 00-42-000-101	IRELAND 1-800-550-000	SPAIN◊ 900-99-00-11
DENMARK................8001-0010	ISRAEL.................177-100-2727	SWEDEN...............020-795-611
FRANCE...............0 800 99 0011	ITALY● 172-1011	SWITZERLAND● ..0-800-550011
GERMANY................0130-0010	MEXICO◊ 95-800-462-4240	U.K.▲ 0800-89-0011

*Non-operator assisted calls to the U.S. only. **Based on customer preference testing. ●Public phones require coin or card deposit. ◊Public phones require local coin payment through call duration. ◊From this country, AT&T Direct calls terminate to designated countries only. ▲May not be available from every phone/pay phone. ✖Not available from public phones. ◊When calling from public phones, use phones marked "Ladatel." ▶Additional charges apply when calling outside of Moscow.

Can't find the Access Number for the country you're calling from? Just ask any operator for AT&T Direct Service.

Greetings from LET'S GO

With pen and notebook in hand, a change of clothes in our backpack, and the tightest of budgets, we've spent our summer roaming the globe in search of travel bargains.

We've put the best of our research into the book that you're now holding. Our intrepid researcher-writers went on the road for months of exploration, from Anchorage to Angkor, Estonia to Ecuador, Iceland to India. Editors worked from spring to fall, massaging copy into witty and informative prose. A brand-new edition of each guide hits the shelves every fall, just months after it is researched, so you know you're getting the most reliable, up-to-date, and comprehensive information available.

We try to make this book an indispensable companion, but sometimes the best discoveries are the ones you make on your own. If you've got something to share, please drop us a line. We're Let's Go Publications, 67 Mount Auburn Street, Cambridge, MA 02138 USA (e-mail: fanmail@letsgo.com). Good luck and happy travels!

London are measured from it), it is no longer the pulsing heart of London life it once was. "Why, Sir, Fleet Street has a very animated appearance," Samuel Johnson once remarked, "but I think the full tide of human existence is at Charing Cross." The full tide of traffic now engulfs the place, and the bronze statue of King Charles drowns in the ebb and flow of automobiles. The statue escaped the cross's fate with the aid of one wily John Rivett. He bought the statue "for scrap" and did a roaring trade in brass souvenirs supposedly made from the melted-down figure; it was in fact hidden and later sold, at a tidy profit, to Charles II.

■ Piccadilly

All of the West End's major arteries—Piccadilly, Regent Street, Shaftesbury Avenue, The Haymarket—merge and swirl around Piccadilly Circus, the bright, gaudy hub of Nash's 19th-century London. Today the Circus earns its place on postcards with lurid neon signs, hordes of tourists, and a fountain topped by a statue everyone calls "Eros," though it was intended to be the Angel of Christian Charity in memory of the Earl of Shaftesbury. Akin to New York's Times Square, Picadilly overflows with glam, glitz, and commerce, but lacks the grit and grime of its American counterpart.

The Circus was ground zero for Victorian popular entertainment, but only the façades of the great music halls remain, propped up against contemporary tourist traps. **London Pavilion,** 1 Piccadilly Circus, is a historic theatre recently converted into a mall (across the street from the Lillywhite's and Sogo stores). Inside the Pavilion lurks the nefarious **Rock Circus** (tel. 734 7203), an ultracheesy waxwork museum and revolving theatre dedicated to the history of rock-and-roll. Elvis, the Beatles, Tina Turner, and, more recently, Jon Bon Jovi and Gloria Estefan, stand among the 50 rock and pop artists eerily recreated as wax effigies. Infrared headsets pick up a CD soundtrack as you wander past each display (open Sun.-Mon.,Wed.-Thurs. 11am-9pm, Tues. noon-9pm, Fri.-Sat. 11am-10pm; admission £7.50, students and seniors £7, children £6, family £20). The massive **Trocadero,** 13 Coventry Street (tel. 439 1791), also specializes in charging hapless tourists exorbitant sums for contrived entertainments. Watch for the virtual reality amusement park **Segaworld,** opening here in late 1996.

For an escape from the world of the gaudy and the touristy, check out Piccadilly, a broad mile-long avenue once lined with aristocratic mansions, stretching from Regent St. in the east to Hyde Park Corner in the west. The name derives from Piccadilly Hall, the 17th-century home of Robert Baker, an affluent tailor who did brisk business in the sale of "pickadills," frilly lace collars that were much in fashion in his day. The only remnant of Piccadilly's stately past is the showy **Burlington House** (across from 185 Piccadilly), built in 1665 for the Earls of Burlington and redesigned in the 18th century by Colin Campbell to accommodate the burgeoning **Royal Academy of Arts** (tel. 439 7438; tube: Piccadilly or Green Park). Founded in 1768, the Academy consists of 40 academicians and 30 associates who administer the exhibition galleries and a massive annual summer show, and maintain a free school of art (see Museums, p. 222). The ambitious **Museum of Mankind** (p. 226) backs onto Burlington House behind the Royal Academy.

An easily overlooked courtyard next to the Academy opens onto the **Albany,** an 18th-century apartment block renowned as one of London's most prestigious addresses. Built in 1771 and remodeled in 1812 to serve as "residential chambers for bachelor gentlemen," the Albany evolved into an exclusive enclave of literary repute. Lord Byron wrote his epic "Childe Harold" here. Other past residents include Macaulay, Gladstone, Canning, "Monk" Lewis, and J.B. Priestley.

Piccadilly continues past imperious Bond Street, past the Ritz Hotel with its distinctive arcade and light-bulb sign, past the Green Park tube station, and past a string of privileged men's clubs on the rim of Green Park. At the gateway of the **Wellington Museum** in **Apsley House,** described by its first owner as "No. 1, London," the avenue merges into the impenetrable Hyde Park corner. Apsley House was built by Robert Adam in the 1780s as the home of the Duke of Wellington.

Running north from Piccadilly Circus are the grand façades of (upper) **Regent Street,** leading to Oxford Circus. The buildings and street were built by John Nash in the early 19th century as part of a processional route for the Prince Regent to follow from St. James's Park through Oxford Circus to his house in Regent's Park. The façades have changed since Nash's time, and today the street is known for the crisp cuts of Burberry raincoats and Aquascutum suits.

■ Soho, Leicester Square, & Chinatown

For centuries, **Soho** was London's red-light district of prostitutes and sex shows. Though most of the prostitutes were forced off the streets by 1959 legislation, the peep shows and porn shops concentrated along Brewer St. and Greek St. honor this licentious tradition. Far from defining its flavor, however, the sex industry adds merely one small ingredient to the cosmopolitan stew which is today's Soho. It's a young and vibrant area with narrow streets lined by cool cafés, classic pubs, unpretentious shops, and theatres. Many Londoners agree that some of the city's best cafés and restaurants (especially for those on a budget who still care how their food tastes) are to be found here.

Loosely bounded by Oxford St. in the north, Shaftesbury Ave. in the south, Charing Cross Rd. in the east, and Regent St. in the west (tube: Leicester Sq., Piccadilly Circus, or Tottenham Ct. Rd.), Soho first emerged as a discrete area in the 1681 with the laying out of **Soho Square,** originally King's Square (tube: Tottenham Ct. Rd., just off of Oxford St.). Grand mansions quickly sprang up as the area became popular with the fashionable set, famous for throwing extravagant parties. By the end of the 18th century, however, the leisure classes had moved out, replaced by the leisure industries. Today, the square is a center of the film-making industry.

Today, a statue of Charles II (1681), blurred by weather and cracked with age, presides over the **Soho Square Gardens** (tel. 798 2064). His illegitimate son, the Duke of Monmouth, who rebelled against (and was beheaded by) uncle James II, once commissioned a palatial house on this site; according to local legend, the district's current name comes from his rallying cry at the battle of Sedgemoor, *"Soe-hoe."* Gardens open daily 10am-dusk.

Soho has a history of welcoming all colors and creeds to its streets. The district was first settled by French Huguenots fleeing religious persecution after the revocation of the Edict of Nantes in 1685. In more recent years, an influx of settlers from the New Territories of Hong Kong have built London's Chinatown south of Soho. A strong Mediterranean influence can also be detected in the aromas of espresso, garlic, and sizzling meats wafting through the area's maze of streets.

Perhaps contemporary Soho's most salient feature, especially on sunny days, is its vibrant **sidewalk café** culture, a recent development marking an intentional departure from Soho's pornographic past. An *al fresco* mecca, today's Soho overflows with media types (mostly in the film and TV industries), artists, writers, club kids, and posers. The area has a significant and visible gay presence; a concentration of gay-owned restaurants and bars has turned the region's central avenue, **Old Compton Street,** into the throbbing gay heart of London.

Like the other SoHo in New York, Soho has become almost too stylish. A recent renaissance, funded by Soho café and restaurant owners, has swept away some of the rubbish and sleaze to make room for London's hippest cafés and bars. Attracted by the scent of money, large corporations and chain stores are moving in for the kill, threatening to destroy the area's distinct character and turn it into another Covent Garden. Nevertheless, today's Soho manages to skillfully tread the line between the sleazy grit of the sex industry and boring corporate sanitization. The eerie ruins of **St. Anne's Soho** (tel. 437 5006) on Wardour Street, which runs north through the offices of Britain's film industry from Shaftesbury Ave., remain from World War II. Leveled by German bombers in 1940, only Wren's anomalous tower of 1685 and the ungainly, bottle-shaped steeple added by Cockerell in 1803 emerged unscathed. Church gardens open daily 8am-dusk.

Since the 1840s, **Berwick St. Market** (parallel to the north end of Wardour St.) has rumbled with trade and far-flung Cockney accents. Famous for the widest and cheapest selection of fruits and vegetables in central London, the market has expanded to include cheap electrical appliances and a small selection of clothes (open Mon.-Sat. 9am-6pm). Nearby **Meard Street** offers up an impression of Soho in its earlier, more residential days.

Running parallel to Regent St. is **Carnaby Street,** a notorious hotbed of 60s sex, fashion, and Mods. It witnessed the rise of youth culture and became the heart of what *Time* magazine called "Swinging London." Although the chic boutiques and parading celebrities of the mid-1960s have long since left the area, which has lapsed into a lurid tourist trap crammed with stalls of junky souvenirs, some of its more traditional denizens (like **Luderwicks**, the oldest pipe-makers in London), have weathered storms of fads and tourists alike.

Soho also has a rich literary past: Blake and Defoe lived on Broadwick St. (off Wardour St.), Thomas de Quincey *(Confessions of an English Opium Eater)* had bad trips in his houses on Greek and Tavistock St., and John Dryden lived at no. 43 Gerrard St. (in Chinatown). To the north, a blue plaque above the Quo Vadis restaurant at **28 Dean Street** locates the austere two-room flat where the impoverished Karl Marx lived with his wife, maid, and five children while writing *Das Kapital.*

Leicester Square, just south of Shaftesbury Ave., between Piccadilly Circus and Charing Cross Rd. (the pedestrian-only streets perpendicular to Charing Cross Rd. all lead to the square itself) is an entertainment nexus. Amusements range from very expensive, mammoth cinemas, to the free performances provided by the street entertainers, to the glockenspiel of the **Swiss Centre** (its 25 bells ring Mon.-Fri. at noon, 6, 7, and 8pm, Sat.-Sun. at noon, 2, 4, 5, 6, 7, and 8pm; ringing is accompanied by a moving model of herdsmen leading their cattle through the Alps). Not to mention the constant cacophony of tourist harangues produced by the throngs of visitors. (Though there's safety in crowds and plenty of police, watch out—the square is a notorious hotbed of bag snatchers and drug offenders.)

On the north side of the square, at Leicester Place, the French presence in Soho manifests itself in **Notre-Dame de France** (tel. 437 9363). This church may not be architecturally distinguished, but those who venture inside will be rewarded with the exquisite Aubusson tapestry lining the inner walls. The tiny chapel built into the western wall features an arresting 1960 Jean Cocteau mural. On the south side of the square, a large queue marks the **half-price ticket booth,** where (surprise!) theatre tickets are sold for half price on the day of the show (see Theater, p. 228).

Cantonese immigrants first arrived in Britain as cooks on British ships, and London's first Chinese community formed around the docks near Limehouse. Today, London's **Chinatown** (known in Chinese as *Tong Yan Kai,* "Chinese Street") lies off the north side of Leicester Sq. Chinatown swelled with Hong Kong's immigrants in the 50s; further immigrations are expected as the colony changes hands in 1997. Between Shaftesbury Ave.'s theatres and Leicester Sq.'s cinemas, the streets sprout Chinese language signs and pagoda-capped telephone booths. **Gerrard Street,** the main thoroughfare, runs closest to the Leicester Sq. tube station. The street where poet John Dryden once lived is now a pedestrian avenue framed by scrollworked dragon gates.

Chinatown is most vibrant during the year's two major festivals: the **Mid-Autumn Festival,** at the end of September, and the **Chinese New Year Festival,** during the beginning of February. For further information on festivals or Chinatown call the **Chinese Community Centre** at 44 Gerrard St., 2nd floor (tel. 439 3822; open Mon.-Thurs. 1:30-5pm, Sun. 11am-5pm). Those thirsty for eastern newspapers (in English or Chinese) should check out the bustling bookshop **Guanghwa,** at 7 Newport Pl. (see Bookstores, p. 253). The otherwise classical church of St. Martin-in-the-Fields in Trafalgar Sq. conducts a Chinese service every Sunday afternoon at 2:45pm.

SIGHTS

■ Covent Garden

The outdoor cafés, upscale shops, and slick crowds animating Covent Garden today belie the square's medieval beginnings as a literal "covent garden" where the monks of Westminster Abbey grew their vegetables. When Henry VIII abolished the monasteries in 1536, he granted the land to John Russell, first Earl of Bedford. The Earl's descendants developed it into a fashionable *piazza* (designed by Inigo Jones) in the 1630s, giving London its first planned square.

Today Covent Garden is filled with street performers who swallow swords, juggle flaming torches, or sketch other street performers as they perform. With lots of pubs, cafés, and nice shops, Covent Garden attracts all kinds, but especially the young and vibrant. The streets are constantly bustling—Friday and Saturday nights are downright hectic as theatre crowds converge with pub crawlers.

Jones's **St. Paul's Church** now stands as the sole remnant of the original square, although the interior had to be rebuilt after bring gutted by a fire in 1795. Known as "the actor's church," St. Paul's is filled with plaques commemorating the achievements of Boris Karloff, Vivien Leigh, Noel Coward, and Tony Simpson ("inspired player of small parts"), among others. The connection to the theater dates back to the mid-17th century when this was the center of London's theatrical culture. (Open Mon.-Fri. 9am-4pm; services Mon.-Wed. 8:30am; Holy Communion services Sun. 11am, Wed. 1:10pm, and Thurs. 8:30am. Evensong is sung on the second Sunday of each month at 4pm. For more information call 836 5221.)

The misleading east portico facing the Covent Garden Piazza never served as a door, but rather as a stage; an inscription marks it as the site of the first known performance of a Punch and Judy puppet show, recorded by Samuel Pepys in 1662.

During the 1800s, a glass and iron roof was built to shelter the fruit, vegetable, and flower market centered in the Piazza. Though the wholesalers' carts left Covent Garden in 1974 for Nine Elms, south of the Thames, the Victorian architecture has remained to house the fashionable shops and expensive restaurants that sprouted during a tourist-oriented redevelopment. The Victorian Flower Market building in the southeast corner of the piazza now contains the **London Transport Museum** (see Museums, p. 221). Markets selling crafts and antiques, madding crowds, and omnipresent street performers re-enact the jostling marketplace of yore.

Two of London's most venerable venues, the **Theatre Royal** and the **Royal Opera House,** lend a feeling of civility to the area, adding pre-theater and pre-concert-goers to the throng of visitors. These venues represent a long tradition of theatre in the Covent Garden area. The Theatre Royal (entrance on Catherine St.) was first built in 1663 as one of two legal theatrical venues in London. Four previous incarnations burnt down; the present building dates from 1812. The Royal Opera House (on Bow St.) began as a theater for concerts and plays in 1732 and currently houses the Royal Opera and Royal Ballet companies. (For information on how to see performances, see Entertainment, p. 237.)

Right across the street from the Royal Opera House stands **Bow Street Magistrates' Court** (which closed in 1992), the oldest of London's 12 magistrates' courts and home of the Bow Street Runners, predecessors of the city's present-day police. In the courthouse, novelist Henry Fielding and his brother Sir John presided over a bench famed for its compassion (in a time when compassion meant sentencing the perpetrator of petty theft to 14 years deportation to Australia rather than hanging).

The **Theatre Museum** sits to the south, on the corner of Russell and Wellington streets (see Museums, p. 227). Nearby, a blue plaque at 8 Russell St. marks the site of James Boswell's home, where he first met Dr. Johnson in 1763.

Even outside the renovated central market area, Covent Garden buzzes with activity. Curious stage-design shops cluster near the Opera House, and moss-covered artisans' studios stud the surrounding streets, interspersed with an odd assortment of theatre-related businesses. Rose St. (between Garrick and Floral streets) leads to the notorious **Lamb and Flag** (see Pubs, p. 126), supposedly the only timber building left in the West End. In this lively pub, Dryden was attacked and nearly murdered by an angry mob hired by the Duchess of Portsmouth (Louise de Keroualle, Mistress of Charles II) who held him responsible for "certain scurrilous verses and lampoons then published concerning her behavior." This attempted murder is commemorated each December 19th (called **Dryden Night**).

On Great Newport St. to the west, **The Photographers' Gallery** holds its reputation as one of London's major venues for contemporary photographic exhibitions. Long Acre and Neal St. bustle with diverse specialty shops, similar only in their high prices. But many of these stores are great for browsing. The building at the corner of Earlham and Neal Streets houses **Contemporary Applied Arts,** a showcase for contemporary British crafts, including furniture, ceramics, and jewelery (sporadic hours, generally between 10am-6pm daily).

Further along, Neal St. leads to **Neal's Yard,** a healthy hub of stores selling whole foods, cheeses and yogurts, herbs, fresh-baked breads, and homeopathic remedies. At the northern section of St. Martin's Lane, six streets converge at the **Seven Dials** monument (the seventh dial is the monument itself as a sundial). A replica of a 17th-century monument, it has recently been restored, and is back standing tall.

■ Mayfair

The long-time center of London's blue-blooded *beau monde* was—in a delightful twist of fate—named for the 17th-century May Fair, held on the site of Shepherd's Market, a notorious haunt of prostitutes. Modern Mayfair has a distinctly patrician atmosphere; it is the most expensive property in the British version of *Monopoly.* In the 18th and 19th centuries, the aristocracy kept houses in Mayfair where they lived during "the season" (the season for opera and balls), retiring to their country estates in the summer. Mayfair is bordered by Oxford St. to the north, Piccadilly to the south, Park Lane to the west, and Regent St. to the east (tube: Green Park, Bond St., or Piccadilly Circus).

Near what is now the Bond St. tube station, Blake saw mystical visions for 17 years on South Molton St. On busy Brook St., home to ritzy **Claridge's Hotel,** Handel wrote the *Messiah.* The reigning queen was born in a house (recently demolished) at no. 17 Bruton St. Laurence Sterne ended his life on haughty Bond St. (no. 39). Back in the 60s, on Davies Mews, **Vidal Sassoon** revolutionized hair styles at his first salon (now the **Vidal Sassoon School**—see Entertainment, p. 243).

Bond St. itself is the traditional address for the oldest and most prestigious shops, art dealers, auction houses, and hair salons in the city. It is divided into Old and New Bond St. Not surprisingly—in this most historically snobbish of cities—Old Bond is the locale of choice for the area's most expensive shops. Cartier, Armani, Brioni, Bally, and Chanel display their lavish wares in elaborately prepared window displays. Alongside these Continental extravagances, long-established homegrown shops—sporting crests indicating royal patronage—sell everything from handmade shotguns to emerald tiaras to antique furniture to *objets d'art.* Every store is watched over by one or several bored, white-shirted guards. Art dealers and auctioneers with public galleries frequently offer special shows of exceptional quality.

Starting at the New Bond St. end, **Sotheby's,** 34 New Bond St. (tel. 408 5397 or 5400), displays everything from Dutch masters to the world's oldest condom before they're put on the auction block. Dress smartly—not too smartly, though, as real art dealers affect a slightly shabby appearance—and spend a wonderful (and free) hour perusing the collections which you can't afford. The pieces up for bids are displayed in the honeycomb of galleries. A typical collection will include originals by artists like Picasso, Miro, Chagall, Warhol, and other luminaries you thought you'd only see in museums. And yes, the tag on some of the pieces *does* say that bids begin at £1,000,000. (Open for viewing Mon.-Fri. 9am-4:30pm, Sun. noon-4pm.) The cafe offers a non-astronomically priced tea (£3.75) from 2:30-5pm during the week. Don't be a wiseguy and try bidding low on the scones, though—the serious looking guards will probably throw you out, wrong end first. You can get a catalog with high quality pictures of the pieces in a particular offering for £5-20, or pick up old catalogs for half price.

Modern art aficionados should note the rugged Henry Moore frieze high up on the crest of the **Time/Life Building,** corner of Bruton St. At the **Marlborough Gallery,** the biggest contemporary names are sold (entrance by Albemarle St.); **Agnew's,** 43 Old Bond St., and **Colnaghi's,** 14 Old Bond St., deal in Old Masters.

Running west off Bond St., Grosvenor St. ends at **Grosvenor Square,** one of the largest of its breed in central London. The square, occasionally known as "little America," has gradually evolved into a U.S. military and political enclave since future President John Adams lived at no. 9 while serving as the first American ambassador to England in 1785. Almost two centuries later, General Eisenhower established his wartime headquarters at no. 20, and memory of his stay persists in the area's postwar nickname, "Eisenhowerplatz." From here you can see the humorless and top-heavy **U.S. Embassy** rising to the west. West of Grosvenor Sq., a walk down **Park Lane,** the western border of Mayfair at Hyde Park, will take you by the legendary hotels of yesteryear.

In the opposite (northeast) corner of Mayfair (tube: Oxford Circus), tiny **Hanover Square** provides a gracious residential setting for **St. George's Hanover Church,** where the *crème de la crème* of London society have been married. Percy Bysshe Shelley, George Eliot, Benjamin Disraeli, and the soft-speaking Teddy Roosevelt came here to tie the bonds of holy matrimony beneath the radiant barrel vault. To the south, off Conduit St., you may window-shop the finest in men's threads. The name **Savile Row** is synonymous with the elegant and excessively priced "bespoke" tailoring that has prospered there for centuries.

At 28 Bond St. you'll find the oldest chocolate shop in London, opened in 1875 by request of Kind Edward VII (then Prince of Wales). He encouraged Mme. Charbonnel to leave her Parisian chocolate house and to join Mrs. Walker in opening a shop on Bond St. Chocolate lovers will swoon inside **Charbonnel et Walker.** The delicious smell of truffles being crafted of fresh cream, by the same recipe upon which Mme. Charbonnel once relied, is overwhelming. An expensive sampler of these delectable treats will teach you why the Queen herself nibbles on this choclatier's magical yummies. (open Mon.-Fri. 9am-6pm, Sat. 10am-5pm; tel. 491 0939). A delicate (tiny) truffle will run you a decadent 50p.

■ Marylebone

Located between Regent's Park and Oxford St., the grid-like district of Marylebone (MAR-lee-bun) is dotted with decorous late-Georgian town houses. The name derives from "St. Mary-by-the-bourne," the "bourne" referring to the Tyburn or the Westbourne stream, both now underground. The eternally dammed Westbourne now forms the Serpentine in Hyde Park.

There's little to see in this well-kept, well-bred region of residences and office buildings, but Marylebone has had its share of notable denizens. Wimpole Street saw the reclusive poet Elizabeth Barrett write the fabulous *Sonnets from the Portuguese* before she eloped and moved in with Robert Browning. At different times, 19 York St. has been the home of John Milton, John Stuart Mill, and William Hazlitt. **Harley Street** is the address for Britain's most eminent doctors and specialists.

The area's most fondly remembered resident is Sherlock Holmes who, although fictitious, still receives about 50 letters per week addressed to his 221b Baker St. residence. The Abbey National Building Society currently occupies the site and employs a full-time secretary to answer requests for Holmes's assistance in solving mysteries around the world. The official line is that Holmes has retired from detective work and is keeping bees in the country. The **Sherlock Holmes Museum,** located at 239 Baker St. (marked "221b") will thrill Holmes enthusiasts with the meticulous re-creation of the detective's lodgings (see Museums, p. 214).

Ever since the redoubtable **Madame Tussaud,** one of Louis XVI's tutors, trekked from Paris in 1802 carrying wax effigies of French nobles decapitated in the

Revolution, her eerie museum on Marylebone Rd. (with an adjacent Planetarium) has been a London landmark (see Museums, p. 225).

Oxford Street, the southern border of Marylebone, passes through Oxford Circus, Bond St., and Marble Arch tube stations. Arguably London's major shopping boulevard, it's jam-packed with shops (ranging from cheap chain stores to the posh boutiques around Bond St.), crowds, and fast-food stands. Off Oxford St., pleasant **James's St.** (tube: Bond St.) lures passersby with one café after another—a good place for people-watching from a sidewalk table. Manchester Sq. holds the **Wallace Collection,** a must-see for fans of Dutch art (see Museums, p. 214). **Hertford House,** the ancestral mansion which contains the Wallace Collection, is worth a visit even by those indifferent to Dutch art, if such people truly exist.

■ Hyde Park and Kensington Gardens

Totalling 630 acres, **Hyde Park** and the contiguous **Kensington Gardens** constitute the largest open area in the center of the city, earning their reputation as the "lungs of London." Henry VIII used to hunt deer here. Cricketers and picnic baskets now dot the park's sprawling green fields. At the far west of the Gardens, you can drop your calling card at **Kensington Palace** (tel. 376 2858; tube: Kensington High St. or Queensway), originally the residence of King William III and Queen Mary II and recently of Princess Margaret. Although always a hotbed of tabloid activity, Kensington became especially famous after a certain heir to the throne moved out. Currently, the Princess of Wales, the little princes, and other stray members of the royal family live in the palace. A museum of uninhabited royal rooms (the State Apartments) and regal memorabilia includes a Court dress collection. A former centerpiece of the display, Princess Di's wedding gown has since been removed. (Palace open daily May-Sept. only through tours leaving every hr. Mon.-Sat. 9:30am-3:30pm.; admission £5.50). **Orangery Gardens,** an exquisite flower display studded by young couples getting mushy, lines the eastern side of the palace. A walk west of the palace along Kensington Palace Gdns., one of London's most opulent thoroughfares, reveals embassies and the homes of a crew of millionaires.

Be careful when crossing through Kensington's pathways—the park is now filled with in-line skaters who are not so keen on stopping for camera-toting tourists. Skate rentals park themselves on the main pathways if you want to try a pair yourself. The statue of Peter Pan, actually modeled from a girl, stands near the **Italian Fountains** on the Serpentine's west bank. The **Serpentine,** a lake carved in 1730, runs from these fountains in the north, near Bayswater Rd., south towards Knightsbridge. From the number of people who pay the £6 per hour to row in the pond, one would think the water was the fountain of youth. Perhaps not: closed to swimmers after a pollution scare, the pond has only recently reopened, but don't be afraid to bring your costume. **Harriet Westbrook,** P.B. Shelley's first wife, numbers among the famous people who have drowned in this human-made "pond." A bone-white arch derived from a Henry Moore sculpture stands on the northwest bank, but the best view is from across the water.

The **Serpentine Gallery** (tel. 402 6075), in Kensington Gardens, hosts interesting exhibitions of contemporary works and art workshops. (Gallery open daily during exhibitions only 10am-6pm; Kensington Gardens open daily, dawn-dusk. Free.)

On the southern edge of Kensington Gardens, the Lord Mayor had the **Albert Memorial** built to honor Victoria's beloved husband. Considered a great artistic achievement when first unveiled in 1869, the extravagant monument now seems an embarrassing piece of imperial excess. You may soon be able to judge for yourself—after years under scaffolding, the revitalized monument should be unveiled in late 1997. Across the street, the **Royal Albert Hall,** with its ornate oval dome, hosts the Promenade Concerts (Proms) in summer (see Music, p. 235). Also built to honor the Prince Consort, the hall is simpler than the memorial, and features a frieze of the "Triumph of the Arts and Sciences" around its circumference. Rotten Row (a corruption of *Route du Roi,* "king's road") was the first English thoroughfare to be lighted to prevent crime. However, this east-west path through southern Hyde Park, like the rest of the park, remains dangerous at night. There is a police station about 300 yards north of the Serpentine.

Speakers' Corner, in the northeast corner of Hyde Park (tube: Marble Arch, not Hyde Park Corner), is the finest example of free speech in action anywhere in the world. The **Marble Arch** is built on the exact site where the public gallows of Tyburn rested until 1783. Hangings here drew immense crowds who jeered and threw stones and rotting food at the unfortunate criminals (some of whom had done as little as steal a shilling's worth of goods) as they rolled in carts to the "Triple Tree," which stood at the present corner of Bayswater and Edgware Rd. Nowadays, on Sundays from late morning to dusk, and on summer evenings, soapbox revolutionaries, haranguers, madmen, and evangelists scream about anything from Kierkegaard to masturbation to aliens. At the southern end of Hyde Park cluster a group of statues: a Diana fountain, the "family of man," a likeness of Lord Byron, and a fig-leafed Achilles dedicated to Wellington (Hyde Park open daily 5am-midnight). Royal park band performances take place in the bandstand 200 yards from Hyde Park Corner, in the direction of the Serpentine (June-Aug. Sun. 3 and 6pm)

Beefcake Wellington

Before television, film, and Hugh Grant, British women culled their sex symbols from the military, and few soldiers set pulses racing faster then Arthur Wellesley, Duke of Wellington. Charlotte Brontë fancied the victor at Waterloo so much as a child that she modeled *Jane Eyre's* Rochester after him. Countess Lavinia Spencer showed her affection in another way, by launching a women-only public subscription to raise funds for a memorial statue. The result was the "Ladies' Trophy," Hyde Park's nude statue of Achilles, cheekily referred to as the ladies' fancy. The statue, London's first nude, was embroiled in controversy from its creation. Lady Holland wrote saucily: "A difficulty has arisen, and the artist had submitted to the female subscribers whether this colossal figure should preserve its antique nudity or should be garnished with a fig leaf. It was carried for the leaf by a majority…The names of the *minority* have not transpired." Those eager to accuse British women of prudery should be advised that it was in fact the gentleman head of the statue committee who insisted on the fig leaf.

■ Kensington, Knightsbridge, & Belgravia

Kensington, a gracious and sheltered residential area, reposes between multi-ethnic Notting Hill to the north and chic Chelsea to the south. **Kensington High Street,** which pierces the area, has become a shopping and scoping epicenter. Obscure specialty and antique shops fill the area along Kensington Church Street to the north, Victorian-era museums and colleges dominate South Kensington, and the area around Earl's Court has mutated into something of a tourist colony while retaining a substantial gay population.

Take the tube to High St. Kensington, Notting Hill Gate, or Holland Park to reach **Holland Park,** a gracious peacock-peppered garden. Holland House (see Accommodations, p. 78), a Jacobean mansion built in 1606, lies on the park's grounds. Destroyed in WWII, the house has since been restored and turned into a youth hostel. Holland Park also contains formal gardens, an open-air amphitheater, and a number of playgrounds. The park boasts cricket pitches, public tennis courts, and the Kyoto Gardens, a traditional Japanese garden.

Two petite exhibition galleries, the **Ice House** and the **Orangery,** blossom in the middle of the park. They mount free displays of contemporary painting and ceramics by local artists. The flag-ridden **Commonwealth Institute** stands by the park's southern entrance on the High St. (see Museums, p. 223).

The curious **Leighton House,** 12 Holland Park Rd. (tel. 602 3316), lies a block west. Devised by the imaginative painter Lord Leighton in the 19th century, the

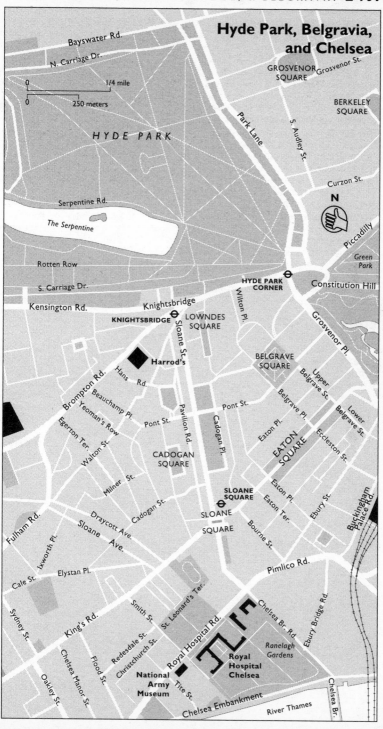

Hyde Park, Belgravia, and Chelsea

Bayswater Rd.

N. Carriage Dr.

GROSVENOR SQUARE

Grosvenor St.

BERKELEY SQUARE

0   1/4 mile
0   250 meters

HYDE PARK

Park Lane

S. Audley St.

Curzon St.

N

Piccadilly

Serpentine Rd.

The Serpentine

Green Park

Rotten Row

S. Carriage Dr.

HYDE PARK CORNER

Constitution Hill

Kensington Rd.

Knightsbridge

Wilton Pl.

KNIGHTSBRIDGE

LOWNDES SQUARE

Grosvenor Pl.

Sloane St.

Hans   Rd.

Harrod's

BELGRAVE SQUARE

Upper Belgrave St.

Lower Belgrave St.

Brompton Rd.

Beauchamp Pl.

Yeoman's Row

Pont St.

Pavilion Rd.

Pont St.

Belgrave Pl.

Eccleston St.

Egerton Ter.

Walton St.

CADOGAN SQUARE

Cadogan Pl.

EATON SQUARE

Eaton Pl.

Milner St.

Cadogan St.

SLOANE SQUARE

Eaton Pl.

Eaton Ter.

Ebury St.

Fulham Rd.

Draycott Ave.

Sloane   Ave.

SLOANE SQUARE

Bourne St.

Buckingham Palace Rd.

Cale St.

Ixworth Pl.

Elystan Pl.

Pimlico Rd.

Sydney St.

King's Rd.

Smith St.

St. Leonard's Ter.

Royal Hospital Rd.

Chelsea Br. Rd.

Ranelagh Gardens

Ebury Bridge Rd.

Redesdale St.

Christchurch St.

Royal Hospital Chelsea

Chelsea Manor St.

Flood St.

National Army Museum

Tite St.

Chelsea Embankment

Chelsea Br.

Oakley St.

River Thames

SIGHTS

house is a presumptuous yet amusing *pastiche*. The thoroughly blue **Arab Hall,** with inlaid tiles, a pool, and a dome, is an attempt to recreate the wonders of the Orient in proper, thoroughly Occidental, Kensington. Now a center for the arts, Leighton House features concerts, receptions, and other events in the evenings, as well as frequent contemporary art exhibitions. An excellent taped commentary (£2.25) helps you find your way around (house open Mon.-Sat. 11am-5:30pm; free).

To reach the grandiose **South Kensington museums,** take the tube to the South Kensington station or Bus 49 from Kensington High St. The **Victoria and Albert Museum** and the **Natural History Museum** (both on Cromwell Road), and the **Science Museum** (on Exhibition Road) all testify on a grand scale to the Victorian mania for collecting, codifying, and cataloguing. The Great Exhibition of 1851 funded many of these monumental buildings, built between 1867 and 1935.

Brompton Oratory, just east of the V&A, is a showpiece of Italian art and architecture. H. Gribble built the aggressively Roman Baroque edifice in 1884 and cluttered its interior with Italian statues; the enormous Renaissance altar in the Lady Chapel came from Brescia. The church affirms its reputation for fine music during its Sunday Latin Masses (oratory open 6:30am-8pm, mass at 11am on Sun.). One of the altars was considered by the KGB to be the best dead drop in all of London—until 1985 agents left microfilms and other documents behind a statue for other agents to surreptitiously pick up.

Christie's, the internationally famous auction house, sells off its less valuable trinkets at 85 Old Brompton Rd., its second branch. (Its first is near St. James Palace, see p. 145.) Still, it's no *Everything's a pound!!!;* objects in these collections cost up to £2000. Various royal institutions of learning and culture are located north of Cromwell Rd., including the Imperial College of Science, the Royal College of Music, the Royal College of Art, the rotund **Royal Albert Hall** (see Entertainment, p. 235), the **Royal School of Needlepoint,** and the **Royal Geographical Society.**

Patrician **Knightsbridge** manages to seem wealthy and groomed without appearing forbidding. Knightsbridge is defined most of all by London's premier department store, **Harrods.** Founded in 1849 as a grocery store, by 1880 Harrods employed over 100 workers. In 1905 the store moved to its current location; today it requires 5000 employees to handle its vast array of products and services. Extravagance is their specialty. Besides an encyclopedic inventory, Harrods also contains a pub, an espresso bar, a salt beef bar, a champagne and oyster bar, a juice bar, and, naturally, a tourist information center (open Mon.-Tues. and Sat. 10am-6pm, Wed.-Fri. 10am-7pm; see Shopping, p. 249). Its dominating five-story megastructure might easily be mistaken for a cathedral, except for the giant flag proclaiming "sale."

Belgravia was first constructed to billet servants after the building of Buckingham Palace in the 1820s, but soon became the haughty bastion of wealth and privilege it is today. Belgravia lies south of Hyde Park, ringed by stately Sloane St. to the west, Victoria Station to the south, and Buckingham Palace Gardens to the east. The spacious avenues and crescents of the district surround **Belgrave Square,** 10 acres of park surrounded by late Georgian buildings that were the setting for *My Fair Lady.* Nearby **Eaton Square** was one of Henry James's favorites. Residential Belgravia exhibits a quieter, more dignified mien than busier Knightsbridge or Mayfair.

■ Chelsea

Chelsea has always been one of London's flashiest districts—Thomas More, Oscar Wilde, and the Sex Pistols have all been residents at one time or another. It used to be that few streets in London screamed louder for a visit than the **King's Road.** Mohawked UB40s (a reference to the unemployed: it's the form they must fill out to get benefits) and pearl-necklaced Sloane Rangers (the awfully loose English equivalent of preppies) gazed at trendy window displays and at each other. While the hordes still flock here on Saturday afternoons to see and be seen, the ambience is drastically muted; most current scenesters look like they are desperately trying to recapture a past they have only read about.

South Kensington and Chelsea

QUEENSWAY ⊖
Bayswater Rd.

KENSINGTON GARDENS

HYDE PARK

The Broad Walk

Kensington Park Gardens

The Serpentine

Round Pond

Kensington Palace

Albert Memorial

W. Carriage Dr.

S. Carriage Rd.

Kensington High St.
Kensington Rd.
Kensington Gore
Royal Geographical Society
Kensington Rd.

■ St. Mary Abbots Church
⊖ HIGH ST KENSINGTON

DeVere Gdns.
Palace Gate
Victoria Rd.
Launceston Pl.

Holy Trinity Church
Prince Consort Rd.
Royal Albert Hall
Exhibition Rd.
Prince's Gdns.
Ennismore Gdns.
S. Carriage Rd.

Stanford Rd.

Elvaston Pl.
Imperial College of Science & Technology

Imperial College Rd.

Science Museum

Brompton Oratory

Gloucester Rd.

Cornwall Gdns.

Natural History Museum

Victoria & Albert Museum

Brompton Rd.

GLOUCESTER ROAD ⊖

Queen's Gate

Cromwell Rd.
Cromwell Rd.

Thurloe Pl.
Thurloe St.

Knaresboro Pl.
Collingham Rd.
Courtfield Rd.
Harrington Gdns.

Stanhope Gdns.

Harrington Rd.
⊖ S. KENSINGTON
Pelham St.

Pelham Cres.

Sloane Ave.

Earls Court Rd.
Wetherby Gdns.
Hereford Sq.

Old Brompton Rd.
Onslow Gdns.
Sumner Pl.
ONSLOW SQUARE

Ixworth Pl.

Bolton Gdns.
Old Brompton Rd.

Little Boltons
The Boltons

Drayton Gdns.
Cranley Gdns.

Neville Terr.
S. Parade
Fulham Rd.

Cale St.
Sydney St.
St. Luke's Church ■
Britten St.

REDCLIFFE SQUARE

Harcourt Terr.
Tregunter Rd.

Gilston Rd.

Elm Park Gdns.

Old Church St.
Manresa Rd.

King's Rd.

Finborough Rd.
Redcliffe Gdns.
Hollywood Rd.

Fulham Rd.

Beaufort St.
Park Walk

Chelsea College

Oakley St.

Brompton Cemetery

PAULTONS SQUARE

N

Cheyne Row
Beaufort St.

Carlyle's House ■

Chelsea Old Church ■
Cheyne Walk

King's Rd.

0 — 1/4 mile
0 — 1/4 kilometer

Symbolic of the street's recent metamorphosis from the center of a dynamic youth culture into a respectable shopping district is the chameleonic storefront at 430 King's Road, **World's End.** At this address in the 70s, impressario Malcolm McLaren and designer Vivienne Westwood masterminded a series of trendy boutiques that capitalized on the subcultural fashions then in vogue, like the Teddy Boy look. Let it Rock, Too Young To Live Too Fast To Die, and Seditionaries were some of the shop's various incarnations; the shop's most important incarnation was **Sex,** the punk clothing store in which the Sex Pistols (and, some would argue, punk rock) were born. Ripped clothing, safety pins, and bondage gear as fashion originated here. While Westwood still displays her designs in a boutique at this address, she now sells fabulously expensive couture garments. Ironically, the boutique's current neighbor is the Chelsea Conservative Club.

Any proper exploration of Chelsea begins at **Sloane Square.** The square takes its name from Sir Hans Sloane (1660-1753), whose collection comprised the whole of the first British Museum. The nearby **Royal Court Theatre** debuted many of George Bernard Shaw's plays. Until 1829, King's Rd., stretching southwest from Sloane Sq., served as a private royal thoroughfare from Hampton Court to Whitehall. Today the street is a commercial thoroughfare where overpriced restaurants, historic pubs, and the **Chelsea Antique Market** (253 King's Road) lurk amid many boutiques. The recent presence of three supermodeling agencies in the square fills many of the boutiques with London's most fashionable women. Be aware that the tube is practically nonexistent around here, so you'll have to rely on **buses** (11 or 22).

Off King's Rd., Chelsea becomes cozier, the closest thing to a village that central London now possesses. Totally immune to the ever-changing world of King's Rd. are the commandingly militaresque buildings of Wren's **Royal Hospital** (1691), founded by Charles II for retired soldiers and still inhabited by 400 army pensioners. Former soldiers, in Royal Hospital uniform, welcome visitors to the spacious grounds and splendid buildings. The North wing of the hospital has borne war's scars quite directly in the last century. In 1918 a German 500-lb. bomb destroyed the wing, killing five residents. After the war it was rebuilt only to be destroyed toward the end of WWII by a German V-2 rocket, again killing five retired soldiers.

East of the Hospital lie the **Ranelagh Gardens** (usually open until dusk). Here 18th-century pleasure-seekers spent their evenings watching pageants and fireworks and imbibing to excess (open till dusk; free). The **Chelsea Flower Show** blooms here the third week in May (Tues.-Fri.), but even Royal Horticultural Society members have trouble procuring tickets for the first two days. Next door is the lovely **Chelsea Physic Garden** (tel. 352-5646); you can wander through this jungle-like garden on Wed. 2pm-5pm and Sun. 2pm-6pm during April through October (admission £3.50, concessions £1.80, wheelchair accessible).

Cheyne (pronounced "CHAY-nee") **Walk, Cheyne Row,** and **Tite Street** formed the heart of Chelsea's artist colony at the turn of the century. Watch for the blue plaques on the houses; J.M.W. Turner moved into a house in Cheyne Walk, and Edgar Allan Poe lived nearby. Mary Ann Evans (a.k.a. George Eliot) moved into no. 4 just before her death. Dante Gabriel Rossetti kept his disreputable *ménage* (which included peacocks and a kangaroo) in no. 16, where he doused himself with chloral hydrate. Nos. 19 to 26 cover the ground that used to be Chelsea Manor, where Queen Elizabeth I once lived. Both Mick Jagger and Keith Richards got satisfaction on the Walk in the 60s. The area's arbiter of the aesthetic, Oscar Wilde, reposed stylishly at 34 Tite St. from 1884-1895 and was arrested for homosexual activity at Chelsea's best-known hotel, the Cadogan (75 Sloane St.). John Singer Sargent, James MacNeill Whistler, Radclyffe Hall, and Bertrand Russell also lived on Tite St. Today, fashionable artists' and designers' homes line the street, though the area is too expensive to remain a true bastion of bohemian culture.

At the west end of Cheyne Walk lies the **Chelsea Old Church,** partially designed by Sir Thomas More. Henry VIII is reported to have married his third wife here before the official wedding took place. The friendly verger will point out **Crosby Hall** down the street, a 15th-century hall that was More's residence in Bishopsgate before it was moved, stone by stone, to its present position in 1910.

Chelsea's famed resident Thomas Carlyle crafted his magnificent prose on Cheyne Row. On this miraculously quiet street colored by flowers and tidy houses, **Carlyle's House,** 24 Cheyne Row (tel. 352 7087), has remained virtually unchanged since the Sage of Chelsea expired in his armchair. Family portraits and sketches ornament the walls—which he had doubled in thickness, vainly hoping to keep out noise. Be sure to read the letters between Disraeli and Carlyle which are displayed in the upstairs study. Disraeli wanted to give Carlyle the Grand Cross of the Bath—heretofore reserved only for those in direct service of the state—as well as a sizeable pension. Carlyle replied that he would always cherish such a compliment from a man as great as Disraeli, but declined, saying that the rest of such an honor would be pure "sorrow." (Open April-Oct. Wed.-Sun. 11am-5pm. Last admission 4:30pm. Admission £2.90, children £1.50.)

■ Notting Hill

Notting Hill is one of London's most diverse neighborhoods—a variety of racial and ethnic groups currently call the area home, as do many hipsters. On the area's lively streets, trendy places to eat and shop ply their trade among dilapidated stores, wafts of incense, and Bob Marley posters. The region explodes with exuberant festivity every summer during the **Notting Hill Carnival,** Europe's biggest outdoor festival (Aug. 24-25, 1997). Around 500,000 people line Portobello Road to watch and walk in a parade of steel drummers, fantastic costumes, skanking followers, and dancing policemen while Afro-Caribbean music reverberates through the streets.

The scenery that surrounded the village of Notting Hill in the mid-19th-century (a few cornfields, a meadow, an occasional lane) has changed drastically since the Great Western Railway opened up North Kensington to development in 1838. The Ladbroke family commissioned high society architects to develop the area, whereupon upper middle class families quickly took up residence in spacious Neoclassical mansion houses.

Commercial **Portobello Road,** the area's lively main thoroughfare, runs parallel to **Ladbroke Grove.** In its present form, the **Portobello Market** (see also p. 257) dominates the scene. Starting on the southern end near Notting Hill Gate, various antique stores and thriving galleries line this bustling thoroughfare. As the idler wanders farther north, antiquarians give way to fresh produce and baked goods stalls. Finally, near Lancaster Road and the Westway (the overhead highway), stalls vend secondhand clothing, collector's vinyl, and various desirable trinkets. The name "Portobello" may evoke childhood memories, even if you've never been to London—one of the market's most famed patrons is **Paddington Bear,** whose purchases here always landed his paws in pot of trouble. Portobello has hosted freakshows, fortune-tellers, conjurers, and charlatans selling miracle elixirs since the early Victorian age. A look at the tattoo parlors or juice bars hawking Gusto herbal drink today should convince cynics that some things never change.

Fortunately, some things do. The area has a checkered past of racial conflict, which it is gradually putting to rest. Irish and Jewish immigrants were the first to occupy the poor areas of "Notting Dale" in the late 19th century, but the 1930s saw the arrival of Fascist demonstrations against Jews and local immigrant groups. Inter-ethnic tension re-emerged in the 1950s when Teddy-Boy gangs engaged in open warfare against Afro-Caribbean immigrants—the devastating riots that ensued are depicted in Colin MacInnes's novel *Absolute Beginners* (later made into a movie musical starring David Bowie). Amy Garvey (Marcus's widow) helped the Black community on Notting Hill survive various onslaughts. Today the multi-ethnic area sees little racial animosity, a fact London's novelists have not overlooked. The only vice the area's most recent literary resident—loathesome dartsman Keith Talent of Martin Amis's *London Fields*—did *not* indulge was bigotry. (He cheated and swindles everyone, regardless of color or creed.)

■ Camden Town

Contemporary Camden Town is a stomping ground for trendy youth of all subcultural affiliations. Every Sunday thousands of merchants set up stands offering everything from vintage pornography to antique sewing machines at the **Camden Markets,** drawing swarms of bargain-seeking Londoners and curious, often bewildered, tourists each weekend (tube: Camden Town; see Shopping, p. 257). The market has become fertile ground for new-age religions to distribute literature, incense sellers to be worshipped by wide-eyed teens, and tattoo artists to find willing patients for experimentation. Opened in 1974 with only four stall holders, the market now crams in hundreds of bohemian vendors catering to an international youth culture. On Sundays, almost anything can be found here. One tip is to head towards the stalls at the back of the market, off Camden High Street. Here students of popular culture will find crates of yesterday's toys, books, lighters, and other unfamiliar knick-knacks. Other stores offer truly bizarre devices, including exotic instruments such as the Russian theremin. Straggly-haired neo-hippies, black-clad goths, pierced punks, clean-cut preppies, and even thirtysomething couples (little kids in tow) all add to the madness of the markets.

On weekdays, you can avoid the elbows and boots of your fellow shoppers. Beggars and scurrying students are the worst you'll have to contend with. Though the markets will be closed, the area's restaurants, cafés, and specialty shops (including one of London's best left-wing bookstores, a gay sex and fetish-wear shop, London's only store dedicated to folk music, and the **three-story emporium of the-artist-formerly-known-as-Prince,** owned by His Royal Badness himself) still offer plenty of fodder for more relaxed browsing. Of course few, if any, of the stalls will be there then. A visitor may find Camden High Street dominated by a series of almost identical shops: each offers a few flavors of Dr. Martens, a few cheap leather jackets, some well-worn corduroy and velvet blazers, and a selection of fruit-print shirts (or whatever is sweeping the club scene). In front of the shop will invariably stand several salesmen wearing bored expressions. After visiting a few of these shops you may find yourself wearing a similar expression.

Camden is connected to nearby Regent's Park and Little Venice by a series of canals and locks. Camden High Road, near its intersection with Chalk Farm Road, crosses over the main canal. From this bridge one can see the occasional **barge** being lowered or raised in the lock.

Although parts of Camden Town have turned into genteel residential enclaves, the area has for the most part resisted gentrification, as the scruffy storefronts on High St. and dilapidated warehouses along Regent's Canal will attest, not to mention the recurrent wake of litter left by the crowds. Despite the area's fame, Camden Town's restaurants and pubs remain dingy gathering places for rising indie stars and rock sensations. Sweat-laden band members and drunk fans stumble into local hangouts after gigs for a last taste of Saturday night fever; even in the grungiest places you can still find stars like Morrissey and Björk mellowing out.

In the 18th century, Camden Town was still only farmland and cattle fields owned by the Lord Chancellor Charles Pratt, Earl of Camden. Though he began some minor building projects in the area around Camden High St., the town really started to develop with the opening of the Regent's Canal in 1820, bringing with it timber and coal wharves, family-run breweries, saddlers, picture-framers, and the like. By the 19th century, Camden Town was a solid working-class district, spliced with railways and covered in soot. Charles Dickens spent his childhood here, crowded in a four-room tenement with his extended family at 16 (now 141) Bayham St. The experience served as the model for the Cratchit family in *A Christmas Carol.* Dylan Thomas found inspiration on Delancey St. Waves of Irish, Cypriot, Greek, Italian, and Portuguese immigrants brought a diversity to the area that persists to this day.

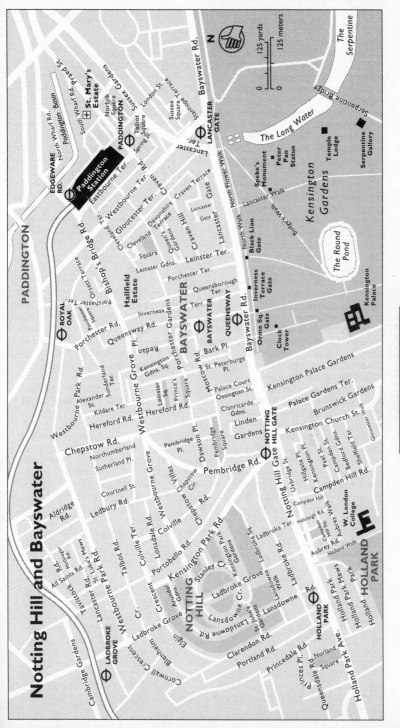

Notting Hill and Bayswater

PADDINGTON

St. Mary's Estate

EDGEWARE RD.
North Wharf Rd.
South Wharf Rd.
Paddington Basin

Paddington Station

PADDINGTON

Norfolk Square
Talbot Square
Spring St.
London St.
Sussex Gardens
Sussex Square
Sussex Terrace

Bishop's Bridge Rd.
Eastbourne Ter.
Westbourne Ter.
Gloucester Ter.
Cleveland Ter.
Cleveland Square
Cleveland Terrace
Craven Ter.
Devonshire Terrace
Craven Terrace
Craven Hill
Craven Hill Gdns
Lancaster Gate
Lancaster Gate

LANCASTER GATE
Lancaster Ter.
Bayswater Rd.
Bayswater Rd.

Leinster Gdns.
Leinster Ter.
Porchester Ter.

Halffield Estate
Orsett Terrace
Porchester Terrace
Porchester Square
Porchester Ter.

ROYAL OAK
Porchester Rd.
Queensway Rd.
Inverness Pl.
Queensway
Redan Pl.
Kensington Gdns. Sq.
Porchester Gardens

BAYSWATER
BAYSWATER
QUEENSWAY
Queensborough Ter.
Inverness Ter.

Inverness Terrace Gate

North Flower Walk
Lancaster Walk
North Walk
Black Lion Gate

Speke's Monument
Peter Pan Statue

The Long Water

Serpentine Bridge
The Serpentine

Temple Lodge
Serpentine Gallery

Kensington Gardens

The Round Pond

Bridge's Walk

Bayswater Rd.
Bark Pl.
Orme Sq. Gate
Clock Tower

Kensington Palace

Kensington Palace Gardens
Palace Gardens Ter.
Brunswick Gardens
Kensington Church St.
Gloucester Walk

Westbourne Park Rd.
Alexander St.
Sunderland Ter.
Kildare Ter.
Hereford Rd.
Westbourne Grove
Hereford Rd.
Leinster Sq.
Prince's Square
Moscow Rd.
St. Peterburge Pl.
Palace Court
Ossington St.
Clanricarde Gdns.
Linden Gardens

NOTTING HILL GATE
Notting Hill Gate
Uxbridge St.
Hillgate St.
Hillgate Pl.
Kensington Pl.
Peel St.
Camden Gdns.
Bedford Ter.
Sheffield Ter.

Campden Hill Rd.
Campden Hill
Campden Hill Walk
Hillsleigh Rd.
Aubrey Walk
W. London College

Chepstow Rd.
Northumberland Pl.
Sutherland Pl.
Courtnell St.
Ledbury Rd.
Chepstow Pl.
Pembridge Pl.
Pembridge Villas
Chepstow Villas
Dawson Pl.
Pembridge Square
Pembridge Rd.
Chepstow Cr.
Chepstow Rd.

Aldridge Rd.
All Saints Rd.
McGregor Rd.
Lancaster Rd.
St. Luke's Mews
Tavistock Cr.
Talbot Rd.
Colville Ter.
Colville Gardens
Lonsdale Rd.
Westbourne Grove
Portobello Rd.

Kensington Park Rd.
Stanley Cr.
Kensington Park Gardens
Ladbroke Sq.
Ladbroke Gardens
Ladbroke Ter.
Ladbroke Rd.
Ladbroke Grove

LADBROKE GROVE
Cambridge Gardens
Cornwall Crescent
Blenheim Cr.
Elgin Cr.
Arundel Gdns.
Westbourne Grove
Ladbroke Grove

NOTTING HILL
Ladbroke Grove
Ladbroke Sq.
Lansdowne Cr.
Lansdowne Rd.
Lansdowne Walk
St. John's Gdns

Clarendon Rd.
Portland Rd.
Princes Rd.
Princes Pl.
Queensdale Rd.
Norland Square

HOLLAND PARK
HOLLAND PARK
Holland Park Ave.
Holland Park
Holland Park Mews
Holland Walk
Aubrey Rd.
Holland Park Rd.

HOLLAND PARK

N
125 yards
125 meters
0
0

■ Regent's Park

Just south of Camden Town lies the 500-acre **Regent's Park** (tel. 486 7905; tube: Regent's Pk., Great Portland St., Baker St., or Camden Town; open 5am-dusk,). Full of lakes, gardens, promenades, and Londoners, it is one of London's most beautiful spaces. The park contains well-kept lawns, broad walkways (including **Broad Walk**), and sunbathers. During the mid-morning and early afternoon it attracts a large number of senior citizens—battalions of retired crumb dispensers sustain a vibrant pigeon community.

The true heart of the park is the 30 or so acres circumscribed by the drive with the veddy, veddy British title, the **Inner Circle.** This area plays home to the park's best-groomed lawns in a town (and country for that matter) with a well-known fetish for well-groomed lawns. Within are found the **Queen Mary's Gardens,** which were dedicated to this royal lady in 1938 simply because she liked them, rather than for some special achievement in gardening or elsewhere. Be sure to stroll by the rather overdone fountain at the center which is flanked by a stunning display of exotic flora. On Sundays from June through August you can hear tubas and trumpets honking away at the bandstand or see performances in the **Open Air Theatre** (tel. 486 2431/1933) near Queen Mary's Gardens (see Entertainment, p. 231). This outdoor theatre puts on Shakespearean plays every summer, as well as more contemporary dramaticks. Tickets cost £7.50-18.50, but students may purchase remaining tickets two hours before the show for only £6 (call the theatre day of show). Saturday matinees (2:30pm) are generally a sure bet for these reduced price tickets. Ticketmaster (tel. 344 4444) sells tickets and adds a maddeningly steep surcharge.

Just outside of the Inner Circle is the park's largest lake. Take a boat ride on the motorized barge (£1.25), or if you're feeling hale, navigate your own (rowboat for max. 4 people £6; available daily 10am-dusk; call 486 4759 for info.). Children, or the vertically challenged, may toot around in small paddleboats in a miniature, calmer lake right next door to the full-size lake (keep in mind the British lakes are quite civilized, i.e. really small) for £2.50/hr. These lakes were designed for the pleasure of the self-consciously elegant upper crust. As it happens the whole park was once envisioned as a playground for the well-born.

The area was cleared in 1650 when Cromwell felled 16,000 trees to raise cash for his cavalry's payroll. In 1812 the scrappy architect John Nash drew up plans ordered by the Prince Regent (the future George IV) for a park dotted with 40 luxury villas. It was to be a project for "the wealthy and the good" which would separate the fine districts from the less-fashionable ones to the east. Due to some admirable liberal sentiment this plan was not realized. Parliament was concerned that too much of London would become the province of the wealthy and the park was, in stages, opened to the public. The 40 villas were never built. Nash's mark is still evident—the park is edged on three sides by majestic Nash terraces. The recently restored Regency terraces present a magnificent façade. The cream-colored, porticoed, and pillared buildings have been home to the likes of H.G. Wells (17 Hanover Terrace) and Wallis Simpson (7 Hanover Terrace).

The park's most popular attraction has historically been the privately owned **London Zoo** (tel. 722 3333; tube: Camden Town, or Baker St.; Bus 274 from either station takes you almost to the door), located in the northeast quadrant. Despite a long period of near financial collapse, the zoo—Britain's largest—survived, and today you can see rare tigers (**Martin, Mira,** and cute little **Hari**), as well as elephants, snakes, et al. The 36-acre park was once the storage ground for zoological specimens collected by members of a learned society; Charles Darwin was perhaps its most illustrious fellow. **Jumbo the Elephant** was the parks biggest attraction in 1882, until cynical Yankee showman P.T. Barnum bought him and carted the big-eared celebrity from burg to burg. Proceeds from the sale were considerable enough to pay for the construction of an entire reptile house. The **Charles Clore Pavilion** displays "small mammals," including a large underground display of nocturnal small mammals. This dank, cave-like exhibit is pitch black except for lighted arrows which are intended to keep view-

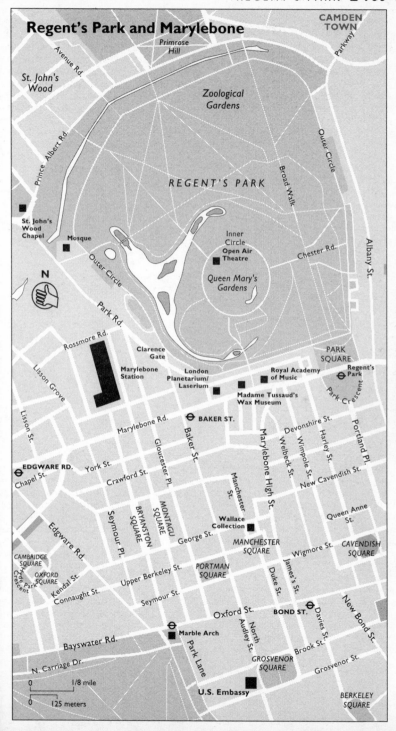

Regent's Park and Marylebone

CAMDEN TOWN

Parkway

Avenue Rd.

Primrose Hill

St. John's Wood

Zoological Gardens

Prince Albert Rd.

Outer Circle

REGENT'S PARK

Broad Walk

St. John's Wood Chapel

Mosque

Inner Circle

Open Air Theatre

Chester Rd.

Albany St.

Outer Circle

Queen Mary's Gardens

N

Park Rd.

Rossmore Rd.

Clarence Gate

PARK SQUARE

Lisson Grove

Marylebone Station

London Planetarium/ Laserium

Royal Academy of Music

Regent's Park

Park Crescent

Madame Tussaud's Wax Museum

Lisson St.

Marylebone Rd.

BAKER ST.

Devonshire St.

Portland Pl.

EDGWARE RD.

York St.

Gloucester Pl.

Baker St.

Marylebone High St.

Welbeck St.

Wimpole St.

Harley St.

New Cavendish St.

Chapel St.

Crawford St.

Manchester St.

Queen Anne St.

Seymour Pl.

BRYANSTON SQUARE

MONTAGU SQUARE

Wallace Collection

MANCHESTER SQUARE

CAVENDISH SQUARE

Edgware Rd.

George St.

Wigmore St.

CAMBRIDGE SQUARE

OXFORD SQUARE

Hyde Park Crescent

Kendal St.

Upper Berkeley St.

PORTMAN SQUARE

Duke St.

James's St.

Connaught St.

Seymour St.

Oxford St.

BOND ST.

Davies St.

New Bond St.

Bayswater Rd.

Marble Arch

Park Lane

North Audley St.

GROSVENOR SQUARE

Brook St.

Grosvenor St.

N. Carriage Dr.

0   1/8 mile

0   125 meters

U.S. Embassy

BERKELEY SQUARE

SIGHTS

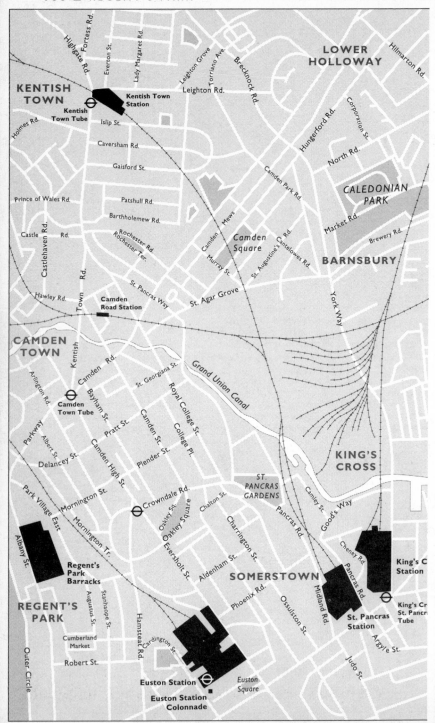

LOWER
HOLLOWAY

KENTISH
TOWN

Highgate Rd.
Fortess Rd.
Everton St.
Lady Margaret Rd.

Kentish Town
Station

Kentish
Town Tube

Islip St.

Leighton Grove
Torriano Ave.
Brecknock Rd.
Leighton Rd.

Hungerford Rd.
Corporation St.
North Rd.

Hilmarton Rd.

Caversham Rd.

Gaisford St.

Camden Park Rd.

CALEDONIAN
PARK

Holmes Rd.

Prince of Wales Rd.

Patshull Rd.

Bartholemew Rd.

Market Rd.

Brewery Rd.

Castle   Rd.

Castlehaven Rd.

Rochester Rd.
Rochester Ter.

Camden Mews

Camden
Square

C. Rd.
St. Augustine's Cantelowes Rd.

BARNSBURY

Town   Rd.

Murray St.

Hawley Rd.

St. Pancras Way

St. Agar Grove

York Way

Camden
Road Station

CAMDEN
TOWN

Kentish

Camden Rd.

Arlington Rd.

Bayham St.

St. Georgiana St.

Royal College St.

College Pl.

Grand Union Canal

Camden
Town Tube

Parkway

Albert St.

Pratt St.

Camden St.

Delancey St.

Camden High St.

Plender St.

KING'S
CROSS

Camley St.

Good's Way

Mornington St.

Crowndale Rd.

Chalton St.

ST.
PANCRAS
GARDENS

Pancras Rd.

Park Village East

Mornington Tr.

Oakley Sq.

Oakley Square

Eversholt St.

Charrington St.

Cheney Rd.

King's C
Station

Albany St.

Regent's
Park
Barracks

Augustus St.

Stanhope St.

Aldenham St.

SOMERSTOWN

Phoenix Rd.

Ossulston St.

Midland Rd.

Pancras Rd.

King's Cr
St. Pancr
Tube

St. Pancras
Station

REGENT'S
PARK

Cumberland
Market

Robert St.

Hampstead Rd.

Cardington St.

Euston Station

Euston Station
Colonnade

Euston
Square

Judo St.

Argyle St.

Outer Circle

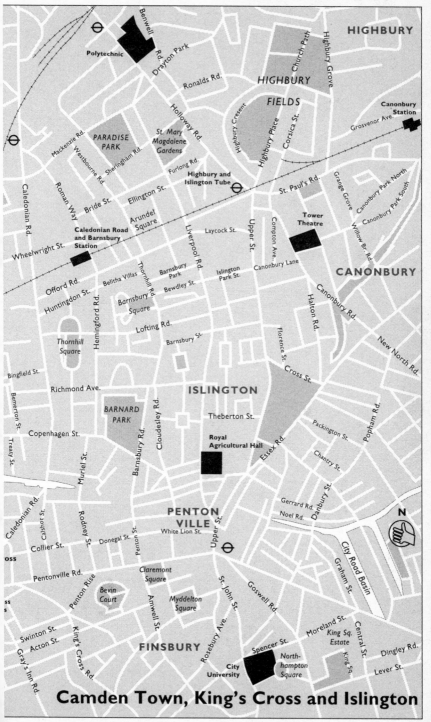

Camden Town, King's Cross and Islington

ers from getting disoriented and lost. Many walk headlong into the hard stone walls which define the narrow, twisted passage. A sign at the door warns patrons to beware of pickpockets. The inside is smelly and dizzying to one entering the blackness from the brightly lit outside. Still the creatures o' the night are eerily arresting and worth seeing. The zoo also has a **snake house** which—according to the £2 guide—somewhere contains a freezer with an antidote to every resident's venom. The snakes are nice little critters—the guide assures readers that only one snakekeeper has died from snakebite in 162 years.

The **Snowdon Aviary** is a striking structure, reminiscent of a nylon stocking stretched over a giant child's jack. Various other exhibits are architecturally notable as well. The **Aquarium** houses a fairly colorless bunch of fish which still seem to enchant the kiddies. Ominous posted warnings at the entrance talk of **biting squirrels.** (Open daily 10am-5:30pm; Oct.-March 10am-4pm. Last admission 1hr. before closing. Admission £7.50, students £6.50, families £22.50.)

Regent's Park Canal, part of the Grand Union Canal, flows though the zoo. The **London Waterbus Company** (tel. 482 2550) offers canal rides April through October to Camden markets (see Street Markets, p. 257; £1.40, £2.20 return) and to "Little Venice" (£2.60, £3.40 return; tube: Warwick Avenue).

■ Bloomsbury

During the first half of the 20th century, Bloomsbury gained its reputation as an intellectual and artistic center, due largely to the presence of the famed Bloomsbury Group, which included biographer Lytton Strachey, novelist E.M. Forster, economist John Maynard Keynes, art critic Roger Fry, painter Vanessa Bell (sister of Virginia Woolf), and hovering on the fringe, T.S. Eliot, the eminent British poet from St. Louis. Although very little of the famed intellectual gossip and high modernist argot currently emanates from 51 Gordon Square, where Virginia Woolf lived with her husband Leonard, the area maintains an earnestly intellectual atmosphere. Even after the Bloomsbury Group's disintegration, young artists and radicals populated the area, giving rise to the term "Bloomsbury bluestockings" to describe modern young women who smoked, drank, and defied the period's restrictive rules.

Today, the British Museum and the University of London guarantee a continued concentration of cerebral activity in the area. The **British Museum** makes an appropriate Bloomsbury centerpiece; forbidding on the outside but quirky and amazing within, it contains the remains of thousands of years worth of world history and civilization, in addition to sheltering the enthralling British Library until construction is completed on its new home, hopefully in late 1997 (see Museums, p. 214).

Buildings of the **University of London** pepper the streets to the north of the Museum. Excluded from the Anglican-dominated universities at Oxford and Cambridge, Jeremy Bentham and a group of dissenters founded **University College** on Gower St. in 1828. They modeled the curriculum after those of German research universities, banned the teaching of theology, and admitted Catholics and Jews. University College was chartered (along with King's College in The Strand) as the University of London in 1836, making London the last major European capital to acquire a university. In 1878, the University became the first to admit women to its degree courses. The university's administrative headquarters and library reside in **Senate House,** the white concrete tower (1933) dominating Malet St. Just up Gower St. at the University College campus, the eerie **remains of Jeremy Bentham** sit proudly in the South Wing. The entrance is in the southwest corner of the quad as you enter from Gower St. (open Mon.-Fri. 9am-5pm).

To the north, close by Strachey and Keynes's former homes, stands the **Percival David Foundation of Chinese Art,** 53 Gordon Sq. (tel. 387 3909; tube: Russell Sq. or Goodge St.), a connoisseur's hoard of fabulously rare ceramics. Sir David presented his ceramics collection to the University of London in 1950; it is currently administered by **SOAS** (School of Oriental and African Studies). The ground floor of the museum resembles a high school trophy case, but the top floors offer more eccentric delights. (Open Mon.-Fri. 10:30am-5pm. Free.)

To the northeast, along Euston Rd., **St. Pancras Station** (tube: King's Cross/St. Pancras) is a monument to Victorian prosperity rising over a currently shabby neighborhood. This red-brick Neo-Gothic fantasy, completed in 1867, opened in 1874 as the Midland Grand Hotel. In 1890 the hotel opened the first smoking room for women in London. After serving as an office building from 1935 until the early 1980s, the now abandoned building faces an uncertain future. Next door, the sprawling new (and controversially ugly) **British Library** is still under construction, although it is due to be completed in late 1997.

Up St. Pancras Rd., past the station's red brick effluvia, **St. Pancras Old Church** sits serenely in its large and leafy garden. Parts of the church date from the 11th century. Mary Godwin first met Shelley here in 1813 by the grave of her mother, Mary Wollstonecraft. Rumor has it that believing her mum died during her birth, Godwin insisted Shelley make love with her on the grave. Moving right along, directly northeast of the British museum, **Russell Square** squares off as central London's second-largest, after Lincoln's Inn Fields. T.S. Eliot, the "Pope of Russell Square," hid from his emotionally ailing first wife at no. 24 while he worked as an editor and later director of Faber and Faber, the famed publishing house.

Bernard Street leads east to Brunswick Square, sight of the **Thomas Coram Foundation for Children** (40 Brunswick Square; tel. 278 2424; tube: Russell Square). Thomas Coram, a retired sea captain, established the Foundling Hospital for abandoned children here in 1747. In order to raise funds, he sought the help of prominent artists, including William Hogarth, who, in addition to serving as a governor of the hospital, donated paintings and persuaded his friends to do the same. The composer Handel also lent a hand, giving the hospital an organ and performing in a number of benefit concerts. Although the hospital was torn down in 1926, its art treasures remain, displayed in a suite of splendidly restored 18th-century rooms. Several canvases by Hogarth mingle with works by Gainsborough, Benjamin West, and Roubiliac, a cartoon by Raphael, and a signed manuscript copy of the *Messiah*. The adjacent Governor's Court Room, with its ornate ceilings and rococo plaster work, houses a poignant collection of tokens and trinkets left with the foundlings admitted to the hospital before 1760 (open by appointment only; admission £2).

Across from the Foundation lies **Coram's Fields** (93 Guilford St.; tel. 837 6138), seven acres of old Foundling Hospital grounds that have been preserved as a children's park, complete with a menagerie of petting animals, an aviary, and a paddling pool for tykes under five. No dogs allowed—no adults, either, unless accompanied by a child (open Easter-Oct. daily 9am-8pm, Nov.-March daily 9am-5pm; free). Although there are no sheep to pet, the adjacent parks are open to the public.

Charles Dickens lived at 48 Doughty St. (east of Russell Sq., parallel to Gray's Inn Rd.) from 1837 to 1839, scribbling parts of *The Pickwick Papers, Nicholas Nickleby, Barnaby Rudge,* and *Oliver Twist.* Now a four-floor museum and library of Dickens paraphernalia, the **Dickens House** (tel. 405 2127; tube: Russell Sq. or Chancery La.) holds an array of prints, photographs, manuscripts, letters, and personal effects. What it lacks in pizzazz, it makes up for by being extremely informative. The rusty iron grill mounted on a basement wall was salvaged by the author from the Marshalsea Jail, a notorious debtor's prison where Dickens's father did time for three months in 1824 while his young son labored in a shoeblack factory (open Mon.-Sat. 10am-5pm, last entry 4:30pm; admission £3.50, students £2.50, children £1.50, families £7).

To the south of the British museum, the shrapnel-scarred Corinthian portico of Hawksmoor's 18th-century church, **St. George's, Bloomsbury** looms in Bloomsbury Way. Completed in 1730 according to Nicholas Hawksmoor's design, a statue of George I crowns the heavy steeple, which was modelled on the tomb of King Mansolos in Turkey. Inside, novelist Anthony Trollope was baptized before the gilded mahogany altar, where Dickens set his "Bloomsbury Christening" in *Sketches by Boz.* (Open Mon.-Sat. 9:30am-5:30pm.)

SIGHTS

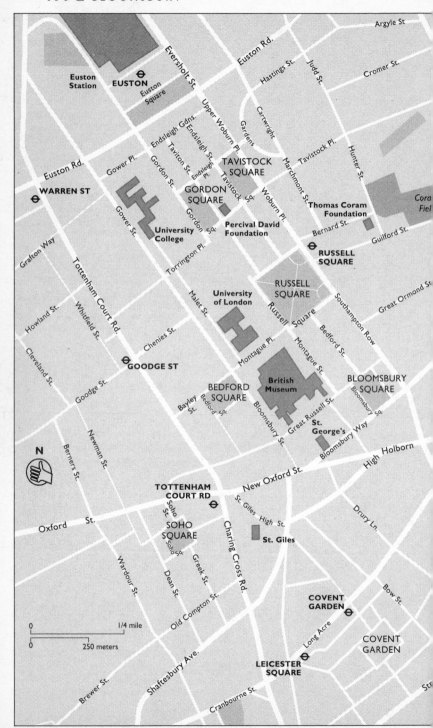

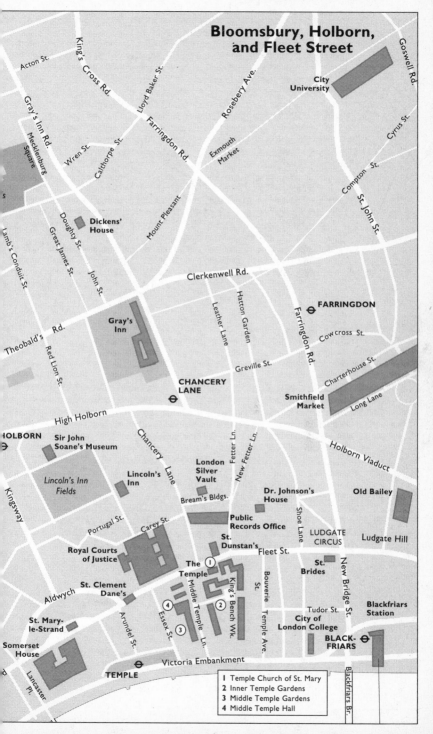

Bloomsbury, Holborn, and Fleet Street

Acton St.

King's Cross Rd.

Lloyd Baker St.

Roseberry Ave.

Goswell Rd.

City University

Cyrus St.

Gray's Inn Rd.

Mecklenburg Square

Wren St.

Calthorpe St.

Farringdon Rd.

Exmouth Market

Compton St.

St. John St.

Doughty St.

Great James St.

Mount Pleasant

Dickens' House

Lamb's Conduit St.

Clerkenwell Rd.

FARRINGDON

Theobald's Rd.

John St.

Gray's Inn

Leather Lane

Hatton Garden

Farringdon Rd.

Cowcross St.

Red Lion St.

Greville St.

Charterhouse St.

CHANCERY LANE

Smithfield Market

Long Lane

High Holborn

Chancery Lane

Fetter Ln.

New Fetter Ln.

Holborn Viaduct

HOLBORN

Sir John Soane's Museum

Lincoln's Inn Fields

Lincoln's Inn

London Silver Vault

Dr. Johnson's House

Old Bailey

Kingsway

Portugal St.

Carey St.

Bream's Bldgs.

Public Records Office

Shoe Lane

LUDGATE CIRCUS

Ludgate Hill

St. Dunstan's

Fleet St.

St. Brides

New Bridge St.

Royal Courts of Justice

The Temple

Middle Temple Ln.

King's Bench Wk.

Bouverie St.

Blackfriars Station

St. Clement Dane's

Aldwych

Temple Ave.

Tudor St.

City of London College

BLACK-FRIARS

St. Mary-le-Strand

Arundel St.

Essex St.

Somerset House

Lancaster Pl.

Victoria Embankment

TEMPLE

Blackfriars Br.

1 Temple Church of St. Mary
2 Inner Temple Gardens
3 Middle Temple Gardens
4 Middle Temple Hall

Directly west of the museum, Bedford Square remains one of London's best-preserved 18th-century squares. All the doorways are framed with original pieces of Coade Stone, an artificial stone manufactured outside of London. Further west, the residential calm is interrupted by Tottenham Ct. Rd., lined with furniture and electronics shops. To the north, the 580-ft. **Telecom Tower** looms over Fitzrovia.

Despite the historical aura that suffuses the area today, Bloomsbury is still a locus of innovation. Several community centers provide venues and resources for alternative cultural activity. Particularly noteworthy are the **Drill Hall** (see Entertainment, p. 232), **The Place** (p. 237), and the **October Gallery** (24 Old Gloucester St., off of Queen St.), a small venue that mounts the works of young, international artists (tel. 242 7367; open Tues.-Sat. 12:30-5:30pm). Similarly, **Gay's The Word Bookshop** (p. 261) adds its own slant to the collection of traditional, secondhand, and rare bookstores that recall Bloomsbury's historical role as a center of book trade.

Jeremy Bentham's "Auto-Icon"

Jeremy Bentham's utilitarianism and religious iconoclasm have resulted in a truly bizarre last request. His organs were donated to science, a highly controversial move in a world dominated by notions of Christians rising from the grave, bodies and all. He hoped for a similarly utilitarian use of his body, and ordered it to be dressed in his customary suit and favorite cane. Bentham hoped that such "auto-icons" of himself and other inspiring individuals might be put on display as encouragement to their successors. After the body was donated to University College and put on display, its head corroded to such a state that it was removed from the body and placed between his legs. Eventually, the powers that be realized just how creepy this was (check the picture to see for yourself) and finally removed it to a University safe. It is rumored that the Auto-Icon sits in on board meetings, always noted as "present, but abstaining."

■ Islington

Lying in the low hills just north of the City of London, Islington (tube: Angel or Highbury and Islington) began as a royal hunting ground. Islington was first absorbed into London by fugitives from the Plague, and later by industrialization and trade along Regent's Canal. Islington first became "trendy" during the late 17th century, when its ale houses and cream teas made it a popular hang-out for wealthy scene-makers. A century later, however, the rich began to move out, leaving the area to deteriorate. In more recent times, Islington was one of London's first areas to undergo regentrification; it established itself as an academic and artistic haven by the 1930s, serving as home to writers such as George Orwell, Evelyn Waugh, Douglas Adams, and Salman Rushdie. Current Labour Party leader Tony Blair also calls this area home.

Today, Islington is one of the hottest neighborhoods in London. The area is favored by trendy, style-conscious, and well-to-do Londoners. It is often spoken of as a district on the verge of becoming the next Covent Garden or Soho. Many of the more stylish University of London students and professors live here, alongside several ethnic communities including Turkish, Irish, Italian, and Bengali residents. As the number of gay pubs in the area attests, Islington is also home to a large gay community. (Chris Smith, one of the few voluntarily out Members of Parliament, was elected from this area.) Islington now puts on a summer display of its artistic resources through the annual **Islington International Festival** during the last week of June (1995 was the inaugural year). **Upper St.**, the area's main drag, is closed for the festival (call 833 3131 for info.). **Angel St.,** which intersects Upper St., in the most happenin' part of town is home to a number of quirky, mod shops.

A refurbished 19th-century chapel at 44a Pentonville Road now houses the **Crafts Council,** the national organization for the promotion of contemporary crafts. In addition to the Crafts Council Gallery, the building also contains a picture library with slides of British works, a reference library, a gallery shop, and a café. The council sponsors fantastic temporary exhibitions. Take advantage of the free admission; not only are the main exhibition galleries wonderfully air-conditioned, but the building's lighting fixtures, furniture, clocks, floors, door handles, and lettering have been designed by contemporary artisans, creating an aesthetically appealing exhibition space. (Tel. 278 7700. Tube: Angel, exit the station to the left and take the first right onto Pentonville Rd. Open Tues.-Sat. 11am-6pm, Sun. 2-6pm. Wheelchair accessible.)

The **Business Design Centre** at 52 Upper St. is hard to miss. The modern-looking glass façade belies its origin as the Royal Agricultural Hall, completed in 1861. Known as "the Aggie," the Hall's large, enclosed space served as the site for a wide range of crafts exhibitions, animal shows, meetings, Christmas *fêtes*, military tournaments, circuses, and the World's Fair. All was happy and glorious until the start of World War II, when the government took over the Hall to use it as an office building. In the 1970s, the Hall was sold to a property developer who hadn't realized that the historic building could not legally be demolished; apparently is was permissible to add skylights and huge, box-like windows which totally update the buildings appearance. Annual exhibits include Fresh Art, a showcase for recent fine arts graduates, and New Designers, a springboard for commercial and consumer design students. (Call 359 3535 or 288 8666 for info. and details; many exhibitions charge admission.)

■ Holborn and The Inns Of Court

There's no law like English law. The historical center of English law lies in an area straddling the precincts of Westminster and the City and surrounding long and litigious precincts of High Holborn, Chancery Lane, and Fleet Street. The Strand and Fleet St. meet at the **Royal Courts of Justice** (tel. 936 6000; tube: Temple), a wonderfully elaborate gothic structure—easily mistaken for a cathedral—designed in 1874 by architect G.E. Street for the Supreme Court of Judicature. At the Strand entrance there are a helpful set of displays explaining the court system. Today's not the day to wear that plated Mercedes medallion—security here is tight, metal detectors here are highly sensitive. The biggest draw for tourists who sit in on proceedings are the **wigs** the justices and barristers wear. On hot days the judge may allow everyone to remove their wigs, but newer weaves have made this indecorous allowance rare. (Courts and galleries open to the public Mon.-Fri. 9am-4:30pm; court cases start at 10-10:30am, but they break for lunch 1-2pm). The first floor contains an otherwise dreary cafeteria which permits patrons to determine the size of their own orders of chips (90p)—some daredevils test the bounds of self service by emptying the pan onto a tray. Rules are rules, *and barristers know this,* so let your appetite guide you.

Barristers in the City are affiliated with one of the famous **Inns of Court** (Middle Temple, Inner Temple, Lincoln's Inn, and Gray's Inn), four ancient legal institutions that provide lectures and apprenticeships for law students and regulate admission to the bar. The tiny gates and narrow alleyways that lead to the Inns are invisible to most passersby. Inside, the Inns are organized like colleges at Oxford, each with its own gardens (great for sunbathing or picnicking), chapel, library, dining hall, common rooms, and chambers. Most were founded in the 13th century when a royal decree barred the clergy from the courts of justice, giving rise to a new class of professional legal advocates. Today, students may seek their legal training outside of the Inns, but to be considered for membership they must "keep term" by dining regularly in one of the halls.

South of Fleet St., the labyrinth of the **Temple** (tube: Temple) encloses the prestigious and stately Middle and Inner Temple Inns. They derive their name from the clandestine, elusive, crusading Order of the Knights Templar, who embraced this site as their English seat in the 12th century. The secretive, bellicose order dissolved in 1312 and this property was eventually passed on to the Knights Hospitallers of St. John, who leased it to a community of common law scholars in 1338. Virtually leveled by the Germans in the early 1940s, only the church, crypt, and buttery of the Inner Temple survive intact from the Middle Ages.

SIGHTS

Held in common by both the Middle and Inner Temples, the **Temple Church** is made of an older round church (1185 AD) and a newer addition of a rectangular nave (1240 AD). The older portion is the finest of the few round churches left in England. It contains gorgeous stained-glass windows, a handsome 12th-century Norman doorway, an altar screen by Wren (1682), and 10 arresting, armor-clad stone effigies of sinister Knights Templar dating from the 12th and 14th centuries. Be sure to note the grotesque heads lining the circular wall surrounding the effigies.

According to Shakespeare *(Henry VI)*, the red and white roses that served as emblems throughout the War of the Roses were plucked from the Middle Temple Garden. On Groundhog Day in 1601, Shakespeare himself supposedly appeared in a performance of *Twelfth Night* in **Middle Temple Hall,** a grand Elizabethan dining room in a building on Middle Temple Lane, just past Brick Ct. (not open to the public). **Fountain Court** contains its 1681 namesake, restored in 1919. Nearby, a handful of London's last functioning gas lamps illuminate Middle Temple Lane.

Back across Fleet St., on the other side of the Royal Courts, **Lincoln's Inn** (tube: Holborn) was the only Inn to emerge unscathed from the Blitz. The lawyers of Lincoln's Inn were mocked by John Donne's rhyming couplets in his *Satire: On Lawyers.* **New Square** and its cloistered churchyard (to the right as you enter from Lincoln's Inn Fields) appear today much as they did in the 1680s. The **Old Hall,** east of New Sq., dates from 1492; here the Lord High Chancellor presided over the High Court of Chancery from 1733 to 1873. The best-known chancery case is that of Jarndyce and Jarndyce, whose life-sapping machinations are played out in the many pages of *Bleak House.* Dickens knew well what he described, having worked as a lawyer's clerk in New Court just across the yard. To the west, Tudor-style **New Hall** houses a 19th-century mural by G.F. Watts and a lugubrious collection of legal portraits. Built in 1497, the adjacent library is London's oldest. John Donne, William Pitt, Horace Walpole, and Benjamin Disraeli number among the many luminaries associated with Lincoln's Inn. The only portion of the grounds open to visitors is the grassy quadrangle and the **New Chapel,** which features a spectacular red roof (open Mon.-Fri. noon-2:30pm). **Sir John Soane's Museum** sits on the north side of Lincoln's Inn Fields, London's largest square; it's the house bedecked with sculpture amidst a row of plain buildings (see Museums, p. 222).

Gray's Inn (tube: Chancery La.), dubbed "that stronghold of melancholy" by Dickens, stands at the northern end of Fulwood Pl., off High Holborn. Reduced to ashes by German bombers in 1941, Gray's Inn was restored during the 1950s. The **Hall,** to your right as you pass through the archway, retains its original stained glass (1580) and most of its ornate screen. The first performance of Shakespeare's *Comedy of Errors* took place here in 1594. Francis Bacon maintained chambers here from 1577 until his death in 1626, and is the purported designer of the gardens.

Of the nine Inns of Chancery, only **Staple Inn's** building survives (located where Gray's Inn Rd. meets High Holborn; tube: Chancery La.). The half-timbered Elizabethan front, with its easily recognized vertical striping, dates from 1586. Devoted son Samuel Johnson wrote "Rasselas" here in one week to pay for his mother's funeral. For those who can't get enough of the fascinating Inns of Court, "Legal London" **walking tours** are held every Monday at 2pm and Wednesday at 11am departing from the Holborn tube station (tel. 624 3978; £4.50, students £3.50).

▓ The Strand

Hugging the embankment of the River Thames, **The Strand** (tube: Charing Cross, Temple, or Aldwych—rush hours only) has fared ill throughout London's growth. The street was built to connect the City with the Westminster Palace and Parliament. Once lined with fine Tudor houses, today this major thoroughfare curves from Trafalgar Square through a jumbled assortment of dull commercial buildings. All the sights are at the Aldwych and Temple end of the street.

Somerset House, a magnificent Palladian structure built by Sir William Chambers in 1776, stands on the site of the 16th-century palace where Elizabeth I resided during the brief reign of her sister Mary. Formerly the administrative center of the Royal Navy, the building now houses the exquisite and intimately-housed **Courtauld Collection** (see Museums, p. 221).

Just east of the Courtauld, **St. Mary-le-Strand's** slender steeple and elegant portico rise above an island of decaying steps in the middle of the modern roadway. Designed by James Gibbs and consecrated in 1724, the church overlooks the site of the original Maypole, where London's first hackney cabs assembled in 1634. Parishioner Isaac Newton laid claim to the pole for a telescope stand. Inside, the baroque barrel vault and altar walls reflect not only the glory of God but also Gibbs' architectural training in Rome. The mesmerizing blue windows are another reminder of things more temporal; they are replacements of those blown out in WWII (open Mon.-Fri. 11am-3:30pm). Across the street, newsreaders intone "This is London" every hour from **Bush House,** the nerve center of the **BBC's** radio services.

To the east stands handsome **St. Clement Danes** (tel. 242 8282), whose melodious bells get their 15 seconds of fame in the nursery rhyme "Oranges and lemons, say the bells of St. Clement's." Children get their 15 minutes of fruit when oranges and lemons are distributed in a ceremony near the end of March. (The bells still ring at 9am, noon, 3, and 6pm every day.) Designed by Wren in 1682, the church was built over the ruins of an older Norman structure reputed to be the tomb of Harold Harefoot, leader of a colony of Danes who settled the area in the 9th century. In 1720, Gibbs replaced Wren's original truncated tower with a slimmer spire. Although German firebombs gutted the church in 1941, the ornately molded white stucco and gilt interior has been restored. Today it is the official church of the Royal Air Force—evident in the many plaques and monuments which honor these bold airmen. A crypt-cum-prayer-chapel houses an eerie collection of 17th-century funerary monuments. Samuel Johnson worshipped here—a statue of the Doctor strikes a bizarre pose outside the church. The good doctor looks like a portly high school football coach urging the team on to victory. (Open daily 8am-5pm.)

The nearby gothic giant houses the Royal Courts of Justice (see Holborn and Inns of Court, p. 173). **Twining's Teas** (tel. 353 3511) honors the leaf which started a war at 216 The Strand, near the Fleet St. end of the road. After nine generations of Mr. Twinings, it is both the oldest business in Britain still on original premises and the narrowest shop in London (open Mon.-Fri. 9:30am-4:30pm). Because of fire regulations they can't brew tea on premises, so they feature only iced tea (served lukewarm). Just east stands the only Strand building to avoid the Great Fire, the **Wig and Pen Club,** 229-230 The Strand, which was constructed over Roman ruins in 1625. Frequented by the best-known barristers and journalists in London, the Wig and Pen is the ultimate old-boys hangout, although women of the legal and newspaper professions are now permitted to join. The club is open to members only, though a passport-toting overseas traveler can peek upstairs. If you have the nerve, walk up the ancient, crooked staircase—the only remnant of the original 17th-century house—and take note of the photographs of Prince Charles dining at the club, as well as signed photos of Nixon, Reagan, and former Chief Justice Burger. Backpackers beware: the doorman will haughtily reject denim-bedecked budget travelers. Displayed on the street is a set of photographs of previous parties, including one of a distinguished-looking bewigged fellow enmeshed in the long limbs of a far younger woman holding an ostrich feather pen and saucily taking dictation.

The **Temple Bar Monument** stands where The Strand meets Fleet St., marking the boundary between Westminster and the City. The Sovereign must obtain ceremonial permission from the Lord Mayor to enter the City here.

To the south, the **Embankment** (tube: Charing Cross or Embankment) runs along the Thames, parallel to The Strand. Between the Hungerford and Waterloo Bridges stands London's oldest (though non-indigenous) landmark, **Cleopatra's Needle,** an Egyptian obelisk from 1450 BC, stolen by the Viceroy of Egypt in 1878. A sister stone stands in Central Park in New York. Fairly near Trafalgar Sq., the **Queen's Chapel of the Savoy** (1505) on Savoy Hill—an appendage of Savoy Palace, inhabited after 1268 by John of Gaunt—provides a respite from the traffic and sensationalistic journalism of Fleet St. (tel. 836 7221; open Tues.-Fri. 11:30am-3pm, and for services Sun. 11am).

■ Fleet Street

Named for the one-time river (now a sewer) that flows from Hampstead to the Thames, Fleet Street (tube: Blackfriars or St. Paul's) was until recently the hub of British journalism. Fleet Street is now just a famous name and a few (vacated) famous buildings. Following a stand-off with the printing unions in 1986, the *Times* moved to cheaper land at Wapping, Docklands, and initiated a mass exodus from the street. The *Daily Telegraph* soon abandoned its startling Greek and Egyptian revival building, moving to Marsh Wall in 1987. The *Daily Express,* once the occupant of an Art Deco manse of chrome and black glass on Fleet St., now headlines in Blackfriars. Rupert Murdoch's *The Sun* also moved to Wapping at this time. (In looking for addresses of the following sights, beware that, like many English streets, Fleet St. is numbered up one side and down the other.)

The tiered spire of Wren's **St. Bride's** (1675), near 89 Fleet St., became the inspiration for countless wedding cakes thanks to an ingenious local baker. Dubbed "the printers' cathedral" because the first printing press with moveable type was housed here in 1500, it has long had a connection with newspapermen. In fact, church officials seem to have taken a lesson from the tabloids in creating their sign board, covered with catchy (and somewhat misleading) *Did you know?* facts about the church. One listing asks (paraphrasing): Did you know that a German bomb falling in 1940 caused the discovery of ancient ruins below the church? The full story is that in 1952, 12 years after the bomb fell, during foundation inspections made before rebuilding the church, a set of skeletons were found below the church. Bodies buried in a crypt which were sealed off in the 19th century during a cholera epidemic. The current church is sparklingly clean and quite beautiful inside. (Open Mon.-Fri. 8am-5pm, Sat. 9am-5pm.) Next to St. Brides stands Reuters, one of the last remaining media powerhouses left on Fleet St.

A few blocks down the street, opposite 54 Fleet St., a large white sign labels the alleyway entrance (through Hind Ct.) to Johnson's Court. Inside the alley, more discreet signs point the way to **Samuel Johnson's House,** 17 Gough Square (tel. 353 3745). Follow the signs carefully; Carlyle got lost on his way here in 1832. A self-described "shrine to the English language," this dark brick house was Dr. Johnson's abode from 1748 to 1759. Here he completed his *Dictionary,* the first definitive English lexicon, even though rumor falsely insists that he omitted "sausage." He compiled this amazing document by reading all the great books of the age and marking the words he wanted included in the *Dictionary* with black pen. He was assisted by six clerks—the books he used were unreadable by the project's end. The knowledgeable curator is eager to supplement your visit with anecdotes about the Great Cham and his hyperbolic biographer, James Boswell (open May-Sept. Mon.-Sat. 11am-5:30pm; Oct.-April Mon.-Sat. 11am-5pm; admission £3, concessions £2, children £1; audio tour 50p).

A few more blocks down Fleet St., the neo-Gothic **St. Dunstan-in-the-West** holds its magnificent lantern tower high above the banks surrounding it. The chimes of its curious 17th-century clock are sounded on the quarter hour by a pair of hammer-wielding mechanical giants. A statue of Elizabeth I (one of the few contemporary likenesses of the Queen) rises above the vestry door. The three 16th-century effigies leaning against the porch may represent King Lud, the mythical founder of London, and his sons.

■ The City of London

Until the 18th century, the City of London was London; all other boroughs and neighborhoods now swallowed up by "London" were neighboring towns or outlying villages. Enclosed by Roman and medieval walls, the City had six gates: Aldersgate, Aldgate, Bishopsgate, Cripplegate, Newgate, and Ludgate.

Today, the 1-sq.-mi. City of London is the financial center of Europe. Each weekday 350,000 people surge in at 9am and rush out again unfailingly at 5pm, leaving behind a resident population of only 6000. Today's City hums with activity during the work week, is dead on Saturdays, and seems downright ghostly on Sundays. At the center of the City, the massive **Bank of England** controls the nation's finances and the **Stock Exchange** makes the nation's fortune (see City: Bank to Tower, p. 180). International banks surrounding the Greek-columned buildings appear in homage to these giant structures. Proliferating cranes, office building sites, and rising share indices bore witness to the British "economic resurgence" of the late 80s, while the panic in such City stalwarts as Lloyd's of London is testimony to the precariousness of the early 90s. Terrorist attacks in the recent past have prompted the government to regulate traffic into the City; although all roadblocks are no longer manned, vehicles must still enter from one of the eight streets where they are sometimes checked for bombs. These security measures have exacerbated traffic congestion, which was already considered horrendous by most city dwellers. London's air quality is among the poorest in the world, and many Londoners hope that the roadblocks will be maintained as a weapon against excessive traffic and pollution regardless of political climate.

Behind this array of modern chaos rest pieces of another city: old London. Aged churches, friaries, and pubs, many of them still in use, dwell behind small alleys and above the roofs of steel office buildings. **St. Paul's Cathedral,** the most glorious and significant of these structures, anchors London's memory to its colorful past (see St. Paul's Cathedral, p. 182). The City owes much of its graceful appearance to Sir Christopher Wren, who was the chief architect working after the **Great fire of 1666** almost completely razed the area. In his diary, Samuel Pepys gives a moving firsthand account of the fire that started in a bakery in Pudding Lane and leapt between the overhanging houses to bring destruction upon the City. In a classic case of locking the barn door after the barn has burned down, Charles II issued a proclamation afterwards that City buildings should be rebuilt in brick and stone, rather than highly flammable wood and thatch. Wren's studio designed 52 churches to replace the 89 destroyed in the fire, and the surviving 24 churches are some of the only buildings in the City from the period immediately following the Great Fire. A host of variations on a theme, they gave Wren a valuable chance to work out design problems that would come up as he rebuilt St. Paul's Cathedral. The original effect of a forest of steeples surrounding the great dome of St. Paul's must be his greatest contribution to London's cityscape; unfortunately, modern skyscrapers now obscure that effect. Some churches and old buildings have not withstood the collision with modernity. Many old structures were totally gutted by the German blitz in 1941, while others have taken on a bombed-out and blackened appearance as a result of coal fires during the 1960s and today's thickening air pollution.

Perhaps the most important secular structures of the City are the buildings of the **Livery Companies.** The companies began as medieval guilds representing specific trades and occupations, such as the Drapers and the Fishmongers. New guilds, like the information technologists, have formed to keep up with changing times. The 84 **livery halls** are scattered around the square mile. Most halls do not open to the public; those that do require tickets. The City of London Information Centre (see below) receives a batch of tickets in February, but they disappear rapidly. Some halls sponsor spring celebrations and a few hold fascinating exhibits—for example, a showing of the finest products of London's goldsmiths.

The **City of London Information Centre,** St. Paul's Churchyard, EC4 (tel. 606 3030; tube: St. Paul's), specializes in information about the City of London but answers questions on all of London. A helpful, knowledgeable staff are worth speaking to before exploring this part of the city. (Open daily 9:15am-5pm; Nov.-March Mon.-Fri. 9:15am-5pm, Sat. 9:15am-12:30pm.) The oldest part of London, the City is home to many municipal traditions. One of the largest is the **Lord Mayor's Show,** on the second Saturday of November, a glittering parade of pomp and red velvet to the Royal

The Lord Mayor

The Lord Mayor's position has not always been entirely ceremonial, nor has it always been lordly. The job originally consisted in running the affairs of the City 900 years ago. The wily merchants of the City used their financial leverage to win increasing amounts of autonomy from the monarchy throughout the years culminating in the construction of Guildhall—the Lord Mayor's official worshipping site—and the move from just plain Mayorship to Lord Mayorship. While the position today is ceremonial, it retains its pomp and grandeur. The Lord Mayor is the Chief Magistrate, Chairman of the Court of Aldermen, and the Court of Common Council, and in the City is second only to the Queen, although the Queen—and only the Queen—has to ask his permission before entering the city gates.

Courts of Justice in celebration of London citizens' right to elect their Lord Mayor. Information and street plans are available from the City of London Information Centre starting in mid-October. One of the newer traditions is July's **City of London Festival,** which jam-packs the churches, halls, squares, and sidewalks of the area with music and theater (see Entertainment, p. 236).

The area is filled with architecturally stunning churches—beware, opening times are often changed without notice due the small staffs in many of these financially strapped houses of worship. The sights in the City area are helpfully marked by distinctive brown signs which direct you from Tube stations.

CITY (WESTERN SECTION): BANK TO ST. PAUL'S

The few remaining stones of the Roman **Temple of Mithras,** Queen Victoria St. (tube: Bank or Mansion House), dwell incongruously in the shadow of the Temple Court building. Discovered during construction work and shifted a few yards from its original location, what remains are 2ft.-tall walls in the shape of the original temple. Down Queen Victoria St., **St. Mary Aldermary** (so called because it is older than any other St. Mary's church in the City) towers over its surroundings. (Open Thurs. 11am-3pm.) A rare Gothic Wren, it is especially notable for its delicate fan vaulting. The bells that recalled Mayor Dick Whittington to London rang out from St. Marie de Arcubus, replaced by Wren's **St. Mary-le-Bow,** Cheapside, in 1683. The range of the Bow bells' toll is supposed to define the extent of true-blue Cockney London. (Open Mon.-Thurs. 6:30am-6pm, Fri. 6:30am-4pm.)

St. James Garlickhythe, on Upper Thames St., gets its name from the garlic once sold nearby. Its modest Hawksmoor steeple is dwarfed by the huge Vintners Place development across the street. (Open Mon.-Fri. 10am-4pm) To the west on Queen Victoria St. stands a rare red-brick Wren church with an elegant cupola, **St. Benet's.** (Open by arrangement.) Just across the street, the **College of Arms** (tel. 248 2762) rests on its heraldic authority behind ornate gates. The College regulates the granting and recognition of coats of arms, and is directed by the Earl Marshal, the Duke of Norfolk. The officer-in-waiting can assess your claim to a British family coat of arms. (Open Mon.-Fri. 10am-4pm.) Farther west, at 146 Queen Victoria, **St. Andrew-by-the-Wardrobe** (tube: Blackfriars) was originally built next to Edward III's impressive Royal Stores. Now the church cowers beneath the Faraday building, the first building allowed to exceed the City's previously strict height limit. (Open Mon.-Fri. 10am-6pm, closed during Aug.)

Queen Victoria St. meets New Bridge St. in the area known as Blackfriars, in reference to the darkly clad Dominican brothers who built a monastery there in the middle ages. Shakespeare acted in James Burbage's theatre here in the late 1500s. Ludgate Circus, to the north, has recently received a major facelift. A peaceful haven is offered by **St. Martin Ludgate,** a Wren church on Ludgate Hill untouched by the Blitz. The square interior boasts some fine Grinling Gibbons woodwork, and the slim spire still pierces the dome of St. Paul's when seen from Ludgate Circus, just as Wren intended. (Open Tues.-Fri. 11am-3pm.)

Around the corner, the **Old Bailey** (tel. 248 3277; tube: St. Paul's), technically the Central Criminal Courts, crouches under a copper dome and a wide-eyed figure of justice on the corner of Old Bailey and Newgate St.—infamous as the site of Britain's grimiest prison. Trial-watching persists as a favorite occupation, and the Old Bailey fills up whenever a gruesome or scandalous case is in progress. You can enter the public Visitors' Gallery and watch bewigged barristers at work (Mon.-Fri. 10am-1pm and 2-4pm; entrance in Warwick Passage off of Old Bailey). Even women wear wigs so that they too may look like wise old men. Cameras and large bags may not be taken inside. The Chief Post Office building, off Newgate to the north, envelops the enthralling **National Postal Museum** (see Museums, p. 226). **Postman's Park,** nestled behind obscuring gates and church walls, provides wonderful space for a quick snooze or picnic. The park was once the churchyard of St. Leonard's Cathedral and the graveyard for Christ Church; haunted-house-like gravestones still line its southern perimeter. Toward the back of the park rests a 19th-century memorial to firefighters, police officers, and good samaritans killed in the line of duty.

Further east on Angel St. and Gresham St., going left up Aldermanbury, huddles the **Guildhall** (tel. 606 3030), a cavernous space where dignitaries were once tried for treason. An improbable mix of high Gothic and modish 60s concrete, the building currently serves as the City's administrative center and houses the town clerk, a library, offices, and the **Guildhall Clock Museum** (see Museums, p. 224). Its **Great Hall,** lined with monuments to national figures like Nelson and Wellington, hosts monthly city council meetings and banquets. On the balcony stand the 9-ft. gilded statues of the ancient giants **Gog** and **Magog.** Visitors are welcome every third Thursday to watch the Lord Mayor of London, bedecked in traditional robes and followed by a sworded entourage, preside over council meetings. He ranks above the Queen when she enters the city. (Open daily May-Sept. 10am-5pm; Oct.-April Mon.-Sat. 10am-5pm.) The **Guildhall Library** on Aldermanbury St. specializes in the history of London—holdings include City church manuscripts, family genealogies, and early maps. Visitors are free to browse through the collection of books as well as to visit the library's quadrennial exhibitions in the Print Room. In 1997 the library will exhibit *Thames Frostfares,* a collection of pictures taken of Londoners frolicking on the frozen river. Visitors are not permitted to take books out of the library. (Library and print room open Mon.-Sat. 9:30am-5pm.) For a quick respite after Guildhall, visit **Finsbury Park.** (On Finsbury Circus around the corner from Moorgate Tube.) Surrounded by round-faced, Georgian office buildings, this circular park's colorful flower bed and jungle-green bowling area offer delightful spots for picnics, free summer concerts, and bowling, British style.

Next to the Guildhall is the Wren-designed **St. Lawrence Jewry,** the official church of the Corporation of London. This seemingly absurd title reflects the fact that the church was, in days of yore, the sole Christian house in a predominately Jewish area. It was rebuilt after the war, due to damage from what the sign outside formally refers to as "action by the King's Enemies," namely a German bomb. (Open Mon.-Fri. 7:30am-2pm.)

CITY: BARBICAN AND NORTHERN SECTION

While housing some of England's greatest cultural treasures, this 35-acre urban complex seems like a shopping mall that never ends (tube: Barbican or Moorgate). The **Barbican Centre** is an unmatched maze of apartment buildings, restaurants, gardens, and exhibition halls, described at its 1982 opening as "the city's gift to the nation." The Royal Shakespeare Company, the London Symphony Orchestra, the Museum of London, the Guildhall School for Music and Drama, and the Barbican Art Gallery (See Entertainment, p. 228, and Museums, p. 223) call this complex home, as do the many politicians and actors who reside in the Barbican's distinctive apartment buildings. St. Giles Church and the City of London School for Girls stand in the complex's unexpectedly verdant central courtyard, whose artificial lakes and planned gardens temper the Barbican's relentless urbanity.

Most visitors enter the Barbican Centre through the Silk St. entrance, where statues of nine golden muses bespeak the Barbican's dazzling elegance. Once inside, though, the Barbican can be daunting. To help visitors successfully navigate the Centre's labyrinthine walkways and vast interior, a reception desk has been installed at the front entrance. In addition, Barbican's floors have been renumbered, so that the ground floor is now called Level 0, not Level 5. Pick up a free pocket guide by the Lakeside Terrace to find your way through the Barbican's wonders, including the Centre's third floor conservatory, second floor library, and ground-floor foyers, where free concerts are held daily. (Library is open Mon. and Wed.-Fri. 9:30am-5:30pm, Tues. 9:30am-7:30pm, Sat. 9:30am-12:30pm.)

In order to reach **St. Bartholomew the Great,** continue past the Barbican tube on Beech St. and make a left on Little Britain. One must enter through an exceedingly narrow Tudor house to reach this architectural jewel. Parts of the church date from 1123, although 800 years of alteration have much embellished it. The tomb near the central main altar belongs to Rahere, who allegedly founded the church after he was cured from malaria through prayer (open Mon.-Fri. 8:30am-5pm, Sat.-Sun. 8am-8pm). Party people anxious to begin a day of drinking should try one of the pubs around **Smithfield Market,** an ancient meat and poultry trade market—the pubs around here are licensed to ale starting at 7am. Smithfield's associations with butchery antedate the meat market. Scotsman William Wallace and rebel Wat Tyler rank among those executed here in the Middle Ages. It was also among the tolerant Queen Mary's favorite Protestant-burning sites.

Charterhouse (tel. 253 3260), a peculiar institution first established as a priory and converted in 1611 to a school and hospital for poor gentlemen, stands on the edge of Charterhouse Sq. The school has moved, but the fine group of 15th- to 17th-century buildings still houses around 40 residents, who must be bachelors or widowers over 60 (tours April-July Wed. at 2:15pm; a small donation is expected).

Just north of the square, up St. John's St. and off Clerkenwell Rd., stands **St. John's Gate** (tel. 253 6644). The gate holds the headquarters of the British Order of the Hospital of St. John, the last vestiges of the medieval crusading order of Knights Hospitallers. Exhibits within relate the order's tumultuous history, from their rise as healers (their 12th-century priory was one of Europe's first hospitals), through their crusading and subsequent dissolution under Henry VIII, and their reemergence in the 19th Century as a volunteer community service organization chartered by Queen Victoria. (Open Mon.-Fri. 10am-5pm, Sat. 10am-4pm. 1-hr. tours of the 1504 gate, the church, and the 12th-century crypt Tues. and Fri.-Sat. 11am and 2:30pm; £2.50 donation requested.)

CITY (EASTERN SECTION): BANK TO THE TOWER

The massive windowless walls and foreboding doors of the **Bank of England** enclose four full acres (tube: Bank). The present building dates from 1925, but the 8-ft.-thick outer wall is the same one built by eccentric architect Sir John Soane in 1788. The only part open to the public is the plush **Bank of England Museum** (see Museums, p. 214). Its neighbors, the Greek-columned Royal Exchange, Stock Exchange, and Lloyd's financial building remain, relics of the days when this block stood as the financial capital of the world. After recent terrorist attacks, all three are no longer open to visitors, but there is not much to see in them anyway. The grand trading pit of the Royal Exchange has been vacated by traders using office-based computers. The room is so empty, in fact, that the government has considered turning it into a gymnasium for local employees. (Head to the Futures Market on Cannon St. to see frenetic traders in brightly-colored jackets continue the Exchange's bustling tradition.) **St. Margaret Lothbury** (down Throgmorton St.), Wren's penultimate church, contains a sumptuous carved wood screen (1689). Most of the church's furnishings have been conglomerated from demolished City churches. (Open Mon.-Fri. 8am-5pm.) A couple of blocks north, the **National Westminster Tower** hovers at over 600ft. Until recently, it was Britain's tallest skyscraper, now displaced by the distant Canary Wharf.

The 1986 **Lloyd's** building and **Leadenhall Market,** off Leadenhall St., supply the most startling architectural clash in the City. The ducts, lifts, and chutes of Lloyd's are straight out of the 21st century. This futuristic setting houses the **Lutine Bell,** which is still occasionally rung—once for bad insurance news, twice for good. In contrast, across a narrow alley behind Lloyd's stretches the ornate red canopies and dazzling gargoyles of Victorian **Leadenhall Market.**

Behind the imposing **Mansion House,** home of the Lord Mayor, stands **St. Stephen Walbrook** (on Walbrook St.). Arguably Wren's finest, and allegedly his personal favorite, the church combines four major styles: the old-fashioned English church characterized by nave and chancel; the Puritan hall church, which lacks any separation between priest and congregation; the Greek-cross-plan church; and the domed church, a study for St. Paul's. The Samaritans, a social service group that advises the suicidal and severely depressed, was founded here in 1953 by rector Chad Varah. In one corner you can see the phone he used, in another is an honorific phone given him by British Telecom. The mysterious cheese-like object ringed by the psychedelic lime, orange, purple, and pink cushion in the center is actually the altar. Sculpted by Henry Moore, it is as controversial as you think it is. (Open Mon.-Thurs. 10am-4pm, Fri. 10am-3pm.)

The church of **St. Mary Woolnoth,** at King William and Lombard St., may look odd without a spire, but the interior proportions and the black and gilt reredos confirm the talents of Wren's pupil Nicholas Hawksmoor. It appears almost wider than it is long. The upper reaches are light and airy; lower portions filled with dark wood. The only City church untouched by the Blitz, it "kept the hours" in T.S. Eliot's *The Waste Land.* (Open Mon.-Fri. 8am-5pm.) **St. Mary Abchurch,** off Abchurch Lane, provides a neat domed comparison to St. Stephen's—its mellow, dark wood and baroque paintings contrast with St. Stephen's bright, airy interior. (Open Mon.-Thurs. 10am-2pm.)

Before even the most basic rebuilding of the city, Wren designed a tall Doric pillar. Completed in 1671, the simply-named **Monument** lies at the bottom of King William St. (tube: Monument). Supposedly, the 202-ft. pillar stands exactly that many feet from where the Great Fire broke out in Pudding Lane on September 2, 1666, and "rushed devastating through every quarter with astonishing swiftness and worse." High on Fish Street Hill, the column offers an expansive view of London. Bring stern resolution and £1 to climb its 311 steps. Upon successfully descending the tower you'll be given a free certificate announcing your feat, signed by the City Secretary. (Open April-Sept. Mon.-Fri. 9am-6pm, Sat.-Sun. 2-6pm; Oct.-March Mon.-Sat. 9am-4pm.)

Over the river near the Monument the current **London Bridge** succeeds a slew of ancestors. The famed version crowded with houses stood from 1176 until it burned in 1758. The most recent predecessor didn't fall down; in 1973 it was sold to an American millionaire for £1.03 million and shipped, block by block, to Lake Havasu City, Arizona. **St. Magnus Martyr,** on Lower Thames St., stands next to the path to the 12th-century London Bridge, and proudly displays a chunk of wood from a Roman jetty. (Open Tues.-Fri. 10:30am-4:30pm.) According to Eliot, the walls of the church "hold inexplicable splendor of Ionian white and gold," a soothing contrast to the forlorn (and former) Billingsgate fish market next door.

St. Mary-at-Hill, Lovat Lane, is a typical Wren church with a surprisingly convincing reworking of the old interior by early Victorian craftsmen, and an even more convincing contemporary reconstruction project. (Open Mon.-Fri. 10am-3pm.) **St. Dunstan-in-the-East,** St. Dunstan's Hill, suffered severe damage in the Blitz; only Wren's amazing spire remains. The ruins have been converted into a gorgeous little garden that makes a fine picnic spot. Covered in green, the remaining walls demarcate a secluded oasis in the middle of the City.

Pepys witnessed the spread of the Great Fire from atop **All Hallows by the Tower,** at the end of Great Tower St. Just inside the south entrance is an arch from the 7th-century Saxon church, discovered in 1960. To the left, the baptistry contains a striking wood font cover by Grinling Gibbons. At the tiny **St. Olave's** in Hart St., an

SIGHTS

annual memorial service is held for Pepys, who is buried here with his wife. According to a 1586 entry in the church's Burial Register, Mother Goose is also interred here.
(Open Mon.-Fri. 9am-5pm.)

■ St. Paul's Cathedral

An extraordinary Anglican spinoff of the Vatican, St. Paul's is arguably the most stunning architectural sight in London. It dominates its surroundings, even as modern
usurpers sneak up around it. St. Paul's has become a physical and spiritual symbol of
London. Prince Charles and Lady Diana broke a 200-year tradition of holding royal
weddings in Westminster Abbey so they could celebrate their ill-fated nuptials here.
The current edifice is the third cathedral to stand on the site; the first was founded in
604 and destroyed by fire in 1089. The second and most massive cathedral was a
medieval structure, one of the largest in Europe, topped by a spire ascending 489 ft.
Falling into almost complete neglect in the 16th century, the cathedral became more
of a marketplace than a church, and plans for its reconstruction were in the works
well before the Great Fire. Wren had already started drawing up his grand scheme in
1666 when the conflagration demolished the cathedral, along with most of London,
and gave him the opportunity to build from scratch.

Both the design and the building of the cathedral were dogged by controversy. Like
his Renaissance predecessors, Wren preferred an equal-armed Greek cross plan,
while ecclesiastical authorities insisted upon a traditional medieval design with a long
nave and choir for services. Wren's final design compromised by translating a Gothic
cathedral into baroque and classical terms: a Latin Cross floor plan with baroque
detailing. Wren's second model received the King's warrant of approval (and is thus
known as the "Warrant Model"), but still differed from today's St. Paul's. The shrewd
architect won permission to make necessary alterations as building proceeded and,
behind the scaffolding, Wren had his way. The cathedral was topped off in 1710; at
365 ft. above the ground, the huge classical dome is the second-largest free-standing
dome in Europe. Queen Victoria, believing the cathedral's cream and wooden interior to be too dull, flooded it with gold before her death in 1901.

In December 1940, London burned once again. On the night of the 29th, at the
height of the Blitz, St. Paul's was engulfed by a sea of fire. This time it survived. Fifty-
one firebombs landed on the cathedral, all swiftly put out by the heroic volunteer St.
Paul's Fire Watch; a small monument in the floor at the end of the nave honors them.
Two of the four high-explosive bombs that landed did explode, wrecking the north
transept; the clear glass there bears silent testimony. Today, St. Paul's serves as a center for state functions, including Winston Churchill's funeral in 1965 (a plaque marks
the spot in front of the choir where the coffin stood) and VE-Day ceremonies in 1994.

Dotted with sculptures, bronzes, and mosaics, St. Paul's makes a rewarding place
for a wander. Above the choir, three neo-Byzantine glass mosaics by William Richmond, done in 1904, tell the story of Creation. The stalls in the **Choir,** carved by Grinling Gibbons, narrowly escaped a bomb, but the old altar did not. It was replaced
with the current marble High Altar, covered by a St. Peter's-like *baldacchino* of oak,
splendidly gilded. Above looms the crowning glory, the ceiling mosaic of *Christ
Seated in Majesty.* A trial mosaic adorns the east wall of **St. Dunstan's Chapel,** on
the left by the entrance. On the other side of the nave in the **Chapel of St. Michael
and St. George** sits a richly carved throne by Grinling Gibbons, made for the coronation of William and Mary in 1710. Along the south aisle hangs Holman Hunt's third
version of *The Light of the World,* allegedly the most well-traveled picture in the
world. Monuments to the mighty abound—Wellington, Nelson, Kitchener, and Samuel Johnson are all remembered here.

The **ambulatory** contains a statue of poet John Donne (Dean of the Cathedral
1621-1631) in shrouds, one of the few monuments to survive from old St. Paul's. Also
in the ambulatory is a modern, abstract sculpture of the Virgin Mary and Baby Jesus
by **Henry Moore.** One month after the arrival of Moore's sculpture, entitled *Mother
and Child,* guides insisted a name plaque be affixed to the base, as no one knew what

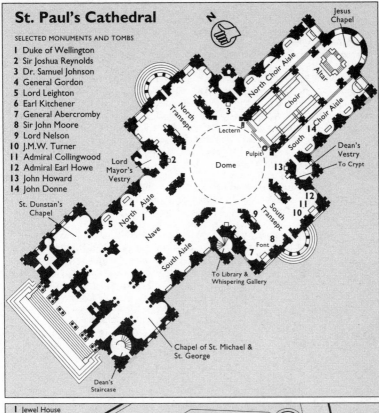

St. Paul's Cathedral

SELECTED MONUMENTS AND TOMBS

1 Duke of Wellington
2 Sir Joshua Reynolds
3 Dr. Samuel Johnson
4 General Gordon
5 Lord Leighton
6 Earl Kitchener
7 General Abercromby
8 Sir John Moore
9 Lord Nelson
10 J.M.W. Turner
11 Admiral Collingwood
12 Admiral Earl Howe
13 John Howard
14 John Donne

Jesus Chapel

Altar

North Choir Aisle

Choir

South Choir Aisle

North Transept

Lectern

Pulpit

Dome

Dean's Vestry

To Crypt

Lord Mayor's Vestry

St. Dunstan's Chapel

North Aisle

Nave

South Aisle

South Transept

Font

To Library & Whispering Gallery

Chapel of St. Michael & St. George

Dean's Staircase

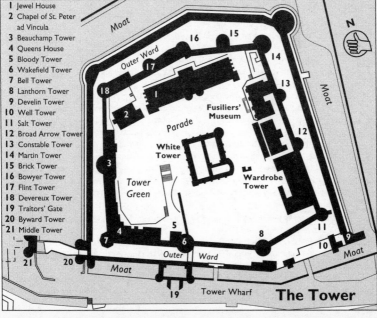

1 Jewel House
2 Chapel of St. Peter ad Vincula
3 Beauchamp Tower
4 Queens House
5 Bloody Tower
6 Wakefield Tower
7 Bell Tower
8 Lanthorn Tower
9 Develin Tower
10 Well Tower
11 Salt Tower
12 Broad Arrow Tower
13 Constable Tower
14 Martin Tower
15 Brick Tower
16 Bowyer Tower
17 Flint Tower
18 Devereux Tower
19 Traitors' Gate
20 Byward Tower
21 Middle Tower

Moat

Outer Ward

Fusiliers' Museum

Parade

White Tower

Wardrobe Tower

Tower Green

Moat

Outer   Ward

Moat

Tower Wharf

The Tower

it was meant to represent. Britain restored the former **Jesus Chapel** after the Blitz and dedicated it to U.S. soldiers who died during World War II. The graceful and intricate choir gates were executed by Jean Tijou early in the 18th century.

The **crypt,** saturated with tombs and monuments, forms a catalogue of Britain's officially "great" figures of the last two centuries, including Florence Nightingale and sculptor Henry Moore. (A few remnants made it through the Great Fire, including a memorial to Francis Bacon's father Nicolas.) The massive tombs of the Duke of Wellington and Nelson command attention; Nelson's coffin, placed directly beneath the dome, was originally intended for Cardinal Wolsey. A bust of George Washington stands opposite a memorial to Lawrence of Arabia. Around the corner lounges Rodin's fine bust of poet W.F. Henley (1849-1903). **Painter's Corner** holds the tombs of Sir Joshua Reynolds, Sir Lawrence Alma-Tadema, and J.M.W. Turner, along with memorials to John Constable and the revolutionary William Blake. Nearby, a black slab in the floor marks Wren's grave, with his son's famous epitaph close by: *Lector, si monumentum requiris circumspice* (roughly, "If you seek his monument, just look around you"). Outside the entrance to the Crypt you will find the **"Loo of the Year,"** as judged by the British Tourist Authority. Sure enough, the WC is sparkly clean and best of all, free.

The display of **models** of St. Paul's details the history of the cathedral in all of its incarnations. Creating the great model of 1674, the star exhibit, cost as much as constructing a small house. In these models you can see how the upper parts of the exterior walls are mere façades, concealing the flying buttresses which support the nave roof (audiovisual presentations every ½hr. 10:30am-3pm; crypt open Mon.-Sat. 8:45am-4:45pm).

The best place to head in St. Paul's is straight up. A visitor may ascend to whichever of three different levels in the dome his legs, heart, and courage will allow. Going up St. Paul's proves more challenging than going down: 259 steps lead to the vertiginous **Whispering Gallery,** on the inside base of the dome. During your ascent, look for the 18th-century grafitti carved into the stairwell. Words whispered against the wall whizz round the sides. A further 119 steps up, the first external view glitters from the **Stone Gallery,** only to be eclipsed by the uninterrupted and incomparable panorama from the **Golden Gallery,** 152 steps higher at the top of the dome. Before descending, take a peek down into the cathedral through the glass peephole in the floor; Nelson lies buried more than 400 ft. directly below. (Tube: St. Paul's. Cathedral open for sightseeing Mon.-Sat. 8:30am-4pm. Galleries and ambulatory open Mon.-Sat. 8:45am-4:15pm. Admission to cathedral, ambulatory, and crypt £3.50, students £3, children £2. Admission to cathedral, ambulatory, crypt, *and* galleries £6, students £5, children £3. Guided supertours of crypt and cathedral leave at 11, 11:30am, 1:30, and 2pm. £3, £2 students. Audio tours are shorter and cost £2.50, students £2, available from opening until 3pm.)

Evensong is performed Monday through Saturday at 5pm. This lovely Anglican ceremony—celebrating Christ's assumption of mortal form and reaffirming the majesty of the religion—will give visitors a chance to hear the cathedral's superb choir. Five minutes before the singing begins worshippers will be allowed to sit in the choir, a few feet from the singers, though this means you must stay for the duration (about 40min.). **St. Paul's Churchyard,** a fine picnic spot popular since Shakespeare's day, is surrounded by railings of mostly unappreciated interest; they were one of the first applications of cast iron. The modern St. Paul's Cross marks the spot where the papal pronouncement condemning Martin Luther was read to the public.

■ The Tower of London

The Tower of London, palace and prison of English monarchs for over 500 years, is soaked in blood and history. Its intriguing past and striking buildings attract over two million visitors per year. The oldest continuously occupied fortress in Europe, "The Tower" was founded by William the Conqueror in 1066 to provide protection for and from his subjects. Not one but 20 towers stand behind its walls, though many associate the image of the **White Tower,** the oldest one, with the Tower of London. Completed in 1097, it overpowers all the fortifications that were built around it in the following centuries. Originally a royal residence, the last monarch it housed was James I. Since then it has served as a wardrobe, storehouse, public records office, mint, armory, and prison.

The various towers are connected by massive walls and gateways, forming fortifications disheartening to visitors even today. Richard I, the Lionheart, began the construction of defenses around the White Tower in 1189. Subsequent work by Henry III and Edward I brought the Tower close to its present condition.

Two rings of defenses surround the White Tower. On the first floor of the White Tower nests the **Chapel of St. John,** dating from 1080, the finest Norman chapel in London. Stark and pristine, it is the only chapel in the world with an "aisled nave and encircling ambulatory," a balcony where women were allowed to join the otherwise men-only chapel services. Failed arsonist Guy Fawkes of the Gunpowder Plot was tortured beneath this chapel. Currently under renovation and open only by Yeoman tour, the chapel will likely be closed to the public when the renovations are completed. The White Tower also houses an expansive display from the **Royal Armouries** and a display of **Instruments of Torture.** If all this won't slake your thirst for violence, visit the **New Armouries** to the east to gorge on even more armor and weaponry.

On the **Inner Ward,** the **Bell Tower** squats on the southwest corner. Since the 1190s, this tower has sounded the curfew bell each night. Sir Thomas More, "the king's good servant but God's first," spent some time here, courtesy of his former friend Henry VIII, before he was executed on **Tower Hill,** the scaffold site just northwest of the fortress where thousands gathered to watch the axe fall.

Along the curtain wall hovers the **Bloody Tower,** arguably the most famous, and certainly the most infamous, part of the fortress. Once pleasantly named the Garden Tower, due to the officers' garden nearby, the Bloody Tower supposedly saw the murder of the Little Princes, the uncrowned King Edward V and his brother (aged 13 and 10), by agents of Richard III. The murder remains one of history's great mysteries; some believe that Richard was innocent and that Henry VII arranged the murders to ease his own ascent. Two children's remains found in the grounds in 1674 (and buried in Westminster Abbey) have never been conclusively identified as those of the Princes. Sir Walter Raleigh did some time in the prison here off and on for 13 years and occupied himself by writing a voluminous *History of the World Part I.* Before he got around to writing Part II, James I had him beheaded.

Henry III lived in the adjacent **Wakefield Tower,** largest after the White Tower. The crown kept its public records and its jewels here until 1856 and 1967 respectively, although Wakefield also has its own gruesome past. Lancastrian Henry VI was imprisoned by Yorkist Edward IV during the Wars of the Roses and was murdered on May 21, 1471, while praying here. Students from King's College, Cambridge—founded by Henry—annually place lilies on the spot of the murder.

Counterclockwise around the inner **Wall Walk** come the **Lanthorn, Salt, Broad Arrow, Constable,** and **Martin** towers. In 1671, the self-styled "Colonel" Thomas Blood nearly pulled off the heist of the millennium. Blood befriended the ward of Martin tower, where the crown jewels were kept and visited him late at night with some "friends," who subdued the guard and stuffed their trousers with booty, only to be caught at the nearby docks. Surprisingly, Blood wasn't executed, and was later awarded a privileged spot in the court of Charles II, the moral being, of course, that crime does pay (*Let's Go* does not recommend stealing state treasures). The inner ring comes full circle, completed by the **Brick, Bowyer, Flint, Devereux,** and **Beauchamp** towers.

Within the inner ring adjoining the Bell Tower lurks the Tudor **Queen's House** (which will become the King's House when Prince Charles ascends to the throne). The house has served time as a prison for some of the Tower's most notable guests: both Anne Boleyn and Catherine Howard were incarcerated here by charming hubby Henry VIII; Guy Fawkes was interrogated in the Council Chamber on the upper floor;

and in 1941, Hitler's henchman Rudolf Hess was brought here after parachuting into Scotland. The only prisoners remaining today are the clipped ravens hopping around on the grass outside the White Tower. Legend has it that without the ravens the Tower would crumble and a great disaster would befall the monarchy; the ravens even have a tomb and gravestone of their own.

Although more famous for the prisoners who languished and died here, the Tower has seen a handful of spectacular escape attempts. The Bishop of Durham escaped from Henry I out a window and down a rope. The Welsh Prince Gruffydd ap Llewe-lyn, prisoner of Henry III in 1244, was unfortunate in more than name—his rope of knotted sheets broke and he fell to his death.

Prisoners of special privilege sometimes received the honor of a private execution, particularly when their public execution risked escape or riot. A block on the Tower Green, inside the Inner Ward, marks the spot where the axe fell on Queen Catherine Howard, Lady Jane Grey, Anne Boleyn, and the Earl of Essex, Queen Elizabeth's rejected suitor. All these and More (Sir Thomas) were treated to unconsecrated burial in the nearby **Chapel of St. Peter ad Vincula** (St. Peter in Chains; entrance to the chapel by Yeoman tour only, see below.)

For many, a visit to the Tower climaxes with a glimpse of the **Crown Jewels.** The queue at the **Jewel House** (lasting 15-30min.) is a miracle of crowd-management—as tourists file past room after room of rope barriers, video projections on the walls show larger-than-life depictions of the Jewels in action, including stirring footage of Queen Elizabeth II's coronation. Finally, the crowd is ushered into the vault and onto "people-movers" which whisk them past the dazzling crowns and insure no awe-struck gazers hold up the queue. Oliver Cromwell melted down much of the original royal booty; most of the collection dates from after Charles II's Restoration in 1660. The **Imperial State Crown** and the **Sceptre with the Cross** feature the Stars of Africa, cut from the Cullinan Diamond. Scotland Yard mailed the precious stone third class from the Transvaal in an unmarked brown paper parcel, a scheme they believed was the safest way of getting it to London. **St. Edward's Crown,** made for Charles II in 1661, is only worn by the monarch during coronation.

The Tower is still guarded by the Yeomen of the Guard Extraordinary, popularly known as the "Beefeaters," who live in the fortress. The name does actually derive from "eaters of beef"—well-nourished domestic servants. To be eligible for Beefeater-hood, a candidate must have at least 22 years honorable service in the armed forces, as well as a strong appetite for flash photography.

Visitors enter the Tower through the **Byward Tower** on the southwest of the **Outer Ward,** which sports a precariously hung portcullis. The password, required for entry here after hours, has been changed every day since 1327. German spies were executed in the Outer Ward during WWII. Along the outer wall, **St. Thomas's Tower** (after Thomas à Becket) tops the evocative **Traitors' Gate,** through which boats once brought new captives. The whole castle used to be surrounded by a broad **moat** dug by Edward I. Cholera epidemics forced the Duke of Wellington to drain the stagnant pond in 1843. The filled land became a vegetable garden during World War II but has since sprouted a tennis court and bowling green for the Yeomen who live and work in the Tower.

The free hour-long tours, given every half-hour by Yeomen, provide an amusing and dramatic introduction to the tower, but are by no means comprehensive. Signs are posted inside the tower for similar free tours highlighting other points of interest. Come early (the biggest crowds come in the afternoon, particularly on Sundays) and stay long; the Tower is one of London's priciest sights, don't go if you're pressed for time. (Tube: Tower Hill; open Mon.-Sat. 9am-6pm, Sun. 10am-6pm (last ticket sold at 5pm); Nov.-Feb. Mon.-Sat. 9am-5pm (last ticket sold at 4pm), Sun. 10am-5pm; admission £8.30, students and seniors £6.25, children £5.50, families £21.95. For inquiries, tel. 709 0765.) For tickets to the **Ceremony of the Keys,** the nightly ritual locking of the gates, write six weeks in advance to Resident Governor, Tower of London, EC3, with the number and date of tickets.

Tower Bridge, a granite and steel structure reminiscent of a castle with a drawbridge, is a familiar sight. The **Tower Bridge Experience** (tel. 403 3761), an exhibition nearly as technologically elaborate as the bridge itself, explains the bridge's genesis through the eyes of its painters, designers, and ghosts in cute but expensive 75-min. tours. The view from the upper level, hampered by steel bars, is far less panoramic than it seems from below. (Open daily April-Oct. 10am-6:30pm, Nov.-March 10am-5:15pm. Admission £5.50 children £3.75.)

▧ The East End

Today's East End eludes the simple characterization that earlier times would have allowed. Once it was Jewish center of London, the Huguenot center, and later the center for a number of more recent immigrant groups—Irish, Somalis, Chinese, and Muslim Bangladeshi. By now all that can be said of the area is that it has never been a province of the fashionable or monied.

Marked today by an invisible line across Bishops Gate St., London's East End continues to serve, as it always has, as a refuge for those who either aren't welcome in the City or who don't want to be subject to the City's jurisdiction. During the 17th century, this included political dissenters, religious orders, and the French Huguenots (Protestants fleeing religious persecution in France). By 1687, 13,000 Huguenots had settled in Spitalfields, the area northeast of the City of London (which takes its name from a long-gone medieval priory, St. Mary Spital). The silk-weaving Huguenots soon built a reputation for high-quality cloth—but as they attracted rich customers, they also attracted resentment. A large working-class population moved into the district during the Industrial Revolution, followed by a wave of Jewish immigrants fleeing persecution in Eastern Europe who settled around **Whitechapel.** Success attained as clothing manufacturers drew the attention of the British Union of Fascists, who instigated anti-Semitic violence that culminated in the "Battle of Cable Street" in 1936. A mural on **St. George's Town Hall** 236 Cable St. (tube: Shadwell) commemorates the victory against bigotry won in the streets that day.

In 1978, the latest immigration wave brought a large Muslim Bangladeshi community to the East End. At the heart of this community is **Brick Lane** (tube: Aldgate East), a street lined with Indian and Bangladeshi restaurants (see Food and Drink, p. 117), colorful textile shops, and grocers stocking ethnic foods. (To reach Brick La., head left up Whitechapel as you exit the tube station; turn left onto Osbourne St., which turns into Brick La.) Most street signs in the area are written in both Arabic and English. On Sundays, vibrant market stalls selling books, bric-a-brac, leather jackets, and salt beef sandwiches flank this street and Middlesex St., better known as **Petticoat Lane**—its original name, drawn from the street's historical role as a center of the clothing trade; a prudish Queen Victoria gave the street the more respectable, official name it bears today (see Shopping, p. 257). At Fournier St., a former church now holds a mosque; it is not uncommon to hear the Islamic call to prayer bellowed from the loudspeakers of numerous local mosques, compete with honking cars. The **East London Mosque,** 82-92 Whitechapel Rd. (tel. 247 1357; tube: Aldgate East), was London's first to have its own building. Its towering minarets and grand building testify to the size of London's Muslim community.

Even the communities that have since moved out of the East End have not vanished without leaving some trace behind. **Christ Church,** Commercial St., E1 (tel. 247 7202; tube: Aldgate East; left on leaving the station, left again onto Commercial St.; open Mon.-Fri. noon-2:30pm), in any other London neighborhood would be just another ancient building; here it is an island of Anglicanism amongst a diverse spectrum of other traditions. The church was begun by Hawksmoor in 1714 as part of Parliament's Fifty New Churches Act of 1711. The Act had been created to combat nonconformism against the Church of England; in this case, the Protestantism of the Huguenots. Today, the church sponsors the **Spitalfields Festival** of classical music during the last three weeks of June (box office tel. 377 1362; tickets £4-25); the church's crypt also serves as a rehabilitation center for alcoholics.

At the **Dennis Severs House,** 18 Folgate St. (tel. 247 4013; left off Commercial St.), you can visit the home of a native Southern Californian experiencing the life of a 19th-century Huguenot family by living without electricity, running water, and other modern conveniences. "New wave art," he calls it (open first Sun. of each month 2-5pm or by appointment; admission £5).

Most of the Jewish community has moved on to suburbs to the north and west of central London, like Stamford Hill and Golders Green (see Greater London, p. 199), taking along even such landmarks as the renowned kosher restaurant **Bloom's.** The city's oldest standing synagogue, **Bevis Marks Synagogue** (tel. 626 1274; Bevis Marks and Heneage La., EC3; tube: Aldgate: from Aldgate High St. turn right onto Houndsditch; Creechurch La. on the left leads to Bevis Marks), remains and is well worth a visit. Bevis Marks prides itself upon being situated in the heart of London, but its congregants undoubtedly came from the outcast East End neighborhood. Rabbi Menashe Ben Israel founded the synagogue in 1701, 435 years after the Jews were first expelled from England and 44 years after they were permitted to return by Oliver Cromwell. Recently, the Archbishop of Canterbury and several major politicians attended VE-Day ceremonies in this ancient synagogue. Rothschilds, Montefiores and Disraelis have been members of this most distinguished congregation. (Organized tours Sun. and Tues. 11:30am, Mon., Wed., and Fri. noon; building open Sun., Mon. and Thurs. from 11:30am-1pm, Tues. 10am-4pm and Fri. 11:30am-12:30pm; suggested donation £1.) Another major synagogue on Fieldgate St., marked by the remaining Hebrew letters above its entrance, has been amalgamated into the East London Mosque, underscoring the racial layering of this area.

The most recent wave of immigrants to join this cultural milieu consists of City artists. In today's East End, scattered deserted warehouse spaces and airy studios house the brushes and oils of over 6000 painters and "new wave" creators. Some of their work, much of which focuses on the experience of the East End's nonwhite population, occasionally hangs on the high white walls of the **Whitechapel Art Gallery** (tel. 522 7888) on Whitechapel High St., which holds temporary exhibitions of such artists as Frida Kahlo and Piotr Nathan (see p. 223). Their cutting-edge, urban tone mixes strangely with the area's growing South Asian presence. The Bangladeshi community's shift towards Islamic traditionalism has pulled the neighborhood ever further away from the neighboring financial districts, while the East End's artists are slowly sewing new ties with the City of London.

Spitalfields Farm, Weaver/Pedley St., E1 (tel. 247 8762; tube: Shoreditch), is a genuine working farm in the middle of the city where you can buy produce and plants. During the summer and on Sundays, enjoy the farm and crafts activities, go for a pony ride or feast at a barbecue (open Tues.-Sun. 10am-1pm and 2-6pm; free). The **Spitalfields Market** at Commercial and Brushfield St. (tel. 247 6590; tube: Liverpool) offers craft and antique stalls, special retail shops, an international food hall (including London's first organic food market), indoor sports including roller hockey, a large-scale train display, and changing art exhibitions under three acres of glass-covered space (open Mon.-Fri. 11am-2pm, Sun. 9am-5pm; Sun. is the best time to go). It combines the East End's artistic flair with Bohemian simplicity and tastefulness. The Sunday morning flower and plant market on **Columbia Road** (tube: Old St. or Shoreditch; take Old St. to Hackney Rd., Columbia Road is on the right) is also worth a visit (open Sun. 8am-2pm).

An overdramatized aspect of the East End's history is its association with London's most notorious criminals. Jack the Ripper's six murders took place in Whitechapel; you can tour his trail with a number of different guided walk companies, all of which offer a Jack the Ripper tour every evening (see London Walks, p. 135). More recently, cockney Capone twins Ron and Reggie Kray ruled the 1960s underworld from their mum's terraced house in Bethnal Green. Ron wiped out an ale-sipping rival in broad daylight in 1966 at the **Blind Beggar** pub at Whitechapel Rd. and Cambridge Heath Rd. (see East End Pubs, p. 129).

Along Cambridge Heath Rd. lies the **Bethnal Green Museum of Childhood** (see Museums, p. 223). North past Bethnal Green and beyond the wafts of curry on Brick

Ridley Rd. Amhurst Rd.
Hackney Downs Station
Dalston Station
Dalston Lane
Ball's Pond Rd. Graham Rd.
Tottenham Rd.
Hackney Central Station
Morning Lane
HACKNEY WICK
Wick Rd.

KINGSLAND Forest Rd.
Queensbridge Rd.
Richmond Rd.
Greenwood Rd.
Navarino Rd.
Kenton Rd. Cassland Rd.
Gascoyne Rd.

Culford Rd.
De Beauvoir Rd.
Kingsland High St.
Holly St.
Middleton Rd.
London Fields
HACKNEY
London Fields Station
Well St.
Well Street Common
Yacht Pond

Whitmore St.
Kingsland Rd.
Stonebridge Gardens
Victoria Fountain
Bathing Pond
Victoria Park

Pitfield St.
Hoxton St.
Grand Union Canal
Haggerston Park
Goldsmiths Sq.
Cambridge Heath Rd.
Bishops Way
Boating Lake
Old Ford Rd.

Geffrye Museum
HAGGERSTON
Cremer St. Hackney Rd.
Cambridge Heath Station
Baths
Bethnal Green Museum of Childhood
Temple St.
Old Ford Rd.
Roman Rd.
Meath Gardens
Grove Rd.
Tredegar Sq.
Mile End Tube

Pearl St.
Old St.
Curtain Rd.
Shoreditch High St.
Gr. Eastern London St.
SHOREDITCH
Columbia Rd.
Gosset St.
BETHNAL GREEN
Old Bethnal Green Rd.
Vallance Rd.
Bethnal Green Rd.
Weavers Fields
Bethnal Green Station
Cephas Rd.
Globe Rd.
Jews Burial Ground
Mile End Park
Mile End Rd.
Burdett Rd.
Copperfield Rd.
Rhodeswell Rd.
King George's Fields

Worship St.
Commercial St.
Brick Lane
Quaker St.
Buxton St.
Burial Ground
Brady St.
Whitechapel Tube
Mile End Rd.
Stepney Green
Ben Johnson Rd.

Liverpool St. Station
Hanbury St.
Spitalfields Heritage Center
Spitalfields Market
SPITALFIELDS
Whitechapel Art Gallery
Petticoat Lane Market
Royal London Hospital
Raven Row
E. Mount St.
Royal London Hospital Archives
Stepney Way
Jubilee St.
Sidney St.
STEPNEY
Aylward St.
Bromley St.
Whitehorse Rd.

Liverpool St. Tube
Middlesex St.
Gouldston St.
Synagogue
East London Mosque
New Rd.
Cannon St.
Commercial Rd.
Limehouse Station

Nat. Westminster Tower
Bevis Marks Synagogue
Leadenhall St.
Bishopsgate
Duke St.
Aldgate East Tube
Osborn St.
Bigland St.
Sutton St.
Butcher Row

Lloyd's
Minories
Vine St.
Mark La.
Braham St.
Christian St.
Shadwell Station
SHADWELL
Narrow St.

Gracechurch St.
Fenchurch St.
Fenchurch St. Station
Prescot St.
Royal Mint St.
Cable St.
Shadwell Tube
King Ed. VII Mem. Park
Horseferry Stairs

Tower Hill
Royal Mint
The Highway
Wapping Lane
Garnet St.
Globe Pier

Old Billingsgate Market
Tower of London
Smithfield
World Trade Center
Thomas More St.
Ensign St.
Horseferry Stairs

London Dungeon
London Bridge Museum
Tower Bridge
London Bridge Station
Horseleydown Old Stairs
Georges Stairs
Mill Stairs
East Lane Stairs
Fountain Dock
Cherry Garden Pier
River Thames
Rotherhithe St.
Salter Rd.
Surrey Water Rd.
Limehouse Beach

Tooley St.
Tower Bridge Rd.
Druid St.
Bermondsey Wall Chambers
Hull St.
Jacob St.
West Lane
Paradise St.
Bermondsey St.
BERMONDSEY
Jamica Rd.

N

The East End

SIGHTS

Lane stretch the expanses of **Hackney** (home of the Geffrye Museum, p. 224), which mesh into **Clapton,** and farther north, **Stoke Newington.** Traditionally known as a community of "Londoners' stock," Hackney now ever-adapts to its growing Caribbean, African, and Turkish populations—Brixton without the hype and the tube line. West Indian beef patty shops, thumping night clubs, and discount clothing, food, and shoe stores line main drags Mare St. and Lower Clapton Rd.

■ The South Bank

A hulk of worn concrete and futuristic slate, the South Bank gestures defiantly at the center of London from across the Thames. Housing the British terminus of the imminent **Channel Tunnel,** this region is currently poised to become one of London's most dynamic. Major commercial development, which anticipates the Chunnel's eventual flourishing, is currently underway. Waterloo station has been designated the London terminus of the "Chunnel," and Nicholas Grimshaw's spectacular new blue and silver international terminal has become many visitors' introduction to Britain. To the untutored eye, this area initially appears confusing and dismal, especially on the average cloudy London day. The massive **South Bank Centre** is the predominant architectural eyesore; yet behind this hulking facade lurks London's most concentrated campus of artistic and cultural activity (tube: Waterloo, then follow signs for York Rd.; or Embankment and cross the Hungerford footbridge).

The region south of the Thames has long been home to entertainment, much of it bawdy—until the English Civil Wars, most of this area fell under the legal jurisdiction of the Bishop of Winchester, and was thus protected from London censors. The region stayed almost entirely rural until the 18th-century Westminster and Blackfriars bridges were built. Until the post-WWII development began, the area was a den of working-class neighborhoods, dark breweries, smoky industry, and murky wharves through which suburbanites passed on their way into the city.

Contemporary development began in 1951 during the Festival of Britain, the centenary of the Great Exhibition of 1851, when the **Royal Festival Hall** was built. A veritable eruption of construction ensued, producing the many concrete blocks that comprise the Centre: the **National Film Theatre,** the **Hayward Gallery** and **Queen Elizabeth Hall** complex, and the **Royal National Theatre.** Recent calls for the demolition and replacement of the Queen Elizabeth Hall and the Hayward Gallery have prompted many to declare their fondness for the complex. More recent additions to the South Bank landscape include the **Jubilee Gardens,** planted for the Queen's Silver Jubilee in 1977, which stretch along the Embankment.

The 3000-seat Royal Festival Hall and its three auditoriums (Olivier, Lyttleton, and Cottesloe) are home to the Philharmonia and London Philharmonic Orchestras, the English National Ballet, and host to countless others; its chamber-musical sibling is the Queen Elizabeth Hall (see Entertainment, p. 235). The **National Theatre** (p. 228), opened by Lord Olivier in 1978, promotes "art for the people" through convivial platform performances, foyer concerts, lectures, tours, and workshops. The **Hayward Gallery** (p. 224) on Belvedere Rd. houses imaginative contemporary art exhibitions. Multicolored posters displaying Russian titles and Asian warriors distinguish the entrance to the **National Film Theatre** (p. 234), directly on the South Bank. The Film Theatre also operates the **Museum of the Moving Image** (p. 221).

The most colorful recent changes in the South Bank landscape result from the unflagging efforts of a non-profit development company, **Coin Street Community Builders (CSCB).** Since 1984 CSCB has converted 13 previously derelict acres into a park and riverside walkway, seven housing cooperatives, and a designer crafts market at **Gabriel's Wharf** (tel. 620 0544). Gabriel's Wharf is a great place to watch original crafts being fashioned while grabbing a snack after a visit to the National Theatre (craft fair open Tues.-Sun. 11am-6pm). During the summer, take advantage of sporadic free festivals (call the Wharf for information).

CSCB's next renovation project, the OXO Tower, is adjacent to Gabriel's Wharf. Formerly the headquarters of a company that produced meat extract, the Art Deco

Lambeth, South Bank and Southwark

River Thames

Tower of London

Tower Bridge

Tower Bridge Museum

Gainsford St.

Lafone

Horsely Down St.

Spa Rd.

Ascot Rd.

Bermondsey Spa

Maltby St.

Abbey St.

Druid St.

Tower Bridge Rd.

W. Curtis Ecological Park

St. Olave's Estate

Grange Rd.

Willow Walk

Pages Walk

London Dungeon

Tooley St.

London Bridge Tube

London Bridge

London Bridge Station

St. Thomas St.

Bermondsey St.

Leather-market Gardens

Leathermarket St.

Tanner St.

Long Lane

Old Kent Rd.

Townsend St.

NEWINGTON

Weston St.

Southwark Cathedral

Kipling St.

Newcomen St.

High St.

Toubard Gardens

Tabard St.

Great Dover St.

New Kent Rd.

Chatham St.

Southwark Bridge

Southwark Bridge Rd.

Emerson St.

Great Guildford St.

Sumner P.

Park St.

Southwark St.

SOUTHWARK

Sessions House

Trinity St.

Swan St.

Falmouth Rd.

Harper Rd.

Ingham St.

Rodney Rd.

Haygate St.

Copperfield St.

Lant St.

Collinson St.

Newington Gardens

Rocki

Elephant & Castle Tube

Elephant & Castle Station

Newington Butts

Blackfriars Bridge

Blackfriars Rd.

St.

Hatfields

Nelson Square

Surey Row

Pocock St.

Lancaster St.

Borough Rd.

London Rd.

Polytechnic

Oswin St.

Stamford St.

Upper Ground

Cornwall

Roupell St.

The Cut

Webber St.

Garden Row

Hayles St.

West Sq.

Brook Drive

Walcott Sq.

Waterloo Bridge

National Theatre

London Weekend TV

Hayward Gallery

Royal Festival Hall

Greet St.

Waterloo Rd.

Morley St.

Gladstone St.

Geraldine Mary Harmsworth Park

Kennington Rd.

Embankment Tube

Queen Elizabeth Hall

Charing Cross Station

Hungerford Bridge

SOUTH BANK

Jubilee Gardens

Waterloo Tube

Belvedere Rd.

York Rd.

Old Vic Theatre

Waterloo Station

Frazier St.

Pearman St.

Baylis Rd.

Westminster Bridge Rd.

Lambeth Rd.

Imperial War Museum

Hercules Rd.

Walnut Tree Walk

Fizzulen St.

Victoria Embankment Gardens

Westminster Bridge

LAMBETH

Lambeth Palace Rd.

Lambeth Palace Gardens

Lambeth Palace

Museum of Garden History

Paradise St.

Lambeth Walk

Lambeth High St.

Black Prince

Houses of Parliament

Thames

Albert Embankment

Lambeth Bridge

River

tower is notable for its clever subversion of rules prohibiting permanent advertising on buildings—architects built the tower's distinct windows in the shape of the company's logo. CSCB boasts that the meticulously planned potpourri of rooftop cafés, retail outlets, designer workshops, performance spaces, and flats that opened last summer at the **OXO Tower Wharf** will make it a hub of London activity.

Numerous pedestrian pathways are being planned for the region, which will make it easier to get to the jumbled stalls of the **Cut Street Market** near Waterloo station. The market's old character has waned as ambitious development projects consume more of the area's residential neighborhoods, but prices have stayed low, and used-book sellers and curiosity stands have maintained the district's flavor.

Farther along Waterloo Rd., the magnificently restored **Old Vic,** former home of Olivier's National Repertory Theatre, now hosts popular seasons of lesser-known classics and worthy revivals. The smaller **Young Vic** is just a bit farther down the road (see Theater, p. 231, 233).

The **Christ Church Tower** of 1876 rises above a mundane block of office buildings at the corner of Kennington Rd., directly across from Lambeth North tube station. **Lambeth Palace** (tube: Lambeth North), on the Embankment opposite the Lambeth Bridge in Archbishops Park, has been the Archbishop of Canterbury's London residence for seven centuries. Although Archbishop Langton founded it in the early 13th century, most of the palace dates from the 1800s. The palace's notable exterior includes the entrance at the 15th-century brick Morton's Tower, and Lollard's Tower, where John Wyclif's followers were thought to be imprisoned (open by prior arrangement only; contact Lambeth Palace, Lambeth Palace Road, SE1). Next door to the Palace's southernmost entrance stands the Museum of Garden History, complete with a replica of a 17th-century garden (tel. 633 9701; open mid-March to mid-Dec. Mon-Fri. 10:30am-4pm, Sun. 10am-5pm; free). East on Lambeth Road is the **Imperial War Museum** (see Museums, p. 224).

■ Southwark and Bankside

Historically a hotbed of prostitution, incarceration, and bear-baiting, Southwark (across London Bridge from the city) seems an unlikely location for a new cradle of London high culture (tube: London Bridge). The area around the **Borough High St.,** "the Borough," has persisted—with a few minor changes—for nearly 2000 years. Until 1750, London Bridge was the only bridge over the Thames in London, and the highway leading to it hosted many travelers who liked to stop at the inns lining the road. The neighborhood has historically been associated with entertainment from the days of bear-baiting to the even more vicious pleasures of Defoe's *Moll Flanders.* **Bear Gardens,** located along the bank of the Thames, received its name from the bear-baiting arena that stood there in Elizabethan times, where bears and bulls were pitted against mastiffs for sport.

But Southwark's greatest "vice" has always been theatre. Shakespeare's and Marlowe's plays were performed at the **Rose Theatre,** built in 1587 and rediscovered during construction in 1989. The remnants are to be preserved and displayed underneath a new *Financial Times* office block at Park St. and Rose Alley. The remains of Shakespeare's **Globe Theatre** were discovered just months after those of the Rose.

A project spearheaded by actor Sam Wanamaker is underway to build a "new" Globe on the riverbank. This Globe replica was scheduled to open on Shakespeare's birthday, April 23, 1995, but a dearth of funds has pushed the opening date back several months. After brief "prologue" seasons in late August 1995 and 1996, the theatre is scheduled (keep your fingers crossed!) to begin its first full season in the summer of 1997, performing the works of Shakespeare, Jonson, and other contemporaries. The replica will be part of the **International Shakespeare Globe Centre,** a vast complex that will ultimately contain a second theatre, an exhibition gallery, an archival library, an auditorium, and various shops, scheduled for completion in 2000. Entertaining, informative tours of the complex are available, but hours, admission, and content are constantly changing, call 620 0202 for an update.

An awesome architectural monolith looms menacingly over the Clink and the new Globe construction site. The huge, terrible **CEGB Power Station's** windowless tower rises to the height of 325 ft. Closed due to its obsolescence in 1980, the tower will become the new home of the Tate Gallery's **Modern Art Museum,** housing the foreign works of the Tate collection. To date, the Tate has poured over £100 million into the project, and expects it to be completed around 2000.

Before the "hoose-gow," the "big house," or the "state-funded vacation," there was "the Clink," living testament to Southwark's less rosy past. The **Liberty of the Clink** comprised 70 acres of bankside land, under the jurisdiction of the Bishop of Winchester's Court. "The Clink" was the Bishop's private prison for London's criminals. Henry Barrowe and John Greenwood, the early Separatists, were imprisoned here before being hanged. The **Clink Prison Exhibition,** 1 Clink St. (tel. 378 1558), a poor man's London Dungeon, attempts to recreate the "glory days" of the prison with eerie choral soundtrack and hands-on restraining and torture devices (open daily 10am-6pm; admission £2.50, students £1.50).

A more endearing remnant of ecclesiatical power is the **Southwark Cathedral** (tel. 407 3708). Probably the most striking Gothic church in the city after Westminster Abbey, it is certainly the oldest. Mostly rebuilt in the 1890s, only the church's original 1207 choir and retro-choir survive. The glorious altar screen is Tudor, with 20th-century statues. The church is dotted with interesting stone and wood effigies which have explanatory notes. Edmund Shakespeare, brother of Bill, was buried in the church in 1607. Medieval poet John Gower is buried here in a colorful tomb. This was the parish church of the Harvard family, and a chapel was dedicated in 1907 to the memory of John Harvard, benefactor (but not founder) of Harvard College, who was baptized in here 300 years before. (Open Mon.-Fri. 10am-4pm).

Just a couple of blocks southeast, your hair will rise and your spine will chill at **St. Thomas's Old Operating Theatre,** 9a St. Thomas St. (tel. 955 4791), a carefully preserved 19th-century surgical hospital. Rediscovered in 1956, it is the only known example of a pre-Victorian operating theatre. See the wooden table where unanesthetized patients endured excruciatingly painful surgery, or travel through the herb garret and museum (open daily 10am-4pm and "most Mondays too"; admission £2).

If your appetite for the macabre is not sated by the minutiae of early medicine, the **London Dungeon** awaits buried beneath the London Bridge Station at 28 Tooley St. (see Museums, p. 225). Not for the squeamish, this dark maze of more than 40 exhibits recreates horrifying historical scenarios of execution, torture, and plague.

Moored on the south bank of the Thames just upstream from Tower Bridge, the WWII warship **HMS Belfast** (tel. 407 6434) led the bombardment of the French coast during D-Day landings. The labyrinth of the engine house and the whopping great guns make it a fun place to play sailor. Mind your head, matey. You can take the ferry that runs from Tower Pier on the north bank to the Belfast whenever the ship is open, or take the tube to London Bridge. Follow Tooley St. from London Bridge, past the London Dungeon, and look for the signs. (Open March 1-Oct. 31 daily 10am-6pm, last admission 5:15pm; Nov. 1-Feb. 28 10am-5pm, last admission 4:15pm. Admission £4.40, children £2.20, students and disabled £3.30. Ferry every 15min. to and from Tower Pier April-Sept., restricted in winter; 50p, £1 return, students 30p, 60p return.) East of Tower Bridge, the bleached *Bauhaus* box perching on the Thames is the **Design Museum** (see Museums, p. 224).

Hundreds of stalls selling antiques have been located at **Bermondsey Market** on Bermondsey Abbey St. since 1949. Go early (the serious traders arrive at 5am) on Friday morning to catch the best bargains. **Hay's Galleria** (tel. 626 3411), Bankside between Hay's Lane, Battlebridge Lane and Tooley St. (tube: London Bridge), occupies the reconstructed Hay's Wharf. Underneath the glass and steel barrel-vaulted roof, the galleria houses restaurants, shops, and a giant kinetic sculpture by David Kemp called *The Navigators* that combines water jets and all the accoutrements of Britain's nautical past. The Galleria also houses the **Southwark Tourist Information Centre,** Hay's Galleria, Tooley St., SE1 (tel. 403 8299), which books rooms and pro-

SIGHTS

vides information on the area's sights. (Open April-Sep. Mon.-Fri. 10:30am-5pm, Sat.-Sun. 11am-5pm; Oct.-March Mon.-Fri. 11am-4om, Sat.-Sun. noon-4pm.)

▓ Brixton

The genteel Victorian shopping and residential district of SW9 (tube: Brixton) became the locus of a Caribbean and African community following large-scale Commonwealth immigration in the 1950s and 1960s. Brixton gained notoriety in mid-April 1981, when fierce riots broke out pitting locals against police. Headlines screamed about "The Battle of Brixton," and alarmist copy spoke of "Bloody Saturday," simmering fires, charred buildings, molotov cocktails, and widespread looting. The backs-against-the-wall desperation of these times was captured in the Clash's anthem "The Guns of Brixton" as well as Hanif Kureishi's film *Sammie and Rosie Get Laid.*

There has been much *ex post* speculation as to the cause of the riots. Some locals argue that as the black population in Brixton grew, so did police harassment, and boiling resentment finally turned to aggression. Many compare the Brixton riots to the race-related riots that rocked major American cities in the 1960s.

One optimistic theory asserted that a vibrant commerce would emerge from the post-riot shambles. Brixton has certainly revived since 26 of its buildings were destroyed by fire that April. The firms "Backing Brixton" on the railway bridge testify to this revitalization.

Yet radicalism still thrives in Brixton. (Tourists should be careful in the area, especially at night.) Outside the tube station revolutionaries distribute a thousand different militant newspapers. Meetings of dub poets, Black Muslims, neo-Marxists, and Rastafarians continuously transpire here. Posters advertising these events confront you as you exit the station; as compelling as these posters are the aromas of baked meat patties, incense, and coco bread that emanate from the market.

Most of the activity in Brixton centers around the **Brixton Market** at Electric Ave., Popes Rd., and Brixton Station Rd. (see Shopping, p. 257). Step out of the station and you're practically at the market's heart. One of the market's main arteries inspired Eddie Grant to "take it higher" in the early-Eighties techno-reggae hit, "Electric Avenue." Shoppers from all over London mix with local crowds among vendors of food, clothing, and junk. Street preachers preach, performers busk, and waves of music pour out of the record shops. Choose from among the stalls of fresh fish, vegetables, and West Indian cuisine, or browse through the stalls of African crafts and discount clothing. And don't miss the delicious hard dough breads and tropical pastries produced by the abundant local bakeries.

Nearby, on the corner of Coldharbour and Atlantic, stand the **Black Cultural Archives,** 378 Coldharbour Lane, SW9 (tel. 738 4591; fax 738 7168). Begun by black parents who were concerned that their children's history curriculum in school taught them nothing about blacks' achievements, the archives mounts small but informative exhibits on black history and local issues in a downstairs gallery (open Mon.-Sat. 10am-6pm). Upstairs, books, documents, clippings, and photographs relating to the black presence in Britain are catalogued and stored (open Mon.-Fri. 10am-4pm and the first Sat. of each month 10am-3pm).

A bit lacking in the sort of history that you build monuments to and museums around, Brixton is nonetheless a fascinating neighborhood for aimless wandering. For information on upcoming concerts and festivals in the Brixton area, stop by the **Lambeth Town Hall,** located at Brixton Hill and Coldharbour La., which compiles a list of community groups' meetings (open Mon.-Fri. 9am-5pm).

Greater London

Lo, where huge London, huger day by day,
O'er six fair counties spreads its hideous sway.
—Jane Austen, *The Golden Age*

London is the world's largest capital in area, but what is popularly considered part of this city changes quickly. Far-flung villages, once thought of as distinct, separate cities, are being swallowed up by London's creeping spread. Places like Hampstead are now mainstream night spots, and don't even think about finding a cheap, quiet drinking spot in distant Richmond. This growth, however, has been met by iron resolve among outlying burgs to maintain their own identities amidst sheets of mundane commuter housing. London Transport and British Rail cover Greater London thoroughly; most areas are accessible without a car. If you plan to discover Greater London—and it would be a shame not to—a Travelcard covering the appropriate areas will save you a great deal of money.

▓ Hampstead and Highgate

Foliage in London traditionally pulls in well-heeled and artistic residents, and the twin villages of "Ham and High," surrounding the gorgeous Hampstead heath, offer no exception. Keats, Dickens, and (more recently) Emma Thompson and Kenneth Branagh have all called the area home. The tidy streets lined with Jaguars, designer boutiques, and Georgian townhouses provide a window on the theory and practice of being idly rich, which may help explain Karl Marx and former Labour Party leader Michael Foot's past residencies. Such affluence gives rise to curiosities, making the area worth a visit—even the McDonald's has slick Italian black-lacquered chairs. To get to Hampstead, take the tube to Hampstead or British Rail to Hampstead Heath. To reach Highgate, take the tube to Archway, then Bus 210 or 217 to Highgate Village. Either trip takes around 30 minutes from the center of London.

This dual legacy of art and wealth shines through in the area's many restored houses, most notably the **Keats House,** Keats Grove (tel. 435 2062), one of London's finest literary shrines. To get there from the Hampstead tube station, head left down High St. for several blocks, turn left down Downshire Hill, and then take the first right onto Keats Grove. (The BR Hampstead Heath station is much closer.) Before dashing off to Italy to breathe his last consumptive breath in true Romantic style, John Keats pined here for his next-door fianceé, Fanny Brawne. He allegedly composed "Ode to a Nightingale" under a plum tree here; one wonders what the arch-Romantic would have made of the "keep off the grass" signs in the garden today. The house's decor and furnishings stay true to the Regency style of the early 19th century, providing an evocative showcase for manuscripts, letters, and contemporary pans of Keats' works by critics dead and forgotten. (Open April-Oct. Mon.-Fri. 10am-1pm and 2-6pm, Sat. 10am-1pm and 2-5pm, Sun. 2-5pm; Nov.-March Mon.-Fri. 1-5pm, Sat. 10am-1pm and 2-5pm, Sun. 2-5pm. Free.) The **Keats Memorial Library** (tel. 794 6829) next door contains 8500 books on the poet's life, family, and friends (open by appointment to accredited researchers only).

Among the delicate china, furniture, and early keyboard instruments exhibited in the **Fenton House,** Hampstead Grove (tel. 435 3471), sits a prototype 18th-century "double guitar," proving that Britain's fascination with excessively stringed instruments predates the meaty guitar hooks of the young Jimmy Page. If you're lucky, area musicians will be strumming, plucking, and tickling as you stroll through, or if you fancy yourself a musical type, you may audition with the curator to play them yourself. For permission, apply in writing to Mimi Waitzman, 11 Sprowston Rd., Forest Gate, London E7 9AD. You can see the walled garden and orchard free of charge. Note the boarded windows of Fenton House—the revenue man tried to levy a tax

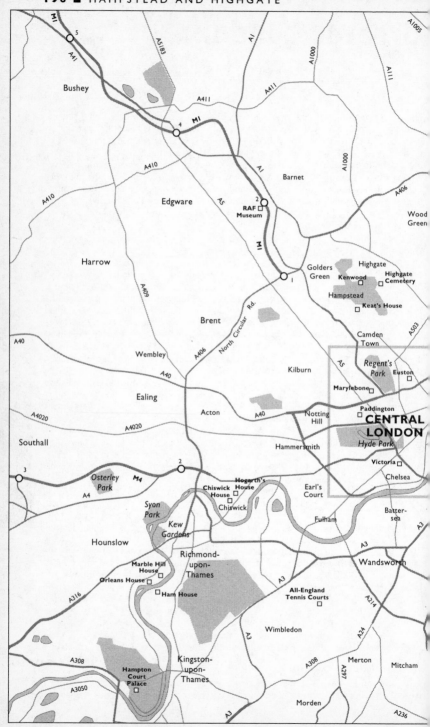

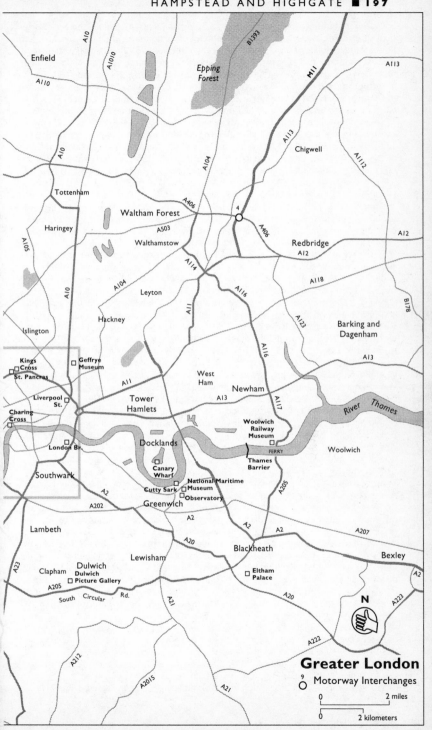

Greater London

○ Motorway Interchanges

0 ——— 2 miles

0 ——— 2 kilometers

upon the number of windows in people's homes, leading people like the Fentons to board up their glass, setting a fine example of tax evasion for the area's well-heeled denizens to emulate. To get there, cross the street onto Holly Bush Hill, then bear right at the fork onto Hampstead Grove (house open March Sat.-Sun. 2-5pm; April-Oct. Wed.-Fri. 2-5:30pm, Sat.-Sun. 11am-5:30pm; admission £3.60, children £1.80).

Farther up Hampstead Grove and a left turn onto Admiral's Walk takes visitors to the **Admiral's House.** The house fails in its attempt to simulate a steam ship but earned celluloid immortality as the home of the nutty admiral in *Mary Poppins.*

The idyllic walk to the **Burgh House,** New End Sq. (tel. 431 0144), is much more satisfying than the exhibitions of the **Hampstead Museum** inside (open Wed.-Sun. 11am-5:30pm). Just a few narrow streets and cobblestone sidewalks away from High St., the town is transformed into a country village with flowers everywhere and birds chirping in the boughs of commandingly large trees. Stop for a peaceful cup of tea at **The Buttery** in the basement. Head left from the Hampstead tube on Hampstead High St. and take the first left onto Flask Walk.

Church Row, off Heath St., assiduously guards its 18th-century style and dignified terraces. The narrow alleyways off the Row hark back to the days of Mary Poppins, complete with small, overflowing secret gardens. The painter John Constable lies buried in St. John's Churchyard down the row.

Hampstead Heath (tube: Hampstead or BR Hampstead Heath) separates Hampstead and Highgate from the rest of London. Once a haunt for outlaws, health nuts, and other undesirables, it now attracts docile picnickers, kite flyers, and anglers. Central Park it ain't, but *it's unadvisable to wander the heath alone at night.*

The pile of ground on the southeastern tip of the heath is called **Parliament Hill,** but rather deceptively—no Parliament, no hill. It was toward this "hill" that Guy Fawkes and his accomplices fled after planting explosives under the House of Commons in 1605, hoping for a good view of the explosion. He was later caught and tortured in the Tower of London (p. 184). Visitors who journey here for the same view may be similarly disappointed; the heath is worth a visit for other reasons, but the view is overrated. What little elevation exists reputedly owes much to the piles of corpses left here during the Plague. The bones of Queen Boudicca—who after a flogging by the Romans raised an army and sacked London—reputedly lie here too.

On a hot day, take a dip in **Kenwood Ladies' Pond, Highgate Men's Pond,** or the *outré* **Mixed Bathing Pond.** Women may expose their upper halves at the Ladies' Pond as long as they remain lying down. In July, 1994, gay protestors held a "strip-off" demonstration at the men's pond to protest the Corporation of London's introduction of a "trunks-on" policy. In all, the heath boasts six ponds.

Kenwood House, Hampstead La., a picture-perfect example of an 18th-century country estate, presides over the heath. This airy mansion now houses the **Iveagh Bequest** (see Museums, p. 225). Chief justice Lord Mansfield, the original owner of Kenwood, decreed an end to slavery on English soil. Mansfield's progressive policies did not win him universal popularity and, after destroying his abandoned townhouse in Bloomsbury, the Gordon Rioters pursued him north to Hampstead. Luckily for him (and for Kenwood House), his pursuers stopped for a drink at the **Spaniard's Inn** on Spaniards Rd. (see Pubs, p. 130), where a responsible publican plied them with drink until the militia could seize them. In summer, Kenwood hosts a hugely popular series of **outdoor concerts** (see Music, p. 236) in which top-flight orchestras play from a bandshell across the lake (tube: Archway or Golders Green, then Bus 210 to Kenwood). From Hampstead High St., Bus 268 goes to Golders Green (grounds open daily 8am-8:30pm or dusk, whichever comes first).

To get from Hampstead to Highgate, walk across the heath (an easy way to get lost but very scenic) or up Hampstead La. Both take about 45 minutes. You can also take Bus 210 from Jack Straw's Castle junction or take the tube to Archway.

Highgate Village stands 424 ft. above the River Thames. You can climb Highgate Hill for a breathtaking panoramic view of London. From Archway tube station, exit onto Highgate Hill, which goes up .75km. to the village, or wait there for Bus 210.

Once in Highgate Village, turn left onto South Grove at the triangular bus depot. Here hides **The Grove,** an avenue of late-17th-century houses secluded behind magnificent elms. Poet and critic Samuel Taylor Coleridge lived at No. 3 for the last 11 years of his life, entertaining Carlyle, Emerson, and other literary luminaries.

Highgate Cemetery, Swains La. (tel. (0181) 380 1834), is a remarkable monument to the Victorian fascination with death. Curiously, the most famous resident of this deathbed of Victoriana is Karl Marx, buried in the **Eastern Cemetery** in 1883. The larger-than-life bust placed above his grave in 1956 is hard to miss, though the number of visits to Marx's tomb has declined noticeably in recent years. Death and politics make strange bedfellows—Herbert Spencer, who vehemently opposed socialism, shares Highgate with socialism's most influential proponent, Marx. On a more harmonious note, Spencer's bones lie near those of his reputed lover, the novelist George Eliot (Mary Ann Evans, buried in the Western section). Resist the temptation to dance on the grave of Communism—this is, after all, a private cemetery. Be aware that the cemetery closes its gates to visitors during funerals (open Mon.-Fri. 10am-4:45pm, Sat.-Sun. 11am-4:45pm; admission £2, but varies nominally). Though its guest list lacks the same notoriety, the western section, appropriately termed the **Western Cemetery,** provides rest for Michael Faraday, the Dickens family, and ornate tombs and mausolea worth seeing regardless of their occupants. (Access by guided tour only Mon.-Fri. at noon, 2, and 4pm, Sat.-Sun. every hr. 11am to 4pm. Admission around £3. Camera permit £1, valid in both sections.)

■ Golders Green

Located north of Hampstead, Golders Green on first view seems a bland suburb, but a watchful walk along its main street reveals a richer texture. Here is the center of today's London Jewish community. Kosher restaurants, men in black hats, and *yarmulke*-covered youths dot the large sidewalks of this suburb. Regrettably, places of interest are spread out over a large area poorly served by public transport. The tube to Golders Green, Bus 268 from Hampstead High St., and Bus 210 from Archway tube, deposit visitors at the intersection of North End Way and **Golders Green Road**. This wide shopping strip houses some mundane stores and a surprising number of Chinese restaurants. Jewish eateries and Hebrew/English signs begin to appear several blocks away from the station.

At no. 130, busy **Bloom's** restaurant and take-away is one of several shops on the block selling kosher foodstuffs supervised by the London *Beth Din*. "Think Tradition! Remember—Kosher!" admonishes Bloom's motto. Neil Diamond, Bob Dylan, Golda Meir, and various royals have sampled *kneidlach* soup, *latkes,* and *gefilte* fish at this *fleischig* (non-dairy) haven (tel. (0181) 455 3303/1338); open Sun.-Thurs. 9:30am-2am, Fri. 9:30am-3pm, Sat. sundown-4am). Israeli-owned **Carmelli's Bagel Bakery,** 126-128 Golders Green Rd., is a late-night wonderland of delicious kosher sweets and bagels (bagels 24p; open daily 7am-1am). Upscale *glatt* kosher Israeli cuisine can be had at **Dizengoff,** 118 Golder's Green Rd. (tel. (0181) 458 7003). Also on Golder's Green Rd. are stores selling "Elite" and "Osem" brand foodstuffs imported from Israel—this is the place to find Bazooka gum with Hebrew cartoons. During the summer, when the Jewish sabbath terminates past sunset at 10:30pm, many restaurants remain open on Sat. nights until 4am, making Golders Green a popular place for starving late-night teens. **The Jewish Chronicle,** the world's oldest Jewish newspaper, provides information on local Jewish events (40p; tel. 405 9252).

The ashes of Freud, in his favorite Greek vase, rest near those of ballerina Anna Pavlova at the **Golders Green Crematorium,** 62 Hoop La., NW11 (tel. (0181) 455 2374; open daily 8am-7pm). Other celeb ashes and memorials include Marks and Spencer founder and Zionist Lord Sieff, Marc Bolan (of T-Rex and "Get It On" fame), and *Dracula* creator Bram Stoker. To pay your respects, walk under the tube's bridge, then turn right at the first traffic light (at the church) onto Hoop Lane Rd. To prevent disgruntled psychology students' vandalism, the good doctor's ashes are locked away in the Ernest George Columbarium—ask an attendant to let you in.

GREATER LONDON

The grassy collection of fields, intricate gardens (including a Japanese display) and exotic zoo of **Golders Hill Park** rests on the other side of the tube station (off North End Rd.). A horticulturalist's dreamland, the park attracts both avid plant watchers and young kite-flyers looking for green space in suburbia (open daily 7:30am-dusk).

■ Docklands

London Docklands, the largest commercial development in Europe, is the only section of London built wholly anew—a total break from the city's typically slow architectural evolution. Developers have poured tons of steel, reflective glass, and money onto the banks of the Thames east of London Bridge. A new Fleet Street and a heavyweight financial center have risen from the ruins of London's docks. Rarely does the economic world so easily lend itself to such gross symbolic interpretation—London's future lies not in shipping and manufactured goods but in the financial services it can provide the world. There is another, more sobering, bit of imagery to be found here as well. The areas surrounding the glass and steel monuments to commercial success are some of London's poorest; the skyscrapers sprout from centers of grinding poverty. Every weekday evening the city's executive class boards trains, cars, and private motor launches to leave this grim reality behind.

The center of the new 8.5-sq.- mi. development is on the **Isle of Dogs,** the spit of land defined by a sharp U-shaped bend in the Thames. To the east lie the **Royal Docks,** once the center of one of history's proudest trading empires. The 800-ft. **Canary Wharf** building, Britain's tallest edifice and the jewel of the Docklands, is visible to the east from almost anywhere in London. The pyramid-topped structure, which contains shops, restaurants, and a concert hall, is virtually the emblem of the Docklands. Below the towering Canary Wharf sprouts a huge fountain which during the lunch hour is carpeted by an expanse of conservative colors, starched fabrics, power ties, and tightly-pulled-back hair—anyone not bedecked in office wear will stick out like a sore thumb. The nearby shopping area has approximately 10 stores selling (you guessed it) well-cut suits, neckties, shirts, and the rest of the uniform.

Docklands covers a huge expanse, from the Tower to Greenwich (55 mi. of waterfront to be exact). The best way to see the region is via the **Docklands Light Railway (DLR)**, a driverless, totally automatic elevated rail system (tel. 918 4000). The DLR is slow but smooth and affords a panoramic view that helps you put the huge expanse of the Docklands into perspective. All tickets, Travelcards, and passes issued by London Transport, London Underground, and BritishRail are vaild on the DLR, provided they cover the correct zones.

The DLR can be accessed from the Bank and Tower Hill tube stops. The route between these City locations and the shining new commercial developments passes through East London's depressed housing blocks. Gradually the dirty brick apartments and laundry lines give way to dramatic glass and steel office spaces. In homage to past architectural traditions these towers sport an occasional cornice, moulding or pilaster—in general however the buildings are smooth expanses of mirror unbroken by a single line. The area is awesome, in both the sense that teenagers use the word and in the sense that religious figures use it. It is spectacular in its scope, but also a bit overwhelming and imposing.

On the southern end of the Isle of Dogs, the pastoral expanses of **Mudchute Park** come as a relief after the human-made modernity of the new Docklands (DLR: Mudchute). Here are 32 acres of grassy knolls, plus horses to ride and farm animals to pet at **Mudchute Farm,** Pier St., E14 (tel. 515 5901; open daily 9am-5pm). Note the round stone pathways leading into the park from West Ferry St. These odd markings run parallel to the Prime Meridian, which is defined by the green-domed observatory just visible across the river. Also note the cement walls and ditches at the entrance to the park. These were WWII anti-aircraft gun sites installed just before the Battle of Britain. For a sweeping view of Greenwich, follow the DLR southern line to its endpoint at Island Gardens. You can walk through the chilly foot tunnel (the steps at either end are quicker than waiting for the lift) and take in some of the sights (see Greenwich and Blackheath, p. 202).

Getting off at **Shadwell** station, you'll see the old dock community: drab brick housing, dusty streets, traditional pubs, caffs, and pie-and-mash shops. Southwest of the station, down Cannon St. Rd. and a right onto The Highway, is the turreted **St. George in the East** (1714-26), whose plain façade and tower can be seen from afar (tel. 481 1345; open daily 9am-5pm). Designed by Wren's disciple Nicholas Hawksmoor, it was bombed and, in 1964, restored with a modern interior.

From the Westferry stop, turn left onto West India Dock Rd., then left onto Three Colt St. for another Hawksmoor church, **St. Anne's** (built 1712-24), presiding over a leafy churchyard. The sister church of St. George in the East, its clock face comes from the workshop that provided Big Ben's face. The church's Victorian organ won the organ prize at the Great Exhibition of 1851 (tel. 987 1502; open daily 2-4pm).

The Limehouse and Westferry stops cover the historic **Limehouse** neighborhood, where dock and factory workers once lived. The legacy of Limehouse's 19th-century Chinese community can be seen in the Chinese restaurants along West India Dock Rd. The famous Narrow Street along the Thames is an official conservation area, where many Georgian houses can be seen. At 76 Narrow Street, **The Grapes,** the pub Dickens described in *Our Mutual Friend* maintains its original ambience. Just east of Narrow street on Ropemaker's Fields lies **The House They Left Behind,** (tel. 538 5102) a pub famed as a Joseph Conrad haunt.

The first stop for any tour of the Docklands should be the **Docklands Visitors Centre** (tel. 512 1111; DLR: Crossharbour, then left up the road). Loads of brochures hide behind the reception, the most useful being the *DLR Tourist Guide,* which includes a map, points of interest, and DLR info. A huge room is devoted to informing visitors about the history of the Docklands and its future, using photos, charts, maps, architects' plans, and a tearfully inspiring propaganda video (open Mon.-Fri. 8:30am-6pm, Sat.-Sun. 9:30am-5pm). Other Docklands information desks are at the Tower Hill/Gateway and Island Gardens stops. A separate **Museum of Docklands** is in the works; until then, a section in the Museum of London counts as the Docklands museum (call the Museum of Docklands Project, tel. 515 1162, for an update). London has a long history as a maritime gateway—Londinium was already a prominent port in Roman times—and by the Middle Ages the city's wharves and quays had creeped east from the City.

The **Royal Dockyards** were established at Deptford and Woolwich in 1515. As London grew in importance, the docks grew with it, stretching miles down the Thames, until they had become the powerful trading center of the British Empire. During World War II, the Blitz obliterated much of the dockland area, while the war seriously diminished Britain's world influence. As the sun set on the empire, the docks continued to do brisk business until the early 60s. Then the advent of container transport and modern shipping methods rapidly rendered the docks obsolete—by 1982 all had closed, leaving sweeping tracts of desperate dereliction.

As part of the Thatcher government's privatization program, redevelopment of the area was handed over to the private sector—in the form of the **London Docklands Development Corporation (LDDC)**—along with a generous helping of public funds. Since then, the LDDC has been at the helm of what it calls "the most significant urban regeneration program in the world." The all-powerful company is answerable only to Parliament and the Department of the Environment; however, local councils retain responsibility for housing, highway, and education decisions.

The LDDC's first mission was to convince Londoners that this blossoming area was an organic part of the city and not a distant, capitalistic wasteland. The Docklands' original investors, Olympia and York Co. of Toronto, poured millions of pounds into British Telecom to ensure that the Docklands received coveted city area codes and not suburban numbers, despite the area's peripheral location.

Since then, building has taken place on a phenomenal scale, but the task of populating new office space with businesses initially lagged behind. Hesitantly at first but now more steadily, big businesses have begun to take up residence in the area, filling in the previously empty floors of shiny new skyscrapers. In 1993, when Canary Wharf remained largely unoccupied due to the recession, Spiral Tribe, an underground rave-coordinating organization, attempted to use the building as a rave venue but were thwarted by the police. Now the Docklands is not only populated by wealthy entrepreneurs ferried to work every day on executive launch motorboats that zoom across the Thames. After a disastrous recession slump, the Docklands are poised for a new housing boom. Low-cost housing communities are springing up all over the southern bank, especially on the Isle of Dogs. Hopefully this housing will also benefit the local residents.

But healthy capitalism has an eerie effect on the Docklands, and it may be a bit too early to celebrate this area's rebirth. Canary Wharf and the stark newness of many buildings is striking, if not chilling; it is quite easy to see the Docklands as a futuristic city conceived in a test tube. Still, the area is a potent political symbol of London's bid to remain a center of commercial activity in the new, unified Europe, a fact which likely motivated the IRA **bomb attack** here on February 9, 1996. The bomb killed two, injured dozens, and caused £150 million worth of damages.

Many of the ancient Dockland wharfs have now been turned into major leisure spots. Six sailing centers, three pools, a go-karting racetrack, and an artificial ski mountain currently stand where ships and toxic waste used to rest. For sailing call **Docklands Sailing and Watersports Center** (tel. 537 2626) or **The Royal Victoria Dock Watersports Center** (tel. 511 2326). **Racepro European Karting** houses a track along Royal Albert Dock Basin, off Woolwich Way DLR (tel. (0181) 317 3657 or 426 9572). These are really fast cars, not like the putt-putts at the amusement park; they cost £10 for a quarter hour.

The year-round **Beckton Alps Ski Centre** is a one-run hillock rising 45m above the surrounding supermarkets and electronics superstores. It is covered with a specially designed carpet upon which water is sprayed to make it slippery. The carpet is similar to white astroturf; you definitely don't want to fall, as it would be truly unpleasant at any speed. The 300m-long run is served by a rope tow. Amateurs may not have much luck turning heads, but the regulars who pay £300 per season manage to look like Killy. The center is owned and operated by a former Austrian olympic skier, he bills it as "London's Premiere Ski Centre," which by force of logic it of course is. (Tel. 511 0351; take DLR to Beckton; adults £6/3hr. during the weekday, £7/3hr. including equip. rental. Open most days, but call to check on conditions— cold rainy days are the best. Pants, long sleeves, and gloves required.) The Docklands Visitors Centre has a list of all sport and leisure facilities.

■ Greenwich and Blackheath

London's love affair with the Thames and Britain's love affair with the sea climax in Greenwich (GREN-idge), at a point where the Thames runs wide and deep. Although the village functioned historically as the eastern water approach to London, Greenwich is synonymous with time in modern-day minds. After Charles II authorized the establishment of a small observatory here in 1675 "for perfecting navigation and astronomy," successive royal astronomers perfected their craft to such a degree that they were blessed with the Prime Meridian in 1884.

When industrialization hit Britain in the 18th century, Greenwich somehow managed to stay above the fracas. As a result, the streets around the pier feel quaint (if somewhat touristy), with their tiny storefronts, pubs, and cafés. Greenwich also offers numerous corner markets. On summer Sundays, the village streets are taken over by the young, old, bold, and beautiful seeking the ultimate bargain at the **Greenwich Market,** at Greenwich Church St. and College Approach (open in summer Sat.-Sun. 9am-6pm; in winter Sat. 9am-5pm). In addition to this covered crafts market, Greenwich boasts an **Antique Market** on Burney St., where peddlers hawk antiques, books, and various bric-a-brac (open Sat.-Sun. 8am-4pm). Come in the summer—the number of stalls and bargains dwindle during the winter months.

The splendid **Greenwich Park,** used as a burial ground during the 1353 plague, contains most of the major sights. The shriveled trunk of the **Queen Elizabeth Oak** on the east side of the park (now fenced off and covered in ivy) marks the spot where Henry VIII frolicked with an 11-fingered Anne Boleyn. The garden in the southeast corner of the park combines English garden and fairy tale, with a wild deer park thrown in for good measure. In summer, bands perform at Greenwich Park as a part of the **Royal Park Band** performance series. Free shows begin at 3 and 6pm (every Sun. June-Aug.) in the bandstand north of the gardens. The Children's Boating Pool next to the playground gives kids a chance to unleash pent-up seafaring energy accumulated in the nearby museums. (Open Apr.-Oct. daily 9am-dusk; £1.50/person/20min., or £2.50/boat/20min. for 2-3 child crafts.)

At the top of the hill in the middle of the park stands the **Old Royal Observatory** (tel. (0181) 858 1167), designed by Sir Christopher Wren. Only select parts are open to the public. Flamsteed House—remarkable for its unique, octagonal top room—contains Britain's largest refracting telescope and also an excellent collection of early astronomical instruments—astrolabes, celestial globes, and orreries—displayed with nearly comprehensible explanations. The **Prime Meridian** is marked by a brass strip in the observatory courtyard. Jump from west to east in an instant. Greenwich Mean Time, still the standard for international communications and navigation, is displayed on a clock over 120 years old. The red time ball, used since 1833 to indicate time to ships on the Thames, drops, quite unspectacularly, daily at 1pm. In 1894, an anarchist blew himself up while trying to destroy the observatory, and Polish sailor Joseph Conrad used the bizarre event as the seed for his novel *The Secret Agent.* (Open Mon.-Sat. 10am-6pm, Sun. 2-6pm; in winter Mon.-Sat. 10am-5pm, Sun. 2-5pm. Admission to the Old Royal Observatory, National Maritime Museum, and the Queen's house includes a free return visit within a year; adults £5.50, concessions £4.50, children (5-16) £3, family £16. Admission to the Observatory alone; adults £4, concessions £3, children £2, family £12, not much of a bargain. Planetarium usually features a show Mon.-Sat. 11:30am, noon, 12:30, 2, 2:30, 3, 3:30, and 4pm; tickets £1.50, children £1. 45min. sound guide to the observatory £2.)

Just outside the observatory, you can share a splendid view of the Thames with a statue of General Wolfe (conqueror of French Canada) kindly donated by the Canadian government. At the foot of the hill is the delightful **National Maritime Museum** (see Museums, p. 226).

The museum forms the west addition to **Queen's House** (tel. (0181) 858 4422), the 17th-century home that was started for James I's wife, Anne of Denmark, who unfortunately died before construction was completed. The house was finished for Henrietta Maria, the wife of Charles I. Designed by the age's master architect, Inigo Jones, it is England's first Palladian villa, known to the Queen as her "house of delights." The renovated house's 17th-century furnishings and rich silk hangings are as swank as a Vegas hotel's, but the art collection makes the effect slightly less garish. Free maps are available, and a display in the basement guides you through the house's muddled jumble of commissioners, architects, and occupants. (Open daily 10am-5pm. No separate entry, see prices for observatory.)

Ranger's House (tel. (0181) 868 2608) overlooks the cricket pitch in the park's southwest corner. Built for an admiral in 1688, it was given to the Park Ranger in 1815. Today it contains the Suffolk Collection of Jacobean portraits and the Dolmetsch Collection of antique musical instruments. The **Architectural Study Centre** holds a substantial collection of architectural details from 18th- and 19th-century London dwellings. (Open April-Oct. daily 10am-1pm and 2-6pm; Nov.-March daily 10am-1pm, 2-4pm. Admission and taped tour £2, concessions £1.50, children £1.)

Charles II commissioned Wren to tear down the Royal Palace of Placentia and to construct the **Royal Naval College** (tel. (0181) 858 2154) in its place. Because it was situated directly between the Queen's House and the river, the College was constructed in two halves to leave the Queen's view unobstructed. James Thornhill's elaborately frescoed ceiling in the Painted Hall and Benjamin West's painting of a shipwrecked St. Paul in the chapel provide excellent opportunity to view breathtaking art in its original location. (Open daily 2:30-5pm, last entrance 4:30pm. Free. Services Sun. 8:30am holy communion, 11am sung eucharist.)

By the River Thames in Greenwich, the **Cutty Sark,** one of the last great tea clippers, anchors in dry dock. The ship (whose name, meaning "short shift," comes from Burns's poem "Tam O'Shanter") carried 1.3 million pounds of tea on each 120-day return trip from China. In the prime of its sea-going days, between 1869 and 1938, it set new records for speed. The decks and crews' quarters have been restored, and exhibits describing the history of the Pacific trade have been added. The vessel is also filled with the largest collection of ships' figureheads in the world (tel. (0181) 858 2698; open Mon.-Sat. 10am-6pm, Sun. noon-6pm; in winter Mon.-Sat. 10am-5pm, Sun. noon-5pm. Admission £3.25, concessions £2.25, families £8). The **Gipsy Moth IV** rests nearby. In this tiny 54-ft.-long craft, the 66-year-old Sir Francis Chichester spent 226 days sailing solo around the globe in 1966-67 (tel. (0181) 853 3589; open April-Oct. Mon.-Sat. 10am-6pm, Sun. noon-6pm, but closed 1-2pm Mon.-Fri. for lunch; last entry ½hr. before closing; admission 50p).

A show at the **Greenwich Theatre,** on Croom's Hill, can be a relaxing conclusion to a day spent traipsing about galleries. For more information, see Off West End and Fringe Theaters p. 232. At 12 Crooms Hill, across from the theater, you'll find the **Fan Museum** (tel. (0181) 305 1441 or 858 7879), which opened in 1991 as the first and only museum in the world dedicated to the history, craft, and coquetry of the fan. Do-it-yourselfers can emulate what they've seen in the fan-making classes held on the first Saturday of every month. (Open Tues.-Sat. 11am-4:30pm, Sun. noon-4:30pm. Admission £3, children £2; Tues. 2-4:30pm free for the disabled and seniors. Wheelchair accessible.)

The most picturesque (and appropriate) passage to Greenwich is by boat. Cruises to Greenwich pier depart from the Westminster (tel. 930 4097), Charing Cross, and Tower (tel. 987 1185 for both) piers (see Boats, p. 71, for times and prices). The crew provides valuable commentary on the major sights along the voyage. Trains leave from Charing Cross, Waterloo East, and London Bridge for Greenwich (less than 20min., day return £3). The DLR whizzes from Tower Gateway to Island Gardens (16min.). From there, Greenwich is just a 7-minute walk through the foot tunnel. When the DLR is not in service, Bus D9 runs from the Island Gardens station to Bank Station. Bus 188 runs between Euston and Greenwich, stopping at Kingsway and Waterloo. The friendly **Greenwich Tourist Information Centre,** 46 Greenwich Church St., SE10 (tel. (0181) 858 6376; open daily 10:15am-4:45pm, in the winter (usually) 11am-4pm), will go out of their way to arrange a variety of afternoon tours (£4, concessions £3 under 14 free, 1-1½hr; call (0181) 858 6169 for info).

Just on the south side of Greenwich Park, the sloping fields of **Blackheath** offer a checkered history of love, rebellion, and golf. Wat Tyler and his fellow peasants revolting over a poll tax congregated on the heath in 1381. Henry VII fought Cornish rebels here, while Henry VIII had a similarly unfortunate experience—it was here that he meet his betrothed Ann, the "mare of Cleves." Henry choose his bride, sight unseen, based on a flattering portrait by Holbein, but repeatedly commented on her equine features when life failed to imitate art. The **Royal Blackheath Golf Club** was founded on the common—James I was known to take an occasional bash here with his three wood. A traditional site for royal celebrations, Blackheath still holds fairs on Bank Holidays, and is the starting point every spring for the **London Marathon,** the world's largest.

A bit farther down the river, the steel and concrete **Thames Barrier** (tel. (0181) 854 1373, 1 Unity Way, Woolwich SE18), the world's largest movable flood barrier, is the reason that London no longer enjoys the exciting high tides of yesteryear. Constructed during the 1970s, the barrier spans 520m and consists of 10 separate movable steel gates; when raised, the main gates stand as high as a five-story building. A visitors center has a working model of the barrier, in addition to exhibits explaining its history (open Mon.-Fri. 10am-5pm, Sat.-Sun. 10:30am-5:30pm; admission £3.40, seniors and children £2, families £7.50). From Charing Cross take BR to Charlton Station; from there it's a 15-minute walk. Alternatively take the boat from Greenwich pier (30min.; 75min. from Westminster pier). Call 930 3373 for details of Westminster service; (0181) 305 0300 for Greenwich.

■ Kew Gardens

The perfect anodyne or alternative to days of sight-seeing in central London, the **Royal Botanic Gardens** (tel. (0181) 940 1171) at Kew provide a restorative breath of fresh air. Yet another example of the Empire's encyclopedic collecting frenzy, the Royal Botanic Gardens display thousands of flowers, plants, bushes, fruits, trees, and vegetables from the world over, spread over 300 perfectly maintained acres. Founded in 1759 by Princess Augusta, Kew gradually grew in size until it became a royal park in 1841.

The wonders of the gardens comprise several buildings and sections, and demand several hours to be seen properly. The moist and tropical **Palm House,** a unique masterpiece of Victorian engineering built in 1848, will stun you with the revelation that bananas are in fact giant herbs. Still reeling from this blow, climb the white spiral stairs to the upper gallery for the toucan's-eye view. The beautifully lit aquariums of the basement **Marine Display** let you watch batfish and porcupine puffer fish interact with colorful sea kelp.

Although replete with voluptuous fronds, the Palm House is dwarfed by its younger Victorian sibling, the **Temperate House.** The climate here nurtures 3000 species, arranged according to geographical origins in its 50,000 square feet. The lush South American Rainforest Species section surpasses all others.

The **Evolution House** leads you through 3.5 billion years of plant history, from the primeval mud stages to the exciting moment when flowering plants appeared. Its misty waterfalls and dinosaur footprints in the path make it seem like a cross between "Land of the Lost" and Biosphere II.

On the opposite side of the park from William Chambers' 1762 **pagoda,** the **Princess of Wales Conservatory** allows you to browse through 10 different tropical climates; it's just a few steps from a rainforest to an arid desert. Its award-winning pyramidal design allows it to both remain innocuous among the foliage and conserve energy. While the pineapple family displayed within is quite amiable, the gargantuan lilypads inspire a holy terror of the absent frogs that must roost here.

In the northeastern section of the gardens stands **Kew Palace.** Built in 1631 but leased as a royal residence since 1730, this inconspicuous summer home of King George III and Queen Charlotte contains a small museum depicting the vagaries of late 18th-century monarchical life. (Palace open daily 11am-5:30pm. Admission £1.)

Other points of interest at the gardens include the **Marianne North Gallery,** a small but interesting collection of 19th-century paintings, the **Rhododendron Dell** (built by Capability Brown), and the **Waterlily House.**

The calming way to reach Kew is by boat from Westminster pier (boats from Westminster daily 10:15 and 11am, 1, 2, and 2:30pm; from Kew at 12, 12:30pm, and every hr. from 3:30-6:30 £5, return £8) and the cheapest way is by tube or BR North London line (Kew Gardens station, zone 3). Should you opt to drive, plenty of parking is available outside the gardens. (Gardens open Mon.-Fri. 9:30am-6:30pm, last admission 6pm, Sat.-Sun. and bank holidays 9:30am-7:30pm, last admission 7pm. Conservatories close at 5:30pm. Call to confirm closing times as they may vary by season. Admission £5, student and seniors £3, children 5-16 £2.50, late admission from 4:45pm £3. Tours leave Victoria Gate daily at 11am and 2pm, £1.) Kew hosts jazz and classical music concerts sporadically in the summer; ticket prices run £14-19. Call for more information.

■ Syon Park

Syon Park (tube: Gunnersbury, zone 3, then Bus 237 or 267), just across the Thames from Kew in Brentford (walk across Kew Bridge and left along London Rd., or BR:

Syon Lane), harbors stately **Syon House** (tel. (0181) 560 0881). Syon Park was originally founded as part of a religious order—hence the phonetic reference to Zion in the Holy Land. The castellated exterior of the house is Tudor, built to incorporate the buildings of a monastery where Queen Catherine Howard was imprisoned before her execution in 1542. In 1553 ownership of the house passed to the Duke of Northumberland, who offered the crown to his daughter-in-law Lady Jane Grey here. Not a week later, Mary Tudor took back the house, and the Duke's head. The house reverted to the Northumberlands in 1594, and they still own it today, making this the last mansion left in London still under its original hereditary ownership. The 11th Duke of Northumberland calls this 200-acre parkland home, and many of the rooms open for viewing serve as private entertaining areas at night.

The mansion's exquisite interior was created by Robert Adam in 1766. The Anteroom, a green marble and gilt extravaganza, is dazzling; the Long Gallery has a more balanced elegance The highlight of the stately gardens around Syon House is the six-acre rose garden, landscaped by Capability Brown. (House open Wed.-Sun. 11am-5pm, Oct.-March Sun. 11am-5pm, last admission 4:15pm. Garden open daily 10am-dusk. Admission for both £5, concessions £4; garden only £2.50, concessions £2.)

Though the rarified delights of Syon House appeal to almost every eye, most other aspects of the Syon Park complex cater to the younger set. This is where Londoners take their little'uns on the weekends. At **London Butterfly House** (tel. (0181) 560 7272), over 1000 butterflies fly "free," and the tykes can pet "giant spiders and other creepy crawlies" (open April-Oct. 10am-5pm; Nov.-March 10am-3pm; admission £2.50). The **London Aquatic Experience** (tel. (0181) 847 4730) next door purveys critters of a more amphibious sort, which the children won't be permitted to touch—piranhas, snakes, frogs, and the like. (Open daily April-Sept. 10am-5pm, Oct.-March 10am-3:30pm. Admission £2.90, students £2, kids and seniors £1.85.) Outside the main gate and to the left, toddlers will squeal at **Snakes and Ladders**, a warehouse full of kids' toys, battery-operated kiddy cars, and a three-tiered adventure playground (tel. (0181) 847 0946; open daily 10am-8pm; £3.65, weekends £4.25; under 5 £2.65, weekends £3.25).

■ Richmond

Ever since Henry I came up the Thames in the 12th century, Richmond has preened its royal pedigree. Although Henry VII's Richmond Palace, built in 1500, was demolished during Cromwell's Commonwealth, the town has not lost its dignified sheen—the sprawling grounds of the 18th-century riverside houses and pathways beneath **Richmond Hill** make this area possibly the most serene in or around London. Richmond is where the banks along the Thames become rural, with trendy shops giving way to luscious fields and forests along the river.

The **Richmond Tourist Information Centre,** in the old Town Hall on Whittaker Ave., has complete information on Richmond and surrounding areas (tel. (0181) 940 9125; BR or tube: Richmond; open Mon.-Sat. 10am-6pm, Sun. 10:15am-4:15pm, Nov.-April open Mon.-Sat. 9am-5pm). The **Museum of Richmond** (tel. (0181) 332 1141) in the same building is an excellent local museum with exhibits on famous inhabitants, from actor Edmund Kean to writers George Eliot and Virginia Woolf (open Tues.-Sat. 11am-5pm, Sun. 2-5pm, closed Sun. Oct.-April; admission £1, children 50p). The **Richmond Festival** (tel. (0181) 332 0534) in the first week of July explodes with music, dance, and children's activities, much of it free.

Most of Richmond's sights are scattered around the actual village. The town itself is perched above the river valley. Richmond Hill provides an extraordinary view of the snake-like Thames and its bankside 18th-century Georgian mansions. So many English paintings have copied this view that Parliament declared it a protected site. The road leads up to more beautiful parkland before descending Thamesward. **Richmond Park,** atop Richmond Hill, is Europe's largest city park. A former royal hunting ground, its 2500 acres are still home to several hundred nervous deer who share the grounds with tourists and the Royal Ballet School, housed in the Palladian White

Lodge. The Isabella Plantation woodland garden, deep inside the park, bursts with color in the spring, when its azaleas and rhododendrons bloom.

Descend Richmond Hill and follow Bridge St. across the Thames. From here it's a 10-minute walk left along the river (follow the signs and the tourists) to the **Marble Hill House** (tel. (0181) 892 5115; Bus 33, 90B or 290 from the station). Perched on the Thames amid vast trimmed lawns, this Palladian house was built in 1729 for Henrietta Howard, George II's mistress. The Great Room, on the first floor, is lavishly decorated with gilt and carvings by James Richards and original Panini paintings of ancient Rome. During the summer, a series of outdoor concerts are held on the grounds. (See Entertainment, p. 236. House open daily April-Oct. 10am-1pm, 2-6pm; Nov.-March Wed.-Sun. 10am-1pm, 2-4pm. Admission £2, concessions £1.50.)

Exit left from Marble Hill House along the path until a brick wall across the road. Turn left, then find a gated entrance concealed in the wall that leads you to the remains of the 18th-century **Orleans House** (tel. (081) 892 0221). This Georgian, geometrically intriguing house holds a gallery of art and artifacts of local history. Only the Octagon Room survives from the original building, which put up with the Duc D'Orleans (the future King Louis Philippe) for three years in the 19th century. The grounds surrounding the house remain untrimmed wildland (open Tues.-Sat. 1-5:30pm, Sun. 2-5:30pm; Oct.-March Tues.-Sat. 1-4:30pm, Sun. 2-4:30pm; free).

On summer days (April-Aug. Sat.-Sun. 10am-6:30pm, Mon.-Fri. 10am-6pm), a small passenger ferry (40p, kids 20p) runs between Marble Hill Park (next to Orleans House) and **Ham House,** on Ham Street. Built in 1610, this house boasts artwork and room designs that are almost as beautiful as the grounds outside. The Duke of Lauderdale inherited the house from his wife's father, Charles I's "whipping boy." (As part of his "reward" for taking all the future king's punishments whenever he misbehaved, he received the lease to the Ham estate when he became an adult.) Rooms filled with family portraits of royalty, including Charles II and his loyal servants, overlook Ham House's recently restored gardens and sprawling riverfront fields. Don't be too surprised to see some recent touch-ups, however; the house was lavishly "modernized" during the 1960s. Have tea (90p) and scones (65p) in the Orangery and enjoy the surrounding meadows. (tel. (0181) 940 1950; Bus 65 or 371 from Richmond station. Gardens open Sat.-Thurs. 10:30am-dusk; free. House open April-Oct. Mon.-Wed. 1-5pm, Sat.-Sun. noon-5:30pm; Nov. to mid-Dec. Sat.-Sun. 1-4pm. Admission £4, children £2.) On Sundays from May through September, visitors can catch a match at the **Ham Polo Club** west of the house (beginning around 2pm).

During the summer, Richmond can also be reached by a boat from Westminster (see Boats, p. 71) which stops at Richmond on its way to Hampton Court. Boats leave Westminster Pier at 10:30am, 11:15am, and noon; last boat returns at 5pm (2-3hr.; adult £6, return £9).

■ Hampton Court Palace

Although a monarch hasn't lived here since George II packed it in over 200 years ago, Hampton Court Palace (tel. (0181) 781 9500) continues to exude regal charm. Located 6 mi. down the Thames from Richmond, the brown-bricked palace housed over 1500 court members at its height. Cardinal Wolsey built it in 1514, showing Henry VIII by his example how to act the part of a splendid and all-powerful ruler. Henry learned the lesson well—he confiscated the Court in 1525 when Wolsey fell out of favor. Today, the palace stands in three distinct parts, each bearing the mark of one of its strong-willed inhabitants.

To help tourists make sense of the chaos of the chaotic and schizophrenic arrangement of the palace, it is divided into six "routes" through which tourists may meander. Fans of Henry VIII have a myriad of options for discovering how the king lived, reigned, and ate his way to a size 54 waist. **Henry VIII's State Apartments,** the first of the palace routes, allows would-be sycophants a chance to reenact some Tudor brown-nosing. Every morning, courtiers would gather in the **Great Watching Chamber,** clamoring for a chance to kiss some royal tuckus as Henry proceeded to morning services in the Chapel Royal (currently held at 8:30am). A nine-minute video starring Sir Ian McKellen describes the origin and function of each room of the apartments, down to the Chapel's remarkably preserved Tudor ceiling.

For those curious as to how Henry acquired his massive girth in the days before the deep-fat fryer, the **Tudor Kitchens,** another palace route, provide the answer. The numerous vast rooms demonstrate, with the aid of fake animal carcasses, pies, and a bubbling cauldron, how one of England's most colorful kings got his grub on.

If the style of Henry's rooms strikes you as a bit vulgar, you're not alone. When William III (of William and Mary fame) sailed up from the Netherlands to ascend to the throne with his wife, he declared the palace a "gothic monstrosity," and commissioned Wren to demolish the entire structure and build a palace to rival Louis XIV's Versailles. Though lack of funds and the death of his queen sapped William's energy and the project was never completed, Wren's work can be seen in the opulent **King's and Queen's Apartments,** two complementary palace routes. Newly restored after a 1986 fire, the King's Apartments held courtiers who watched in rapture as William III publicly dressed, dined, and took the occasional powder. Along the ceiling of the **King's Guard Chamber,** almost 3000 guns and weapons arranged in six repeating patterns reminded visitors that the man they were about to see, no matter which throne they found him on, was not to be trifled with. As you pass through the public and private bedchambers and down the stairs, don't miss the plush **velvet-covered toilet** in a small enclave on your left. This petite chamber served as the "office" for the Groom of the Stool, William's most trusted servant, who received a royal sum for attending the king's toilet.

George II was the last monarch to rule from Hampton Court. **The Georgian Rooms,** significantly more exciting with the audio guide, recreate a tumultuous day in his scandal-ridden court.

The legacies of all the palace's past residents can be felt in the **Wolsey Rooms.** Chambers that housed Cardinal Wolsey before he fell from favor now house some of the finest treasures of the Royal Collection, including **tapestries** woven from the Raphael cartoons in the Victoria and Albert Museum (p. 219), and a roomful of grisaille work originally by Mantegna but poorly repainted in the 18th century.

The walls of the Palace are steeped in more royal lore and anecdotes than can possibly be discovered during a quick stroll through. If you do pay the hefty admission fee, allow yourself plenty of time. Stop by the information center to pick up **free audio guides** for the Georgian Rooms, Kitchens, and Kings apartments. The free **costumed guided tours** of Henry's Apartments and the King's Apartments, given by guards and courtiers in period costumes, teach you Stuart drinking toasts and explain how the English attained world renown for **poor dental hygiene.**

The exterior of the palace holds nearly as many delights, mostly free. Note the black, spiked steel railings along the Clock Court; these were installed in 1850 to keep **public urinators** from defacing palace walls. Sixty marvelous acres of Palace gardens are open and free, and contain some highly celebrated amusements, including the **maze** (open March-Oct.), a hedgerow labyrinth first planted in 1714 that inspired the hedges a crazed Jack Nicholson dashed through at Stanley Kubrick's Overlook Hotel. "Solve" the maze by getting to the benches in the middle, and back.

By following the signs on the grounds to the Tudor Tennis Court, you may be lucky enough to catch a match of **"Real Tennis"** in progress on the indoor tennis court (1529). The rules, including playing off the terraces and the baffling "chases" are posted for all to see, but make cricket seem downright comprehensible. According to legend, Henry VIII was chasing lobs on this court whilst the executioner lobbed off the head of Anne Boleyn. Henry's is one of only four courts of its kind left in England (open March-Oct.). Also note the exhibit of Tijou's ironwork gates, left freestanding for the most part, and admirable from all sides. (Palace open March to late Oct. Mon. 10:15am-6pm, Tues.-Sun. 9:30am-6pm; late Oct. to March Mon. 10:15am-4:30pm, Tues.-Sun. 9:30am-4:30pm. Last admission 45min. before closing. Gardens open at the same time, but close at 9pm or dusk, whichever comes first (free). All-encompassing admission £8, concessions £5.75, under 16 £4.90, under 5 free, families £19.50.

Admission to maze or Privy Garden only £1.70, under 16 £1.00. Admission to tennis court 50p, children 20p. Wheelchair accessible.)

To reach Hampton Court by tube, take the district line to Richmond (zone 3), Bus R68 runs from the station to Hampton court (80p). BR runs trains from Waterloo to Hampton Court every half-hour (day return £3.60). From the first Monday before Easter until the end of September, a boat runs from Westminster Pier (See Boats, p. 71) to Hampton Court, leaving in the morning at 10:30, 11:15am, and noon, and returning from Hampton Court at 3, 4, and 5pm. The trip takes three to four hours one way (adult one-way £7, return £10).

■ Chiswick

Six miles west of central London, the riverside village of Chiswick was long ago engulfed by London's suburban sprawl. Today, two houses of great historical and artistic interest stand off from the undistinguished dwellings of this busy village.

Chiswick House (tel. (0181) 995 0508; BR: Chiswick or tube: Turnham Green, Gunnersbury, or Chiswick Park), built by Lord Burlington in 1729, studs the heart of Chiswick with 68 acres of luscious gardens, ponds, and wild forests. Heavily influenced by Andrea Palladio's ancient Italian forms, architect William Kent took English society by storm with his creation. Lord Harvey, a contemporary freelance critic, sneered, "You call it a house? Why? It is too small to live in, and too large to hang from one's watch." But the day's notables were more than happy to see and be seen when Burlington entertained at Chiswick.

As exquisite as Chiswick's architecture are the 67 acres of gardens and manicured fields surrounding the house itself. The sixth Duke of Devonshire—an eccentric fond of horticulture and exotic animals—built up the mansion's grounds in order to house his pet elephant, giraffe, and kangaroo. Next to the house are an Italian garden as well as a conservatory. The beautiful fields provide perfect staging grounds for annual summer Shakespeare plays hosted by the National Heritage. (Call (0181) 577 6969 for info. House open daily 10am-1pm, 2pm-6pm, winter Wed.-Sun. 10am-4pm. Grounds open 8am-dusk. Admission £2.50, concessions £1.90.)

Just northeast of the Chiswick House grounds, on Hogarth La., the modest abode of artist and social critic William Hogarth stands as a subtle jab to Lord Burlington's extravagance. Rumor has it that the two hated each other. Hogarth, the great moralist, saw Lord Burlington as a sycophant who imported "foreign" trends to England. **Hogarth's House** (tel. (0181) 994 6757; follow Burlington La. north to Chiswick Sq. and go left at the Hogarth Roundabout; the house is about 200 yards down Hogarth La., next to a very busy road), which Hogarth called his "country box by the Thames," will be closed for extensive renovations between September 1996 and February 15, 1997. It will reopen featuring more informative plaques and a greater focus on historical and biographical detail. Though we haven't seen the new exhibits, it's worth noting that the museum's previous incarnation, relative to other restored houses, was quite scholarly and detailed (open Tues.-Fri. 1pm-5pm, Sat. and Sun. 1pm-6pm, closes one hour earlier Nov.-March.; free).

■ Windsor and Eton

Windsor Castle (tel. (01753) 868 286 or (01753) 831 118 for 24-hour information line) proves beyond a doubt that, borrowing from Mel Brooks, it's good to be the Queen. Within these ancient stone walls lie some of the most sumptuous rooms in Europe and some of the rarest artworks in the Western world. It is odd that Windsor castle and all its elegant treasures should have been made possible through centuries of bloody, sweaty struggle. But beyond the velvet and fine art, this castle's essence is its strategic location high in the hills above the Thames and the thousands of hauberks, swords, pistols, rifles, and suits of armor which bedeck its walls.

The castle dominates this river town of cobbled lanes and tea shops surrounded by the 4800-acre Great Park, far away from London in the farming country of Surrey.

Built by William the Conqueror as a fortress rather than as a residence, it has grown over nine centuries into the world's largest inhabited castle. Saunter blithely in and out of its labyrinthine terraces and enjoy dreamlike views of the Thames Valley.

Be aware that Windsor is a working castle, which may sound a little strange in this day and age, but it only means that various members of the Royal Family reside here on weekends and for various special ceremonies. The practical consequence of the Royal's residence is that, often without warning, large areas of the castle will be unavailable to visitors. The steep admission prices will be lowered, but it is wise to call before visiting to check that the areas you want to see are open.

The 13 acres covered by the castle are organized into the lower, middle, and upper wards. The **Round Tower** dominates the middle ward. The **Moat Garden,** filled not with water but with roses and well-attended grass, surrounds the tower.

On passing through Norman Tower and Gate (built by Edward III in 1359-1360) you enter the upper ward, where many of the rooms are open to the public. You can visit the elegantly furnished **state apartments,** which are mostly used for ceremonial occasions and official entertainment. The rooms are richly decorated with artwork from the massive Royal Collection, including works by Holbein, Rubens, Rembrandt, and an entire room of Van Dycks. The rooms are covered with all manners of the instruments of war, bearing witness to the more savage side of the Royal history. In the same wing is **Queen Mary's dolls' house,** an exact replica of a palace on a tiny scale. Sadly, the room displaying the house is kept very dark, which makes viewing difficult. The Queen's collection of 20,000 drawings and 10,000 watercolors includes works by da Vinci, Michelangelo, and more recent artists.

A stroll down to the lower ward will bring you to **St. George's Chapel,** a sumptuous 15th-century building with delicate fan vaulting and an amazing wall of stained glass dedicated to the Order of the Garter. Here Henry VIII rests in a surprisingly modest tomb near George V, Edward IV, Charles I, and Henry VI. A ceremonial procession of the Knights of the Garter, led by the Queen, takes place here in June. Windsor's **Changing of the Guard** takes place in front of the Guard Room at 11 am (Mon.-Sat. during summer, alternate days Mon.-Sat. during winter).

Windsor is notorious to contemporary visitors as the site of a fire that helped make 1992 an *annus horribilis* for the royal family. The fierce conflagration blazed for nine hours on November 20, 1992, and was only extinguished through the efforts of 225 firefighters and 39 fire engines. Six rooms and three towers were destroyed or badly damaged by smoke and flames, although 80% of the state rooms escaped harm. Projections indicate that the rooms will be restored by 1998

Windsor is open daily from 10am to 5:30pm; last admission is at 4pm. From November to March, it closes one and a half hours earlier and last admission is at 3pm. Call (01753) 868 286 or (01753) 831 118 for a 24-hour. information line. Admission is for adults is £8.50, over 60 £6, under 17 £4.50, family tickets £19.50. To see Queen Mary's doll house, pay an extra pound, which, according to Queen Mary's original 1924 request, is still donated to charity. The majority of the castle is accessible to disabled visitors—call (01753) 868 286 ext. 2235 for details.

Follow the road that bears left around royal grounds to come to the entrance to **Windsor Great Park,** a huge expanse of parkland where deer graze and royals ride. The park follows the 3-mi. **Long Walk,** which passes by a couple of former hunting lodges, one of which houses the Queen Mum (on weekends). The town of Royal Windsor is directly across the road from the castle gate. Built up around the castle during the Middle Ages, it is filled with specialty shops, tea houses, and pubs.

About 10 minutes down Thames St. and across the river is **Eton College,** the preeminent public (that is, private) school founded by Henry VI in 1440. Eton boys still wear tailcoats to every class and solemnly raise one finger in greeting to any teacher on the street. Wellington claimed that the Battle of Waterloo was "won on the playing fields of Eton"—catch a glimpse of the uniquely brutal "Wall Game" and see why. Eton has molded some notable dissidents and revolutionaries—Percy Bysshe Shelley, Aldous Huxley, George Orwell, and even former Liberal Party leader Jeremy Thorpe. The Queen is the sole (honorary) female Old Etonian.

More than a Toy

Built on a scale of 12:1, Queen Mary's dolls' house was designed by Sir Edwin Lutyens and given to Queen Mary in 1924. There are two working lifts, a running water system, and electric lights. The furniture was made by the best furniture manufacturers of the time, the paintings commissioned by well-known artists, and the books in the library written by Rudyard Kipling and Thomas Hardy, among others. Even the wine cellar is real. Berry and Bros. Wine Merchants in London contributed to the project—the tiny bottles are filled with genuine vintage wines and are labeled correctly. Don't miss the garden—it is fully outfitted with beautiful flowers and, of course, all the necessary garden tools.

Wander around the schoolyard, a central quad where Eton boys have frolicked for centuries. A statue of Henry VI and the school's chapel, an unfinished cathedral, occupy this space. The central area is surrounded by the 25 houses that shelter approximately 1250 students; those with the best exam results get the best rooms (tel. (01753) 671 177; open July and Aug. and first 3 weeks of April from 10:30am-4:30pm, other times 2-4:30pm; tours leave at 2:15pm and 3:30pm daily; admission £2.50, children £1.90; tours £3.50, children £2.90.)

A more recent (1996) and whimsical addition to the area is **Legoland Windsor** (tel. (0990) 62 63 64, for advance bookings (0990) 62 63 75). This bizarre playfield is directed mainly at the 13-and-under set, but adults will be amazed by **Miniland,** which 100 workers spent three years and 25 million blocks to build. The replica of the City of London includes a 6-ft. high St. Paul's as well as every other major building or landmark in the city. The Lego buses which motor along the city's streets without hitting a car or building are a marvel. The rest of Miniland offers superbly detailed buildings and sights from other European cities. (Open April-Sept., and Oct. weekends; 10am-6pm (July and Aug. until 8pm). Admission £15, children £12, seniors £11, £1 cheaper if booked in advance.)

British Rail (tel. 262 6767) serves Windsor and Eton Central station and Windsor and Eton Riverside station, both of which are near Windsor Castle (follow the signs). Trains leaving Victoria or Paddington go via a change in Slough to Windsor and Eton Central Station. Trains for Waterloo go directly to Windsor and Eton Riverside station (every 30min., 50min. Day return £5.40). Green Line **coaches** (tel. (0181) 668 7261) 700 and 702 also make the trip from their station on Eccleston Bridge, behind Victoria Station (50-90min., day return £4.35-5.50).

■ Great Views

"Your architects were madmen, your builders sane but drunk," Shane MacGowan sang of London's "planners." The best way to experience the strange appeal of this aged city's disheveled *mien* and endless sprawl is from above. The following are roosts which permit a comprehensive view of this oddly beautiful muddle.

Monument, King William St. Tube: Monument. A fantastic 332-step view of the Thames, Tower of London, and St. Paul's from one of Wren's most famously ramrod buildings. Right in the middle of the Bank District. £1 (see City (Western Section): Bank to St. Paul's, p. 178).

St. Paul's. Tube: St. Paul's. Set in the heart of the City of London, this cathedral's inner elegance can only be matched by the view from its 271-step dome. Unrivalled views of ye olde City, the modern financial district, the distant weirdness of the Docklands, and the chic West End (p. 176).

Primrose Hill, Regent's Park. Tube: Camden Town, Great Portland Baker Street and Baker Street. You're up to your head in urban slime, and suddenly, by the grace of Primrose Hill's grassy surroundings, you rise above the city to a wonderful view of London. On a good day you can see past the Surrey Downs (p. 164).

Anywhere along the South bank of the Thames at night. Tube: Tower Hill or Tower Gateway. Cross Tower Bridge and look upon the city's skyscrapers floodlit in evening colors. A wonderful place for dinner or an evening walk.

■ Parks

> *The tulip-beds across the road flamed like throbbing rings of fire. A white dust, tremulous cloud of orris-root it seemed, hung in the panting air. The brightly-coloured parasols danced and dipped like monstrous butterflies.*
> —Oscar Wilde on Hyde Park

London's parks have always been the refuge of the happy and sad. There is no better place to luxuriate in the sun or stroll away a languid evening. And the splendor of flaming gardens and unmovable trunks cannot fail to comfort the weary and heavy-hearted.

During the mid-morning the unoccupied—chiefly the very young, the very old, and, of course, travelers—enjoy the park's early glory. By lunchtime the green fields are dotted with office workers enjoying a take-away lunch. In the summer evenings Londoners flock to the curving walks to stroll, blade, and revel in the open-air performances put on in these graceful collections of lawns and gardens. With the exception of Hyde Park's midnight closing, London's parks are generally open from 7am-dusk, which comes to London extraordinarily late in the summer.

Battersea Park. Tube: Sloane Sq., then a walk to the Thames and over the Chelsea or Albert Bridge. On the south bank of the Thames, across from Chelsea, this lovely park is one of the city's best kept secrets. Don't miss the small walled garden in the center of the park.

Green Park. Tube: Green Park. Green Park is an expanse of grounds which would suit a palace—which is fitting because it forms Buckingham Palace's backyard. This set of well-kept lawns and open walks is located between the southeast corner of Hyde Park and the northwest corner of St. James.

Hampstead Heath. Tube: Hampstead, Belsize Park, BR: Hampstead Heath. A delightfully vast sprawl of wilderness sandwiched between two tony neighborhoods. Hampstead Heath boasts over 6 ponds (you can swim in three of them), the Iveagh Bequest (see p. 195) and summer concerts (see Music: Kenwood, page 236), and acres of lush hiking ground. This gorgeous area is more rustic than other city parks; the term city sanctuary might fit better.

Hyde Park and Kensington Gardens. Tube: South Kensington, Hyde Park Corner. This park's luscious 600 acres make up the "lungs of London." Skaters streak past the park's art gallery, huge man-made pond, and Princess Di's Kensington Palace. Speaker's Corner invites the lunatic and loquacious to practice their art in the northeast corner of Hyde Park (tube: Marble Arch). More citified than other parks but still exquisite (see Hyde Park and Kensington Gardens, p. 155).

Mudchute. DLR: Mudchute. Escape the Docklands' futuristic weirdness in this classic London park. Contains a "city farm" (see p. 242) and locals' veggie gardens.

Postman's Park. Tube: St. Paul's. Wonderful old men's hangout and sanctuary for local businessmen. This petite park dwells across the street from the Central Post Office, surrounded by church walls on one side and a graveyard on the other.

St. James's Park. Tube: St. James's Park. Many think that this is London's most beautiful park. Weeping willows bend over mirror-surfaced ponds; lush greenery and immaculate lawns makes this a welcome respite from the nearby offices. During lunch hour London's office workers lose their office pallor here (p. 144).

Regent's Park. Tube: Camden Town, Great Portland St., Regent's Park, Baker St. The largest of London's parks (though the contiguous Ken. Gardens/Hyde Park space is larger), Regent's Park boasts vast football and cricket fields for its adoring Sunday visitors. It is also the home of the London Zoo and beautiful Primrose Hill, and it shelters the gorgeous Queen Mary's gardens (p. 164).

Richmond Park. Tube: Richmond. Standing on this vast, hilly garden spot overlooking a splendid view of the Thames below, one feels like the king of England. Particularly if you're Henry VIII, who used to hunt deer in this vast park (p. 206).

Waterlow Park. Tube: Archway. Sweetly donated by Sidney Waterlow to the people of London to provide "a garden for the gardenless." This park's sloping hills provide a splendid vista of the city below. Towering trees and duck-dotted ponds line the path. Highgate Cemetery, Marx's resting place, lies nearby (p. 199).

■ Notable Gardens

Gardening is the English national obsession—in the hinterlands and the capital alike. It is no surprise then that London has some of the world's most lovingly manicured lawn and best trimmed topiary. Here are short descriptions of the best. Refer to the longer write-ups in our Sights section for more information.

Chelsea Physic Garden. Tube: Sloane Square. A beautiful patch of green near the Chelsea bank of the Thames. The smallish garden is filled with glorious wispy fauna, making it a perfect place for a Wednesday or Sunday afternoon stroll. Why Wednesday or Sunday you ask? Because the park is open to visitors only April-Oct. Wed. 2-5pm and Sun. 2-6pm. Admission £3.50, concessions £1.80 (p. 160).

Hampton Court Palace. A palace this impressive needs a helluva backyard to match, and King William's gorgeous Privy Gardens turn the trick. Also the site of a well-known and well-loved hedge maze and the world's oldest vine (p. 208).

Kew Gardens. A 300-acre wonderland that takes lush where it's never gone before. Field after greenhouse after pond of botanical treasures from around the world. London's most famous garden (p. 205).

The Orangery Gardens in Kensington Gardens. Tube: Bayswater or Queensway. The gorgeous gardens outside Lady Di's window are open for commoners to stroll about, though the prettiest part is walled off and may be seen only by peeking through the hedge in a few niches designed for such a purpose. Next door is a field covered with what appear to be scampering squirrels—on closer examination they reveal themselves to be a fleet of pet rabbits. Free (p. 155).

Queen Mary's Gardens at Regent's Park. Tube: Baker St. The area of Regent's Park within the Inner Circle is a symphony in color. The roses are famous. Nearby one may rent a rowboat or lawn chair. Free (p. 164).

Ranleagh Gardens at the Royal Hospital. Tube: Sloane Sq. Here 18th-century pleasure-seekers spent their evenings watching pageants and fireworks and imbibing to excess. Today aging army veterans from the nearby hospital seek peace of mind here, and no wonder. The site of the Chelsea Flower Show during the third week of May. Free (p. 160).

Syon Park. The name is a phonetic reference to Zion, and the foliage, including a rose garden designed by Capability Brown, is appropriately divine (p. 205).

Museums

A couple of centuries as capital of one of the world's richest and most powerful countries, focus of an empire upon which the sun never sets, advanced navigation combined with something of a wanderlust, and a decidedly English penchant for collecting have given London a spectacular set of museums. Art lovers, history buffs, and amateur ethnologists will not know which way to turn when they land. London will inevitably frustrate those who vow to see all that is displayed—the city suffers from an embarrassment of riches. It would be impossible, in less than a year, to see everything in the British Museum, let alone view the whole of this city's varied and excellent collections.

Museums tend to be the most peaceful on weekday mornings. Admission to major collections is usually free, but many museums, no longer heavily subsidized by the government, now charge or request a £1-2 donation. Most charge for special exhibits and offer student and senior citizen discounts **("concessions")**. The last few years have witnessed the birth of a number of expensive theme museums, with elaborate sound systems and computers supplementing more traditional exhibits. Expect to meet your fellow countrymen-on-holiday here.

The **London White Card** is a discount card that allows unlimited access to 13 participating museums for a period of three or seven days. The card can be purchased at any of the participating museums, including the V&A, the Science Museum, the Natural History Museum, the Royal Academy of Arts, the Hayward Gallery, the Design Museum, the London Transport Museum, the Museum of London, the Museum of the Moving Image, and the Courtauld Institute. The card will only afford you substantial discounts if you plan to visit *many* museums, or if you plan to visit a particularly expensive museum more than once (3-day card £15, families £30; 7-day card £25, families £50).

■ British Museum

The sheer volume of the British Museum's collections is a fascinating document of the political, military, and economic power of the British Empire. Founded in 1753, the museum began with the personal collection of the physician Sir Hans Sloane. In the following decades, the museum became so swollen with gifts, purchases, and Imperialist spoils that a new building had to be commissioned. Robert Smirke drew up the design in 1824. Constructed over the next 30 years, his Neo-classical building is still home to the museum today.

The British Museum's national archaeological collections recapitulate the glory days of Egypt, Asia, Greece, Rome, and prehistoric and medieval Europe. The museum also houses superb temporary exhibitions of its coin and medal and its print and drawing collections. The **British Library's** galleries share the building now, but its most famous manuscripts (the *Magna Carta*, the Gutenberg Bible, etc.) and most current stacks are due to move with the rest of the library to a new building in St. Pancras in 1997.

Wandering through 2½ mi. of galleries may frustrate even the most die-hard museum-goer. To catch the main attractions, buy the £3 short guide; for a more in-depth look, introductory books on specific parts of the collection are available for about £5. If you're interested in a little human interaction and just want to see the basics, avail yourself of a **guided tour** (Mon.-Sat. 10:45, 11:15am, 1:45, 2:15pm; Sun. 3, 3:20, 3:45pm; £6, children under 16 £3; 1½hr.). You also might get lucky and be able to catch one of the occasional free tours or gallery talks offered by the museum (call for info. or pick up a "Current Events" leaflet at the information desk).

The British Library galleries, to the right of the main entrance, showcase scrawling from Lenin to Lennon, and that's just the 20th-century offerings. In the **Manuscript Saloon,** the **English Literature** displays contain the bane of the high school English student: manuscripts from *Beowulf* (c. 1000) and the *Canterbury Tales* (1410), as well as the scrawlings of Jonson, Jane Austen, Elizabeth Barrett Browning, James Joyce, Virginia Woolf, Philip Larkin, and more. **Biblical displays** include ravishing illuminated texts and some of the oldest surviving fragments (the *Codex Sinaiticus* and the *Codex Alexandrinus*), 3rd-century Greek gospels, and the Celtic **Lindesfarne Gospels.** The **Historical Documents** section proffers epistles by Henry VIII, Elizabeth I, Churchill, Napoleon, and Jeremy Bentham, among others. Two copies of the *Magna Carta* get their very own cases. The wily Lenin's application for a reader's ticket is signed under the pseudonym "Jacob Richter." **Music displays** show off works by Handel, Beethoven, and Stravinsky, as well as lyric drafts by Lennon and McCartney. Other cases offer curious **maps** from ancient times to the 18th century. The "Manuscript of the Month" case offers a rare chance to view a manuscript of current pertinence not normally on display.

The **King's Library,** built between 1823 and 1826 to house George III's library, now contains (in addition to his books) an exhibit on early printing history and displays of printed books, most notably a Gutenberg Bible and Shakespeare's First Folio. Manuscripts from around the world fill the display cases in the south end of the gallery. Samples of Chinese calligraphy, early Japanese printed books, manuscripts in Hebrew and Arabic, and Sanskrit scriptures provide glimpses into the role of books in various cultures. Although you'll need a reader's pass in order to study in here, check out the circular **Reading Room** where Marx wrote *Das Kapital.*

The outstanding **ancient Egypt** collection occupies rooms on the ground and upper floors. Entering the ground floor gallery, one is greeted by two of the many imposing statues of Amenophis III. To the left rests the **Rosetta Stone,** discovered in 1799 by French soldiers. Its Greek text enabled Champollion to finally crack the hieroglyphic code. The head of Ramses II, famed for his arrogance towards Joseph and higher beings in Exodus, dominates the northern section of Room 25. Among the sculptures, the sublime royal head in green schist (1490 BC) stands out. The asexual representation of the latter has left scholars to debate whether it represents dominatrix Queen Hatshepsut or her successor, King Tuthmosis. In the side gallery 25a, don't miss three of the finest and best-known Theban tomb paintings. While famed as one of the most "human" of the daunting sculptures in the collection, the black granite Sesostris III remains more noteworthy for its ears than its warmth. To the right of the virile Ramses (reputed father of 150), in a side gallery, glistens the gold of the inner coffin of priestess Henutmehit. The central gallery is filled with tributes to the animal world, including the tiny blue hippo. The upstairs Egyptian gallery contains brilliant sarcophagi, grisly mummies, and an ancient body "desiccated by the dry, hot sand." Delicate papyri include the *Book of the Dead of Ani.*

The **Assyrian galleries,** wedged between Egypt and Greece, are renowned for the reliefs from Nineveh (704-668 BC), illustrating a campaign in southern Iraq. Room 16's entrance is guarded by the enormous, five-legged, human-headed bulls, made to look stationary from the front, mobile from the side.

The **Greek antiquities** exhibits are dominated by the **Elgin Marbles,** 5th-century BC reliefs from the Parthenon, now residing in the spacious Duveen Gallery. In 1810, Lord Elgin procured the statues and pieces of the Parthenon frieze while serving as ambassador to Constantinople. The museum claims that Elgin's "agents removed many sculptures from the Parthenon with the approval" of unnamed "authorities" for the price of £75,000. Later, for reasons of financial necessity, he sold them to Britain for £35,000. Every so often, the Greeks renew their efforts to convince the British government to return the marbles. Carved under the direction of ancient Greece's greatest sculptor, Phidias, the marbles comprise three main groups: the frieze, which portrays the most important Athenian civic festivals; the metopes, which depict incidents from the battle of the Lapiths and Centaurs (symbolizing the triumph of "civilization" over "barbarism"); and the remains of large statues that stood in the east and west pediments of the building.

Other Greek highlights include the complete Ionic façade of the **Nereid Monument,** one of the female caryatid columns from the Acropolis, and two of the Seven

Wonders of the Ancient World. Once crowded by a four-horse chariot, the **Mauso-leum at Halicarnassus** gained such fame in antiquity that it coined the word "mau-soleum" in many European languages. Frieze slabs and some freestanding sculpture commemorate the second wonder—the **Temple of Artemis,** built to replace the one buried by Herostratus in 356 BC to perpetuate his name in history.

Among the many sculptures of the **Roman antiquities,** the dark blue glass of the **Portland Vase** stands out. The inspiration for ceramic designer Josiah Wedgwood, the vase has tenaciously survived a series of mishaps and reconstructive operations that took place even before the vase was dug up in 1582. When it was discovered, the base had already been broken and replaced. In 1845, it was shattered by a drunken museum-goer; when it was put back together, 37 small chips were left over. Since then, the vase has been beautifully reconstructed twice, with more left-over chips being reincorporated each time— don't touch! The scene depicted is an enigma; controversy still rages among experts over a Ph.D. student's recent interpre-tation of it as the depiction of an ancient poem.

The **Roman-Britain** section includes the **Mindenhall Treasure,** a magnificent col-lection of 4th-century silver tableware. With a diameter of almost two feet and weigh-ing over 18 pounds, the aptly named Great Dish impresses with its size and elaborate decorations. Nearby crouches **Lindow Man,** an Iron Age Celt supposedly sacrificed in a gruesome ritual and preserved by peat bog. The **Sutton Hoo Ship Burial,** an Anglo-Saxon ship buried (and subsequently dug up) in Suffolk complete with an unknown king, is the centerpiece of the **Medieval** galleries. Other fascinating high-lights of these allegedly dark ages include a display of elaborate clocks, and the **Lewis Chessmen,** an 800-year-old ivory set more elaborately carved than anything offered by Franklin Mint.

The majority of the museum's **Oriental Collections** reside in the recently refur-bished Gallery 33. The gallery's eastern half is dedicated to the Chinese collection, renowned for its ancient Shang bronzes and fine porcelains, and the western half is filled by Indian and Southeast Asian exhibits, which include the largest collection of Indian religious sculpture outside of India. Upstairs, the collection continues with a series of three galleries displaying Japanese artifacts, paintings, and calligraphy.

The most recent gallery additions are **Renaissance to the 20th Century,** featuring housewares from Bach to *Bauhaus,* and the **Mexican Gallery,** highlighted by exquis-ite masks, weapons, and ornaments coated with a mosaic of turquoise.

In addition to their prodigious permanent collections, the British Museum and Brit-ish Library both also put on a number of temporary exhibits. The museum is located at Great Russell St., WC1 (tel. 323 8299 for the information desk, or 580 1788 for recorded information; tube: Tottenham Ct. Rd., Goodge St., Russell Sq., or Holborn). The rear entrance, with access to certain galleries, is on Montague St. For recorded information on wheelchair accessibility, call 637 7384. Persons who are blind or visu-ally-impaired should enquire about the tactile exhibits; a **touch tour** of Roman sculp-tures is given in room 84 in the basement—ask about it at the main information desk. (Open Mon.-Sat. 10am-5pm, Sun. 2:30-6pm. Free, suggested donation £1. The larger, special exhibits cost £3, concessions £2.)

▓ National Gallery

The National Gallery maintains one of the world's finest collections of Western paint-ing, especially strong in works by Rembrandt, Rubens, and Renaissance Italian paint-ers. The Tate Gallery has joint custody of the British Collection, and is a better bet if you are more interested in 20th-century works.

You can spend days in this maze of galleries, renovated and rehung in 1992. A help-ful guide is the **Micro Gallery,** a computerized (though easy-to-use) illustrated cata-logue that cross references works any way you want and prints out (at £1/5 pages) a personal tour mapping out the locations of the paintings you want to see (open Mon.-Sat. 10am-5:30pm, Sun. 2-5:30pm). If you prefer a more personal touch, take advantage of the free hour-long tours. (Tours depart twice each day from the Sainsbury Wing Mon.-Fri. 11:30am and 2:30pm, Sat. 2 and 3:30pm.)

The National's collection is chronologically divided into four color-coded sections, each comprising one wing of the museum; paintings within these sections are arranged by school or artist. The collection starts in the new **Sainsbury Wing,** to the west of the main building, designed by postmodern Philadelphian Robert Venturi. Amid fake ceiling supports and false perspectives hang works painted from 1260 to 1510. Early Italian paintings such as Botticelli's *Venus and Mars,* Raphael's *Crucifixion,* and da Vinci's famous *Virgin of the Rocks* are framed by the arches and columns of the new building. Though Van Eyck's *Arnolfini Marriage* appears to be a depiction of a medieval "shotgun wedding," the bride is merely holding up the hem of her dress as per the style of the day. More mystery surrounds the mysterious figures reflected in the mirror—many believe one of them to be Van Eyck himself.

Paintings from 1510 to 1600 are found in the **West Wing,** to the left of the Trafalgar Sq. entrance. Titian's *Bacchus and Ariadne* displays his mastery of contrast. Stormy El Grecos are featured here as well. Holbein's *The Ambassadors* (the focus of a special exhibition Nov.-Dec. 1997) contains a cunning blob that resolves itself into a skull when viewed from the right. Strong Rembrandt and Rubens collections adorn the **North Wing** (devoted to works from the 17th century)—Rembrandt's young and old self-portraits make a fascinating contrast. Placid Claude and Poussin landscapes are routed by the unabashed romanticism of Caravaggio and Velázquez. Van Dyck's *Equestrian Portrait of Charles I* headlines the State Portrait room.

The **East Wing,** to the right of the main entrance, is devoted to painting from 1700 to 1920, including a strong English collection. The natural light provides the perfect setting for viewing the paintings; many, such as Turner's *Rain, Steam, and Speed* (note the tiny jackrabbit running alongside the train), seem to acquire a special luminosity. Gainsborough's tight *Mr. and Mrs. Andrews* and Constable's rustic *The Hay Wain* whet the appetite before the Impressionists clamor for attention. Impressionist works include a number of Monet's near-abstract waterlilies, Cézanne's *Old Woman with Roses,* and Rousseau's rainswept *Tropical Storm with a Tiger.* Picasso's *Fruit Dish, Bottle, and Violin* (1914), the National Gallery's initial foray into the abstract, has since been joined by another room of Picasso's work.

The National Gallery holds frequent special exhibitions in the basement galleries of the Sainsbury Wing, which sometimes cost £2-4, but are often free. *Making and Meaning: Rubens's Landscapes* (through Jan. 19),*Seurat: Impressions of the Seine* (July 2-Sept. 28), and *Themes and Variations: Sleep* (July 16-Sept. 14) highlight the 1997 calendar. The National shows free films about art every Monday at 1pm in the lower-floor theater, and lectures take place in the afternoons (Tues.-Fri. at 1pm, Sat. at noon). During the summer months (June-Aug.) there are musical performances from 5:30-7:30pm in the Sainsbury foyer.

The gallery is located in Trafalgar Sq., WC2 (tel. 839 3321 or 747 2885 for recorded info.; tube: Charing Cross, Leicester Sq., Embankment, or Piccadilly Circus). Disabled access is on the north side at the Orange St. entrance. (Open Mon.-Tues., Fri.-Sat. 10am-6pm, Wed. 10am-8pm. Sun. noon-6pm. Free.)

■ National Portrait Gallery

This unofficial *Who's Who in Britain* began in 1856 as "the fulfillment of a patriotic and moral ideal"—namely to showcase Britain's most officially noteworthy citizens. The museum's declared principle of looking "to the celebrity of the person represented, rather than to the merit of the artist" does not seem to have affected the quality of the works displayed—portraits by Reynolds, Lawrence, Holbein, Sargent, and Gainsborough that have stared up from countless history books segue easily into Warhol's depictions of Queen Elizabeth II and Annie Leibovitz's classic photos of John Lennon and Yoko Ono.

Over 9000 works have been arranged more or less chronologically. The earliest portraits hang in the top story—solemn Thomas More, maligned Richard III, venerated Elizabeth I, and canny Henry VII. Charles II is here, surrounded by his wife and mistresses. Follow the flow of British history through the galleries: from the War of the Roses (Yorks and Lancasters), to the Civil War (Cromwell and his buddies), to the American Revolution (George Washington), to imperial days (Florence Nightingale), and on to modern times (Margaret Thatcher).

Level four, dedicated to Henry VIII and predecessors, cherishes the Holbein cartoon of the king. Famous geologists, politicians, reformers, and fops populate the Victorian section, along with literary figures, among them Tennyson, Thackeray, and Dickens. Charming "informal" portraits of the royal family are displayed on the mezzanine; check out the incredibly unflattering portrait of Prince Charles.

The first floor is jammed with displays of the 20th century, from Churchill to Peter Gabriel; the modern works take more amusing liberties with their likenesses, (but then again, we never saw the old guys).

The gallery often mounts temporary displays. 1997 will bring exhibits on Ignatius Sancho (Jan. 24-May 11), British Composers (Feb. 7-May 26), and August Sander (Feb. 28-June 8). Admission averages £5, concessions £3. The annual British Petroleum Portrait Award brings out a selection of works from England's most promising portrait artists (on display June 27–Oct. 1).

Informative lectures lasting about an hour begin at 1:10pm Tuesday and Thursday, 3pm on Saturday. Check the monthly schedule for locations. Wednesday evening lectures, some of which have an entrance fee (£2), relate to the temporary exhibitions and begin at 6:30pm.

The gallery displays its works at St. Martin's Pl., WC2, just opposite St.-Martin's-in-the-Fields (tel. 306 0055; tube: Charing Cross, Leicester Sq., Piccadilly, or Embankment; open Mon.-Sat. 10am-6pm, Sun. 12-6pm; free, excluding temporary exhibits). The new Orange St. entrance has a wheelchair ramp and there is a lift to all floors. Sign-interpreted talks are now a regular feature: for more info, call extension 216.

■ Tate Gallery

The Tate Gallery opened in 1897 expressly to display contemporary British art, though a modern visitor could hardly divine this original intent from today's collection. Since then, the gallery has widened its scope, obtaining a superb collection of British works from the 16th century to the present and a distinguished ensemble of international modern art. The Tate also shows an admirable commitment to education—audio guides (£2, concessions £1.50, for either the main collection or Clore galleries; £3, concessions £2, for both) allow the visitor to hear a 5-10 minute discussion on several of the most significant or interesting pieces in each room. The guide allows you to punch in the number of the painting in which you are interested, freeing you from the need to hear about every piece or to follow a set route.

The exhibits in the main galleries change frequently. Each room contains related works, either by the same artist or by members of similar movements. About 10-15% of the collection is displayed at any one time.

The Tate's **British collection** starts with a room at the far end of the gallery devoted to 16th- and 17th-century painting. The parade of Constables includes the famous views of Salisbury Cathedral, and a number of Hampstead scenes dotted with the requisite red saddle splashes. George Stubbs's enlivening landscapes and sporting scenes lead to Gainsborough's landscapes and Sir Joshua Reynolds's portraits. Don't miss the visionary works of poet, philosopher, and painter William Blake, or the haunting images of Sir John Everett Millais, one of the three founding members of the Pre-Raphaelite Brotherhood.

The paintings in each of the 30 rooms of the main gallery are organized chronologically and grouped by theme, offering a clear perspective on the development of British art, from early landscapes and portraits through Victorian, Pre-Raphaelite, and Impressionist paintings. At this point, the rooms begin to emphasize the relationship between British and foreign art movements, thus providing the perfect segue into the Tate's outstanding **modern collection** of international 20th-century art. Sculptures by

Henry Moore, Epstein, Eric Gill, and Barbara Hepworth, in addition to Rodin's **The Kiss,** are found in the **Cuveen Sculpture Galleries,** the central hall of which leads to the start of the British collection. Modern paintings and sculptures are displayed in subsequent rooms: the works of Monet, Degas, Van Gogh, Beardsley, Matisse, and the Camden Town Group (Sickert, Bevan) hang to the left of the entrance. Paintings by members of the Bloomsbury Group, Picasso, Dalí, and Francis Bacon, sculptures by Modigliani and Giacometti, and samples of the styles that have dominated since the 1950s—Constructivism, Minimalism, Pop, Super-realism, and Process Art—lie to the right of the central hall.

The Tate's 300-work J.M.W. Turner collection resides in the **Clore Gallery.** Architect James Stirling designed the annex to allow natural light to illuminate both the serenity of *Peace—Burial at Sea* and the raging brushstrokes of gale-swept ocean scenes. The collection covers all of Turner's career, from early, dreamy landscapes such as *Chevening Park* to the later visionary works, in which the subject is lost in a sublime array of light and color.

The Tate hosts a series of temporary exhibits in the downstairs galleries. In 1997 the Tate will host exhibitions on Corinth (Feb. 20-May 4), Ellsworth Kelly (June 12-Sept. 7), and Symbolism in Britain (Oct. 16-Jan. 1998). Admission varies.

Free tours run Monday-Friday at 11am for British Old Masters: Van Dyck to the Pre-Raphaelites, noon for the Turner Collection, 2pm for Early Modern Art, 3pm for Conceptual Art, and, on Saturday only, 3pm for the General Tour: The Essential Tate. The Tate is located at Millbank, SW1 (tel. 887 8000; tube: Pimlico; open Mon.-Sat. 10am-5:50pm, Sun. 2-5:50pm; free).

▓ **Victoria and Albert Museum**

Housing the best collection of Italian Renaissance sculpture outside Italy, the greatest collection of Indian art outside India, and the world center for John Constable studies, the mind-bogglingly inclusive V&A has practically perfected the display of fine and applied arts. Founded in 1899 by Queen Victoria, the museum took on its eclectic contours when the original curators were deluged with objects donated for exhibition from every epoch and region of the world. Easily one of the most enchanting museums in London, the V&A lets you saunter through the histories of art, design, and style in its 12 acres of galleries.

The vast scope of the museum's permanent collection is astonishing, but this fact does not stop the V&A from putting up consistently ground-breaking **temporary exhibitions;** watch for *American Photography,* the best pictures from New York's Museum of Modern Art (Nov. 1996-Jan. 1997) including works by Steicher, Evans, Adams, and Stieglitz; *British Fashion 1947-1997* which opens in Spring 1997; and a showing of Carl Larsson work projected for October 1997-January 1998.

While there are a million possible trajectories through the V&A's corridors, you might consider beginning your visit with the ground floor galleries. Reopening in October 1996, after extensive renovation, are the stars of the **Renaissance collection:** the famed **Raphael Cartoons**—seven of the 10 large, full-color sketches (scenes from the Acts of the Apostles) done by Raphael and his apprentices as tapestry patterns for the Sistine Chapel. The endless galleries of Italian sculpture include Donatello's *Ascension* and *Madonna and Child.* The **Medieval Treasury,** in the center of the ground floor, features well-displayed vestments, plate, stained glass, and illuminations. The most spectacular treasure is the domed Eltenburg Reliquary.

Plaster cast reproductions of European sculpture and architecture (the 80-ft. Trojans column from Rome; the façade of the Santiago Cathedral in Spain; Michelangelo's *Moses, Dying Slave, Rebellious Slave,* and *David*) occupy rooms 46A-B on the ground floor. These are the remnants of an unfortunately abandoned movement, popular in the 1800s, to place casts of the great works of Western art in the major European cities. Next door, test the knowledge you've gained here to distinguish impostors from the real things in the **Fakes and Forgeries Gallery.**

The **dress collection,** also on the ground floor, traces popular and elite clothing fashions from 17th-century shoes to the latest John Galliano confection. Focused primarily on Western women's garb, this exhibit documents the vagaries of sartorial design and textile technology—and implicitly documents changing gender roles. Expansive and edifying, this collection displays both the mantua, a mid-18th century dress so restrictive that women who wore it had trouble walking through doorways, and the metallic nylon "longest minidress" that underfed Kate Moss wore to the British Design Awards. Women can count their fully intact ribs in thankful glee that they are no longer subject to the corsets and stays of 200 years ago; however, lest they think that fashion has become emancipatory, the precipitous purple mock-crocodile platform shoes that tripped Naomi Campbell up during a recent Vivienne Westwood runway show are also displayed.

The V&A's formidable **Asian collections** have recently been supplemented by the Nehru Gallery of Indian Art and the T.T. Tsui Gallery of Chinese Art. The **Nehru gallery** contains splendid examples of textiles, painting, Mughal jewelry and decor, and revealing displays on European imperial conduct. You can see Tippoo's Tiger, a life-sized wooden musical automaton that simulates groans and roars while consuming a European gentleman, alluded to by John Keats in his poem *The Cap and Bells.* The simply elegant **Tsui gallery** divides its 5000-year span of Chinese art into six areas of life—Eating and Drinking, Living, Worship, Ruling, Collecting, and Burial. Objects are displayed in the context in which they were originally used. Treasures include the Sakyamuni Buddha and an Imperial Throne. The **Toshiba Gallery of Japanese Art** has a prime collection of lacquer art, as well as traditional armor and intriguing contemporary sculpture.

The V&A's displays of **Islamic Art** are punctuated by the intricacies of Persian carpets and Moroccan rugs. The collection's most breathtaking carpet, completed in Azerbaijan in 1540, is perhaps the largest carpet that you will ever see.

The first floor holds the sizable collection of **British art and design.** Shakespeare immortalized the immense Great Bed of Ware (room 54) in *Twelfth Night.* Cool, dim room 74, "1900-1960," exhibits the best in modern British design, including works by Wyndham Lewis, Charles Rennie Mackintosh, and Eric Gill. International design classics—mostly chairs—grace "Twentieth Century Design."

The **jewelry collection** (rooms 91-93—actually a pilfer-proof vault!), so unwieldy that it has been annotated in bound catalogues instead of posted descriptions, includes pieces dating from 2000 BC. The **National Art Library,** located on the first floor, houses numerous Beatrix Potter originals as well as first editions of Winnie the Pooh adventures.

The new **Frank Lloyd Wright gallery** on the second floor of the Henry Cole Wing illustrates Wright's philosophy of Organic Architecture. The Wright-designed interior of the Kauffmann Office, originally commissioned for a Pittsburgh department store, is the V&A's first 20th-century period room.

The exquisitely redesigned **Glass Gallery** recently reopened in room C-131. Vases, bowls, pipes, and brandy bottles provide a colorful and shiny assault on visitors' eyes. A sophisticated electronic labeling system allows visitors to retrieve extensive details about any piece in the gallery by entering a code into a computer.

Photography aficionados will want to visit the **Print Room** (#503 in the Henry Cole Wing), a provisional home for photography until the V&A opens a full-fledged photography gallery in 1998. The print collection encompasses both the incipient stages of the medium and its most contemporary products. Sander, Arbus, and Freidlander are all represented here.

John Constable's prodigious collection of weather studies resides on the sixth floor of the Henry Cole Wing. For those whose tastes run smaller, room 406 showcases English and Continental **portrait miniatures** (including Holbein's *Anne of Cleves* and *Elizabeth I*).

The V&A offers scores of special events. One-hour introductory museum tours meet at the Cromwell entrance information desk at 12:15, 2, and 3pm on Monday and 11am, noon, 2, 3pm Tuesday-Sunday. On Wednesday evenings during the summer the V&A hires a few musicians, set up a wine bar, opens a few galleries for museum patrons between 6:30pm-9:15pm and allows visitors in this swanky atmosphere for only £2. Experts give lectures on select pieces in these open galleries; attendance costs £5-7. Call 938 8407 for more information or to make (required) reservations. Individual lectures of V&A summer courses can be attended for partial tuition: contact the Education Services Department (tel. 938 8638). Free gallery talks are given throughout the summer at 2:30pm covering anything from Impressionism to Japanese quilt technique.

The **New Restaurant,** on the ground floor of the Henry Cole Wing, serves a wide range of meals. On Sunday mornings the restaurant hosts a jazz brunch, which features live music and full English breakfast or lunch (11am-3pm; £8).

The V&A is located on Cromwell Rd., SW7 (tel. 938 8500, 938 8441 for 24-hr. recorded information, or 938 8349 for current exhibitions; tube: South Kensington or Buses C1, 14, and 74; open Mon. noon-5:50pm, Tues.-Sun. 10am-5:50pm; beginning Oct. 1996 the museum will begin charging a not-as-yet-determined fee, promotional materials assure us it will be "in the region of £5"; mercifully students and under-18s will be free.) Most of the museum is wheelchair accessible; wheelchair users are advised to use the side entrance on Exhibition Rd. Gallery tours and taped tours are available for the visually impaired.

▓ Recommended Collections

These collections are the few that, in addition to the five heavyweights mentioned above, simply must be seen. In our researchers' judgement, the following collections are so gripping or well-presented that visitors of almost every persuasion and predilection will find a trip worthwhile.

The Courtauld Institute, Somerset House, the Strand, WC2 (tel. 873 2526), across from the corner of Aldwych and the Strand. Tube: Temple, Embankment, Charing Cross, or Covent Garden. This intimate 11-room gallery in Somerset House is an ideal place to see some world-famous masterpieces. Mostly Impressionist and post-Impressionist works, including pieces by Cézanne, Degas, Gauguin, Seurat, and Renoir, plus Van Gogh's *Portrait of the Artist with a Bandaged Ear,* and Manet's *Bar aux Folies Bergère.* The Institute's other collections include early Italian religious paintings—key works by Botticelli, Rubens *(Descent from the Cross),* Bruegel, Cranach *(Adam and Eve),* and Modigliani. Frequent special free student exhibitions. Lectures about the exhibits are offered throughout the year (call 873 2143 for info). If this is not enough education for you, attend one of the free Afternoon Gallery Talks offered Tues., Wed., and Sat. at 3pm. Open Mon.-Sat. 10am-6pm, Sun. 2-6pm. Admission £3, concessions £1.50. Free for UK students. Wheelchair accessible.

London Transport Museum, Covent Garden, WC2 (tel. 379 6344, recorded information 836 8557). Tube: Covent Garden. On the east side of the Covent Garden piazza. Wildly revamped in 1993, the museum now boasts two new mezzanine floors, two new air-conditioned galleries, and a variety of interactive video displays. Although much of the ground floor traffic flows through a maze of historic trains, trams, and buses, the museum offers much more than a history of London's public transport vehicles. Low-tech exhibits provide a thought-provoking cultural history: see how the expansion of the transportation system fed the growth of suburbs (one of the reasons Hampstead is wealthier than Islington). High-tech simulators allow you to recklessly endanger the lives of scores of cyber-commuters as you take the helm of a subway train, a feat requiring more finesse than tube-weary tourists might think. Don't miss the excellent temporary exhibits, drawn largely from the museum's photo, map, and poster archives. First-class museum shop sells London Transport posters and postcards. Open Sat.-Thurs. 10am-6pm, Fri. 11am-6pm, last admission 5:15pm. Admission £4.50, concessions £2.50, families £11, special group rates available. Wheelchair accessible. MC, Visa.

Museum of the Moving Image (MOMI), South Bank Centre, SE1 (tel. 928 3232 or 401 2636 for 24-hr. information). Tube: Waterloo, or Embankment and cross the

Hungerford footbridge. MOMI and the National Film Theatre, both appendages of the British Film Institute, are housed in a phenomenal building on the South Bank. The entertaining museum charts the development of image-making with light, from shadow puppets to film and telly. Costumed actor-guides are stationed at interactive exhibits—act out your favorite western, read the TV news, or watch your own superimposed image fly over the River Thames. The camera-shy will enjoy countless clips and props, from the slapstick of the silents to the gaudy days of "Dr. Who." Open daily 10am-6pm; last entry 5pm, but allow around 2hrs. Admission £5.95, students £4.85, handicapped, seniors, children £4, family £16.

National Maritime Museum, Romney Rd., Greenwich, SE10 (tel. (0181) 858 4422). BR: Greenwich. Set in picturesque Greenwich, the museum's loving documentation of the history of British sea power can have even the staunchest land-lubber longing to sail the bounding main. The highlight, by far, is the "All Hands" hands-on gallery, where visitors can play sailor, firing the cannon, operating the loading crane, or practicing their underwater diving techniques. But drink too much grog on shore-leave, and it's into the scuppers with a hose-pipe for ye! Arrr! Admission £5.50, concessions £4.50, children £3, families £16 (also good for Old Royal Observatory and the Queen's house, see p. 202).

Royal Academy, Piccadilly, W1 (tel. 494 5615), across from no. 185. Tube: Green Park or Piccadilly Circus. The academy hosts traveling exhibits of the highest order. Space for these shows has recently been enlarged by high-tech architect Norman Foster. The whopping annual summer exhibition (June 1-Aug. 10, 1997) is a London institution—the works of established and unknown contemporary artists festoon every square inch of wall space and are for sale (at non-budget prices). The architectural models offered are often spectacular. 1997 will see a Braque exhibition (Jan.-March) and the ambitiously titled *The Age of Modern Art* (Sept. to mid-Dec.). Open daily 10am-6pm. Admission varies by exhibition; average £5, concessions £4. Advance tickets often necessary for popular exhibitions.

Royal Air Force Museum, Grahame Park Way, NW9 (tel. 0181 205 6867 or 24-hr. info line 0181 205 2266). Tube: Colindale. Exit left and head straight for about 15min. until the giant missile battery and Spitfires inform you of your arrival at the museum, or take the Bus 303 from the tube station. Even those uninterested in aerial combat will have a tough time being bored in Britain's Smithsonian-like national museum of aviation. The RAF has converted this former WWI airbase into a hangarful of the country's aeronautic greatest hits. WWI Bristols, Korean War submarine hunters, and Falkland War Tornados display the dignified history of the RAF, while Gulf War footage and high-tech weapons exhibits hint to the future of Britain's air defense. Glance inside the cockpit of an F-4 or test fly a flight simulator (£1.50) in the cavernous Main Aircraft Hall, then prepare to be awed by the Bomber Command Hall, where nuclear bombers appear hauntingly poised for take-off. Open daily 10am-6pm, last admission 5:30pm. Admission £5.20, students £2.60, family £12.60. Wheelchair accessible.

Science Museum, Exhibition Rd., SW7 (tel. 938 8008 or 938 8080). Tube: South Kensington. Closet science geeks will be outed by their orgasmic cries as they enter this wonderland of diagrammed motors, springs, and spaceships. This superbly arranged five-story collection rivals the best science museums around. The museum's introductory exhibit romps through a "synopsis" of science since 6000 BC and lingers (a bit unseemingly) over the steam-powered Industrial Revolution that vaulted Britain to imperialist world domination. Launch Pad, a special hall of child-run experiments on the first floor, is irresistible to kids of all ages. Other permanent exhibits include "Food for Thought," which demonstrates the impact of technology on food, and the excellent Flight Gallery of aeronautics. The "Glimpses of Medical History" exhibit is not for the squeamish. Open daily 10am-6pm. Admission £5, concessions £2.90, under 5 and people with disabilities free. Free daily 4:30-6pm. Once inside check out the large board behind the admissions desk which will list the day's special events and tours.

Sir John Soane's Museum, 13 Lincoln's Inn Fields, WC2 (tel. 405 2107). Tube: Holborn. Soane was an architect's architect, but the idiosyncratic home he designed for himself will intrigue even lay-persons. Window-sized, inset, and convex mirrors placed strategically throughout the house for lighting effects create skewed angles and weird distortions. The columns in the Colonnade room support a room-within-a-room above. Famous artifacts on display include Hogarth paintings, the massive sarcophagus of Seti I, and casts of famous buildings and sculptures from around the world. Look for the little numbers on the objects and art works; Soane catalogued everything himself. Open Tues.-Sat. 10am-5pm. Free. Tours (restricted to 22 people) leave at 2:30pm on Sat., tickets are offered on a first-come, first-serve basis at 2pm on day of tour.

The Wallace Collection, Hertford House, Manchester Sq., W1 (tel. 935 0687). Tube: Bond St. Founded by various Marquises of Hertford and the illegitimate son of the fourth Marquis, Sir Richard Wallace, this mansion defines the adjective "sumptuous." The wall of the entire first floor are covered in red velvet patterned wallpaper. Ceilings and mouldings are drizzled with gold. Outstanding works include Hals's *The Laughing Cavalier,* Delacroix's *Execution of Marino Faliero,* Fragnard's *The Swing,* and Rubens' *Christ on the Cross.* Landscapes, interiors, portraits, and genre scenes from the major Dutch Golden Age artists hang near a number of Rubens oil sketches (drafts of some of his most famous works). Also home to the largest armor and weaponry collection outside of the Tower of London. Open Mon.-Sat. 10am-5pm, Sun. 2-5pm. Guided tours Mon.-Tues. 1pm, Wed. 11:30am and 1pm, Thurs.-Fri. 1pm, Sat. 11:30am, Sun. 3pm. Free.

■ Other Outstanding Collections

Bank of England Museum, Threadneedle St., EC2 (tel. 601 5792 or 601 5545). Tube: Bank. Entrance on Bartholomew La., left off Threadneedle St. Housed in the Bank of England. Enter the museum through a grandly domed entrance foyer with a mosaic floor where an attendant in red tails waits to receive you. A cultural history of banknotes and check-writing. See a £1,000,000 note and a display of arms once used to defend the bank. Sit at a trading desk (not operational) with three monitors displaying pretty-colored graphs explaining the minutely-detailed happenings of almost all of the major financial markets (looks like just a bunch of numbers, but oh how they flash and move!). Open Mon.-Fri. 10am-5pm.

Barbican Galleries, Barbican Centre, EC2 (tel. 638 8891). Tube: Barbican. A community arts center, the Barbican hosts free concerts, art exhibitions, and library displays in its labyrinthine network of foyers. Open Mon. and Wed.-Sat. 10am-6:45pm, Tues. 10am-5:45pm, Sun. and holidays 10am-6:45pm. Admission to the Barbican Gallery £4.50, students and seniors £2.50, Mon.-Fri. after 5pm £2.50.

Bethnal Green Museum of Childhood, Cambridge Heath Rd., E2 (tel. (0181) 980 3204 or info line (0181) 980 2415). Tube: Bethnal Green. Colorful toy store entrance leads into elegant Victorian warehouse full of toys, dolls, board games, and puppets. Displays also include children's books, costumes, and nursery furniture. The doll houses provide interesting architectural and social history. Open Mon.-Thurs. and Sat. 10am-6pm, Sun. 2:30-6pm. Free.

Bramah Tea and Coffee Museum, The Clove Building, Maguire St., Butlers Wharf, SE1 (tel. 378 0222). Tube: Tower Hill or London Bridge, or DLR: Tower Gateway. Follow Design Museum directions and turn right on Maguire St. Appropriately located in the spot on Butlers Wharf that used to see 6000 chests of tea unloaded each day. See anti-decaf propaganda, teapots in the shape of Playboy bunnies, and other tasteful vessels. The jasmine aroma steaming around the entrance leaves you thirsting for a drink at the teashop (£1/pot). Admission £3, concessions £1.50, family £5. Group discounts. Open daily 10am-6pm.

Cabinet War Rooms, Clive Steps, King Charles St., SW1 (tel. 930 6961). Tube: Westminster. Follow the signs from Whitehall. Churchill and his cabinet ran a nation at war from this secret warren of underground rooms. Free (but slow) cassette guides lead you through the room where Churchill made his famous wartime broadcasts and point out the transatlantic hotline disguised as a loo. Open April-Sept. daily 9:30am-6pm, Oct.-March 10am-6pm. Last entrance 5:15pm. Admission £4.20, students £3.10, seniors £3.20, under 16 £2.10, disabled ½ price.

Commonwealth Institute, Kensington High St., W8 (tel. 603 4535). Tube: High St. Kensington. This organization of the 53 Commonwealth states normally has a well-regarded gallery celebrating the member states' culture and resources, from Malaysian paper crafts and Indian musical instruments to Asian film. Currently the exhibits are closed, with a projected reopening in April 1997. Call for reports.

The Design Museum, Butlers Wharf, Shad Thames, SE1 (tel. 403 6933 or 407 6261). Tube: London Bridge, then follow signs on Tooley St. or Tower Hill and cross the Tower Bridge. Housed in an appropriately *Bauhaus*-y box on the river, this museum is dedicated to mass-produced classics of culture and industry. Young artsy visitors peruse exhibits of modern art and suburban history. Happily, you *can* sit in some of the century's most influential chairs. Simulators demonstrate the design process—help dashing young Euro-designer "Doug" craft a hip toothbrush for the 12- to 15-year-old set. Around half of the space is devoted to excellent changing exhibitions. Library open by appointment. Open Mon.-Fri. 11:30am-6pm, Sat.-Sun. noon-6pm. Admission £4.75, concessions £3.50.

Dulwich Picture Gallery, College Rd., SE21 (tel. (0181) 693 5254). BR: West Dulwich (15min. from Victoria, day return £1.80), then right from the station and follow the signs (15min.), or tube: Brixton and take the P4 bus to the door. If the National Galleries (above) fail to satisfy your appetite for English Portraiture and Dutch landscapes, get another Gainsborough, Reynolds, and Rembrandt fix here. Thieves fancied Rembrandt's *Jacob III de Gheyn* so much that it was stolen on four separate occasions (it has since been recovered). Open Tues.-Fri. 10am-5pm, Sat. 11am-5pm, Sun. 2-5pm. Free Fri., otherwise £2, concessions £1, children free.

Freud Museum, 20 Maresfield Gdns., NW3 (tel. 435 2002). Tube: Finchley Rd. Head right from the tube station down Finchley Rd. Take the fifth left onto Trinity Walk; Maresfield Gdns. is at the end of the street. A re-creation of the home where Freud spent a year after escaping Nazi Vienna in 1938. The museum includes the library, study, and, of course, couch, where he completed some of his most influential works. Open Wed.-Sun. noon-5pm. Admission £2.50, students £1.50.

Geffrye Museum, Kingsland Road, E2 (tel 739 9893). Tube: Liverpool St., then Bus 22A or 22B north. Set in a large former poorhouse founded and funded by the rags-to-riches Sir Geffrye, the current incarnation of this building traces the history of English interior design. Outside are a large courtyard and a lovely herb garden. The Geffrye meticulously chronicles the English home interior, from the well-appointed formalities of the 1600s to the height of the Linoleum and Bakelite Age in the 1950s. Excellent temporary exhibits. Open Tues.-Sat. 10am-5pm, Sun. 2-5pm. Wheelchair accessible. Free.

Guildhall Clock Museum, in the Guildhall Library, Aldermanbury, EC2 (tel. 260 1858). Tube: Bank, St. Paul's, or Moorgate. "The Worshipful Company of Clock-makers" presents a well-labeled collection of pocket watches, jeweled watch keys, and a few curiosities. Mary Queen of Scots' macabre silver skull-shaped watch is notable—she checked the time by opening the jaw and looking inside its mouth. The watch Sir Edmund Hilary wore on the first ascent of Everest now rests here, in a less dramatic setting. Watery ticking of old grandfather clocks creates swell Pink Floyd effect. Mon.-Fri. 9:30am-4:45pm. Free.

Hayward Gallery, at Royal Festival Hall, Belvedere Rd., SE1 (tel. 928 3144; recorded info 261 0127). Tube: Waterloo. A fixture of the South Bank Centre, this six-room gallery hosts high-powered exhibitions of 20th-century art. On tap for 1997: pieces from the Prinzham collection of art by the mentally ill (through March), and an exhibit on British painter Howard Hodgkin (beginning in Feb.). Gallery talks and events correspond with current exhibits—call for info. Open daily 10am-6pm, Tues.-Wed. until 8pm. Admission £5, concessions £3.50, family ticket £12, children under 12 free with adult.

Imperial War Museum, Lambeth Rd., SE1 (tel. 416 5000). Tube: Lambeth North or Elephant & Castle. Don't be misled by the jingoistic resonance of the name; this museum is a moving reminder of the brutal human cost of war. The atrium is filled with tanks and planes; the eloquent testimony to war's horror is downstairs. Gripping exhibits illuminate every aspect of two world wars, in every medium possible. The Blitz and Trench Experiences recreate every detail (even smells); veterans and victims speak through telephone handsets. The powerful Bergen-Belsen exhibit documents the genocide of the concentration camps and the story of the rescue and rehabilitation of survivors. Don't miss the "peace in our time" agreement Neville Chamberlain triumphantly brought back from Munich in 1938, or Adolf Hitler's "political testament," dictated in the chancellery bunker. Upstairs, the art galleries keep fine examples of war painting, such as Sargent's *Gassed, 1918*. A new permanent exhibit called *Secret War* reveals Britain's enigmatic world of espionage. Open daily 10am-6pm. £4.50, students £3.50, children (5-16yrs.) £2.25, families £11. Disabled ½ price. Free daily 4:30-6pm.

Institute of Contemporary Arts, the Mall, SW1 (tel. 930 3647 or 930 6393 for 24-hr. recorded information). Tube: Charing Cross. Entrance is located on the Mall at the foot of the Duke of York steps. Vigorous hipper-than-thou outpost of the avant garde of visual and performance art. Three temporary galleries, a cinema featuring first-run independent films (£6.50, concessions £5), experimental space for film and video, and a theater. "ICA Talks" feature intellectuals like Bruno Latour (£6.50, concessions £5). Open Sat.-Thurs. noon-7:30pm, Fri. noon-9pm. Mon.-Fri admission £1.50, concessions £1; Sat.-Sun. £2.50, concessions £1.50.

The Iveagh Bequest, Kenwood House, Hampstead La., NW3 (tel. (0181) 348 1286). Tube: Archway or Golders Green, then Bus 210 to Kenwood. An impeccable recreation of an 18th-century Neoclassical villa, beautifully located on the Kenwood Estate overlooking Hampstead Heath. Fine works by Dutch masters, including Vermeer's *Guitar Player* and the last of Rembrandt's self-portraits. Plenty of Sir Joshua Reynolds for his fans. Open daily 10am-6pm; Oct. to mid-April 10am-4pm. Free. Admission charged for special visiting exhibitions.

Jewish Museum, 129-31 Albert St., NW1 (tel. 284 1997). Tube: Camden Town. Exit the station to the right and head left. Take the first right onto Parkway; Albert St. will be on the left. A collection of antiques, manuscripts, and paintings documenting Jewish history set inside an elegant museum with Jerusalem stone walkways. Intimate setup focuses on the history of Jews in London from 1066 to the present. Open Sun.-Thurs. 10am-4pm. Admission £3, £1.10 concessions.

London Dungeon, 28-34 Tooley St., SE1 (tel. 403 0606). Tube: London Bridge. An inexplicably popular spectacle. At first, you think it's a cheesy haunted house capable of scaring only little kids. But terrifying groans that accompany scenes of drowning, disembowelment, head crushing, and body stretching freak out adults as well. Plague, decomposition, and anything else remotely connected to horror and British history thrown in for effect. Even the Pizza Hut and ice cream shop at the end of the museum can't make the chills go away. Takes at least 1¾hrs. Open daily April-Sept. 10am-6:30pm, last entrance 5:30pm. Nov.-Feb. 10am-5:30pm, last entrance 4:30pm. Admission £7.75, under 14 £4.50, students £6.50.

Madame Tussaud's, Marylebone Rd., NW1 (tel. 935 6861). Tube: Baker St. The classic waxwork museum, founded by an *emigré* aristocrat who manufactured life-size models of French nobility who met their demise at the guillotine. Figures are disconcertingly lifelike, with a tendency towards being flattering (see Bogart) with some exceptions (see Prince Charles). Diana has been placed off to the side of the Royal family's display, and Sarah Ferguson has been effaced. The more macabre exhibits, like the display of famous psychopaths and wife-murderers from English history, are eerily powerful. Be warned: this is one of London's most popular attractions, which translates into huge lines and high prices—visitors should think carefully about whether the museum is worth 9 quid and an hour-long wait. Madame Tussaud's is best visited in the morning to get a good view of the most popular collections. To avoid the horrific queues, form a group with at least nine fellow sufferers and use the group entrance, or go either when they first open or in the late afternoon. Open Mon.-Fri. 10am-5:30pm (last admission, actually stays open later), Sat.-Sun. 9:30am-5:30pm. A distinctive green dome shelters the adjacent **Planetarium.** Ride the Space Trail through a model universe and watch a Star Show. Admission to Madame Tussaud's £8.75, children £5.75, seniors £6.60. Planetarium £5.45, children £3.60, seniors £4.30. Both museum and planetarium £10.95, children £6.95, seniors £8.50.

Museum of London, 150 London Wall, EC2 (tel. 600 3699, 24-hr. info 600 0807). Tube: St. Paul's or Barbican. Comprehensive is an understatement: this fabulously engrossing museum tells the story of the metropolis from the beginning of time, through its origins as Londinium, up to the 1996 European Soccer Championships hosted here. Exhibits including reconstructed industrial-age streets and 17th-century royal carriages outline London's domestic, political, religious, cultural, indus-

MUSEUMS

trial, sartorial, and natural histories. An oasis flourishes at the museum's center: the Nursery Garden, a living history of the flora trade in London (the garden closes at 5:20pm). The new London Now gallery opens in 1997, accompanied by the special exhibit *In Royal Fashion* (May 20-Nov. 23). Free historical lectures given Wed.-Fri. 1:10pm. Open Tues.-Sat. and Mon. Bank Holidays 10am-5:50pm, Sun. noon-5:50pm, last entry 5:30pm. Admission £3.50, concessions £1.75, families £8.50, free after 4:30pm. Wheelchair accessible.

Museum of Mankind, 6 Burlington Gdns., W1 (tel. 323 8043). Tube: Green Park or Piccadilly Circus. The Burlington Arcade next to the Royal Academy leads right to the museum. The ethnographic collection of the British Museum, it includes a mass of engrossing artifacts, primarily from non-Western cultures. Annual exhibits recreate the lifestyles of ancients and moderns, featuring everything from everyday tools to ritual objects. Latest exhibits include *Paradise: Change and Continuity in the New Guinea Highlands* and *The Power of the Hand: African Arms and Armour*. Useful introductory gallery tour gives a cross-section of the permanent collection, which includes Mexican turquoise mosaics, African pipes, British Columbian stone carvings, and Sioux war bonnets. Check out the "Treasures" room, which displays changing highlights from the permanent collection. Often there are free special events that continue themes of special exhibitions. Open Mon.-Sat. 10am-5pm, Sun. 2:30-6pm. Free.

National Army Museum, Royal Hospital Rd. SW3 (tel. 730 0717). Tube: Sloane Sq. Set next to the dignified buildings of the Royal Hospital for army pensioners, this 4-story building presents the more personal side of serving in the Royal Majesty's army. Not the slickest museum, but clean, efficient and decent—much as a good armed forces should be. That includes weapons (2 centuries of swords in the chillingly titled *Cut, Thrust, Swagger* room) uniforms, and medals, huge war paintings and battle drums of Britain's cleanly shaven, beefeating soldiers (they had to shave daily, even on the beaches of Normandy), as well as random artifacts like the skeleton of Napolean's horse at Waterloo. Open daily 10am-5:30pm. Free.

Natural History Museum, Cromwell Rd., SW7 (tel. 938 9123 or 938 9242 for group bookings). Tube: South Kensington. A tremendous cathedral of a museum, combining monumental medieval styling with a modern iron and steel framework. The museum's personality is split between a glorious but ultimately dull Victorian past (the encyclopedic frenzy is only slightly diluted—see the world's largest collection of metalliferous ores) and a high-tech present (buttons, levers, and microscopes galore). Permanent exhibits include "Discovering Mammals," "Creepy Crawlies," "Ecology: A Greenhouse Effect," "Primates" (the lifestyle and behavior of everything from the lemur to the human being), and the superb dinosaur exhibits, with tantalizing computer displays and relatively realistic life-size models. The interactive Discovery Centre for children and other hands-on enthusiasts is matchless. Open Mon.-Sat. 10am-6pm, Sun. 11am-6pm. Admission £5.50, concessions £3, families (up to 2 adults and 4 children) £15, children £2.80. Free Mon.-Fri. 4:30-6pm, Sat.-Sun. 5-6pm. Wheelchair accessible.

National Postal Museum, London Chief Post Office, King Edward Building, King Edward St., EC1 (tel. 239 5420). Tube: St. Paul's. A stamptastic array of postal memorabilia sure to delight dedicated post fiends and Johnny-come-philatelies alike. See everything from the "Penny Black," the world's first adhesive postage stamp, to the ludicrous five-wheeled bikes used by Victorian postmen. The astute visitor will learn about the legendary connection between the Post Office and military service, and the untutored will be initiated into the mysteries of pneumatic postage and stamp security. Open Mon.-Fri. 9:30am-4:30pm. Free.

Pollock's Toy Museum, 1 Scala St. (entrance on Whitfield St.), W1 (tel. 636 3452). Tube: Goodge St.; head west on Goodge St. then right onto Whitfield St. Housed above a modern toy shop in a maze of tiny, 18th-century rooms congested with antique playthings of every size and description. Highlights include Eric, the oldest known teddy bear (b. 1905), and German "saucy Fraulines," who expose their britches at the tug of a string. Elaborate toy theaters take center stage in one room. The histories and anecdotes which accompany the collection often astound—who'd've thought "Chutes and Ladders" was originally a tool for Hindu religious instruction?

Open Mon.-Sat. 10am-5pm, last admission 4:30pm. Admission £2, under 18 75p, under 18 free on Sat. AmEx.

Royal Festival Hall Galleries, Royal Festival Hall, South Bank Centre, SE1 (tel. 928 3002). Tube: Waterloo, or Embankment and cross the Hungerford footbridge. In what is essentially the lobby of the Royal Festival Hall (see p. 235), a creative display space for contemporary art exhibits. Photography and architecture are this gallery's primary art forms. A necessary part of any stroll along the South Bank. Open daily 10am-10:30pm. Free.

Saatchi Gallery, 98 Boundary Rd., NW8 (tel. 624 8299). Tube: Swiss Cottage. This is art. *This* is beauty! The holdings of enormously influential art-collector Charles Saatchi (he of the eponymous advertising firm). Hot modern art! Open Thurs.-Sun. noon-6pm. Admission £3.50, free on Thurs.

The Sherlock Holmes Museum, 239 Baker St. (marked "221b"), W1 (tel. 935 8866). Tube: Baker St. Sir Arthur Conan Doyle actually occupied this small house in the late 1800s. Students of Holmes' deductive method will be intrigued by the museum's meticulous re-creation of his storied lodgings. Upstairs is a display of "artifacts" from the stories. Leaf through a hilarious selection of letters Holmes has received in the last few years. You are encouraged to try on the deerstalker cap and cloak; a museum employee will snap a picture if you'd like. Open daily 9:15am-6pm (last admission). Admission £5, under 17 £3.

British Telecom (BT) Museum, 145 Queen Victoria St., EC4 (tel. 248 7444). Tube: Blackfriars. If anyone's ever told you to "go fax yourself," you can comply at this two-story display of British technological know-how. Interspersed with displays of Victorian phones, publicity ads from the 1920s and 30s, and optical fibre technology are a number of cacophonous hands-on exhibits popular with children—send faxes and telegrams within the museum, or pit your technological know-how against their computers. Open Mon.-Fri. 10am-5pm. Wheelchair accessible with prior arrangement. Free.

Theatre Museum, 1e Tavistock St., WC2 (tel. 836 7891 or 836 2330 for box office). Tube: Covent Garden. Public entrance on Russell St., off the east end of the Covent Garden piazza. This branch of the V&A contains Britain's richest holding of theatrical memorabilia; see numerous 19th-century Shakespearean daggers before you. Exhibits also include models of historical and present-day theaters, as well as other stage-related arts, such as ballet, opera, puppetry, the circus, and rock music. Evocative photograph collection and eccentric temporary exhibits. Box office just inside the door sells tickets to West End plays, musicals, and concerts with negligible mark-up in most cases. Box office and museum open Tues.-Sun. 11am-7pm. Admission £3.50, concessions £1.50.

Wellington Museum, Apsley House, on the north side of Hyde Park Corner at 149 Piccadilly, W1 (tel. 499 5676). Tube: Hyde Park Corner. Following a three-year renovation, this 19th-century mansion built for the First Duke of Wellington has been restored to its original glory and glitz. Built between 1771 and 1778, the Apsley House is popularly known as Number One, London, as it is just past the toll gate into the capital when approached from the west. The Duke's collection of paintings, silver, porcelain, sculpture, and furniture is housed here, and is displayed in its full and wholly ostentatious splendor. Open Tues.-Sun. 11am-5pm. Admission £3, concessions £1.50, families (2 adults and 4 or fewer children) £7.

Whitechapel Art Gallery, Whitechapel High St., E1 (tel. 377 7888). Tube: Aldgate East. The high-ceilinged and sunny galleries of the Whitechapel contain no permanent collection, but host some of Britain's (and the Continent's) most daring exhibitions of contemporary art. Exhibits are informal and sometimes outright weird and reflect the East End community. In 1997 look for *Inside the Visible*, a showing of Tony Cragg's work, and a showing of Cathy de Monchaux's. Open Tues. and Thurs.-Sun. 11am-5pm, Wed. 11am-8pm. Free. Wheelchair accessible.

Winston Churchill's Britain at War, 64-66 Tooley St., SE1 (tel. 403 3171). Tube: London Bridge. Confusingly macabre reconstruction of underground life in London during the Blitz. Jitterbug with mannequin GIs in a club, then step into a bombed-out street with bodies flung all over. Fun. Open daily 10am-5:30pm; Oct.-March 10am-4:30pm. Admission £5, concessions £3.75, family £13.

Entertainment

When a man is tired of London, he is tired of life; for there is in London all that life can afford.

—Samuel Johnson, 1777

On any given day or night, Londoners and visitors can choose from the widest range of entertainment a city can offer. Suffering competition only from Broadway, the West End is the world's theater capital, supplemented by an adventurous "fringe." Music scenes range from the black ties of the Royal Opera House to Wembley mobs and nightclub raves. The work of British filmmakers like Derek Jarman, Sally Potter, and Mike Leigh—often available in the States only on video—is shown in cinemas all over the city. Dance, comedy, sports, and countless unclassifiable happenings can leave you poring in bewilderment over the listings in *Time Out* (£1.60) and *What's On* (£1.20). Their recommendations are usually dead on. **Kidsline** (tel. 222 8070) answers queries on children's events (Mon.-Fri. 4-6pm). **Artsline** (tel. 388 2227) provides information about disabled access at entertainment venues across London (Mon.-Fri. 9:30am-5:30pm).

▓ Theater

The stage for a national dramatic tradition dating from Shakespeare, London maintains unrivaled standards in theater. The renowned Royal Academy for the Dramatic Arts draws students from around the globe. Playwrights such as Tom Stoppard and Alan Ayckbourn premier their works in the West End, class-conscious political dramas, younger writers, and performance artists sustain a vibrant fringe theater scene, and classic tragedies are revived everywhere. Tickets are relatively inexpensive; the cheapest seats in most theaters cost about £8, progressing upward to £30 for orchestra seats. Previews and matinees cost a few pounds less, and many theaters offer dirt-cheap **student/senior standbys** (indicated by "concs," "concessions," or "S" in newspaper and *Time Out* listings)—around £7 shortly before curtain (come two hours beforehand to be sure of a seat and bring ID). **Day seats** are sold to the public from 9 or 10am on the day of the performance at a reduced price, but you must queue up earlier to snag one. If a show is sold out, returned tickets may be sold (at full price) just before curtain. Most theaters also offer senior citizen discounts on advance ticket purchases for weekday matinees. For the latest on standbys for West End shows, call the **Student Theatreline** (tel. 379 8900; updated from 2pm daily).

Stalls are orchestra seats. **Upper Circle** and **Dress Circle** refer to balcony seats above the stalls. **Slips** are seats along the top edges of the theater; usually the cheapest, they often have restricted views of the stage. The **interval** is the intermission. Programs are never free; these large, glossy booklets cost £1.50-2. Matinees are on weekdays and Saturday between 2-3pm. Evening performances start between 7:15 and 8pm.

The **Leicester Square Half Price Ticket Booth** sells tickets at half-price (plus £1.50-2 booking fee) on the day of the performance, but carries only tickets for the West End, Barbican (and Pit), and National Theatres. Tickets are sold from the top of the pile, which means you can't choose a seat and the most expensive seats are sold first. Lines are the worst on Saturday (open Mon.-Sat. noon-6:30pm; cash only; max. 4/person). Accept no imitations: the peculiar structure with the small tower on the south side of Leicester Sq. is the only discount booth sanctioned by the **Society of London Theater,** but doesn't offer tickets to the huge musicals (*Cats, Phantom,* etc.). If you do get burned by bogus vendors, or have other problems with ticket vendors, contact the Society at 836 0971. Your next best bet for the lowest prices is to schlep to a box office in person and select your seats from the theater seating plan

The Theatre District

Theatres 1

Adelphi, 56
Alberry, 50
Aldwych, 8
Ambassadors, 19
Apollo, 25
Apollo Victoria, 32
Barbican Centre, 6
Cambridge, 17
Comedy, 41
Criterion, 35
Donmar Warehouse, 16
Duchess, 10
Duke of York's, 51
Fortune, 12
Garrick, 52
Globe, 24
Haymarket, 39
Her Majesty's, 38
Lyric, 26
Mayfair, 30
National Theatre, 60
New Arts, 48

New London, 13
Old Vic, 63
Palladium, 1
Phoenix, 20
Piccadilly, 28
Players, 55
Prince Edward, 22
Queens, 23
The Ritz, 31
Royal Court, 32
Royalty, 7
Sadler's Wells, 5
Savoy, 58
Shaftesbury, 15
St. Martin's, 18
Strand, 9
Theatre Royal, 11
Vaudeville, 57
Victoria Palace, 32
Westminster, 32
Whitehall, 54
Wyndhams, 49

Cinemas 1

Cannon Haymarket, 37
Cannon Moulin, 27
Cannon Oxford St., 2
Cannon Panton St., 40
Cannon Piccadilly Circus, 33
Cannon Premiere, 42
Cannon Tottenham Court Rd., 3
Curzon Mayfair, 29

Curzon West End, 21
Dominion, 4
Empire, 45
National Film Theatre, 59
Odeon, 36
Odeon Leicester Sq., 44
Odeon West End, 43
Plaza 1 2 3 & 4, 34
Prince Charles, 46
Warner, 47

Concert Halls ◇

Coliseum, 53
Queen Elizabeth Hall, 61

Royal Festival Hall, 62
Royal Opera House, 14

N

Lincoln's Inn Fields
Holborn
Kingsway
Aldwych
ALDWYCH
TEMPLE
Embankment
Waterloo Bridge
River Thames
Hungerford Br. (rail & foot)
Embankment
Victoria
Charing Cross Station
Northumberland Ave.
Craven St.
National Gallery
TRAFALGAR SQUARE
Whitehall
Whitehall
St. James's Park
The Mall
Pall Mall
Lwr. Regent St.
Haymarket
PICCADILLY CIRCUS
Piccadilly
Jermyn St.
Regent St.
Savile Row
Argyll St.
Bond St.
St. James's St.
OXFORD CIRCUS
Great Marlborough St.
Oxford St.
Wardour St.
Dean St.
SOHO SQUARE
Old Compton St.
Brewer St.
Shaftesbury Ave.
CAMBRIDGE CIRCUS
LEICESTER SQUARE
LEICESTER SQUARE
Charing Cross Rd.
TOTTENHAM COURT RD.
ST. GILES CIRCUS
Charing
New Oxford St.
High Holborn
Holborn
Great Queen St.
Drury Lane
COVENT GARDEN
COVENT GARDEN
Bow St.
Long Acre
Maiden Lane
Wellington St.
The Strand
Chandos Pl.
William IV St.

ENTERTAINMENT

(box offices usually open 10am-8pm). Reserve seats by calling the box office and then paying by post or in person within three days.

Legitimate ticket agencies will get you real seats but no real bargains—they include the **First Call booking office** (tel. 497 9977), **Keith Prowse** (tel. 493 0130), London's largest ticket agency, and **Ticketmaster** (tel. 344 4444). All sell tickets to most major West End shows, as well as larger concert venues. Credit card holders can charge tickets over the phone but must produce the card to pick up tickets.

Patronize ticket agencies only if you're desperate—they can, and will, charge whatever they like. Avoid package deals cooked up for tourists, and be aware that many shows around Piccadilly are tawdry farces and sex shows. For big-name shows, try to get tickets months in advance. Write or call the theater box office first.

Aside from what's going on inside them, many West End theaters themselves form part of the city's fabric. The **Theatre Trust** has protected many historic theaters from demolition; landmarks include the Theatre Royal, Haymarket, the Albery, the Palace, the Criterion, the Duke of York, Her Majesty's, the Shaftesbury, the Savoy, and the Palladium. Shakespeare's **Globe Theatre,** exists only as a carefully preserved excavation site and foundation. The Shakespeare Society of America has constructed a replica down the street. This **Shakespeare's Globe** will begin its first regular season in June of 1997 (see p. 233).

Barbican Theatre, Barbican Centre, EC2 (tel. 628 2295 for 24-hr. information or call 638 8891 for reservations). Tube: Barbican or Moorgate. London home of the Royal Shakespeare Company. Tickets for the main stage, £7.50-22.50; weekday matinees £6-12; Sat. matinees and previews £8-17. Student and senior citizen standbys bookable in person or by telephone from 9am on the day of the performance, £6 (1/person). Fascinating futuristic auditorium showcases the Bard's work in style; each row of seats has its own side door (there are no aisles). Forward-leaning balconies guarantee that none of the 1100 seats sit farther than 65ft. from center stage, and every seat gives a clear view. Stick around at the interval to watch the shiny metal safety curtain seal off the stage. **The Pit**—the 200-seat second theater—showcases Jacobean, Restoration, and experimental contemporary works in a more intimate setting. Evenings and Sat. matinees £9-24.50, previews £6-13.50, midweek matinees £12. Student and senior citizen standbys available from 9am the day of the performance for £6.50. There are always several signed and audio-described performances during the run of each show. Box office (Level 0 of the Centre) open daily 9am-8pm. Visa, MC, AmEx.

Royal National Theatre, South Bank Centre, SE1 (tel. 928 2252). Tube: Waterloo, or Embankment and cross the Hungerford footbridge. The brilliant repertory companies in the **Olivier** and **Lyttleton** theatres (£4-22.50) put on classics from Shakespeare to Ibsen as well as mainstream contemporary drama. The smaller **Cottesloe** (£6.50-14.50) plays with more experimental works like Kushner's *Angels in America*. All 3 theaters are well-raked and have widely spaced rows, so even the rear balcony seats offer an unobstructed view of the stage. 40 day seats in each of the 3 theaters reduced to £7-13 at 10am on day of performance. General standby seats sold from 2hr. before performance a (£8-12); student and senior standby 45min. before show £6.50; senior citizen matinees £9. The complex features live music, exhibitions, and other free activities. The National's outstanding **bookshop** has the widest selection in London for plays and books about theater (open Mon.-Sat. 10am-10:45pm; tel. 928 2033; ask for the bookstore). **Backstage tours** Mon.-Sat. £3.50, concessions £3; call 633 0880 for times. **Box office** open Mon.-Sat. 10am-8pm.

WEST END THEATERS

In a country where Andrew Lloyd Webber is a knight, it's not surprising that *Phantom of the Opera* remains the hardest show in town for which to find seats. Similar fare dominates the theaters of the West End, the London theater district that out-Broadways Broadway. To guarantee a seat for the big musicals, comedies, and thrillers that constitute West End fare, book a week or two ahead.

Adelphi Theatre, The Strand, WC2R (tel. 379 8884). Tube: Charing Cross. Lloyd Webber's latest—*Sunset Boulevard* through '97. £15-32.50.

Albery Theatre, St. Martin's La., WC2N (tel. 369 1730). Tube: Leicester Sq. Newer musicals and comedies, seats £10-30. Concessions receive 2 for 1 ticket deals on £24 and up seats.

Aldwych Theatre, The Strand, WC2B (tel. 416 6003). Tube: Covent Garden. Musicals, comedies, and Stoppard, £10-30.

Apollo Victoria Theatre, Wilton Rd., SW1 (tel. 828 8665). Tube: Victoria. Venue for big musicals. Starlight Express, Lloyd Webber on roller skates, just finished a 13-year run. £12.50-30.

Criterion Theatre, Piccadilly Circus, W1 (tel. 369 1747). Tube: Piccadilly Circus. Top notch comedies. £5.50-20.

Dominion Theatre, Tottenham Ct. Rd., W1 (tel. 416 6060). Tube: Tottenham Ct. Rd. *Scrooge* running through March '97. £5.50-22.50.

Drury Lane Theatre Royal, Catherine St., WC2B (tel. 494 5000). Tube: Covent Garden. *Miss Saigon* continues through '97. £5.75-32.50.

Duke of York's Theatre, St. Martin's La., WC2 (tel. 836 5122). Tube: Leicester Sq. During renovations, the Duke will be hosting the challenging, inventive company from the **Royal Court Theatre.**

Gielgud Theatre, 33 Shaftesbury Ave., W1 (tel. 494 5065). Tube: Piccadilly Circus. Straight plays, mainly comedies; seats £10.50-24.

Her Majesty's Theatre, Haymarket, SW1 (tel. 494 5400). Tube: Piccadilly Circus. Seemingly invincible freak-makes-good musical *Phantom of the Opera.* £9-32.50. Book before you arrive, at least a month ahead if you want Sat. night tickets.

London Palladium Theatre, Argyll St., W1 (tel. 494 5020). Tube: Oxford Circus. *Oliver!,* sadly minus Jonathan Pryce, continues into '97. £10-32.50.

Lyric Hammersmith, King St., W6 (tel. (0181) 741 2311.) Tube: Hammersmith. High-quality repertory comedies and drama from Ibsen to Coward. More experimental fringe-type doings in the Studio Theatre £7.50-15. Mon. all seats £5.

Lyric Shaftesbury Theatre, Shaftesbury Ave., W1 (tel. 494 5045). Tube: Piccadilly Circus. The West End will be watching breathlessly to see how they'll top '96's wildly popular *Tap Dogs,* a troupe of tap-dancing Australian beefcakes. £7.50-26.

New London Theatre, Pirker St., WC2 (tel. 405 0072). Tube: Covent Garden. *Cats.* Singing, dancing cats, because hey, that's how T.S. Eliot would've wanted it. £10.50-32.50.

Old Vic, Waterloo Rd., SE1 (tel. 928 7616). Tube: Waterloo. Historic, famed repertory company in one of the most beautiful performance spaces in London. *The Wind in the Willows* through Feb. of '97. £14-24.

Open Air Theatre, Inner Circle, Regent's Park, NW1 (tel. 486 2431). Tube: Baker St. or Regent's Park. Mostly Shakespeare; sit in the front to catch every word. Bring a blanket and a bottle of wine. £5.50-18.50.

Palace Theatre, Shaftesbury Ave., W1 (tel. 434 0909). Tube: Leicester Sq. *Les Misérables.* Singing, dancing French peasants, because hey, that's how Hugo would've wanted it. £7-30.

Prince Edward Theatre, Old Compton St., W1 (tel. 734 8951). Tube: Leicester Sq. *Martin Guerre* through March '97. £16.50-32.50.

Prince of Wales Theatre, Coventry St., W1 (tel. 839 5987). Tube: Piccadilly Circus. Musicals showcasing everybody from Elvis to Manilow, occasional ½-price Friday matinee. £12.50-27.50.

St. Martin's Theatre, West St., WC2 (tel. 836 1443). Tube: Leicester Sq. Agatha Christie's *The Mousetrap* in its 5th decade. Not the original cast. £8-20.

Savoy Theatre, The Strand, WC2 (tel. 836 8888). Tube: Charing Cross. Varied—plays, musicals, and some ballets, mostly contemporary. £12-24.

Victoria Palace Theatre, Victoria St., SW1 (tel. 834 1317). Tube: Victoria. *Jolson,* the musical biography of Al Jolson in '97. £12.50-30.

Wyndham's Theatre, Charing Cross Rd., WC2 (tel. 369 1746). Tube: Leicester Sq. *Art,* with Albert Finney, through March '97. £9.50-25.

ENTERTAINMENT

OFF-WEST END AND FRINGE THEATERS

"The fringe" is what Londoners dub the dozens of smaller, less commercial theaters that nurture unrefined talents and stage the city's most cutting-edge productions. Born in the avant-garde late 1960s, the fringe today runs the gamut from amateur community productions to top-notch experimental dramas. Ticket prices are much lower than in the West End (£4.50-10). All offer student and senior citizen's discounts in advance or at the door—no standby necessary. Off-West End theaters tend to be larger than the fringe performance spaces, but smaller than the grand West End spaces.

Almeida Theatre, Almeida St., N1 (tel. 359 4404). Tube: Angel or Highbury & Islington. A highly notable theater. The summer new opera series generates rave reviews from critics. 1997 performances will include Checkov's *Ivanov* starring recent Hollywood star (former RSC star) Ralph Fiennes. Box office open Mon.-Sat. 10am-6pm.

Trinity Arts Center London, 17 Gloucester Terr., W2 (tel. 262 1629). Tube: Paddington, then Bus 27. Also served by Bus 7, 23, 36. Community theater based in Paddington—everything from local kid's productions to guest companies. Student discounts. £2.50-7.

Battersea Arts Centre (BAC), Old Town Hall, 176 Lavender Hill, SW11 (tel. 223 2223). BR: Clapham Junction. One of the top fringe venues, with innovative productions and talented new playwrights. Main and 2 studio stages with "mainstream" (radical corruptions of Shakespeare and other canonical texts) and experimental works, plus improv in the Arts Café. In Oct. holds British Festival of Visual Theatre. Pay what you can on Tues. £6-8.50.

The Bush, Bush Hotel, Shepherd's Bush Green, W12 (tel. (0181) 743 3388). Tube: Goldhawk Rd. or Shepherd's Bush. Above a busy old English pub. Well-known for producing innovative plays by new writers. Telephone booking Mon.-Sat. 10am-7pm. Box office open Mon.-Fri. from 6:30pm, Sat. from 7pm. £9.50, concessions £6.

Café Theatre, Wilde Ct. off of 65 Kings Way, WC2 (tel. 240 9582). Tube: Covent Garden. Home of the Artaud Theatre Company, which presents Artaudian shows on one stage; on the other stage, Sartre's comedy *Intimacy* is the longest-running show on the fringe. All shows £5, concessions £4.

Donmar Warehouse, Earlham St., WC2 (tel. 369 1732). Tube: Covent Garden. Mainstream contemporary works. £12-18.

Drill Hall, 16 Chenies St., WC1 (tel. 637 8270). Tube: Goodge St. Politically active productions, often with a gay slant. Vegetarian restaurant downstairs. Also workshops, darkroom, bar.

Etcetera Theatre, Oxford Arms, 265 Camden High St., NW1 (tel. 482 4857). Tube: Camden Town. Don't expect a lot of seating room in this super-small theater, but do look forward to frequent presentations of inventive, experimental plays by new playwrights. £5-7. Box office open Mon.-Sat. 10am-8pm.

The Gate, The Prince Albert, 11 Pembridge Road, W11 (tel. 229 0706). Tube: Notting Hill Gate. This pub-theater with a big reputation hosts an international array of mostly new plays. £10, concessions £5. Box office open Mon.-Fri. 10am-6pm.

Greenwich Theatre, Croom's Hill, SE18 (tel. (0181) 858 7755). This friendly 423-seat venue mixes West End quality with fringe adventurousness. £9.25-15.50, concessions £5.50-6.50. Call ahead for wheelchair access.

Hampstead Theatre, Avenue Rd., Swiss Cottage Centre, NW3 (tel. 722 9301). Tube: Swiss Cottage. One of London's oldest small theaters: notable alumni like "Mr. Sunshine" John Malkovich. Much new writing. Shows change every 6-8 weeks. £8-13.50. Box office open Mon.-Sat. 10am-7pm.

Holland Park Open Air Theatre, Holland Park, W8 (tel. 602 7856). Tube: Holland Park or High St. Kensington. Open-air stage with opera and ballet in the summer. £20, concessions £14.50.

King's Head, 115 Upper St., N1 (tel. 226 1916). Tube: Highbury & Islington or Angel. A Very Big Deal. The slightly ramshackle atmosphere of this pub theater is well known among dedicated London theater-goers as the first dinner-theater since

Shakespeare's time. Kenneth Branagh and Ben Kingsley are alumni. Occasional lunchtime performances. £9-10.

Man in the Moon, 392 Kings Rd., SW3 (tel. 351 2876). A small pub-theater on its way to greatness. Last year's performances included the British premiere of *Oh What a Bloody Circus.* Open 6 nights a week, with 2 shows every night.

New End Theatre, 27 New End, NW3 (tel. 794 0022). Tube: Hampstead. New and classic works presented by local and touring companies. £5-10.

Old Red Lion, St. John's St., N1 (tel. 837 7816). Tube: Angel. Yet another of Islington's gems, the Lion is one of the top fringe theaters and usually presents intriguing plays by new writers. Box office open daily 10am-11pm.

Oval House, 52-54 Kennington Oval, SE11 (tel. 582 7680). Tube: Oval. Flamboyant, provocative productions by Black, Asian, lesbian, and gay playwrights. £6.50, concessions £3. Box office open Mon.-Fri. 2-5:30pm.

Shakespeare's Globe, Bear Gardens, Bankside, SE1 (tel. 620 0202). Tube: London Bridge. A gala opening in June 1997 will kick off the first season of Shakespeare at this reconstruction of the bard's stage. Exact schedule was undecided at press time, so call for details. Standing tickets £5 (groundlings will be expected to yell and throw vegetables at the players). Unreserved gallery seats £12, reserved £16.

Theatre Royal Stratford East, Gerry Raffles Sq., E15 (tel. (0181) 534 0310). Tube: Stratford. Acclaimed and popular new drama in a classic Victorian theater. £5-15. Box office open Mon.-Fri. 10am-6pm, Sat. 10am-3pm.

Tricycle Theatre, 269 Kilburn High Rd., NW6 (tel. 328 1000). Tube: Kilburn. A favorite among locals—some good avant-garde performances. Best-known for new Black and Irish playwrights. £7.50-13. Box office open Mon.-Sat. 10am-8pm.

Young Vic, 66 The Cut, SE1 (tel. 928 6363). Tube: Waterloo. Inland from the actual river bank, across from the Old Vic. One of London's favorite and most acclaimed Off-West End venues. Presents theater in the round. £6-18. Box office open Mon.-Sat. 10am-6pm (by telephone) or curtain (in person).

Lunchtime theater productions are generally less serious than evening performances, but at £2-4 they're a great way to start the afternoon. (Most productions start around 1:15pm.) Check the lunchtime listings at the end of *Time Out*'s theater section. The **King's Head** (see above) is probably the most successful at daytime shows. **St. Paul's Church,** at the central marketplace in Covent Garden, often has lunchtime theater on its steps.

▓ Film

London's film scene offers everything from Arnold Schwarzenegger to French existentialism, from Hollywood dramas to Asian documentaries. The degenerate heart of the celluloid monster is Leicester Square, where the most recent hits premier a day before hitting the chains around the city. West End first-run screens include the **Empire** (tel. 437 1234), **Odeon Leicester Sq.** (tel. 930 3232), the **Warner West End** (tel. 437 4347), all at Leicester Sq. tube; the **Odeon Haymarket** (tel. 839 7697; tube: Piccadilly Circus), and the **MGM Trocadero** (tel. 434 0031; tube: Piccadilly Circus or Leicester Sq.).

Thousands of films pass through the capital every year, old and new. Newspapers have listings, while *Time Out* covers both commercial films and the vast range of cheaper alternatives—late-night films, free films, "serious" films, and repertory cinema clubs. Also worth perusing are the ICA and NFT monthly schedules, available on-site (see below). Cinema clubs charge a small membership fee. This fee (usually 30p-£1.50) entitles cardholders and one guest to reduced admission; some cards work at more than one cinema. Fees and cards make cinemas "clubs," and "clubs" can legally serve liquor—most cinemas have bars and many have restaurants. For evening performances buy your ticket early or book in advance, especially on weekends. Many cinemas have assigned seating; ushers will help you find your place. Big theaters often charge different prices for different seats. Most London moviehouses charge £5-9, but many charge £3 all day Monday and for first shows Tuesday through Friday. Repertory and other cinemas include:

The Prince Charles, Leicester Pl., WC2 (tel. 437 8181 or 437 7003). Tube: Leicester Sq. A Soho institution: 4 shows/day (cheerily deconstructed on the recorded phone message); generally second runs and a sprinkling of classics for only £1.75-2.25. Every Fri., the **Rocky Horror Picture Show** struts in, complete with biscuit throwing and a live troupe for £6, concessions £3.

Everyman Cinema, Hollybush Vale, Hampstead, NW3 (tel. 435 1525). Tube: Hampstead. Double and triple bills based on either a theme or a classic celluloid figure. Special seasonal runs; membership 60p per year. Mon.-Fri. £4.50, Sat.-Sun. £5, students Mon.-Fri. £3.50.

Gate Cinema, Notting Hill Gate, W11 (tel. 727 4043). Tube: Notting Hill Gate. Art house films, with a repertory on Sun. Featured directors include Wim Wenders, Jane Campion, and Derek Jarman. £6, Mon.-Fri. before 6pm and late shows £3, Sun. matinee £4, concessions £3.

Goethe Institute, 50 Prince's Gate, Exhibition Rd., SW7 (tel. 411 3400). Tube: South Kensington. German classics and a sprinkling of U.S. favorites. £2.

Institute of Contemporary Arts (ICA) Cinema, Nash House, The Mall, W1 (tel. 930 3647). Tube: Piccadilly Circus or Charing Cross. Cutting-edge contemporary cinema, plus an extensive list of classics. Frequent special programs celebrating the work of a single director; recent tributes have lauded Rainer Fassbinder and Peter Greenaway. £6.50, concessions, Mon. screenings, and first screenings Tues.-Fri. £5. Experimental films and classics in the *cinémathèque* £4.

London Film-maker's Co-op Cinema, 12-18 Hoxton St., N1 (tel. 586 8516). Tube: Camden Town or Chalk Farm. Devoted to avant-garde and British films. Some double bills. Membership £5 per year, 50p per day. £3.50. Screenings fluctuate between Tues. and Fri. evenings.

MGM Swiss Centre, Leicester Sq., WC2 (tel. 439 4470). Tube: Leicester Sq. or Piccadilly Circus. New French films with subtitles, as well as artsy films not shown in other theaters. Hidden around the left side of the centre. £6.20, concessions £3.60.

Minema, 45 Knightsbridge, W1 (tel. 369 1723). Tube: Knightsbridge or Hyde Park Corner. Small screen behind a tiny door, showing recent art classics and popular foreign films as well as "commercial art." £6.50, Mon.-Fri. 1st show £4.

National Film Theatre (NFT), South Bank Centre, SE1 (tel. 928 3232 for box office). Tube: Waterloo, or Embankment and cross the Hungerford footbridge. The NFT is one of the world's leading cinemas, screening a mind-boggling array of film, TV, and video in its three auditoria. Program changes daily but is arranged in seasonal series. Home of the London Film Festival, held in Nov. For ticket availability, call 633 0274. Annual membership gives discounted tickets, mailings, and priority bookings (£12). Most main screenings £5.50, members £4.50.

Phoenix, 52 High Rd., N2 (tel. (0181) 883 2233 or 444 6789). Tube: East Finchley. Double bills mix and match European, American, and Asian mainstream hits and classics. Comfortable auditorium. Children's cinema club on Sat. mornings. £4.50, all day Mon. and afternoons £3, students (except Sat. night) £3, children £2, seniors £2.50.

▨ Music

London doesn't produce many musicians, but its abundant venues showcase them by the score. Unparalleled classical resources include five world-class orchestras, two opera houses, two huge arts centers, and countless concert halls. Additionally, London serves as the port of call for popular music: any rocker hoping to storm the British Isles, or conquer the world from Liverpool, Dublin, or Manchester, must first gig successfully in the one of the capital's numerous clubs.

Check the listings in *Time Out.* Keep your eyes open for special festivals or gigs posted on most of the city's surfaces and for discounts posted on student union bulletin boards. Many of the most famous troupes take the summer off.

CLASSICAL

London's world-class orchestras provide only a fraction of the notes that fill its major music centers. London has been the professional home of some of the greatest conductors of the century—Sir Thomas Beecham, Otto Klemperer, and Andre Previn.

Barbican Hall, Barbican Centre (tel. 638 4141 or tel. 638 8891 for box office). Tube: Barbican or Moorgate. Houses the venerable **London Symphony Orchestra.** The Barbican also welcomes a number of guest artists. £6-30, student and senior standby tickets sold shortly before the performance £6-8.
Blackheath Concert Halls, 23 Lee Rd., Blackheath, SE3 (tel. (0181) 463 0100). BR (from Charing Cross): Blackheath, then left from the station. Attracts top performers year-round, and serves as a venue for the Greenwich and Docklands Festival (see below). £3.50-20.
Royal Albert Hall, Kensington Gore, SW7 (tel. 589 8212). Tube: South Kensington. Exuberant and skilled, the **Proms** (BBC Henry Wood Promenade Concerts) never fail to enliven London summers. Every day for 8 weeks between the end of July and mid-Sept., an impressive roster of musicians routinely performs outstanding programs, including annually commissioned new works. Camaraderie and craziness develop in the long lines for standing room outside. The last night of the Proms traditionally steals the show, with the massed singing of "Land of Hope and Glory" and "Jerusalem." Don't expect to show up at the last minute and get in; a lottery of thousands determines who will be allowed to paint their faces as Union Jacks and "air-conduct" in person. Eric Clapton also calls this his London home. Gallery £2 (the tippy-top of the theatre), arena £3 (the floor of the hall, best seats in the house but you gotta stand)—join the queue around 6pm; £4-18, sometimes £4-23 or £4-30 for special performances. Box office open daily 9am-9pm, or try Ticketmaster at 379 4444.
South Bank Centre, (box office tel. 960 4242). Tube: Waterloo, or Embankment and cross the Hungerford footbridge. 3 venues here host classical shows. The 2500-seat **Royal Festival Hall** often houses the **London Philharmonic** and the **Philharmonia Orchestra.** Highlights for the '96-'97 season (Sept.-May) include visits from the Vienna Philharmonic and *The Nutcracker Suite* (Dec. '96, of course). The 2 other venues in the South Bank Centre, the **Queen Elizabeth Hall** and the **Purcell Room** also host some classical shows. Summer season booking begins in early May. Tickets for the RFH £5-35, for the QEH and PR £8-12. Students, seniors, and children receive a discount of around £2 for advance tickets, and can queue for standbys (usually a little over ½ price) from 5pm on the night of performances. Box office open daily 10am-9pm.
St. John's, Smith Square, converted church just off Millbank (box office tel. 222 1061). Tube: Westminster. A schedule weighted toward chamber groups and soloists. £6-20, occasional concessions for students and seniors.
Wigmore Hall, 36 Wigmore St., W1 (tel. 935 2141). Tube: Bond St. or Oxford Circus. Small, elegant, and Victorian. Many young artists debut here. Master concerts and chamber music series. Tickets £6-20. 1-hr. standbys at lowest price. In summer, Sun. morning coffee concerts begin at 11:30am; £7, coffee free. Closed end of July through Aug. Box office open 10am-7pm, until 8:30pm in person.

The two main locations of the Barbican and the Royal Festival Hall, as well as the South Bank's smaller halls, the **Queen Elizabeth Hall** and the **Purcell Room,** play host to a superb lineup of groups, including the **Academy of St. Martin-in-the-Fields,** the **London Festival Orchestra,** the **London Chamber Orchestra,** the **London Soloists Chamber Orchestra,** the **London Classical Players,** and the **London Mozart Players,** as well as diverse national and international orchestras. Vladimir Ashkenazy's **Royal Philharmonic Orchestra** performs at both the Barbican and the South Bank, and the **BBC Symphony Orchestra** pops up around town as well. Although the regular season ends in mid-July, a series of festivals on the South Bank in July and August take up the slack admirably, offering traditional orchestral music along with more exotic tidbits (tickets £3-20). Festivals include:

City of London Festival, box office at St. Paul's Churchyard, London EC4 (tel. 377 0540). Tube: St. Paul's. Explosion of activity around the city's grandest monuments: music in the livery halls, singing in churches, plays at various venues, grand opera, art exhibitions, and a trail of dance winding among the monuments. '97 dates: June 22-July 10. Box office open Mon.-Fri. 9:30am-5:30pm. Many events free, most others £10-25. Information from early May at box office.

Greenwich and Docklands International Festival (tel. (0181) 305 1818). Opening night ceremonies culminate in a fireworks show so big it shuts down the river. Other events include free concerts in Greenwich Park (see Greenwich and Blackheath, p. 202). and other area venues. '97 dates: May 24- June 1. Free-£14.

Kenwood Lakeside Concerts, at Kenwood, on Hampstead Heath (tel. (0181) 348 1286, 973 3427, or 379 4444 for Ticketmaster booking with an unpleasant £1 service charge). Tube: Golders Green or Archway, then Bus 210; or East Finchley, then take a free shuttle bus to Kenwood (5-7:50pm, and after concerts until 10:45pm). The concerts are on the North side of Hampstead Heath. The National Symphony Orchestra, the English National Opera, and others offer top-class outdoor performances, often graced by firework displays and laser shows. Every summer Sat. (mid-June to early Sept.) at 7:30pm and sporadic Sundays at 7pm, music floats to the audience from a performance shell across the lake. Reserved deck chairs £11-25, students and seniors £9-20. Grass admission £8.50-15, students and seniors £8.50-12. If "outdoor" is more important than "concert," you can listen from afar for free. Limited free parking available.

Lufthansa Festival of Baroque Music, main site at St. James's Church, Piccadilly (tel. 437 5053). Tube: Piccadilly Circus. One of the top period music festivals in the world. Held yearly in June and July. Baroque tunes from Germany, France, Spain, and England. £5-15.

Marble Hill House (tel. 413 1443 for booking). Tube/BR: Richmond, then Bus R70. Hosts outdoor concerts in summer Sun. at 7:30pm. Bring a blanket and picnic on the grounds of this stately house (mid- July to late Aug.). £11-12, students and seniors £9-12.

Medieval and Renaissance music still commands a following in England; many London churches offer performances, often at lunchtime. Premier among them are **St. Martin-in-the-Fields,** Trafalgar Sq. (tel. 839 8362; tube: Charing Cross); **St. James's Piccadilly** (see above); **St. Bride's,** Fleet St. (tel. 353 1301; tube: Blackfriars). **St. Paul's boys' choir** sings at the Sunday 5pm service. Concerts are usually free. Watch for the **Academy of Ancient Music,** the **Early Music Consort of London,** and the **Praetorius Ensemble.**

Artists from the **Royal College of Music,** Prince Consort Rd., SW7 (tel. 589 3643) and the **Royal Academy of Music,** Marylebone Rd., NW1 (tel. 935 5461) play at their home institutions and at the main city halls. Concerts at these schools are often free—call for details. Check with the **University of London Union,** 1 Malet St., WC1 (tel. 580 9551; tube: Goodge St.) for on-campus music there.

OPERA AND BALLET

Victoria Embankment Gardens. Tube: Embankment. Popular, free *al fresco* opera in the Victoria Embankment gardens summer Wed.-Sat. at 6pm.

Holland Park Theatre, box office in the Visitor Centre (tel. 602 7856). Tube: Holland Park. Open-air opera from a number of companies early June to late Aug., in both English and the original languages. Some dance and classical music, too. £20, children, seniors, and students £14.50.

London Coliseum, St. Martin's La., WC2 (tel. 632 8300 or fax 379 1264 for credit card bookings). Tube: Charing Cross or Leicester Sq. The **English National Opera's (ENO)** repertoire leans towards the contemporary, and all works are sung in English. Seats reserved in advance range £6.50-55. The Half-Price Ticket Booth sells tickets the day of the show if available (see p. 228) or you can show up at the box office weekdays (and Sat. matinees) from 10am to claim the 100 day seats in the balcony for £5. Standby seats also available 3hr. before the performance, the best seats go first. Weekdays, students and senior get the best seat available (1/person) £18. Saturdays, anyone can get standby tickets but they cost £28. If all of these tickets are sold out, they will also sell a few standing room tickets on the day of performance for £5. From mid-July to Sept., when the ENO is off, various visiting ballet companies perform. The Kirov Ballet, American Ballet Theatre, and Royal Swedish Ballet are among recent guests.

The Place, 17 Duke's Rd., WC1 (tel. 387 0031). Tube: Euston. Britain's national contemporary dance center. Four seasons showcasing new/experimental dance, independent British dance, Continental dance, and Oriental dance, but no Safety Dance. Put on your boogie shoes for the evening dance classes (around £4, call 388 8430 for details). Performances £4-10.

Royal Festival Hall, see South Bank Centre, above. Visiting ballet companies and the English National Ballet grace the stage year-round. £10-35.

Royal Opera House, at Covent Garden, Box St., box office at 48 Floral St., WC2 (tel. 304 4000, fax 497 1256). Tube: Covent Garden. Ticket prices at this grand old venue do much to keep ballet and opera an amusement of the idle rich. If the word "ballet" conjures images of a circus bear driving a toy car, seek your fun elsewhere. Tickets for the resident companies, the **Royal Opera** and the **Royal Ballet** come in a bewildering variety of prices and flavors. "Upper slip" tickets with seats on uncomfortable benches and a view of about half the stage are the cheapest, costing £4 for the opera and £2 for the ballet. 65 "Day seats" in the amphitheater are available the day of every show, and provide a decent, if distant, view. Available from 10am on performance day; £7.50-29 opera, £7.50-12.50 ballet. Standby seats, which also tend to be in the amphitheater, are available more sporadically 1½hr. before curtain-up (1hr. for matinees and performances starting at 6:30pm and earlier); opera £15, ballet £12. 1997 season features opera by Mozart and Wagner, as well as a continuation of their summer spotlights on Verdi. Box office open Mon.-Sat. 10am-8pm.

Sadler's Wells Theatre, Rosebery Ave., EC1 (tel. 278 8916). Tube: Angel. This stage, generally a host for visiting dance troupes, is officially closed until 1998, but might be hosting some temporary events, call for info.

ROCK, POP, JAZZ, AND FOLK

London generates and attracts almost every type of performer under the sun: the clubs and pubs of the capital offer a wide, strange, and satisfying variety of musical entertainment. Often, thrash metallists play the same venue as Gaelic folk singers: check weekly listings carefully. *Time Out* and *What's On* have extensive listings and information about bookings and festivals. Also try the Friday *Evening Standard's* insert *Hot Tickets*. You can make credit card reservations for major events by calling **Ticketmaster** (tel. 344 4444); if you do not buy your tickets directly from the venue's box office, you may be charged a booking fee.

Rock and Pop

Major venues for rock concerts include the indoor **Wembley Arena** and the huge outdoor **Wembley Stadium** (tel. (0181) 900 1234; tube: Wembley Park or Wembley Central), the **Royal Albert Hall** (see Classical Music, p. 235), and the **Forum** (see below). In the summer, many outdoor arenas such as **Finsbury Park** become venues for major concerts and festivals.

Apollo Hammersmith, Queen Caroline St., W6 (tel. 416 6080). Tube: Hammersmith. Mainstream rock. £11-25. Box office phones answered Mon.-Sat. 8am-10pm, Sun. 10am-9pm.

Astoria, 157 Charing Cross Rd., WC2 (tel. 434 0403). Tube: Tottenham Ct. Rd. Hot and sweaty hard rock, but the patrons don't seem to mind. Capacity 1800. £7-16.

Borderline, Orange Yard, off Manette St., WC2 (tel. 734 2095). Tube: Tottenham Ct. Rd. British record companies test new rock and pop talent in this basement club. £5-8. Live music Mon.-Sat. 8:30-11pm, dancing Mon.-Sat. 11pm-3am.

Brixton Academy, 211 Stockwell Rd., SW9 (tel. 924 9999). Tube: Brixton. Time-honored and rowdy venue for a wide variety of music including rock, reggae, rap, and "alternative." 4300 capacity. £8-25. Box office takes cash only—book ahead with a credit card.

Dublin Castle, 94 Parkway St. (tel. 485 1773). Tube: Camden Town. Irish pub façade hides one of London's most infamous indie clubs. This is a no-holds-barred joint. 3-4 bands a night, usually starting at 9pm. £3-5.

Forum, 9-17 Highgate Rd., NW5 (tel. 284 1001). Tube: Kentish Town. Night bus N2. Top-notch audio system in a popular venue that was formerly the Town-and-Country Club. Open Sun.-Thurs. 7-11pm, Fri. and Sat. 7pm-2am. £7.50-17.50.

Garage, 20-24 Highbury Corner, N5 (tel. 607 1818). Tube: Highbury and Islington. Night bus N92 or N65. Club/performance space with decent views. Rock, pop, and indie bands most nights. £4-11. Music starts 9pm.

Hackney Empire, 291 Mare St., E8 (tel. (0181) 985 2424). Tube: Bethnal Green then Bus 253 north or BR: Hackney Central. Not much to look at, but its East End location attracts reggae and roots lovers for live tunes and wicked DJs. Lots of community theater. Also host to popular comic routines like the Caribbean duo Bello and Blacka. £3-12. Hours vary by show.

Half Moon Putney, 93 Lower Richmond Rd., SW15 (tel. (0181) 780 9383). Tube: Putney Bridge. Rocking pub with a mix of rock, jazz, and folk. £3-6. Music starts at 8:30 or 9pm (see Hammersmith and Putney, p. 131).

London Palladium, 8 Argyll St., W1 (tel. 494 5020). Tube: Oxford Circus. They've hosted Lou Reed. Serves primarily as a theater venue, but hosts big name concerts on some Sundays. Music usually starts at 7:30pm. Capacity 2312. £10-30.

Mean Fiddler, 24-28 Harlesden High St., NW10 (tel. (0181) 961 5490). Tube: Willesden Junction. Night Bus N18. Cavernous club with high balconies and good bars, strangely mixing country & western, folk, and indie rock. Tues.-Thurs. 8pm-2am, Fri. and Sat. 8:30pm-3am, Sun. 8pm-1am. £10-15.

Rock Garden, The Piazza, Covent Garden, WC2 (tel. 836 4052). Tube: Covent Garden. A variety of great new bands play nightly £5—rock, indie, acid jazz, soul. Happy hour Mon.-Sat. 5-8pm, cover £2, all drinks £1. Open Mon.-Thurs. 5pm-3am, Fri. 5pm-6am, Sat. 4pm-4am, Sun. 7-3am.

Royal Albert Hall, Kensington Gore, SW7 (tel. 589 8212). Tube: South Kensington. Elton John, Elvis Costello, Eric Clapton, and others. Box office open daily 9am-9pm. (See Royal Albert Hall, p. 235.)

Shepherd's Bush Empire, Shepherds Bush Green, W12 (tel. (0181) 740 7474). Tube: Shepherds Bush. Hosts dorky cool musicians like David Byrne, the Proclaimers, and Boy George. 2000 capacity, with 6 bars. £6-20.

Wembley Stadium and **Wembley Arena,** Empire Way, Wembley (tel. (0181) 900 1234). Tube: Wembley Park or Wembley Central. A football (soccer) stadium. Take a pair of binoculars. Open 7:30pm-11pm selected nights. £14-25. The **Arena** is the largest indoor venue in London, serving high-priced refreshments. Open 6:30-11pm selected nights. £12-28.

The Venue, 2A Clifton Rise, New Cross, SE14 (tel. (0181) 692 4077). Tube: New Cross, Night Bus N77. Getting to be a big indie scene. Dancing goes late into the night. Open Fri.-Sat. 8pm-3am; music starts 9:30pm. £5-6.

Jazz

In the summer, hundreds of jazz festivals appear in the city and its outskirts, including July's **City of London Festival** (tel. 638 8891) and the **JVC Capital Radio Jazz, Funk, and Soul Festival** (Royal Albert Hall box office tel. 589 8212). Ronnie Scott's, Bass Clef, and Jazz Café are the most popular clubs. Jazz clubs often stay open much later than pubs.

100 Club, 100 Oxford St., W1 (tel. 636 0933). Tube: Tottenham Ct. Rd. Strange mix of traditional modern jazz, swing, and blues. Staged one of the Sex Pistols' first London gigs. Discount for groups of 5 or more. £5-8. Open Mon.-Wed. 7:30pm-midnight, Thurs. 8pm-1am, Fri. 7:30pm-3am, Sat. 7:30pm-1am, Sun. 7:30-11:30pm.

606 Club, 90 Lots Rd., SW10 (tel. 352 5953). Tube: Fulham Broadway. Blossoming talent bops along with household names in diverse styles. Open Mon.-Sat. 8:30pm-

2:30am, Sun. 8:30-11:30pm. Music begins Mon.-Wed. 9:30pm, Thurs.-Sat. 10pm, Sun. 9pm. Cover Sun.-Thurs. £4, Fri.-Sat. £4.50.

Blue Note, 1 Hoxton Sq., N1 (tel. 729 8440). Tube: Old St., night bus N96. New ownership of one of London's most P-funkified jazz houses has maintained the club's soulful reputation. Modern funk jazz Tues.-Wed. Dance club nights Mon. and Thurs.-Sat. (see p. 241). Hours vary with shows but usually are Tues. 10pm-3am for jazz. £3-8, concession prices available for some shows.

Bull's Head, Barnes Bridge, SW13 (tel. (0181) 876 5241). Tube: Hammersmith, then Bus 9. A waterside pub renowned for good food and modern jazz and funk. £3-7. Open Mon.-Sat. 11am-11pm, Sun. noon-10:30pm. Music starts at 8pm and at lunchtime on Sun.

Jazz Café, 5 Parkway, Camden Town, NW1 (tel. 344 0044). Tube: Camden Town, Night Bus N93. Top new venue in a converted bank. Classic and experimental jazz. £5-15. Open Sun.-Thurs. 7pm-midnight, Fri. and Sat. 7pm-2am.

Jazz at Pizza Express, 10 Dean St., W1 (tel. 437 9595). Tube: Tottenham Ct. Rd. or Leicester Sq. Packed, dark club hiding behind a pizzeria. Fantastic groups and occasional greats; get there early. £4-18. Music begins Sun.-Thurs. at 8:30pm, Fri. and Sat. at 9pm. Doors daily 11:30am-12:30am.

Pizza on the Park, 11 Knightsbridge, Hyde Park Corner, SW1 (tel. 235 5550). Tube: Hyde Park Corner. Another Pizza Express branch that hosts mainstream jazz musicians. Open daily 8am-midnight. Music starts 9:15pm.

Ronnie Scott's, 47 Frith St., W1 (tel. 439 0747). Tube: Leicester Sq. or Piccadilly Circus. The most famous jazz club in London. Expensive food (but don't overlook the cheese and biscuits £2.20 or the various starters £2.10-5) and great music. Ronnie, himself a legend in his own time, still hosts. Waiters masterfully keep noisy clients from ruining the music by politely telling them to shut up. Open fabulously late—the music just keeps going. Mon.-Thurs. £12, Fri. and Sat. £14. Book ahead or arrive by 9:30pm. Box office open Mon.-Sat. 11am-6pm. Music 9:30-2am. Open Mon.-Sat. 8:30pm-3am. On Sun. different promoters rent out the space to put on world music (prices vary).

Folk and Roots

To a large extent, folk music in London means Irish music. But aside from the Celtic variety, the term "folk" covers a whole host of musical hybrids including acoustic folk rock, political tunes, folky blues, and even English country & western. Some of the best are free, but welcome donations.

Acoustic Room, at The Mean Fiddler, 24-28 Harlesden Hight St., NW10 (tel. (0181) 961 5490). Tube: Willesden Junction. Superb performers, with a decidedly "alternative" slant. Open daily 8pm-2am. £4.

Africa Centre, 38 King St., WC2 (tel. 836 1973). Tube: Covent Garden. Music and dance from Africa. More like a cultural center than a club. African music Fri. nights 9pm-3am. £5-6. (See Dance Clubs, p. 240.)

Archway Tavern, Archway Roundabout, N19 (tel. 272 2840). Tube: Archway. Across the street from the station. Hard-core Irish sessions in appropriately green-painted Victorian building every night. Mon.-Thurs., music 8pm-12:30am, Fri.-Sun. until 2am (see Pubs and Bars, p. 131).

Bunjie's, 27 Litchfield St., WC2 (tel. 240 1796). Tube: Covent Garden. Packed vegetarian restaurant with folk and almost-folk groups; lively, dancing audience. £3-3.50, students £2. Open Mon.-Sat. noon-11pm. Folk music Mon.-Wed. and Sat. 8:30-11pm. Fri. is poetry night 8-11pm. Thurs. is comedy 8-11pm.

Cecil Sharpe House, 2 Regent's Park Rd., NW1 (tel. 485 2206). Tube: Camden Town, Night Buses N2, N29, or N93. Regents canal-side view. Happening folk scene with singing and dancing. £3-5. Open Tues. 7-11pm, Thurs.-Sat. 7:30pm-11pm, but events take place throughout the week.

Halfway House, 142 The Broadway, West Ealing, W13 (tel. (0181) 567 0236). Tube: Ealing Broadway. Irish, Cajun, and blues. Open Mon.-Thurs., Fri.-Sat. 11am-midnight, Sun. noon-10:30pm. Free.

Troubadour Coffee House, 265 Old Brompton Rd., SW5 (tel. 370 1434). Tube: Earl's Ct. Acoustic entertainment is served up in a warm café. Bob Dylan and Paul

ENTERTAINMENT

Simon played here early in their careers. On Wed. the café becomes the "Institute for Acoustic Research" and on Mon. it attracts some of the best poets around. Folk and jazz Fri.-Sat. Offering classical now as well. £4.50, concessions £3.50. Open 8pm-11pm.

Weavers, 98 Newington Green Rd., N1 (tel. 226 6911). Tube: Highbury and Islington. Head straight along St. Pauls, left on Newington Green, or take Bus 70 or 277 to Newington Green. Well-respected folk and country acts. £2-6. Open Mon.-Sat. 8:30pm-midnight, Sun. 8-10:30.

■ Nightclubbing

London pounds to 100% Groovy Liverpool tunes, ecstatic Manchester rave, hometown soul and house, imported U.S. hip-hop, and Jamaican ragga. Fashion evolves and revolves, but **black** (and simple) **is always in,** and dress codes (denoted in listings as DC), when they exist, are rarely more elaborate than standard London wear.

In a scene striving to exude effortless extravagance, budget clubbing is a bit difficult. If you must go out with the rest of the city on Friday and Saturday, **show up before the pubs close**—perverse things happen to cover charges after 11pm. Though it's always cooler to slide in fashionably late, earlier's cheaper and the beautiful people will glare enviously at your table when they slink in after midnight.

Take advantage of your tourist status and **party during the week**—though there are fewer options, London has enough tourists, slackers, and devoted party people to pack a few clubs even on Sunday through Wednesday. On these nights, covers rarely top £4, and drink specials abound. Many clubs host a variety of provocative weekly, fortnightly, or monthly one-nighters (e.g. "Horny"), where the club is rented out to independent DJs and promoters. Travelers with fewer scruples than pounds will often call clubs during the day and try to weasel their way onto the guest list, often by expressing a desire to hire the club for such purposes. If you see a cover price prefixed by "NUS (National Union of Students)," an ISIC card or halfway legit-looking college ID should fetch a discount.

For the discriminating clubber, planning is important—**look before you leap, and especially before you drink.** Wandering around drunk after the pubs close looking for a disco is the surest way to end up paying £10 to drink £5 beers and dance the Macarena with prepubescent Essex kids in some glitzy tourist trap (fun at the time, but so much physical, financial, and legal regret in the morning). *Time Out* is the undisputed scene cop, their starred picks of the day are usually a safe bet, and will inevitably be crowded with *Time Out* readers (a generally young, hip, and slightly spendy crowd). Don't let bouncers sweat you. If they tell you "members and regulars only," they don't think you'll fit in, but persist and you can get past (the clientele are on average much less pretentious than the doorman). If there's no queue and it's less than two hours before closing, you shouldn't have to pay full cover, so try to strike a deal. Remember that the tube shuts down two or three hours before most clubs and that taxis can be hard to find in the wee hours of the morning. Some late-night frolickers catch "minicabs," little unmarked cars that sometimes wait outside clubs (see Essentials, p. 69). Arrange transportation in advance or acquaint yourself with the extensive network of night buses (tel. 222 1234 for information). Listings include some of the night bus routes that connect to venues outside of central London, but routes change and a quick double-check is recommended.

For gay and lesbian clubs, see Bisexual, Gay, and Lesbian London, p. 261.

Africa Centre, 38 King St., WC2 (tel. 836 1973). Tube: Covent Garden. Art center by day, psychedelic, blacklit den of funk by night. Live music most Fridays, but Saturday's "Funkin' Pussy" lets Funkateers shake booty to vintage funk and hip-hop. Spontaneous breakdancing is not uncommon. Fri. 9pm-3am, £5 in advance, £6 at the door. Sat. 9pm-3am, £3 before 11pm, otherwise £7, concessions £5. (See Folk and Roots, p. 239.)

Bar Rumba, 36 Shaftesbury Ave., W1 (tel. 287 2715). Tube: Piccadilly Circus. *¡Muy caliente!* The legion of industrial fans aren't enough to keep things cool at this basement bar and dancefloor. At Tuesday's excellent "Salsa Pa'Ti," a seemingly random crowd of all ages and nationalities are fused into one nation under a salsa groove. The dancing is somewhat formal, so if you can't tango, cha-cha, or pachanga, arrive at 7pm for instruction (£6, cover included), or look forlorn and one of the fledgling Romeos will volunteer to "teach you." Dancing is informal other nights, but the Latin flavor persists, the bar serves til three, and the cover's low, making this a popular late-night watering hole for non-dancers. £2-7. Open most nights 9pm-3:30am, Fri. til 4am, Sat. til 6am.

The Underworld, 174 Camden High St. NW1 (tel. 482 1932). Tube: Camden Town. Across the street from the tube. Huge fire station-like pub leads into soul center and techno training camp downstairs. Thurs. night is "Hazzard County," with indie DJ and moshers. £2-5.

Blue Note, 1 Hoxton Sq., N1 (tel. 729 8440). Tube: Old St. A new club on the cutting edge of the London dance scene, where DJs searching for the perfect beat nightly perfect genres most Americans have never heard of, taking dub, drum 'n' bass, house, and garage to other levels. £5-8, concessions £4-6. Open Mon., Thurs. 9pm-3am, Fri.-Sat. 10pm-5am, Sun. 7pm-midnight.

The Camden Palace, 1a Camden High St. NW1 (tel. 387 0428). Tube: Camden Town. Night Bus N2, N29, or N90. Huge and hugely popular with tourists and Brits alike. Friday's "Peach" packs 'em in with house and garage, while Tuesday's "Feet First" does the same with indie, Brit pop, and the occasional live act. £2-10. Open Tues.-Thurs. and Sat. 9pm-2:30am, Fri. 9pm-6am.

Club 414, 414 Coldharbour Ln., SW2 (tel. 924 9322). Tube: Brixton. Groove to melodic deep house, underground, and garage at this lesser-known dance venue. Downstairs offers laser lights; upstairs is "melo melo" chill-out floor. Open Fri.-Sat. 10pm-6am, Sun. 6pm-1am.

The Electric Ballroom, 184 Camden High St., NW1 (tel. 485 9006). Tube: Camden Town. Night Bus N2, N29, N90, or N93. Cheap and fun. *Time Out* described Sat. as "probably London's best rock, Gothic, and Glamour punk night." Most of the clientele refuse to wear natural fibers. £5, members £4.

The Fridge, Town Hall Parade, Brixton Hill, SW2 (tel. 326 5100). Tube: Brixton. Night bus N2. A serious dance dive with a stylish multi-ethnic crowd. Telly psychedelia, twisting dance cages, and Saturday's "Love Muscle," the ultimate London one-nighter, pack in a beautiful and shocking mixed-gay clientele. Every Fri. is a different theme night—call for the latest update. £10, with flyer £8.Open Fri.-Sat. 10pm-6am.

Hippodrome, Charing Cross Rd., WC2 (tel. 437 4311). Tube: Leicester Sq. Infamously enormous, loud, and tourist-ridden; leave your blue jeans and trainers behind. Mon. night is "PSST!!"—the biggest U.K. students' night around. £2 before 11pm, £3 before midnight with U.K. student ID. Pints go for £1.50 all night. Thurs. and Fri. party with "BUSH!" Dance it up to the house/party mix. Professional dancers and laser shows. Open Mon.-Sat. 9pm-3:00am.

Iceni, 11 White Horse St., W1 (tel. 495 5333). Tube: Green Park. Off Curzon Street. 3 beautiful floors of deep funk entertainment in this stylish Mayfair hotspot. They also have board games for those who can't keep the beat. £5-8. Open Wed.-Sat. 10pm-3am.

Jazz Bistro, 340 Farringdon St., EC1 (tel. 236 8112). Tube: Farringdon. With a handle like "Jazz Bistro" it's amazing how unpretentious this place is. A refreshing enclave of Farringdon bohemian on the fringe of the decidedly un-boho City, this joint serves up the freshest beats in town, both live and canned. On weekends, Bright Young People pack into the alcove-filled basement and intimate dance floor to boogie among the trippy visual projections. Cover never tops £4. Open nightly 10pm-3am.

Legends, 29 Old Burlington St., W1 (tel. 437 9933). Tube: Green Park, Piccadilly Circus, or Oxford Circus. Excellent one-nighters in this dark chrome-lined dance club. Thurs. is "Horny" with garage grooves and a "devilish, wicked, and horny" dress code. Bring your pheromones and bump and grind with the sleek, beautiful, and friendly people of Mayfair. £3-15. Open Wed.-Sat. 10pm-3:30am.

Ministry of Sound, 103 Gaunt St., SE1 (tel. 378 6528). Tube: Elephant & Castle. Night Bus N12, N62, N65, N72, N77, or N78. Another south of the Thames megaclub, with the long queues, beefy covers, beautiful people, and pumping house tunes. An excellent way to while away a Sunday morning. Fri. £10, Sat. £15. Open Fri. 11pm-8am, Sat. 11pm-9am.

RAW, 112a Great Russell Street, WC1. Tube: Tottenham Ct. Rd. Music? Atmosphere? How about cheap beers—for one glorious ½hr. on Thursdays beer sells for 50p a bottle. 'Nuff said. £3-5. Open 10:30pm-3am.

Subterania, 12 Acklam Rd., W10 (tel. (0181) 960 4590). Tube: Ladbroke Grove. This is where it's at—directly beneath the Westway flyover. Relaxed, multi-ethnic crowd comes to dance to wicked house and garage music. Club classics and "90s disco." £5-8. Open daily 9pm-3:30am.

United Kingdom, Buckhold Rd., SW18 (tel. (0181) 877 0110). BR: Wandsworth Town or night Bus N88. A hot, young club far removed from the kitsch of the West End—go if you feel the need for a long trip. Hard house, Euro-style techno and trance. £9-11. Open Fri.-Sat. 10pm-6am.

Velvet Underground, 143 Charing Cross Rd., (tel. 439 4655). Tube: Tottenham Ct. Rd. Half velvet-soaked leisure lounge, half pumping house and techno dance floor. Particularly cheap and juicy in the early week—Monday's "World Recession" lures party people with a low (£4) cover and £1 drinks. Open Sun.-Thurs. 10pm-3am, Fri.-Sat. 10pm-4:30am.

The Wag Club, 35 Wardour St., W1 (tel. 437 5534). Tube: Piccadilly Circus. Funky multi-level complex with bars and an eatery amongst throngs of dancers. The two dancefloors and wildly random mixing guarantee a little groove for everyone's tastes. Mon.-Thurs. £3-5, Fri. £6, Sat. £8. Open Mon.-Thurs. 10:30pm-3:30am, Fri. 10:30pm-4:30am, Sat. 10:30pm-5:30am.

■ Offbeat Entertainment

London, that great cesspool into which all the loungers and idlers of the Empire are irresistibly drained.
—Sir Arthur Conan Doyle, *"A Study in Scarlet"*

If you've got the cash, you can indulge in luxuries like rowing boats in the pond at Regent's Park or being wrapped by beauty consultants in the latest combination of mud, seaweed, and turtle spit. If you haven't, there are other options for entertainment that won't break the budget traveler's bank.

City Farms: Goats, ducks, rabbits, sheep, poultry, and sometimes cattle, horses, and donkeys bleat, quack, baa, moo, and cluck at **Kentish Town,** 1 Cressfield Close, off Grafton Rd., NW5 (tel. 916 5420; tube: Kentish Town; open daily 9:30am-5:30pm; **pony rides** on Sun. 1:30-2:30pm); **Freightliners,** Sheringham Rd., N7 (tel. 609 0467; tube: Highbury & Islington; open Tues.-Sun. 9am-1pm, 2-5pm); **Hackney,** 1a Goldsmith's Row, E2 (tel. 729 6381; tube: Bethnal Green; open Tues.-Sun. 10am-4:30pm); **Stepping Stones,** Stepney Way, E1 (tel. 790 8204; tube: Stepney Green; open Tues.-Sun. 9am-6pm); and **Surrey Docks,** Rotherhithe St., SE16 (tel. 231 1010; tube: Surrey Quays; open Tues.-Thurs., Sat.-Sun. 10am-1pm, 2-5pm). Call to confirm times. All are free.

The College of Psychic Studies, 16 Queensberry Pl., SW7 (tel. 589 3292). Tube: South Kensington. Increase your psychic sensitivity through lectures (£2-4), musical events (free-£7), and evening courses (£35-70) dealing with healing and spiritual awareness. Open Mon.-Thurs. 10am-7:30pm, Fri. 10am-4:30pm.

Daily Mail and **Evening Standard,** Tour the plants of one of these tabloids. Witness an actual press run, and finally get your chance to (ineffectually) yell "Stop the presses!" For information write at least a month in advance to Managing Director John Bird, Harmsworth Quays Printers Ltd., Surrey Quays Rd., SE16 1PI.

House of Hemp, 31-39 Redchurch St., E2 (739 8953). Tube: Shoreditch, right on Brick La., left on Cheshire, as you turn right onto Bishopsgate from Cheshire, Redchurch is the first right. Small museum lovingly chronicles the history, industrial uses, and "medicinal" properties of *cannabis sativa*, relating the hemp fixations of U.S. presidents from Washington to JFK (the White House's first burner). Shop sells hemp goods. Open Wed. 11am-7pm, occasionally Sun. 2pm-6pm. Admission £3, students and seniors £2, includes info pack with stickers and cannabis goods.

Islington Arts Factory, 2 Parkhurst Rd., N7 (tel. 607 0561). Tube: Holloway Rd. Exit left onto Holloway Rd. Turn left onto Camden Rd., which leads to the corner of Camden and Parkhurst. Music, art, and dance studios available for hire. (The Factory itself offers classes and sponsors free small exhibitions; they also have a darkroom.) For £3.50-6.50/hour (in the daytime) you can rent a music room fully equipped with a drum set, P.A., and mikes. (£3 annual membership fee required to enroll in classes.) Open Mon.-Fri. 10am-10pm, Sat. 10am-6pm.

London College of Fashion, 20 John Povices St., W1 (tel 514 7400). Tube: Oxford Circus. If you want some pampering and have a few quid and a few hours to spare, offer yourself to the students at the LCF's beauty-therapy department, where they learn how to give everything from cathiodermie to pedicures. Prices (to cover the cost of products used) start from £2.50. Open Oct.-June Mon.-Fri. 9am-8pm, but call to make an appointment—no walk-ins.

Old Bailey, corner of Old Bailey and Newgate St. (tel. 248 3277) Tube: St. Paul's. Technically the Central Criminal Courts, Old Bailey crouches under a copper dome and a wide-eyed figure of justice on the corner of Old Bailey and Newgate St.—infamous as the site of Britain's grimiest prison. Trial-watching persists as a favorite occupation, and the Old Bailey fills up whenever a gruesome or scandalous case is in progress. You can enter the public Visitors' Gallery and watch bewigged barristers at work. Even women wear the wigs so that they too may look like wise old men. Cameras, large bags, and backpacks may not be taken inside. Open Mon.-Fri. 10am-1pm and 2-4pm; entrance in Warwick Passage off of Old Bailey.

Porchester Spa, Queensway, W2 (tel. 792 3980). Tube: Bayswater or Royal Oak. In the Porchester Centre. A Turkish bath with steam and dry heat rooms and a swimming pool. Built in 1929, the baths are a newly refurbished Art Deco masterpiece of gold and marble. Rates are high (3hr. £17.50), but devoted fans keep taking the plunge. Open daily 10am-10pm. Men bathe Mon., Wed., and Sat.; women bathe Tues., Thurs., and Fri. On Sun. women may bathe from 10am-4pm, and couples may bathe together from 4-10pm at the special rate of £23.50 per couple for 3hr.). Swimwear required for mixed couples night.

Speakers' Corner, in the northeast corner of Hyde Park. Tube: Marble Arch. Crackpots, evangelists, political activists, and more crackpots speak their minds every Sun. 11am-dusk. (See Hyde Park, p. 155.)

Radio and TV Shows. Become part of a live studio audience. Get free tickets for the endless variations on "Master Mind." Write to the **BBC Ticket Unit,** Broadcasting House, Portland Pl., W1; **Thames TV Ticket Unit,** 306 Euston Rd., NW1; or **London Weekend Television,** Kent House, Upper Ground, SE1.

The Rocky Horror Picture Show, at the Prince Charles Cinema (see p. 234). This ain't *Cats* anymore, boys. Witness the legend in its hometown, complete with a live troupe and biscuit throwing. Fri. 11:30pm. £6, concessions £3.

Vidal Sassoon School of Hairdressing, 56 Davies Mews, W1 (tel. 318 5205). Tube: Bond St. Become your own offbeat entertainment. Cuts, perms, and colorings at the hand of *un petit* Sassoony. Cut and blow dry £11 (concessions £5.50), which includes lengthy consultations with an experienced stylist before the students do their worst. Actually most "students" have spent time styling at lesser studios before even being allowed to study with the maestro. Make sure you have about 2-2½hr. to spare. Appointment recommended. Open Mon.-Fri. 9:30am-4pm.

▓ Sports

SPECTATOR SPORTS

Association Football

Many evils may arise which God forbid.
—King Edward II, banning football in London, 1314

ENTERTAINMENT

Football (soccer) draws huge crowds—over half a million people attend professional matches in Britain every Saturday. Each club's fans dress with fierce loyalty in team colors and make themselves heard with uncanny synchronized cheering. Mass violence and vandalism at stadiums have dogged the game for years. Ninety-five people were crushed to death in Sheffield in 1989 after a surge of fans tried to push their way into the grounds. The atmosphere in the stands has become a bit tamer now that most stadiums sell only seats rather than spaces in the once infamous "terraces." In 1996, during England's turn at hosting the European Championships, a small-scale riot broke out in Trafalgar Square.

The season runs from mid-August to May. Most games take place on Saturday, kicking off at 3pm. Allow time to wander through the crowds milling around the stadium. London has been blessed with 13 of the 92 professional teams in England. The big two are **Arsenal,** Arsenal Stadium, Avenell Rd., N5 (tel. 226 0304; tube: Arsenal) and **Tottenham Hotspur,** White Hart Lane, 748 High Rd., W17 (tel. (0181) 365 5000; BR: White Hart Lane). But the football scene is very partisan and favorites vary from neighborhood to neighborhood. Tickets are available in advance from each club's box office; many have a credit card telephone booking system. Seats cost £10-35. England plays occasional international matches at Wembley Stadium, usually on Wednesday evenings (tel. (0181) 900 1234; tube: Wembley Park).

Rugby

The game was spontaneously created when a Rugby College student picked up a soccer ball and ran it into the goal. Rugby has since evolved into a complex and subtle game. **Rugby League,** a professional sport played by teams of 13, has traditionally been a northern game. Wembley Stadium (tel. (0181) 900 1234) stages some of the championship matches in May. A random *melee* of blood, mud, and drinking songs, "rugger" can be incomprehensible to the outsider, yet aesthetically exciting nonetheless. The season runs from September to May. The most significant contests, including the Oxford vs. Cambridge varsity match in December and the springtime five nations championship (featuring England, Scotland, Wales, Ireland, and France) are played at **Twickenham** (tel. (0181) 892 8161; BR: Twickenham). First-rate games can be seen in relaxed surroundings at one of London's premiere clubs such as **Saracens,** Dale Green Rd., N14 (tel. (0181) 449 3770; tube: Oakwood), and **Rosslyn Park,** Priory La., Upper Richmond Rd., SW15 (tel. (0181) 876 1879; BR: Barnes).

Cricket

Cricket remains a confusing spectacle to most North Americans. The impossibility of explaining its rules to an American has virtually become a national in-joke in England. Once a synonym for civility, cricket's image has been dulled. The much-used phrase "It's just not cricket" has recently taken on an ironic edge. While purists disdain one-day matches, novices find these the most exciting. "First class" matches amble on rather ambiguously for days, often ending in "draws."

London's two grounds stage both county and international matches. **Lord's,** St. John's Wood Rd., NW8 (tel. 289 1300/1611; tube: St. John's Wood), is *the* cricket ground, home turf of the Marylebone Cricket Club, the established governing body of cricket. Archaic stuffiness pervades the MCC; women have yet to see the inside of its pavilion. **Middlesex** plays its games here (tickets £7 for summer matches). Tickets to international matches cost £15-37 (booking required for major matches). **Foster's Oval,** Kennington Oval, SE11 (tel. 582 6660; tube: Oval), home to **Surrey** cricket club (tickets £7-8), also fields Test Matches (tickets for internationals £21-36; book ahead).

Rowing

The **Henley Royal Regatta,** the most famous annual crew race in the world, conducts itself both as a proper hobnob social affair (like Ascot) and as a popular corporate social event (like Wimbledon). The rowing is graceful, though laypeople are often unable to figure out what on earth is going on. The event transpires from July 2-

6, 1997. Saturday is the most popular and busiest day, but some of the best races are the finals on Sunday. Public enclosure tickets (£5 for the first three days, £6 for the last two) are available by the river (the side opposite the train station) or write to the Secretary's Office, Regatta Headquarters, Henley-on-Thames, Oxfordshire, England RG9 2LY (tel. (01491) 572 153).

The **Boat Race,** between eights from Oxford and Cambridge Universities, enacts the traditional rivalry between the schools. The course runs from Putney to Mortlake on Saturday, March 29, 1997. Old-money alums, fortified by strawberries and champagne, sport their crested blazers and college ties to cheer the teams on. Bumptious crowds line the Thames and fill the pubs (tube: Putney Bridge or Hammersmith; BR: Barnes Bridge or Mortlake). Call 379 3234 for info.

Tennis

From June 23, 1997 until July 6, 1997, tennis buffs all over the world will focus their attention on Wimbledon. This village-like suburb annually converts itself into a tennis lovefest where top tennis stars are gently applauded by the toffs (English slang meaning upper crust). If you want to get in, arrive early (6am); the gate opens at 10:30am (get off the tube at Southfields or take one of the buses from central London that run frequently during the season). Entrance to the grounds (including lesser matches) costs £7-8, £5-6 after 5pm. If you arrive in the queue early enough, you can buy one of the few show court tickets that were not sold months before. Depending on the day, center court tickets cost £21-47, No.1 court tickets £12-33, No.2 court tickets £14-22. Other courts have first-come, first-served seats or standing room only. Get a copy of the order of play on each court, printed in most newspapers. If you fail to get center or No. 1 court tickets in the morning, try to find the resale booth (usually in Aorangi Park), which sells tickets handed in by those who leave early (open from 2:30pm; tickets only £2). Also, on the first Saturday of the championships, 2000 extra center court tickets are put up for sale at the "bargain" price of £25. Call (0181) 946 2244 for ticket information.

For details on the 1997 championships send a self-addressed stamped envelope between September 1 and December 31, 1996 to **The All England Lawn Tennis and Croquet Club,** P.O. Box 98, Church Rd., Wimbledon SW19 5AE. Topspin lob fans mustn't miss the **Wimbledon Lawn Tennis Museum** (tel. (0181) 946 6131), located right on the grounds (open Tues.-Sat. 10:30am-5pm, Sun. 2-5pm; during the tournament daily 10:30am-7pm for ticketholders only).

Horses

The **Royal Gold Cup Meeting** at **Ascot** takes place each summer in the second half of June. An "important" society event, it is essentially an excuse for Brits of all strata to indulge in the twin pastimes of drinking and gambling while wearing silly hats. The Queen takes up residence at Windsor Castle in order to lavish her full attentions on this socio-political vaudeville act. (The enclosure is open only by invitation; grandstand tickets £24, Silver Ring £6; tel. (01344) 222 11). In July, the popular George VI and Queen Elizabeth Diamond Stakes are run here, and during the winter Ascot hosts excellent steeplechase meetings (BR from Waterloo to Ascot). Top hats, gypsies, and Pimms also distinguish the **Derby** ("darby"), run on June 7, 1997 at **Epsom** Racecourse, Epsom, Surrey (tel. (01372) 726 311; grandstand tickets £9-20). More accessible, less expensive summer evening races are run at **Royal Windsor Racecourse,** Berkshire (tel. (01753) 865 234; BR: Windsor Riverside; admission to tattersalls and paddock £8), and **Kempton Park Racecourse,** Sunbury-on-Thames (tel. (01932) 782 292; BR: Kempton Park; grandstand £12, Silver Ring £6).

In late June, **polo** aficionados flock to the **Royal Windsor Cup,** The Guards Polo Club, Smiths Lawn, Windsor Great Park (tel. (01784) 437 797; BR: Windsor & Eton Central; admission £15 per car). You can stand on the "wrong" side of the field for free, or hobnob in the clubhouse (one-day membership £12).

The Lottery

George Orwell's apocalyptic vision of the future, *1984,* predicted that the Lottery would be the one event which would continue to delight the masses even when all else had been eradicated by Big Brother.

Following the introduction of the National Lottery many fear that Orwell is being proved right. The choosing of the winning numbers has become the highest rated television program, and Britain does indeed seem to be in Lottery fever. The first multi-million pound pay-outs first brought joy, and then ruined many families not able to bear the full glare of tabloid intrusion and the stress that large undeserved bounty seems to induce.

The lottery has created a furor not just because it's brash and American, but also because it represents a radical departure from how taxes used to be raised in Britain. Surplus funds are to go to the *Millennium Fund* which is supposed to oversee a program of beautification and public works to prepare Britain for the year 2000. The administration of the funds, however, has also been controversial, with some suggesting that subsidies to the Opera are unwarranted when evidence suggests that it is the poorest and least educated Britons who are contributing most to this *fin-de-siècle* project.

Greyhound Racing

Greyhound racing—a.k.a. "the dogs"—is the second most popular spectator sport in Britain, after football. It's a quick and easy way to lose money—races last all of 20 seconds. Almost all races start at 7:30pm. Races are held year-round at **Walthamstow** (tel. (0181) 531 4255), and **Wembley** (tel. (0181) 902 8833). In late June, Wimbledon hosts the **Greyhound Derby,** nephew to its horseracing uncle (tel. (0181) 946 5361). Admission starts at £2.50.

PARTICIPATORY SPORTS

Time Out's section on Sports, Mind, and Body can give you more complete information on the sports listed below and many others. Another outstanding resource is **The Sportsline**, which answers queries Mon.-Fri. from 10am-6pm (tel. 222 8000). A live operator can give information on an unbelievable range of sporting opportunities in your area.

For general fitness during your visit, **London Central YMCA,** 112 Great Russell St., WC1 (tel. 637 8131; tube: Tottenham Ct. Rd.), has a pool, gym, weights, and offers weekly membership for £30. (Open Mon.-Fri. 7am-10pm, Sat.-Sun. 9:30am-9pm.)

Swimming

Dive into the **Britannia Leisure Centre,** 40 Hyde Rd., N1 (tel. 729 4485; tube: Old Street), an unashamedly sensational aquatic playground replete with a towering flume, fountains, and monstrous inflatables (open Mon.-Fri. 9am-10pm, Sat.-Sun. 9am-6pm; admission £2.50, children £1.25). The Britannia also offers various women-only swimming times. Outdoor bathers may prefer the popular **Serpentine Lido** (tel. 262 3751; tube: Knightsbridge or Hyde Park Corner), a chlorinated section of the Serpentine lake in Hyde Park with surprisingly luxurious changing rooms and a kiddie pool and sandpit for children (open May-Sept. daily 9am-5pm; admission £2, concessions £1, sunloungers £2). The pool at the **University of London Union,** Malet St., WC1, is closer to the center of town; a £30 Community user membership will enable you to use the pool and other fitness facilities for a small surcharge (tel. 580 9551 (ext. 205) for more information). Also see the sports centers listed below, most of which have pools.

Tennis

Public courts vary in quality; all cost about £3-6 per hour. You can call ahead and book in advance, though walk-ons are sometimes available. Hard courts include **Bat-**

tersea Park (tel. (0181) 871 7542; BR: Battersea Park); **Hyde Park** (tel. 262 3474; tube: Hyde Park Corner or Knightsbridge); **Lincoln's Inn Fields** (tel. 580 2403; tube: Holborn); and **Regent's Park** (tel. 486 7905; tube: Regent's Park).

Squash

While London is honeycombed with squash courts, the vast majority reside within private health and racket clubs that charge £200-400 for membership plus steep court fees. Visitors and casual players can, however, use the courts maintained by the city's numerous sports centers on a "pay as you play" basis; most charge around £6/hour. Call the **Chelsea Sports Centre,** Chelsea Manor St., SW3 (tel. 352 6985); the **Queen Mother's Sports Centre,** 223 Vauxhall St., SW1 (tel. 630 5522); and the **Saddlers Sports Centre** (for details, see Health and Fitness Centers below).

Health and Fitness Centers

London is blessed with over 200 public sports and fitness centers; consult the yellow pages under "Leisure Centers" for more exhaustive listings or call the local borough council for a list of centers near you.

Chelsea Sports Centre, Chelsea Manor St., off Kings Rd., SW3 (tel. 352 6985). Tube: Sloane Sq. or South Kensington. Activities: aerobics, badminton, basketball, bowls, canoeing, dance, football, lacrosse, martial arts, racquetball, roller skating, squash, swimming, tennis, volleyball, weight training, and yoga. Special facilities: sauna, solarium, and spa baths. No membership or admission charge. Gym card £7.20 annually for use of weights, with a fee of £2.80 per use. Swimming £2.10. Classes and other activities £2.50-4. Open Mon.-Fri. 7:30am-10pm, Sat. 8am-10pm, Sun. 8am-6:30pm.

Jubilee Hall Recreation Centre, 30 The Piazza, WC2 (tel. 836 4835), on the south side of Covent Garden. Tube: Covent Garden. Regular classes and activities include weight lifting, yoga, martial arts, gymnastics, dance, badminton, and aerobics. Special facilities include a sauna, solarium, and an alternative sports medicine clinic. Crowded with West End office workers at lunchtime. Monthly membership £47. Admission free to members; day membership £6. All memberships require 2-passport sized photos. Open Mon.-Fri. 7am-10pm, Sat.-Sun. 10am-5pm.

Queen Mother Sports Centre, 223 Vauxhall Bridge Rd., SW1 (tel. 630 5522). Tube: Victoria. Activities: aerobics, badminton, basketball, bowls, canoeing, diving, gymnastics, martial arts, racquetball, squash, swimming, trampolining, volleyball, and weight lifting. Equipment rental. Activities (£2-5.85/hour) and full use of facilities on a pay-per-use basis are open to non-members, but membership (£33.15/year) entitles one to lower prices. Use of weight gym requires completion of a 1-hr. course (£25.90) on the weights, and costs £5.85 per use thereafter for non-members. Pool £2.05/use, £1.65 for members. Open Mon.-Fri. 7:30am-10pm, Sat. 8am-6pm, Sun. 9am-6pm.

Saddlers Sports Centre, 12 Goswell Rd., EC1 (tel. 253 9285). Tube: Barbican. Activities: aerobics, badminton, basketball, body conditioning, canoeing, cricket, fencing, racquetball, squash, swimming, tennis, volleyball, weight training, and yoga. Young, casual clientele. No membership or admission charge but activities are quite expensive. Squash £8.20/hr., badminton £6.80. Open Mon., Wed., and Fri, 7:30am-9pm, Tues. and Thurs. 9am-9pm.

ENTERTAINMENT

Shopping

London Transport's handy *Shoppers' Bus Wheel* instructs Routemaster shoppers on the routes between shopping areas (available free from any London Transport Information Centre). *Nicholson's Shopping Guide and Streetfinder* (£3) should suit bargain hunters seeking further guidance. Serious shoppers should read *Time Out's* massive *Directory to London's Shops and Services* (£6) cover to cover.

Budget shoppers should keep a keen eye out for the London **sales.** These anxiously awaited affairs involve substantial discounts on large portions of the merchandise as well as extended shopping hours. Most stores have both a winter and a summer sale, usually around January and July. This is the time to pick up designer fashions at almost reasonable prices. The London sales reward the shopper who begins early and wades through rack after rack looking for the diamond in the rough. *Time Out*'s "Sell Out" section has listings of stores offering markdowns.

Tourists who have purchased anything over £50 should ask about getting a refund on the 17.5% VAT. Another option is to save receipts and to send off for a refund at the airport. Each shopping area has a late night of shopping. Kings Rd. and Kensington High St., for example, stay open late on Wednesday, while the West End shops open their doors to the night on Thursday. Many stores may be closed on Sunday.

▓ Shopping Districts

Stores change lines each year, and the trendsetting boutiques of yesteryear may offer clothes which inspire nothing but yawns and sneers from today's shoppers. Fortunately, one can be sure that certain areas of the city will offer exciting threads even if one or two shops have missed the mark—the best way to shop may be by strolling along the main boulevards and checking out what's in the windows.

Oxford St. Tube: Bond St., Oxford Circus, or Tottenham Ct. Rd. This bustling thoroughfare may be the busiest pedestrian street in all of London. Venerable department stores like **Selfridges,** discount chains, and trendy boutiques offer options for every shopper. The districts to the south of Oxford St. (**Bond St.** and **Regent St.**) feature absurdly expensive couture while the areas to the north offer pretty dismal wares. The area is such a shopping mecca that larger stores pack branches within 5-6 blocks of each other to lure as many shoppers as possible.

Regent St. Tube: Oxford Circus or Piccadilly Circus. This elegant, Nash-designed street intersects Oxford St. at the Oxford Circus tube. The section south of Oxford St. is the home of some of the city's oldest and best known stores, including **Liberty's of London.** The stores here tend to have in elegance what they lack in affordability.

Jermyn St. Tube: Piccadilly Circus or Green Park. The last refuge of the English gentleman. Known for well-tailored shirtings, this street also offers conservative ties, well-turned shoes, expensive cigars, and fine spirits. Hardly budget territory, but a fun place to window shop nonetheless. Running parallel to Jermyn St., just north, is Piccadilly St.—the home of **Fortnum & Mason** as well as several other luxury shops.

Knightsbridge. Tube: Knightsbridge. This famous shopping area is anchored by the city's most celebrated department stores, **Harvey Nichols** and **Harrods.** Sloane St., Knightsbridge, and Brompton Rd. radiate outwards from the tube station. The district is also filled with expensive boutiques and trendy chain stores. During the day, the streets are filled with sidewalk vendors hawking jewelry and perfumes to the milling tourists.

Kensington High St. Tube: High St. Kensington. A fairly heterogeneous district at the southwest corner of Kensington Gardens offering a couple of camping outfitters, a few boutiques, and a wealth of trendy chains. This is another of London's busiest streets. Those who hate crowds will hate Kensington High Street as well.

Covent Garden. Tube: Covent Garden. Emerging as the hottest proving ground for new designers, Covent Garden is filled with small boutiques vending off-the-wall fashion. Much of the clothing is too outrageous to be worn anywhere but to the clubs, but the tamer stuff is what everyone will be wearing in a few years. The small boutiques are inexpensive when compared to the pieces created by the top rank of designers, but compared to chain stores, boutique clothing is still insanely expensive. As always, look for sales and clearances.

Bond St. Tube: Bond St. The heart of couture and unjustifiable excess. Old and New Bond St., extending south of Oxford St., are the most prestigious shop addresses in all of London. Old Bond street is particularly glitzy—a cloudy Rodeo Drive. For more on Bond St. and its Mayfair surroundings, see p. 153.

King's Rd. Tube: Sloane Sq. Extending west of Sloane Sq., this busy Chelsea street is lined with small stores offering everything from high fashion to cheap knockoffs of so-called American fashion (mostly jeans, Hawaiian prints, and bowling shirts). The stores here are generously interspersed with pubs and cafés, making it a less concentrated dose for true shopaholics.

Camden High St. Tube: Camden Town. Filled with shoe stores, the shops here are geared to the Sunday market crowds looking for cheap used jeans and leather jackets. Some stores sell trend-conscious new clothes as well, making it a good place to pick up clubwear at reasonable prices. Still, it's a good policy to compare the prices here with those at the chain stores found along Oxford St. and Covent Garden before buying anything.

■ Department Stores

Fortnum & Mason, 181 Piccadilly, W1 (tel. 734 8040). Tube: Green Park or Piccadilly Circus. Liveried clerks vend expensive foods in red-carpeted and chandeliered halls at this renowned establishment. Look out for rare free samples of the food court's exquisite wares. Queen Victoria naturally turned to Fortnum & Mason when she wanted to send Florence Nightingale 250 lbs. of beef tea for the Crimean field hospitals. The upper floors carry clothing, jewelry, shoes, etc., in a posh and truly sophisticated setting. The St. James Restaurant on the 4th floor serves a mean high tea (see Tea, p. 132). Expensive but fun to sniff around. Open Mon.-Sat. 9:30am-6pm.

Harrods, 87-135 Brompton Rd., SW3 (tel. 730 1234). Tube: Knightsbridge. Simply put, this is *the* store in London, perhaps the world—English gentlemen keeping a stiff upper lip in African jungles and savannahs dream of the Harrods food court. Their humble motto *Omnia Omnibus Ubique* ("All things for all people, everywhere") says it all. They can do everything from finding you a live rhinoceros to arranging your funeral. They stock more than 450 kinds of cheese, and pour an elegant afternoon tea. Harrods' sales (mid-July and after Christmas) get so crazy that the police brings out a whole detail and combat operations truck to deal with the shoppers. Shorts, ripped clothing, and backpacks are forbidden in this quasi-museum of luxury—nevertheless, the downstairs seems like a tourist convention at times. Elegance has a price, though the improbable downstairs grocery store offers the cheapest can of Coca-cola (40p, 55p for the immense 500mL Supercan) anywhere in Knightsbridge. Elaborate security cameras in the ceiling follow suspicious looking shoppers. Luxury washrooms (£1) offer fluffy towels and an almost unimaginable selection of fragrant washes and wipes—an affordable extravagance. Open Mon.-Tues., Sat. 10am-6pm, Wed.-Fri. 10am-7pm.

Harvey Nichols, 109-125 Knightsbridge, SW3 (tel. 235 5000). Tube: Knightsbridge. The trendiest of London's huge department stores, also one of the most expensive. Known for wacky and avant-garde window displays which change frequently. Stupendous sale in early July. Outrageous prices at downstairs bar *Foundations* (cocktails from £6) and the chic, well-known 5th floor cafe (entrees from £10) should give you an idea of how deep most Harvey Nichols shoppers' pockets are. Clothing is priced accordingly. Open Mon.-Tues., Thurs.-Fri. 10am-7pm, Wed. 10am-8pm, Sat. 10am-6pm.

John Lewis, 278-306 Oxford St. (tel. 629 7711). Tube: Oxford Circus. Giant department store offering merchandise in various price ranges. Sister shop, **Peter Jones**

on Sloane Sq. (tel. 730 3434; tube: Sloane Sq.) is equally wide-ranging. Both have a price guarantee similar to Selfridges's. Both open Mon.-Wed., Fri. 9:30am-6pm, Thurs. 10am-8pm, Sat. 9am-6pm. Accepts only their own credit card.

Liberty's of London, south of Oxford Circus on Regent St. and Great Marlborough St. (tel. 734 1234). Tube: Oxford Circus. A prime exponent of the 19th-century arts and crafts movement, this is the home of the famous Liberty prints, ranging in form from entire bolts of fabric to silk ties. The faux-Tudor building also houses a large variety of Eastern imports. They host giant, store-altering sales in early July and December. Open Mon.-Tues., Fri.-Sat. 9:30am-6pm, Wed. 10am-6pm, Thurs. 9:30am-7:30pm. Major credit cards.

Marks & Spencer, 458 Oxford St., W1 (tel. 935 7954). Tube: Bond St. Also at 113 Kensington High St. (tel. 938 3711); 85 Kings Rd. (tel. 376 5634; tube: Sloane Sq.) and literally hundreds of other locations. Brits know it as Marks & Sparks or M & S. Sells British staples in a classy but value-conscious manner. The clothes err on the side of frumpy. Everyone British, including Margaret Thatcher, buys her underwear here. Open Mon.-Wed., Sat. 9am-7pm, Thurs.-Fri. 9am-8pm. Hours vary slightly in more far-flung regions. Major credit cards.

Selfridges, 400 Oxford St. (tel. 629 1234). Tube: Bond St. An enormous pseudo-Renaissance building with a vast array of fashions, homewares, foods, and a tourist office. The food hall is amazing, with cheeses, meats, produce, a deli, a bakery, and even an oyster bar. Look out for free samples. The kind folks at Selfridges will refund the difference on any item found for less elsewhere. Huge mid-July sale. Open Mon.-Wed., Fri.-Sat. 9:30am-7pm, Thurs. 9:30am-8pm. Major credit cards.

■ Clothing

Smaller stores in London also cluster around the main shopping districts. Some of the most revolutionary new styles are first offered in these boutiques, and some of the best bargains are to be found here.

Aquascutum, 9-13 Brompton Rd., SW3 (tel. 581 4444). Tube: Knightsbridge. Vends classic English tailoring with a modern twist. Usually absurdly expensive, the prices fall during the winter sale (early Jan.) and summer sale (June to late July). Also at 100 Regent St., W1 (tel. 734 6090; tube: Oxford Circus). Open Mon.-Thurs. 10am-6pm, Wed.-Fri. 10am-7pm., Sat. 9:30am-7pm.

Big Apple, 96 Kensington High St., W8 (tel. 376 1404). Tube: High St. Kensington. Also at 70 Neal St., WC2 (tel. 497 0165; tube: Covent Garden). Tiny t-shirts and spandex minis galore. Open Mon.-Sat. 10am-7:30pm, Sun. 11am-7pm.

Cornucopia, 12 Upper Tachbrook St., SW1 (tel. 828 5752). Tube: Victoria. The grande dame of period clothing shops, selling women's attire from 1910-1960. Ball gowns start at £35. Open Mon.-Sat. 11am-6pm.

The Designer Second Hand Store, 132 Long Acre, WC2 (tel. 240 8765). Tube: Covent Garden. Used clothes in good condition bearing labels of the world's most famous designers. Some men's stuff, but the real bargains are among the more extensive collection of women's wear. Open Mon.-Wed., Fri. 11am-7pm, Thurs. 11am-8pm, Sat. 10:30am-7pm, Sun. noon-6pm.

Hennes & Mauritz (aka H&M or Hennes), 261-271 Regents St., W1 (tel. 493 4004). Tube: Oxford Circus. At the intersection of Oxford and Regent St. This discount chain sells fairly fashion-conscious, inexpensive women's wear. Somewhere on these 2 floors is an inexpensive piece to suit every taste. Open Mon.-Wed., Fri.-Sat. 10am-6:30pm, Thurs. 10am-8pm, Sun. noon-6pm.

Kensington Market, 49-53 Kensington High St., W8. Tube: High St. Kensington. 3 floors of stalls with some vintage threads, some fanciable clubwear, some military surplus, and much that is cheap. Permanent shops and a punky hair salon on the upper floor. Zandra Rhodes had a stall here in the 60s. Open Mon.-Sat. 10am-6pm.

Sam Walker, 41 Neal Street, WC2 (tel. 240 7800). Tube: Covent Garden. A wonderful, if expensive, collection of immaculately restored men's vintage clothing. Tears are mended and linings replaced. True, the prices here are higher than other vintage clothing shops, but so is quality, and a restored vintage corduroy blazer is still much cheaper than a new one. Also sells a line of own-make dress shoes. Offers a nice selection of funky cufflinks and tie-bars as well as sleeve garters. Open daily 10am-7:30pm.

Scotch House, 2 Brompton Rd., SW1 (tel. 581 2151). Tube: Knightsbridge. A luxurious collection of silky sweaters and Tartan woolens. A bespoke kilt will cost you £425, but more affordable duds are available around Christmas and from late June to mid-July during the very extensive sale. Also contains a **Burberry** store vending very expensive and well tailored menswear. Open Mon.-Tues., Thurs.-Fri. 9:30am-6pm, Wed. 9:30am-7pm, Sat. 9am-6pm.

Top Shop/Top Man, 214 Oxford St., W1 (tel. 636 7700). Tube: Oxford Circus. An absolute must-visit for a wannabe club kid on a budget. Multi-story megastore right at Oxford Circus with the trendiest of inexpensive fashions for men and women (in the basement), with something to suit one's flamboyant side. Aspiring Topmen must be sure to spend some time perusing the sale racks on the first floor towards the back. These racks often have fabrics and cuts quite similar to the more expensive wares upstairs. Aspiring Topwomen should also check out the less inspiring sale racks in the basement. Open Mon.-Wed., Fri.-Sat. 10am-7pm, Thurs. 10am-8pm, Sun. noon-6pm. Major credit cards.

These **chain stores** specialize in relatively affordable, yet very trendy, duds for lads and ladies. They appeal to a younger crowd interested in sleek, tight clothing. In truth, there is not much that is particularly English about the following stores—they take their cues from European and other trends in international fashion. We have given several of the larger locations for each of the listings; check the phone books for smaller stores which may be nearer. Beware that not all of the smaller locations have both the men's and women's lines.

Burton Menswear and Dorothy Perkins, 379 Oxford St., W1 (tel. 495 6282). Tube: Bond St. In the West One shopping center which straddles the tube stop. Burton handles conservative casualwear for men, while Dorothy takes care of slightly less sober (but still responsible) casuals for women. Many other locations. Open Mon.-Wed., Fri.-Sat. 10am-7pm, Thurs. 10am-8pm, Sun. noon-5pm.

French Connection, 99-103 Long Acre, WC2 (tel. 379 5650). Tube: Covent Garden. Also at 249-251 Regent St., W1 (493 3124; tube: Oxford Circus); 140-144 King's Rd., SW3 (tel. 225 3302; tube: Sloane Sq.). An unfailingly current collection of men's and women's wear. As the name implies, the cuts and fabrics are heavily influenced by the latest Gallic fashions. Prices are a bit upscale, but there are some less expensive pieces. There is a huge sale during mid-July. Open Mon.-Wed., Sat. 10am-7pm, Thurs.-Fri. 10am-8pm, Sun. 11am-6pm.

Kookai, 5-7 Brompton Rd., SW3 (tel. 581 9633). Tube: Knightsbridge. Also at 362 Oxford St., W1 (tel. 499 4564; tube: Bond St.). Also at 123 Kensington High St., W8 (tel. 938 1427); 27a Sloane Sq., SW1 (tel. 730 6903); 124 King's Rd., SW1 (tel. 589 0120; tube: Sloane Sq.); numerous other locations. Slinky, sexy women's clothes at almost reasonable prices. Stores throb with funky dance tunes. Hip, yet elegant. Open Mon.-Sat. 10am-7pm, Sun. noon-5pm. Major credit cards.

Jigsaw, 31 Brompton Rd., SW3 (tel. 584 6226). Tube: Knightsbridge. Also at 21 Long Acre, WC2 (tel. 240 3855; tube: Covent Garden); 65 Kensington High St., W8 (tel. 937 3573); 124 Kings Rd., SW3 (tel. 589 5083; tube: Sloane Sq.); and numerous others. Purveyors of somewhat expensive women's threads in a variety of luscious fabrics and muted, subtle colors. Some stores have smallish men's departments as well. The Covent Garden location has a large men's only store next door. Open Mon.-Sat. 10am-7pm, Sun. noon-5pm.

Next, 33 Brompton Rd., SW3 (tel. 584 0619). Tube: Knightsbridge. Also at 327 Oxford St., W1 (tel. 494 3646; tube: Oxford Circus); 54 Kensington High St., W8 (tel. 938 4211). A sort of cross between The Limited and J. Crew—bright, sporty, almost whimsical casual clothes for a wide range of ages. Open Mon.-Tues. Thurs.-Sat. 10am-6:30pm, Wed. 10am-7:30pm. Major credit cards.

Warehouse, just off Oxford St. at Unit G13/F12, The Plaza, Oxford St., W1 (tel. 436 4179). Tube: Oxford Circus and Bond St. Also at 24 Long Acre, WC2 (tube: Covent Garden); 63-67 Kensington High St., W8; 96 King's Rd., SW3, and 19-21 Argyll St. Stretchy pants with flared bottoms in pastels, neons, and of course basic black.

Women's clothes only, fashionable stuff at fair prices. Open Mon.-Wed., Fri.-Sat. 10am-7pm, Thurs. 10am-8pm. Major credit cards except Diners Club.

Some of the better-known British fashion designers and their ateliers:

Hyper-Hyper, 26-40 Kensington High St., W8 (tel. 938 4343). Tube: High St. Kensington. A mall of small boutiques exhibiting the work of more than 70 young British designers. Garments sold here have appeared in the pages of *Vogue* and *Elle*. So icy the store needs no air-conditioning. Open Mon.-Wed., Fri.-Sat. 10am-6pm, Thurs. 10am-7pm.

Paul Smith, 23 Avery Row, W1 (tel. 493 1287), off of Brook St. Tube: Bond St. The seconds and out-of-season outlet for the witty yet elegant menswear store. Emphasis here tends towards stylish casual wear, with savings of up to 50% off regular retail prices. Open Mon.-Wed., Fri. 10:30am-6:30pm, Thurs. 10:30am-7pm, Sat. 10am-6pm.

▓ Shoes

Devout shoppers come to London for shoes, where they find the coolest soles at decent prices. Shoe venders take a cue from Henry Ford—you can get a shoe in any color so long as it's black. Actually, this a bit of an overstatement—faux black and white snakeskin, fur, and pastelly patent leather often adorn newer styles.

Dr. Martens Dept. Store Ltd., 1-4 King St. WC2 (tel. 497 1460). Tube: Covent Garden. Tourist-packed 6-tiered mega-store showcases watches, sunglasses, candles, a café, and a hair salon, but surprisingly few Dr. Martens shoes, which can be bought in less chaotic environs elsewhere. Open Mon.-Wed., Fri.-Sat. 10am-7pm, Thurs. 10am-8pm, Sun. noon-6pm. Major credit cards.

Dolci's, 333 Oxford St., W1 (tel. 493 9626). Tube: Bond St. Also at 40 Kensington High St., W8. Just as hip as Shelly's (see below), but also stocks more conventional styles, foul-weather footwear, and dressy pumps. Very popular with young hipsters on a budget. Open Mon.-Wed., Fri. 10am-7pm, Thurs. 10am-8pm, Sat. 9:30am-6:30pm, Sun. noon-6pm. Major credit cards.

Office, 43 Kensington High St., W8 (tel. 937 7022). Tube: High St. Kensington. Also at 57 Neal St., WC2 (tel. 379 1896; tube: Covent Garden); men's shoes only at 59 So. Molton St., W1 (tel. 493 0051; tube: Bond St.); and 221 Camden High St., NW1 (tel. 267 9873; tube: Camden Town). Ultra-trendy mid-range chain patronized by chic black-clad types. Carries well-known designers and a hip collection of own-label stompers as well. Open daily 9:30am-6:30pm.

Red or Dead, 36 Kensington High St., W8 (tel. 937 3137). Tube: High St. Kensington. Also at 33 Neal St., WC2 (tel. 379 7571; tube: Covent Garden); 1 Sloane St. (tel. 235 1335; tube: Sloane Sq.) They were hawking platforms long before the 70s revival. Not for budgeteers. Also carries a line of predominately spandex and polyester clothes. Open Mon.-Wed., Fri. 9:30am-6pm, Thurs. and Sat. 9:30am-7pm.

Airwair

Dr. Marten was once Dr. Maerten. Although the omnipresent clodhoppers are identified with the U.K., they were born a half-century ago in war-time Munich. Dr. Klaus Maerten designed them after a skiing accident so that he might walk more comfortably. The air-cushioned shoes were marketed to elderly women with foot trouble all over Germany. The shoes gained in popularity, and soon production was extended to Britain. With the move across the Channel, the name lost an "e," and what was once a healing sole became a youth icon. At the same time, the less stylish "bovver boots" became popular among the working men and women of England, and the Marten invasion was complete. The shoes have been spotted on everyone from Pete Townsend and the Clash to Madonna and Pope John Paul II.

Shelly's, 159 Oxford St., W1 (tel. 437 5842). Tube: Oxford Circus. Also at 14-18 Neal St., WC2 (tel. 240 3726; tube: Covent Garden); 40 Kensington High St., W8 (tel. 938 1082; tube: Kensington High St.); 124b King's Rd., SW3 (tel. 581 5537; tube: Sloane Sq.). Shelly's reverses the preppie ethic of sensible shoes at outrageous prices—they offer outrageous shoes at sensible prices. Always displaying the most current styles. Open Mon.-Wed., Fri.-Sat. 9:15am-6:15pm, Thurs. 9:15am-7:15pm, Sun. noon-6pm. Major credit cards.

■ Bookstores

In London, even the chain bookstores are wonders. An exhaustive selection of book-shops lines **Charing Cross Rd.** between Tottenham Ct. Rd. and Leicester Sq. and many vend secondhand paperbacks. Cecil Ct., near Leicester Sq., is a treasure trove of tiny shops with specialty bookstores for dance, Italian, travel, etc. Establishments along Great Russell St. stock esoteric and specialized books on any subject from Adorno to the Zohar.

You may find maps and other travel literature at **Stanford's,** 12 Long Acre (tel. 836 1321; tube: Covent Garden; open Mon. and Sat. 10am-6pm, Tues.-Fri. 9am-7pm); also try the travel sections at the larger bookstores (Waterstones and Dillons) and the YHA shop in Covent Garden (see p. 78).

GIANT BOOKSTORES

Dillons, Trafalgar Sq., Grand Building, WC2 (tel. 839 4411). Tube: Charing Cross or Leicester Sq. This is the branch open latest, the largest is at 82 Gower St., WC2 (tel. 636 1577). Numerous other branches. One of London's best. Strong on academic subjects, particularly history and politics. Fair selection of reduced-price and sec-ondhand books, plus classical CDs and tapes. Open Mon.-Sat. 10am-9pm, Sun. noon-6pm.

Foyles, 119 Charing Cross Rd., WC1 (tel. 437 5660). Tube: Tottenham Ct. Rd. or Leicester Sq. A giant warehouse of books—you'll get lost. Open Mon.-Sat. 9am-6pm, Thurs. 9am-7pm. Major credit cards.

Hatchards, 187 Piccadilly, W1 (tel. 439 9921). Tube: Green Park. Oldest of Lon-don's bookstores. Come in for 10min., stay for 2hr. Open Mon.-Sat. 9am-6pm, Sun. noon-6pm. Major credit cards.

Waterstone's, 121-125 Charing Cross Rd., WC1 (tel. 434 4291), next door to Foyles. Tube: Leicester Sq. It's a chain, but a good one. It even carries the New York Review of Books. Many branches including 193 Kensington High St., W8 (tel. 937 8432); 101 Old Brompton Rd., SW7 (tel. 581 8522). Open Mon.-Sat. 9:30am-8pm, Sun. noon-6pm. Major credit cards.

ANTIQUE AND USED BOOKSTORES

Bell, Book and Radmall, 4 Cecil Ct., WC2 (tel. 240 2161). Tube: Leicester Sq. A small antiquarian bookstore with a zippy staff, an exceptional selection of Ameri-can and British first editions, and an impressive supply of sci-fi and detective nov-els. Open Mon.-Fri. 10am-5:30pm, Sat. 11am-4:30pm. Major credit cards.

Bookmongers, 439 Coldharbour La., SW9 (tel. 738 4225). Tube: Brixton. A second-hand bookstore with a healthy selection of works by African and Caribbean authors. Significant gay and lesbian novels section, and a section of modern classics by women authors. Open Mon.-Sat. 10:30am-6:30pm. No credit cards.

Harrington Bros., 253 Kings Road, SW (tel. 352 5689) Tube: Sloane Sq. Head west along Kings Rd. from Sloane Sq. Not much is affordable here, but browsing through such a wonderful collection of first editions is a pleasure (and free). Open daily 10am-6pm.

Maggs Brothers Ltd., 50 Berkeley Sq., W1 (tel. 493 7160). Tube: Green Park. A bib-liophile's paradise housed in a haunted (so the story goes) 18th-century mansion. Tremendous selection of 19th-century travel narratives, illuminated manuscripts, militaria, orientalia, maps, and autographs. Open Mon.-Fri. 9:30am-5pm. Major credit cards.

Skoob Books, 15-17 Sicilian Ave., Southampton Row and Vernon Pl., WC1 (tel. 405 0030). Tube: Holborn. The best used bookstore in Bloomsbury; academic and general interest. Students receive a 10% discount. Open Mon.-Sat. 10:30am-6:30pm. Major credit cards.

Southeran's of Sackville Street, 2-5 Sackville St., W1 (tel. 439 6151). Tube: Piccadilly Circus. Founded in 1815, Southeran's has established itself as an institution of literary London. Dickens frequented these unnervingly silent stacks, and the firm handled the sale of his library after his death in 1870. Strong departments include architecture and literary first editions. If you want to know how people traveled before the *Let's Go* era, check out their antiquarian travel narratives. Not cheap, but museum-like. Open Mon.-Fri. 9:30am-6pm, Sat. 10am-4pm (closed Sat. preceding major bank holidays).

ART BOOKS

Dillons Arts Bookshop, 8 Long Acre, WC2 (tel. 836 1359). Tube: Leicester Sq. or Covent Garden. This branch of Dillon's carries a very browsable selection of art books. Covers the performing arts as well as poetry, art theory, art history, and design. Open Mon.-Sat. 9:30am-10pm, Sun. noon-6pm.

National Theatre Bookshop, South Bank Centre, SE1 (tel. 928 2033 ext. 600). Tube: Waterloo. The widest selection in London for plays and books about theater. Open Mon.-Sat. 10am-10:45pm.

Offstage Theatre and Film Bookstore, 37 Chalk Farm Rd. (tel. 485 4996). Tube: Chalk Farm. A theater converted into bookstore that serves as an actors' hangout. Ground floor houses new theater, film, and cultural literature, downstairs offers used books and scripts. Open daily 10am-6pm.

Pleasures of Past Times, 11 Cecil Ct., WC2 (tel. 836 1142). Tube: Leicester Sq. A friendly, fascinating shop crammed with the stuff of youthful enchantment: early children's books with exquisite color plates, adventure stories, fairy tales, antique postcards, Victorian valentines, and other vintage juvenalia. Open Mon.-Fri. 11am-2:30pm and 3:30-5:45pm, Sat. by appointment. Major credit cards.

Samuel French's, 52 Fitzroy St., W1 (tel. 387 9373). Tube: Warren St. Deals in books on the theater. Open Mon.-Fri. 9:30am-5:30pm. Major credit cards.

Thomas Heneage & Co., 42 Duke St., SW1 (tel. 930 9223). Tube: Green Park. A truly outstanding collection of art books. Close to Christie's. Open Mon.-Fri. 10am-6pm. Major credit cards.

Zwemmers, 24 Litchfield St., WC2 (tel. 379 7886). Tube: Leicester Sq. A multi-store art book empire, headquartered at the Litchfield St. The store here, just east of Charing Cross Rd., specializes in books on art, architecture, and design. A Stone's throw to the south at 80 Charing Cross Rd., the focus is on graphics, film, and photography. The final branch in the immediate vicinity is at 72 Charing Cross Rd., which sells diverse offerings published by the Oxford University Press. All three open Mon.-Fri. 9:30am-6pm, Sat. 10am-6pm.

SPECIAL INTERESTS

Angel Bookshop, 102 Islington High St., N1 (tel. 226 2904). Tube: Angel. A well-read staff and a nice selection make this small bookstore worth checking out if you're in Islington for the market or for dinner. Open Mon.-Sat. 9:30am-6pm.

Bookshop Islington Green, 76 Upper St., N1 (tel. 359 4699). Tube: Angel. Small store with excellent selection of paperbacks and pleasant staff. Open Mon.-Sat. 10am-10pm, Sun. noon-6pm.

Books for Cooks, 4 Blenheim Crescent, W11 (tel. 221 1992 or 221 8102). Tube: Ladbroke Grove. The definitive cookbook shop. Titles range from *Classic Austrian Cooking* to *Exotic Cuisine of Mauritus*. Cuisines of many countries are covered with extensive works on Italy and France. Wholefood and vegan section. Budget cookery section with secondhand books. Test kitchen in the rear serves samples from different books. Open Mon.-Sat. 9:30am-6pm. Major credit cards.

Compendium, 234 Camden High St., NW1 (tel. 485 8944). Tube: Camden Town. A good general selection, but specializes in postmodern literature, the left, occult, and the all-around avant-garde. "Male fiction" shelved apart from "Women's fiction." Open Mon.-Sat. 10am-6pm, Sun. noon-6pm.

Gay's the Word, 66 Marchmont St., WC1N 1AB (tel. 278 7654). Tube: Russell Sq. Widest stock of gay and lesbian literature in England. Open Mon.-Wed., Fri.-Sat. 10am-6pm, Thurs. 10am-7pm, Sun. 2-6pm. (see Bisexual, Gay, and Lesbian London, p. 261.)

Guanghwa, 7 Newport Pl., WC2 (tel. 437 3737). Tube: Leicester Sq. The sweet smell of incense enhances the exotic feel of this bookstore, which specializes in Eastern literature, dictionaries, and periodicals, with a smattering of English offerings. Open Mon.-Sat. 10:30am-7pm.

Kilburn Book Shop, 8 Kilburn Bridge, Kilburn High Rd., NW6 (tel. 328 7071). Tube: Kilburn. Features politically correct reading material. Open Mon.-Sat. 9:30am-5:30pm. Major credit cards except AmEx.

Silver Moon, 68 Charing Cross Rd., WC2 (tel. 836 7906). Tube: Leicester Sq. A radical feminist bookstore and the largest women's bookshop in Europe. An exhaustive selection of books by and about women (fiction by women, non-fiction about women written by either sex), the largest lesbian department in Britain, a complete stock of all Virago books, and a nice travel section. Open Mon.-Wed., Fri.–Sat. 10am-6:30pm, Thurs. 10am-8pm, Sun. noon-6pm. Major credit cards.

Sportspages, Caxton Walk at 94-96 Charing Cross Rd., WC2 (tel. 240 9604). Tube: Leicester Sq. Specializes in books for both sports fans and professionals on practically every sport imaginable. Also sports an impressive selection of the merchandise of local football and rugby clubs, from jerseys to videotapes of classic matches. A chalk board posts recent event results. Open Mon.-Fri. 9:30am-7pm. Major credit cards.

Timbuktu Bookshop, in the Black Cultural Archives, 378 Coldharbour Ln., SW9 (tel. 737 2770). Tube: Brixton. Features a small collection of both academic and spiritual books relating to people of African origin in the diaspora. Also carries local crafts and African clothing. Open (usually) Mon.-Sat. 10am-6pm.

Vintage Magazine Market, 39-43 Brewer St., on the corner of Brewer and Great Windmill St. near Piccadilly Circus (tel. 439 8525). 50s magazines and film posters, hip postcards and t-shirts clutter this store. A good stop for a last minute birthday need. Open Mon.-Wed. 10am-7pm, Thurs.-Sat. 10am-10pm, Sun. noon-8pm. Major credit cards.

▓ Record Stores

If a record can't be found in London, it's probably not worth your listening time. London, for years the hub of the English music scene, has a record collection to match. Corporate megaliths **HMV, Virgin,** and **Tower Records** fall over each other claiming to be the world's largest record store. Don't expect any bargains or rarities, and remember that when it comes to records, "import" means "rip-off." CDs will seem expensive to Americans. The best bargains, just as in the states, are found in vinyl, although the record market is frustratingly efficient. At **Camden Town, Brixton, Ladbroke Grove,** or Soho's **Hanway Street** record stores tempt collectors and intimidate browsers with rare vinyl and memorabilia at rock star prices. The shops surrounding the intersection of **D'Arblay** and **Berwick Streets** in Soho provide listening booths for DJs to sample the latest 12-in. singles. Dig deep in the bargain bins. Think about how British tastes differ from your own, and shop accordingly: early LPs and singles by British bands aren't as rare and dear here as they are elsewhere, and the endearing popularity of jazz is also reflected in the wide collections of many stores.

Black Market, 25 D'Arblay St., W1 (tel. 437 0478). Tube: Oxford Circus. This Soho institution flirts with "Hard Rock Cafe" tourist trap oblivion by hawking logoed merchandise, but if you're looking for the latest hip-hop, techno, house, or garage 12-inches, they've got the goods. Listening booths. Open Mon.-Sat. 11am-7pm.

Cheapo Cheapo Records, 53 Rupert St., W12 (tel. 437 8272). Tube: Piccadilly Circus. A warren of 70s and early 80s records at rock bottom prices. Open Mon.-Fri. 11am-10pm, Sat. 10:30am-10:30pm.

Honest Jon's, 276-8 Portobello Rd., W10 (tel. (0181) 969 9822). Tube: Ladbroke Grove. Newly refurbished but still fonkay. 276 holds an impressive jazz collection where Blakey, Parker, and Mingus are only the tip of the iceberg. 278 sports a wide selection of hip-hop LP's and some decent 12-inch singles, as well as funk holdings from A to Zapp. Collector prices, unfortunately. Open Mon.-Sat. 10am-6pm, Sun. 11am-5pm. Major credit cards.

Intoxica!, 231 Portobello Rd., W11 (tel. 229 8010). Tube: Ladbroke Grove. Enviable collection of surf-rock and rockabilly, with a smattering of punk and soul. All vinyl. Open Mon.-Fri. 10:30am-6:30pm, Sat. 10am-6:30pm, Sun. noon-4pm.

Music and Video Exchange, 229 Camden High St., NW1 (tel. 267 1898). Tube: Camden Town. Branch at 95 Berwick St., W8 (tel. 434 2939). Dirt-cheap 70s stuff in the basement. Strong offerings in rap (esp. old-school), acid jazz, and trip-hop. If your head is still throbbing from some house or techno groove, you can scratch that itch in the recently renovated house room. Open daily 10am-8pm.

Ufo Music, 18 Hanway St., W1 (tel. 636 1281). Tube: Tottenham Ct. Rd. Broad but shallow collection of indie, rock, pop, blues, jazz, and techno LPs and CDs. Open Mon.-Sat. 10am-6:30pm.

Out on the Floor, 10 Inverness, NW1 (tel. 267 5989). Tube: Camden Town. A well-stocked used-CD and vinyl shop. CDs from £7.50-12; vinyl £6 and up. Upstairs mostly jazz and funk, downstairs indie and new wave punk. Open Mon.-Fri. 11am-6pm, Sat.-Sun. 11am-7pm. Visa, MC, Access, Eurocard.

Red Records, 500 Brixton Rd., SW2 (tel. 274 5896). Tube: Brixton. Though it touts itself as "the Black Music Store of the 90s," Red Records' collection of jazz, hip-hop, reggae, soul, and garage will appeal to loose booties of all colors. Open Mon.-Sat. 9:30am-8pm, Sun. noon-4pm. Major credit cards.

Rhythm Records, 281 Camden High St., NW1 (tel. 267 0123). Tube: Camden Town. Modern, clean shop offers secondhand reggae, ska, and dub; proudly offers no top 40 discs at all. CDs begin at about £9. Open daily 10:30am-6:30pm.

Rough Trade, 130 Talbot Rd., W11 (tel. 229 8541). Tube: Ladbroke Grove. Birthplace of the legendary independent record label. Original snapshots of Johnny Rotten are casually tacked up on the wall next to old posters advertising concerts for Rough Trade bands like The Smiths, The Raincoats, and the X-Ray Spex. Another London Branch at 16 Neal's Yard (tel. 240 0105; tube: Covent Garden). Open Mon.-Sat. 10am-6:30pm. Major credit cards.

Sister Ray, 94 Berwick St., W1 (tel. 287 8385, fax 287 1087). Tube: Piccadilly Circus or Tottenham Ct. Road. The loud music competes with the shouts from nearby Berwick St. Market. Not as much Velvet Underground as you'd expect, but a strong collection of 90s indie and 70s rock and punk. Open Mon.-Sat. 10:30am-7pm. Major credit cards.

Soho Records, 3 Hanway St., W1 (tel. 580 4805). Tube: Tottenham Ct. Road. Lots of 60s and 70s memorabilia gems, and priced accordingly. 3 for £5 bargain section is an checklist of sensitive 70s sounds—Cat Stevens, James Taylor, Jim Croce, Carole King, and, oddly enough, 2 Live Crew. Open Mon.-Sat. 10am-7pm.

▓ Specialty Shops

Hamley's, 188-189 Regent St., W1 (tel. 734 3161). Tube: Oxford Circus. Even safer than giving a wee tot a plastic bag to play with is taking them to Hamley's. London's largest toy shop offers 6 floors of every conceivable toy and game, not to mention an arcade, soda fountain, and sandwich bar. Bring a leash for the kids. Open Mon.,Wed., and Fri. 10am-7pm, Thurs. 10am-8pm, Sat. 9:30am-7pm, Sun. noon-6pm. Major credit cards.

Honour, 86 Lower Marsh, SE1 (tel. 401 8220). Tube: Waterloo. One of the few places in England where rubber isn't just another word for an eraser: the first floor stocks wigs and all sorts of rubber and PVC gear for fetish trendies, the second floor features the sort of bondage gear you wouldn't wear to a club. A good resource for information on upcoming gothic, pagan, and fetish happenings. Open Mon.-Fri. 10:30am-7pm, Sat. 11:30am-5pm.

Into You, 144 St. John St., EC1 (tel. 253 5085). Tattooing, body-piercing, and related literature and items. If pain is pleasure for you, and permanency doesn't bother you, then take the plunge. Open Tues.-Fri. noon-7pm, Sat. noon-6pm.

Mrs. Price's Junk Shop, 2 White Conduit Rd., NW1 (tel. 833 3518). Tube: Angel. Exit station, cross street to Chapel Market, then right onto White Conduit. Even Fred and Lamont Sanford would be dismayed by this place. Piles of junk and other stuff surround old bookcases and chests. You might get lucky and find something swell. Open daily 10am-6pm.

The New Power Generation, 21 Chalk Farm Rd., NW1 (tel. 267 7951). Tube: Chalk Farm. One man's profit-making shrine to himself and his creations. The first floor sells the owner's (artist formerly known as Prince) merchandise, like symbol-adorned purple goblets; the basement sells Prince CDs; and at the top you'll find a funky snack bar overlooking Chalk Farm Rd. A Prince interactive computer setup, as well as the former royalty's purple rain coat hanging in the café, makes this self-worshipping spot a trippy place to hang out. Everybody Gett Off. Open daily 10am-5:30pm.

G. Smith and Sons Snuff Shop, 74 Charing Cross Rd., WC2. Tube: Leicester Sq. Established in 1869 by George Smith, this is the main snuff shop in London. Buy a can of snuff for £4.50. A pocket tin (only 75p) will keep you sneezin' through London. They sell 1 ton each year, in addition to offering a host of pipes, lighters, and cigars from around the world. Open Mon.-Fri. 9am-6pm, Sat. 9:30am-5:30pm. Major credit cards.

Snow and Rock Ski and Mountain Specialists, 188 Kensington High St., W8 (tel. 937 0872). Tube: High St. Kensington. Small but adequate collection of ropes and climbing hardware, rock shoes, tents, packs, and camping gear. Also stocks a wide selection of expensive outerwear by North Face, Patagonia, and Berghaus. Downstairs has skis for those who dream of the Alps and in-line skates for sunnier, warmer London days. Open Mon.-Wed., Fri. 11am-6pm, Thurs. 11am-7pm, Sat. 9am-6pm, Sun. 11am-5pm.

■ Markets

STREET MARKETS

Time spent bopping around London's street markets means 99% perspiration and 1% inspiration. There are wonderful bargains and must-have gems thrown in with what seems like a bunch of awful garbage. No matter your budget, it is likely that you can find the perfect gift or knick-knack that you didn't know you needed somewhere in the miles of stalls which magically appear on market day. Remember, many prices (even posted ones) are merely a first offer—a clever bargainer can shave prices down with a bit of haggling.

London's markets attract all sorts of vendors. Many well-appointed shops lining the market streets (especially along **Portobello Rd.** and **Camden Passage**) offer extremely rare and expensive antiques. Next door, hastily-constructed stalls sell to the young and penniless looking for an absurdly cheap pair of used jeans or a vintage Ronson. Still other stalls display exotic wares appealing to immigrants who have retained a taste for traditional foods, music, and languages. In many of the markets listed below, all these stalls and more do business side by side, making the markets a wonderful place to see different types of people as well as goods.

Pages in parentheses feature comprehensive descriptions of the areas containing these markets. In all of these crowded markets, *watch out for pickpockets.*

Brick Lane, E1. Tube: Aldgate East. Market with a South Asian flair: food, rugs, spices, bolts of fabric, and strains of sitar. Open Sun. 6am-1pm (p. 188).

Brixton Market, Electric Ave., Brixton Station Rd. and Popes Rd., SW2. Tube: Brixton. Covered market halls and outdoor stalls sprawl out from the station. The wide selection of African and West Indian fruit, vegetables, fabrics, and records make Brixton one of the most vibrant, and hippest markets. Open Mon.-Tues., Thurs.-Sat. 8:30am-5:30pm, Wed. 8:30am-1pm (p. 194).

Camden Markets, by Regent's Canal and along Camden High St., NW1. Tube: Camden Town. One of the most popular, and therefore crowded, places to find almost anything old or funky at discount prices. The best collection of stalls crops up on Sundays. Wed.-Sun. 9:30am-5:30pm (p. 162).

Camden Passage, Islington High St., N1. Tube: Angel. Right from the tube, then right on narrow, pedestrian-only Islington High St. One of the biggest antique markets, plus prints and drawings. Open Wed. and Sat. 8:30am-3pm (p. 162).

Greenwich Market, Covered Market Sq., SE10, near the Cutty Sark. BR: Greenwich. A popular crafts market in a pastoral setting frequented by London lawyers on day-trips down the river. On Greenwich High Rd., the Open-Air Second-hand Market proffers vintage print dresses. Open Sat.-Sun. 9am-6pm (p. 203).

Petticoat Lane, E1. Tube: Liverpool St., Aldgate, or Aldgate East. A London institution—street after street of stalls, mostly cheap clothing and household appliances. The real action begins at about 9:30am. Open Sun. 9am-2pm; starts shutting down around noon (p. 188).

Portobello Road, W11. Tube: Notting Hill Gate or Ladbroke Grove. High-quality antiques at high prices at the Notting Hill end of the street. A popular and very old London market, immortalized by Paddington Bear. Antique market Sat. 7am-5pm. Clothes market Fri.-Sat. 8am-3pm (p. 161).

Spitalfields Market, E1. Tube: Liverpool St. This soaring indoor market has a ceiling so high it feels like the great outdoors. A somewhat smaller market, this is the place to find a really special item at a reasonable price. Lots of fresh veggies and produce are sold here. Inside, beside the stalls, one will find small-scale Astro turf football pitches. Oi! (p. 188).

TRADE MARKETS

London's fresh produce comes in through massive wholesale markets. These markets don't exactly roll out the red carpet for visitors, but they have wall-to-wall atmosphere. You won't find a more fascinating place to have a pint at 6:30am than near the trading. The new **Billingsgate** market (tel. 987 1118; DLR: Canary Wharf or Poplar; open Tues.-Sat. 5:00-8:30am) removed its fishy smells from the old site by St. Magnus Martyr in the City. **Smithfield,** Charterhouse St., EC1 (tel. 248 0367; tube: Farringdon or Barbican; open Mon.-Fri. 5-9am), allegedly the largest meat market in the world, sells wholesale only. The market's name is derived from the "smooth field" upon which cattle were sold here in the mid-1800s. Pubs in the area wake up as early as the meat mongers and serve correspondingly flesh-filled breakfasts.

Bisexual, Gay, and Lesbian London

Travelers coming to London will be delighted by the range of London's very visible gay scene, which covers everything from the flamboyant to the cruisy to the mainstream. London presents a paradoxical mix of tolerance and homophobia. On the one hand, gay culture is so visible that an entire section of the general entertainment weekly *Time Out* is dedicated to Gay Listings; on the other, queer bashings and police arrests of cruisers are not uncommon occurrences.

Britain suffers from a number of regressive laws, most notably **Section 28,** which prohibits local governments from "promoting" homosexuality. Additionally, the age of consent law for male homosexuals is 18 (recently lowered from 21), in contrast to the age of consent for heterosexuals, which is 16. Another developing issue involves the National Health Secretary's recent move to ban lesbian mothers and single women from the NHS's artificial insemination treatment.

Despite this negative political climate, gay communities thrive in London. Heavily gay-populated areas like Earl's Court, Islington, and Soho attest to the liveliness of the social scene; London also boasts an active network of political groups. Section 28 sparked an immediate call to action within the gay community, and the spirit of political activism has not died out; July 1994 witnessed the launch of London's first Lesbian Avengers branch. The Labour Party has committed itself to repealing Section 28 as soon as it returns to power.

With so many bisexual-, gay-, and lesbian-specific **periodicals** in London, it's easy to educate yourself to the current concerns of London's many gay communities. *Capital Gay* (free) mostly caters to men. The *Pink Paper* is a free newspaper covering stories of interest to the pink community. Its bimonthly sister publication, *Shebang,* covers all aspects of lesbian life. *Gay Times* (£3) is the British counterpart to the *Advocate; Diva* (£2) is a monthly lesbian lifestyle magazine with an excellent mix of political and entertainment features, and good listings. Also check out *Time Out* each week for the latest from clubs to community groups.

▓ Information and Advice Lines

Bisexual Helpline: tel. (0181) 569 7500. Tues.-Wed. 7:30-9:30pm.
Jewish Lesbian and Gay Line: tel. 706 3123. Mon. and Thurs. 7-10pm.
Lesbian and Gay Switchboard: tel. 837 7324. A 24-hr. advice, support, and information service. Minicom facility for the deaf.
Lesbian Line: tel. 251 6911. Advice, information, and support. Mon. 6-10pm, Tues.-Thurs. 7-10pm, Fri. 3-6pm.

▓ Bars, Cafés, Pubs, and Restaurants

The Box, Seven Dials, 32-34 Monmouth St., WC2 (tel. 240 5828). Tube: Covent Garden. Small, intimate, and stylish gay bar and brasserie in a removed section of Covent Garden. Popular women-only "Girl Bar" every Sunday attracts nice girls, entice girls, shock girls, frock girls, cute girls, and boot girls. Be a part of the scene and listen to the DJs' funky, eclectic mixes for only £1. Open Mon.-Sat. 11am-11pm, Sun. 7pm-midnight.
Balans, 60 Old Compton St., W1 (tel. 437 5212). Tube: Leicester Square. Fiery flower arrangements and feral zebra-print lampshades create a ruthlessly glamorous ambience for the mostly gay, male clientele in this brasserie/bar. Lots of veggie options, and it never closes. Another branch at 239 Old Brompton Rd. (tel. 244 8838).

The Black Cap, 171 Camden High St., NW1 (tel. 485 1743). Tube: Camden Town. North London's best-known drag bar. Live shows every night attract a mixed male and female crowd. When the shows aren't on, a DJ plays top 40. Especially crowded Sunday afternoon. Open Mon-Thurs. 9pm-2am, Fri.-Sat. 9pm-3am, Sun. noon-3pm and 7pm-midnight. Cover Tues.-Sat. £2-3.

Comptons of Soho, 53 Old Compton St., W1 (tel. 437 4445). Tube: Leicester Sq. or Piccadilly Circus. Soho's "official" gay pub, always busy with a large crowd of all ages. Horseshoe-shaped bar encourages the exchange of meaningful glances. The upstairs offers a mellower scene, where patrons can gaze at a big screen TV instead of each other. Open Mon.-Sat. noon-11pm, Sun. noon-10:30pm.

Colherine, 261 Old Brompton Rd. (tel. 373 9859). Tube: Earl's Court. Take a right out of the station, then another right at Old Brompton Rd. A center of the glam, glitz, and leather scene. A bit more hard-core than other local gay bars. Open daily noon-11pm; upstairs bar noon-midnight.

Drill Hall Women-Only Bar, 16 Chenies St., WC1 (tel. 631 1353). Tube: Goodge St. A much anticipated one-nighter located in the lobby of one of London's biggest alternative theatres. Dim lighting and red walls. Crowded and laid back. Open Mon. 6-11pm.

The Edge, 11 Soho Sq., W1 (tel. 439 1313). Tube: Tottenham Ct. Rd. Possibly the prime café/bar in which to pose and socialize in Soho; gay or straight, the clientele is uniformly gorgeous, particularly the ones spilling out onto the sidewalk tables. Purple walls, plenty of metal trim, and a brassy bar decorate the 2 floors inside. Pricey food served until 3pm. Open Mon.-Sat. noon-1am, Sun. 2-10:30pm.

Earl's, 180 Earl's Court Rd. (tel. 835 1826). Tube: Earl's Court. Arch Puritan Oliver Cromwell himself was reportedly born in this pub that now hosts male strippers several nights a week. Gay and straight crowd. Pub open Mon.-Sat. 4pm-midnight, Sun. 2pm-midnight.

Freedom, 60-66 Wardour St., W1 (tel. 734 0071). Tube: Piccadilly or Leicester Sq. This hyper-trendy Soho haunt sports a basement theater and a predominantly gay crowd. Stark white walls are covered with arresting safe-sex propaganda. The pricey cocktails include the Heroin Rush (£4.75) and the Lesbian Nun (£4.25). Open daily 9am-3am. Cover after 11pm £3.

Fridge Café/Bar, Town Hall Parade, Brixton Hill SW2 (tel. 326 5100). Tube: Brixton. A refuge from the throbbing music and gyrating bodies of one of London's biggest nightclubs, this café's downstairs dancefloor becomes a women-only alternative to "Love Muscle" Saturdays 10pm-4am (cover £5). Open Mon.-Wed. 10am-11pm, Thurs. 10pm-2am, Fri.-Sat. 10am-4am.

Old Compton Café, 35 Old Compton St., W1 (tel. 439 3309). Tube: Leicester Sq. Open 24hr. in the geographic epicenter of Soho, this is *the* gay café. Tables and people (mostly twenty- and thirty-something males) overflow onto the street.

Substation Soho, Falconberg Ct., W1 (tel. 287 9608). Tube: Tottenham Ct. Rd. For gay men who find the Old Compton St. scene too tame, a cruisy, late-night testosterone fest—one popular one-nighter is the underwear-only grope-a-thon "Y Front" (changing rooms provided). Open Mon.-Thurs. 10pm-3am, Fri.-10pm-4am, Sat. 10:30pm-6am. If it's Sunday, you can't wait for 10pm, or you live south of the Thames, **Substation South,** 9 Brighton Terr., SW9 (tel. 732 2095; tube: Brixton) provides a similar scene in Brixton, but is open at 6pm, and on Sun. 6pm-1am. Cover for either £2-4.

Wilde About Oscar, 30-31 Philbeach Gdns., SW5 (tel. 373 1244 before 5pm or 835 1858 after 5pm). Tube: Earl's Ct. In the garden of a gay B&B. A definite splurge (entrees about £10), but it's worth it—dine in a manicured garden. Candles, flowers, and few tables make for an intimate dining encounter. Main courses are mostly French dishes. Open daily 7pm-midnight.

"Wow Bar," Saturdays from 8-11pm at Glasshouse St., Piccadilly (tel. (0956) 514574 for info and free membership). Tube: Piccadilly. Newly transplanted "lipstick lesbian" haunt whose former guests include Martina Navratilova. Cover before 9pm and for members £2; otherwise £3.

■ Dance Clubs

The Fridge, Town Hall Parade, Brixton Hill, SW2 (tel. 326 5100). Tube: Brixton. "Love Muscle" on Sat. is one of the biggest, most popular one-nighters in all of London. Totally packed. Lesbians have replaced thespians on the former theater's cavernous dance floor but women seeking refuge from the pumping house music can chill in the adjacent Fridge café/bar (see above). Open Fri.-Sat. 10pm-6am. £10 before midnight with flyer or after 3am; £12 otherwise.

Heaven, Villiers St., WC2 (tel. 839 3852), underneath The Arches. Tube: Embankment or Charing Cross (Villiers is off the Strand). Still the oldest and biggest gay disco in Europe. Three dance floors, high-tech lighting, pool tables, bars, and a capacity of nearly 4000 means you'll never get bored. Wed.'s "Fruit Machine" (10pm-3:30am; £4, after 11:30pm £6) sometimes features a drag bar. Bumping garage music Fri. 10pm-3:30am, Sat. 10pm-4am. Fri. £6, after 11:30pm £7.50. Sat. £7; after 11:30pm £8.

"G.A.Y.," at London Astoria 1 (Sat.), and 2 (Thurs. and Mon.), 157 Charing Cross Rd., WC2 (tel. 734 6963). Tube: Tottenham Ct. Rd. A 3-nights-a-week pop extravaganza amidst chrome and mirrored disco balls. Emphatically unpretentious clientele (very mixed, in both gender and orientation). Mon. 10:30pm-3am, Thurs. 10:30pm-4am, Sat. 10:30pm-5am. Mon. £3; £1 if student or with flyer. Thurs. £3, free with flyer. Sat. £6, with flyer £5.

"Mis-shapes", Sun. at the Crossbar, 257-259 Pentonville Rd., N1 (tel. 837 3218). Tube: King's Cross/St. Pancras. Most days, the Crossbar is a free nightspot for the backpackers crashing in the King's Cross area, but on Sundays it turns into a haven for other emphatically non-Beautiful People: "all those mis-shapen types bullied at school, and rejected by the fashion/attitude side of the gay scene." Music is a suitably non-trendy blend of cheese-pop and straight-ahead rock. Open 4pm-midnight. £3, after 8pm £4.

"Popstarz," Fridays at the Leisure Lounge, 121 Holborn, EC1 (tel. 738 2336). Tube: Chancery La. This weekly gay indie one-nighter proved so popular during its 1996 inception that it moved to this larger venue at the swank Leisure Lounge. Open 10pm-5am. £5, after 11pm £6. Student discount £1.

Turnmills, 63B Clerkenwell Rd., EC1 (tel. 250 3409). Tube: Farringdon. Walk up Turnmill St. and turn right onto Clerkenwell Rd. Sat. nights at 3am, "Trade" gets kickin' and keeps on kickin' until noon. Get there early or late to avoid long queues, or call and get an advance ticket. Open Fri.-Sat. 3am-noon. £10.

■ Shopping and Services

Gay's the Word, 66 Marchmont St., London WC1N 1AB (tel. 278 7654). Widest stock of gay and lesbian literature in England; mail order service available. Noticeboard, discussion groups, readings, coffee, and tea. Free newspapers provide info on other happenings. Open Mon.-Wed. and Fri.-Sat. 10am-6pm, Thurs. 10am-7pm, Sun. 2-6pm.

Clone Zone, 64 Old Compton St., W1 (tel. 287 3530). Tube: Piccadilly or Leicester Sq. Well-stocked shop for cards, books, club wear, and enough fatigues and biker gear to outfit 40% of the Village People. Sex toys and bondage gear in the basement. Also at 266 Old Brompton Rd. Both shops open Mon.-Sat. 10:30am-10:40pm, Sun. 1-6:40pm. AmEx, MC, Visa.

SH!, 46 Coronet St., N1 (tel. 613 5458). Tube: Old St. Head east on Old St. and turn left onto Pitfield St, Coronet St. will be off the right. A sex shop run by women, for women. Men cannot even get in unless escorted by a lady. Open Mon. and Wed.-Sat 11:30am-6:30pm.

Daytrippers

London is a splendid place to live for those who can get out of it.
—Lord Balfour, *Observer Sayings of the Week*, 1 Oct. 1944

■ Getting Out of It

Trains and Buses

In general, most sites of general interest are served by both rail and bus services. Buses tend to be cheaper and slower. For information on the cheapest way to get in and out of the city by bus or train, see Getting In and Out of London, p. 57.

Cars

The advantage of car travel is that you have a car. If three or four people pool resources, it's a cheap and quick way to traverse the Isles. Disadvantages include high gasoline prices, the unfamiliar laws and habits associated with foreign driving, and the heinous exhaust that results from lax British emissions standards. It's not our place to criticize cultural peculiarities, but it's pretty hard to say that Brits drive on the right side of the road. Be particularly cautious at roundabouts (rotary interchanges): give way to traffic from the right. British law requires drivers and front-seat passengers to wear seat belts; rear-seat passengers also should buckle up when belts are provided. Speed limits are always marked at the beginning of town areas; upon leaving, you'll see a circular sign with a slash through it, signaling the end of the speed restriction. Speed limits are strictly enforced, and note that many British roads are sinuous and single-track; drivers should use common sense.

   Hiring (renting) an automobile is the least expensive option if you drive for a month or less. For more extended travel, you might consider **leasing.** Rental prices are £150 to £300 a week with unlimited mileage plus VAT; for insurance reasons, renters are required to be over 21 and under 70. **Europe by Car** (see below), however, will rent to younger people if the paperwork is done, in advance, in the U.S. All plans require sizable deposits unless you pay by credit card. Make sure you understand insurance before you rent; some agreements make you pay for damages you may not have caused. Expect to pay more for an automatic than for a stick.

   Several U.S. firms offer rental or leasing plans for Britain; try **Kemwel Group,** 106 Calvert St., Harrison, NY 10528-3199 (tel. (800) 678 0678) or **Europe by Car,** 1 Rockefeller Plaza, New York, NY 10020 (tel. (800) 223 1516 or (212) 581 3040; student and faculty discounts available).

■ Oxford

King Henry II founded Oxford University (England's first) in 1167. Until then, the English had traveled to Paris to study. After his tiff with Thomas à Becket, Archbishop of Canterbury, Henry ordered the return of English students studying in Paris, so that "there may never be wanting a succession of persons duly qualified for the service of God in church and state." Graduates include John Donne, Indira Gandhi, and Thomas Hobbes; Christ Church alone has produced 13 prime ministers.

   The tourist office guide *Welcome to Oxford* (£1) and the tourist office map (20p) list the colleges' public visiting hours (usually for a few hours in the afternoon; often curtailed without prior notice or explanation). Some colleges charge admission; others may impose mercenary fees during peak tourist times. At Christ Church, don't bother trying to sneak in (even after cleverly hiding your backpack and bright yellow *Let's Go*): elderly bouncers sporting bowler hats (porters) stationed 50 feet apart will squint at you and kick you out. Other colleges have been known to be less vigilant near the back gates. Coddle the porters or you will get nowhere.

Day Trips from London

DAYTRIPPERS

North Sea

English Channel

Strait of Dover

River Thames

N

20 miles

20 kilometers

FRANCE

CHANNEL TUNNEL

Calais

Boulogne

Harwich

Ipswich

Bury St. Edmunds

Colchester

Saffron Walden

Anglesey Abbey

Cambridge

Bedford

Luton

Watford

Northampton

Warwick

Warwick Castle

Stratford-upon-Avon

Alcester

Worcester

Gloucester

Cheltenham

Woodstock

Blenheim Castle

Bladon

Oxford

High Wycombe

Reading

Windsor

Guildford

LONDON

Chelmsford

Southend

Rochester

Maidstone

Leeds Castle

Canterbury

Chilham Castle

Margate

Broadstairs

Ramsgate

Sandwich

Deal

Dover

Folkestone

Romney Marsh

Hastings

Rye

Battle

Pevensey

Eastbourne

Royal Tunbridge Wells

Crawley

Lewes

Brighton

Newhaven

Worthing

Arundel

Amberley

Littlehampton

Chichester

South Downs

SOUTH DOWNS WAY

Winchester

Southampton

Portsmouth

Isle of Wight

Bournemouth

Weymouth

Salisbury

Stonehenge

Avebury

Lacock

Bath

Bristol

Cheddar Gorge

Wells

Glastonbury

M1

M11

M25

M23

M2

M20

M4

M5

M50

M3

A1

A11

A12

A120

A130

A127

A13

A2

A20

A28

A257

A21

A259

A22

A23

A24

A25

A3

A32

A27

A31

A33

A34

A303

A30

A36

A46

A4

A40

A41

A6

A5

A45

A10

A428

A43

A49

A35

Start your walking tour at Carfax, the center of activity, with a hike up the 99 spiral stairs of **Carfax Tower** (tel. 792 653) for an overview of the city. Before hitting the heights, get a free map of the rooftops from the attendant at the bottom (open late March-Oct. daily 10am-6pm; £1.20, children 60p).

Just down St. Aldates St. stands **Christ Church** (tel. 276 150), an intimidating pile of stone dwarfing the other colleges. "The House" has Oxford's grandest quad and its most socially distinguished, obnoxious students. (Open Mon.-Sat. 9am-6pm, Sun. 11:30am-6pm. Admission is a scandalous £3, concessions £2, families £6.) Christ Church's chapel is also Oxford's **cathedral,** the smallest in England. In 730 AD, Oxford's patron saint, St. Frideswide, built a nunnery on this site in thanks for two miracles: the blinding and subsequent recovery of an annoying suitor. The cathedral contains a stained glass window (c. 1320) depicting Thomas à Becket kneeling in supplication, just before being hacked apart in Canterbury Cathedral.

Curiouser and curiouser, the adjoining **Tom Quad** sometimes becomes the site of undergraduate pond dunking. The quad takes its name from **Great Tom,** the seven-ton bell in Tom Tower, which has faithfully rung 101 strokes (the original number of students) at 9:05pm (the original undergraduate curfew) every evening since 1682. Nearby, the fan-vaulted **college hall** bears imposing portraits of some of Christ Church's most famous alums— Charles "Lewis Carroll" Dodgson, Sir Philip Sidney, John Ruskin, John Locke, and W.H. Auden—in the corner by the kitchen.

Through an archway (to your left as you face the cathedral) lies **Peckwater Quad,** encircled by the most elegant Palladian building in Oxford. Look here for faded rowing standings chalked on the walls and for Christ Church's library (closed to visitors). The adjoining **Canterbury Quad** houses the **Christ Church Picture Gallery** (enter on Oriel Sq. and at Canterbury Gate), a fine collection of Italian, Dutch, and Flemish paintings. (Open April-Sept. Mon.-Sat. 10:30am-1pm and 2-5:30pm, Sun. 2-5:30pm; Oct.-March closes at 4:30pm. £1, students 50p. Visitors to gallery only should enter through Canterbury Gate off Oriel St.) The **Museum of Modern Art** (tel. 722 733), across St. Aldates at 30 Pembroke St., which showcases changing exhibitions. (Open Tues.-Wed. and Fri.-Sun. 11am-6pm, Thurs. 11am-9pm. £2.50, seniors and students £1.50, children free; free for all (but rarely a free-for-all) Wed. 11am-1pm and Thurs. 6-9pm. Wheelchair accessible.)

Merton College, off Merton St. (tel. 276 310), features a fine garden and a 14th-century library holding the first printed Welsh Bible. The college also houses the **Mob Quad** (Oxford's oldest and least impressive), and some of the University's best gargoyles (college open Mon.-Fri. 2-4pm, Sat.-Sun. 10am-4pm).

The soot-blackened **University College** on High St. (tel. 276 602), up the crooked Logic La. from Merton St., dates from 1249 and vies with Merton for the title of oldest college, claiming Alfred the Great as its founder. Percy Bysshe Shelley was expelled from University for writing *The Necessity of Atheism,* but has since been immortalized in a prominent godless monument inside the college (to the right as you enter from High St.). Bill Clinton spent his Rhodes days here; his rooms at 46 Leckford Rd. are an endless source of smoked-but-didn't-inhale jokes for tour guides (open July-Aug. daily 10am-6pm). Down High St. on the right lies the **Botanic Garden,** a sumptuous array of plants that have flourished for three centuries (open daily 9am-5pm; glasshouses open daily 2-4pm; free).

Picking up where the Botanic Garden across the street left off, extensive verdant grounds surround the flower-laced quads of **Magdalen College** (MAUD-lin; tel. 276 000), traditionally considered Oxford's handsomest. The college's spiritual patron is alumnus Oscar Wilde—the place has always walked on the flamboyant side. Edward Gibbon declared the 14 months he spent here "the most idle and unprofitable of my whole career" (open daily 11am-6pm; admission £2, concessions £1).

Just up High St. toward Carfax, a statue of Queen Caroline (wife of George II) crowns the front gate of **Queen's College** (tel. 279 121). Wren and Hawksmoor went to the trouble of rebuilding Queen's in the 17th and 18th centuries with a distinctive Queen Anne style. A boar's head graces the Christmas table—supposedly commemorating an early student of the college who, attacked by a boar on the outskirts of

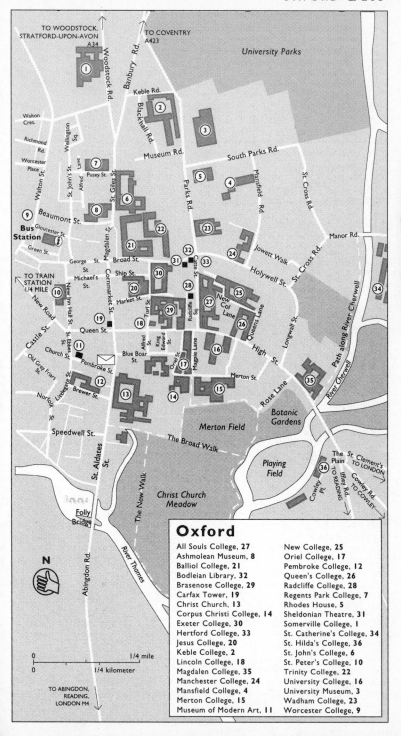

TO WOODSTOCK,
STRATFORD-UPON-AVON
A34

TO COVENTRY
A423

University Parks

Woodstock Rd.

Banbury Rd.

Keble Rd.

Blackhall Rd.

Museum Rd.

Walton
Cres.

Richmond
Rd.

Worcester
Place

Walton St.

Wellington Sq.

St. John's St.

Alfred Lane

Pusey St.

St. Giles St.

Parks Rd.

South Parks Rd.

Mansfield Rd.

St. Cross Rd.

Beaumont St.

Bus
Station

Gloucester St.

Green St.

Magdalen St.

George St.

Broad St.

St. Michael's St.

Ship St.

Cornmarket St.

Manor Rd.

Jowett Walk

Holywell St.

Gate St.

TO TRAIN
STATION
1/4 MILE

New Road

New Inn Hall St.

Market St.

Turl St.

Radcliffe Sq.

New Col Lane

Queen's Lane

Longwall St.

Path along River Cherwell

River Cherwell

Castle St.

Bulwarks Lane

Church St.

Queen St.

Pembroke St.

Blue Boar St.

Alfred St.

King Edward St.

Oriel St.

Magpie Lane

High St.

Old Grey Friars

Brewer St.

Lincoln St.

Merton St.

Norfolk

Speedwell St.

St. Aldates St.

Merton Field

The Broad Walk

Botanic Gardens

Rose Lane

Playing Field

The New Walk

River Thames

Christ Church
Meadow

Folly
Bridge

Abingdon Rd.

The Plain

St. Clement's
TO LONDON

Cowley Pl.

Iffley Rd.
TO READING

Cowley Rd.
TO COWLEY

N

TO ABINGDON,
READING,
LONDON M4

0 — 1/4 mile
0 — 1/4 kilometer

Oxford

All Souls College, 27
Ashmolean Museum, 8
Balliol College, 21
Bodleian Library, 32
Brasenose College, 29
Carfax Tower, 19
Christ Church, 13
Corpus Christi College, 14
Exeter College, 30
Hertford College, 33
Jesus College, 20
Keble College, 2
Lincoln College, 18
Magdalen College, 35
Mansfield College, 4
Merton College, 15
Museum of Modern Art, 11

New College, 25
Oriel College, 17
Pembroke College, 12
Queen's College, 26
Radcliffe College, 28
Regents Park College, 7
Rhodes House, 5
Sheldonian Theatre, 31
Somerville College, 1
St. Catherine's College, 34
St. Hilda's College, 36
St. John's College, 6
St. Peter's College, 10
Trinity College, 22
University College, 16
University Museum, 3
Wadham College, 23
Worcester College, 9

Oxford, choked his assailant to death with a volume of Aristotle (closed to the public, except for authorized tours).

Next to Queen's stands **All Souls** (tel. 279 379), a graduate college with a prodigious endowment. Candidates who survive the admission exams get invited to dinner, where it is ensured that they are "well-born, well-bred, and only moderately learned" (open April-Oct. Mon.-Fri. 2-4:30pm; Nov.-March 2-4pm; closed in August).

Turn up Catte St. to the **Bodleian Library** (tel. 277 165), Oxford's principal reading and research library with over five million books and 50,000 manuscripts. Sir Thomas Bodley endowed the library's first wing in 1602; the institution has since grown to fill the immense **Old Library** complex, the **Radcliffe Camera** next door, and two Broad St. buildings. There are four guided tours on weekdays and two on Saturdays (in winter 2 tours daily, £3). Admission to the reading rooms is by pass only. A student ID (and optimally a letter of introduction from your college), two passport photos (available on the spot), and £2 can get you a two-day pass. To get to the manuscripts division you must be "formally enrolled in a graduate degree program" and/or have a letter from your institution explicitly specifying the necessity of the Oxford archives. No one has ever been permitted to take out a book, not even Cromwell. Well, especially not Cromwell (open Mon.-Fri. 9am-6pm, Sat. 9am-12:30pm). On Broad St., across from the Bodleian, you can browse at **Blackwell's,** the famous bookstore.

The **Sheldonian Theatre** (tel. 277 299), set beside the Bodleian, is a Roman-style jewel of an auditorium designed by Wren when he was a teenager. Graduation ceremonies, conducted in Latin, take place in the Sheldonian and can be witnessed with permission from one of the "bulldogs" (an "affectionate" term for porter). The cupola of the theatre affords an inspiring view of the spires of Oxford (open Mon.-Sat. 10am-12:30pm, and 2-3:30pm, subject to change; admission £1, children 50p).

The gates of **Balliol College** (tel. 277 777), across Broad St., still bear scorch marks from the immolations of 16th-century Protestant martyrs. The pyres were built near the college, look for the small cross set into Broad St. This monument is often identified to gullible tourists as Oxford's "famous sunken cathedral." Matthew Arnold, the poet Swinburne, Aldous Huxley, and Adam Smith were all sons of Balliol's spires (open daily 10:30-noon and 1:45-5pm; admission £1, children 50p).

Balliol students preserve a semblance of tradition by hurling bricks over the wall at their arch-rival, conservative **Trinity College** (tel. 279 900), on Broad St. Founded in 1555, Trinity's baroque chapel features a limewood altarpiece, cedar lattices, and angel-capped pediments (open daily 9am-7pm; admission £1, concessions 50p).

Across Catte St. from the Bodleian, New College La. leads inevitably to **New College** (tel. 279 555). Founded by William of Wykeham in 1379, New College has become one of Oxford's most prestigious colleges. The multiple layers of the front quad (compare the different stones of the first and second stories) reveal the architectural history of the college. Look for the exquisitely detailed misericords, carved into the pews by sympathetic carpenters to support monks' bottoms. A peaceful croquet garden is encircled by part of the **old city wall,** and every few years the mayor of the City of Oxford visits the college for a ceremonial inspection to ascertain the wall's good repair. A former head of the college, Rev. Warden Spooner, is now remembered as the unintentional inventor of the "spoonerism." This stern but befuddled academic would raise a toast to "our queer old dean" or rebuke students who had "hissed all the mystery lectures" and "tasted the whole worm" (open daily 11am-5pm; £1).

Turn left at the end of Holywell St. and bear right on Manor Rd. to see **St. Catherine's** (tel. 271 700). Built between 1960 and 1964 by the Danish architect Arne Jacobsen, the chapel-less "Catz" is one of the most striking colleges (no set hours, call and ask; free). At the corner of St. Cross and South Parks Rd., the **Zoology and Psychology Building** looms like a great concrete ocean liner. Many colleges hold sporting matches on the nearby **University Parks.**

Walk through the **University Museum** (tel. 272 951), Parks Rd. (open Mon.-Sat. noon-5pm; free) to the **Pitt Rivers Museum** (tel. 270 949) and behold a wonderfully eclectic ethnography and natural history collection that includes shrunken heads and rare butterflies (open Mon.-Sat. 1-4:30pm; free). Just up Banbury Rd. on the right, the

Balfour Buildings house 1400 musical instruments from all over the world, including a working black leather violin (open daily 1-4:30pm; free).

Keble College (tel. 272 727), across from the University Museum, was designed by architect William Butterfield to stand out from the museum's sandstone background; the intricate and multi-patterned red brick, known as "The Fair Isle Sweater," was deemed "actively ugly" by Sir Nikolaus Pevsner (open daily 2-5pm).

The imposing **Ashmolean Museum**, Beaumont St. (tel. 278 000), opened in 1683, is Britain's first public museum. Van Gogh, Michelangelo, and Monet convene in the permanent collection (open Tues.-Sat. 10am-4pm, Sun. 2-4pm; free). The **Cast Gallery** behind the museum stores over 250 casts of Greek sculptures (normally open Tues.-Sat. 10am-4pm, Sun. 2-4pm; free).

A few blocks up St. Giles, as the street becomes Woodstock Rd., stands **Somerville College** (tel. 270 600), Oxford's most famous women's college. Somerville's alumnae include Dorothy Sayers, Indira Gandhi, and Margaret Thatcher. Women were not granted degrees until 1920, and they comprise only about 38% of today's student body (open daily 10am-5:30pm).

ORIENTATION AND PRACTICAL INFORMATION

Queen St., High St., St. Aldates St., and **Cornmarket St.** meet at right angles in **Carfax,** the town center. The colleges surround Carfax to the east along High St. and Broad St.; the bus and train stations lie to the west. Past the east end of High St. over Magdalen Bridge, the neighborhoods of **East Oxford** stretch along **Cowley Rd.** (marked "To Cowley" on some maps) and **Iffley Rd.** (marked "To Reading"). To the north along **Woodstock** and **Banbury Rd.,** leafier residential areas roll on for miles past some of the more remote colleges.

Getting There: Local trains run hourly from London. **Intercity** trains leave from Paddington (1hr.; day return £12.40). The **Oxford Tube** (tel. 772 250) sends buses from London's Grosvenor Gardens (1-6/hr.; 1½hr.; day return £6.50, concessions £6).

Getting About: The **Oxford Bus Company** (tel. 711 312) operates the red and green "Park & Ride" buses and the yellow, blue, and white "Citylinks" buses. Rival **Thames Transit**'s (tel. 772 250) rigs are purple, white and blue. Most local services board on the streets adjacent to Carfax; some longer-distance buses depart from the bus station. Abingdon Rd. buses are often marked "Red Bridge," and some Iffley Rd. buses are marked "Rose Hill." Fares are low (around 50p single). Some companies issue **Compass** tickets good for one day's travel (about £4), but companies disdain each other's tickets. You can also purchase weekly bus passes at the bus station.

Tourist Office: The Old School, Gloucester Green (tel. 726 871; fax 240 261). From Carfax, follow signs up Cornmarket St., left on George St., and right on Gloucester Green. Books rooms for £2.50 and a 10% deposit. Bureau de change. Accommodations list 45p. The 60p street map and guide includes a valuable index. Open Mon.-Sat. 9am-5pm, Sun. 10am-3:30pm.

Tours: Slightly dry 2-hr. walking tours leave 7 times daily from the tourist office from 10:30am-4pm (£4, children £2.50). **Spires and Shires** (tel. 513 998) runs livelier 1½hr. tours every hr. 11am-4pm from the Trinity College gate on Broad St. (£3, children £2). **The Oxford Tour** charges £6, students £4, seniors £4.50, children £2 (tel. 790 522). Many **student groups** lead tours from the tourist office hourly between 9am-5pm; some regale you with stories you won't hear on the official tours and several offer money back guarantees (prices vary).

Train Station: Park End St., west of Carfax (tel. 722 333; for timetable tel. 794 422). Office open Mon.-Fri. 5:50am-8pm, Sat. 6:20am-8pm, Sun. 7:45am-8pm.

Bus Station: Gloucester Green (follow arrows from Carfax). **Oxford Tube** (tel. 772 250) desk open Mon.-Fri. 7:15am-7:15pm, Sat. 8:30am-noon and 12:30-5pm, Sun. 9am-noon and 12:30-5pm. **Oxford CityLink** (tel. 785 400 or 772 250 for timetable) desk open Sun.-Fri. 8am-6pm, Sat. 8am-5pm. **National Express** (tel. (0990)

808 080), office open daily 8am-5:30pm. **Luggage storage** at the Pensioners' Club in Gloucester Green (tel. 242 237; 9am-4:45pm; £1/bag).

Taxi: Radio Taxi, tel. 242 424. **ABC,** tel. 770 681 (easy as 1-2-3).

Bike Rental: Pennyfarthing, 5 George St. (tel. 249 368). The closest to the town center. Rental £5/day; £10/week; deposit £25. Open Mon.-Sat. 8am-5:30pm.

Boat Rental: Magdalen Bridge Boat Co., Magdalen Bridge (tel. 202 643), east of Carfax along High St. (£7/hr.; £20 plus ID deposit; open March-Nov. daily 10am-9pm) will supply you with a punt for navigating the "Isis."

Pharmacy: 10 O'Clock Pharmacy, 59 Woodstock Rd. Open daily 9am-10pm.

Hospital: John Radcliffe Hospital, Headley Way (tel. 741 166). Take Bus 10 or 11.

Emergency: Dial 999; no coins required. **Police:** St. Aldates St. (tel. 266 000).

Postal Code: OX1 1ZZ. **Telephone Code:** 01865.

ACCOMMODATIONS

Book at least a week ahead, especially for singles, and expect to mail in a deposit. B&Bs line the main roads out of town, all of them a vigorous walk (15-20min.) from Carfax. The No. 300s on **Banbury Road,** fern-laced and domestic, stand miles north of the center (catch a Banbury bus on St. Giles St.). You'll find cheaper B&Bs in the 200s and 300s on Iffley Rd. and from No. 250-350 on **Cowley Rd.,** both served frequently by Buses 3 and 40 from Carfax. **Abingdon Road** in South Oxford, is about the same price and distance, though less colorful (served by Bus 30). If it's late and you're homeless, call the Oxford Association of Hotels and Guest Houses at one of the following numbers: 774 083 (East Oxford), 862 138 (West Oxford), 510 327 (North Oxford), or 722 995 (South Oxford).

HI Youth Hostel, Jack Straw's Lane, Headington (tel. 62997). Moving in late '96 or early '97—call YHA's National Office (tel. 844126) for updates. Catch any minibus from the post office south of Carfax (every 15min., last bus 11:10pm; 95p return). Close quarters and large lounges promote chatter. 114 beds, kitchen, lockers. £8.80, under 18 £6. June-Aug. book at least a week ahead.

Tara, 10 Holywell St. (call (toll-free) at (4451) 494 2022; within the U.K. (0800) 515 152; give the operator Tara's phone number (01865) 202 953; fax 200 297). A lark-charmed dream among the spires on the oldest medieval street in Oxford. Kind hearing-impaired proprietors, Mr. and Mrs. Godwin, lip-read and speak clearly. Desks, basins, TVs, and refrigerators in every room; kitchenette on 2nd floor. Single £25. Double £39. Triple £50. Open July-Sept.; other times it fills up with students, but check anyway. Reserve at least 2 weeks in advance.

Heather House, 192 Iffley Rd. (tel. and fax 249 757). Bus 3 or 40 (50p) from Carfax or walk 15min. Sparkling rooms and proprietor remind you why you love to travel. Private phones, facilities. English or "healthy" breakfast (featuring home-made mueslix). Single £20, larger rooms £18-20/person.

FOOD

The swank, bulging swagger of Oxford's eateries seduces students fed up with fetid college food. For fresh produce, deli goods, breads, and shoe leather, visit the **Covered Market** between Market St. and Carfax (open Mon.-Sat. 8am-5:30pm).

Eat and run at one of the better take-aways: **Bret's Burgers,** in a shack on Park End St. (tel. 245 229), near the train station, fries delectable burgers and chips (open Sun.-Thurs. noon-11pm, Fri.-Sat. noon-11:30pm). **Harvey's of Oxford,** 58 High St. near Magdalen College, recognizable by the line out the door, serves cherry flapjacks (80p), and mighty sandwiches (£1.40-2.75); open Mon.-Fri. 8:30am-5:30pm, Sat. 8:30am-6:30pm, Sun. 9:30am-6:30pm).

Chiang Mai, in an alley at 130A High St. (tel. 202 233). Spicy Thai food in half-timbered surroundings. Extensive vegetarian menu for £5-7. Try the sticky rice dessert for £3.50. Reserve ahead. Open Mon.-Sat. noon-2:30pm and 6-10:30pm.

The Nosebag, 6-8 St. Michael's St. (tel. 721 033). More wholesome than the name suggests. Cafeteria-style gourmet-grade dishes served for under £5 (lunch), or £7 (dinner). Veggie options come with choice of salads. Open Mon. 9:30am-5:30pm, Tues.-Thurs. and Sun. 9:30am-10pm, Fri.-Sat. 9:30am-10:30pm.

Heroes, 8 Ship St. (tel. 723 459). Student clientele pack in for superfresh sandwiches (£1.70-3.30). Open Mon.-Fri. 8am-7pm, Sat. 8:30am-6pm, Sun. 10am-5pm.

Dhaka, 186 Cowley Rd. (tel. 200 203). Distinctive Bangladeshi dishes will make your palate do things it's never done before. Main dishes from £4-6.50, Chicken Kashmir with banana £3.80. Open daily noon-2:30pm and 6pm-midnight.

PUBS

Pubs far outnumber colleges in Oxford; many consider them the city's prime attraction. Most pubs are open all afternoon and begin to fill up around 4pm. Be ready to crawl—some pubs are so small that a single band of merry students will squeeze out other patrons. *Good Pubs of Oxford* (£3 at bookstores and tourist office) is an indispensable guide to the town's beer dungeons. Buy it, use it, keep it dry.

The Bear, Alfred St. 5000 ties from England's brightest and most boastful cover every flat surface but the floor; you can buy your own "The Bear 1242-1992" tie for £6.50. Food served daily noon-3pm, Tues.-Sat. also 6-8pm.

The Eagle and Child, 49 St. Giles St. Known to all as the Bird and Baby, this archipelago of paneled alcoves moistened the tongues of C.S. Lewis and J.R.R. Tolkien. *The Chronicles of Narnia* and *The Hobbit* were first read aloud here.

Turf Tavern, 4 Bath Pl., off Holywell St. Intimate 13th-century cavern stays relaxed until the student crowd turns it into a mosh pit. Many, many drinks: beers, punches, ciders, and country wines—mead, elderberry, and red-and-white currant. Open Mon.-Sat. 11am-11pm, Sun. noon-10:30pm.

The Kings Arms, Holywell St. (tel. 242 369). Oxford's unofficial student union, with a few refugee scholars from the New Bodleian across the street. Open Mon.-Sat. 10:30am-11pm, Sun. 10:30am-10:30pm.

ENTERTAINMENT

Public transit shuts down at midnight. For information on what's happening, check the bulletin boards at the tourist office or pick up a free copy of *This Month in Oxford.* The tourist office prints a daily event sheet in summer.

Oxford cherishes music; try to attend a concert or an Evensong service at one of the colleges, or a performance at the **Holywell Music Rooms.** The **City of Oxford Orchestra,** the city's professional symphony orchestra (tel. 252 365), plays Sunday coffee concerts and a subscription series in the Sheldonian Theatre and college chapels throughout the summer (shows at 8pm; tickets £12-15; student discount 25%). Buy your tickets at **Blackwell's Music Shop,** 38 Holywell St. (tel. 261 384; open Mon. and Wed.-Sat. 9am-6pm, Tues. 9:30am-6pm, Sun. noon-5pm).

The **Apollo Theatre,** George St. (tel. 244 544), presents a wide range of performances, ranging from lounge-lizard jazz to the Welsh National Opera (tickets from £7, senior and student discounts). The **Oxford Playhouse,** 11-12 Beaumont St. (tel. 798 600), is a venue for bands, dance troupes, and the Oxford Stage Company (tickets from £7, student and senior discount £2, same-day standby tickets for seniors and students £5). The **Oxford Union,** St. Michael's St., shows student productions. **The Old Fire Station** on George St. (tel. 794 494) features more avant-garde work.

Two of Oxford's late-night clubs are well worth a visit. Open until 2am (Wed.-Sat.), **Freuds** on Walton Street has live bands and an even livelier student crowd. Come early— there's a £3 cover after 10pm. The **Westgate Pub,** 190 Cowled Rd. (tel. 250 099) is the best option for late-night live jazz and comedy (open Mon.-Thurs. until 1am, Fri. and Sat. until 2am; shows £7, students £6).

A favorite pastime in Oxford is **punting** on the River Thames (known here as the Isis) or on the River Cherwell (CHAR-wul). Watch for **Parson's Pleasure,** a small riverside area where men sometimes sunbathe nude. Female passersby are expected to open their parasols and tip them at a discreet angle to obscure the view. For information on punt rental, see Boat Rental, p. 268.

The university celebrates **Eights Week** at the end of May, when all the colleges enter crews in the bumping races and beautiful people gather on the banks to nibble strawberries and sip champagne. In early September, **St. Giles Fair** invades one of Oxford's main streets with an old-fashioned carnival, complete with Victorian round-about and whirligigs. Daybreak on May 1 brings one of Oxford's loveliest moments: the Magdalen College Choir greets the summer by singing madrigals from the top of the tower to a crowd below, and the town indulges in morris dancing, beating the bounds, and other age-old rituals of merrymaking—pubs open at 7am.

▨ Stratford-upon-Avon

It is something, I thought, to have seen the dust of Shakespeare.
—Washington Irving

The past few decades have seen an unprecedented cutting-up of Shakespeare in Strat-ford-upon-Avon: everyone, it seems, wants a piece of him. The indoctrinated have paid him worship since David Garrick's 1769 Stratford jubilee—England and this town have made an industry of Shakespeare, emblazoning him on £20 notes and affirming there's no business like Bard business.

Stratford's sights are best seen before 11am or after 4pm—Bardolatry peaks at 2pm. Five official **Shakespeare properties** grace the town: Shakespeare's Birthplace, Anne Hathaway's cottage, the so-called Mary Arden's House and Countryside Museum, Hall's Croft, and New Place/Nash's House. Diehard fans should purchase the **combination ticket** (£9, students £7.50, children £4), a savings of £6 if you make it to every shrine. If you don't want to visit them all, buy a **Shakespeare's Town Her-itage Trail ticket,** which covers only the three in-town sights (the Birthplace, Hall's Croft, and New Place) for £6 (students £5, children £2.75). The cheapest way to pay homage to the institution himself is to visit his grave, his little, little grave in **Holy Trinity Church,** Trinity St. The trite epitaph is credulously attributed by some to Shakespeare himself (admission 50p, students and children 30p).

In town, begin your walking tour at **Shakespeare's Birthplace** on Henley St. (tel. 269 890; enter through the adjoining museum) a combination period recreation and Shakespeare life-and-work exhibition. On High St., you can see another example of humble Elizabethan lodgings in the **Harvard House.** Period pieces sparsely punctu-ate this authentic Tudor building, vaguely connected with the man who lends his name to the American college that runs it (open late May to Sept. daily 10am-4pm; admission £1, students and children 50p). Shakespeare bought **New Place,** down the road in 1597 after writing some hits in London. The site's disappointing red brick wall is only accessible through admission to the adjacent **Nash's House,** which holds Tudor furnishings and a local history collection. (Open Mon.-Sat. 9:30am-5pm, Sun. 10:30am-5:30pm; Nov.-Feb. Mon.-Sat. 10am-4pm, Sun. 1:30-4pm. £2, children £1.) View the **Great Garden** and the exterior at New Place for free from the leafy bowers in back.

Shakespeare learned his "small Latin and less Greek" at the **Grammar School,** on Church St. To visit, write in advance to the headmaster, N.W.R. Mellon, King Edward VI School, Church St., Stratford-upon-Avon, CV37 6HB (tel. 293 351). The 13th-cen-tury **guild chapel** next door is open daily. Shakespeare's eldest daughter once lived in **Hall's Croft,** Old Town Rd.; though painstakingly furnished, Bardolaters will find no relics here. (Hours and admission match those of Nash's House.)

The violets have not withered in the **Royal Shakespeare Theatre Gardens,** on the pilgrim's progress between the theatre and Holy Trinity (free). The riverbank between the RST and Clopton Bridge is a sight in itself. The **RST Summer House** in the gardens contains a **brass-rubbing studio** (free, but frottage materials cost around £3; open April-Sept. daily 10am-6pm; Oct. daily 11am-4pm). The RSC offers **back-stage tours** that cram camera-happy groups within the wooden "O"s of the RST and the Swan. Entertaining guides let you play with fake blood and soliloquize with Olivier's ghost (tel. 412 602 for bookings, or go to the Swan's shop; tours daily at 1:30, 5:30pm, and after performances; £4, students £3).

Anne Hathaway's Cottage, (tel. 292 100), the birthplace of Shakespeare's wife, lies about 1 mi. from Stratford in Shottery; take one of the footpaths north. (Open March-Oct. Mon.-Sat. 9am-6pm, Sun. 9:30am-6pm; Nov.-Feb. Mon.-Sat. 9:30am-4:30pm, Sun. 10am-4:30pm; £2.30, children £1.10.) **Mary Arden's House,** a farmhouse restored in the style of Shakespeare's mother's home, stands 4 mi. from Stratford in Wilmcote. A footpath connects it to Anne Hathaway's Cottage. (Open March-Oct. Mon.-Sat. 9:30am-5pm, Sun. 10:30am-5pm; Nov.-Feb. Mon.-Sat. 10am-4pm, Sun. 1:30-4pm. £3.20, children £1.40, family £8.)

PRACTICAL INFORMATION

Getting There: Stratford (pop. 22,000) struts a fretful 2¼hr. from Paddington Station by **Thames Trains** (tel. 579 453). **National Express buses** run from Victoria Station (3/day; 3hr.; £12 day return). Consider the discount rail/theater combo packages offered by **Theatre and Concert Travel** (tel. 414 999) if you plan to visit the theater while in Stratford.

Tourist Office: Bridgefoot (tel. 293 127). Cross Warwick Rd. at Bridge St. toward the waterside park. Books accommodations for a 10% deposit.

Tours: Guide Friday, 14 Rother St. (tel. 294 466) operates tours of Stratford departing daily 4/hr. from various spots (£7, seniors £5, children under 12 £2).

Royal Shakespeare Theatre Box Office, Waterside (tel. 295 623; 24-hr. recorded information 269 191; fax 261 974). Standby tickets for seniors and students (£11-14) available immediately before the show at the RST, the Swan, and The Other Place. Open Mon.-Sat. 9:30am-8pm, closes at 6pm when there is no performance.

Train Station: off Alcester Rd. (for train information call (0345) 484 950). Call **Guide Friday, Ltd.** (tel. 294 466) in advance if you plan travel on the late-night Shakespeare Connection.

Bus Station: The corner of **Waterside** and **Bridge St.,** in front of or opposite McDonald's, is as close to a bus station as Stratford gets; **National Express** and **Midland Red South** buses stop here. Local **Stratford Blue** service also stops on **Wood St.** You can buy tickets for National Express buses at the tourist office.

Taxi: Main Taxis (tel. 414 514) or **007 Taxis** (tel. 414 007), both 24-hr. service.

Bike Rental: Clarke's Cycle Rental, Guild St. (tel. 205 057), at Union St.; look for the Esso sign. £6/day, £25/week; deposit £50. Open daily 9am-5:30pm.

Hospital: Stratford-upon-Avon Hospital, Arden St. (tel. 205 831).

Emergency: Dial 999; no coins required. **Police:** Rother St. (tel. 414 111).

Postal Code: CV37 6AA. **Telephone Code:** 01789.

ACCOMMODATIONS

To B&B or not to B&B? In summer, 'tis nobler to make advance reservations by phone. Guest houses (£13-20) line **Grove Road, Evesham Place,** and **Evesham Road.** Standards are high, as the guest houses cater to overseas tourists used to amenities. (From the train station, walk down Alcester Rd., take a right on Grove Rd., and continue to Evesham Place, which becomes Evesham Rd.) If these fail you, try **Shipston** and **Banbury Road** across the river. The nearest youth hostel is more than 2 mi. out of town, and with a return bus fare costs as much as a cheaper B&B. The tourist office will put you in touch with local farms that take paying guests (£12.50-16); they'll also book B&Bs.

Greensleeves, 46 Alcester Rd. (tel. 292 131), on the way to the train station. Mrs. Graham loves her job but loves her guests even more—she's a surrogate grandmother who serves delicious food. TVs in every room. £15, students £14.

Nando's, 18 Evesham Pl. (tel. 20907; fax reservations to the same number). More and more ensuites monthly! Friendly owners, bright, comfortable rooms—all have TVs and most have private facilities. Single £18-25. Double £28.

The Hollies, 16 Evesham Pl. (tel. 266 857). Truly warm and attentive proprietors for whom the guest house has become a labor of love. TV and tea-making facilities in every room. Spacious doubles; no singles. £17.50, with bath £22.50.

Field View Guest House, 35 Banbury Rd. (tel. 292 694). Quiet, peaceful rooms with a welcoming owner. Only an 8-min. walk to town, but less convenient to the train station. Tea- and coffee-making facilities in each room. Vegetarian options at breakfast. Single £15. Double £30.

FOOD

Vintner Bistro and Café Bar, 5 Sheep St. (tel. 297 259). Satisfying salads (£5), a large vegetarian selection, and uncommon desserts. Open Mon.-Sat. 10:30am-11pm, Sun. 10:30am-10:30pm.

Hussain's Indian Cuisine, 6a Chapel St. Probably Stratford's best Indian cuisine. 3-course lunch £6. Open Mon.-Thurs. noon-2pm and 5:15-11:45pm, Fri.-Sat. noon-2pm and 5pm-midnight, Sun. 12:30-2:30pm and 5:30-11:45pm.

Dirty Duck Pub, Southern La. River view outside, huge bust of Shakespeare within. Pub lunch £2-4.50; dinners. Ask for sack. Open Mon.-Sat. 11am-11pm, Sun noon-10pm.

ENTERTAINMENT

Show! Show! Show! He was born on Henley St., died at New Place, and lives at the **Royal Shakespeare Theatre.** One of the world's most acclaimed repertories, the **Royal Shakespeare Company** boasts such recent sons as Kenneth Branagh and Ralph Fiennes. Get thee to a performance; to reserve seats (£5-£42) call the box office (tel. 295 623; 24-hr. recording tel. 269 191; fax 261 974; disabled should call in advance to advise box office of their needs). Without payment, they'll only hold seats for three days. The box office, in the foyer of Swan Theatre, is open from 9:30am-6pm every day (phones open at 9am). A group gathers outside around 9am for same-day ticket sales. Restricted view or, occasionally, good matinee seats are available on the day of the performance. A happy few get customer returns and standing-room tickets later in the day for evening shows (line up 1-2hr. before curtain). Student and senior standbys (£11) are available just before curtain—be ready to pounce. Season runs from November to September.

The **Swan Theatre,** has been specially designed for RSC productions of plays written by Shakespeare's contemporaries. The theater is located down Waterside, behind the Royal Shakespeare Theatre, on the grounds of the old Memorial Theatre (tickets £12-26.50, standing room £5). It's smaller and often more crowded than the RST; line up early for tickets. The Swan also reserves a few same-day sale tickets (£12-14.50); standbys are rare. **The Other Place,** the RSC's newest branch, stages modern and avant garde works (reserved seats £13.50-17, standbys £12).

Astonishingly, the **Stratford Festival** (for two weeks in July) celebrates artistic achievement other than Shakespeare's. Tickets (when required) can be purchased from the Civil Hall box office (tel. 414 513), on Rother St. The modern, well-respected **Shakespeare Centre,** Henley St. (tel. 204 016) hosts the annual **Poetry Festival** throughout July and August every Sunday evening. Those putting in appearances at the festival over the past few years include Leo McKern, Seamus Heaney, Elaine Feinstein, Ted Hughes, James Fenton, and Derek Walcott (tickets £5.50-6.80).

■ Cambridge

The town of Cambridge has been around for over 2000 years, but the University got its start 785 years ago when rebels "defected" from nearby Oxford to this settlement on the River Cam. In recent years, Cambridge has ceased to be the exclusive preserve of upper-class sons, although roughly half of its students still come from independent schools and only 40% are women.

The University itself exists mainly as a bureaucracy that handles the formalities of lectures, degrees, and real estate, leaving to individual colleges the small tutorials and

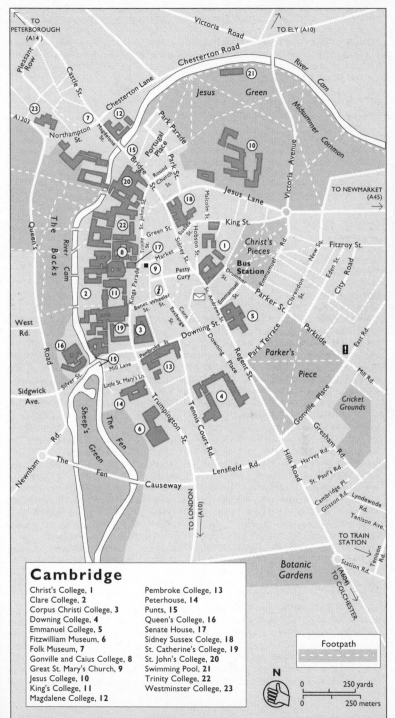

TO PETERBOROUGH (A14)

TO ELY (A10)

Victoria Road

Chesterton Road

River Cam

Pleasant Row

Castle St.

Chesterton Lane

Jesus Green

Midsummer Common

(23)

A1303

(7)

(12)

Northampton St.

Magdalene St.

(15)

Portugal Place

Park Parade

Round Church St.

(21)

(10)

Victoria Avenue

TO NEWMARKET (A45)

(20)

Park St.

(18)

Jesus Lane

Malcom St.

King St.

Christ's Pieces

Fitzroy St.

New Sq.

The Backs

River Cam

(22)

Green St.

Trinity St.

(17)

Sussex St.

Sidney St.

Hobson St.

(1)

Bus Station

Emmanuel Rd.

Eden St.

City Road

Queen's

(8)

(9)

Market

Petty Cury

Drummer St.

Parker St.

Clarendon St.

(2)

(11)

(i)

Benet St.

Wheeler St.

Corn Exchange St.

St. Andrew's St.

(5)

Emmanuel St.

Park Terrace

Parker's

Parkside

East Rd.

West Rd.

(19)

(3)

Downing St.

Downing Place

Regent St.

Piece

Mill Rd.

(16)

(15)

Mill Lane

Pembroke St.

(13)

Silver St.

Little St. Mary's Ln.

Trumpington St.

Tennis Court Rd.

(4)

Gonville Place

Cricket Grounds

Sidgwick Ave.

Sheep's Green

The Fen

(14)

(6)

Gresham Rd.

Harvey Rd.

St. Paul's Rd.

Newnham Rd.

The Fen

Causeway

Lensfield Rd.

Hills Road

Cambridge Pl.

Glisson Rd.

Lyndewode Rd.

Tenison Ave.

TO LONDON (A10)

TO TRAIN STATION

Station Rd.

Tenison Rd.

TO COLCHESTER (A604)

Botanic Gardens

Cambridge

Christ's College, 1
Clare College, 2
Corpus Christi College, 3
Downing College, 4
Emmanuel College, 5
Fitzwilliam Museum, 6
Folk Museum, 7
Gonville and Caius College, 8
Great St. Mary's Church, 9
Jesus College, 10
King's College, 11
Magdalene College, 12

Pembroke College, 13
Peterhouse, 14
Punts, 15
Queen's College, 16
Senate House, 17
Sidney Sussex Colege, 18
St. Catherine's College, 19
St. John's College, 20
Swimming Pool, 21
Trinity College, 22
Westminster College, 23

Footpath

N

0   250 yards

0   250 meters

seminars that comprise a Cambridge education. At exams' end, Cambridge explodes with gin-soaked glee, and May Week (in mid-June, naturally) launches a dizzying schedule of cocktail parties; in the middle of the week, students down a health-threatening number of toddies on aptly named Suicide Sunday.

Cambridge is an architect's fantasia, packing some of the most breathtaking monuments to English aesthetics over the last 700 years into less than one square mile. The soaring grandeur of King's College Chapel and the postcard-familiar St. John's Bridge of Sighs are sight-seeing staples, but if you explore some of the more obscure courts (quads), you'll discover delicacies untasted by most visitors.

If you are pressed for time, visit at least one chapel (preferably King's College), one garden (try Christ's), one library (Trinity's is the most interesting), and one dining hall (though many dining halls are emphatically closed to visitors). Most historic university buildings line the east side of the Cam between Magdalene Bridge and Silver St. On both sides of the river, the gardens, meadows, and cows of the **Backs** bring a pastoral air to Cambridge. If you have time for only a few colleges, **King's, Trinity, Queens', Christ's, St. John's,** and **Jesus** should top your list. Five of the most photographed colleges (King's, Trinity, Queens', St. John's, and Clare) charge admission; planning can help you allocate your precious pence.

The University of Cambridge has three eight-week terms: Michaelmas (Oct.-Dec.), Lent (Jan.-March), and Easter (April-June). Visitors can gain access to most of the college grounds daily from 9am to 5:30pm, though many close to sightseers during the Easter term, and virtually all are closed during exam period (mid-May to mid-June). Plump bowler-bedecked ex-servicemen called Porters maintain security. Look and act like a (resident) student, and you should be able to wander freely through most college grounds even after hours. Some university buildings shut down off term.

King's College, on King's Parade, possesses the university's most famous chapel, a spectacular Gothic monument. In 1441, Henry VI cleared away most of the center of medieval Cambridge for the foundation of King's College, and he intended this chapel to be England's finest. Although Hank wanted the inside to remain unadorned, his successors spent nearly £5000 carving an elaborate interior. If you stand at the southwest corner of the courtyard, you can see where Henry's master mason John Wastell left off and where work under the Tudors began. The earlier stone is off-white, the later, dark. The interior of the chapel consists of one huge chamber cleft by a carved wooden choir screen, one of the purest examples of the early Renaissance style in England. Wordsworth described the fan-vaulted ceiling as a "branching roof self-poised, and scooped into ten thousand cells where light and shade repose." Stained-glass windows depicting the life of Jesus were preserved from the iconoclasm of the English Civil War, allegedly because John Milton, then Cromwell's secretary, groveled on their behalf. Behind the altar hangs Rubens' magnificent *Adoration of the Magi* (1639). Free musical recitals often play at the chapel—pick up a schedule at the entrance. (College open June-Oct. Mon.-Fri. 9:30am-4:30pm, Sun. 9am-5pm. Admission £2.50, students and children £1.50, under 12 free with adults. Guided 45-min. **tours** £1.50, under 12 free. Check notices in the chapel for daily times. Chapel open term-time Mon.-Sat. 9:30am-3:30pm, Sun. 1:15-2:15pm and 4:45-5:15pm; chapel and exhibitions open college vacations 10am-5pm; free.) Enjoy the classic view of the chapel and of the adjacent **Gibbs Building** from the river. Take a picnic down by the water and think on those who have gone before you: E.M. Forster was an undergraduate at King's, basing *The Longest Journey* and the posthumous *Maurice* on his Cambridge days; Salman Rushdie walked the King's courts before running from the Court of Allah.

In early June the university posts the names and final grades of every student in the Georgian **Senate House** opposite the King's College chapel, designed by Gibbs and built in the 1720s; about a week later, degree ceremonies are held here. Cambridge graduates are eligible for incredibly easy master's degrees: after spending three and one-third years out in the Real World, a graduate sends £15 to the university. Provided that said graduate is not in the custody of one of Her Majesty's Gaols, the grad receives an M.A. without further ado, making Cambridge the world's easiest correspondence school.

Trinity College, on Trinity St. (tel. 338 400), holds the largest purse at the University. The college's status as the wealthiest at Cambridge has become legendary—myth-mongers claim that it was once possible to walk from Cambridge to Oxford without stepping off Trinity land. Founded in 1546 by Henry VIII, Trinity once specialized in literati (alums include John Dryden, Lord Byron, and Lord Tennyson) but in this century has spat forth scientists and philosophers (Ernest Rutherford, Ludwig Wittgenstein, and Bertrand Russell). Byron used to bathe nude in a florid fountain (1602) inside the courtyard. The eccentric young poet lived in Nevile's Court and shared his rooms with a pet bear, whom he claimed would take his fellowship exams for him. Generations later, Prince Charles earned average marks in anthropology. The expanse of Trinity's **Great Court** encompasses an area so large you can almost overlook its utter lack of straight lines and symmetry. The courtyard race in *Chariots of Fire* is set here, although it was filmed at Eton College (see p. 210). What William Wordsworth called the "loquacious clock that speaks with male and female voice" still strikes 24 times each noon. Sir Isaac Newton, who lived on the first floor of E-entry for 30 years, first measured the speed of sound by stamping his foot in the cloister along the north side of the court. Underneath the courtyards lie the well-hidden, well-stocked Trinity wine cellars. The college recently purchased over £20,000 worth of port that won't be drinkable until 2020.

Amble through the college toward the river to reach the reddish stone walls of the stunning **Wren Library.** Treasures in this naturally lit building include A.A. Milne's handwritten manuscript of *Winnie the Pooh* and less momentous works such as John Milton's *Lycidas.* The collection also contains works by Byron, Tennyson, and Thackeray. German speakers certain of the existence of books might look for Wittgenstein's journals. His phenomenal *Philosophical Investigations* was conceived here during years of intense discussion with G.E. Moore and students in his top-floor K-entry rooms. (£1.50; library open Mon.-Fri. noon-2pm; hall open 3-5pm; chapel and courtyard open 10am-6pm; college and library closed during exams.)

Established in 1511 by Lady Margaret Beaufort, mother of Henry VIII, **St. John's College** (tel. 338 600) is one of seven Cambridge colleges founded by women. The striking brick and stone gatehouse bears Lady Margaret's heraldic emblem. St. John's centers around a paved plaza rather than a grassy courtyard, and its two most interesting buildings stand across the river from the other colleges. A copy of Venice's Bridge of Sighs connects the older part of the college to the towering neo-Gothic extravagance of New Court. (Chapel open Mon.-Fri. 10am-5:30pm, Sat. and Sun. 9:30am-5:30pm; Evensong at 6:30pm most nights. College open daily during vacation. Admission £1.50, seniors and children 75p, families £3.) Next door, you can see the modern **Cripps Building,** with clever bends that create three distinct courts under the shade of a noble willow. The **School of Pythagoras,** a 12th-century pile of wood and stone rumored to be the oldest complete building in Cambridge, hides in St. John's Gardens (courtyard and some buildings open until 6pm).

Queens' College (tel. 335 511), was founded not once, but twice—by painted Queen Margaret of Anjou in 1448 and again by Elizabeth Woodville in 1465. It possesses the only unaltered Tudor courtyard in Cambridge, containing the half-timbered President's Gallery. The **Mathematical Bridge,** just past Cloister Court, was built in 1749 without bolts or nails. A meddling Victorian took the bridge apart to see how it worked and couldn't put it back together without using a steel rivet every two inches. (College open daily 1:45-4:30pm; during summer vacation also 10:30am-12:45pm; closed during exams. Admission £1, under 14 free.)

Clare College (tel. 333 200), founded in 1326 by the thrice-widowed, 29-year-old Lady Elizabeth de Clare, has preserved an appropriate coat of arms: golden teardrops on a black border. Across Clare Bridge lie the **Clare Gardens** (open Mon.-Fri. 2-4:45pm; during summer vacation also 10am-4:30pm). Walk through Clare's **Old Court** (open during exams after 4:45pm to groups of less than 3) for a view of the University Library, where 82 mi. of shelves hold books arranged by size rather than subject. George V called it "the greatest erection in Cambridge"; more recently it appeared in the film *Brazil* (college open daily 10am-5pm; £1.50, under 10 free).

Christ's College (tel. 334 900), founded as "God's-house" in 1448 and renamed in 1505, has won fame for its gardens (open Mon.-Fri. 10:30am-12:30pm and 2-4pm; summer Mon.-Fri. 9:30am-noon) and its association with the poet John Milton; a mulberry tree reputedly planted by the "Lady of Christ's" still thrives here. To reach the gardens, walk under the lovely Neoclassical Fellows Building dubiously accredited to Inigo Jones. Charles Darwin studied here, but his rooms on G staircase in First Court are unmarked and closed to visitors. **New Court,** on King St., is one of the most stunning modern structures in Cambridge. Bowing to pressure from aesthetically offended Cantabridgians, a new wall has been built that blocks the view of the building from all sides except the inner courtyard of the college. The college closes during exams, save for access to the chapel (inquire at the porter's desk).

Cloistered on a secluded site, **Jesus College** (tel. 339 339) has preserved an enormous amount of unaltered medieval work, dating from 1496. Beyond the long, high-walled walk (the "Chimny") lies a three-sided court fringed with colorful gardens. Through the archway on the right lie the remains of a gloomy medieval nunnery. The Pre-Raphaelite stained glass of Burne-Jones and ceiling decorations by William Morris festoon the chapel. Alums included Coleridge, Thomas Malthus, and Alistair *"Masterpiece Theatre"* Cooke (courtyard open until 6pm; closed during exams).

Inhabiting buildings from a 15th-century Benedictine hostel, **Magdalene College** (MAUD-lin; tel. 332 100), founded in 1524, has acquired an aristocratic reputation. Don't forget to take a peek at the **Pepys Library** (labeled **Bibliotheca Pepysiana**) in the second court; the library displays the noted statesman and prolific diarist's collection in their original cases. (Library open Mon.-Sat. 2:30-5:30pm; Easter-Aug. 11:30am-12:30pm and 2:30-3:30pm. Free. Courtyards closed during exams.)

Peterhouse, on Trumpington St., is Cambridge's oldest and smallest college, founded in 1294. **Robinson College,** across the river on Grange Rd., is its newest. Founded in 1977, this brick pastiche sits just behind the university library. The college chapel features some fascinating stained glass and bronzed flowers.

Corpus Christi College (tel. 338 000), founded in 1352 by the common people, contains the dreariest and oldest courtyard in Cambridge. The library maintains the snazziest collection of Anglo-Saxon manuscripts in England, including the Parker Manuscript of the *Anglo-Saxon Chronicle.* Alums include Sir Francis Drake and Christopher Marlowe. The 1347 **Pembroke College** next door harbors Sir Christopher Wren's earliest architectural effort and counts Edmund Spenser, Ted Hughes, and Eric Idle among grads (courtyards open until 6pm; closed during exams).

A chapel designed by Sir Christopher Wren dominates the front court of **Emmanuel College.** Emmanuel, founded in 1584, on St. Andrew's St. at Downing St., and **Downing College,** founded in 1807, just to the south along Regent St., are both pleasantly isolated (courtyards open until 6pm; chapel open when not in use). Downing's austere Neoclassical buildings flank an immense lawn (open daily until 6pm; dining hall open when not in use; closed during exams). John Harvard, benefactor (though not the founder) of another Cambridge university, attended Emmanuel; a stained-glass panel depicting Harvard graces the college chapel. Among alumni with more tangible accomplishments is John Cleese.

The **Round Church (Holy Sepulchre),** Bridge St. and St. John's St., one of five circular churches surviving in England, was built in 1130 (and later rebuilt) on the pattern of the Church of the Holy Sepulchre in Jerusalem. The pattern merits comparison with **St. Benet's Church,** a rough Saxon church on Benet St. The tower of St. Benet's, built in 1050, is the oldest structure in Cambridge.

For a choice ogle at this mind-boggling collection of colleges, climb the tower of the **Church of St. Mary the Great,** just off King's Parade (tower open Mon.-Sat. 9:45am-4:45pm, Sun. 12:30-4:45pm).

The **Fitzwilliam Museum,** Trumpington St. (tel. 332 900), a 10-minute walk down the road from King's College, dwells within an immense Romanesque building. Inside, an opulent marble foyer leads to an impressive collection including paintings by da Vinci, Michelangelo, Dürer, Renoir, Degas, Monet, and Seurat. A goulash of Egyptian, Chinese, Japanese and Greek antiquities bides its time downstairs, coupled with an extensive collection of 16th-century German armor. Check out the illuminated manuscripts under protective cloths. The drawing room displays William Blake's books and woodcuts (Open Tues.-Sun. 10am-5pm. Free, but suggested donation £3. Call to inquire about lunchtime and evening concerts. Guided tours Sat.-Sun. at 2:30pm, £1.50.) The **Museum of Zoology** (tel. 336 650), off Downing St., houses a fine assemblage of wildlife specimens in a modern, well-lit building (open Mon.-Fri. 2:15-4:45pm; free; wheelchair access). Across the road, on Downing St. opposite Corn Exchange St., the **Museum of Archaeology and Anthropology** (tel. 333 516) contains an excellent display of prehistoric artifacts from American, African, Pacific, and Asian cultures, as well as exhibits from Cambridge through the ages. (Open Mon.-Fri. 10am-1pm and 2-5pm, Sat. 10am-12:30pm; free; wheelchair access, but call ahead.) The **Folk Museum,** 2-3 Castle St. (tel. 355 159) by Northampton St. (near Magdalene College), features an appealing collection dating from the 17th century (open Mon.-Sat. 10:30am-5pm, Sun. 2-5pm; £1, seniors, students, and children 50p). **Kettle's Yard,** at the corner of Castle and Northampton St. (tel. 352 124), houses early 20th-century art (house open daily April-Sept.; Oct.-March Tues.-Sun.; gallery open Tues.-Sat. 12:30-5:30pm, Sun. 2-5pm; free). The **Scott Polar Research Institute,** Lensfield Rd. (tel. 336 540), commemorates icy expeditions with photos, art, and memorabilia (open Mon.-Sat. 2:30-4pm; free).

The **Botanic Gardens** (tel. 336 265; enter from Hill Rd.) become an olfactory delight when the winds blow. (Open daily 10am-4pm or 6pm, varies by season. Mar.-Oct. Wed. free; Nov.-Feb. Mon.-Fri. free; otherwise £1.50, under 18 £1.)

ORIENTATION & PRACTICAL INFORMATION

Cambridge (pop. 100,000), about 60 mi. north of London, has two main avenues. The main shopping street starts at **Magdalene Bridge** and becomes **Bridge St., Sidney St., St. Andrew's St., Regent St.,** and finally **Hills Rd.** The other—alternately **St. John's St., Trinity St., King's Parade, Trumpington St.,** and **Trumpington Rd.**—is the academic thoroughfare, with several colleges lying between it and the River Cam. The two streets merge at **St. John's College.** From the bus station at **Drummer St.,** a hop-skip-and-jump down **Emmanuel St.** will land you right in the shopping district near the tourist office. To get to the heart of things from the train station, go west along **Station Rd.,** turn right onto **Hills Rd.,** and continue straight.

Getting There: Trains to Cambridge run from King's Cross and Liverpool St. Stations (2/hr.; 1hr.; £14.50). **National Express** coaches connect Victoria Station and Drummer St. Station in Cambridge (1/hr.; 2hr.; from £7.50).

Tourist Office: Wheeler St. (tel. 322 640; fax 463 385), a block south of the marketplace. Mini-guide 30p, town maps 10p-£2. Books rooms for a £3 fee and a 10% deposit. Open April-Oct. Mon.-Tues. and Thurs.-Fri. 9am-6pm, Wed. 9:30am-6pm, Sat. 9am-5pm, Sun. 10:30am-3:30pm; Nov.-March closes at 5:30pm. Information on Cambridge events also available at **Corn Exchange box office,** Corn Exchange St. (tel. 357 851), adjacent to the tourist office.

Tours: Informative 2-hr. walking tours of the city and some colleges leave the main tourist office daily mid-June to Sept. 10:30, 11:30am, 1:30, and 2:30pm; Oct. and April to mid-June 11:30am and 1:30pm; Nov.-March 11:30am. Admission including entrance to 1 college £5.75, children £3.75. Tours are well narrated but cover limited ground (usually entering only one college—probably King's). Special **Drama Tour** (Tues. at 6:30pm) led by guides in period dress (£3.90). **Guide Friday** (tel. 362 444) runs its familiar **bus tours** every 15 or 30min. from April through Oct. (£7, seniors and students £5, children £3).

Train Station: Station Rd. (tel. (0345) 484 950). Ticket desk open daily 5am-11pm. Help desk open Mon.-Sat. 8:30am-6:30pm, Sun 11am-7pm.

Bus Station: Drummer St. Station. National Express (call (0990) 808 080 for information). **Cambus** (tel. 423 554) handles city and area service (40p-£1). National Express agent open Mon.-Sat. 8:15am-5:30pm.

Taxis: Cabco, tel. 312 444. **Camtax,** tel. 313 131. Both open 24hr.
Bike Rental: Geoff's Bike Hike, 65 Devonshire Rd. (tel. 365 629), near the railway station, behind the youth hostel. £6/day; June-Aug. £15/week; Sept.-May £12/week. **University Cycle,** 9 Victoria Ave. (tel. 355 517). £7/day, £15/week; cash deposit £25. Open Mon.-Sat. 9am-5:45pm.
Hospital: Addenbrookes, Hills Rd. (tel. 245 151). Catch Cambus 95 from Emmanuel St. (95p).
Emergency: Dial 999; no coins required. **Police:** Parkside (tel. 358 966).
Postal Code: CB2 3AA. **Telephone Code:** 01223.

ACCOMMODATIONS

Book ahead. Check the tourist office window, or pick up their guide (50p). Cambridge B&Bs tend to be pricier and a bit more worn-down than their counterparts throughout England.

YHA Youth Hostel, 97 Tenison Rd. (tel. 354 601; fax 312 780), entrance on Devonshire Rd. Relaxed, welcoming atmosphere. 105 beds, mostly in 3- to 4-bed rooms; a few doubles. Couples may share a room, space permitting. Well-equipped kitchen, laundry room, TV lounge. Small lockers to store valuables available in some rooms. Bureau de change. No curfew or lockout. Crowded March-Oct.; call a week ahead in the summer with a credit card or mail a deposit. £10, students £9, under 18 £6.80.
Mrs. McCann, 40 Warkworth St. (tel. 314 098). A jolly hostess with comfortably lived-in twin rooms in a quiet neighborhood near the bus station. Rates go down after 3 nights. Breakfast included. Single £15. Double £26.
Warkworth Guest House, Warkworth Terrace (tel. 363 682). Fifteem sunny rooms near the bus station. Kitchen access; TV in every room. Breakfast included, packed lunch on request. Single £20. Double £35. Family £50.

FOOD

Market Sq. has bright pyramids of fruit and vegetables for the budgetarian (open Mon.-Sat. usually 8am-5:30pm). For vegetarian and wholefood groceries, try **Arjuna,** 12 Mill Rd. (tel. 364 845; Mon.-Fri. 9:30am-6pm, Sat. 9am-5:30pm). South of town, **Hills Rd.** and **Mill Rd.** brim with good, cheap restaurants.

Tatties, 26-28 Regent St. Yummy baked potatoes in roof garden over Downing College. Hot potato with butter (£2), more studly spuds (pineapple or curry potatoes) are £3.25. Open daily 10am-10:30pm.
Rainbow's Vegetarian Bistro, 9A King's Parade (tel 321 551). Duck under the rainbow sign on King's Parade. A tiny burrow of a place with delicious vegan and vegetarian fare, at £4.75 each. Try the Cypriot *moussaka.* Open daily 9am-9pm.
Nadia's, 11 St. John's St. (tel. 460 961). An uncommonly good bakery at commoner's prices. Wonderful flapjacks and quiches (55p-£1.50). Take-away only; sit outside Trinity across the street or try the branches on King's Parade and Silver St. Open Mon.-Sat. 7:30am-5:30pm, Sun. 7:30am-5pm.
The Little Tea Room, 1 All Saints' Passage, off Trinity St. As hopelessly precious as it sounds; tip-top teas served in a teeny basement room opposite Trinity. "Post-tutorial tea" (pot of tea, scone, cucumber sandwich, jam, and choice of cake £5). Open March-Dec. Mon.-Sat. 9:30am-5:30pm, Sun. noon-6pm.

PUBS & NIGHTLIFE

Cantabrigian hangouts offer good pub-crawling year-round, though they lose some of their character and their best customers in summer. The local brewery, Greene King, supplies many of the pubs with the popular Abbott bitter. Students drink at the **Anchor,** Silver St. (tel. 353 554), and the **Tap and Spile (The Mill),** Mill La. (tel. 357 026), off Silver St. Bridge. The **Pickerel** on Bridge St. (tel. 355 068), where it turns into Magdalene St., holds the grand distinction of being Cambridge's oldest pub. **The Eagle,** Benet St. (tel. 301286) off King's Parade, was the spot where Nobel Laureates

Watson and Crick first rushed in breathless to announce their discovery of the DNA double helix. The barmaid insisted they settle their four-shilling back-tab before she'd serve them a toast. The **Sir Isaac Newton,** Castle St. (tel. 324 238), is one of the few pubs in town with facilities for travelers with disabilities. The **Burleigh Arms,** 9-11 Newmarket Rd. (tel. 316 881), serves up beer and lager to its primarily gay clientele. **Flambard's Wine Bar,** 4 Rose Crescent (tel. 358 108), has live blues and jazz on weekends, with occasional Saturday-night dance parties. To the east, **The Geldart,** 1 Ainsworth St. (tel. 355 983), features Irish folk, rock, and R&B. **The Junction,** Clifton Rd. (tel. 412 600), off Cherry Hinton Rd. south of town, proves a popular alternative dance venue on Friday nights and hosts top local bands. The tourist office can give you a free *Cambridge Nightlife Guide* with a map of the spots, but leave the map at home.

ENTERTAINMENT

During the first two weeks of June, students celebrate the end of the term with **May Week** (a May of the mind), crammed with concerts, plays, and elaborate balls that feature everything from hot air balloon rides to sleeping dead drunk in the street. Along the Cam, the college boat clubs compete in an eyebrow-raising series of races known as the **bumps.** Crews line up along the river (rather than across it) and attempt to ram the boat in front before being bumped from behind. Visitors may enjoy the annual fireworks from the vantage of one of the city's bridges. May Week's artistic repertoire stars the famous **Footlights Revue,** a collection of comedy skits; Pythons John Cleese, Eric Idle, and Graham Chapman are all alums.

The third week of June ushers in the **Midsummer Fair,** which dates from the early 16th century and appropriates the Midsummer Common for about five days. The free **Strawberry Fair** offers games and music the first Saturday in June. Address all festival inquiries to the tourist office; for information on the Strawberry Fair, call 560 160. The **Summer in the City** and **Camfest** brighten the last two weeks of July with concerts and special exhibits culminating in the weekend-long **Cambridge Folk Festival** (for the main festival call the Corn Exchange box office, tel. 357 851). Tickets for the weekend (around £38) should be booked well in advance. **Camping** on the grounds costs £5-18.

Don't Miss the Punt

On sunny afternoons, bodies sprawl on the lush banks of the Cam and the river fills with **punts,** England's answer to the gondola. Punting is the sometimes stately, sometimes soggy pastime of propelling a narrow flat-bottomed boat (the punt) by pushing a long pole into the river bottom. If your pole gets stuck, leave it in the mud lest you take a plunge. Punters seeking calm and charm can take two routes—one from Magdalene Bridge to Silver Street, and the other from Silver Street along the River Granta (as the Cam is called when it passes out of town) to Grantchester. On the first route—the shorter, busier, and more interesting of the two—you'll pass the colleges and the Backs. **Punt-bombing,** in which students jump from bridges into the river next to a punt (thereby tipping its occupants into the Cam) has been raised to an art form, hindered only slightly by increased river policing. **Scudamore's Boatyards,** at Magdalene Bridge or Silver St. (tel. 359 750), charges £8 per hour for punts, rowboats, and canoes, plus a £30 cash deposit, and chauffeured trips from £20 per group (open daily 9am-6pm). **Tyrell's,** Magdalene Bridge (tel. 352 847), has punts, rowboats, and a canoe for £8 per hour, plus a £30 deposit. They also offers chauffeured rides (45min.) from £20 per group. Boats must be returned by 9pm. Most renters accept credit cards. Expect long lines for punts on weekends, particularly on Sunday. To avoid bumper-punting, go late in the afternoon when traffic dwindles. Student-punted **guided tours** (about £10), are another option for those unwilling to risk a plunge. Inquire at the tourist office.

The Arts Box Office, Market Passage (tel. 352 001) handles ticket sales for the newly reopened **Arts Theatre,** which stages travelling productions, the **ADC Theatre** (Amateur Dramatic Club), Park St., which offers lively performances of student-produced plays, and the **Cambridge Shakespeare Festival,** four plays in open-air repertory throughout July and August (tickets £8, concessions £5). The **Cambridge Corn Exchange,** at the corner of Wheeler St. and Corn Exchange provides a venue for band, jazz, and classical concerts (box office tel. 357 851; tickets £7.50-16).

■ Brighton

In Lydia's imagination, a visit to Brighton comprised every possibility of earthly happiness.

—Jane Austen, *Pride and Prejudice*

The undisputed home of the "dirty weekend," Brighton (pop. 145,000) sparkles with a risqué, tawdry luster all its own. According to legend, the future King George IV sidled into Brighton for some hanky-panky around 1784. Having staged a fake wedding with a certain "Mrs. Jones" (Fitzherbert), he headed off to the farmhouse known today as the Royal Pavilion and the Royal rumpus began. Brighton turns a blind eye to some of the more outrageous activity occurring along its shores; holiday-goers and locals alike peel it off—all off—at England's first bathing beach. Kemp Town, among other areas of Brighton, thrives with what is collectively one of the biggest gay and lesbian populations in Britain. Foreign students flock to the southern coast (ostensibly to learn English) and join an already immense student population to set the town abuzz with mayhem and frivolity.

A must see is the wild **Royal Pavilion.** Originally a plain-Jane farmhouse in a dull Brighton, the Pavilion on Pavilion Parade next to Old Steine has come to resemble an English princess in a *sari.* Brighton itself had become fashionable when Royalty graced its streets in the form of George, Prince of Wales, who requested that the Pavilion undergo its third round of cosmetic surgery. Reflecting England's longtime fascination with the Far East, Chinese decorations clutter every inch of floor and wall space, with the exceptions of the King's apartments, which contain bland Regency furniture. A full nine yards high, the chandelier in the opulent, pink Banquet Room sports a silver dragon. Rumor has it George wept tears of joy upon first entering it, proving that having money does not give one taste. Queen Victoria was less thrilled by the Pavilion, proving that having money does not exclude one from having taste either (tel. 603 005; open June-Sept. daily 10am-6pm; Oct.-May 10am-5pm; £4, seniors and students £3, children £2.35; partial wheelchair access).

Around the corner from the Pavilion stands the **Brighton Museum and Art Gallery** on Church St. (tel. 713 287), featuring paintings, English pottery, and an Art Deco collection which recalls the glamour of the inter-war years. The museum occupies the same buildings as the fantastic **Public Library**. Go leer at Salvador Dalí's incredibly sexy, red, pursing sofa, *Mae West's Lips.* (Open Mon.-Tues. and Thurs.-Sat. 10am-5pm, Sun. 2-5:30pm; free; limited wheelchair access.)

Before heading to the seafront, stroll through the **Lanes**—a hodge-podge of 17th-century streets, some no wider than three feet, filled with shops, restaurants, and nightspots. The **Palace Pier,** 100 years old and recently painted, offers a host of garish video games and food vendors near the waterfront.

The main attraction in Brighton is, of course, the **beach.** Those who associate the word beach with sand and sun may be sorely disappointed—the weather can be quite nippy even in June and July, and the closest thing to sand on the beach are the fist-sized brown rocks. At least with rocks like these, no one optimistic hostel owner observes, no one tracks sand into their rooms at night. In fact, the whole town seems to revolve around this sort of glass-is-half-full spirit. Even in 70° weather with overcast skies beach-goers gamely strip to bikinis and lifeguards don sunglasses.

ORIENTATION & PRACTICAL INFORMATION

The train stands at least 10 minutes from the town center and seafront. To reach the tourist office in Bartholomew Sq. opposite the town hall, walk south along **Queen's Rd.** towards the water. Turn left onto **North St.** (not to be confused with North Rd.) and continue until you reach **Ship St.;** then turn right onto Ship and proceed along to **Prince Albert St.,** which leads up to that dandy little mecca, the tourist office.

Tourist Office: 10 Bartholomew Sq. (tel. 323 755; http://www.pavilion.co.uk/ vbrighton/tourist.html). The enthusiastic staff will thrust materials on practically any subject down your gullet. Book-a-bed-ahead service £1 plus deposit. Free street map available. Open Mon.-Fri. 9am-5pm, Sat. 10am-5pm, Sun. 10am-4pm. **Walking tours** leave the tourist office on Sundays (June-Aug. 2:30pm; £3).

Bus Station: National Express buses stop at Pool Valley, at the southern angle of Old Steine. Ticket and information booth at the south tip of Old Steine Green. For information call 674 881. Open Mon.-Sat. 9am-5pm.

Public Transportation: Local buses are operated by over 6 different companies. To get to **Hove** hop on any of the buses travelling westward along Western Rd. (just a few blocks off the beach, continuation of North St., running parallel to waterfront). The Tourist Information Office can give helpful advice and a sheet containing route and price information for all buses tourists are likely to use. All carriers in the central area charge 60p.

Bike Rental: Freedom Bikes, 96 St. James's St. (tel. 681 698). £8/day for a snazzy mountain bike, £20/week, £40/month. Open Mon.-Sat. 9:30-5:30.

Hospital: Royal Sussex County, Eastern Rd., parallel to Marine Parade (tel. 696 955).

Emergency: Dial 999; no coins required. **Police:** John St. (tel. 606 744).

Postal Code: BN1 1BA. **Telephone Code:** 01273.

ACCOMMODATIONS

Brighton's best bets for budget lodging are its two hostels. B&Bs and cheaper hotels begin at £17. Shabbier B&Bs and hotels collect west of West Pier and east of Palace Pier. A huge number of B&Bs are located in **Kemp Town,** the neighborhood which runs perpendicular to the sea east of Palace Pier a bit farther from the town center.

Brighton Backpackers Hostel, 75-76 Middle St. (tel. 777 717). An unforgettably painted independent hostel that bubbles with international flavah. *The* place to meet other backpackers in Brighton. Most nights large groups of guests leave in search of the cheapest fun. Clean but somewhat cramped rooms overlook the ocean. Innovative artwork—courtesy of previous guests—graces most of the walls. Great location (50m. from seafront and the fringe of the Lanes) and no curfew. TV lounge and jungle-colored café with spectacularly-plumed parakeets under a skylight; free pool table. Kitchen, laundry facilities available. 4- to 8-bed dorm (mixed and/or single sex) £9. Weekly £50. Sheets £1. £5 key deposit. Winter discount. The newly opened annex faces the ocean and provides a quieter environment. Annex £10-12.50/person depending on room size.

Baggies Back-packers, 33 Oriental Pl, near West Pier (tel. 733 740). Go west of West Pier along King's Rd.; Oriental Pl. will be on your right. Owners have been known to spin a little jazz and take a turn on the floor in the cool bar with a blue mosaic floor; the hostel takes its clue from these groovy vibes. Exquisite murals and moon crescents line the walls of this clean, casual hostel. Mixed- and single-sex dorms available as well as an odd assortment of doubles. Laundry facilities. No lock-out, no curfew. £8-9. Weekly: £45. Double £23. Luxurious duvet and bedding £1 first night only. Key deposit £5.

Friese Greene, 20 Middle St. (tel. 747 551). Bohemian, family-run hostel situated in the heart of Brighton's nightlife. Great location attracts serious partiers and seasoned travelers looking for a cheap place to crash. Clean, decent rooms are comfortably dishevelled. £9. Weekly: £45. Sheets £1.

FOOD & PUBS

The area around the Lanes is filled with trendy and expensive places waiting to gobble up tourist dollars. For cheaper fare try the fish and chip shops along the beach or north of the Lanes.

Food for Friends, 17a Prince Albert St. (tel. 202 310). Cheap, well-cooked, well-seasoned vegetarian food in a breezy, youthful atmosphere. Daily specials, but the salads send the taste buds straight to heaven. Handwritten menus daily. Salads £2-3.25, various hot meals around £3-6. Large slices of fresh bread 50p. Open daily 8am-10pm.

Terre à Terre, 7 Pool Valley (tel. 729 051). When backpackers want to splurge, this is often the place they do it. Well-prepared vegetarian dishes cheerfully dispensed. Entrees around £6. Open Tues.-Sun. noon-11pm, Mon. 6-11pm.

Buddies, 4-8 King's Rd. (tel. 323 600). An American-themed restaurant cursed with too many ferns and too much yellow wallpaper. Redeemed by the fact that they never close. Entrees around £4.

ENTERTAINMENT

Brighton brims with nightlife options, earning it the nickname "London-by-the-Sea." And as surely as the tide turns, clubs and venues go in and out of fashion. The local monthly, *The Punter* (70p), details evening events and can be found at pubs, newsagents, and record stores. *What's On* (£1.20), a poster-sized flysheet, points the hedonist towards hot-and-happening scenes. Gay and lesbian venues can be found in the latest issues of *Gay Times* (£2.20) or *Capital Gay.*

Brighton is a student town, and where there are students there are inevitably cheap drinks somewhere. Many pubs and clubs offer fantastic drink specials during the week—some budget-minded backpackers find no reason to go out on weekends when most places are crowded and expensive. **Fortune of War,** 157 King's Rd. Arches (tel. 205 065; open Mon.-Sat. 11am-11pm, Sun. noon-10:30) and **Cuba,** 160 King's Rd. Arches (tel. 770 505; open Sun.-Wed. 11am-11pm, Thurs. 6pm-2am, Fri. 6pm-3am, Sat. 6pm-4am; cover after midnight £3-6) are both on the beach between West and Palace Pier. Revelers congregate in front of these two pubs and drink on the beach until about 11pm.

Most clubs open from 10pm-2am every day except Sunday. The most technically armed and massively populated are **Paradox** (tel. 321 628) and **Event II** (tel. 732 627), both on West St. Paradox gets a bit dressy towards the end of the week; Monday is gay night. Event spent over £1 million adding all of the electric trimmings to its already immense dance floor. **The Escape Club** (tel. 606 906) near the Pier at 10 Marine Parade has a trendy mix of gay and straight dancers. The arches of old WWII tunnels-turned-**Zap Club,** King's Rd. (tel. 821 588), provide space for dark rendezvous and dirty dancing; come here for hardcore pounding to rave and house music. The club hosts frequent gay nights. The gaydar blips hard and fast at **Zanzibar,** St. James St. (tel. 622 100), and at **Revenge** on Old Steine, Brighton's largest gay dance club. **Gloucester,** at Gloucester Plaza (tel. 699 068) provides good cheap fun with music varying nightly. Slightly unsightly **Casablanca** on Middle St. (tel. 321 817) delivers live jazz to a largely student crowd. Get ready to sweat.

The **Queen's Arms,** 8 George St. (tel. 696 873), packs an enthusiastic gay and lesbian crowd into its Sunday night cabaret. On Wednesday and Saturday nights the disco ball also sees some action. Bedsteads and vodka bottle chandeliers make **Smugglers** on Ship St. a raucous place to drink. Pirate theme makes you thirst for more ale; happy hour from Monday to Friday (6-8pm) pumps pints for £1.50. The **Berlin Bar,** also on Ship St., pulls internationals toward its huge MTV screens, lights, and now's-the-time-when-we-dahnce floor.

Hang loose just west of Brighton Marina at the **nude bathing** areas. Be sure to stay within the limits. **Telescombe Beach,** nearly 4½ mi. to the east of Palace Pier, is frequented for the most part by a gay crowd. Look for a sign before Telescombe Tavern marked "Telescombe Cliffs." Numerous sailing opportunities crop up in summer; check bulletin boards at the tourist office.

■ Canterbury

With pilgrims coming and going for nearly a millennium, the soul of Canterbury is a flighty thing, wedged somewhere between a cathedral and the open road. Archbishop Thomas à Becket met his demise here after an irate Henry II remarked, "Not one will rid me of this troublesome priest," and a few of his henchmen proved him wrong. Subsequent healings and miracles were attributed to "the hooly blisful martir," and thus "to Canterbury they wende." Chaucer's winking satire of materialism on the pilgrimage trail remains ever-relevant. Seek out the city's nomad charms and soaring, grand cathedral, but follow Geoff's example: don't take Canterbury's carefully cultivated soul too seriously.

Canterbury Cathedral has drawn the faithful—or the macabrely curious—since 1170, when Archbishop Thomas à Becket was gruesomely beheaded here with a strike so forceful it broke the blade of the axe. A kind of permanent "police line" surrounds the murder site, the **Altar of the Sword's Point.** Nearby, a 15-minute audiovisual presentation (shown continuously 10am-4pm; 90p, seniors, students 60p, children 50p) gives a concise history of the cathedral; it's worthwhile if you don't have time for a **guided tour** (4/day, fewer off-season; admission £2.80, seniors and students £1.80, children £1.10; check nave or visitors centre for times). In a building beset with fire and rebuilt again and again, the **Norman crypt** remains a huge, intact 12th-century chapel. (Cathedral open Easter-Oct. Mon.-Sat. 8:45am-7pm, Sun. 12:30-2:30pm and 4:30-5:30pm; Nov.-Easter 8:45am-5pm; choral Evensong Mon. 5:15pm, Sat.-Sun. 3:15pm; closed for 2 days in mid-July. Admission £2, concessions £1.)

The remainder of Chaucer's medieval Canterbury crowds around the branches of the River Stour on the way to the **West Gate,** through which pilgrims entered the city. The **West Gate Museum** (tel. 452 747) holds armor and prison relics, and commands broad views of the city. (Open Mon.-Sat. 11am-12:30pm and 1:30-3:30pm; 70p, seniors and students 45p, children and disabled 35p.) For a quiet break, walk over to Stour St. and visit the riverside gardens of the **Greyfriars,** the first Franciscan friary in England, built over the river in 1267. The friary contains a small museum and chapel (open in summer Mon.-Fri. 2-4pm; free). The nearby medieval **Poor Priests' Hospital,** now houses the **Canterbury Heritage Museum** (tel. 452 747; open Mon.-Sat. 10:30am-5pm; June-Oct. Mon.-Sat. 10:30am-5pm, Sun. 1:30-5pm; £1.70, seniors and students £1.10, children 85p).

At 1 St. Peter's St. stand the famous **Weaver's Houses,** where Huguenots lived during the 16th century. An authentic ducking stool (a medieval test for suspected witches) swings above the garden. **Weaver's River Tours** (tel. 450 912) runs cruises from here several times daily (½hr.; £3.50, children £2.50).

The **Royal Museum and Art Gallery** on High St. (tel. 452 747) showcases struggling local talent. Its angst-ridden Gallery of the "Buffs" retells the history of the oldest regiments of the British army (open Mon.-Sat. 10am-5pm in the public library building; free). If all the museum-going and gallery-hopping has tired you out, head to **The Great Stour Brewery and Museum**, 75 Stour St. (tel. 763 579), a "new concept in brewing" that allows visitors to brew their very own pints for just 40p. Your visit will be a truly happy hour (scheduled to open in late 1996).

Near the medieval city wall lie the massive, solemn remnants of the Norman **Canterbury Castle,** built for Conquering Bill himself. A statue of Christopher Marlowe stands in the garden. To the north on St. Dunstan's St., **St. Dunstan's Church** allegedly contains the head of Sir Thomas More (free). Outside the city wall near the cathedral, **St. Augustine's Abbey** (598 AD) holds little more than Roman ruins and the site of St. Augustine's first tomb (605 AD). Some sprucing up is planned for 1997, the 1400th anniversary of Augustine's arrival in Canterbury (tel. 767 345; open daily 10am-6pm; off-season Mon.-Sat. 10am-4pm; admission £1.50, students £1.10, children 80p). Around the corner on North Holmes St. stands the **Church of St. Martin**, where Joseph Conrad's heart rests in darkness.

ORIENTATION & PRACTICAL INFORMATION

Canterbury is roughly circular, enclosed by a ring road around an eroding city wall. An unbroken street crosses the circle from west to east, taking the names **St. Peter's St.**, **High St.**, and **St. George's St.** The cathedral rises from the northeast quadrant. To reach the tourist office from East Station, cross the footbridge, go left down the hill, and right on Castle St., which becomes St. Margaret's St. From West Station, go right on Station Rd. West, left on St. Dunstan's St., through Westgate Tower onto St. Peter's St. (which becomes High St.), and then, after about six blocks, make a right. Watch for St. Margaret's St. on your right.

Getting There: A pilgrimage from London to Canterbury? How original. **Trains** run from Victoria Station to Canterbury East Station (the stop nearest the youth hostel) and from Charing Cross and Waterloo stations to Canterbury West Station (1/hr.; 1½hr.; £12.90). Ask those in your compartment to tell one story each way. **National Express buses** leave Victoria Bus Station hourly (1¾hr.; £12).

Tourist Office: 34 St. Margaret's St. CT1 2TG (tel. 766 567). Book-a-bed ahead for £3.50 or 10% deposit of first night's stay. Guided tours leave April-Nov. daily at 2pm; (1½hr.) £3, concessions £2.50, families £7.50, under 14 free with parent. Open daily 9:30am-5:30pm; Nov.-March 9:30am-5pm.

Train Stations: East Station, Station Rd. East, off Castle St., southeast of town. Ticket window open Mon.-Sat. 6:10am-8pm, Sun. 6:30am-9pm. **West Station,** Station Rd. West, off St. Dunstan's St. (regional tel. (01732) 770 111). Open Mon.-Fri. 6:15am-8pm, Sat. 6:30am-8pm, Sun. 7:15am-9:30pm.

Bus Station: St. George's La. (tel. 472 082). Open Mon.-Sat. 8:15am-5:15pm. Get there by 5pm to book National Express tickets.

Taxis: Longport (tel. 464 800), 24hr.

Bike Rental: House of Agnes Hotel, 71 St. Dunstan's St. (tel. 422 185; fax 464527). £5/day, £25/week. £50 deposit. Open daily 7:30am-11pm.

Hospital: Kent and Canterbury Hospital, off Ethelbert Rd. (tel. 766 877).

Emergency: Dial 999; no coins required. **Police:** Old Dover Rd. (tel. 762 055).

Postal Code: CT1 2BA. **Telephone Code:** 01227.

ACCOMMODATIONS AND FOOD

Book ahead in summer or arrive by mid-morning to secure rooms recently vacated. B&Bs bunch by both train stations and on London and Whitstable Rd.

YHA Youth Hostel, 54 New Dover Rd. (tel. 462 911; fax 470 752), ¾mi. from East Station and ½mi. southeast of the bus station. Turn right as you leave the station and continue up the main artery, which becomes Upper Bridge St.; at second rotary, turn right onto St. George's Pl., which becomes New Dover Rd. Lockers free with deposit. July-Aug. £9.40, under 18 £6.30. Doors open 7-10am and 1-11pm. Book a week in advance Open Feb.-Dec. daily; call for off-season openings.

Kingsbridge Villa, 14-15 Best La. (tel. 766 415). Nondescript exterior belies interior elegance. You can't beat the location: a few steps off the main street. Full English breakfast. Single £18. Double £36, with private facilities £46.

The Tudor House, 6 Best La. (tel. 765 650), off High St. Ideal location in town center; eat breakfast in front of a Tudor fireplace in this lovely 450-year-old house, largely antique-furnished. Agreeable owners have bikes and boats for hire to guests. Single £17. Double with bath £40.

Let's Stay, Mrs. Connolly, 26 New Dover Rd. (tel. 463 628), on the way to the hostel. Hostel-style accommodation in Irish hostess's immaculate home. 2 rooms with 2 wooden bunks each; 2 bathrooms. Backpackers get preference at the door. Full English breakfast included; vegetarian options. £9. Copyright free.

Whether or not you are generally carnivorous, visit the vegetarian **Fungus Mungus,** 34 St. Peter's St. (tel. 781 922). Sit on a trippy mushroom stool; you may think the giant spicy beanburger (£4) is a hallucination. The pasta and pizza dishes at **Ask,** 24 High St. (tel. 767 617), provide budget sophistication (main dishes about £5; open daily 11:30am-11pm). **Marlowe's,** 55 St. Peter's St. (tel. 462 194) presents an eclectic mix of vegetarian and beefy English, American, and Mexican food. Choose from eight toppings for 8-oz. burgers (£6), or stuff down a burrito for 15p more (open daily 11am-11pm). **The White Hart,** Worthgate Pl. (tel. 765 091) near East Station, is a congenial pub with homemade luncheon specials (£3-6). Ask to eat in the rose garden (open for lunch Mon.-Sat. noon-2pm).

ENTERTAINMENT

Around Canterbury provides an up-to-date calendar of events in Canterbury; *Fifteen Days,* published biweekly, describes entertainment in all its urban guises. Call 767 744 for the recorded "Leisure Line."

The task of regaling pilgrims with stories today falls upon the **Marlowe Theatre,** The Friars (tel. 787 787), which stages London productions and variety shows (tickets £6.50-27.50; discounts available for seniors, students, and children). The **Gulbenkian Theatre,** at the University of Kent, University Rd. (tel. 769 075) stages a series of amateur and professional productions. (Box office open Sept.-Dec. Mon. noon-4pm, Tues.-Fri. 10:30am-6pm, until 8pm performance evenings. Tickets £6-10; ask about senior and student discounts.)

For information on summer arts events and the **Canterbury Festival**—two full October weeks of artistic revelry—call 452 853, or write to Canterbury Festival, Christ Church Gate, The Precincts, Canterbury, Kent CT1 2EE. The **Chaucer Festival Spring Pilgrimage** in late April ushers in a medieval fair and period-costumed performers. Call the Chaucer Centre (tel. 470 379) for more information.

▨ Bath

Immortalized by Fielding, Smollet, Austen, and Dickens, Bath once stood second only to London as the social capital of England. Queen Anne's visit to the natural hot springs here in 1701 established Bath as one of the great meeting places for 18th-century British artists, politicians, and intellectuals.

You'll be unable to come clean about having been to Bath until you visit its namesake, the **Roman Baths** (tel. 461 111). Sewer diggers inadvertently uncovered the site in 1880, and recent excavation have unearthed a splendid model of advanced Roman engineering. Audio guides (included with admission) do an admirable job of revealing little-known facts about Roman life, some explicated with *dramatis personae*. Alternatively, free guided tours (1/hr.) run from the main pool. (Open April-July and Sept. daily 9am-6pm; Aug. 9am-6pm and 8-10pm; Oct.-March Mon.-Sat. 9:30am-5pm, Sun. 10:30am-5pm. Partial wheelchair access. £5.60, children £3.30, family £14.30; or buy a joint ticket to the Museum of Costume, £7.50, children £4, family £17.60. Avoid crowds by arriving when the museum opens, or an hour and a half before closing.)

Situated next door to the Baths, the 15th-century **Bath Abbey** towers over its neighbors. The abbey saw the crowning of King Edgar, "first king of all England," in 973 AD. A stone just inside the entrance remembers Reverend Dr. Thomas Malthus (1766-1834), founder of modern demographics and inspiration to family planners everywhere. (Open April-Sept. daily 9am-7pm; Oct.-March daily 9am-4:30pm; £1.50 suggested donation.) The Abbey's **Heritage Vaults** below detail the millennia-spanning history of the stone giant. (Open Mon.-Sat. 10am-4pm. £2, seniors, students, and children £1; wheelchair accessible.)

The **Museum of Costume,** Bennett St. houses a dazzling fashion parade of 400 years of catwalks. Cynics may deem the museum a collection of giant Barbie dolls sporting Barbie Dream Outfits from the Renaissance to the 80s, but examining these cultural specimens proves far more intriguing than flipping through the pages of

Vogue. (Open Mon.-Sat. 10am-5pm, Sun. 11am-5pm. £3.20, 18 and under £2, 9 and under free; joint ticket with Roman Baths available (see above). Wheelchair accessible.) The clothes are closeted in the basement of the **Assembly Rooms** (tel. 477 789), which staged fashionable social events in the late 18th century (open Mon.-Sat. 10am-5pm, Sun. 11am-5pm; free).

A few blocks over on the Paragon, the **Building of Bath Museum** (tel. 333 895) recounts how this Georgian masterpiece progressed from the drawing board to the drawing room. (Open March-Nov. Tues.-Sun. 10:30am-5pm. £3, seniors and students £1.50, children £1.) Up Broad St., the **National Centre of Photography** (tel. 462 841), features a history of photography and contemporary exhibits. (Open Mon.-Sat. 10am-5pm, Sun. 11am-5pm. £2.50, concessions £1.75, disabled free.)

In the city's residential northwest corner, Nash's contemporaries John Wood, father and son, made the Georgian rowhouse a design to be reckoned with. From Queen Sq., walk up Gay St. to **The Circus,** which has attracted illustrious residents for two centuries. Proceed from there up Brock St. to **Royal Crescent.** The interior of **One Royal Crescent** (tel. 428 126) has been painstakingly restored by the Bath Preservation Trust to a near-perfect replica of a 1770 townhouse, authentic to the last teacup and butter knife. (Open March-Oct. Tues.-Sun. 10:30am-5pm; Nov.-mid-Dec. Tues.-Sun. 10:30am-4pm. £3.50, concessions £2.50.) **Royal Victoria Park,** next to Royal Crescent, contains one of the finest collections of trees in the country, lush botanical gardens with 5000 species of plants from all over the globe, and an aviary (park open Mon.-Sat. 9am-dusk, Sun. 10am-dusk; free).

Amble back down the hill to **Beckford's Tower,** Lansdown Rd. (tel. 338 727), for 156 steps and stupendous views. (Open April-late Oct. Sat.-Sun., and bank holidays 2-5pm. Admission £1.50, concessions 75p.) Those with a discerning eye might consider the **Victoria Art Gallery,** Bridge St. (tel. 477 000, ext. 7244). The gallery holds a diverse collection of Old Masters and contemporary British art (open Mon.-Fri. 10am-5:30pm, Sat. 10am-5pm; free; wheelchair accessible).

Homesick Yanks and those who want to visit the United States vicariously but haven't yet found a McDonald's should stop by the **American Museum** (tel. 460 503), perched above the city at Claverton Manor. Inside is a fascinating series of furnished rooms transplanted from historically significant American homes. (Museum open late March to early Nov. Tues.-Sat. 2-5pm; also Sun. and Mon. on bank holiday weekends 11am-5pm. Gardens open Tues.-Fri. 1-6pm, Sat.-Sun. noon-6pm; house, grounds, and galleries £5, seniors and students £4.50, children £2.50. Grounds, Folk Art, and New Galleries only £2, children £1.) Climb Bathwick Hill to reach the manor. Bus 18 (£1.20) can save you the steep 2-mi. trudge.

ORIENTATION & PRACTICAL INFORMATION

The **Pulteney Bridge** and **North Parade Bridge** span the **River Avon,** which runs through the city from the east. The **Roman Baths,** the **Abbey,** and the **Pump Room** are all in the city center. The **Royal Crescent** and the **Circus** lie to the northwest. The train and bus stations are near the south end of **Manvers St.,** at the bend in the river. From either terminal, walk up Manvers St. to the Orange Grove roundabout and turn left to the tourist office in the Abbey Churchyard. Be aware that many of Bath's "streets" are not streets as such, but blocks of houses.

Getting There: Bath is served by direct Intercity **rail** service from Paddington (1/hr.; 1½hr.; £26) and Waterloo Stations (2/day; 2¼hr.; £22.50). **National Express buses** run from Victoria Station (9/day; 3hr.; £9.75 return).

Tourist Office: Abbey Chambers (C4; tel. 462 831). Booking fee £2.50 plus a 10% room deposit. Office gets crowded in summer. Map and mini-guide 25p. Pick up a free copy of *This Month in Bath.* Open June to end of Sept. Mon.-Sat. 9:30am-7pm, Sun. 10am-6pm; Oct.-May Mon.-Sat. 9:30am-5pm, Sun. 10am-4pm.

Tours: Free guided **walking tours** depart from the Abbey Churchyard Mon.-Fri. 10:30am and 2pm, Sat 10:30am, Sun 10:30am and 2:30pm; May-Sept. also Tues., Fri., and Sat. 7pm. Tours range from good to excellent, depending on your guide.

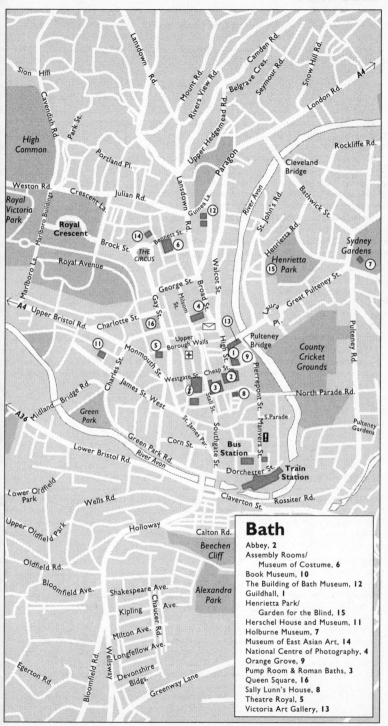

Bath

Abbey, **2**
Assembly Rooms/
    Museum of Costume, **6**
Book Museum, **10**
The Building of Bath Museum, **12**
Guildhall, **1**
Henrietta Park/
    Garden for the Blind, **15**
Herschel House and Museum, **11**
Holburne Museum, **7**
Museum of East Asian Art, **14**
National Centre of Photography, **4**
Orange Grove, **9**
Pump Room & Roman Baths, **3**
Queen Square, **16**
Sally Lunn's House, **8**
Theatre Royal, **5**
Victoria Art Gallery, **13**

Open-topped, narrated **bus tours** by Guide Friday pump exhaust every 15-min. from 9:25am to 5pm, departing from the bus station (tel. 464 446; £6.50, seniors and students £5, children £2; no booking required).

Train Station: Railway Pl., at the south end of Manvers St. Office open Mon.-Fri. 5:30am-8:30pm, Sat. 6am-8:30pm, Sun. 7:45am-8:30pm. Travel Centre open Mon.-Fri. 8am-7pm, Sat. 9am-6pm, Sun. 9am-6pm. If open, **lockers** available for £1-3. For train information call Bristol at (0117) 929 4255.

Bus Station: Manvers St. (tel. 464 446). Office open Mon.-Fri. 9am-5pm. **Lockers** available for £2.

Taxis: Abbey Radio (tel. 465 843) or **Orange Grove Taxis** (tel. 447 777).

Bike Rental: Avon Valley Bike Hire (tel. 461 880), behind train station. £3-6/hr., £12-18/day; deposit £100. Open daily 9am-6pm.

Boating: Bath Boating Station, at the end of Forester Rd. (tel. 466 407), about ½mi. north of town. Punts £3.50/person for 1hr., £1.50/person each additional hr. Canoes £9.50/day single. Open daily 11am-6pm weather permitting.

Hospital: Royal United Hospital, Coombe Park, in Weston (tel. 428 331). Take Bus 14,15,16, or 17 from the rail or bus station.

Emergency: Dial 999; no coins required.

Police: Manvers St. (tel. 444 343), just up from the train and bus stations.

Postal Code: BA1 1AA. **Telephone Code:** 01225.

ACCOMMODATIONS

Bath's well-to-do visitors drive up the prices of the B&Bs; expect to pay £16-18. B&Bs cluster on **Pulteney Road** and **Pulteney Gardens.** From the stations, walk up Manvers St., which becomes Pierrepont St., right onto N. Parade Rd. and past the cricket pitch to Pulteney Rd.

YHA Youth Hostel, Bathwick Hill (tel. 465 674). From N. Parade Rd., turn left onto Pulteney Rd., then right onto Bathwick Hill (a steep 20-min. walk, or take Badgerline "University" Bus 18 (5/hr. until 11pm; £1.15 return) from the bus station or the Orange Grove roundabout. Secluded and clean Italianate mansion overlooking the city. 125 beds; TV, laundry. No lockout, no curfew. June-Aug. £9.10, under 18 £6.10; Sept.-May £8.25, under 18 £5.55. Breakfast £2.80.

Mrs. Guy, 14 Raby Pl. (tel. 465 120; fax 465 283). From N. Parade, turn left onto Pulteney Rd., then right up Bathwick Hill; Raby Pl. is the first row of buildings on the left. Savor your stay in this Georgian home, one of Britain's most elegant B&Bs. Generous English breakfast. No smoking. Single £17. Double £34-36.

Lynn Shearn, Prior House, 3 Marlborough La. (tel. 313 587). Convenient location and great value on the west side of town. Easy walk, or take Bus 14 from bus station (4/hr.). Warm proprietors will welcome you as friends. No smoking; no singles. Double with full English breakfast £26, with bath £30.

Bath Backpackers Hostel, 13 Pierrepont St. (tel. 446 787; fax 446 305). Extremely good location, 2 blocks from the train and bus stations and the town center. Clean rooms, friendly atmosphere. Few showers; self-catering kitchen; continental breakfast £1.50. No curfew, no lockout; reception open 9am-11:30pm. £9.50. One twin and one double for £25.

FOOD & PUBS

For fruits and vegetables, visit the **Guildhall Market,** between High St. and Grand Parade (open Mon.-Sat. 9:30am-5:30pm). On Sundays when food is hard to come by, hit the pubs; many offer Sunday three-course lunches at bargain prices.

Demuths Restaurant, 2 North Parade Passage, of Abbey Green (tel. 446 059). Creative vegetarian and vegan dishes even the most devoted carnivore would enjoy. Specials change daily (about £5-6). Yum. Open Mon.-Thurs. 9am-9pm, Fri.-Sat. 9am-about 10:30pm, Sun. 10am-9pm.

The Walrus and The Carpenter, 28 Barton St. (tel. 314 684), uphill from the Theatre Royal. Basic bistro dishes served alongside candle-stuffed wine bottles. Good burgers (£6-8) and vegetarian entrees (£5-8). No oysters. Open Mon.-Sat. noon-2:30pm and 6-11pm, Sun. 6-11pm.

The Canary, 3 Queen St. (tel. 424 846). Airy tea house serving tasty twists on light meals. Somerset rabbit from an 18th-century recipe £4. Open Mon.-Fri. 9am-10pm, Sat. 9am-7pm, Sun. 11am-5:30pm.

The Boater, 9 Argyle St., overlooks the river with outdoor seating and a stunning view of the lit-up Pulteney Bridge (open daily 11am-11pm). **The Garrick's Head** attracts a largely gay crowd. Sit outside and scope the stage door of the Theatre Royal. An inspiration for Dickens's *Pickwick Papers,* the **Saracen's Head,** 42 Broad St., is Bath's oldest pub, dating from 1713.

ENTERTAINMENT

In summer, buskers (street musicians) perform in the Abbey Churchyard, and a brass band often graces the Parade Gardens. The magnificent **Theatre Royal,** Sawclose (tel. 448 844), at the south end of Barton St., sponsors a diverse theatrical program. (Matinees £7-20, student discounts available Mon.-Thurs. evenings and Sat. matinees. Box office open Mon.-Sat. 10am-8pm, Sun. 1hr. before show.)

The **Bizarre Bath Walking Tour** (tel. 335 124; no advance booking required) begins at the Huntsman Inn at North Parade Passage nightly at 8pm. Punsters lead locals and tourists alike around Bath pulling pranks for about one and a quarter hours; like all improv, tours vary from mildly amusing to hysterical (£3, students £2.50). Bath nights wake up at **The Bell,** 103 Walcot St. (tel. 460 426), an artsy pub featuring live jazz and blues (open Mon.-Sat. 11am-11pm, Sun. 11am-3pm and 6:30-11pm). **The Hat and Feather,** farther down Walcott St. at London St. (tel. 425 672), rocks with two levels of funk and indie (open daily 11am-11pm). **The Hub** (on the Paragon at Lansdowne Rd.; tel. 446 288; open Wed.-Sat; cover £3-6) and **The Swamp,** N. Parade (tel. 420 330; open daily; no cover Wed.) provide dance venues for young Bathians. Check the tourist office or shop windows for club schedules.

The renowned **Bath International Festival of the Arts,** over two weeks of concerts and exhibits, induces merriment all over town from late May to early June. It includes the world maestri of the **Bath International Music Festival** (box office tel. 463 362; open Mon.-Sat. 9:30am-5:30pm, Sun. 10:30am-4pm), the British art of the **Contemporary Art Fair,** and the bizarre theatrics of the **Fringe Festival.** For a complete festival brochure and reservations, write to the Bath Festival Office, No. 2 Church St., Abbey Green, Bath BA1 1NL.

▓ Dover

The grating roar of the English Channel has been drowned out by the puttering of ferries, the hum of hovercraft, and the squabbling of French families *en vacances.* Yet Dover has retained its identity despite the hum of tourist traffic.

The edifice which makes Dover worth a visit, **Dover Castle,** famed for its magnificent setting, its historic cachet, and its impregnability. Many have launched assaults on it by land, sea, and air: the French tried in 1216, the English during the Civil Wars in the 17th century, and the Germans in World Wars I and II. All efforts failed until 1994, when a phalanx of cyclists under the banner of the *Tour de France* invaded the castle, starting the British leg of cycling's greatest event here. The **castle keep** showcases an odd medley of trivia and relics from the 12th century to the present, including an exhibit entitled "Live and Let Spy," a tribute to the gadgets and genius of Charles Fraser-Smith, on whom the character Q in Ian Fleming's James Bond novels was based. The **Queen's Regimental Museum,** also in the castle complex, which houses a bombastic display of every major British military war and conquest. The ruins of the **Church of St. James,** destroyed by German "doodle-bugs" (V-1 and V-2 rocket bombs) rest at the base of Castle Hill. The **Pharos,** the only Roman lighthouse still in existence (43 BC), sits alongside **St. Mary's,** a Saxon church. **Hell Fire Corner** is a 3½-mi. labyrinth of secret **tunnels** only recently declassified. Originally built in the late 18th century to defend Britain from attack by Napoleon, the tunnels were the base for the evacuation of Allied troops from Dunkirk in WWII. Graffiti covers most of the passageways. Though most date from the 1940s, a few inscriptions from the 19th century are visible (accessible only by hourly tours). (Hourly buses from the town center run daily April-Sept., 45p. The entire complex open April-Oct. daily 10am-6pm; Nov.-March 10am-4pm. £5.50, seniors and students £4.10, children £2.80, family £15. Partial wheelchair access.)

Recent excavation has unearthed a remarkably well preserved **Roman painted house**, New St. (tel. 203 279), off Cannon St. near Market Sq., the oldest Roman house in Britain, complete with wall paintings and an under-floor central heating system (open April-Oct. Tues.-Sun. 10am-5pm; £1.50, seniors and children 50p).

The **Dover Museum**, Market Sq. (tel. 201 066) displays curious bits of Dover history and Victoriana. (Open March to mid–Nov. daily 10am-6pm; mid-Nov. to Feb. 10am-5:30pm. £1.50, seniors, students, and children 75p. Wheelchair access.)

A few miles west of Dover (25min. by foot along Snargate St.) sprawls the whitest, steepest, most famous, and least accommodating of the Dover's famed **White Cliffs**. Known as **Shakespeare Cliff** (look for the signs), it is traditionally identified with the cliff scene in *King Lear*. Closer to town on Snargate St. is the **Grand Shaft** (tel. 201 200), a 140-ft. triple spiral staircase shot through the rock in Napoleonic times to link the army on the Western Heights and the city center. The first stairwell was for "officers and their ladies," the second for "sergeants and their wives," the last for "soldiers and their women." (Choose your stairwell and ascend July-Aug. Wed.-Sun. 2-5pm; on bank holidays 10am-5pm. £1.20, seniors and children 70p.)

ORIENTATION & PRACTICAL INFORMATION

To reach the tourist office from the railway station, turn left onto **Folkestone Rd.** Continue until **York St.;** turn right and follow it to the end. where you turn left onto **Townwall St.;** the tourist office is on the left. From the bus station, turn left from Pencester onto **Cannon St.** Proceed through the pedestrian friendly city to Townwall St. and turn left. York St., which becomes **High St.** and eventually **London Rd.,** borders the center of town. **Maison Dieu Rd.** braces the town's other side.

Getting There: Trains roll to Dover's Priory Station from Victoria, Waterloo East, London Bridge, and Charing Cross Stations approximately every 45min. (2hr.; £18.40). **Buses** run regularly from Victoria Bus Station (2/hr.; 2¾hr.; £12).

Tourist Office: Townwall St. (tel. 205 108; fax 225 498), a block from the shore. They post a list of accommodations after hours and supply ferry and hovercraft tickets. Open daily 9am-6pm.

Train Station: Priory Station, off Folkestone Rd.

Bus Station: Pencester Rd., which runs between York St. and Maison Dieu Rd. (tel. 240 024; information (01813) 581 333). Purchase tickets on the bus or in the ticket office. Open Mon.-Fri. 8:30am-5:30pm, Sat. 8:30am-2pm.

Hospital: Buckland Hospital (tel. 201 624), on Coomb Valley Rd. northwest of town. Take Bus D9 or D5 from outside the post office.

Police: Ladywell St., right off High St. (tel. 240 055).

Postal Code: CT16 1BA. **Telephone Code:** 01304.

ACCOMMODATIONS

Several of the hundreds of B&Bs on **Folkestone Rd.** (by the train station) stay open all night; if the lights are on, ring the bell. During the day, try the **Castle St.** B&Bs near the center of town. A "White Cliffs Association" plaques outside homes indicate quality, moderately priced rooms. Most B&Bs ask for a deposit.

YHA Charlton House Youth Hostel, 306 London Rd. (tel. 201 314; fax 202 236), with overflow at **14 Goodwyne Rd.** (closer to town center). Hostel is a ½-mi. walk from the train station; turn left onto Folkestone Rd., left onto Effingham St., past the gas station onto Saxon St., and left at the bottom of the street onto High St., which becomes London Rd. 70 beds; rooms with 2-10 beds. Kitchen, showers, lockers available. Lockout 10am-1pm, curfew 11pm. Overflow building has 60 beds with bathrooms in each room; kitchen and lounge area. Both hostels £9.10, under 18 £6.15. Breakfast £2.80, 3-course dinner £4.15.

YMCA, 4 Leyburn Rd. (tel. 206 138); turn right off Goodwyne Rd. Rough it with a pallet on the floor (perfect if you have a sleeping bag). Men and women accepted. 47 mattresses in a coed room on a dance floor; also separate rooms for women. Get yourself clean (showers available), have a good meal (coffee and cornflakes included)—hell, do whatever you feel. Reception open Mon.-Fri. 8:30am-noon and 6-10pm, Sat.-Sun. 6-10pm. Curfew 10pm. £5.

Victoria Guest House, 1 Laureston Pl. (tel. and fax 205140). The Hamblins (and on Sun. their very extended family) extend a friendly, family welcome to their international guests. Gracious Victorian rooms in an excellent location. Double £28-40, family room £48-54. Special 5-day rates available.

FOOD

Chaplin's, 2 Church St. (tel. 204 870). Pictures of the famous expatriate compliment the classic feel of this Dover diner. Specials like roast chicken, 3 vegetables, and potatoes (£4). Open Mon.-Sat. 8:30am-9pm, Sun. 11am-9pm.

Jermain's Café, 18 Beaconsfield Rd. (tel. 205 956), on a quiet street off London Rd., just past the hostel; turn onto Beaconsfield Rd.; its on the left. An inexpensive quality British dining experience. Open daily 11:30am-2pm.

Curry Garden, 24 High St. (tel. 206 357). Aching for a change from Dover's British diners? Tandoori chicken £4.20. Open daily noon-3pm and 6pm-midnight.

■ Stonehenge

Stonehenge is a potent reminder that England seemed ancient even to the Saxons and Normans. The much-touted stones, some of which are 45 tons and 22 ft. high, are surrounded by imperturbable cows and swirled by winds exceeding 50mph. The stones were lifted by a simple but infinitely tedious process of rope-and-log leverage. Buffeted by sensationalistic theories and outlandish fantasies, Stonehenge has yielded none of its ageless mystery.

Admission to Stonehenge includes an entertaining and worthwhile 40-minute audio tour. Personal tours are also offered throughout the day; ask the helpful guides. (Stonehenge (tel. (01980) 624 715) open June-Aug. daily 9am-7pm; Sept. 1-Oct. 15 and March 16-May 9:30am-6pm; Oct. 16-March 15 9:30am-4pm. £3.50, seniors, students, and unemployed £2.60, ages 5-15 £1.80. Wheelchair accessible.) If you'd rather not get stoned by the price of admission, admire the stones from the roadside or from Amesbury Hill, 1½ mi. up the A303. Even if you do see Stonehenge up close, it's worth the walk to view the coterie of giants looming in the distance.

The most scenic **walking** or **cycling** route from Salisbury to Stonehenge (about 10mi.) follows the **Woodford Valley Route** through Woodford and Wilsford. Go north from Salisbury on Castle Rd., bear left just before Victoria Pk. onto Stratford Rd., and follow the road over the bridge through Lower, Middle, and Upper Woodford. After about 9 mi., turn left onto the A303 for the last mile. If Stonehenge doesn't quench your thirst for rock, keep your eyes peeled when you reach Wilsford for the Jacobean mansion that belongs to singer **Sting,** on the right-hand side in the fields of gold. Don't go inside the gates or you'll meet the police, not The Police.

London to Stonehenge takes two jumps. **Trains** (1/hr.;2hr.; £19.50) and **National Express buses** (3/day; 3hr.; £13) run between Salisbury (80mi. southwest of London) and London Victoria. **Wilts & Dorset** (tel. (01722) 336 855) runs several buses daily from the Salisbury train station to Stonehenge (30min.; £4.25 return). The first bus leaves Salisbury at 8:45am (Sun. 10:35am; though times vary seasonally), and the last leaves Stonehenge at 4:20pm (Sun. 3:50pm). Some private operators run **tours** to Stonehenge and Avebury (£15-20) from Salisbury.

Appendix

▨ Weights and Measures

1 meter (m) = 1.09 yards	1 yard = 0.92m
1 kilometer (km) = 0.621 mile	1 mile = 1.61km
1 gram (g) = 0.04 ounce	1 ounce = 25g
1 kilogram (kg) = 2.2 pounds	1 pound = 0.45 kg
1 "stone" (weight—of man or beast only) = 14 pounds	1 pound = .071 stone
1 liter = 1.057 U.S quarts	1 U.S quart = 0.94 liter
1 liter = 0.88 Imperial quarts	1 Imperial quart = 1.14 liter
1 Imperial gallon = 1.193 U.S. gallons	1 U.S. gallon = 0.84 Imperial gallon
1 British pint = 1.19 U.S. pint	1 U.S. pint = 0.84 British pint

Though Greenwich Mean Time (GMT) is the standard by which much of the rest of the world sets its clocks, the British have a system of their own, with Winter Time (=GMT) and British Summer Time (late March-late Oct.; 1hr. later than GMT). This time change is a week out of sync with other daylight savings time changes, but British time is usually five hours ahead of Eastern North American time.

▨ Average Temperature and Rainfall

Temp in °C Rain in cm	January Temp	Rain	April Temp	Rain	July Temp	Rain	October Temp	Rain
London	6/2	5.4	13/6	3.7	22/14	5.9	14/8	5.7

▨ Telephone Codes

Britain (including Northern Ireland	44
Northern Ireland (from the Republic of Ireland only)	08
Republic of Ireland	353
USA and Canada	1
Australia	61
New Zealand	6
South Africa	27

▨ Speaking British

aubergine	eggplant
bap	a soft bun, like a hamburger bun
bed-sit, or bedsitter	one-room apartment
bevvy; bevvied	a drink, an alcoholic beverage; drunk
biscuit	if sweet, a cookie; if not, a cracker
boozer	pub
brilliant	cool, excellent
busker	street musician
cheers, cheerio	thank you, good-bye
chemist	pharmacist
chips	french fries

chuffed	excited; or disappointed
concession, "concs"	discount on admission
courgette	zucchini
crisps	potato chips
dicey, dodgy	problematic, sketchy
dosh	money
dustbin, rubbish bin	trash can
fag	cigarette
fanny	female sexual organs
fortnight	two weeks
grotty	grungy
hire	rental
hoover	vacuum cleaner
iced lolly	popsicle
jelly	gelatin
jumper	sweater
kit	clothes (get one's kit off means to strip)
knickers	underwear
leader (in newspaper)	editorial
to let	to rent
lift	elevator
loo	restroom
lorry	truck
pensioner	senior citizen
phone box, or call box	telephone booth
piss (take the piss out of, on)	make fun of
pissed	drunk
pull	to "score"
punter	a guy, an average joe, a bar patron
public school	private school
queue; queue up, Q	a line; line up
return ticket	roundtrip ticket
ring up	telephone, call
rubber	eraser
self-catering	(accommodations with) kitchen facilities
shag, shagging, "fancy a shag?"	sexual intercourse
stroppy	crabby, grumpy
sultanas	raisins
swish	swanky
tights	pantyhose
tosser	loser, jerk
trainers	sneakers
wanker	jerk, tool
way out	exit
W.C. (water closet)	restroom
zed	the letter "Z,"

COCKNEY RHYMING SLANG

To keep from arousing police suspicion over their dodgy exchanges, East End merchants devised a rhyming slang. Few words of this amusing slang are commonly used, but it's a cultural phenomenon every visitor should be aware of. Observe:

word	example	rhyme	meaning
dog	"I'm on the dog"	dog and bone	phone
trouble	"the trouble's at home"	trouble and strife	wife

| rhythms | "Nice rhythms" | rhythm and blues | shoes |
| porky | "Don't tell porkies" | pork pies | lies |

■ Bank Holidays

January 1	New Year's
April 4	Good Friday
April 7	Easter Monday
May 6	May Day Holiday
May 27	Spring or Whitsun Holiday
August 26	Late Summer Holiday
December 25	Christmas
December 26	Boxing Day

■ Blue Plaque Houses

Matthew Arnold	poet and essayist	2 Chester Sq., SW1
Hector Berlioz	composer	58 Queen Anne St., W1
James Boswell	author	8 Russell St., WC2
Elizabeth B. Browning	poet	99 Gloucester Pl., W1
Beau Brummell	dandy	4 Chesterfield St., W1
Thomas Carlyle	essayist and historian	24 Cheyne Walk, SW3
Frederic Chopin	composer	4 St. James's Pl., SW1
Sir Winston Churchill	statesman and soldier	28 Hyde Park Gate, SW7
Joseph Conrad	novelist	17 Gillingham St., SW1
Charles Darwin	naturalist	UCL Science Building
Charles Dickens	novelist	48 Doughty St., WC1
Benjamin Disraeli	statesman	19 Curzon St., W1
T.S. Eliot	poet and critic	3 Kensington Ct., W8
Benjamin Franklin	statesman and inventor	36 Craven St., WC2
Thomas Gainsborough	portrait artist	82 Pall Mall, SW1
Edward Gibbon	historian	7 Bentinck St., W1
George Frederick Händel	composer	25 Brook St., W1
Henry James	writer	34 De Vere Gdns., W8
Samuel Johnson	author / lexicographer	17 Gough Sq., EC4
Rudyard Kipling	poet and writer	43 Villiers St., WC2
Gugliemo Marconi	inventor of the wireless	71 Hereford Rd., W2
Karl Marx	economist/philosopher	28 Dean St., W1
Somerset Maugham	novelist and playwright	6 Chesterfield St., W1
Samuel Morse	inventor and painter	141 Cleveland St., W1
Wolfgang A. Mozart	composer	180 Ebury St., SW1
Sir Isaac Newton	physicist/mathematician	87 Jermyn St., SW1
Florence Nightingale	Crimean war nurse	10 South St., W1
Samuel Pepys	diarist	14 Buckingham St., WC2
Sir Joshua Reynolds	portrait painter	Leicester Sq., WC2
Dante Gabriel Rossetti	poet and painter	16 Cheyne Walk, SW3
George Bernard Shaw	playwright and critic	29 Fitzroy Sq., W1
Percy Bysshe Shelley	Romantic poet	15 Poland St., W1
Vincent Van Gogh	impressionist painter	87 Hackford Rd., SW9
James A. McNeil Whistler	painter and etcher	96 Cheyne Walk, SW10
Oscar Wilde	wit and dramatist	34 Tite St., SW3

Index

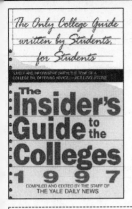

★ Let's Go 1997 Reader Questionnaire ★

Name: _____ **What book did you use?** _____

Address: _____

City: _____ **State:** _____ **Zip Code:** _____

How old are you? under 19   19-24   25-34   35-44   45-54   55 or over

Are you (circle one)   in high school   in college   in grad school
employed   retired   between jobs

Have you used Let's Go before?   yes   no

Would you use Let's Go again?   yes   no

How did you first hear about Let's Go?   friend   store clerk   CNN
bookstore display   advertisement/promotion   review   other

Why did you choose Let's Go (circle up to two)?   annual updating
reputation   budget focus   price   writing style
other: _____

Which other guides have you used, if any?   Frommer's $-a-day   Fodor's
Rough Guides   Lonely Planet   Berkeley   Rick Steves
other: _____

Is Let's Go the best guidebook?   yes   no

If not, which do you prefer? _____

**Which part of Let's Go do you feel needs most to be improved, if any
(circle up to two)?**   packaging/cover   practical information
accommodations   food   cultural introduction   sights
practical introduction ("Essentials")   directions   entertainment
gay/lesbian information   maps   other: _____

How would you like to see these things improved?

_____

_____

How long was your trip?   one week   two weeks   three weeks
one month   two months or more

Have you traveled extensively before?   yes   no

Do you buy a separate map when you visit a foreign city?   yes   no

Have you seen the Let's Go Map Guides?   yes   no

Have you used a Let's Go Map Guide?   yes   no

If you have, would you recommend them to others?   yes   no

Did you use the internet to plan your trip?   yes   no

Would you buy a Let's Go   phrasebook   adventure/trekking guide
gay/lesbian guide

**Which of the following destinations do you hope to visit in the next three
to five years (circle one)?**   Australia   China   South America   Russia
other: _____

Where did you buy your guidebook?   internet   chain bookstore
independent bookstore   college bookstore   travel store
other: _____